# Introduction to
# Islamic Banking
# & Finance

## Principles and Practice

**M. Kabir Hassan, Ph.D.**
University of New Orleans,
United States of America

**Rasem N. Kayed, Ph.D.**
Arab American University Jenin,
Palestine

**Umar A. Oseni, Ph.D.**
International Islamic University,
Malaysia

**Acquisitions Editor:** Rasheed Roussan
**Senior Development Editor:** Sophie Bulbrook
**Project Editor:** Jeanette Hewitt
**Copy-editor:** Louise Bolotin
**Proofreaders:** Paul Stirner, Stephen York
**Design Manager:** Sarah Fach
**Permissions Editor:** Rachel Thorne
**Picture Researchers:** Iman Naciri, Zohir Naciri

**Indexer:** Indexing Specialists (UK) Ltd
**Marketing Manager:** Sue Mainey
**Production Controller:** Christopher Crow
**Cover Designer:** Sarah Fach
**Typesetter:** Tech-Set Ltd, Gateshead
**Typeface:** 9/14pt The Serif HP3 Light

Printed in China (CTPSC/01)

**Pearson Education Limited**
Edinburgh Gate
Harlow
Essex CM20 2JE
England

and Associated Companies throughout the world

First published 2013

21 20 19 18 17 16 15 14 13
IMP 10 9 8 7 6 5 4 3 2 1

ISBN: 978-0-2737-3731-5

**PEARSON**

This textbook is dedicated to our respective families who have stood behind us during the course of writing this pioneering work. They have been a constant source of inspiration. With renewed zeal, we have pursued the goal of producing a textbook for the global Islamic finance industry that will enhance the Islamic finance pedagogy.

## About the Authors

### M. Kabir Hassan

Dr. M. Kabir Hassan is a financial economist with consulting, research, and teaching experience in development finance, money and capital markets, Islamic finance, corporate finance, investments, monetary economics, macroeconomics, and international trade and finance. He has provided consulting services to the World Bank (WB), International Monetary Fund (IMF), Islamic Development Bank (IDB), African Development Bank (AfDB), USAID, Government of Bangladesh, Organization of Islamic Conferences (OIC), Federal Reserve Bank, USA, and many corporations, private organizations, and universities around the world. Dr. Hassan received his BA in Economics and Mathematics from Gustavus Adolphus College, Minnesota, USA, and MA in Economics and PhD in Finance from the University of Nebraska-Lincoln, USA, respectively. He is now a tenured Full Professor in the Department of Economics and Finance at the University of New Orleans, Louisiana, USA. He has 135 papers published in refereed academic journals to his credit. Dr. Hassan has published in the *Journal of Banking and Finance*, *Pacific Basin Finance Journal*, *Journal of Financial Services Research*, *Financial Review*, *Quarterly Review of Economics and Finance*, *Journal of Business*, *Finance and Accounting*, *Journal of Economics and Finance*, *Global Finance Journal*, *World Development*, *Thunderbird International Business Review*, *African Development Review*, *Islamic Economic Studies*, *Review of Islamic Economics*, *Journal of King Abdul Aziz University* and *Journal of Developmental Entrepreneurship*. Dr. Hassan supervised 27 doctoral theses, and many of his students are now well placed in the academia, government and private sectors. He is editor of *The Global Journal of Finance and Economics* and *Journal of Islamic Economics, Banking and Finance*, *International Journal of Islamic and Middle Eastern Finance and Management*, and co-editor of *Journal of Economic Cooperation and Development*. Dr. Hassan has edited and published many books along with articles in refereed academic journals. He is co-editor (with M. K. Lewis) of *Handbook of Islamic Banking and Islamic Finance*, *The International Library of Critical Writings in Economics* (Edward Elgar, 2007), and co-editor (with Michael Mahlknecht) of *Islamic Capital Market: Products and Strategies* (John Wiley and Sons, 2011). He is co-author of *Islamic Entrepreneurship* (Routledge UK, 2010). A frequent traveler, Dr. Hassan gives lectures and workshops in the USA and abroad, and has presented more than 257 research papers at professional conferences and has delivered 91 invited papers/seminars.

### Rasem N. Kayed

Dr. Rasem N. Kayed is currently the Head of Business Administration and Marketing Departments and Deputy Dean of the Faculty of Administrative and Financial Sciences at the Arab American University-Jenin (AAUJ) in Palestine. Prior to his appointment at the AAUJ, he was a lecturer in international business at the College of Business at Massey University, New Zealand, and an adjunct senior lecturer at the New Zealand School of Export. Dr. Kayed received both his undergraduate degrees as well as his MBA degree from Jacksonville State University, USA, and his PhD in Development Studies from Massey University. His doctoral thesis explored the entrepreneurial phenomenon from an Islamic perspective and argued for profit and loss sharing (PLS) contracts as viable alternatives to conventional interest-based financing instruments. Dr. Kayed is co-author (with Kabir Hassan) of *Islamic Entrepreneurship* (UK: Routledge, Durham Modern Middle East and Islamic World Series, 2011). He has published a number of peer-reviewed papers in preferred academic international journals and chapters in books. He has also participated in a variety of seminars, forums and workshops, and presented various empirical and analytical research papers at several high-profile international conferences. Dr. Kayed sits on the editorial advisory board of a number of internationally renowned journals of Islamic banking and finance. His research activities are currently twofold: his first research activity explores the developmental role that entrepreneurship could play in advancing the wellbeing of the Muslim *ummah*; his second major research theme focuses on the global financial crisis and the resilience of the Islamic financial services industry, and its ability to present itself as a more reliable alternative to the conventional financial system. Dr. Kayed has more than 25 years' experience in both the commercial and academic worlds in the USA, Saudi Arabia, New Zealand, and Palestine.

**Umar A. Oseni**

Umar Oseni is currently an Assistant Professor at the Ahmad Ibrahim Kulliyyah (Faculty) of Laws, International Islamic University Malaysia. Prior to this, he was a visiting fellow at the Islamic Legal Studies Program of Harvard Law School, USA. He received his LLB (Hons) in Common and Islamic Law from the University of Ilorin, Nigeria; Master of Comparative Laws (*with Distinction*), and PhD from the International Islamic University Malaysia. His doctoral research was on the legal framework for alternative dispute resolution in courts with Sharī'ah jurisdiction in Nigeria, Malaysia, and Singapore, where he proposed a new framework for dispute resolution in the Islamic finance industry. He was a resource person on Islamic microfinance at the *UN-Habitat Workshop on Land Development in Islam*, jointly organized by the UN-Habitat, International Islamic University Malaysia and the University of East London in 2009. His areas of interest include the law and regulation of Islamic finance, contemporary issues in Islamic law, alternative dispute resolution, and international commercial arbitration. He is a member of the following professional bodies: the Chartered Institute of Arbitrators UK; the International Centre for Dispute Resolution Young & International (ICDR Y&I); the Young International Arbitration Group (YIAG); the London Court of International Arbitration; the Nigerian Bar Association; and the Association of Professional Negotiators and Mediators. Umar Oseni has written widely on current legal and regulatory issues in Islamic finance. He is a co-editor (with Engku Rabiah Adawiah Engku Ali) of *Essential Readings in Legal and Regulatory Issues in Islamic Finance* (Kuala Lumpur: CERT Publications, 2012).

# Brief Contents

# Expanded Contents

# Expanded Contents

# Preface

Islamic banking and finance is becoming one of the most significant aspects of the modern global financial system. Why? Because it is a fast-growing industry that has developed rapidly within a few years from a niche industry to a global force to be reckoned with in the international arena. However, with the worldwide spread of Islamic financial products and the growing interest of students and financial experts in Islamic finance, numerous books, monographs, and academic articles are being produced to explain the significance of this new industry to the global financial system. Nevertheless, there has not been much focus on a professional textbook on Islamic banking and finance for students of higher education who require case studies and practical examples in their programs. This seemingly neglected aspect of Islamic financial literature is the gap that this book seeks to fill, focusing on the principles and practice of Islamic banking and finance in the modern world. In this dynamic industry, there is a need to present a textbook for the ever-increasing academic and professional institutions offering Islamic finance as a course.

## Approach

We have tried to simplify the discussion through practical case studies and other helpful pedagogical features. Underpinning this are three major principles that have guided our approach to the presentation of the book.

- *Practice-oriented approach.* The pedagogical features embedded in the book—ranging from Professional Perspectives, Islamic Finance in Practice, Global Islamic Finance and Islamic Finance in the News, to problems and activities, marginal challenges, and marginal definitions—are meant to facilitate the understanding of the underlying principles. These practice-oriented features provide a hands-on experience for the students in understanding the dynamics of the Islamic finance industry.
- *The need for more sustainable practices.* We believe that in order to sustain the tremendous growth recorded in the Islamic finance industry, a dedicated textbook that addresses key issues should be made readily available for the students and practitioners alike. While there are numerous monographs on Islamic banking and finance, this textbook provides both the theory and practice, which is necessary to prepare the future professionals in the industry for the rewards and challenges they are bound to face in their careers.
- *Towards the standardization of Islamic finance.* As the pioneering textbook on Islamic banking and finance that seeks to fulfill the academic and professional needs of both students and practitioners, it also seeks to standardize the principles and practices of Islamic finance, bearing in mind the notable differences in the use of some products between jurisdictions in South-East Asia, the Middle East, and North African countries.

We have tried to present complex Islamic financial transactions in a manner that is easy to grasp, particularly for students who are new to the field of Islamic finance. Our goal in writing this book is to help students understand the underlying principles of

Islamic banking and finance and be able to translate such principles into practice in their professional lives. This seeks to bridge the gap between theory and practice of Islamic banking and finance.

## Chapter Organization

The chapters are organized as follows.

- *Chapter 1: An Introduction to Islamic Banking and Finance.* This chapter introduces the underlying principles of Islamic banking and finance with specific focus on its conceptual basis, historical development, components and structures, and the current size and worldwide spread of the industry.
- *Chapter 2: Islamic Contract Law.* This chapter builds upon Chapter 1 by discussing the underlying principles of Islamic contract law that form the basis of Islamic financial transactions. It discusses the following four main issues, which it must be emphasized form the basis of the modern practice of Islamic banking and finance: the philosophy of business transactions in Islam; the meaning of contract and its types based on the legal concepts and theories of Islamic law; different classification of contracts and the significance of the contract of sale; and the main forbidden contracts in Islamic commercial transactions.
- *Chapter 3: Financial Instruments of Islamic Banking and Finance.* This chapter puts the above theories and blueprint into action through the practical application of different forms of contracts in Islamic law in the modern Islamic banking and finance industry. It shows how exchange-based contracts, service-based contracts, partnership contracts, and supporting contracts are transformed into viable financial instruments and used by Islamic financial institutions.
- *Chapter 4: Financial Accounting for Islamic Banking Products.* This chapter provides a general introduction to financial accounting of Islamic banking products based on the framework of the Accounting and Auditing Organization for Islamic Financial Institutions (AAOIFI). It draws most of its examples from the AAOIFI Standards with a view to presenting a basic understanding of the principles of Islamic accounting. Included are sections on the significance of financial decision-making, the relevance of International Financial Reporting Standards (IFRS) in international accounting regulation, basic principles of accounting from both the conventional and the Islamic perspectives, the differences between the accrual and cash flow accounting methods, and samples of financial statements for Islamic finance products.
- *Chapter 5: Corporate Governance for Islamic Financial Institutions.* This chapter provides a discussion on the principles and practice of corporate governance in the Islamic banking and finance industry. It highlights the uniqueness of the corporate governance framework of Islamic financial institutions when compared with their conventional counterparts. Emphasis is placed on the Sharī'ah governance body of the total corporate governance framework in Islamic financial institutions. It also highlights the different models of corporate governance and Sharī'ah governance, and the different approaches adopted by Islamic different financial institutions.

- *Chapter 6: Islamic Asset and Fund Management.* This chapter examines Islamic asset and fund management in the light of current developments in the Islamic finance industry. It focuses on the following issues: fundamentals of Islamic asset and fund management; the criteria for the selection of Islamic stocks for investing, and reviewing the performance of Islamic funds; the structure, marketing and distribution of Islamic funds; Sharī'ah governance for Islamic funds; the importance of Islamic fund management; and the meaning and importance of risk management issues in Islamic funds.

- *Chapter 7: Islamic Bonds.* This chapter offers a comprehensive discussion on Islamic bonds or Islamic investment certificates (*sukuk*), while focusing on the types, characteristics, structuring, rating, and the AAOIFI standards on Islamic bonds. In addition, it provides a comparison between Islamic bonds and conventional bonds in order to highlight some key differences between the two, and the underlying concepts of Islamic bonds. The chapter further examines the most important elements of *sukuk* and some of the key issues involved in the securitization of Islamic products.

- *Chapter 8: Islamic Insurance (Takaful).* This chapter puts forward the discussion on the basic concepts and practice of Islamic insurance as an alternative to conventional insurance. It describes the innovative Sharī'ah-approved models and structures of *takaful*, the main *takaful* products and their expansion into the global insurance market, the process of determining and allocating surplus or deficit as proposed by AAOIFI, and the relevance of reinsurance and *retakaful* in the modern practice of *takaful* business.

- *Chapter 9: Islamic Microfinance.* This chapter examines Islamic microfinance, with its unique features and its similarities to conventional micro-credit initiatives. It provides a discussion on some Islamic microfinance products that are being used for microfinance, the differences between Islamic microfinance institutions and their conventional counterparts, an overview of some major Islamic microfinance institutions in the modern world, and the corporate social responsibility role of Islamic banks in financing micro-enterprises. Using specific case studies, it focuses on the role of Islamic banks and financial institutions in promoting Islamic microfinance as part of their general functions, with specific reference to corporate social responsibility.

- *Chapter 10: Risk Management in Islamic Finance.* This chapter provides a general introductory discussion on risk management in Islamic finance through the analysis of key guidelines on risk management issued by internationally recognized standard-setting bodies such as that of the Islamic Financial Services Board (IFSB). It discusses the following four main issues: the concept of risk management from the Islamic perspective with particular reference to Islamic commercial transactions; the types and characteristics of risk exposure and the Islamic banking risks under the IFSB guiding principles; the risk management techniques in Islamic banks and how such risks can be avoided, absorbed or transferred; and risk management techniques such as hedging through the use of Sharī'ah-compliant derivatives.

The outline covers almost every aspect of Islamic banking and finance and each of the chapters reflects current practices in the industry through appropriate case studies and figures that will aid the understanding of the theories, concepts, and practices of Islamic banking and finance.

## Key Features

Every chapter contains a set of learning features to help students grasp the key concepts in Islamic finance and banking.

## Chapter opener

**Learning Objectives:** These are presented at the beginning of every chapter, to provide students with clear learning goals. The chapter is organized around these objectives, and they are linked to the summary points at the end of the chapter.

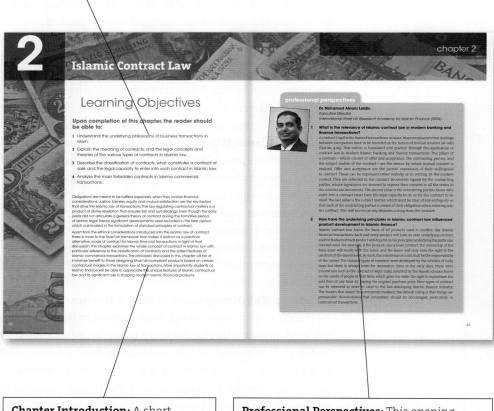

**Chapter Introduction:** A short introduction to each chapter sets the scene and tells students what will be covered in the chapter.

**Professional Perspectives:** This opening feature enables students to see the 'face of the industry' and also how the chapter theory connects with practice in the real world.

# Preface

## In chapter

**Marginal Challenges:** Thought-provoking questions are scattered throughout the text to make students stop and think, engage with the material and to apply what they have learnt.

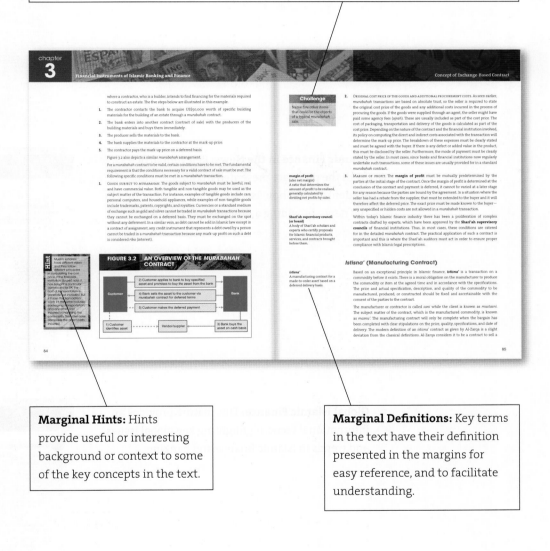

**Marginal Hints:** Hints provide useful or interesting background or context to some of the key concepts in the text.

**Marginal Definitions:** Key terms in the text have their definition presented in the margins for easy reference, and to facilitate understanding.

xv

**Islamic Finance in Practice:** This feature reinforces the theory by providing an interesting and relevant application to a real Islamic bank or financial institution, allowing students to see how Islamic banking and finance are practiced.

**Islamic Finance in the News:** Relevant articles from the press are presented in full, allowing students to see how Islamic Finance is reported in the news, providing a different perspective.

**Global Islamic Finance:** This feature provides an international focus, highlighting key global issues and trends in Islamic finance and banking.

## End of chapter

**Key Terms:** At the end of each chapter, a list of the key terms presented in bold throughout the chapter is presented, allowing for an easy recap of the key concepts. These terms and their definitions can also be found in the glossary at the end of the book.

**Questions and Activities:** Each chapter ends with a set of review questions and class activities. The questions require students to apply what they have learned in the chapter, while the activities encourage them to continue their learning outside the class and textbook.

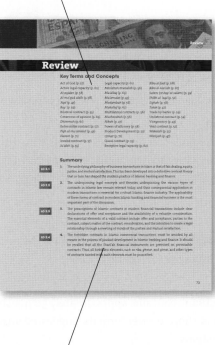

**Chapter Summary:** Summary points are linked to the learning objectives at the beginning of the chapter, providing a brief overview of the key concepts covered in the chapter, enabling students to check they have achieved the chapter goals.

**Further Reading:** A list of key references that students may find useful is presented at the end of each chapter, providing an easy reference point for any research they may need to carry out.

### English-Arabic Terminology

All Arabic terms are first presented with their English equivalent in the text, and these are reinforced by the Arabic term presented with its English equivalent on fold-out cover flaps that students can refer to at any point in the chapter. This serves as a quick reference so that Arabic terms can be quickly translated and do not need to be looked up in the chapter or the glossary.

## Instructor Resources

Instructors can download the instructor resources from www.pearsoned.co.uk/Hassan.

### Instructor's Manual

This comprehensive supplement provides extensive instructional support. The instructor's manual (IM) includes a breakdown of chapter content—including a chapter outline, lecture notes, answers to questions posed in the text, activity notes and places for the instructor's notes.

### PowerPoint Slides

The PowerPoint slides that accompany the book can be used by instructors for class presentation, or by students for lecture review.

### Test Bank

A computerized TestBank contains approximately 50 questions per chapter in multiple choice, true/false and short answer formats. Suggested answers and page numbers are included for all questions.

# Acknowledgments

We would like to take this opportunity to thank several individuals and institutions from both the public sector and the academic industry for their advice, encouragement and moral support. Special thanks go to Dr. Naser Hamad, the Vice President for Academic Affairs at the Arab American University, Jenin (AAUJ) and Dr. Zahran Daraghmeh, the Head of the Accounting Department at the AAUJ for their positive comments and constant encouragement throughout this project. We also thank our family and friends who were with us during the entire process of writing this book.

We appreciate the helpful reviews from the following Islamic finance instructors around the world:

> Dr. Hussein A. Abdou, The University of Salford Business School, UK.

> Salah Fahd AlShalhoob, King Fahd University of Petroleum & Minerals, Kingdom of Saudi Arabia.

> Dr. Abdel-Maoula Chaar, Ecole Supérieure des Affaires, Lebanon.

> Said Sami al Hallaq, Yarmouk University, Jordan.

> Professor Roszaini Haniffa, Hull University Business School, UK.

> Associate Professor Dr. Rusni Hassan, International Islamic University Malaysia, Malaysia.

> Dr. Nicole van de Locht, Fontys International Business School, The Netherlands.

> Dr. Rosylin Mohd. Yusof, International Islamic University Malaysia, University of Bahrain, Bahrain.

Thanks also go to the Islamic finance professionals who contributed to the Professional Perspectives feature at the beginning of each chapter, offering their personal views on key topics:

> Abdulazeem Abozaid, Associate Professor at Damascus University and advisor to Islamic banks.

> Dr. Mohamad Akram Laldin, Executive Director, International Sharī'ah Research Academy for Islamic Finance (ISRA).

> Dr. Savas Alpay, Director General, Statistical, Economic and Social Research and Training Centre for Islamic Countries (SESRIC).

> Dr. Mohammad Omar Farooq, Head of the Centre for Islamic Finance, Bahrain Institute of Banking and Finance (BIBF).

> Sayd Farook, Global Head of Islamic Capital Markets, Thomson Reuters.

> Dr. Omar Fisher, Managing Director, Khidr Solutions, Bahrain.

> Professor Habib Ahmed, Sharjah Chair in Islamic Law and Finance, Institute of Middle Eastern and Islamic Studies, School of Government and International Affairs, Durham University, UK.

# Acknowledgments

Professor Mustafa Hanefah, Dean, Research and Innovation, Universiti Sains Islam Malaysia.

Dr. Zamir Iqbal, Lead Investment Officer, World Bank, Washington, D.C.

Andreas Jobst, Economist, Monetary and Capital Markets Department, International Monetary Fund (IMF).

Professor Mervyn K. Lewis, University of Southern Australia.

Professor Dr. Volker Nienhaus, Adjunct Professor, INCEIF, Kuala Lumpur.

Rushdi Siddiqui, Global Head, Islamic Finance, Thomson Reuters, USA.

Muhammad Tariq, Partner, Head of Islamic Finance, KPMG UAE.

Professor Rodney Wilson, School of Government and International Affairs, Durham University, UK.

We wish to formally acknowledge the Accounting and Auditing Organization for Islamic Financial Institutions (AAOIFI), the Islamic Financial Services Board (IFSB) and the International Islamic Fiqu Acadamy of the Organization of Islamic Cooperation, whose guidelines and standards were used throughout the book. We received outstanding editorial guidance and support from Sophie Bulbrook, Senior Development Editor at Pearson, and the Editorial Team Leader of the Arab World. We also thank Rasheed Roussan, who actually got us involved in this book project.

— M. Kabir Hassan, Rasem N. Kayed, and Umar A. Oseni

We are grateful to the following for permission to reproduce copyright material:

**Figures**

Figure 1.5 from Standard and Poor's, Islamic Finance Outlook 2010, p.10, Standard & Poor's Ratings Services, 2010. Reproduced by permission of Standard & Poor's Financial Services LLC. Standard & Poor's Financial Services LLC (S&P) does not guarantee the accuracy, completeness, timeliness or availability of any information, including ratings, and is not responsible for any errors or omissions (negligent or otherwise), regardless of the cause, or for the results obtained from the use of ratings. S&P gives no express or implied warranties, including, but not limited to, any warranties of merchantability or fitness for a particular purpose or use. S&P shall not be liable for any direct, indirect, incidental, exemplary, compensatory, punitive, special or consequential damages, costs, expenses, legal fees or losses (including lost income or profits and opportunity costs) in connection with any use of ratings. S&P's ratings are statements of opinions and are not statements of fact or recommendations to purchase, hold or sell securities. They do not address the market value of securities or the suitability of securities for investment purposes, and should not be relied on as investment advice; Figure 3.6 from *Understanding Islamic Finance*, John Wiley & Sons, Ltd (Muhammad Ayub, 2007) p.394. Reproduced with permission of John Wiley & Sons Ltd; Figure 4.1 from "IFRS to Converge with Islamic Accounting Standards", http://www.leoisaac.com/fin/fin004.htm. Reproduced with kind permission of Leo Isaac, Online Learning for Sports Management; Figure 5.1 from *An Advanced Exposition of Islamic Economics and Finance*, Edwin Mellen Press (M. A. Choudury and M. Z. Hoque, 2004) p.86, Reproduced by permission of The Edwin Mellen Press; Figure 5.4 adapted from *IFSB-8 Guiding Principles on Governance for Takaful (Islamic Insurance Undertakings)*, IFSB (2009), copyright © Islamic Financial Services Board; Figure 6.1 from DJ ISLAMIC INDEX, *The Financial Times* (Markets Data, Financial Times), copyright © Thomson Reuters; Figure 6.2 from "Islamic Approach to Venture Capital Finance: An Alternative to Financing MME (Micro and Medium Enterprises)" by M. Kabir Hassan and Ali Ashraf, p.17, University of New Orleans Department of Economics and Finance Working Paper. Reproduced by permission of Ali Ashraf, University of New Orleans, USA; Figure 6.3 from Amanah Trust Income Funds, *The Financial Times*, copyright © The Financial Times Limited. All Rights Reserved; Figure 8.5 from *IFSB-8, Guiding Principles on Governance for Takaful (Islamic Insurance) Undertakings*, IFSB (2009) p.30; and Figure 10.3 from IFSB, IDB, IRTI, Islamic Finance and Global Financial Stability. Being a report of the Task Force on Islamic Finance and Global Financial Stability, April 2010, www.ifsb.org/docs/IFSB-IRTI-IDB2010.pdf, copyright © Islamic Financial Services Board.

**Tables**

Table 1.1 "Islamic banks in the United States: breaking through the barriers", *NewHorizon*, p.3 (Abdi Shayesteh), April-June 2009. Reproduced from NewHorizon Magazine with permission of the Institute of Islamic Banking and Insurance, London; Table 4.1 from http://www.ifrs.org/Use+around+the+world/Use+around+the+world.htm, copyright © 2012 IFRS Foundation. All rights reserved. Reproduced by Pearson Education Limited with the permission of the IFRS Foundation®. No permission granted to third parties to reproduce or distribute; Table 5.1 from *Corporate Governance in Islamic Financial Institutions*, Jeddah: Islamic Development Bank, IRTI (Umar Chapra and Habib Ahmed, 2002) pp.15-16, Reproduced with permission of Islamic Development Bank; Table 7.2 from *Islamic Bonds*, Euromoney (Nathif J. Adam and Adulkader Thomas, 2004) Original source: AAOIFI. Reproduced by permission of Adulkader Thomas; Table 8.1 from 'Takaful: Philosophy, Legitimacy and Operation' in *Humayon a. Dar & Umar F. Moghul, The Chancellor Guide to the Legal and Shari'a Aspects of Islamic Finance*, Chancellor Publications Limited (Dusuki, A W. & Abdullah N. I., 2009), pp.285-313. Reproduced with permission of Chancellor Publications Limited; and Table 8.4 from "Re-takaful (Islamic Re-insurance) Paradigm" by Prof. Dr. Mohd. Ma'sum Billah, http://www.applied-islamicfinance.com/sp_retakaful_1.htm, Reproduced with kind permission.

In some instances we have been unable to trace the owners of copyright material, and we would appreciate any information that would enable us to do so.

# 1

# An Introduction to Islamic Banking and Finance

## Learning Objectives

**Upon completion of this chapter, the reader should be able to:**

1  Describe the conceptual basis of the modern practice of Islamic banking and finance.

2  Explain the historical development of and conceptual arguments for Islamic banking and finance.

3  Understand the components and operating structures of the Islamic banking and finance industry as well as the process of development of Islamic finance products.

4  Describe the current size and worldwide spread of Islamic banking and finance.

Presenting an alternative mode of banking and finance in a world dominated by conventional banks for more than 200 years seems unrealistic but there has been tremendous development in the Islamic banking and finance industry during the past four decades, proving the feasibility of a level playing field for different theories of finance. The exponential growth experienced in this fast-growing industry is unprecedented in modern finance. The first modern financial institutions were created in the late 1950s and 1960s as profit-sharing institutions that later developed into full-blown financial institutions. This chapter provides a general introduction to the theory and practice of Islamic banking and finance in the modern world.

The unprecedented crystallization of Islamic principles of finance and commerce into an Islamic banking system with Shari`ah-compliant financial products and the proliferation of Islamic financial institutions across borders and continents is a testimony to the resilient nature of this industry. The industry has passed significant milestones in its integration into the global economy. Even though the underlying philosophy of Islamic banking and finance is firmly established in the Qur'an and Sunnah, its practice transcends faith-based rituals as it has now been accepted as an alternative to the conventional system, which may be explored by anyone. This has resulted in a new crop of non-Muslim experts and professionals in Islamic banking and finance.

The three major components of Islamic banking and finance are Islamic banking, *takaful* (insurance) and capital markets. These three major aspects of Islamic banking and finance have experienced tremendous growth as many economies are opening up to accept this alternative system running parallel to conventional banking.

## professional perspectives

**Emeritus Professor Rodney Wilson**
*School of Government and International Affairs*
*Durham University*

**1  How do you view the current status of Islamic finance curriculum taught at universities?**

There is a good choice available. Some institutions offer Islamic finance with courses in *fiqh al-mu'amalat* (transaction law). In other institutions, including Durham University, students take courses in conventional finance, including corporate finance and econometrics for finance, alongside Islamic finance. What best suits individual students depends on their academic background and abilities.

**2  What is the future of Islamic finance? Is it a fad or real?**

Islamic finance is for real. It is based on solid foundations and at a time when many are questioning the morality of conventional debt finance, it offers an attractive alternative. It has been developing for four decades and has an exciting future.

**3  How do you respond to the criticism that Islamic finance is going in the wrong direction?**

This is untrue. The financial needs of Muslims are no different to those of other religions and no religion, but Islamic finance ensures the needs are fulfilled in a just manner. The emphasis is on risk-sharing rather than transferring risks to the weaker party.

**4  What are your thoughts on 'mimicking versus innovation' and 'Sharī'ah-based versus Sharī'ah-compliant'.**

Islamic finance has been innovative and the products do not simply mimic those offered by conventional financial institutions. The purpose of the finance is the same, but the methods of financing are distinct. We need both Sharī'ah-based and Sharī'ah-compliant finance; they are not alternatives. Investing in equities that are Sharī'ah-compliant is desirable for example, but equity finance was unknown in both the east and west until two centuries ago. *Mudarabah* and *musharakah* have equity-type characteristics, and are Sharī'ah-based, but they are not the same as investing in listed companies or private equity.

# Basis of Islamic Banking and Finance

**International Islamic Fiqh Academy (IIFA)**
The central rule-making body of the Organization of Islamic Cooperation (OIC) composed of learned Sharī'ah scholars entrusted to issue legal rulings on contemporary issues, which generally include commercial transactions.

**Sharī'ah**
Embodiment of divine prescriptions in the form of faith and belief, and laws and moral norms that are meant to guide the affairs of Muslims.

We will start by examining the conceptual basis of the modern practice of Islamic banking and finance. The basis of Islamic finance is Islamic law, which is also known as the Sharī'ah. In this section, we shall review some affirmative evidence on Islamic banking and finance in the Qur'an, Sunnah, and the resolutions of the central rule-making body, the **International Islamic Fiqh Academy (IIFA)**. In these sources of the Sharī'ah, there are copious references to the prohibition of interest and excessive risk, permissibility of lawful sales, and Islamic entrepreneurship. These concepts are the underlying principles of the modern Islamic banking and finance industry.

## The Sharī'ah

The practice of Islamic finance is based on a number of moral and legal principles of Islam. As a religion, Islam encompasses the total lifestyle and wellbeing of Muslims: their social, political and economic lives. From the economic perspective, Muslims believe that both general and specific rules are laid down in Islam to guide mankind towards social justice, economic wellbeing and development, and global development. The Islamic concept of Sharī'ah defines the man-to-God and man-to-man relationships. **Sharī'ah** is the divine prescriptions in form of faith and belief, laws and moral norms broadly classified into two strands: *ibadah (*worship and devotional practices) and *mu'amalat* (civil transactions). Figure 1.1 illustrates the overall framework of Sharī'ah as the basis of modern Islamic banking and finance.

**Challenge**

From the broad classification given in Figure 1.1, name two non-banking economic activities in Islam.

## FIGURE 1.1    SHARĪ'AH AS THE BASIS OF ISLAMIC BANKING AND FINANCE

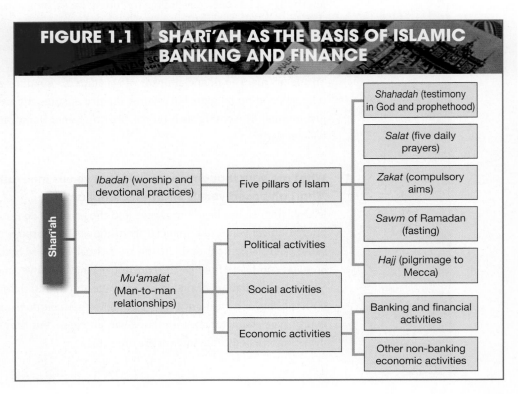

The ethical practices in commercial transactions are based on the legal principles taken and developed from the primary sources of the Sharī'ah. The primary sources of the Sharī'ah are the Qur'an and Sunnah. In order to understand contemporary Islamic banking and finance business, let us consider its basis and justifications. The basis of Islamic banking and finance is the Sharī'ah. Therefore, any form of banking and financial institution that carries out business that is consistent with the principles of the Sharī'ah can simply be referred to as an Islamic bank or financial institution.

## The Qur'an

**gharar**
Excessive risk or absolute uncertainty relating to major elements of a contract, for example, the sale of a commodity that is not present at the time of concluding the contract.

**riba**
Any transaction that has an element of usury or interest in it that is regarded as an unearned and undeserving income.

The first source of the Sharī'ah is the Qur'an, which is an embodiment of general and specific rules on religious, commercial, political, economic, legal, and social norms. It provides the original basis of the permissibility of lawful commercial and financial transactions, with emphasis on mutual consent and consensus among contracting parties. The underlying rule regulating these transactions in the Qur'an is justice and fair dealing. While the Qur'an permits and even encourages commercial transactions, it prohibits exploitative measures such as excessive risk or absolute uncertainty relating to major elements of a contract, known as **gharar**. It also prohibits any transaction that has an element of usury or interest in it that is regarded as an unearned and undeserving income, known as **riba**. This is established in the following verses of the Qur'an:

Qur'an 30:39: "That which you give as *riba* to increase the people's wealth increases not with God; but that which you give in charity, seeking the goodwill of God, multiplies manifold."

Qur'an 4:161: "And for their taking *riba* even though it was forbidden for them, and their wrongful appropriation of other people's property, we have prepared for those among them who reject faith a grievous punishment."

Qur'an 3:130–132: "O you who have believed, take not doubled and redoubled *riba*, and fear God so that you prosper. Fear the fire which has been prepared for those who reject faith, and obey God and the Prophet so that you may receive mercy."

Qur'an 2:275–276: "Those who benefit from *riba* shall be raised like those who have been driven to madness by the touch of the Devil; that is because they say: 'Trade is like *riba*' while God has permitted trade and forbidden *riba*. God deprives interest of all but blesses charity. He loves not the ungrateful sinners."

> Qur'an 2:278-281: "O you who have believed! Fear Allah and give up *riba* that remains outstanding, if you are true believers. If you do not, then be sure of being at war with God and His messenger. But if you repent, you can have your principal. Neither you should commit injustice nor you be subjected to it. If the debtor is in difficulty, let him have respite until it is easier, but if you forego out of charity, it is better for you if you realize."

The prohibition of *riba* developed gradually from an initial moral persuasion to a complete prohibition. While the Lawgiver prohibits exploitative tendencies and unjust dealings. He gives a viable option that emphasizes the significance of entrepreneurship. The above verses establish the following important points:

- Any increase in the principal amount borrowed constitutes *riba*.
- *Riba* leads to unjust enrichment, which further impoverishes the poor.
- Islam prohibits *riba* in unequivocal terms.
- From the religious perspective, God does not bless interest-bearing transactions.
- *Riba* transactions lead to destruction and are prone to economic crisis.
- The alternative to *riba* is ethical commercial transactions that promote mutual benefits.

The Qur'an also prohibits cheating and corrupt practices in the management of funds and does not allow dealings in prohibited products.

## The Sunnah

**Sunnah**
The second primary source of the Shari'ah, which comprises the sayings, practices and tacit approvals of the Prophet Muhammad.

The traditions of the Prophet Muhammad (PBUH) include his habits, words, practices, and tacit approvals that are meant to further explain the injunctions of the Qur'an. For example, there are a number of instances where the Prophet practically explained and demonstrated what constitutes *riba* as mentioned in the above verses of the Qur'an. This further elaboration is always necessary in divine legislation because, as a general rule, the Qur'an only provides the broad principles of law on legal issues while the elaboration of those principles is given in the prophetic traditions otherwise known as the **Sunnah**. Although there are numerous Prophetic traditions that deal with the subject of *riba*, a few examples are given in Box 1.1 to highlight the affirmative evidence on the prohibition of *riba* already mentioned in the Qur'an. There are basically two types of *riba*—*riba al-nasi'ah*, which is the interest on lent money, and *riba al-fadl*, the exchange of superior goods with more inferior ones.

The form of *riba* prohibited in the Qur'an is *riba al-nasi'ah*, interest for delayed payment. It is also known as *riba al-duyun* (*riba* on loans), *riba al-jali* (obvious *riba*), or *riba al-mubashir* (direct *riba*), which generally means an unjustifiable increase for the deferment of repayment of a loan. Apart from these Qur'anic *riba*, there is another category called *riba al-fadl* (interest of an increase in the quantity of one of the counter values), which is clarified in the Sunnah. *Riba al-fadl* is also known as *riba al-buyu'u* (*riba* in trade), *riba ghayr al-mubashir* (indirect *riba*), or *riba al-khafi* (hidden *riba*). This latter category, described in the Sunnah, relates to the exchange of superior goods with a greater quantity of inferior goods. So, while *riba al-nasi'ah* relates to loans, *riba al-fadl* relates to trade.

## BOX 1.1:    PROPHETIC TRADITIONS ON *RIBA*

Abu Sa'id al-Khudri narrated that the Prophet said:

> Do not sell gold for gold, except when it is like for like, and do not increase one over the other; and do not sell silver for silver except when it is like for like, and do not increase one over the other; and do not sell what is away (from among these) for what is ready.[1]

\*   \*   \*

The Prophet was also reported to have said on more than one occasion:

> Gold for gold, silver for silver, wheat for wheat, barley for barley, dates for dates, and salt for salt – like for like, equal for equal and hand to hand (that is, immediate sale); if the commodities differ, then you may sell as you wish, provided that the exchange is hand to hand.[2]

\*   \*   \*

From another narration, Abu Sa'id al-Khudri quoted the following passage:

> Bilal visited the Messenger of God with some high quality dates, and the Prophet inquired about their source. Bilal explained that he traded two volumes of lower quality dates for one volume of higher quality. The Messenger of God said: "This is precisely the forbidden *riba*! Do not do this. Instead, sell the first type of dates and use the proceeds to buy the other."[3]

\*   \*   \*

During the last sermon, Prophet Muhammad declared openly:

> All *riba* is annulled. But you will get back your principal amounts. Neither shall you wrong nor shall you be wronged against. Allah has decried that there shall be no *riba*. The *riba* of Abbas bin Abdul Muttalib is cancelled, all of it.[4]

**hadith**
The sayings, acts, or tacit approvals and disapprovals of the Prophet Muhammad (PBUH).

Apart from verses and **hadith** prohibiting *riba*, all other textual evidence of forbidden transactions involving unjust enrichment, excessive risk, monopoly, hoarding of commodities, embezzlement, trading in unlawful commodities, and corrupt tendencies give credence to Islamic banking and finance business being a just financial system. For instance, the Lawgiver emphatically legislates:

> Qur'an 2:188: "And eat up not one another's property unjustly (in any illegal way), nor give bribery to the rulers (judges before presenting your cases) that you may knowingly eat up a part of the property of others sinfully."

Unlawful appropriation of other people's property through excessive profits is also considered *riba*. *Riba* is a generic term that covers many forms, including the two broad types explained above.

In accordance with these legal texts in both the Qur'an and Sunnah, the IIFA resolved:

- First: Any increase or interest on a debt that has matured, in return for an extension of the maturity date, in case the borrower is unable to pay the increase (or interest) on the loan at the inception of its agreement, are both forms of usury, which is prohibited under the Sharī'ah.
- Second: The alternative, which guarantees the cash flow and financial support for the commercial activity in a form acceptable to Islam, is to trade with each other in conformity with Sharī'ah principles.
- Third: The Academy invites governments of Islamic countries to encourage the financial institutions which operate in accordance with the principles of the Sharī'ah, and to enable them to operate in every Muslim country, so that they may respond to the needs of Muslims and a Muslim does not have to live in contradiction between the demands of his faith and the realities of life.[5]

This resolution of the IIFA summarizes the evidence on the prohibition of interest-based banking and the need to embrace the interest-free banking and finance popularly called Islamic banking and finance. Whether or not the term 'Islamic' is used as a prefix to banking and finance, any form of interest-free banking based on ethical ideals of financial transactions will be recognized as Sharī'ah-compliant. Therefore, within the modern context, the interest element in banking and finance is replaced with profit-sharing through certain Islamic financial products.

# Origins and Historical Overview of Islamic Banking and Finance

In this section, we shall examine the origins and historical development of modern Islamic banking and finance as well as the conceptual arguments and justification of Islamic banking and finance. The history of Islamic finance is generally divided into two major aspects: the early days transactions and the modern-day experiments.

## Early Days Transactions in the Era of the Prophet

The history of Islamic finance cannot be discussed without considering the whole history of Islamic economics as the former is a segment of the latter. The early days transactions comprise the commercial and financial transactions that were prevalent during the Prophet Muhammad's time. During this era, trade and investment activities were prevalent among the Arabs and these took different forms. The financial principles that were in place during this era were based on the economic regime introduced by Islam at the dawn of the 8th century CE. This new economic revolution, introduced through injunctions in the Qur'an and Sunnah, came on the brink of the call to prophethood of the Prophet Muhammad. The Prophet and his companions engaged practically in commercial transactions that involved financial dealings among parties of different nations and tribes. Transregional trade was prevalent in the then Arabian Peninsula, which involved trade caravans from Mecca to Syria and vice versa. Mecca was the centre of interregional trade in the Arabian Peninsula. Ethical trade practices were the norm during this era and the advent of the religion of Islam ushered in a more formalized ethical system of commercial transactions built on fair dealing, justice, and mutual gains.

The truthfulness and uncommon trustworthiness of the Prophet Muhammad in the call to prophethood was significant in him winning the love of both co-traders and customers. He was upright, honest and ingenious in his commercial dealings and this earned him the titles of *Al-Sadiq* (the Truthful One) and *Al-Amin* (the Trustworthy). In his business dealings, he never engaged in unethical transactions, and he did not hoard commercial goods for the purpose of selling at higher prices when such commodities become scarce. Consequently, Khadijah, a rich and reputable merchant in Mecca, engaged the services of the young and reliable Muhammad to assist in the management of her business. After some time, she proposed to Muhammad and the marriage was solemnized. This further boosted the trade of these two merchants, whose basis of transactions was fair dealing. This important feature of trustworthiness for which Prophet Muhammad was known prepared him for the greater responsibility of prophethood. As the people of Arabia never knew him to lie or deceive anybody in commercial transactions, a good number of his acquaintances accepted his call to the religion of Islam.

***shirkah***
Any form of business partnership between two or more individuals.

***sarf***
A contract of exchange of money subject to the mandatory rules of Islamic law.

***Sa'a***
An ancient measure of volume, equivalent to 3 kg, that was widely used in Muslim communities.

## Prevailing Modes of Transactions during the Early Period

The prevailing modes of transactions during this era included **shirkah** (partnership), whether *mudarabah* (trust financing) or *musharakah* (joint venture partnership), both of which were practiced as profit and loss sharing (PLS) transactions. In addition, interregional trade within the Arabian Peninsula involved caravan trades where agents were employed to represent their principals in the business, mostly to carry out specific transactions under the authority of the latter. Agents were sent to Syria and its Mediterranean ports to trade in goods. The agents were compensated either through financial payments or proprietary benefits as agreed by the parties. This form of transaction is known as *wakalah* (agency contract), which has crystallized into an ancillary mode of finance in modern complex Islamic capital market transactions.

Furthermore, *qard* (a benevolent loan) was also common during this era. The Prophet sometimes borrowed money from Jews and facilitated some interest-free loans for his needy companions. This form of transaction is a goodwill loan made without the intention of receiving interest or any benefit in making such a loan. The Prophet's approval of benevolent loans can be found in a passage where he was reported to have said: 'Whoever gives loans would have the reward (equivalent to the reward) of one of them.'[6] In a similar vein, one of the wives of the Prophet, Aishah, told that the Prophet bought some food on credit from a Jew and gave him his chain mail as security for the debt.[7]

Apart from the above modes of transaction, the Prophet also recognized and his companions practically engaged in *salam* (forward) contracts. According to a tale, Ibn 'Abbas, a companion of the Prophet, said that when the latter came to Medina they used to engage in *salam* contracts against cash payment until the season.[8] Other widespread permissible transactions during this period include **sarf** (exchange of money, that is gold for gold and silver for silver at the same sitting) and *ijarah* (leasing). An incident is recorded in the collections of hadith by Al-Bukhari and Muslim, respectively, where Abu Sa'id al-Khudri, a companion of the Prophet, reported that Bilal, another companion, brought some dates to the Prophet, who asked where he had obtained them. Bilal replied: "I had some inferior quality dates so I exchanged two **Sa'a** (a kind of measure) of them for one **Sa'a**." The Prophet responded: "Ah! This is the very essence of *riba* (usury), the very essence of *riba*! Do not do so, but when you wish to buy, sell the dates in a separate transaction, then buy with what you get."[9]

## Mediums of Exchange

The existing mediums of exchange during the advent of Islam in the Arab region were the dinar (gold) and dirham (silver). The former was the Roman Empire's currency (denarius) while the latter was the Persian currency. The Prophet adopted these currencies as mediums of exchange in the then-emergent Muslim community. One of their significant features was their intrinsic value. In a hadith that gives a glimpse into what constitutes money during this golden era, Abu Sa'id al-Khudri told that the Prophet once emphatically explained: "Gold for gold, silver for silver, wheat for wheat, barley for barley, dates for dates, and salt for salt. When a transaction is like for like, payment being made on the spot, then if anyone gives more or asks for more, he has dealt in *riba*, the receiver and the giver are equally guilty."[10] It is clear from Prophet's pronouncements that the mediums of exchange recognized during this era were precious metals such as gold and silver, and other commodities such as wheat, barley, dates and salt, which are regularly consumed by people. These commodities, which were also a measure of value, all have an intrinsic value within themselves.

Since the advent of Islam brought about both socioeconomic and political reforms in the Arabian Peninsula, and by extension the world, Islamic law came to regulate economic policies and transactions through approval of compliant transactions and disapproval of non-compliant forms of transactions. Some of the prohibited transactions prevalent during this era included commercial or financial transactions tainted with interest, excessive risk, or speculation, dealing in prohibited commodities, dealing in stolen goods, exploitation and unjust practices in the market through exorbitant prices, deliberate hoarding of foodstuffs or certain essential commodities, giving short measures, cheating and fraud in business transactions. We shall look into some of these mandatory prohibitions in commercial transactions in more detail in Chapter 3.

## Period of the Noble Companions and the Succeeding Generations

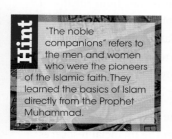

**Hint**

"The noble companions" refers to the men and women who were the pioneers of the Islamic faith. They learned the basics of Islam directly from the Prophet Muhammad.

While the basics of the laws regulating commercial and financial transactions were established during the era of the Prophet, the noble companions had no choice but to adhere tenaciously to the Prophetic precedents. The companions and the succeeding generations of believers built on the reforms introduced by the Prophet, as the Islamic state was gradually expanding to different parts of the world during this period. On top of such reforms, the level of commercial engagements between merchants in the Islamic state and other regions increased tremendously, leading to calls for more reforms in the light of such realities.

The *fiqh* or Islamic jurisprudence was further developed during this period because new socioeconomic questions emerged that had not existed during the time of the Prophet. The successive Caliphs, as the heads of state, had to carry out certain economic reforms based on their own judgment (*ijtihad*) after consultation with the Prophet's leading companions. These reforms were consistent with the general spirit of Islamic law as established by the Qur'an and Sunnah. The period of Orthodox Caliphate covered the period between 632–661 CE with the following four Rightly Guided Caliphs: Abu Bakr (632–634), Umar (634–644), Uthman (644–656) and Ali (656–661). During this 30-year period, there was economic transformation as each succeeding Caliph, at different times and in various degrees, introduced far-reaching reforms that shaped contemporary economic thought, particularly on Islamic banking and finance.

During the period of the first Caliph, Abu Bakr, the major economic problem he encountered was the failure of a segment of the Islamic state to pay the compulsory alms known as *zakat*. Several tribes rebelled against the payment of *zakat*: this subversive act was neither acceptable nor sustainable for the Caliph and the nascent Islamic state. In order to fulfill his promise as the new head of the state, Abu Bakr suppressed the revolt and consolidated the economic policies of the Prophet. The cardinal purpose of the institution of *zakat* is to create and maintain a sustainable society by requesting

*Bait al-mal*

The state treasury who deals
with mall economic matters,
including the revenue and
expenditure of the Islamic state.

those with reasonable means of income to pay a higher percentage in order to assist the less privileged in society. Since *zakat* as a major economic policy introduced by Islam is one of the five pillars of Islam, Muslims consider the denial of it as downright disbelief. The significance of *zakat* as a distributive tool in the process of wealth circulation and social security cannot be overemphasized and this further justified the need to suppress such rebellious tendencies within the budding Islamic state. There was a need to garner enough public funds to build the state and enrich the coffers of the public treasury to boost the state's financial resources. This was one of the major steps taken after the Prophet's demise to reposition the state-organized policy of public finance.

The second Rightly Guided Caliph, Umar, introduced dramatic reforms in economic policy, which have significantly influenced the modern Islamic banking and finance industry. Before his rule, there was no centralized public treasury. Any revenue received during the time of the Prophet was distributed immediately to those in need. Under Abu Bakr, although a place was earmarked as the public treasury, there was no practical need for it because most of the revenues received were distributed immediately. It is on record that Caliph Umar was the first to introduce a centralized and permanent **Bait al-mal**, or treasury house. Run by the state, it was responsible for the management of state treasury including revenue and expenditure. It administered the distribution of revenues from *zakat* and other sources of income that were developed by successive Caliphs. The establishment of this treasury house is a significant milestone in the history of Islamic finance, particularly when envisaging the role of an Islamic central bank in the modern world. All the economic policies of the Islamic state were formulated and implemented by the treasury house.

The continued expansion of the Islamic state during the reign of Caliph Umar simultaneously spurred an increase in state revenue and there was a need to create a central monetary agency to manage and effectively administer the financial resources of the state. Stipends were paid to the needy and the elderly who could not work. A noble companion, Walid bin Hisham, advised the Caliph to set up separate departments for treasury and accounts, just like the Byzantines. After due consultation with other leading companions, the Caliph decided to set up the treasury house in Medina and appointed Abdullah bin Arqam as the first chancellor. During this period, the official mediums of exchange were the dinar and dirham.

During the Caliphate of Uthman (644–656 CE), the first Muslim coins were struck, which ushered in a new economic regime. During this period, the revenue of the state further increased and there was a need to strengthen the management of the treasury house of the state. In order to promote and further consolidate the unprecedented welfare state established by Caliph Umar, Uthman increased the stipends given to the people by 25 percent, which increased living standards. The treasury house was not just a central body for the management of the financial resources of the state. Citizens often applied for benevolent loans, which they paid back on or before the due date. This was considered the right of all Muslims living in the Islamic state. Both the ruler and the ruled had an equal right to borrow any amount of money from the treasury house. In one narration the third Rightly Guided Caliph, Uthman, is reported to have borrowed 100,000 dirhams from the treasury house. Such financial incentives were not just made orally but documented. Uthman's loan from the treasury house was duly notarized by the chancellor Abdullah bin Arqam and witnessed by leading companions such as Ali ibn Abu Talib, Zubair, Talhah, Sa'd ibn Abu Waqqas, and Abdullah ibn Umar.

The Umayyad period witnessed significant development in Islamic financial policies. In 695 CE, the Islamic state minted its first Islamic dirham under the reign of the Umayyad Caliph Abd al-Malik bin Marwan, who had served as chancellor of Medina. With his vast experience in the financial administration of state resources, he introduced landmark economic reforms. A viceroy of the Caliph sent to Kufah, Al-Hajjaj ibn Yusuf Al-Thaqafi, followed suit by minting pure Islamic coins in Kufah and Wasit.[11] Meanwhile, the Umayyad silver coins, though similar to the Persian coins that were in use before these reforms, contained the crescent, the star and *bismillah* ('in the name of God') around the rim. With these new coins, an end was put to the use of human and animal figures in the design.

As the Umayyad Caliphate had its capital in Damascus the treasury house was automatically moved there, where a bigger building was designated as the *Bait al-mal*. The huge amounts of money sent from different states under the wider Islamic state necessitated a proper organization of the central treasury but each state was allowed to establish treasury departments to manage their financial resources. These departments were subsidiaries of the treasury house. Similar economic and financial reforms took place in successive Umayyad caliphates, particularly during the reign of Caliph Umar bin Abd al-Aziz who went to the extent of paying the debts of the insolvent from the treasury house.

As a central financial institution of the Islamic state managed by the successive caliphates, the treasury house retained its significant role during the Abbasid, Andalusia, and the Mamluk eras. The dinar and dirham were still widely used as the mediums of exchange in financial transactions. Later developments such as colonialism and the fall of the last Islamic caliphate, the Ottoman Caliphate, ushered in a new financial regime at the international level and all traces of Islamic banking and finance gradually disappeared. It is, however, important to observe that there are formidable moves in the modern world to reintroduce the dinar and dirham as major mediums of exchange at the micro and macro levels of the world economy. In Malaysia, they have introduced the latest models of gold and silver coins in the state of Kelantan, in the north-east of Peninsula Malaysia, and Perak, the second-largest state in Peninsula Malaysia (see Box 1.2).

The gold dinar (L) and silver dirham (R) introduced in the states of Perak and Kelantan in Malaysia have generated controversy in the progressive Islamic finance industry in Malaysia over what constitutes legal tender.

## BOX 1.2: THE INTRODUCTION OF GOLD AND SILVER COINS IN TWO STATES IN MALAYSIA

In Malaysia, some states have reinvented the Islamic gold dinar and silver dirham as part of reforms towards reintroducing some of the old practices of the Muslim Caliphate. As a result, the Perak and Kelantan state governments in Malaysia have introduced dinars and dirhams, which contain about 99.9 percent of gold and silver purity respectively, equivalent to 24 karats. This state government-backed initiative has continued to generate controversy in the progressive Islamic finance industry in Malaysia. What constitutes legal tender under the relevant laws of Malaysia has been debated in different forums within the country and elsewhere, with the proponents and opponents of the gold dinar initiative holding on to their respective views. According to the Central Bank of Malaysia, the only currency valid in the country is the ringgit.

Meanwhile, the vanguards for a change in the financial system towards the traditional way of carrying out business have argued that the gold dinars and silver dirhams are not meant to replace the ringgit as legal tender but are new financial instruments for savings and investments with stored value that cannot be affected by global financial crises. They are produced in four denominations. The first is half a gold dinar, which weighs 2.125gm and is priced at US$115. The second denomination is one gold dinar, which weighs 4.25gm and is priced at US$230. The third denomination is two gold dinars, which weighs 8.5gm and is priced at US$460. The fourth denomination contains a set of silver dirhams priced at US$86. The table below summarizes the denominations, their weights and corresponding prices.

| Denomination | Weight (grams) | Price in US$ |
|---|---|---|
| Half gold dinar | 2.125 | 115 |
| 1 gold dinar | 4.25 | 230 |
| 2 gold dinars | 8.5 | 460 |
| Silver dirhams | – | 86 |

According to proponents of the initiative, for public entities such as state governments the issuance of gold dinars and silver dirhams is meant to diversify their reserves. At the individual level, people can use the uncommon opportunity to preserve their wealth. So, they consider the initiative as a new form of asset and wealth management in Islamic finance.

## Modern-Day Experiments in Islamic Finance

After the fall of the Ottoman Empire and the fragmentation of Muslim nations into different countries, many of which were colonized by different European powers, the prevailing banking and finance system was interest-based and its dominant effect was felt in Muslim countries across the world. There was a modicum of awareness among these Muslim communities of the need to return to their roots. Muslims are always conscious of the mandatory economic policies in the Sharī'ah through the Qur'an. Therefore, in order to test the modern practicability of some of the rules in the Qur'an and Sunnah within the context of local communities, there were pockets of experiments in Egypt, Malaysia, and Pakistan, which may be referred to as the embryonic stage of modern Islamic banking and finance.

## Initial Regulatory Reforms in the Banking Industry in Pakistan in 1962

This growing awareness triggered some major economic reforms in Pakistan. While Pakistan was on the verge of introducing Islamization policies in every sector in the country, certain reforms were initiated in the banking sector. Sweeping changes were introduced in the Banking Companies Ordinance in 1962, including the subsidiary laws and regulations, to make way for non-interest banking transactions in Pakistan. These actions spurred further developments that subsequently led to banks and financial institutions, including mutual funds, gradually eliminating interest from all transactions in the 1970s and 1980s. With these major reforms, Pakistan led the way for a banking industry that reflects the features of Islamic finance. The 1962 amendments introduced Islamic modes of financing such as PLS, leasing and hire purchase, and mark-up sales.

## Mit Ghamr Local Savings Bank in Egypt, 1963

The Mit Ghamr experiment is considered the first modern-day trial of Islamic banking. The Islamic saving bank, which was premised on PLS, was established in Mit Ghamr in the Nile Delta of Egypt by Ahmad A. El Naggar. The primary objective of establishing this financial institution was to introduce meaningful private initiatives to industrialize Egyptian villages through investment and savings. Box 1.3 presents the underlying considerations of the project.

These pioneering efforts raised awareness, particularly in some other Muslim countries, of the need to experiment with some Islamic modes of financing within communities. The Mit Ghamr savings project gave short-term, interest-free loans specifically for productive purposes. It also attracted funds from investors who wanted to invest their money in Sharī'ah-compliant products based on PLS, whereby profits and losses are shared between investors and the bank in accordance with predetermined ratios. Nine years after the pioneering Mit Ghamr experiment was begun, the bank was integrated into the Nasr Social Bank in Egypt in 1972.

## BOX 1.3: CONSIDERATIONS UNDERLYING THE PIONEERING MIT GHAMR EXPERIMENT

1. The basis of dynamic economic growth is an increase in the volume of savings.

2. The essential role of private savings, education in saving, and of credit expansion in the process of socioeconomic development is fully recognized.

3. Individual savings is primarily a personal matter and reflects a certain way of life. The promotion of thrift must therefore begin by changing current attitudes and habits.

4. There is considerable evidence from successful economic development models to indicate that the effective contribution of the masses in the development process cannot be overlooked. It hardly needs to be stressed that the economy of developing countries cannot be built up strongly and organically solely from the top. Therefore, involving the masses in the process of capital formation is essential.

5. It was obvious from the beginning that it would be somewhat impractical to establish a savings bank, such as those in other countries, owing to wide differences in economic, social and political climate, and to the nature of change in our country [Egypt] in contrast to others. Lack of private initiatives, entrepreneurs' ignorance in dealing with financial institutions, deterioration of the capital market, and lack of experience are instances of such factors.

6. To be most effective, development institutions must not be separated from the environment in which they operate. Their leaders should consider the cultural context in which they operate, so that the institutions reflect the people's needs and aspirations, and are consistent with their beliefs and spiritual virtues.

Source: El Naggar, Ahmad A. (2007). Islamic Banks in Egypt: A Model and the Challenge. In Pramanik, Ataul Huq. 2007. *Islamic Banking—How Far Have We Gone*, Kuala Lumpur: Research Centre, IIUM: p. 249.

**Tabung Haji**
The Malaysian Hajj Pilgrims Fund Board.

**Hint**

It is important to note that the establishment of *Tabung Haji* in Malaysia was inspired by Royal Professor Ungku Aziz, the father of the current Governor of the Central Bank of Malaysia, Dr. Zeti Akhtar Aziz. Dr. Aziz has made a tremendous contribution to the modern transformation of Islamic finance, not only in Malaysia but globally.

## The Malaysian Pilgrims Savings Board, *Tabung Haji* of 1963

The modern Islamic finance industry in Malaysia began with a humble initiative popularly called **Tabung Haji**, which is still in existence today. It started operating on September 30, 1963 and the management board was established in law in 1969. *Tabung Haji* simply means the pilgrims fund managed by the *Lembaga Tabung Haji* or Malaysian Pilgrims Management Fund. Its main functions are presented in Box 1.4. The fund was launched in 1963, the same year the Mit Ghamr experiment was launched in Egypt. The fund's primary objective is to manage the savings of prospective pilgrims by investing them in Sharī'ah-compliant investments within a given period of time. The returns of such investments plus the principal amount invested are used to facilitate their *hajj* (pilgrimage) to Mecca. Rather than distributing the returns to the investors directly, they are used to offset their *hajj* expenses and manage the whole exercise of the pilgrimage from Malaysia to Saudi Arabia and back.

## BOX 1.4: FUNCTIONS OF *TABUNG HAJI*

In accordance with the provisions of Section 4 of the Tabung Haji Act of 1995, these are the functions of the *Lembaga Tabung Haji*:

- general administration of the fund
- administration of all matters concerning the welfare of pilgrims from the planning stage to the execution stage of the pilgrimage
- entry into any partnership, joint venture, undertaking or any other form of cooperation or arrangement for profit-sharing with third parties after the necessary approval from the relevant minister
- acquisition of shares and securities in any corporation, public authority or other corporate bodies
- disposal, sale, hold or reissue of shares or securities
- establishment of a corporation to effectively manage any project or enterprise it embarks upon
- establishment of companies under the Companies Act of Malaysia to engage in an activity that is aimed at boosting the investment fund
- carry out any other duty permitted under the enabling law to facilitate the welfare of the pilgrims.

Source: The Tabung Haji Act 1995 (Act 535) (Laws of Malaysia).

*Tabung Haji* was established as a non-banking Sharī'ah-compliant savings institution under a Special Act of the Malaysian Parliament. The fund is managed by the Prime Minister of Malaysia's office, as statutorily required by the law. The success of *Tabung Haji* and the aim of the Malaysian government to introduce a Sharī'ah-compliant banking system led to the enactment of the Islamic Banking Act in 1983.

The modern Islamic finance industry in Malaysia began with *Lembaga Tabung Haji* (the Malaysian Pilgrims Management Fund). Headquartered in Kuala Lumpur, it was set up to manage the savings of prospective pilgrims by investing them in Sharī'ah-compliant products, with the returns being used to facilitate the pilgrimage to Mecca.

## The Founding of the Islamic Development Bank in 1975

To further the development of Islamic banks and financial institutions, the Islamic Development Bank (IDB) was established in 1974 as a multilateral development financing institution. Its primary role is to foster economic development among the member countries and Muslim communities in non-member countries across the world. The decision to establish the IDB was mooted and subsequently approved during the first meeting of the finance ministers of the Organization of Islamic Cooperation (OIC) on December 18, 1973. The administrative and management infrastructures were set up during a 20-month period and it officially commenced business on October 20, 1975.

At present, membership of IDB consists of 56 countries. The functions of the bank are:

- to participate in equity capital and grant loans for productive projects and enterprises, besides providing financial assistance to member countries in other forms for economic and social development
- to establish and operate special funds for specific purposes, including a fund for assistance to Muslim communities in non-member countries, in addition to setting up trust funds
- to accept deposits and to mobilize financial resources through Sharī'ah-compatible modes
- to assist in the promotion of foreign trade, especially in capital goods, among member countries, provide technical assistance to member countries, and extend training facilities for personnel engaged in development activities in Muslim countries to conform to the Sharī'ah.[12]

In summary, the bank's major financing operations, are loans development credits, equity financing, profit-sharing operations and foreign trade financing operations. The headquarters of the bank is in Jeddah, Saudi Arabia, with four regional offices in Rabat, Morocco; Kuala Lumpur, Malaysia; Almaty, Kazakhstan; and Dakar, Senegal.

## The Dubai Islamic Bank, Established 1975

A few days before the IDB officially commenced its business, the first world Islamic commercial bank was established in the United Arab Emirates—the Dubai Islamic Bank. It began functioning as a public limited company on October 1, 1975 on the basis of mandatory Islamic principles. This bank is the first fully fledged Islamic bank in the world. In contrast to IDB, the DIB is a commercial bank primarily established to perform all activities and undertake all transactions carried out by a conventional bank but streamlining such transactions according to the Islamic principles of finance. Its vision is to be the leading provider of innovative financial services in accordance with the Sharī'ah. In the three-year period from its founding to December 31, 1978, its total deposits reached more than 127 million dirhams. The bank operates five main business groups:

- retail banking
- corporate banking
- real estate

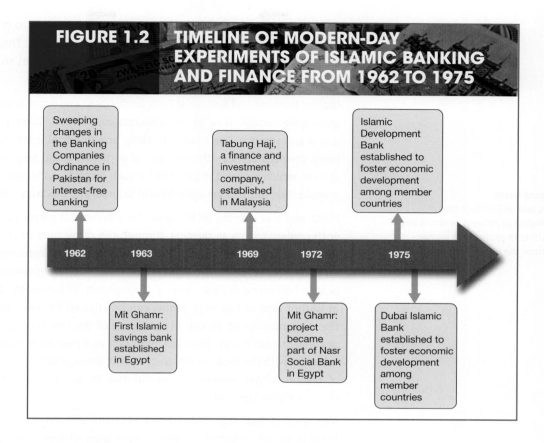

**FIGURE 1.2 TIMELINE OF MODERN-DAY EXPERIMENTS OF ISLAMIC BANKING AND FINANCE FROM 1962 TO 1975**

- investment banking
- proprietary trading investments.

The DIB has continued to grow in leaps and bounds over the years. It is considered one of the leading financial institutions in the modern world. Its current share structure comprises a 30 percent stake for the Dubai government, 4 percent for the UAE Federal Government Pension Fund, and 66 percent free float and others.

The modern experiment in Islamic banking and finance that kicked off in 1962 has developed from a niche industry to a global financial system that is now recognized as an alternative to conventional banking. Figure 1.2 illustrates the timeline from 1962 to 1975 that spearheaded the subsequent development of the industry.

## Conceptual Arguments for Islamic Banking and Finance

The conceptual argument for Islamic banking and finance in the modern world is based on the need to avoid unjust enrichment and appropriation of other people's property. Ethical banking and finance business is fair and just in the light of investors and depositors' funds. As described in Figure 1.1 on page 4, Islamic teaching governs all aspects of the community and goes beyond mere observance of the five daily prayers.

It extends to both the sociopolitical and economic matrixes of the society, which together are responsible for molding the Islamic personality. Thus, banking and financial business must be compliant with the principles of the Sharī'ah and the popular needs of the people.

Islamic banking and finance is both asset-based and asset-backed, which makes it real and viable compared to its conventional counterpart. There must be an exchange of goods and services. The Islamic banking and financial institutions are more than just profit-oriented bodies—the element of corporate social responsibility is built into the system, which makes it imperative for such institutions to also focus on rural areas and provide short-term loans (**qard hasan**) to small and medium enterprises.

**qard hasan**
A benevolent loan that is devoid of interest, without any share in profits that accrue from the use of such funds.

Profit and loss sharing (PLS) allows for a beneficial partnership between a bank and entrepreneurs, such as farmers, through the conversion of all interest-based loans to functional investments under PLS and interest-based consumption loans to interest-free benevolent loans. The contract between the entrepreneurs and an Islamic bank is based on an equity partnership through any of the modes of financing recognized in Islamic law. In this way, profits can be enjoyed by many in society, as opposed to the concentration of wealth in the hands of the few through the low-cost financing of conventional banks. With PLS, both rich and poor have equal access to investment activities with the banks and financial institutions, resulting in an equitable distribution of resources and economic opportunities in society that can enhance a country's economic development.

Moreover, it has been established that interest rates contribute to inflation but there is an anti-inflationary effect when interest-free banking is introduced into an economy. In Islamic banking and finance, inflationary trends do not affect depositors and investors because their funds are invested in lawful transactions that protect these funds from inflationary effects. The value of their money is preserved and even enhanced through equity partnership contracts between them and the financial institution, and yields are usually higher than the inflation rate. However, money deposited in a savings account at a conventional bank will have its value eroded by the inflation rate by the end of the year.

## The Development of Islamic Banking and Finance Industry

The Islamic banking and finance industry has passed through different stages of development in the past five decades. We shall not give its history here but instead discuss the gradual development of the industry from PLS outfits to the modern sophisticated Islamic banking and finance industry. Initially, the modern Islamic banking and finance industry in the 1960s was limited to commercial banking. Between the 1980s and 1990 there was a gradual expansion in Asian markets. This period also saw the introduction of Islamic insurance (**takaful**). Project financing was also introduced, mostly carried out with the support of the Islamic Development

**takaful**
An Arabic word meaning 'guaranteeing one another' is a mutual indemnity scheme in Islamic finance. This Islamic insurance is based on mutual cooperation.

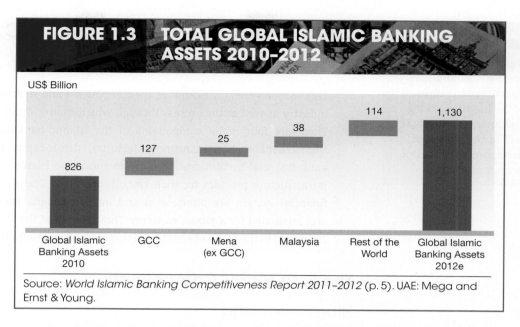

**FIGURE 1.3 TOTAL GLOBAL ISLAMIC BANKING ASSETS 2010–2012**

US$ Billion

Source: *World Islamic Banking Competitiveness Report 2011–2012* (p. 5). UAE: Mega and Ernst & Young.

*sukuk*
Islamic bonds. These are certificates of equal value representing an undivided share in the ownership of tangible assets of certain identified projects, services or usufruct.

Bank. In the 1990s, the oil shocks led to the rapid growth and expansion of the Islamic banking and finance industry as a result of the soaring net revenues derived from the oil boom. There was surplus foreign currency from oil revenues, which needed to be invested in other sectors. During this period, **sukuk** (Islamic bonds) and equities markets were introduced. Subsequently, the new millennium saw rapid growth in the industry, which led to its internationalization. Islamic funds and asset management were created alongside the structured products introduced during the same period. Figure 1.3 shows the estimated growth of total global Islamic banking assets between 2010 and 2012.

The tremendous growth in total global Islamic banking assets contributes to its continued penetration into the global market. Its resilient nature, particularly during the global economic meltdown of the early 21st century, has contributed significantly to this growth. "From a situation nearly 30 years ago when it was virtually unknown, Islamic banking has expanded to become a distinctive and fast-growing segment of the international banking and capital markets."[13]

We have discussed the important developments that have taken place in the Islamic banking and finance industry, but it is important to add that there is room for improvement. The legal and regulatory frameworks need to be developed further to meet the modern challenges it faces. Fortifying the legal and dispute resolution framework will enhance customers' confidence in the industry. The regulatory challenges have to be addressed to improve the level of customer satisfaction in the products and services offered by Islamic banks and financial institutions. In order to ensure socioeconomic development, a socially inclusive financial system is required through public participation in the process as the stability of the financial system is determined by the level of people's confidence and trust in it.

**LEARNING OBJECTIVE 1.3**

Understand the components and operating structures of the Islamic banking and finance industry as well as the process of development of Islamic finance products.

# Components of the Islamic Banking and Finance Industry

This section generally examines the components and structures of the Islamic finance industry as well as the process through which Islamic finance products are developed. There are four major components of the Islamic banking and finance industry—Islamic banking, Islamic insurance (*takaful*), Islamic capital markets, and Islamic non-bank financial institutions. Apart from these, the Islamic financial architecture and infrastructure provides for their smooth operation. These components of the Islamic financial system are interrelated and interdependent. Each needs to be developed and integrated for a robust economy. Though each of the above components is closely examined in the relevant chapters of this book, let us briefly study what they mean here.

## The Four Major Components

### Islamic Banking

The banking component of Islamic financial services comprises deposit-taking and financing institutions strategically established to cater for the needs of Muslim customers and investors who choose ethical banking in the modern world. The Islamic banking component may be fully fledged Islamic banks, or Islamic subsidiaries or 'windows' of conventional banks. The fully fledged Islamic banks are institutions licensed to carry out Islamic banking business alone. Examples of fully fledged Islamic banks include Dubai Islamic Bank, Bank Islam (Malaysia), Islami Bank Bangladesh Limited, Qatar Islamic Bank, Al Rajhi Bank, Islamic Bank of Britain, Bahrain Islamic Bank, Al Baraka Bank, Kuwait Finance House, Bank Melli Iran, and Jaiz Bank plc. In some countries such as Malaysia, these and other categories of Islamic financial institutions (IFIs) are regulated by legislation specifically providing for full-scale Islamic banking operations.

**Challenge**

Aside from those mentioned here, list 10 other fully fledged Islamic banks you know.

Among the Islamic subsidiaries and windows of conventional banks, prominent examples include HSBC Amanah, University Islamic Financial Corporation (based in Ann Arbor, Michigan), Citi Islamic Investment Bank, and Standard Chartered Saadiq. In this last case, the Islamic component of a conventional bank is a subsidiary banking institution of the holding company, which is a conventional bank. Islamic subsidiaries necessarily have their own board of directors, and a unique, exclusive Sharī'ah supervisory board. As reported in the *Financial Times* (see panel opposite), the Qatar Central Bank issued a directive to all conventional banks with Islamic windows to close them by the end of 2011 and this directive was complied with.

The third model of Islamic banking in practice is an Islamic window whereby a division is designated within an existing conventional bank to undertake Islamic banking business. That is, Islamic products are structured and packaged in the conventional bank to attract customers who prefer Islamic banking products. These are not fully fledged subsidiaries or windows but they operate within the same corporate entity of the conventional financial institution. Examples of these banks include most of the conventional banks offering

# ISLAMIC FINANCE IN THE NEWS
## Islamic directive shocks Qatari banks

**February 14, 2011**

**A** directive by Qatar's central bank has perplexed and infuriated bankers and analysts in the gas-rich emirate.

The central bank this month ordered conventional banks to close their Islamic banking operations by the end of 2011. This deadline is less than a year since the regulator's Islamic 'window' rules were sharpened, and six years after it first permitted conventional banks to make Islamic loans.

'The conventional banks are livid about it. It was very unexpected,' says a Dubai-based analyst. 'They're now scratching their heads on why the central bank did this, and how they will deal with it.'

The central bank has argued that with tailored Islamic banking regulations and capital adequacy regimes about to be introduced – based on guidelines by the Malaysia-based Islamic Financial Services Board, an industry standards body – it would be 'very difficult' for commercial banks with mixed operations to follow both these and conventional banking rules.

Some experts argue that the central bank has made a valid point, given the important differences between Islamic and conventional lenders, and say the circular could introduce more clarity and standardization.

'There are clearly issues around supervision and oversight which make Islamic windows more susceptible to risk from a regulator's perspective,' Amjad Hussain, a partner at Eversheds, the law firm, says.

Nonetheless, analysts say the new measures will have a significant short-term effect on Qatari conventional banks.

Moody's Investor Service estimates these banks could lose between 8 percent and 16 percent of their deposit bases, assets and profits. It adds that the move would be 'credit negative' for the conventional bank sector.

Qatar National Bank, the largest commercial bank, would be the worst affected. It has a 20 percent market share in Islamic banking, and its Shari'ah-compliant window contributes about 15 percent of its net profits, assets and deposits.

While only about 4 percent of revenues at Commercial Bank of Qatar, the second-largest lender, are derived from Islamic banking, Doha Bank, the third-largest financial institution in the country, could lose about 9 percent of its net operating income, according to Moody's.

The shares of 'pure' Islamic banks, such as Masraf Al Rayan and Qatar Islamic Bank, have rallied on the central bank's move, but the conventional banks have dipped.

It is uncertain from the circular whether international banks with Islamic arms, such as HSBC Amanah and Standard Chartered's Saadiq, could also be affected. HSBC has said it is 'communicating with the Qatar Central Bank to seek clarification on this issue'.

There are indications that the central bank has softened its stance. Raghavan Seetharaman, the chief executive of Doha Bank, said last week that while the lender would not be taking on new customers, it would not be forced to close its Islamic banking unit, and would continue to meet 'existing obligations'.

Some analysts hope the conventional banks, all of which are partially owned by the government, will be able to persuade the central bank to rescind its directive, or allow banks to spin off their Islamic operations, or at the very least extend the tight deadline.

'Unwinding these deposits, loans and corporate relationships is extremely complicated,' the Dubai-based analyst says. 'Banks will be pushing back, if only to get more time and clarify the details.'

Whatever the outcome, some experts argue the suddenness of central bank's move, and lack of consultation with the commercial banks, raises questions over its ability as a regulator.

'The Qatari regulator has had a good reputation until now, but this was an extreme and abrupt move,' the analyst says.

**Source:** Robin Wigglesworth, "Islamic directive shocks Qatari banks", *Financial Times*, February 14, 2011.

Islamic finance products in the United States of America. These include Devon Bank, Broadway Bank of Chicago and RomAsia Bank. Table 1.1 presents a full list of products offered by these banks as well as other banks within their conventional banking umbrella.

| TABLE 1.1: Islamic Finance Components of Conventional Banks in the USA | | | | |
|---|---|---|---|---|
| Financial Institution | Geographic Presence | Company Structure/Funding Source | Products Offered | Structures Used |
| **BANKS** | | | | |
| University Bank | • Headquarters: Detroit, Michigan<br>• Sharī'ah-compliant products offered in: California, Connecticut, Idaho, Maryland, Michigan, New Jersey, New York, Ohio, Pennsylvania, Virginia | • State chartered bank<br>• Financing products are offered through its wholly owned subsidiary, University Islamic Financial | • Residential real estate financing<br>• Deposit product<br>• Money market product<br>• Mutual funds | • *Murabahah* and *ijarah*<br>• Profit sharing deposits<br>• Mutual funds offered by HSBC Amanah |
| Devon Bank | • Headquarters: Chicago, Illinois<br>• Sharī'ah-compliant products offered in: Alaska, Alabama, Arizona, Arkansas, California, Colorado, Connecticut, Florida, Georgia, Idaho, Indiana, Kansas, Kentucky, Georgia, Idaho, Indiana, Kansas, Kentucky, Louisiana, Massachusetts, Michigan, Minnesota, Missouri, Nebraska, North Carolina, North Dakota, New Hampshire, New York, Ohio, Oklahoma, Oregon, Pennsylvania, Rhode Island, South Carolina, South Dakota, Tennessee, Texas, Utah, Virginia, Washington DC, Wisconsin, Wyoming | • State chartered bank<br>• Financing products are offered through its wholly owned subsidiary | • Residential real estate financing<br>• Commercial real estate financing<br>• Real estate construction financing<br>• Lines of credit<br>• Cash management<br>• Business and trade financing<br>• Institutional deposits products<br>• Investment products<br>• Trust and advisory services | • *Murabahah* and *ijarah*<br>• *Musharakah*<br>• Profit sharing deposits<br>• Mutual funds offered by third party providers |
| Broadway Bank of Chicago | • Headquarters: Chicago, Illinois<br>• Sharī'ah-compliant products offered in Illinois only | • Community bank | • Residential real estate financing<br>• Commercial real estate financing | • *Ijarah* |
| RomAsia Bank | • Headquarters: Monmouth Junction, New Jersey | • State chartered bank | • To be determined | |
| Lincoln State Bank | • Headquarters: Chicago, Illinois<br>• Sharī'ah-compliant products offered in Illinois only | • State chartered bank | • Residential real estate financing | • *Ijarah* |
| Mutual Bank | • Headquarters: Chicago, Illinois<br>• Sharī'ah-compliant products offered in Illinois only | • State chartered bank | • Commercial real estate financing | • *Murabahah* |
| Cole Taylor Bank | • Headquarters: Chicago, Illinois<br>• Sharī'ah-compliant products offered in Illinois only | • State chartered bank | • Commercial real estate financing | • *Murabahah* and *ijarah* |

Source: Shayesteh, A. (2009). Islamic banks in the United States: breaking through the barriers. *New Horizon* (April–June 2009): p. 3.

## *Takaful* (Islamic Insurance)

**retakaful**
The Islamic alternative to reinsurance. It is structured in a Shari'ah-compliant model.

The *takaful* component of Islamic financial services presently comprises Islamic insurance and reinsurance (**retakaful**) products. These play a significant role in managing and mitigating risks in Islamic banking and finance. The *takaful* is based on the principles of mutual cooperation and assistance for the general good of society. Unlike conventional insurance policy, which is individual-centric, communal welfare and mutual assistance are at the core of *takaful*. Other segments of Islamic financial services need *takaful* to mitigate and effectively manage all forms of risks in banking and finance.

*Takaful* is an alternative to the age-long practice of conventional insurance. Despite the fact that certain forms of arrangements existed among earlier Muslim communities for mutual assistance, Islamic insurance was never developed into its modern form until recently, when Muslims realized that this aspect of Islamic finance could also be explored to benefit people in various ways. The majority of contemporary scholars established the validity of Islamic insurance from the perspective of mutual cooperation and mutual social security. The wider application of *takaful* may involve a large number of people, which will necessarily be more than two individuals. Though the definition given here refers to mutual risk, some scholars have extended *takaful* to life insurance.

Insurance is a veritable mechanism in finance generally and it has enough potential in Islamic finance. The development of modern *takaful* began with the debate about the legality or otherwise of conventional insurance schemes. This was resolved by the International Islamic Fiqh Academy in its Resolution No. 9 of 1985, where it held that an insurance contract that conforms to Islamic principles based on cooperative and charitable undertakings is valid under the Shari'ah.

This drove some Muslim countries to come up with the framework for Islamic insurance. Thus *takaful* was developed as a component of Islamic finance, as it grew with other components such as the Islamic banking industry and the Islamic capital markets. Islamic banks and financial institutions require *takaful* to operate, especially when they engage in equity partnership products, which are prone to risk. In order to maintain its tremendous growth in the global economy, the Islamic finance industry needs to scale up its *takaful* component to remain competitive. *Takaful* has become the fastest-growing insurance industry globally, especially during and after the global economic meltdown of the early 21st century. As illustrated in the panel on page 26, Islamic Finance in Practice, at the heart of the meltdown giant insurance companies in the west such as the American International Group (AIG) realized the potential of *takaful*, AIG set up its *takaful* window in Bahrain.

## ISLAMIC FINANCE IN PRACTICE

# American International Group Ventures into *Takaful*

At the peak of the 2008 global financial crisis, the international insurance giant, AIG ventured into Sharī'ah-compliant products. This was not surprising as other international giants such as Allianz, Aviva, and HSBC have also moved into *takaful*. This development, which was met with stiff opposition, spurred much controversy in the United States of America. It even became the subject of litigation, which eventually led to the striking out of the action by the court. Before the global financial crisis emerged, AIG had earlier established AIG Takaful Enaya in April 2006 in Bahrain in order to offer *takaful* products such as auto, accident and health, and energy. AIG Takaful Enaya is incorporated under the Laws of Bahrain and it was licensed by the Central Bank of Bahrain. Just like other Islamic financial institutions, it has a functional Sharī'ah supervisory board which is composed of three prominent Sharī'ah scholars—

Sheikh Nizam Yaquby, Dr. Mohammed Ali Elgari and Dr. Muhammad Imran Usmani.

Further developments took place in the heat of the global economic crisis. In 2009, the Risk Specialists Companies, Inc. (RSC), a subsidiary of AIG, introduced a Sharī'ah-compliant homeowners insurance product. The product is based on mutual insurance advocated under the Sharī'ah. This is the first Sharī'ah-compliant homeowners *takaful* offering in the U.S. and it is available in all the 50 states of the country. The AIG considers the initiative as part of socially responsible investing guided by religious ethics. These developments have help to breach the gap between the East and the West as there is increasing dialogue on different fronts, the most prominent of which is the commercial intercourse between the two civilizations.

Source: Zuriah Abdul Rahman. (2009). *Takaful*: Potential Demand and Growth. *J.KAU: Islamic Econ.* Vol. 22 no. 1: 171-188.

## The Islamic Capital Markets

As a component of the Islamic banking and finance industry, the Islamic capital markets (ICM) are markets where investment activities are carried out in a manner that does not contradict the principles of the Sharī'ah. The market players include brokerage houses, investment banks, fund management institutions, and Islamic asset management institutions. Securities, markets, and products continue to evolve and this has affected the global capital market during the last two decades. The ICM has grown to become a significant segment of the global financial market. There is a growing awareness and demand for Sharī'ah-compliant investments across Muslim communities and this trend has enhanced the relevance of the ICM in the global economy.

The ICM is a special market where investment activities are carried out in ways that do not in any way contradict the requirements of Islamic commercial law. This application of ethical and prudent practices in the capital market is influenced

**interest-bearing** (*ribawi*)
Any product or transaction that has an element of usury or interest that is considered as unearned and undeserving income.

*maysir*
A game of chance or gambling that involves the acquisition of wealth by chance of winning without any form of consideration or compensation for such wealth.

*waqf*
A charitable endowment in perpetuity for a specific purpose. It is meant to assist the poor and the less privileged in the society.

*hajj*
The annual pilgrimage to Mecca enjoined upon able-bodied Muslims.

*zakat* (also written as *zakah*)
The compulsory alms giving to charity in Islam, which is meant for the redistribution of wealth in the society. It is an obligation on all adult Muslims who have wealth above a minimum threshold amount.

by Islamic legal thought and the market is free from prohibited elements such as **interest-bearing** transactions (*ribawi*), transactions that involve excessive risks (*gharar*) and other transactions tainted with elements of gambling (*maysir*). The ICM runs in parallel with the conventional capital market and this offers a unique opportunity for investors to choose the market that best suits their needs. One important regulatory advantage of the ICM is the establishment of international bodies to study, promote, develop and set new standards for the practical application of Islamic finance products. Such bodies include the International Islamic Financial Market (IIFM), Islamic Financial Services Board (IFSB), and Accounting and Auditing Organization for Islamic Financial Institutions (AAOIFI). As a result, investors find it easy to invest their money in Sharī'ah-compliant products, especially because of the resilient nature of the industry.

There are a number of Sharī'ah-compliant capital market products that are no different from the earlier discussed Islamic finance products. However, Islamic finance products have been designed to suit the needs of conventional markets while retaining the true nature of Islamic financial transactions. For a detailed discussion on the ICM and the relevant financial products used for the purpose of financing, turn to Chapter 7.

## Islamic non-bank financial institutions

These are Islamic financial institutions that engage in business activities that do not reflect the customary roles of Islamic banks. They include finance companies, Islamic housing cooperatives, Islamic leasing and factoring companies, Islamic microfinance institutions, **waqf** (charitable endowment) management institutions, private equity/venture capital firms, **hajj** (pilgrimage to Mecca), and **zakat** (compulsory alms) management bodies. These institutions support the liquidity needs of the major agents in the economy. They therefore play a facilitative role in Islamic society to ensure economic development through non-bank financing.

## Islamic Financial Architecture and Infrastructure

The architectural and infrastructural elements supporting the various components of the Islamic banking and finance industry includes:

- payment-settlement systems, legal institutions and framework
- risk management
- liquidity support providers
- corporate governance systems (which includes the Sharī'ah governance structure)
- standard setters for financial supervision and infrastructure
- rating and external credit assessment institutions
- financial statistics and information providers
- knowledge management and human resource development institutions
- research and development institutions.

These supporting institutions are necessary for sustainable practices in the industry.

## Operating Structures of the Islamic Banking and Finance Industry

Let us now examine how Islamic banks and financial institutions operate. The operating structures of the Islamic banking and finance industry in the modern world are founded on the conventional models practiced in Europe and America. The models have similar operating structures, which consist of basic functions, departmental structure, main layout, and mobilization of funds. The main difference is in the modes of financing adopted, which are based on the different underlying principles regulating the conventional banking system on one part and the Islamic banking system on the other part. The modes of financing of Islamic banks and financial institutions are structured within a regulated framework of Islamic finance.

The Islamic banking and finance industry has two key operating mechanisms: fund mobilization and fund utilization. The ways that funds are utilized can be classified under one of three modes: sharing modes, sale modes, and leasing modes (see Figure 1.4). Let's take a look at each of these mechanisms.

### Fund mobilization

**fund mobilization**
The process of raising funds to establish a viable financial institution through the sale of shares to investors and receiving funds from depositors.

**Fund mobilization** involves the positive mobilization of funds from shareholders, savings owners and investors. The funds mobilized are invested in an ethical manner through any of the equity partnership modes. The net equities of the bank are owned by the shareholders while the savings owners, who are the investors, participate in the equity investment activities of the bank. There are two broad categories of deposits utilized in Islamic banks: investment deposits and demand deposits. While the former allow investment account holders to share in a return on investment based on a predetermined ratio and the proportion of the amount invested, the latter do not earn any return as they are usually guaranteed because they are liabilities.

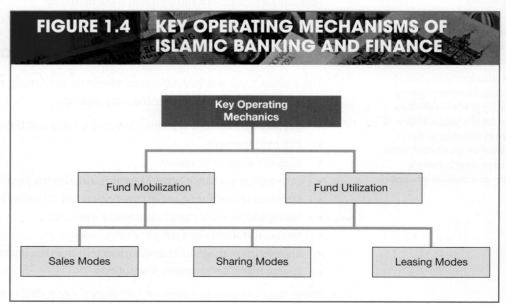

**FIGURE 1.4  KEY OPERATING MECHANISMS OF ISLAMIC BANKING AND FINANCE**

## Fund Utilization

**fund utilization**
The process of using the funds realized in Sharī'ah-compliant business.

The utilization of funds deployed is known as **fund utilization**. The modes of financing used by the Islamic banks are sharing modes, sale modes and leasing modes. All financing in Islamic banking and finance can be conveniently classified under any of these three modes.

### Sharing Modes

**sharing modes**
Partnership where the funds initially mobilized are invested in a Sharī'ah-compliant business and the parties share the profits or loss, whichever is applicable.

**Sharing modes** financing involves either full partnership or a non-voting partnership. In this regard, Islamic banks provide the necessary financing for a project with the anticipation of reasonable return as profits. This mode of financing may be referred to as *mudarabah*. The managerial decisions in the business are fully entrusted to the fund managers or entrepreneurs. Meanwhile, in the event of any loss, the capital provider loses the funds while the entrepreneur potentially loses his business.

### Sale Modes

**sale modes**
A mechanism where the bank purchases an item on behalf of the client and resells it to them either on a deferred basis or immediately.

**Sale mode** financing involves requesting the bank to buy certain commodities whose payment is deferred based on a mark-up price. Though there are different forms of sale modes financing, *murabahah* (cost-plus contract) is the commonly used Islamic financial product. However, this mode of financing can also be used in *istisna'* (manufacturing contract) or construction contracts, which involve deferred delivery of the subject matter of the contract.

### Leasing Modes

**leasing modes**
A financing mechanism that involves the rent of an asset or hire purchase where some form of rental fee is paid for a stipulated period of time mutually agreed by the parties.

The **leasing modes** involve the application of the *ijarah* contract and its different variables. This mode can be used for both medium and long-term financing. The banks may purchase machinery, equipment, or automobiles for the sole purpose of leasing or hire purchase. In a joint-ownership lease contract, the bank would receive a periodic share of the rental value of the asset in addition to the principal. Such assets may need to be insured and usually the parties to the contract share the cost of insurance in accordance with their respective proportions. The lessee becomes the legal owner of the leased asset after the full liquidation of all installments in accordance with the contractual terms.

## The Development of Islamic Banking Products

### Challenge

How relevant is Sharī'ah in the Islamic finance industry?

*ijtihad*
Independent legal reasoning by a competent Sharī'ah scholar who deduces the applicable law on novel issues from the sources of the Sharī'ah.

In practical terms, financial 'products' or 'instruments' are designed to solve a specific problem or attain certain objectives through financial means. Islamic banking products are the financial tools through which the financial institutions carry out their business.

There is a wide range of Islamic financial products being used as a mode of financing in Islamic financial institutions (IFIs) across the world. The classical products, which later became more sophisticated in modern times, form the basis of the development of new products. The early Muslim scholars employed the mechanism of **ijtihad** in deducing and developing new and Sharī'ah-compliant products. *Ijtihad* means independent legal reasoning by a competent Sharī'ah scholar who deduces the applicable law on novel issues from the sources of the Sharī'ah. Islamic finance products were initially based on the idea of equity partnership or partnership modalities generally.

With stiff competition from conventional financial institutions, there is a gradual drift towards debt-based finance products such as *murabahah* (cost-plus contract) and *bay al-salam* (forward contract). The idea of Sharī'ah-compliant products stems from the need to adopt modern financial products that do not contradict the underlying principles of Islamic law. Muslim scholars believe that if conventional finance products do not contradict the Islamic prescriptions, they can be endorsed as a Sharī'ah-compliant product. Islamic law permits the development and subsequent endorsement of financial products that satisfy the objectives of Islamic law and fulfill the interests of all concerned parties. Such products must have the potential to contribute to the general welfare of the people and economic development of the nation.

Without undermining the efforts of the IFIs' Sharī'ah boards in endorsing Sharī'ah-compliant products, it is the duty of Sharī'ah scholars to continue to closely study the classical books on Islamic law to come up with more competitive products that are Sharī'ah-based rather than always relying on conventional products. A comprehensive study conducted on Islamic finance products and instruments reveals about 1,357 products extracted from 14 sources. These products are still relevant in the modern era. Giving blanket approval to conventional finance products, which are not thoroughly scrutinized, would not be in the best interests of the Islamic finance industry because it would have fallen into the trap of product imitation.

Despite the fact that classical Islamic financial products have been limited to a single form of contract that involves equity participation, a careful study of the books on Islamic commercial law reveals a wide range of contracts, which includes exchange contracts (*mu'awadat*), partnerships (*musharikat*), securities (*tauthīqat*) and gratuitous contracts (*tabarru'at*). Practical applications of these forms of contract falls within the scope of Islamic finance products. Thus, any instrument based on a principle or concept of Islamic commercial law that seeks to address a specific problem relating to financial issues and brings mutual benefit to all the parties involved may be appropriately considered a financial product. It is therefore the duty of the scholars to design and develop it into a functional financial product within the framework of the modern practice of Islamic banking and finance.

**tabarru'at**
Gratuitous contracts or donations which include bequests and gifts.

In Islamic law, financial products are not only restricted to profitable dealings. Non-profitable dealings such as *zakat* (compulsory alms), *waqf* (charitable endowment) and **tabarru'at** (gratuitous contracts) may also be designed as financial products to achieve certain economic goals. These are all considered to be financial products in as much as they contribute to the economic development of society as a whole based on the concept of Sharī'ah-oriented policies (*siyasah shar'iyyah*).

In the Islamic financial markets, similar products based on the same principles have been developed for the Islamic capital markets. The products are equity-based and may be structured in the form of redeemable short-, medium-, and long-term partnership instruments that represent ownership in the underlying asset. In addition, Sharī'ah-compliant capital market products have been endorsed by scholars and also form part of the operating instruments in the Islamic capital markets around the world.

**LEARNING OBJECTIVE 1.4**

Describe the current size and worldwide spread of Islamic banking and finance.

# The Growth of Islamic Banking and Finance

In this section, we shall examine the growth of the Islamic banking and finance industry by looking at its size and the worldwide spread of IFIs, with a brief overview of some multinational Islamic banks. Finally, we shall take a brief look at the future of the Islamic finance industry.

Until relatively recently, the world was dominated by conventional banks. The first modern Islamic financial institutions were created in the late 1950s and 1960s as profit-sharing institutions that were later developed into full-blown financial institutions. However, the tremendous growth in the Islamic banking and finance industry in the past four decades presents more opportunities for expansion. The spread of Islamic financial institutions across borders and continents has integrated the industry into the global economy.

Islamic finance, as an ethical, interest-free regime built on PLS, is not only meant for Muslims. Many conventional financial institutions across the world, particularly in Europe and America, have established or are considering Islamic banking windows. Even though the underlying philosophy of Islamic banking and finance is firmly established in the Qur'an and Sunnah, its practice goes beyond faith-based practices, as it has now been accepted as an alternative to the conventional system that may be explored by anyone. This has brought new non-Muslim experts and professionals to Islamic banking and finance.

## Islamic Banking Today: the Size of the Industry

There has been a distinct upsurge of Islamic financial institutions around the world. With a modest beginning as profit and loss ventures, Islamic finance has developed into a competitive and innovative industry in the global economy. The globalization of Islamic banking and finance has greatly contributed to the growth in the industry. The dawn of the 21st century witnessed dramatic transformation in the international landscape of Islamic banking and finance. The many opportunities in the industry have been embraced by both Muslims and non-Muslims across the world. By the end of 2010, it was estimated that the total size of Islamic financial assets was more than US$1 trillion. Sharī'ah-compliant assets rose by 8.85 percent from US$822 billion in 2009 to US$895 billion in 2010, according to a 2010 survey of Islamic financial institutions practicing Islamic banking. By the end of 2011, the total estimate of Sharī'ah-compliant assets was put at US$1.3 trillion. In a similar vein, rapid growth was experienced in the Gulf Cooperation Council (GCC) countries over the last decade. Figure 1.5 shows the tremendous continuous growth recorded between 2003 and 2008, and by the end of 2008, the total assets of the Islamic financial institutions in the GCC countries had risen to US$288.2 billion.[14]

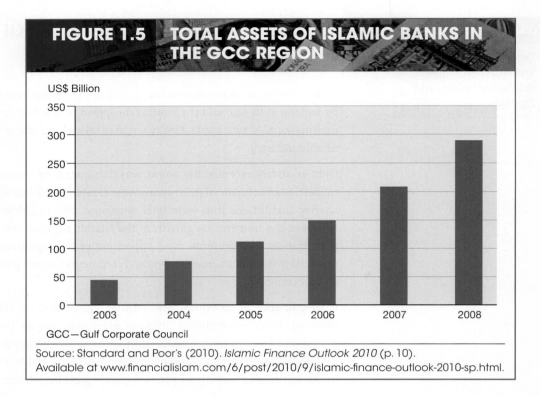

**FIGURE 1.5   TOTAL ASSETS OF ISLAMIC BANKS IN THE GCC REGION**

US$ Billion

GCC—Gulf Corporate Council

Source: Standard and Poor's (2010). *Islamic Finance Outlook 2010* (p. 10).
Available at www.financialislam.com/6/post/2010/9/islamic-finance-outlook-2010-sp.html.

"Islamic assets grew almost 21.5 percent in *The Banker's* 2011 survey, surpassing US$1000 billion for the first time. By contrast, assets in *The Banker's* Top 1000 World Banks survey in July 2011 had risen just 6.4 percent year on year—and that after a decline of almost 1 percent the year before."[15]

## The Worldwide Spread of Islamic Banking

Since the beginning of the 21st century, Islamic commercial banking experienced a dramatic surge in its products and areas of influence across the world. From the single pioneering efforts of the Dubai Islamic Bank in 1975 to the robust modern Islamic finance industry, there has been significant development in the spread of Islamic commercial banking, which has tremendously increased the total assets of the institutions. As shown in Figure 1.6, countries where Islamic finance has strong footprints are highlighted in red. Fully fledged Islamic banks and financial institutions exist in these countries.

The multinational Islamic banks include Al Rajhi Bank, Kuwait Finance House, Faisal Islamic Bank in Egypt and Sudan, and Jordan Islamic Bank. After the successful establishment of the IDB, Prince Muhammad Faisal started a bigger project to establish Islamic financial institutions in key Muslim countries. The necessary financial incentives and technical infrastructure were provided by IDB and banks such as the Dubai Islamic Bank, Jordan Islamic Bank, Faisal Islamic Bank of Sudan, Faisal Islamic Bank of Egypt, Kuwait Finance House, Islamic Bank of Bahrain and Nasser Social Bank

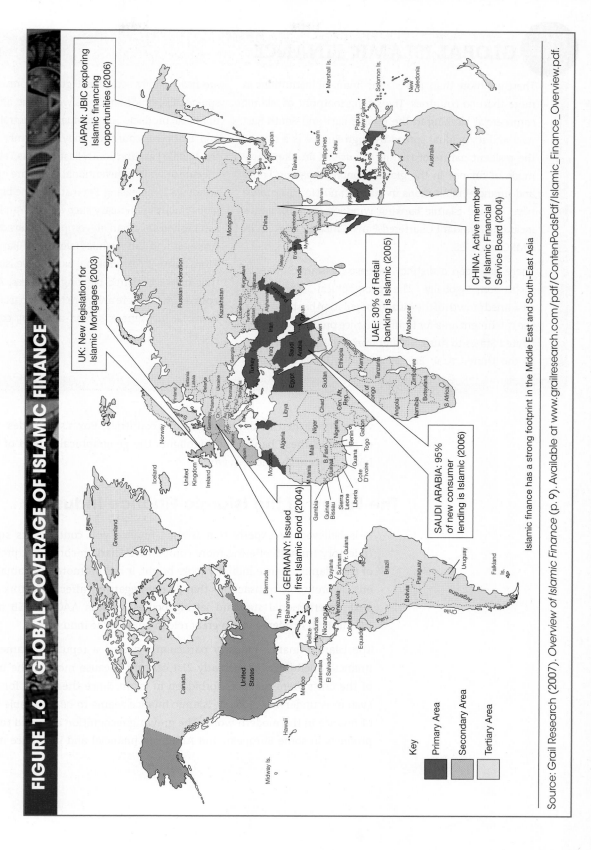

# FIGURE 1.6 GLOBAL COVERAGE OF ISLAMIC FINANCE

JAPAN: JBIC exploring Islamic financing opportunities (2006)

UK: New legislation for Islamic Mortgages (2003)

GERMANY: Issued first Islamic Bond (2004)

CHINA: Active member of Islamic Financial Service Board (2004)

UAE: 30% of Retail banking is Islamic (2005)

SAUDI ARABIA: 95% of new consumer lending is Islamic (2006)

Islamic finance has a strong footprint in the Middle East and South-East Asia

Key

Primary Area

Secondary Area

Tertiary Area

Source: Grail Research (2007). *Overview of Islamic Finance* (p. 9). Available at www.grailresearch.com/pdf/ContenPodsPdf/Islamic_Finance_Overview.pdf.

## GLOBAL ISLAMIC FINANCE

There are more than 300 Islamic financial institutions in more than 50 countries. The strong footprint of Islamic commercial banking in the Middle East and South-East Asia and its gradual spread through Europe is a sign of the resilient nature of Islamic finance as an alternative mode of finance in the global economy. Leading banks and financial institutions in Europe and North America have opened Islamic banking windows or subsidiaries, including Standard Chartered Bank, Citibank, HSBC, ABN AMRO, and UBS.

There has been a distinct increase in Islamic financial institutions globally. The geographical spread and sustained growth of the Muslim population has broadened the catchment area for Islamic finance products. From the United States to Australia and from the United Kingdom to the United Arab Emirates, Islamic finance products

are now readily available. Figure 1.6 presents the global spread of Islamic finance. As we can see, although Islamic financial products are gradually penetrating American and European countries, they are firmly established in the Middle East and South-East Asia. As Table 1.1 suggests, the rate at which conventional banks are opening Islamic windows is increasing. For instance, the big names in the global financial industry such as HSBC and Citibank have established the Sharī'ah-compliant subsidiaries of HSBC Amanah and Citi Islamic Investment Bank, respectively. More than 191 conventional banks have Islamic windows that transact Islamic banking business. According to a 2010 estimate, there are more than 430 Islamic banks and financial institutions spread across 75 countries in the world.

were established in different Muslim countries. Box 1.5 provides a brief overview of some of these banks, and highlights the geographical spread of Islamic financial institutions in the modern world.

## The Future of the Islamic Finance Industry

It is believed by experts that Islamic finance will continue its significant growth trajectory through offering more competitive Sharī'ah-compliant products. The future of the Islamic finance industry looks bright. It has promoted sustainable practices that ensure profitable transactions that do not negatively affect investors and shareholders alike. International standard-setting bodies such as AAOIFI, IFSB and International Islamic Fiqh Academy play a great role in guiding the industry.

The Islamic finance industry particularly gained a reputable name after the global financial meltdown in the early 21st century because most of the underlying causes of the crisis were practices forbidden in Islam. Since the search for a new monetary system is underway globally, Islamic finance seems to be a suitable alternative mode of finance in the modern world. The growing recognition accorded to Islamic financial products in some European and American financial and insurance institutions in the post-financial crisis era attests to this projection. According to a *Financial Times* report of December 2010:

> Islamic finance has weathered the storm. One of the world's fastest-growing asset classes before the financial crisis hit in August 2007 continues to expand, albeit at a slower pace. ... Islamic finance banking assets have risen by 8.9 percent this year, valuing the industry at US$895bn, according to the latest figures from *The Banker* and Maris Strategies. Since 2006, the industry has more than doubled in size, as more individuals and institutions have sought to save or invest in an Islamic, or Sharī'ah-compliant, way. This means avoiding earning money through interest, known as *riba*, which is seen as sinful under Islamic law as the creation of money from money itself is considered immoral.[17]

The future of Islamic finance in Europe has been examined by Rodney Wilson, Emeritus Professor at the University of Durham (featured at the beginning of this chapter), and it is believed that the volume of business among British Muslims will increase, which will invariably boost the Islamic finance industry in the United Kingdom. The global spread of Islamic finance products is expected to reach Latin America and other parts of the world.

## BOX 1.5:    OVERVIEW OF SELECTED MULTINATIONAL ISLAMIC BANKS

### Jordan Islamic Bank

The Jordan Islamic Bank (JIB) was established in 1978 as a public shareholding company in Jordan. It was primarily established to carry out all kinds of banking, financing, and investment business operations in compliance with Islamic law and in accordance with the existing laws in Jordan. The bank officially commenced business on September 22, 1979. One striking part of the JIB is that it is considered to be the first Islamic financial institution established through specific legislation. The bank was established under the Jordan Islamic Bank for Finance and Investment Act, Act No. 13 of the Government of Jordan (1978). In 2010, JIB was named the best Islamic retail bank in the world and the best Islamic bank group in Jordan by *World Finance* magazine in London.

### Faisal Islamic Banks, Egypt and Sudan

The Faisal Islamic Banks in both Egypt and Sudan were named after Prince Muhammad Faisal for his significant efforts in the establishment of IDB and other Islamic banks around the world. The idea of establishing the Islamic bank was adopted at a meeting in May 1977 between Sudanese and Saudi Arabian representatives. Faisal Islamic Bank was registered as a public incorporated company in Sudan on August 18, 1977 and commenced operations in May 1978. The bank was established to conduct all forms of banking activities (financial, commercial, investment) as well as to participate in economic development and social projects. It was also meant to promote transactions

**BOX 1.5** *(continued)*

and cooperation in the field of foreign trade, in conformity with Islamic law, and advance modern, developed banking techniques.

In a similar vein, the Faisal Islamic Bank of Egypt was incorporated under Law No. 48 of 1977 as an economic and social institution operating as a joint-stock company in compliance with Islamic law. This bank is the first Egyptian Islamic and commercial bank. It officially commenced operations on July 5, 1979. The main objective behind the establishment of the bank is carrying out all banking, trade and investment activities, financing economic and urban development projects in addition to performing various social services through the *zakat* fund. The bank thus aims to consolidate the basis of Islamic banking practices and develop it further by deducing and introducing successful practical applications of the legal concepts at the core of Islamic transactional jurisprudence.

### Kuwait Finance House

Kuwait Finance House (KFH) is the first Islamic bank founded in the State of Kuwait. Since its inception in 1977, KFH has recorded remarkable development and established subsidiaries in Bahrain, Turkey and Malaysia. It has also engaged heavily in investment activities in Europe, the United States, South-East Asia and the Middle East. As a market leader, KFH provides a wide range of Sharī'ah-compliant products and services in the area of banking, trade finance, real estate, investment portfolios and corporate, commercial, and retail financial markets. Its corporate values include:

- upholding Islamic principles and values in its organizational activities
- supporting ongoing initiatives of the global Islamic financing industry
- participating in and assisting with constructive socioeconomic endeavors of local communities as a responsible corporate citizen.[16]

### Al Rajhi Bank

The history of Al Rajhi Banking & Investment Corporation dates back to 1957. Al Rajhi Bank was originally established by Saleh bin Abdul Aziz Al-Rajhi and Brothers Co. for the provision of Islamic financial services through money exchange. This family-owned bullion arbitrage and money-changing business was later amalgamated in 1978 to form Al Rajhi Trading and Exchange Corporation. In 1987, it obtained a license to undertake banking operations in addition to its erstwhile transactions. Since then, it has been operating as a fully fledged Islamic bank. To date, Al Rajhi Bank is still controlled by the Al Rajhi family, with several members owning up to 46 percent of its total share capital. With branches in Malaysia, Kuwait, Jordan, and its original headquarters in Saudi Arabia, Al Rajhi Bank provides wholesale, retail and commercial banking, and investment services.

# Review

## Key Terms and Concepts

*Bait al-mal* (p. 12)

fund mobilization (p. 28)

fund utilization (p. 29)

*gharar* (p. 5)

hadith (p. 8)

*hajj* (p. 27)

ijtihad (p. 29)

interest-bearing (*ribawi*) (p. 27)

International Islamic Fiqh Academy (IIFA) (p. 4)

leasing modes (p. 29)

*maysir* (p. 27)

*qard hasan* (p. 20)

*retakaful* (p. 25)

riba (p. 5)

*Sa'a* (p. 10)

sale modes (p. 29)

*sarf* (p. 10)

Sharī'ah (p. 4)

sharing modes (p. 29)

*shirkah* (p. 10)

*sukuk* (p. 21)

Sunnah (p. 6)

*tabarru'at* (p. 30)

*Tabung Haji* (p. 16)

*takaful* (p. 20)

*waqf* (p. 27)

*zakat* (p. 27)

## Summary

**Learning Objective 1.1**

1. The conceptual basis of the modern practice of Islamic banking and finance is firmly rooted in the primary sources of the Sharī'ah—the Qur'an and Sunnah. Its origins lie in early Islamic history but the underlying principles have been developed to suit modern needs.

**Learning Objective 1.2**

2. The underlying principles of Islamic banking and finance in the modern world, from its historical origins to modern competitive products, present an alternative financial system. The crystallization of simple Islamic finance products into sophisticated and competitive products in the modern world has greatly contributed to the spread of Islamic banks and financial institutions.

**Learning Objective 1.3**

3. Though similar to conventional banking, the operating structures and infrastructure are largely influenced by the mandatory prescriptions of the Sharī'ah. The four major components of the Islamic finance industry are the banking sector, the Islamic capital market, Islamic insurance, and non-bank financial institutions. For a robust and sound Islamic finance industry, the Sharī'ah and regulatory framework must be strengthened to remain competitive in the global industry.

**Learning Objective 1.4**

4. The worldwide spread of Islamic banking and finance is evidenced by the establishment of more than 430 Islamic financial institutions in more than 75 countries around the world. The current state of the Islamic finance industry and the global spread of the banks and financial institutions have been graphically presented to indicate the significant progress that has been achieved. It is projected that Islamic finance products will filter through the European economy in the second decade of the 21st century.

## Practice Questions and Activities

## Practice Questions

1. Explain the conceptual basis of the modern practice of Islamic banking and finance.

2. With the aid of relevant Qur'anic verses and traditions from the Sunnah, explain the reason behind the prohibition of interest-bearing (*ribawi*) transactions.

3. Explain the origins of modern Islamic finance by juxtaposing the golden era of the Prophet with the development of Islamic finance in the 20th century.

4. Why should a faith-based banking and finance be introduced into the modern global economy?

5. What are the conceptual arguments for Islamic banking and finance?

6. Critically examine the operating structures and components of the Islamic banking and finance industry.

7. Write a short essay on the modern size of the Islamic banking and finance industry and the worldwide spread of its products.

8. What is the future of the Islamic banking and finance industry?

## Activities

1. Get three newspaper cuttings on the global spread of Islamic finance from your library.
2. Get the profiles of ten Islamic banks or financial institutions around the world.
3. Select three Islamic banks of your choice and get their latest annual reports.
4. Interview an Islamic finance expert on the growth and development of Islamic banking and finance in your country. Prepare the interview report for a 20-minute class presentation.

## Further Reading

Abdul Rahman, Y. (2010). *The Art of Islamic Banking and Finance: Tools and Techniques for Community-Based Banking*. New Jersey: John Wiley & Sons.

Ataul Huq, P. (2005). *Islamic Banking—How Far Have We Gone*. Kuala Lumpur: Research Centre, IIUM.

Ayub, M. (2007). *Understanding Islamic Finance*. England: John Wiley & Sons.

Buckmaster, D. (1996). *Islamic Banking: An Overview*. London: Institute of Islamic Banking & Insurance.

El-Gamal, M. A. (2006). *Islamic Finance: Law, Economics, and Practice*. Cambridge: Cambridge University Press.

Hassan, M. K. and Lewis, M. (2007). *Handbook on Islamic Banking*. United Kingdom: Edward Elgar Publishing.

Kettell, B. (2010). *Islamic Finance in a Nutshell: A Guide for Non-Specialists.* West Sussex, United Kingdom: John Wiley & Sons.

Oseni, U. and Hassan, M. K. (2010). The Emergence and Development of Islamic Banking. In *Islamic Finance: Instruments and Markets* (pp. 113–117). London: Bloomsbury Information.

Warde, I. (2010). *Islamic Finance in the Global Economy* (2nd edn.) Edinburgh: Edinburgh University Press.

Wilson, R. (2012). *Legal, Regulatory and Governance Issues in Islamic Finance.* Edinburgh Guides to Islamic Finance. Edinburgh: Edinburgh University Press.

# 2

# Islamic Contract Law

# Learning Objectives

**Upon completion of this chapter, the reader should be able to:**

1 Understand the underlying philosophy of business transactions in Islam.

2 Explain the meaning of contracts, and the legal concepts and theories of the various types of contracts in Islamic law.

3 Describe the classification of contracts, what constitutes a contract of sale, and the legal capacity to enter into such contract in Islamic law.

4 Analyze the main forbidden contracts in Islamic commercial transactions.

Obligations are meant to be fulfilled especially when they involve financial considerations. Justice, fairness, equity, and mutual satisfaction are the key factors that drive the Islamic law of transactions. The law regulating contractual matters is a product of divine revelation that ensures fair and just dealings. Even though the early jurists did not articulate a general theory of contract during the formative period of Islamic legal theory, significant developments were recorded in the later period, which culminated in the formulation of standard principles of contract.

Apart from the ethical considerations introduced into the Islamic law of contract, there is more to the Shari`ah framework that makes it distinct as a practical alternative mode of contract for Islamic financial transactions. In light of that discussion, this chapter examines the whole concept of contract in Islamic law with particular reference to the classification of contracts and the salient features of Islamic commercial transactions. The principles discussed in this chapter will be of immense benefit to those designing Shari`ah-compliant products based on certain contractual models in the Islamic law of transactions. More importantly, students of Islamic finance will be able to appreciate the unique features of Islamic contractual law and its significant role in shaping modern Islamic financial products.

## professional perspectives

**Dr. Mohamad Akram Laldin**
*Executive Director*
*International Shari'ah Research Academy for Islamic Finance (ISRA)*

**1  What is the relevance of Islamic contract law in modern banking and finance transactions?**

A contract ('*aqd*) is the basis of transactions in Islam. Islam emphasizes that dealings between two parties have to be founded on the notion of mutual consent (*al-rida*) (Qur'an, 4:29). This notion is translated into practice through the application of contract law in modern Islamic banking and finance transactions. The pillars of a contract—which consist of offer and acceptance, the contracting parties, and the subject matter of the contract—are the means by which mutual consent is realized. Offer and acceptance are the parties' expression of their willingness to contract. These can be expressed either verbally or in writing. In the modern context, they are reflected in the contract documents signed by the contracting parties, whose signatures are deemed to express their consent to all the terms in the contractual documents. The second pillar is the contracting parties; those who enter into a contract must have the legal capacity to do so for the contract to be valid. The last pillar is the subject matter, which must be clear of any ambiguity so that each of the contracting parties is aware of their obligation when entering into the contract. This will minimize any disputes arising from the contract.

**2  How have the underlying principles in Islamic contract law influenced product development in Islamic finance?**

Islamic contract law forms the basis of all products used in modern day Islamic financial transactions. Each and every product will have its own underlying contract, and the features of each product will depend on the principles underlying the particular contract used. For example, if the product uses a lease contract, the ownership of the lease asset will reside with the lessor, and the lessee will only have the right to the usufruct of the leased asset. As such, the maintenance costs shall be the responsibility of the owner. The classical types of contracts were developed by the scholars of early days, but there is always room for innovation. Even in the early days, there were innovations such as the contract of *wafa'* (sale), invented by the Hanafi scholars based on the needs of people at that time, which gives the seller the right to repurchase the sold item at any time by paying the original purchase price. New types of contract can be invented in order to cater to the fast-developing Islamic finance industry. The maxim that states '(in commercial matters), the default ruling is that things are permissible' demonstrates that innovation should be encouraged, particularly in commercial transactions.

## professional perspectives

**Abdulazeem Abozaid**
*Associate Professor at Damascus University and advisor to Islamic banks*

**1    What is the relevance of Islamic contract law in modern banking and finance transactions?**

Sharī'ah-nominated contracts represent the basis for all Islamic banking and finance transactions. These contracts are either readily found in the classic books of Islamic law or in modified versions adopted to suit the modern transactions of Islamic finance. Sometimes they are a combination of more than one contract designed to serve a particular financing purpose, such as the contract of *ijarah muntahia bittamlik* where the transaction starts with lease and ends with sale.

However, Islamic financial contract law is flexible enough to give people the freedom to generate totally new contracts provided the principles of the law are observed. It has been noted by Sharī'ah scholars that Sharī'ah texts, namely the Qur'an and Sunnah, merely provide general principles when it comes to financial transactions but rarely the specific details. This is due to the changeable nature of financial transactions, which logically entails laying down general principles and not specific details. Scholars of Islamic law across the history of Islamic legislation have developed many types of financial transactions based on these general principles, but contemporary scholars of Islamic banking and finance have favored working on adjusting existing conventional contracts to fit within the framework of Islamic law. This has, in fact, burdened Islamic banking and finance with some products that fail to reflect the Islamic transactional spirit, and it has also denied this industry the opportunity of achieving an unquestionable excellence.

**2    How have the underlying principles in Islamic contract law influenced product development in Islamic finance?**

Islamic finance derives its credibility from the declared full adherence to Sharī'ah rules embedded in Islamic contracts. However, the principles of Islamic law not only deal with the contracts' forms and structures but also, importantly, with their essence and spirit. Obviously, the two ends of this equation have not been given equal attention in the contemporary development of products in Islamic finance. Extra care has been given to the former at the expense of the latter, which has yielded controversy about some of the structured products. In fact, for the proper structuring of a product under Islamic finance, three aspects of the product must be well taken care of.

First is form, which relates to fulfilling the basic Sharī'ah structural requirements and conditions for contracts and contractors. A contract whose form is invalid has no legal consequences and is considered as null and void.

Second is substance, which is concerned with the essence of the structured product. This applies especially when more than one contract is involved in the structure as this may yield a controversial product, as is the case with *bay al-inah* or *tawarruq*. Two sale contracts are involved herein, each independently valid in essence, but the total outcome of having them consecutively executed is a highly controversial cash financing product.

Third is the spirit of the structured product that has passed the form and substance tests. It is a requirement that the implementation of the structured product does not lead to an evil or have unfavorable or negative impacts.

## Business Transactions in Islam

**LEARNING OBJECTIVE 2.1**

Understand the underlying philosophy of business transactions in Islam.

*fiqh al-mu'amalat*
The jurisprudence concerning transactions regulated by Islamic law. This covers all aspects of Islamic commercial contracts.

**vicegerency**
The concept of the representation of God's ruling on Earth, conferred on mankind.

*mu'amalat*
Commercial transactions between people regulated under the principles of Islamic law.

People are encouraged to earn a living through lawful means to cater for both their spiritual and mundane wellbeing. The Prophet Muhammad (PBUH) was a trader, before the clarion call to prophethood, who engaged in trans-territorial trades. In every trade, it is customary for the parties to conclude a contract, either written or oral. People engage in business transactions that are built on certain forms of contract. This human engagement, which transcends ideological and racial divides, is regulated in Islam through general and specific laws in **fiqh al-mu'amalat**. In pursuing its objectives, Islam encourages business transactions to secure the basic needs for all human beings, and these should be within the general ambit of permissible transactions. In essence, in order to effectively manage the resources that God has bestowed upon the world, transactions are involved.

The concept of **vicegerency** (*khilafah*) necessitates the propensity for the acquisition of property if people are to maintain their dignified status. Thus Islam establishes, through its numerous laws, the need to lawfully acquire property and validates all measures and policies towards the protection of that right. Stringent laws are in place as punitive measures to regulate any distortion in the economic equilibrium and people's freedoms within it. Distortion may be in the form of theft, bribery, unlawful gains that may be considered as usury, deceitful gains, or speculative transactions that amount to unnecessary risks.

Nevertheless, business transactions are a less-regulated aspect of Sharī'ah as they are generally classified under **mu'amalat** and subject to change over time and place even though the underlying philosophy is retained. Accordingly, the principle in *fiqh al-mu'amalat* is that all transactions are permissible unless tainted by prohibited gains or contracts involving usury, deception, speculation, undue profits, or engaging in trade of prohibited items. The underlying philosophy of commercial transactions in Islam is summarized in the following verses of the Qur'an:

> Qur'an 2:275: "Allah has permitted trading and forbidden usury."

> Qur'an 2:188: "And do not eat up one another's property unjustly, nor give bribery to the rulers (judges before presenting your cases) that you may knowingly eat up a part of the property of others sinfully."

Just enrichment through lawful acquisition of property is encouraged in Islam. As discussed in Chapter 1, the mandatory prescriptions of Sharī'ah for commercial transactions constitute an amalgam of ethical business transactions. This regime is an alternative model that has been proved to be efficient in the economic sphere.

## Lawful Earning Under the Sharī'ah

One of the fundamental objectives of the Sharī'ah is the right to lawful acquisition of legitimate property. This right is established, guaranteed, and protected by law. Muslims consider Islam to be a complete way of life that caters for both their mundane affairs and their spiritual requirements. The mundane affairs include the need to earn a living through legitimate means. Regardless of a person's gender Islam gives an unfettered right to the acquisition of property to all, subject to the general rules of the Sharī'ah. As the propensity to earn or acquire property is an innate character of humans generally, Islam regulates this right for the benefit of all. The regulations placed on lawful earnings in Islam are not meant to restrain the legitimate acquisition of property but are there to guide people on the proper manner to do so to avoid rancor and chaos in society.

### The Right to Earn a Livelihood

The right to earn legitimate wages or engage in business transactions is embedded in the higher objectives of the Sharī'ah. As noted above, this right was conferred on everyone —male and female—more than 1,400 years ago through the divine legislation in the Qur'an and Sunnah. Men and women are considered equal in matters of this kind; both have the right to enter into lawful transactions through contracts that are in accordance with the general principle of the Sharī'ah. The Qur'an says:

> Qur'an 4:32: "...For men is the benefit of what they earn. And for women is the benefit of what they earn. And ask Allah of His grace..."

This verse clearly explains the position of Islam on earning, in that people have the right to earn a legitimate means of livelihood. Hence, Islam encourages lawful earning.

In most cases, exercising this right involves a number of commercial transactions that will be discussed in this chapter. The virtues of manufacturing business and commercial transactions have been explained by the Prophet. For instance, Rafi' ibn Khadij narrated: "It was said: 'O Messenger of Allah, what kind of earning is best?' He said: 'For a man to work with his hands and every honest transaction.'"[1] This gives an idea of the nature of business transactions in Islamic law. Business ethics through fair dealings and honesty are highly emphasized in Islamic law. In another narration, Al-Miqdam wrote that the Prophet once said: "No one ever eats anything better than that which he earned with his own hands. Prophet Dawud (peace be upon him) used to eat that which he earned with his own hands."[2] In explaining this hadith, scholars have differed on the best type of work. According to Imam al-Mawardi, the best ways through which one can earn a living are agriculture, trading, and manufacturing. Al-Nawawi prefers a particular means of livelihood whereby people earn their living with their own hands regardless of the type of work, in line with the hadith quoted above.

In accordance with the directives in the above Prophetic traditions, both men and women engaged in commercial transactions, which involved contracts, during the time of the Prophet. In fact, the Prophet's first wife Khadijah was an entrepreneur in Mecca who earlier engaged the services of the Prophet as an experienced trader to manage her businesses. While managing Khadijah's businesses, the Prophet entered into series of contracts with merchants and customers.

Through the divine legislations in the Qur'an and Sunnah, men and women are considered equal regarding the right to earn legitimate wages or engage in transactions.

## Ways in Which the Prophet's Companions Earned their Living

The Prophet's companions earned their living through different legitimate ways. The following glimpse into some of those ways may not be totally applicable to the modern era, but some insights can be taken from these precedents. Every era is different, with its particular ways of earning, but the underlying principle is that whatever way one chooses to earn a living the form and substance must be legitimate, i.e. the method of earning and the object of the process must be lawful in the eyes of Sharī'ah. Leading companions of the Prophet, such as Abu Bakr, Uthman ibn 'Affan and 'Abdul Rahman ibn 'Awf engaged in lawful trade and the proceeds were spent on the development of the Muslim community. Business and trade was the most common form of work during the era but some migrants and helpers in Medina also engaged in agriculture. Some companions were reported to have owned farmland while others were involved in skilled crafts such as smithery and carpentry. There were also professional jobs connected to the state, such as teaching, the giving of compulsory alms (*zakat*), and adjudication of disputes.

Lawful business and trade are considered to be the best mode of earning but must be carried out in accordance with laid-down principles governing any contract concluded by the parties involved. Therefore, legitimate money earned through hard work is rewarding from both the financial and spiritual perspectives.

## Unlawful Earnings

**Challenge**

In your opinion, do you think Islamic banks stipulate excessive charges and fees for services rendered to their customers?

The Qur'an and Sunnah prohibit unlawful gains in strong terms. The right to earn a means of livelihood is limited to the lawful acquisition of property. Any further step towards the appropriation of property belonging to another person or the state as a whole is considered unlawful gains. This includes excessive gains in business transactions and undue profits, which should be avoided in contractual dealings. Excessive commission and service charges by some banks and financial institutions fall under this prohibited list. Through a number of verses in the Qur'an, Allah has prohibited the exploitation of fellow beings while acquiring one's property. The legal text prohibiting excessive gains in the Qur'an says:

> Qur'an 2:188: "And do not eat up one another's property unjustly, nor give bribery to the rulers (judges before presenting your cases) that you may knowingly eat up a part of the property of others sinfully."

This general rule applies to different transactions within a state. It extends to management of state funds and contractual transactions entered into with others. Simply put, excessive gains or undue profits amount to eating other people's property, as pointed out in the verse. Thus, usurping the rights of others through disproportionate and top-heavy charges by financial institutions is prohibited in Islamic law. The Prophet consistently called for fair and just trade dealings to the extent of prohibiting the act of hiding defects in commodities on sale or incorporating ambiguous elements in the underlying trade contract.

Though the forbidden elements in Islamic commercial transactions are discussed in the last part of this chapter, it is important to point out that gains derived from the following sources are prohibited in Islamic law:

- earning a living through money lending that involves usury
- trading in prohibited items such as intoxicating wine, pork, and dead animals
- gambling and lotteries
- offering short measures in trade
- hoarding to inflate prices at a later time
- adulterating commodities and trading in defective items
- earning through prostitution
- misappropriating public funds.

The panel on page 48, *Islamic Finance in Practice*, presents the ruling of the International Islamic Fiqh Academy on undue exploitation of others through the inflation of prices beyond the market value. A common thread in the prohibited list given above is exploitation of other people's financial resources through unhealthy business dealings. This is because commerce plays a significant role in the Islamic economic system. Thus, all business dealings are required to be conducted among contracting parties in a fair and just manner. In light of this, any earnings received from clean and just business dealings or work are permissible in Islam.

Explain the meaning of contract and the legal concepts and theories of the various types of contracts in Islamic law.

**'aqd**
A contractual transaction involving two or more parties.

**talaq**
The legal dissolution of marriage in accordance with Islamic law.

**wasiyyah**
The statement or will of a Muslim testator where it is stipulated how a limited portion (up to one-third) of the testator's estate is to be disposed after their demise.

**nikah**
The marital union between a male and female in accordance with the rules of Islamic law.

# Islamic Contract Law

This section explains the juristic definitions of contract in Islamic law, nature of contracts and affirmative evidence in the prime sources of the Sharī'ah.

## Definition of Contract in Islamic Law

In Arabic philology, the term for a contract is **'aqd**. Though it has a number of meanings, *'aqd* means to tie between two ends, to fasten, to link. In Islamic law, it means an agreement, commercial arrangement, legal transaction, document, or deed. Muslim jurists have given numerous definitions for the word *'aqd* but all are based on two major interpretations of the term one general and one specific. In the general sense, *'aqd* can be defined as any thing or disposition that is intended to be performed by a person of their own will or through mutual agreement. For example, unilateral contracts such as *waqf*, **talaq** (divorce), **wasiyyah** (bequest), or **nikah** (marriage). On the other hand, the word *'aqd* has been given a specific interpretation that has resulted in its restricted usage. According to this specific interpretation, a contract can be defined as an agreement among contracting parties that is concluded through an offer and acceptance with the consequences of binding legal obligation.

A *'aqd* contract is an agreement between two or more parties on a particular subject matter identified by them that is to be concluded through offer and acceptance and

# ISLAMIC FINANCE IN PRACTICE

A daily occurrence in the Islamic finance industry is continuous consultation with the Sharī'ah scholars, who go through different forms of contracts brought before them by Islamic financial institutions to avoid running foul of the provisions of Islamic law. They vet the contracts in detail and advise the financial institution accordingly to uphold the mandatory requirements for every contract in Islamic law. Despite the volume of Islamic finance contracts produced every day, there has been a consistent practice of vetting on the part of the Sharī'ah scholars to ensure compliance. For instance, the International Islamic Fiqh Academy was asked about limiting profit margins for traders. It ruled as follows.

**First:** The basic principle in the Qur'an and the Sunnah of the Prophet is that a person should be free to buy and sell and dispose of his possession and money, within the framework of Sharī'ah, in accordance with the divine command: 'O ye who believe! Consume not each other's property in vanities, unless there is trade based on mutual acceptance'.

**Second:** There is no restriction on the percentage of profit which a trader may make in his transactions. It is generally left to the merchants themselves, the business environment and the nature of the merchant and of the goods. Care should be given, however, to ethics recommended by Sharī'ah, such as moderation, contention, leniency and indulgence.

**Third:** Sharī'ah texts have spelt out the necessity to keep the transactions away from illicit acts like fraud, cheating, deceit, forgery, concealment of actual benefits, monopoly, which are detrimental to society and individuals.

**Fourth:** Government should not be involved in fixing prices except only when obvious pitfalls are noticed within the market and the price, due to artificial factors. In this case, the government should intervene by applying adequate means to get rid of these factors, the causes of defects, excessive price increases and fraud.

This resolution touches on different aspects of Islamic contractual transactions. It enumerates a number of vitiating elements in contractual transactions, which must be regulated to protect consumers. This regular practice of Sharī'ah supervision has been the saving grace of the entire Islamic finance industry.

Source: *Resolutions and Recommendations of the Council of the Islamic Fiqh Academy (1985–2000).* (2000). Jeddah: Islamic Fiqh Academy and Islamic Development Bank: pp. 93–94.

**Majallah al-ahkam al-adliyyah**
(also known as the *Mejelle*)
The famous and often-cited
Islamic civil code of the
Ottoman Empire which
also contains a number of
provisions relating to Islamic
commercial transactions.

triggers an obligation upon them. There must be consensus *ad idem* among the parties before it can be regarded as a binding contract. Contractual agreements are highly regulated by the Sharī'ah to ensure equity and a fair exchange of resources in an open market. According to Articles 103–104 of **Majallah al-ahkam al-adliyyah**, the Islamic civil code of the Ottoman Empire:

> *'Aqd* is the two parties taking upon themselves an undertaking to do something. It is composed of the combination of an offer (*ijab*) and acceptance (*qabul*). The making of *'aqd* is connecting in a legal manner, one's offer (*ijab*) and acceptance (*qabul*) with the other, in a way which will be clear evidence of being mutually connected.[3]

**consideration**
Something that has a value
given by one party to a contract
in return for a benefit or
promise from the other party
of the contract.

Al-Sanhuri defines the term *'aqd*, while approving the definition given by the author of *Murshid al-Hairan*, as "the conjunction of the offer emanating from one of the two contracting parties with the acceptance of the other in a manner that it may affect the subject matter of the contract. It is further explained that as a result of this conjunction both are under obligation to each another. It therefore follows from this that the origin of a contract in Islamic jurisprudence is an obligation."[4] The obligation to undertake certain actions in exchange for some sort of **consideration** represents the underlying spirit behind every valid contract.

It is thus clear that the lexical meaning of *'aqd* is not so different from its juristic meaning as the link or nexus between two things is the definition given for the former while the link or nexus between the disposition of two contracting parties with regards to a particular subject matter is that of the latter. With this analysis, there must always be a link between the two contracting parties or two things to have a valid contract. This is why the meeting of minds among the parties to the contract is considered one of the most important elements of a contract. All Islamic financial operations are carried out through such contractual arrangements.

## Nature of Contract and Related Terms—*Wa'ad, Muwa'adah, and 'Aqd*

**wa'ad**
A unilateral promise that binds
the maker alone.

**muwa'adah**
A bilateral promise in
commercial transactions
that binds both parties when
inculcated into a contract.

Although the general term for contract is *'aqd* in Islamic law, other related terms include *wa'ad* and *muwa'adah*. While **wa'ad** is a binding unilateral promise, **muwa'adah** is a bilateral promise in commercial transactions. Therefore, *'aqd* may be said to be a general term for contract while its different varieties may include both *wa'ad* and *muwa'adah*. *Wa'ad* is a unilateral undertaking and *muwa'adah* is a bilateral undertaking. All forms of contract fall under either of these two classifications.

**murabahah**
Cost-plus financing contract where a sale is made at a specified profit margin.

**Islamic hire-purchase contract (al-ijarah thumma al-bay')**
A lease agreement where the lessee gives a binding commitment or promise to purchase the underlying asset upon expiry of the lease period.

**Hint**
There are four major schools of Islamic jurisprudence among the Sunnis. These are the Maliki (Imam Malik), Shafi'i (Imam Shafi'i), Hanbali (Imam Hanbali) and Hanafi (Abu Hanifah) schools, respectively. While they all utilize the same primary sources of Shari'ah, they differ in some cases on trivial issues relating to the interpretation of some textual evidence.

In simple terms, *wa'ad* may be described as a promise or undertaking by a party to carry out a unilateral contract and signifies their commitment to perform an obligation. The concept of *wa'ad* is based on the principle of fulfillment of promise in all dispositions. In financial transactions, *wa'ad* may be a fundamental requirement through which a customer declares their intention to fulfill a contract which was entered into earlier. For instance, in a cost-plus financing contract where a sale is made at a specified profit margin (**murabahah**), and where the bank is required to purchase the commodity, the customer must give an undertaking to show their commitment to fulfill the contract. This is because if they fail to fulfill their own part of the *murabahah* contract after the bank has purchased the commodity, the latter will definitely suffer financial loss. Therefore, a unilateral promise is required at the outset to avoid future disputes. Another example of *wa'ad* is found in a lease contract (*ijarah*) where a customer gives a binding promise to buy the leased asset upon expiry of the contractual lease period. This situation occurs in a contractual arrangement known as **al-ijarah thumma al-bay'** otherwise known as an **Islamic hire-purchase contract**.

However, Muslim jurists disagree on the binding nature of *wa'ad*. The majority contend that fulfilling *wa'ad* is recommended in financial transactions. The jurists who uphold this view include those of the Shafi'i school, some Maliki jurists, and Abu Hanifah. They believe a promise is like a gift that only becomes binding after it has been delivered. On the other hand, the majority of the Maliki scholars believe that fulfilling *wa'ad* is obligatory and is usually enforceable. Ibn Shubrimah, a Maliki jurist, argues that *wa'ad* is binding and enforceable except in cases where non-fulfillment is otherwise justified. This controversy still rages as jurists continue to hold different views on the binding nature of *wa'ad*. In order to clear the air, the International Islamic Fiqh Academy issued this resolution:

That a unilateral promise (*wa'ad*) (which is issued unilaterally by either the orderer or the client) is by religion binding upon the promisor except where otherwise justified. It is also judicially binding if it is made contingent upon a reason and a promise (*wa'ad*). In such cases, the consequences of the binding character of the unilateral promise (*wa'ad*) are determined by either the fulfillment of the unilateral promise (*wa'ad*) or by reparation for losses actually incurred as a result of the non-fulfillment of the unilateral promise (*wa'ad*) without justification.[5]

On the other hand, *muwa'adah*, which is a derivative of *wa'ad*, is a bilateral promise in a contractual form that may either be conditional or unconditional. In such an arrangement, the bilateral promise may be accompanied with or without a corresponding consideration. The nature of an unconditional bilateral promise is like that of a simple contract where a party undertakes to sell a commodity during a particular time and the other party agrees to buy it at that same time. But the conditional bilateral promise occurs when a party promises to sell a commodity and the other party agrees to buy it if certain conditions occur. The legality of *muwa'adah* has been affirmed by modern jurists as being binding on the orderer of the assets provided the bank owns the goods, the goods are in the bank's possession, the goods are sold to the purchaser with an agreed specification of profit, the bank bears the ownership risk until delivery, and the bank undertakes to accept redelivery if the goods turn out to be defective. This is based on the resolution of the second conference of Islamic banking in Kuwait held in 1983. When an option to rescind the contract is given to one of the parties, a mutual promise becomes permissible and binding. This was emphasized in the relevant resolution of the International Islamic Fiqh Academy, which states:

> Mutual promise (involving two parties) is permissible in the case of *murabahah* sale provided that the option is given to one or both parties. Without such an option, it is not permissible, since in a sale, a mutual and binding promise is like an ordinary sale contract, in which the prerequisite is that the seller should be in full possession of the goods to be sold, in order to be in conformity with the hadith of the Prophet forbidding the sale of anything that is not in one's possession.[6]

According to this, it is clear that the concept and implications of the terms *wa'ad* and *muwa'adah* are closely related to the term *'aqd* because the former are forms of undertaking that are either unilateral or bilateral.

## Affirmative Evidence on Contract

The Qur'an and Sunnah contain a number of legal texts on contractual relationships and terms. Most of the principles in these legal texts form the basis of modern Islamic finance transactions. It is therefore important to review the affirmative evidence on contractual laws in the Sharī'ah with a view to establishing the justification for the various forms of contract. The following verses are often quoted to establish the legality of contracts in Islamic law:

> Qur'an 5:1: "O you who believe! Fulfill (your) obligations."

> Qur'an 17:34: "And fulfill (every) covenant. Verily, the covenant will be questioned about."

> Qur'an 16:91: "And fulfill the Covenant of Allah when you have covenanted, and break not the oaths after you have confirmed them—and indeed you have appointed Allah your surety. Verily! Allah knows what you do."

> Qur'an 9:4: "Except for the idolaters with whom you have a treaty, and who have not subsequently failed you in aught, nor have supported anyone against you. So fulfill their treaty to them for the end of their term. Surely Allah loves the pious."

All these verses emphasize the importance of fulfilling contractual agreements whether they are in form of treaties, commercial contracts, or social obligations.

**LEARNING OBJECTIVE 2.3**

Describe the classification of contracts, what constitutes a contract of sale, and the legal capacity to enter into such contract in Islamic law.

# Classifications of Contract in Islamic Law

The basic Sharī'ah principles of contracts are based on the general wellbeing of the community, economic justice, and equitable distribution of resources. No form of unjustified enrichment is allowed in commercial transactions under the Sharī'ah. When discussing types of Sharī'ah contracts, scholars have classified a contract of sale according to its *nature*, its *circumstances*, and its *legal consequences*. Let's give a brief overview of these categories to shed some light on the different types of Sharī'ah contracts. You should, however, note that these classifications are not necessarily based on the Qur'an and Sunnah because these specifics were not discussed in detail in these primary sources. The primary sources of the Sharī'ah only lay down the general principles for most legal issues. The classification presented here is born out of the forms of contracts practiced in the early period and the way people engaged in such transactions. Though based on general principles of the Sharī'ah, the classification differentiates between valid and void contracts. These classifications are therefore based on the judgments made by learned jurists through independent legal reasoning and deduction (*ijtihad*) on the proper identification of types of contracts practiced.

## Classifications of Contract According to Its Nature

The first classification of contracts is the *nature* of such contracts. This classification includes unilateral contracts (**'aqd infiradi**), bilateral contracts (**'aqd thuna'i**) and quasi contracts (**shibh al-'aqd**). Muslim jurists have classified contracts according to their nature, including whether they are Sharī'ah-compliant or contain some prohibited elements such as interest-bearing, deceptive, speculative, or fortuitous elements.

**'aqd infiradi**
A unilateral contract where a single party, who intends to establish a form of legal relationship with another party, makes a promise which is considered binding to the initiating party alone.

**'aqd thuna'i**
A bilateral contract between two parties where the legal terms and conditions are binding for both parties.

**shibh al-'aqd**
Semblance of a contract or a quasi contract which, although it creates an obligation, lacks elements of a valid contract.

**operation of law**
A right or liability created by law irrespective of the intention of the party or parties involved.

**product development**
A systematic process of developing and structuring Islamic finance products, which are generally used in Islamic financial transactions.

The nature of a contract is considered in line with clear provisions in the texts used to assess the legality or otherwise of certain contractual transactions. This classification generally includes the long list of contracts enumerated in Table 2.1. Note that this list is not exhaustive, as you will learn about many other forms of contracts later. Some bilateral contracts can transform to quasi contracts depending on the manner in which they were created. If any contract was created by the mere **operation of law** without a formal agreement between the parties, it becomes a quasi contract.

A number of these types of contracts according are, to the nature of the transaction, employed widely in Islamic financial transactions. The *Global Islamic Finance* box briefly describes the developments that have taken place in contractual transactions from the Dark Ages to today's modern, complex society. Muslim jurists have transformed most of them into Islamic financial products, and many are hybridized in the process of **product development** in Islamic finance.

**TABLE 2.1: A List of Common Contracts in Islamic Law**

| | Contract | Arabic Term | Nature |
|---|---|---|---|
| 1. | Contract of sale | *'aqd al-bay'* | Bilateral |
| 2. | Contingent contract | *al-'aqd al-ihtimali* | Bilateral |
| 3. | Contract of agency | *'aqd al-wakalah* | Bilateral |
| 4. | Contract of arbitration | *'aqd al-tahkim* | Bilateral |
| 5. | Contract of bailment | *'aqd al-wadi'ah* | Bilateral |
| 6. | Contract of bequest | *al-wasiyyah* | Unilateral |
| 7. | Contract of commission | *'aqd al-ju'alah* | Unilateral |
| 8. | Contract of compromise | *'aqd al-sulh* | Bilateral |
| 9. | Contract of education | *'aqd al-tarbiyyah wa ta'lim* | Bilateral |
| 10. | Contract of employment | *'aqd al-istikhdam* | Bilateral |
| 11. | Contract of guarantee | *'aqd al-daman* | Bilateral |
| 12. | Contract of marriage | *'aqd al-nikah* | Bilateral |
| 13. | Contract of suretyship | *'aqd al-kafalah* | Bilateral |
| 14. | Gift contract | *'aqd al-hibah* | Unilateral |
| 15. | Insurance contract | *'aqd al-ta'min* or *'aqd al-takaful* | Bilateral |
| 16. | Lease contract | *'aqd al-ijarah* | Bilateral |
| 17. | Manufacturing contract | *'aqd al-istisna'* | Bilateral |
| 18. | Mortgage contract | *'aqd al-rahn* | Bilateral |
| 19. | Partnership contracts | *'aqd al-shirkah* | Bilateral |
| 20. | Social contract | *al-'aqd al-ijtima'i* | Bilateral |
| 21. | Trust investment partnership | *'aqd al-mudarabah* | Bilateral |

# GLOBAL ISLAMIC FINANCE

Hundreds of years ago, from the east to the west, commercial transactions were carried out through simple contracts based on prevailing practices in each locality. However, as people's needs increased, transnational transactions emerged amid new forms of contract. As society progressed, people also developed different forms of contracts to meet their needs. Such developments involved reforms or modifications of previous forms of contracts. According to recent statistics released by the World Trade Organization in 2011, the volume of interregional trade has continued to increase since the start of the 21st century. Countries all over the world depend on one another, and the volume of international trade financing has surged to a record high since 2000.

As part of this trend, the Muslim world has not been left behind in global trade financing. As most Muslim countries give preference to Sharī'ah-compliant techniques in trade financing, the Islamic legal concept of commercial contracts has also followed the same line of development. Contracts that were previously very simple gradually became more sophisticated. Simple forms of contracts were gradually hybridized and a situation where two or more contracts are combined in a string of related transactions emerged while maintaining the distinct nature of each.

The cardinal principle in Islamic contract law is ethical investment and the prohibition of elements such as interest and excessive risks. The resilient nature of the Islamic finance industry is reinforced by these faith-based principles. In

Chapter 1, we explained how the modern practice of Islamic banking and finance is premised on various Islamic legal contracts practiced for more than 1,400 years in Muslim communities. Despite a sizeable number of multinational financial institutions being badly affected by the global economic crisis since 2007, most Islamic banks and financial institutions survived. They were able to escape the heat of the crisis unscathed as a result of the contracts used in the Islamic finance industry.

Furthermore, those products and practices that are not necessarily allowed in Islamic law, such as short-selling, credit default swaps, excessive speculation, and complex derivatives, to mention but a few, were the factors that led to this financial crisis. This shifted attention to Islamic finance. The resilience of the Islamic finance industry doesn't mean it is not susceptible to a future financial crisis but proper adherence to the Sharī'ah principles on commercial contracts will help forestall such occurrences.

One major body established to promote Sharī'ah-compliant trade financing, particularly among the Organization of Islamic Cooperation (OIC) countries, is the International Islamic Trade Finance Corporation (ITFC). The Islamic Development Bank (IDB) established the ITFC in 2006 to foster interstate trade and advance economic development in member countries. It formally commenced operations in 2008. As a member of the IDB group, the ITFC adopts Sharī'ah-compliant contracts in its financing undertakings in different countries around the world.

**unilateral contract**
A contract initiated and concluded by a single party which involves some form of benefit being transferred to another party, usually without consideration.

## Unilateral Contract ('aqd infiradi)

A **unilateral contract** is made by a single person who intends to establish a form of legal relationship with another party through a promise. Such a promise becomes binding on the person who makes it. It only becomes binding on the person in whose favor it has been made once he or she accept the promise. A typical example of a unilateral contract

**ju'alah**
(contract of commission)
A contract of promise of reward where the entitlement to compensation is contingent upon the performance of a particular act.

is a promise made by somebody in the form of a reward for whoever does something or finds a missing thing. Such reward (**ju'alah**) is usually open to anyone and whoever finds the thing becomes entitled to the reward and thus may be regarded as accepting the offer. The permissibility of a unilateral contract is approved by the majority of the Muslim jurists based on the event narrated in the Qur'an on what transpired between Prophet Yusuf (Joseph) and his brothers:

> Qur'an 12:72: "They said: 'We have lost the (golden) bowl of the king and for him who produces it is (the reward of) a camel load; and I will be bound by it.'"

This is an open promise that is meant for the whole world. Anybody who comes forward with the golden bowl of the king automatically accepts the open offer. The contract then becomes binding on both parties.

## Bilateral contract ('aqd thuna'i)

**bilateral contract**
A contract between two parties with the necessary legal effect that makes their terms and conditions binding on them.

**Bilateral contracts** are the most prevalent form of contract in modern Islamic financial transactions where you have at least two parties contracting. One party makes an offer, the other accepts and the contract becomes binding on both parties providing the subject matter is ascertained and it falls within the scope of items that are tradable. In this case, there must be consensus among the parties, which is usually based on mutual consent. Once the offer has been accepted, a legal relationship is established between the parties and certain rights and obligations are also established. Bilateral contracts are broadly divided into six by Muslim jurists:

**wakalah**
(contract of agency)
A contract of agency whereby a party appoints an agent to act on his behalf based on certain specified terms of service.

- contracts of exchange (*mu'awadah*)
- contracts of security (*tawthiqat*)
- contracts of partnership (*shirkah*)
- contracts of safe custody (*wadi'ah*)
- contracts relating to the use of an asset (*ijarah*)
- contracts relating to the performance of a work or rendering of specific services (e.g., **wakalah** and *ju'alah*).

## Quasi contract (shibh al-'aqd)

**quasi contract**
(*shibh al-'aqd*)
An arrangement or obligations created by the law despite the absence of a contract.

A **quasi contract** is an arrangement that is not really a contract in its true sense but resembles one. By its very nature it is not a contract, but its legal implication establishes what may be likened to a contract. In essence, a quasi contract is an obligation that originates from the operation of law and not by an agreement between parties. This form of relationship is not a real contract but its effect may create a binding legal relationship. For instance, when a buyer wrongly pays the price of a commodity to the wrong person due to a mistaken identity, such a relationship is a quasi contract, as it is not originally based on mutual consent. As a result, the person receiving the money in error must return the sum paid to the buyer for onward payment to the rightful seller.

## Classification of a Contract According to its Circumstances

**mudarabah**
A trust partnership contract between a capital provider and an entrepreneur where the parties share the profits but in the event of any loss, the capital provider bears the loss.

**musharakah**
A joint business partnership enterprise in which the parties share the profits based on the contractual ratio and losses are borne based on the equity participation ratio.

**multilateral contracts**
Contracts involving more than two parties such as a bank, the client and the agent.

The circumstances of a particular contract determine its legal consequences. Its classification according to its circumstances involves the type of contract being offered, such as whether it is in the form of a sale contract when the circumstance involves mere buying and selling, or a partnership contract when the contract involves a joint venture. Hence, this classification covers the wide range of circumstances in which contracts may be entered into by willing parties. The contracts include contracts of sale, partnership contracts such as **mudarabah** (trust investment partnership), and **musharakah** (joint venture partnership).

Some contracts may be in the form of unilateral contracts or bilateral contracts while others may be in the form of quasi contracts or a combination of both bilateral and unilateral contracts, or **multilateral contracts**. While a unilateral contract is considered as a one-party transaction where the contract is deemed to bind the maker, a bilateral contract involves two parties who establish legal obligations with regard to a subject matter concluded by an offer and its acceptance. The bilateral contract is the most common form of contract in modern society and it is widely practiced by all societies around the world. The difference between the legal effects of unilateral contracts and bilateral contracts is in the pre-contract position of the parties. In a unilateral contract, if the party making a unilateral promise does not fulfill that promise, they are not obliged to do so. However, if the party fulfills the self-imposed contract, they are bound by their actions. When parties in a bilateral contract make a promise, they are both bound by their promises to conclude the contract. The third category in this classification is multilateral contracts, in which a group of people can enter into a valid legal relationship that binds all of them in a joint contract. Such a contract may be a joint contract between the co-owners of a property and a third-party buyer. The fourth category is the quasi contract, which is a form of transaction that may not be validly called a contract but simply resembles one. Quasi contracts can sometimes be enforceable but in other circumstances are not.

### Challenge

Name three examples each for unilateral, bilateral, and multilateral contracts in Islamic finance.

## Classification of a Contract According to its Legal Consequences

**maslahah mursalah**
A branch of the secondary sources of the Sharī'ah, which means unrestricted or unregulated public interest, that is in full harmony with the letter and spirit of the Sharī'ah. An example of *maslahah mursalah* is the publication of the financial report of an Islamic bank bearing the endorsement of the Sharī'ah board.

In Sharī'ah, the legal consequences of a particular contract may be the basis of classification. This classification emphasizes the extent of validity or binding nature of the contract. Thus, the legal consequences of a contract may result in being declared as valid (*sahih*), invalid or deficient (*fasid*), void (*batil*), and binding (*lazim*). While there are different types of contracts, their classification according to their legal consequences is very important to establish their enforceability or otherwise. This classification is generally based on public interest (**maslahah mursalah**), which is explicitly or implicitly confirmed by the Qur'an and Sunnah. The categories of contract under this broad classification are valid contracts (*al-'aqd al-salih*), which are enforceable and

**act of God**
Legal description of an event that is outside human control, usually a destructive type that prevents the performance of a duty under a contract. An example of this is a natural disaster.

**enforceable contract**
A contract where a party has the legal remedy to execute the contract.

**invalid contract**
A transaction where the basis of the contract itself is valid but there are defects in its attributes that make it invalid and thus unenforceable under the Sharī'ah.

**void contract**
An unenforceable contract that is invalid from the very beginning, which cannot be remedied by addressing any missing element in such transaction.

binding on the contracting parties. But although such a contract is valid it may not be enforceable in certain circumstances such as an **act of God**, especially when the subject matter of the contract is destroyed. On the other hand, an **enforceable contract** (*al-'aqd al-nafidh*) is always enforceable. Thus, not all valid contracts are enforceable, but all enforceable contracts are valid. In addition to the foregoing classification, there are invalid contracts (*al-'aqd al-fasid*) and void contracts (*al-'aqd al-batil*). An **invalid contract** is a transaction whereby the basis of the contract itself is valid but there are defects in its attributes that make it invalid and thus unenforceable under the Sharī'ah. In contrast, a **void contract** is a transaction that is void from the very beginning and has no legal effect. The basis of such a contract and all its attributes are defective and cannot be enforced whatsoever. For instance, when the two parties in a bilateral contract who are legally incapable of concluding that contract proceed to execute the contract, it would be held void from the very beginning as if no contract had ever existed between them. The underlying rule in void contracts is that they cannot be validated by the consent of the contracting parties.

## Valid Contract (*Sahih*)

When a contract is concluded in its normal manner with an effective offer and acceptance and the parties have the legal capacity to enter into the contract, it is regarded as a valid contract. The legal consequence of a valid contract is its binding nature since the parties have showed their desire to create a binding legal relationship. The consideration must be valuable to warrant the description of a valid contract.

## Invalid or Deficient Contract (*Fasid*)

Any form of contract short of key elements for a valid contract may be considered invalid or deficient depending on the elements it is missing. A contract may be considered deficient if it is lawful in its substance but unlawful in its description. The substance of a contract comprises the offer, acceptance and its subject matter. Without these three things, a contract will be rendered void from the very beginning. However, the description in a contract may involve the specification of price or the quality of the subject matter. If either of these is missing in the contract, it will be declared deficient, i.e., it can still be validated if the items that make it deficient are duly addressed.

## Void Contract (*Batil*)

A void contract is different from a deficient contract because it cannot be remedied by addressing certain descriptive elements that are missing in the agreement. This is because a void contract is unlawful in both its substance and description. For instance, an agreement to sell pork will be considered void from the very beginning because the contract is unlawful in its substance and description.

## Binding Contract (*Lazim*)

When a contract is sound in its substance and description it becomes binding on the parties and is enforceable under the law. A binding contract can either be revocable or irrevocable. A revocable contract is a binding contract where either of the parties is given an option to revoke the contract at any stage, for example, partnership contracts such as *musharakah* and *mudarabah* are revocable. An agency contract (*wakalah*) is also revocable at the instigation of either of the parties. Irrevocable binding contracts are those that cannot be revoked at any stage once they are concluded. For example, if a valid contract of sale is duly executed while its substance and description are both lawful, none of the parties can rescind the contract without reasonable grounds.

## Enforceable Contract (*Nafidh*)

A binding contract is enforceable under the law. An enforceable contract does not usually affect the rights of a third party. It only relates to the rights of the parties to the contract. Therefore, all binding contracts are enforceable.

## Withheld Contract (*Mawquf*)

**power of attorney**
An authorization by one person to another to act on their behalf or represent them in business or other legal affairs such as a contract.

When a binding contract is concluded by someone who does not own a property, the contract may be dependent on the final approval of the real owner of the subject matter. This may happen when **power of attorney** is given to a person to sell a property subject to the final ratification of the negotiated price. The contract is kept hanging until such ratification is given by the actual owner.

## Pillars of Sharī'ah Contracts

*sighah*
The form of any contract in Islamic law expressed as an offer and an acceptance.

*al-aqidan*
The two contracting parties in a transaction.

*al-ma'qud alaih*
The subject matter of the contract which is usually the object of sale.

1.   FORM (**SIGHAH**): The form of any contract in Islamic law is offer and acceptance (*ijab* and *qubul*). For a contract to be valid there should be an offer followed by its acceptance, made by the use of words or indications that are commonly used in the particular locality.

2.   PARTIES TO THE CONTRACT (**AL-AQIDAN**): The parties to the contract should have the ability or capacity to enter into a valid contract. This means the capacity to acquire and exercise rights and discharge obligations. Subject to certain principles, impediments or incapacity to enter into a valid contractual arrangement include being a minor (*sighar*), insanity (*junun*), forgetfulness, sleep and fainting fits, and terminal illness (*marad al-mawt*).

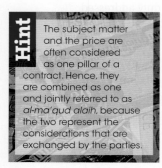

Hint
The subject matter and the price are often considered as one pillar of a contract. Hence, they are combined as one and jointly referred to as *al-ma'qud alaih*, because the two represent the considerations that are exchanged by the parties.

3.   SUBJECT MATTER AND PRICE OF THE CONTRACT (**AL-MA'QUD ALAIH**): The subject matter of a contract must necessarily have a commercial value and must necessarily be something of benefit as permitted under the Sharī'ah. The subject matter, which must be legally owned, must also be capable of possession and should exist at the time of contract. The benefit of the subject matter should be mutual, whereby the buyer acquires the property and the seller receives its monetary value. In addition, the price of the contract is usually in the form of a consideration, which may or may not necessarily be money. There should be some form of consideration in the contract, which should be known to the parties to avoid fraud, deceit, and future disputes. According to Mahmassani, a learned Muslim jurist, the conditions for a valid consideration are as follows:
   a.   the consideration should be in existence
   b.   it must be permissible under the Sharī'ah
   c.   it must be valid
   d.   it should be a valuable commodity.

4. INTENTION TO CREATE LEGAL RELATIONS AND MEETING OF MINDS: The parties should necessarily have the intention to create legal obligations, which involves the meeting of both minds based on mutual satisfaction. This should be based on mutual satisfaction and goodwill, as accentuated by the Qur'an:

> Qur'an 4:29: "O you who believe! Eat not up your property among yourselves unjustly except it be a trade amongst you, by mutual consent."

**majlis al-'aqd**
The session of contract where the parties conclude the terms and conditions of the contract.

The meeting of minds takes place at the formation of the contract where the offer and acceptance are indicated by the parties, and this is usually concluded at a meeting session known as **majlis al-'aqd**. This creates the required unity of time and place for the execution of the contract. Mutual consent and satisfaction is emphasized in all contractual agreements and can be vitiated when the following factors creep in: duress (*ikrah*), mistake (*khata*), fraud (*ghish*), and misrepresentation.

## Contract of Sale

### Meaning of Contract of Sale

A contract of sale involves the exchange of property for a well-defined consideration in accordance with the mutual consent of the parties to the contract. The consideration is usually a property. This is why some scholars prefer to define a contract of sale as the exchange of a property for another property. The term used in Islamic law for a contract of sale is **bay'**. In the proper sense, *bay'* involves the transfer of an ascertained object in exchange for its equivalent based on consensus *ad idem*. A number of contracts in Islamic jurisprudence follow the *bay'* model even though their nature may be different. Most of the contractual transactions in Islamic law are based on this generic term, which has a wider application. Exchange of values can be represented in any form whether in the form of a forward sale (**salam** or *bay' al-salam*), or a cost-plus sale (*murabahah*).

**bay'**
Any transaction in which the ownership of a property is transferred to another party.

**salam** (or *bay' al-salam*)
A forward sale contract where advance payment is made for goods to be delivered later.

### Nature of a Contract of Sale

Trading is encouraged in Islam as a means of lawful earning. There are situations where someone may desire things that are not within their capacity and that alone may call for a kind of exchange of a property for another. Therefore, to engage in buying and selling or an exchange of values through **trade by barter** is a natural propensity of mankind. In as much as such transactions are carried out within the lawful confines of Islamic law, they are highly recommended. The permissibility of such exchanges is proved beyond doubt in the Qur'an where Allah clearly provides that trading is permissible while interest-bearing transactions are forbidden. The Prophet, who was a trader before the call to prophethood, also emphasized the importance of trading as compared to begging for alms: "For one of you to take his rope and then come with a load of wood upon his back and sells is better than to beg of men whether they give or reject him."[7]

**trade by barter**
A simple trade where goods or services are exchanged for a certain amount of other goods or services, subject to the exceptions and general rules of the Sharī'ah.

The Islamic sale of goods is based on the Islamic law of obligations, which provides that Muslims are bound by their agreement and prescriptions. Thus, once a person agrees to exchange certain goods for a definite consideration and this is effectuated, the contract becomes binding on the parties. A contract of sale is usually a bilateral contract because there must be a buyer and a seller. The objects, properties or values being exchanged must have some value, be permissible, and be owned by the parties who intend to trade in them. Mutual consent involves an offer and acceptance. For instance, when the seller says to the buyer 'I sell this item to you', the buyer is required to declare his consent by saying 'I accept the ownership of the item' or 'I buy the item'. This is the simple nature of a contract of sale but, with technological advancement, a sale may be concluded using more sophisticated means such as online purchasing, where the description of the object of the contract is given and the transaction is completed online without any physical meeting. However sophisticated the means adopted in the modern era such as electronic sales, the underlying spirit remains the same, i.e. there must be an offer and a corresponding acceptance with a valuable consideration based on the mutual consent of the parties.

## Essential Elements of a Contract of Sale

For a contract to be valid, certain essential elements must be present. These elements have conditions that must be met to conclude a valid contract of sale. The four elements of a valid contract of sale are offer and acceptance, subject matter, consideration or price, and legal capacity of the parties.

### Offer and Acceptance

For a valid contract, there must be an offer and acceptance. These must be expressed in absolute terms, i.e. in definite and decisive language that leaves no room for any other intention. The language may be in the past or present tense but it cannot be in the future or imperative tenses. Such a contract must not be limited to a certain period. Offer and acceptance flow from voluntary mutual consent, which is an indication of the meeting of the minds of the contracting parties. The contract of sale must be carried out through mutual consent, which is expressed through offer and acceptance. Anything short of this will not be accepted as a valid sale contract. The acceptance must agree with and be directly related to the offer made. Both offer and acceptance should be made at the *majlis al-'aqd*.

### Subject Matter

The subject matter should exist at the time of concluding the contract. However, subject to some difference of opinion regarding this, the object of the contract must be capable of being delivered once the contract is concluded between the parties. That is, it must be free from all encumbrances. This indicates that the ownership of the property must be ascertained—the seller cannot sell what does not belong to him. Once it is ascertained the property belongs to the seller as the true owner, agent, or guardian of the owner, the description and specifications of that property must also be determined. The property should have some sort of beneficial use and, as such, it should be a valuable property from which the buyer will benefit. To this end, the subject matter must be pure and permissible in the eyes of the Sharī'ah. One cannot trade in things that are forbidden in Islamic law, such as carcasses and pigs.

### Consideration or Price

In the modern context, the consideration, popularly known as the price, is usually a form of exchange. The means of exchange should be the prevailing medium of exchange in a particular locality based on customary practices. It must be a valuable commodity such as gold or silver, or a particular kind of money generally acceptable as a valid medium of exchange. The price of the subject matter must be known and the amount determined.

### Legal Capacity of the Parties

An important requirement in Islamic law is that the seller must have the requisite legal capacity to engage in a contract of sale. That is, they must possess a sound mind, have attained the age of majority, not be a declared bankrupt, nor be a **prodigal**. Above all, as a contract of sale is premised on mutual consent, it must be established that the seller is not selling the subject matter under duress or overwhelming coercion. We shall discuss the significance of legal capacity in a contract of sale in more detail next.

## Legal Capacity (*Ahliyyah*)

The **legal capacity** of parties entering into a contract is a major prerequisite for a valid contract. In order to conclude a valid contract, the parties must have the requisite capacity to fully understand the nature of the contract and the implication of their dispositions. This is highly regulated by the Sharī'ah to prevent hardship or harming the weaker parties. Parties who seek to engage in a contract are allowed to conclude it if they are legally fit. Every human being is endowed with legal capacity and the sole criterion is life, whether in the womb or after birth. The fitness of a person to warrant the application of Islamic law through either the acquisition of rights or the discharge of obligations is known as **dhimmah**. This is the concept in which a person becomes fit to enjoy the rights they are entitled to and bear the liabilities they must fulfill. Everyone acquires a juristic personality (*dhimmah*) that is determined and evaluated according to their ability to comprehend the law and understand their responsibilities. The juristic personality of a person confers on them the legal capacity that enables them to enter into a valid transaction.

### What is Legal Capacity in a Contract?

Various authors of books on Islamic jurisprudence have given almost the same definition for the legal capacity of a person to competently enter into a contract. However, it is important to examine the definition of 'legal capacity,' otherwise known as *ahliyyah*, before considering its relevance to the validity of a contract. In the literal sense, *ahliyyah* simply means aptitude, fitness, suitableness, competence, qualification, or absolute fitness.

In the juristic sense, *ahliyyah* has been defined as 'the ability to acquire rights and exercise them and to accept duties and perform them accordingly'.[8] In a similar vein, Al-Sabouni defines *ahliyyah* as 'the ability of a person to oblige, be obliged and conduct one's affairs by oneself'.[9] This is a wider definition than the first one. Meanwhile,

---

**Challenge**

Why do you think legal capacity to enter into a contract is necessary in concluding a valid contract?

**prodigal**
A thoughtless person who exhibits a lack of good sense or judgment.

**legal capacity**
Ability to acquire and exercise rights and at the same time accept duties and perform them accordingly.

**dhimmah**
Fitness of a person to warrant the application of Islamic law through either acquisition of rights or discharge of obligations.

**mukallaf**
(*sui juris*)
A person who is competent enough to acquire rights and discharge obligations accordingly without any encumbrance, and as a result is a subject of the law. To conclude a valid contract, the general rule is that a person must be *sui juris*.

**receptive legal capacity**
The capacity of every human being to acquire rights and obligations subject to certain limitations.

**active legal capacity**
The capacity of a person to acquire rights, responsibilities and discharge obligations absolutely with full capacity.

Al-Zarqa' gives a definition from the viewpoint of the subject of the law as a **mukallaf** by defining legal capacity as 'a description presumed in a person rendering such a person a possible candidate to receive a legislative injunction'.[10] One basic idea derived from the juristic definitions given above is the cardinal qualification of a person to be able to receive rights, and at the same time bear and discharge obligations. These qualities enable them to conduct certain transactions competently in accordance with the state of their legal capacity, which will attract some legal consequences.

## Types of Legal Capacity

There are two main types of legal capacity, particularly with regard to contractual transactions in Islamic law: **receptive legal capacity** (*ahliyyah al-wujub*) and **active legal capacity** (*ahliyyah al-'ada*). Receptive legal capacity gives every person the ability to acquire rights and obligations subject to certain limitations, whereas active legal capacity gives one the ability to acquire rights, responsibilities and discharge obligations absolutely. At every point in time, a person is endowed with a certain legal capacity, by virtue of the *dhimmah*. At birth, and even before then, a baby or fetus acquires a form of receptive legal capacity. For the fetus, as it has not acquired an independent personality, it only enjoys an incomplete receptive legal capacity. The legal implication of this form of capacity with regard to concluding a valid contract in Islamic law is that a fetus can only acquire some rights on a limited scale. For example, a fetus can benefit from the unilateral contract of transfer of property through inheritance. At birth, an infant consequentially acquires a complete receptive legal capacity that allows it to acquire certain rights but not to validly conclude contracts personally.

For example, an infant may conclude contracts for necessaries through a guardian. As the infant cannot understand the legal consequences of such contracts, legal guardians may validly conclude contracts on their behalf. Figure 2.1 shows a child who, unfortunately, is an orphan but has inherited a large amount of liquid wealth, concluding a contract of diminishing partnership with an Islamic financial institution to get shelter.

At every point in time, a person is endowed with certain legal capacity, by virtue of the *dhimmah*. At birth, and even before then, a baby or fetus acquires a form of receptive legal capacity.

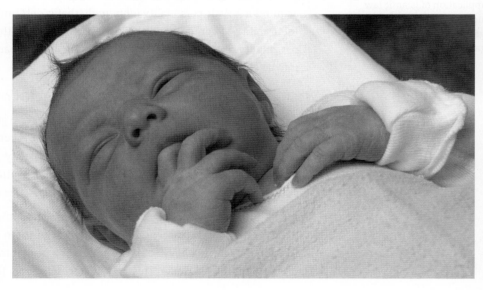

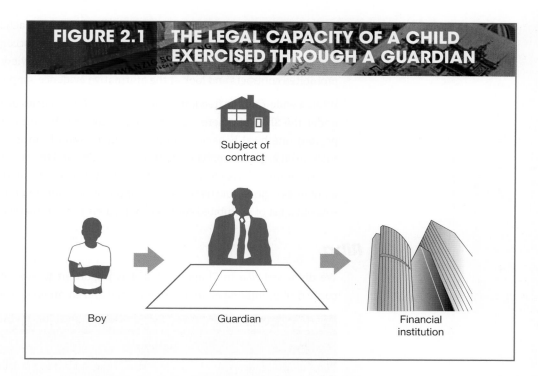

**FIGURE 2.1    THE LEGAL CAPACITY OF A CHILD EXERCISED THROUGH A GUARDIAN**

Subject of contract

Boy

Guardian

Financial institution

Contracts are a necessity in this situation, but the child can only conclude a contract validly through their guardian. In this situation, the child has an incomplete active legal capacity, which only allows them to exercise such a right of purchase through a guardian.

**LEARNING OBJECTIVE 2.4**

Analyse the main forbidden contracts in Islamic commercial transactions.

# The Main Forbidden Contracts in Islamic Commercial Transactions

This section sets out the major forbidden elements in Islamic commercial transactions that form the basis for Sharī'ah screening in the modern Islamic finance industry. For ethical practices and fair trade in the open market, Islamic law prohibits a number of contracts, contractual terms, and practices that may bring about economic crisis in the long run. It is important to add that people engaged in many types of contracts with various contractual terms before the advent of Islam, which brought about a high degree of justice and fairness. The new legal regime introduced sweeping reforms in commercial dealings—it adopted a number of fair contracts and rejected unfair dealings.

**Challenge**

Besides *riba, gharar, and maysir*, what are other prohibited elements in commercial contracts?

There are numerous legal texts in the Qur'an and Sunnah that prohibit certain forms of contracts. The most prominent are those forbidding interest-bearing transactions (*ribawi*), risky or uncertain transactions (*gharar*), and transactions involving gambling or games of chance (*qimar* or *maysir*). Islamic law puts a blanket prohibition on these elements in commercial transactions. To encourage fair dealing and prevent monopoly, exploitation, and undue enrichment at the expense of others in the open market, Islamic law provides a practical mechanism for commercial transactions. To understand why these mandatory prohibitions cannot be compromised according to the underlying philosophy of Islamic law, we will present a brief overview of the main forms of prohibited contracts and look at the affirmative evidence supporting them.

While a wide-ranging freedom is given to contracting parties in a contractual transaction under the Sharī'ah, there are some regulations in the form of limitations in place to prevent unethical behavior and inject a high level of fairness and impartiality. These rules are also there to prevent market exploitation and the creation of market oligarchies in the community. All forms of contracts that involve speculation, exploitation, bribery, gambling or games of chance, and are interest-bearing are prohibited in Islam. Table 2.2 sets out a list of prohibited contracts or elements in commercial transactions.

## Riba

We discussed *riba* in Chapter 1, but it is important to look at the details within the context of prohibited elements in financial and commercial contracts. One of the most

| TABLE 2.2: Forbidden Elements in Commercial Contracts in Islamic Law | |
| --- | --- |
| **Contract** | **Meaning** |
| *Bay' al-Mulamasah* | Sale by touching. A kind of pre-Islamic sale contract where it is agreed that when the prospective buyer touches an item displayed for sale, it becomes binding on him to buy it. |
| *Bay' al-Munabadhah* | A kind of pre-Islamic sale contract where it is agreed that when the seller throws an item to the prospective buyer, it becomes binding on the latter to buy it. It also includes bartering items without inspection. |
| *Bay' al-Hisat* | A kind of sale that involves selling a lot of cloth upon which a thrown stone will fall. The outcome is determined by the throwing of stones. |
| *Bay' al-Habl-al-Hablah* | A kind of sale that involves selling the contents of an animal's womb. |
| *Bay' al-Madhamin* | The sale of an animal fetus. |
| *Bay' al-Malaqih* | The sale of animal sperm. |
| *Bay' al-Gharar* | Speculative or uncertain contracts that involve excessive risks. |
| *Bay' al-Riba* | Lending, borrowing and trading with interest. |
| *Bay' Muzabanah* | A sale contract involving the exchange of fresh fruit for dried fruit, when the quantity of dried fruit is measured and fixed while the quantity of fresh fruit is estimated while still on the tree. |
| *Bay' Muhaqalah* | The sale of still-unharvested grain in exchange for an equal quantity of harvested grain. |

prominent and profoundly prohibited elements in Islamic financial transactions is *riba*. The term literally means usury, interest, or a usurious element in any transaction. The interesting part of this literal definition is the controversy the issue triggered among Muslim jurists on what constitutes *riba*. A majority of scholars believe *riba* indicates that interest is prohibited, while others believe it does not mean interest and that it is part of the gains accruable to a party entitled in a contractual arrangement. Thus, the more general term 'interest-bearing transaction' is used. Although we shall avoid discussing the disagreements between jurists, particularly modern scholars, regarding the interpretation of the legal texts on *riba*, the point of convergence among their respective views will be outlined here in line with the affirmative evidence in the primary sources of the Sharī'ah. Note that the majority of jurists contend that the verses and Prophetic traditions on *riba* have established definitive evidence of what constitutes interest-bearing transactions. This is reflected in the sternness of tone used in prohibiting such transactions in the Qur'an as well as in the Prophet Muhammad's attitude towards such transactions.

The word *riba* is used several times in the Qur'an to refer to interest-bearing transactions, which are prohibited in Islamic law. The prohibition took placely when revelation began. The policy reforms introduced by the Qur'an were orchestrated through gradual, calculated changes. In line with this divine reasoning, the gradualism adopted in the Qur'anic legislation for the prohibition of *riba* followed a five-stage revelation. Table 2.3 enumerates the stages of prohibition, the applicable textual evidence and the degree of prohibition at each stage.

**consensus of opinion**
A secondary source of the Sharī'ah that means the unanimous agreement of the Muslim scholars of a particular period on a Sharī'ah issue. The Arabic term for this concept is *ijma'*.

Without doubt, *riba* is declared forbidden in the Qur'an, Sunnah, and the **consensus of opinion** of the scholars. According to Ibn Abbas and Umar, the last revelation received by the blessed Prophet, shortly before his death, was the passage in *Surah Al-Baqarah* (2:278–281) which dealt with *riba* as quoted in Table 2.3. There is a remarkable Prophetic tradition on the central theme of these last verses on the total prohibition of *riba*. Abu Hurairah narrated that Prophet Muhammad said: "A man used to give loans to the people, and used to say to his servant, 'If the debtor is poor, forgive him, so that Allah may forgive us'. So when he met Allah (after his death), Allah forgave him."[11]

In addition, a number of traditions are often quoted from the Sunnah to justify the prohibition of *riba* in commercial transactions. For instance, Jabir narrated that the Prophet cursed the receiver, the payer of interest, the one who records it, and the two witnesses of the transaction, and said: "They are all alike (in guilt)."[12] During the last sermon of the Prophet, Jabir narrated: "The Prophet said, 'All of the *riba* of *jahiliyyah* (the pre-Islamic era) is annulled. The first *riba* that I annul is our *riba*, that accruing to 'Abbas Ibn Abd al-Muttalib; it is being cancelled completely.'"[13] The term '*riba* of *jahiliyyah*' refers to *riba* of debt, which is the interest prohibited by the Qur'anic legislation. Furthermore, Abu Sa'id Al-Khudri also narrated that the Prophet once said: "Do not sell gold for gold unless equivalent in weight, and do not sell less amount for greater amount or vice versa; and do not sell silver for silver unless equivalent in weight, and do not sell less amount for greater amount or vice versa; and do not sell gold or silver that is not present at the moment of exchange for gold or silver that is present."[14]

| TABLE 2.3: Stages in the Prohibition of *Riba* | | | |
|---|---|---|---|
| **Stage** | **Textual Evidence** | **Verse (Qur'an)** | **Degree of Prohibition** |
| 1st | That which you give as *riba* the people's wealth increases not with God; but that which you give in charity, seeking the goodwill of God, multiplies manifold. | 30:39 | Exhortation |
| 2nd | And for their taking *riba* even though it was forbidden for them, and their wrongful appropriation of other people's property, we have prepared those among them who reject faith a grievous punishment. | 4:161 | Stark warning |
| 3rd | O you who have believed, take not doubled and redoubled *riba*, and fear God so that you prosper. Fear the fire which has been prepared for those who reject faith, and obey God and the Prophet so that you may receive mercy. | 3:130-132 | Total abhorrence |
| 4th | Those who benefit from *riba* shall be raised like those who have been driven to madness by the touch of the Devil; that is because they say 'trade is like *riba*' while God has permitted trade and forbidden *riba*. God deprives interest of all but blesses charity. He loves not the ungrateful sinners. | 2:275-276 | Prohibition |
| 5th | O you who have believed! Fear Allah and give up *riba* that remains outstanding, if you are true believers. If you do not, then be sure of being at war with God and His messenger. But if you repent, you can have your principal. Neither you should commit injustice nor you be subjected to it. If the debtor is in difficulty, let him have respite until it is easier, but if you forgo out of charity, it is better for you if you realize. | 2:278-281 | Total prohibition and repercussions |

## Types of *Riba* Transactions

There are two principal types of *riba* transactions described in the Qur'an and Sunnah and deduced by earlier Muslim jurists from the sources of Islamic law. The two types are:

1. *riba al-nasi'ah* (interest on delayed payment)
2. *riba al-fadl* (interest on excess in countervalue in trade).

Figure 2.2 illustrates this broad classification and gives the other meanings of the two types of *riba*. While *riba al-nasi'ah* relates to loans, *riba al-fadl* relates to trade and commercial transactions generally. *Riba al-nasi'ah* is also known as *riba al-duyun* (*riba* on loans), *riba al-jali* (obvious *riba*), *riba al-mubashir* (direct *riba*), *riba al-jahiliyyah/al-Qur'an* (*riba* prohibited by the Qur'an). *Riba al-fadl* is also known as *riba al-buyu'u* (*riba* in trade), *riba ghayr al-mubashir* (indirect *riba*), or *riba al-khafi* (hidden *riba*).

### Riba Al-Nasi'ah

*riba al-nasi'ah*
An unjustifiable increase in the amount owed in return for the deferment of repayment of a loan, as mentioned in the Qur'an.

*Riba al-nasi'ah* generally refers to an unjustifiable increase in a debt for deferring the repayment of a loan. It means interest on money lent by a creditor to a debtor. It is considered the most common form of *riba* clearly established in the Qur'an. This form of *riba* transaction was common during the pre-Islamic era, where the Arabs would lend money to each other on the agreement that after a specified period of time mutually agreed by the parties, the debtor would pay an excess amount over the principal sum due to the creditor. This is the prohibited form of *riba* in the fifth stage of revelation described in Table 2.3. Hence the name *riba al-jahiliyyah*, which describes the prevalent interest-bearing transactions of that period.

**FIGURE 2.2 CLASSIFICATION OF *RIBA***

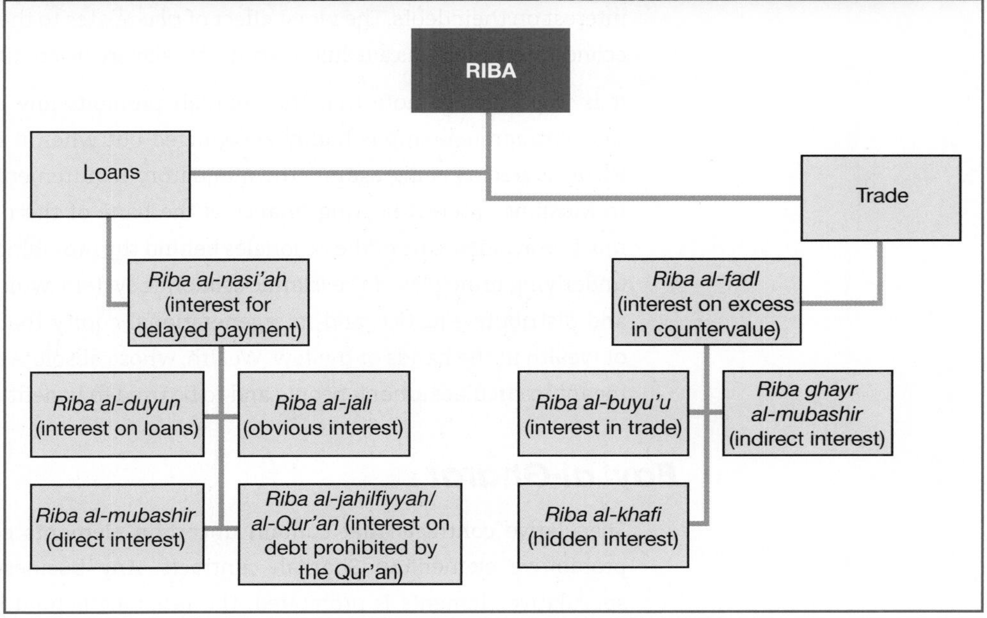

### *Riba al-Fadl*

**Riba al-fadl** is different from *Riba al-nasi'ah* because it involves certain forms of goods of the same kind but of different quality. When someone takes a superior quality of goods in exchange for more of the same kind of goods that are of inferior quality in a transaction, this constitutes *riba al-fadl*. This form of *riba* is prominent in the Sunnah because the Prophet personally witnessed such transactions among his companions and he immediately condemned them. For instance, exchanging dates of superior quality for dates of inferior quality in greater amounts is tantamount to a *riba* transaction. Abu Sa'id Al-Khudri narrated: "Once Bilal brought *barni* [a kind of] dates to the Prophet and the Prophet asked him, 'From where have you brought these?' Bilal replied, 'I had some inferior kind of dates and exchanged two *Sa'a* (measures) of it for one *Sa'a* of *barni* dates, in order to give it to the Prophet to eat.' Thereupon the Prophet said, 'Beware! Beware! This is definitely *riba*! This is definitely *riba*! Do not do so, but if you want to buy (a superior kind of dates) sell the inferior kind of dates for money and then buy the superior kind of dates with that money.'"[15] This typical example of *riba al-fadl* practiced by some companions was prevalent during the pre-Islamic era so the Prophet had to teach his companions that such transactions constitute *riba*.

## Why the Prohibition of *Riba*?

The reason behind the prohibition of *riba* is its resultant harmful effect on the economy, social life, the psychological and spiritual wellbeing of people individually, and the collective social fabric. The economic effects of *riba* are counterproductive as it encourages people to keep money idle and unproductive. In such a situation, financial resources are kept in the hands of a few in society, and this results in the social effects of *riba* whereby enmity is cultivated between rich and poor. When the rich exploit the poor economically, there are resultant psychological and spiritual effects. In such a situation, the rich look down on the poor, who must work tirelessly to pay the compounding interest on their debts. The worst effect of *riba* relates to the state level, where the whole economy crumbles as a result of economic slavery by creditors.

It is important to note that the Sharī'ah prohibits any interest-yielding contract of sale. Entrepreneurship is highly encouraged but when it involves usury or interest, it is considered as being against the mandatory requirements of the Sharī'ah. According to Muslims, interest-bearing finance is the bane of the modern banking system and must be avoided. One of the rationales behind the prohibition of *riba* is found in the core underlying principles of the Islamic economic system, which is based on socioeconomic and distributive justice, and intergenerational equity that prevents the accumulation of wealth in the hands of the few. Wealth, whose absolute ownership belongs to God, is meant to circulate among people and to be used to benefit all.

### *Bay' al-Gharar*

Speculative contracts that contain uncertain elements constitute the second major prohibitive element in Sharī'ah contracts. Any business transaction that involves speculative elements is prohibited. The rationale behind this is to avoid unnecessary risk-taking, which will eventually lead to disputes between the parties. An example of *gharar* is given in a hadith where Abu-Sa'īd Al-Khudrī said: "The Prophet has forbidden the purchase of the unborn animal in its mother's womb, the sale of the milk in the udder without measurement, the purchase of spoils of war prior to their distribution, the purchase of charities prior to their receipt, and the purchase of the catch of a diver."[16] This prohibition is for the avoidance of uncertainties and the associated risks. Such uncertainties are so great and vague that they cannot be ascertained, quantified and conceptualized in a valid contract. Classical examples of *gharar* mentioned in the Sunnah include contracts of sale for the following:

• birds in the sky
• fish in the sea
• an unborn calf in its mother's womb
• unripe fruits on the tree
• a runaway animal
• the semen and unfertilized eggs of camels
• milk in the udder of an animal without measurement.

This is why contracts are required to be drafted in unambiguous terms to avoid future disputes. The *Islamic Finance in the News* box (on page 70) shows the current practices in the Islamic finance industry and the problems caused by ambiguous terms in commercial contracts. The way that Sharī'ah contracts are drafted is important to avoid leaving room for multiple interpretations especially when they are brought before an English court. Any uncertainties or ambiguous terms in a contract that may be subject to different interpretations are to be avoided.

**mu'allaq**
A contingent contract where the contract is only effective upon the actualization of an event or condition that will occur in the future.

Some contemporary forms of financial contracts such as two sales in one sale, financial derivatives, suspended sales (**mu'allaq**), some forms of forward sales, and futures may involve elements of *gharar* that, according to some jurists, are not in accordance with Sharī'ah principles. Therefore, the power to sell is denied in the following circumstances in order to avoid elements of uncertainty:

1. 'Things that, as the object of a legal transaction, do not exist.
2. Things that exist but that are not in possession of the seller or the availability of which may not be expected.
3. Things that are exchanged on the basis of uncertain delivery and payment that may also involve ignorance (*al-jahalah*) of the actual terms of the contract.'[17]

Just as speculative contracts were prohibited in the early days of Islam, there are contemporary financial transactions that involve risks or uncertainties that will bring about economic regression and financial depression. There are stringent rules in Islamic law against uncertain transactions that may result in the deception of one or more parties to the contract. Earlier jurists attempted to define or describe what constitutes *gharar*. According to Ibn Taimiyyah, *gharar* means any transaction or disposition whose consequences are not known to the parties involved. In a similar vein, the definitions given by Al-Shiraazi and Al-Sarakhsi consider *gharar* to be a particular phenomenon, which may be a transaction, whose nature and consequences are concealed and cannot

# ISLAMIC FINANCE IN THE NEWS

## Islamic banks caught between two worlds

**April 20, 2010**

Corporate restructurings were until recently relatively rare in the oil-rich Arab Gulf, but the experience is particularly novel for investment companies and banks that adhere to Islamic, or Sharī'ah, law.

The Islamic finance industry grew exponentially in the years preceding the financial crisis—particularly in the Middle East—boosted by increasing religious awareness and an inflow of billions of dollars of oil revenue into the Gulf. The industry now holds total assets of about US $950bn, according to Moody's.

Yet it has been hit by the economic downturn, which caused several high-profile Islamic investment banks to default and restructure their operations and debt.

Restructurings in the Gulf are already complicated by underdeveloped legal frameworks, a lack of transparency, inexperienced commercial courts and a 'head in the sand' approach, bankers and lawyers say. Adherence to Sharī'ah adds another layer of complexity to the process.

Bridging the gap between religious and secular commercial law—and Islamic financial theory and practice—is often complicated and gives rise to ambiguity and uncertainty, industry figures say.

The difficulties have been highlighted by the US $3.5bn restructuring of The Investment Dar, the Kuwaiti finance house, which is emerging as a key test case for the Islamic finance sector. TID defaulted on an Islamic bond last July and has since been struggling to get its creditors to agree to a restructuring plan.

Other Islamic investment companies in Kuwait and Bahrain have also defaulted, but TID is the largest 'Islamic restructuring' to emerge thus far.

Islamic financial principles ban interest and promote equity-based risk sharing. While all transactions and instruments ostensibly follow Sharī'ah rules, almost all are drafted in accordance with English law.

'One of the main problems is the way in which some Islamic financial contracts are drafted, which causes contentions when things go bad and a default takes place,' says Muddassir Siddiqui, a Sharī'ah scholar and head of Islamic finance at Denton Wilde Sapte, the law firm. 'From a Sharī'ah perspective there is one interpretation, but from a conventional legal perspective, there is often a very different interpretation,' he says.

This has been underscored by an ongoing legal case between TID and one of its creditors, Lebanon's Blom Bank. The investment company has argued that a US $10m 'wakala' instrument the Lebanese lender placed with TID should be judged void since it breaks Islamic law and is therefore outside the company's remit.

An English judge said in December that Blom Bank would likely win the case if it went to a hearing, but controversially conceded that TID at least had 'an arguable case'.

Lawyers warn that this could potentially lead struggling Islamic companies to attempt to overturn contracts on the basis of whether they comply with Islamic law.

No Islamic bank has failed during the crisis, but many have been hurt by the global downturn in real estate—the most popular asset class due to Islamic finance's preference for real assets to back transactions.

Islamic financial theory stipulates that Sharī'ah-compliant banks are agents who invest depositors' money in profitable ventures. Therefore, according to many Sharī'ah scholars, if a bank loses money, depositors should in theory share in the loss.

In reality this has never happened, as it could cause runs in the Islamic finance industry, bankers point out. Yet it is still uncertain what would happen if an Islamic bank were to default.

Governments, particularly in the Middle East, are likely to step in to prevent banks collapsing—Islamic or conventional—but this could pose problems for some clerics due to Sharī'ah's risk-sharing requirements.

'Islamic bank depositors aren't real depositors in the conventional sense, but investors that are supposed to share risks and rewards,' Mr Siddiqui says. 'It's complex. These areas have to be sorted out deal by deal, contract by contract and institution by institution.'

**Source:** Robin Wigglesworth, "Islamic banks caught between two worlds", *Financial Times*, April 20, 2010.

be ascertained. This means all forms of clandestine transactions involving uncertain elements can be easily classified under *gharar*.

**haram**
Strictly forbidden acts, practices or transactions in Islam, which are considered as sins.

Muhammad Ayub, a Pakistani Islamic finance expert, has raised an important issue regarding the nature of uncertainty in business transactions. "Risk-taking is rather a condition for the entitlement to profit in business. The problem, however, was that the extent of uncertainty making any transaction **haram** had not been clearly defined. Lately, scholars have differentiated between *gharar-e-kathir* and *gharar qalil* (too much and nominal uncertainty) and declared that only those transactions that involve too much or excessive uncertainty in respect of the subject matter and the price in a contract should be prohibited."[18] The reason for this line of argument is that profit and risk-sharing businesses such as *musharakah* and *mudarabah*, involve some elements of risk-sharing in a situation when losses are recorded in the joint venture. This position can be reconciled with the definition of *gharar* in the sense that *gharar* involves excessive uncertainty in respect of the subject matter of the contract. On the other hand, a profit and risk-sharing business entails certainty of the subject matter, and the price and parties involved in any contracts. The risk involved in profit and risk-sharing transactions is only determined when the joint venture incurs losses.

The contemporary relevance of these simple prohibitions can be seen in modern financial transactions such as insurance and financial derivatives. Some contemporary scholars have endeavored to validate or make conventional insurance policies Shari'ah-compliant, but many jurists argue that these forms of insurance policies fall under the prohibited list in Islamic commercial jurisprudence. For the juristic views on Islamic insurance (*takaful*) and financial derivatives, see Chapters 8 and 10, respectively.

**qimar (or maysir)**
A game of chance or gambling that involves the acquisition of wealth by chance of winning the game or speculation without any form of consideration or compensation for such wealth.

## *Maysir* or *Qimar* (Gambling or Games of Chance)

Gambling can be defined as 'a contract among two or more persons involving the exchange of money or other valuables depending upon the uncertain outcome of a staged event'.[19] All forms of games of chance (**qimar** or **maysir**), whether contractual or non-contractual, are prohibited by the Shari'ah. This prohibition arises from the premise that the agreement between the parties involves certain immoral and undue benefits based on false hopes in the contract. It involves the lucky chance of acquiring something valuable without actually earning it. Such immoral inducements may lead to bankruptcy for some individuals and the enrichment of others, as experienced in non-Muslim countries that have legalised betting and games of chance with the granting of licenses to casinos.

There is a relationship between *gharar* and *qimar* in terms of the uncertain outcome. Another term for a game of chance is *maysir*, as used in the Qur'an. The references in the Qur'an to games of chance may conveniently be cited to support the prohibition of risky or hazardous transactions. The wisdom behind the prohibition of these forms of transactions is the resultant injustice that flows from undue advantage, deceit, and fraud.

The affirmative evidence for the prohibition of *qimar* in the Qur'an are:

> Qur'an 5:90–91: "O you who have believed! Intoxicants and gambling, sacrificing to stones, and divination are abominable actions of Satan; so abstain from them in order that you may be successful. Satan intends to excite enmity and hatred between you with intoxicants and gambling, and hinder you from the remembrance of Allah and from prayer. So will you not then abstain?"

> Qur'an 2:219: "They ask you concerning wine and gambling. Say: 'In them is great sin and some benefits for people; but the sin is greater than the benefits.'"

The outcome of any game of chance such as gambling or raffles is always uncertain. This is akin to *gharar*, which has been explained. On this basis, authorities from the Qur'an and Sunnah that invalidate all transactions tainted with uncertain or risky elements may be conveniently cited to prohibit *qimar*. Abu Hurairah narrated that the Prophet said: "Whoever takes an oath in which he (forgetfully) mentions *Lat* and *Uzza* (two idols of Arab pagans) should say: 'None has the right to be worshipped but Allah', and whoever says to his companion, 'Come along, let us gamble' must give alms (as an expiation)."[20] This gives an insight into the prohibition of *qimar* from the traditions of the Prophet.

The wisdom behind the prohibition of *qimar* includes reliance on accidental gains or luck. Islam encourages people to earn their means of livelihood in a legitimate manner through hard work and due diligence. In addition, *qimar* destroys the source of families' livelihoods by impoverishing the losers and unfairly enriching the winners through prohibited means. Through this, enmity and hatred is generated among the players.

# Review

## Key Terms and Concepts

act of God (p. 57)

active legal capacity (p. 62)

*al-aqidan* (p. 58)

*al-ma'qud alaih* (p. 58)

*'aqd* (p. 47)

*'aqd infiradi* (p. 52)

*'aqd thuna'i* (p. 52)

*bay'* (p. 59)

bilateral contract (p. 55)

consensus of opinion (p. 65)

consideration (p. 49)

*dhimmah* (p. 61)

enforceable contract (p. 57)

*fiqh al-mu'amalat* (p. 43)

*haram* (p. 71)

invalid contract (p. 57)

Islamic hire-purchase contract (p. 50)

*ju'alah* (p. 55)

legal capacity (p. 61)

*Majallah al-ahkam al-adliyyah* (p. 49)

*majlis al-'aqd* (p. 59)

*maslahah mursalah* (p. 56)

*mu'allaq* (p. 69)

*mu'amalat* (p. 43)

*mudarabah* (p. 56)

*mukallaf* (p. 62)

multilateral contracts (p. 56)

*murabahah* (p. 50)

*musharakah* (p. 56)

*muwa'adah* (p. 49)

*nikah* (p. 47)

operation of law (p. 53)

prodigal (p. 61)

product Development (p. 53)

*qimar* (p. 71)

quasi contract (p. 55)

receptive legal capacity (p. 62)

*riba al-fadl* (p. 68)

*riba al-nasi'ah* (p. 67)

*salam* (or *bay' al-salam*) (p. 59)

*shibh al-'aqd* (p. 52)

*sighah* (p. 58)

*talaq* (p. 47)

trade by barter (p. 59)

unilateral contract (p. 54)

vicegerency (p. 43)

void contract (p. 57)

*wa'ad* (p. 49)

*wakalah* (p. 55)

*wasiyah* (p. 47)

## Summary

**Learning Objective 2.1**

1. The underlying philosophy of business transactions in Islam is that of fair dealing, equity, justice, and mutual satisfaction. This has been developed into a definitive contract theory that in turn has shaped the modern practice of Islamic banking and finance.

**Learning Objective 2.2**

2. The legal concepts and theories underpinning the various types of contracts in Islamic law remain relevant today, and their consequential application in modern transactions is essential for a robust Islamic finance industry. The applicability of these forms of contract in modern Islamic banking and financial business is the most important part of the discussion.

**Learning Objective 2.3**

3. The prescriptions of Islamic contracts in modern financial transactions include clear declarations of offer and acceptance and the availability of a valuable consideration. The essential elements of a valid contract include offer and acceptance, parties to the contract, subject matter of the contract, consideration, and the intention to create a legal relationship through a meeting of minds of the parties and mutual satisfaction.

**Learning Objective 2.4**

4. The forbidden contracts in Islamic commercial transactions must be avoided by all means in the process of product development in Islamic banking and finance. It should be recalled that all the Sharī'ah financial instruments are premised on permissible contracts. Thus, all forbidden elements, such as *riba*, *gharar*, and *qimar*, and other types of contracts tainted with such elements must be proscribed.

## Practice Questions and Activities

### Practice Questions

1. Explain the underlying philosophy of Islamic contract law with special reference to the permissibility of commercial transactions and the proscription of all usurious dealings.

2. How does the right to earn a legitimate means of livelihood relate to contracts in Islamic law?

3. Differentiate between *wa'ad* and *muwa'adah* as they both relate to undertakings or promises in contractual transactions.

4. What is the relevance of Islamic contract law to the modern practice of Islamic banking and finance?

5. What are the essential elements of a valid contract in Islamic law?

6. In product development in Islamic finance, what do Sharī'ah scholars rely on in designing new Islamic financial products?

7. Iskil received a personal loan of US$50,000 from XYZ Bank. In order to cater for the service charges of the bank and other expenses, the parties expressly stipulated in the loan agreement that Iskil will repay the loan to the bank together with 10 percent interest per annum within five years. As a member of the Sharī'ah Advisory Board of XYZ Bank, advise the bank on the prescriptions of Islamic law on financial contracts with particular reference to loans and service charges.

8. Discuss three major prohibited elements in commercial transactions under the Sharī'ah.

### Activities

1. Find a copy of a contractual agreement for any Islamic finance product and identify the major elements of a contract of sale.

2. Prepare a sketch of a contract of sale in Islamic law based on the essential elements of a valid contract.

3. Submit three newspaper cuttings on Islamic finance contracts concluded by any bank or financial institution situated in your locality or elsewhere.

## Further Reading

Al-Maghribi, M. A. M. (1988). *Ahkam al-'Aqd fi al-Sharī'ah al-Islamiyyah-Dirasatun muqaranah*. Beirut, Lebanon: Al-Maktabat al-Hadith.

Ayub, M. (2007). *Understanding Islamic Finance*. England: John Wiley & Sons Ltd.

Habachy, S. (1962). Property, Right, and Contract in Muslim Law. *Columbia Law Review*. Vol. 62: pp. 450–473.

Hassan, H. (2002). Contracts in Islamic Law: The Principles of Commutative Justice and Liberality. 13 *Journal of Islamic Studies*: pp. 257–297.

Kamali, M. H. (2002). *Islamic Commercial Law: An Analysis of Futures and Options*. Kuala Lumpur: Ilmiah Publishers.

Ma'sum Billah, M. (1426/2006). *Sharī'ah Standard of Business Contract*. Kuala Lumpur: A.S. Noordeen.

Niazi, L. A. (1991). *Islamic Law of Contract*. Lahore: Research Cell, Dyal Sing Trust Library.

Nyazee, I. A. (1997). *Islamic Law of Business Organization—Partnerships*. Islamabad, Pakistan: International Institute of Islamic Thought and Islamic Research Institute.

Rayner, S. (1991). *The Theory of Contracts in Islamic Law*. London: Graham and Trotman.

Razali, S. S. (2010). *Islamic Law of Contract*. Singapore: Cengage Learning Asia Pte Ltd.

# Financial Instruments of Islamic Banking and Financ

# Learning Objectives

**Upon completion of this chapter, the reader should be able to:**

1 Describe the sources and uses of funds and the operation of bank accounts by Islamic banks.

2 Understand how exchange-based contracts are utilized as financial instruments in Islamic finance.

3 Understand how service-based contracts are utilized as financial instruments in Islamic finance.

4 Understand how partnership contracts are utilized as financial instruments in Islamic finance.

5 Know the nature of supporting contracts in Islamic finance, including the unilateral supporting contracts.

The Sharī'ah financial instruments derived from the Islamic finance contracts discussed in Chapter 2 form the basis of the business of Islamic financial institutions. They were originally Sharī'ah contracts that have since been transformed into competitive products by the Islamic finance industry. The financial instruments designed by experts and endorsed by the Sharī'ah experts are meant to be used by banks and financial institutions in an interest-free regime. Any financial instrument, whether it originates from the classical Sharī'ah contracts or conventional financial contracts, may be regarded as a Sharī'ah financial instrument if it is compliant with the underlying philosophy of Islamic finance. A financial instrument regardless of its origin is Sharī'ah-compliant if it is devoid of excessive risk, interest, deceit, and other prohibited practices in commercial and financial contracts.

This chapter examines Sharī'ah financial instruments based on the popular forms of contract in Islamic law. The categorisation of these instruments is based on the type of contract, ranging from exchange-based contracts, service-based contracts, partnership contracts, supporting or accessory contracts, to unilateral supporting contracts. This chapter also offers a unique appraisal of how classical contracts have been transformed into competitive Sharī'ah financial instruments that meet the modern challenges faced in the Islamic banking, finance, and *takaful* (insurance) services.

**Dr. Mohammad Omar Farooq**

*Head of the Centre for Islamic Finance, Bahrain Institute of Banking and Finance (BIBF)*

**1    What are the processes/stages of product development in Islamic banking and finance?**

Product development has some common stages, including market study, resource deployment, team formation, as well as relevant R&D. Development of Islamic financial products shares these common stages. However, in certain respects, there are some additional stages and/or some common stages that are relatively more elaborate and complex. The main aspects of Islamic financial product development include Islamic law and jurisprudence based on Sharī'ah, law of the land, tax structure, accounting standards, technicalities/technology, finance, and marketing. The distinguishing aspect of Islamic financial products is that they must all be Sharī'ah-compliant—most importantly, avoiding key prohibitions such as *riba* (commonly equated with interest), *gharar* (excessive uncertainty or speculation) and *maysir* (gambling).

In developing products that are Sharī'ah-compliant, the key role is assigned to Sharī'ah experts who evaluate and then validate a product by issuing a *fatwa* (expert or authoritative religious edict). In some countries, there are national Sharī'ah boards that validate Sharī'ah-compliant products, and Islamic financial institutions (IFIs) depend on them, while in other countries Sharī'ah-compliance validation is done by the Sharī'ah supervisory board of each IFI. Malaysia, for example, has a national Sharī'ah board, while Bahrain and Gulf Cooperation Council (GCC) countries generally leave this matter to an IFI's own Sharī'ah supervisory board. However, even in case of the latter, product development must be based on standards issued by key organizations, such as the Accounting and Auditing Organization for Islamic Financial Institutions (AAOIFI).

**2    What is the procedure adopted by the AAOIFI Sharī'ah Board?**

AAOIFI has a well-established procedure for developing standards, where the Sharī'ah board is responsible for developing Sharī'ah standards and the Accounting and Auditing Standards Board is responsible for accounting, ethics, and governance standards. The process firstly begins with a *preliminary idea* for a potential new standard. Ideas for new standards or a review of existing standards can come from the industry, AAOIFI, or its boards/committees. Next, a *consultation note* is generated in the form of an outline of the major points of the new, or major changes to an existing, standard. Relevant stakeholders, including the industry and the public, are then invited to share their feedback, which leads to an exposure draft. An *exposure draft* is developed in the same format as a final standard for deliberations by the respective standards committees. This document also goes through a feedback process with the industry and the public. This results in a developed *final standard* that needs approval by the respective standard boards. From a publicly-announced specific date of *issuance*, the standard(s) become official and thus binding upon member institutions. Each standard is subject to future review, following the same process.

**3    How can product development in Islamic finance be accelerated?**

During the early stages of the industry, product development was less systematic. Sometimes in a less-regulated environment, it might have taken little time whereas in a highly regulated one, an unusually long time. Factors that constrained product development include the regulatory environment, market practices, lack of expertise, rating issues, etc. Notable progress has been facilitated by the standards—Sharī'ah and accounting—set by AAOIFI, the prudential regulatory standards set by the Islamic Financial Services Board (IFSB), standardizations introduced by International Islamic Financial Markets (IIFM), the establishment of rating institutions, such as the International Islamic Rating Agency (IIRA), as well as availability of ratings from established agencies such as Standard & Poor's and Moody's, and the expanding demand for a wider range of products, particularly in the Muslim world and in countries with significant Muslim minorities.

Unfortunately, product development so far has been narrowly focused on taking products from the conventional shelf and restructuring them as Sharī'ah-compliant products. While this in itself is a creative enterprise, innovative, truly new products that are a genuine contribution to the global shelf of products, rather than products that are of interest to Muslims only, has not been forthcoming. In this area, Islamic financial engineering has been mostly legal engineering, if it has to do with engineering at all.

However, the realization that this industry has a much greater and fundamentally distinctive contribution to make and collaborative efforts among the relevant stakeholders in the Muslim world could significantly accelerate more relevant product development.

Describe the sources
and uses of funds and
the operation of bank
accounts by Islamic
banks.

**dual banking system**
A banking system of a country
or territory that incorporates
both the conventional and
Islamic financial systems.

**Islamic finance windows**
Subsidiaries or branches
of a conventional financial
institution that are specifically
established to operate Sharī'ah-
compliant banking and finance.

**real capital**
Original assets of financial
institutions, such as machinery,
equipment, and real estate.

**equity capital**
Funds invested to acquire real
capital. This generally includes
the funds of shareholders and
investors.

# Sources and Uses of Funds by Islamic Banks

Before we examine the financial instruments of Islamic banking and finance, let us consider the sources and uses of funds. These are based on financial instruments designed to serve customers' specific needs. To this end, this section describes the sources and uses of funds and the operation of current accounts by Islamic banks. Generally, the phrase 'sources and application of funds' refers to the cash inflows and outflows in an Islamic bank or financial institution over a period of time. In a **dual banking system**, where Islamic banking and conventional banking operate concurrently in the same jurisdiction, some ethical issues are often raised regarding the sources and application of the funds of depositors. These are among the concerns addressed in this section.

## Sources of Funds

Remember that some transactions are prohibited in Islamic law, such as interest-bearing and speculative transactions. Therefore, in order to avoid sourcing funds from prohibited means or investing funds in prohibited transactions, most banks with dual banking arrangements manage their Islamic funds separately from conventional funds. Bank customers who opt for Islamic financial products are very sensitive to issues concerning the application of their money. The sources of funds in IFIs include deposits in savings, current, and general investment accounts. It appears, however that concerns about the sources and application of funds in conventional financial institutions with **Islamic finance windows** informed the decision of the Qatar Central Bank in 2011 to close all Islamic finance windows in the country. The *Islamic Finance in the News* box (on page 81) shows the views of different stakeholders on this issue of assets split between conventional and Islamic banking. In fact, global banking leaders, such as HSBC, subsequently closed their Islamic finance subsidiaries at the end of 2011 following the directive.

Although interest is forbidden in Islamic financial transactions, fees and commissions or fixed charges are permissible for banking services performed by either a corporate body or an individual. These are one source of funds for IFIs. Generally, apart from the **real capital** and **equity capital** of Islamic banks, they also rely on the following sources of funds which they use in banking business:

1. TRANSACTION DEPOSITS: These are risk-free funds that do not yield any return, such as current accounts based on the *wadi'ah* concept, whereby a sum of money is deposited with the bank for safekeeping.

2. INVESTMENT DEPOSITS: Investment deposits offer the benefit of making profit or the risk of capital loss, depending on the amount realized by the bank in its investments. For example, in an investment account where the depositor concludes a *mudarabah* contract with the bank, they are entitled to some form of return or loss based on the performance of the investment.

These two major sources of funds come from deposits in three main types of accounts.

1. CURRENT ACCOUNTS: These are accounts opened in the name of individuals, companies, or firms for the deposit of cash, checks, and bills. These bank accounts neither yield any return nor bear any risk. Current accounts operated by Islamic banks are based on the concept of *wadi'ah*, that is, safekeeping of the deposits. As part of the contract between the depositor and the bank, the funds deposited will be guaranteed as they will not be used for any joint-venture business prone to profit and loss. On its own volition, the bank may use the funds for **short-term liquidity** but repayment remains guaranteed at any time when requested.

2. SAVINGS ACCOUNTS: In savings accounts, the funds deposited yield some returns, unlike current accounts, depending on the bank's financial results. This type of deposit is also based on a number of concepts in Islamic finance. These include *wadi'ah*, *mudarabah* (trust investment partnership), and *musharakah* (joint-venture partnership) concepts. In practice, the *wadi'ah* concept is often consolidated with other concepts such as *hibah* (gift), which is a premium sometimes paid to customers who have savings accounts. Some scholars, however, consider this practice of paying a premium to customers to retain them to be a form of *riba*. The payment of such premiums to the holders of savings accounts is at the discretion of the bank. This is different from interest earned in the conventional banking system, where there is a fixed interest payment depending on the amount of funds in the account and the length of time such funds have been deposited.

3. INVESTMENT ACCOUNTS: These are the most important source of funds for Islamic banks. In investment accounts, there is a joint-venture agreement between the customers and the bank. This type of account operates under the *mudarabah* concept where power of attorney is given to the bank to undertake any lawful investment activities that will yield profit or loss. In this partnership agreement, there is an active partner (the bank) and a sleeping partner (the customer), where the former has absolute freedom in the management and investment decisions that affect the business. The uniqueness of Islamic banking is the risk element of a joint venture with the bank. Although banks take every prudent step to manage risk, the depositor must be ready to bear any loss in the event of losses on the part of the bank. For larger investors and corporate bodies, Islamic banks have special investment accounts that are also operated under the *mudarabah* concept, in which the depositor/investor has the right to choose a specified project for the investment.

**short-term liquidity**
Degree by which a corporate body or an individual can meet its short-term cash obligations.

## Application of Funds

Islamic banks apply their funds to raise profits through different means. A bank has the option to either deploy its own funds in a particular business or enter into a joint-venture agreement with customers. The main conduits for the outflow of the funds of the banks include the *musharakah*, *mudarabah*, *murabahah* (cost-plus financing), *ijarah* (lease), *istisna'* (manufacturing contract), *bay al-salam* and *bay al-muajjal* (deferred sale contract) models depending on the structure adopted by a particular bank. Different banks have continued to come up with modified financial instruments that are not only Sharī'ah-compliant but also competitive in global banking. These models through which the funds of the Islamic bank are deployed are financial instruments, which will be explained later in this chapter.

# ISLAMIC FINANCE IN THE NEWS

## Qatar Banks Prepare for Islamic Assets Split

June 6, 2011

In February, Qatar Central Bank issued a circular stipulating that conventional banks must close their Islamic windows by the end of the year.

At issue are the 23.4 percent of the assets of Qatari banks operating under the aegis of the QCB that are classified as Islamic. The likelihood is that the assets that are booked with conventional banks will have to be sold or auctioned to wholly Islamic banks in the emirate, analysts say.

'While there is still some uncertainty regarding required timing, my understanding is that the conventional banks are providing information to potential bidders,' says Khalid Howladar, senior credit officer at Moody's Investors Service, the rating agency.

'Once timings are formalized and institutions are committed, you will likely see more visible signs, such as asset or franchise sales or bids, and branding or branch changes.'

The numbers are far from negligible. The Islamic window at Qatar National Bank, the emirate's largest lender, contributed 16 percent of net profits last year, while Islamic assets formed 14 percent of the total. A QNB official nonetheless says that the impact of the QCB circular on his bank will be 'minimal'.

Raghavan Seetharaman, chief executive at Doha Bank, the third-largest institution, said earlier this year that 89 percent of its assets are conventional and his institution will not be taking a 'big hit'.

HSBC Amanah said in a statement that 'in accordance with central bank requirements, HSBC Amanah will close its Islamic operations in Qatar by 31 December 2011. There will be no impact on staff. HSBC Amanah employees in Qatar will be absorbed into the conventional business.'

Analysts regard the comingling of funds and, in particular, the use of conventional fixed-income deposits to fund Islamic assets as a main reason for the QCB intervention. Financial reporting and capital adequacy concerns have also come into play. The QCB could be aiming to comply with standards issued by the Malaysia-based Islamic Financial Standards Board, the analysts say. 'A lot of this comes down to accounting,' says Andrew Cunningham, head of Darien Middle East, a consultancy. 'How confident are you as a regulator that one set of financial statements can capture valuation and income recognition when two quite different ways of doing business are involved, namely conventional and Islamic?'

Mr Cunningham says that because Islamic transactions are largely asset-based, Islamic banks tend to hold physical assets, such as property and commodities, on their books to a much larger extent than conventional institutions. 'Typically, you don't allow banks to do that but prefer them instead to hold loans or bonds, limited real estate, limited real assets.'

Are other jurisdictions likely to follow the QCB lead?

'No one else has decided to do it,' says Rod Ringrow, senior executive officer at State Street Middle East North Africa. 'Let's see how it works out in practice and what that unleashes on both sides in terms of activity.'

Mr Howladar of Moody's says that bankers in Saudi Arabia and the United Arab Emirates seem confident that there are no plans to follow Qatar and separate Islamic from conventional assets in their jurisdictions in the near future.

'I don't see any global trend away from Islamic windows in conventional banks,' says Mr Cunningham. 'If anything it's the reverse: conventional banks are wanting to do more and more Islamic business.'

Mr Howladar says that the QCB is a member of the IFSB, and that this body is focused on modifications necessary to handle Islamic finance in Basel II. 'Basel III will require more "integration", given some of the asset-deposit idiosyncrasies of Islamic financial institutions, so separation may make regulation at least conceptually easier.'

A Doha-based lawyer says compliance might not be enforced as strictly as originally stated, from a practical point of view, and that the QCB has yet to give its final word on the issue. 'It will be very difficult for conventional banks to transfer all their assets by the end of the year,' he says. In a forced sale of conventional banks' Islamic assets, buyers might demand discounts to book value, further muddying the situation.

**Source:** Peter Shaw-Smith, "Qatar Banks Prepare for Islamic Assets Split," *Financial Times*, June 6, 2011.

In 2011, Qatar Central Bank ordered all Qatari banks operating under QCB to close all Islamic finance windows in the country in order to avoid the comingling of funds and the use of conventional fixed-income deposits to fund Islamic assets.

**LEARNING OBJECTIVE 3.2**

Understand how exchange-based contracts are used as financial instruments in Islamic finance.

# Concept of Exchange-Based Contracts

The exchange-based contracts in Islamic law that have been transformed into viable financial instruments include:

- *murabahah* (mark-up)
- *istisna'* (manufacture sale)
- *salam* (forward sale)
- *bay al-dayn* (sale of debt)
- *tawriq* (securitization)
- *sarf* (sale of currency)
- *tawarruq* (cash financing)
- *bay al-inah* (sale with immediate repurchase).

While some of these contracts have been independently designed into unique financial instruments, others have been merged into hybrid financial instruments. In most cases, the accessory or supporting contracts will always appear to serve their unique purpose by facilitating the underlying contracts. Exchange-based contracts have been developed into **debt-based financing instruments** in the form of securities because they are contracts that create debts. A careful study of each of the exchange-based contracts will reveal a wider latitude for their use as competitive financial instruments. Therefore, to begin with, let's consider the exchange-based contracts used as financial instruments in Islamic finance.

**debt-based financing instruments**
Financial instruments that create a debt-like relationship between the parties.

## *Murabahah* (Cost-Plus or Mark-up Sale)

**murabahah**
Cost-plus financing contract where a sale is made at a specified profit margin.

**Murabahah** is a sale of goods with a profit mark-up that creates a line of credit. Lexically, 'murabahah' is derived from the root word *ribh*, which means profit, gain, or a legal addition. The morphological derivation of the word that establishes a form of mutual contract between two parties where they agree to the mark-up led to the name *murabahah*. In the classical Islamic literature, *murabahah* is a sale where the buyer demands a particular commodity from the buyer. When the commodity is ready for sale, the seller reveals the cost price to the buyer but the commodity is thereafter sold at a mark-up price to the buyer. The additional cost must be agreed upon by the parties at the initial stage of the contract. Such contracts are permissible under the Sharī'ah.

In simple terms, *murabahah* is the sale of a commodity at the cost price at which it was purchased plus an additional profit that has been mutually agreed upon by the parties. As this form of exchange contract involves some element of trust on the part of the parties, particularly the seller, a fundamental condition for the validity of the contract is for the buyer to know the original cost price of the commodity as well as the additional profit that has been added by the seller.

What therefore emerges from the above is the question of whether *murabahah* is meant for the purchase of every commodity one intends to buy. In the classical literature, *murabahah* was used specifically for certain situations. It was intended to protect unsuspecting consumers who might not know much about specific commodities that require knowledge of the trade or industry. The classical sellers in *murabahah* transactions were like brokers who facilitated trade through mark-up arrangements. However, modern practice is restricted to IFIs where standard *murabahah* contracts are signed by the parties and conducted on a deferred payment basis. Although the modern practice of *murabahah* is slightly different from the classical one, it has been hybridized with other permissible concepts of commercial transactions, such as the permissibility of deferred payment.

As explained earlier, the classical practice of *murabahah* has been further designed into a financial instrument for project financing. A typical example is given in Figure 3.1

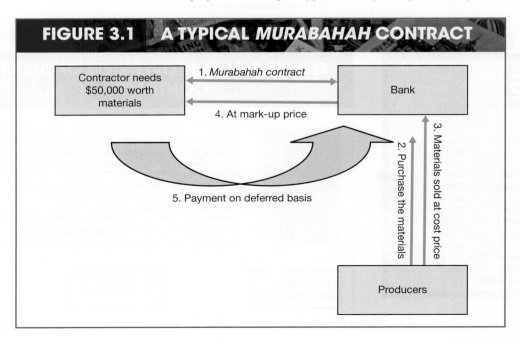

FIGURE 3.1  A TYPICAL *MURABAHAH* CONTRACT

Contractor needs $50,000 worth materials

1. *Murabahah contract*

4. At mark-up price

Bank

5. Payment on deferred basis

2. Purchase the materials

3. Materials sold at cost price

Producers

where a contractor, who is a builder, intends to find financing for the materials required to construct an estate. The five steps below are illustrated in this example.

1.   The contractor contacts the bank to acquire US$50,000 worth of specific building materials for the building of an estate through a *murabahah* contract.

2.   The bank enters into another contract (contract of sale) with the producers of the building materials and buys them immediately.

3.   The producer sells the materials to the bank.

4.   The bank supplies the materials to the contractor at the mark-up price.

5.   The contractor pays the mark-up price on a deferred basis.

Figure 3.2 also depicts a similar *murabahah* arrangement.

For a *murabahah* contract to be valid, certain conditions have to be met. The fundamental requirement is that the conditions necessary for a valid contract of sale must be met. The following specific conditions must be met in a *murabahah* transaction.

1.   GOODS SUBJECT TO *MURABAHAH*. The goods subject to *murabahah* must be lawful, real, and have commercial value. Both tangible and non-tangible goods may be used as the subject matter of the transaction. For instance, examples of tangible goods include cars, personal computers, and household appliances, while examples of non-tangible goods include trademarks, patents, copyrights, and royalties. Currencies or a standard medium of exchange such as gold and silver cannot be traded in *murababah* transactions because they cannot be exchanged on a deferred basis. They must be exchanged on the spot without any deferment. In a similar vein, as debt cannot be sold in Islamic law except in a contract of assignment, any credit instrument that represents a debt owed by a person cannot be traded in a *murabahah* transaction because any mark-up profit on such a debt is considered *riba* (interest).

**Hint**

Muslim scholars have different views and they follow different processes in calculating the cost price. If the financial institution (buyer) says it has *bought* a particular commodity for $X, the cost of transportation is generally not included. But if it says the transaction costs $Y, the price includes packaging, transportation, and any other cost incurred in handling the commodity. This latter case comprises the direct costs incurred.

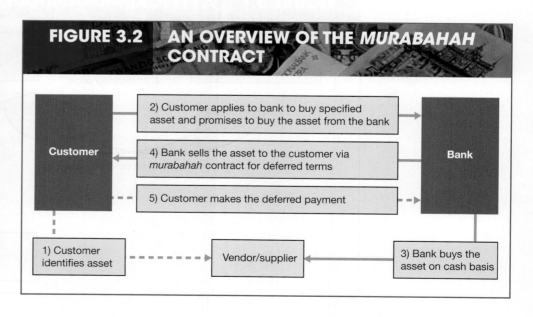

**FIGURE 3.2   AN OVERVIEW OF THE *MURABAHAH* CONTRACT**

2. ORIGINAL COST PRICE OF THE GOODS AND ADDITIONAL PROCUREMENT COSTS. As seen earlier, *murabahah* transactions are based on absolute trust, so the seller is required to state the original cost price of the goods and any additional costs incurred in the process of procuring the goods. If the goods were supplied through an agent, the seller might have paid some agency fees (*ujrah*). These are usually included as part of the cost price. The cost of packaging, transportation and delivery of the goods is calculated as part of the cost price. Depending on the nature of the contract and the financial institution involved, its policy on computing the direct and indirect costs associated with the transaction will determine the mark-up price. The breakdown of these expenses must be clearly stated and must be agreed with the buyer. If there is any defect or added value in the product, this must be disclosed by the seller. Furthermore, the mode of payment must be clearly stated by the seller. In most cases, since banks and financial institutions now regularly undertake such transactions, some of these issues are usually provided for in a standard *murabahah* contract.

**margin of profit**
(also net margin)
A ratio that determines the amount of profit to be realised, generally calculated by dividing net profits by sales.

3. MARGIN OF PROFIT. The **margin of profit** must be mutually predetermined by the parties at the initial stage of the contract. Once the margin of profit is determined at the conclusion of the contract and payment is deferred, it cannot be varied at a later stage for any reason because the parties are bound by the agreement. In a situation where the seller has had a rebate from the supplier, that must be extended to the buyer and it will therefore affect the deferred price. The exact price must be made known to the buyer—any unspecified or hidden costs are not allowed in a *murabahah* transaction.

**Shari'ah supervisory council (or board)**
A body of Shari'ah scholars and experts who certify proposals for Islamic financial products, services, and contracts brought before them.

Within today's Islamic finance industry there has been a proliferation of complex contracts drafted by experts, which have been approved by the **Shari'ah supervisory councils** of financial institutions. Thus, in most cases, these conditions are catered for in the detailed *murabahah* contract. The practical application of such a contract is important and this is where the Shari'ah auditors must act in order to ensure proper compliance with Islamic legal prescriptions.

## *Istisna'* (Manufacturing Contract)

*istisna'*
A manufacturing contract for a made-to-order asset based on a deferred delivery basis.

Based on an exceptional principle in Islamic finance, **istisna'** is a transaction on a commodity before it exists. There is a moral obligation on the manufacturer to produce the commodity or item at the agreed time and in accordance with the specifications. The price and actual specification, description, and quality of the commodity to be manufactured, produced, or constructed should be fixed and ascertainable with the consent of the parties to the contract.

The manufacturer or contractor is called *sani* while the client is known as *mustasni*. The subject matter of the contract, which is the manufactured commodity, is known as *masnu'*. The manufacturing contract will only be complete when the bargain has been completed with clear stipulations on the price, quality, specifications, and date of delivery. The modern definition of an *istisna'* contract as given by Al-Zarqa is a slight deviation from the classical definitions. Al-Zarqa considers it to be a contract to sell a manufactured commodity, already known to the parties, with an undertaking from the seller to manufacture it from his own materials based on the specifications and price mutually agreed upon.[1] This definition is not so different from the classical ones but the dimension introduced here fits with modern realities. In practice, a preview of the subject matter may be available as a model which can be seen by the parties to the contract. Alternatively, an already manufactured model may be shown as a sample for replication based on certain specifications and at an agreed price. The payment arrangement may be by instalments or deferred. The *istisna'* contract can only be concluded on an item that can be manufactured or constructed, such as a house, shirt, trousers, or customised items. Once the manufacturing process has commenced, the contract cannot be unilaterally terminated unless with the consent of the parties involved.

There is no direct reference to *istisna'* contracts in the Qur'an and and Sunnah. However, Muslim jurists have justified the contract through the concept of **istihsan** (juristic preference), which is considered to be a secondary source of the Sharī'ah. On this basis, Muslim jurists have unanimously validated the contract provided it has satisfied other essential elements of a contract of sale. The majority of Muslim scholars have invoked the principle of *istihsan* from the perspective of the need and necessity to validate an *istisna'* contract. Party autonomy does not contradict Islamic law once it is exercised within the confines of mandatory prescriptions of the law.

As a mode of financing that has been developed into a financial instrument, *istisna'* has assumed an important position as a mechanism for financing certain transactions such as the manufacture and design of machinery for specific purposes. It may also be a facility accessed at an Islamic financial institution that deals in the development of real estate. Figure 3.3 illustrates a typical structure of a chain contract of *istisna'* where the Islamic financial institution occupies centre stage.

The *istisna'* structure illustrated in Figure 3.3 is most suited for project financing, such as construction and trade finance, where the client/customer approaches the financial

**istihsan**
A secondary source of Islamic law that simply means juristic preference or equity, used as a legal adaptation mechanism to address people's emerging needs while upholding the general philosophy of the Qur'an and Sunnah.

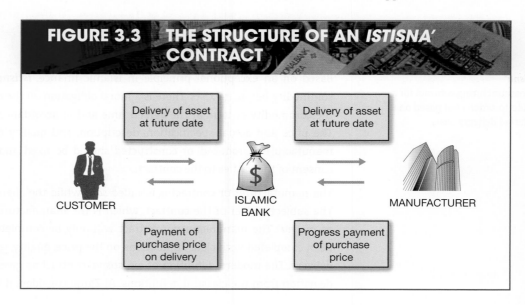

**FIGURE 3.3   THE STRUCTURE OF AN *ISTISNA'* CONTRACT**

Delivery of asset at future date

Delivery of asset at future date

CUSTOMER

ISLAMIC BANK

MANUFACTURER

Payment of purchase price on delivery

Progress payment of purchase price

institution. The bank enters into an *istisna'* contract with the manufacturer and payment may be made immediately or by installments. Delivery of the asset is at a future date but once it is ready, the manufacturer delivers it to the bank and receives the full payment of the purchase price. The bank then delivers the asset to the client and receives the payment of the purchase price, either immediately or on a deferred basis. All processes in this chain of contracts are carried out through agency contracts.

Apart from the use described above, an *istisna'* contract has been further developed into a viable financial instrument for use in the **Islamic capital market** (ICM). *Istisna'* is one of the four major types of Islamic financial instruments used as the basis for Islamic asset securitization. In *istisna'* asset securitization, a project company is created to undertake a specific project that automatically ceases to exist at the completion of the project. The project company in this case is an Islamic **special purpose vehicle** (SPV). The SPV securitizes an asset that is yet to exist, in the form of a project to be developed.

Figure 3.4 shows a typical example of a *sukuk* transaction using the *istisna'* structure that is based on the following five-step composite contract:

1. The established SPV raises funds by issuing *sukuk* certificates to *sukuk*-holders.

2. The proceeds from this fundraising are used to finance the project by paying the contractor on the basis of an *istisna'* contract.

3. The title to the asset is transferred to the SPV.

4. The completed property is leased or sold to the end buyer, who is required to pay for the property by monthly installments.

5. The proceeds from the payment for the property are distributed among the *sukuk*-holders.

**Islamic capital market**
A secondary market where financial and trade activities are carried out in ways that do not contradict Islamic commercial law.

**special purpose vehicle (SPV)**
A corporate entity incorporated for the sole purpose of carrying out a specified investment within a particular period of time. This entity manages the securitization process and handles the issuance of the certificates.

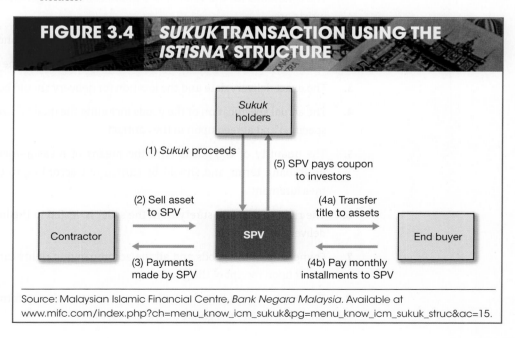

**FIGURE 3.4  *SUKUK* TRANSACTION USING THE *ISTISNA'* STRUCTURE**

Source: Malaysian Islamic Financial Centre, *Bank Negara Malaysia*. Available at www.mifc.com/index.php?ch=menu_know_icm_sukuk&pg=menu_know_icm_sukuk_struc&ac=15.

## *Salam* or *Bay al-Salam* (Forward Sale)

### Definition and Nature

**bay al-salam (or salam)**
A forward sale contract where advance payment is made for goods to be delivered later.

There are two fundamental exceptions to the general condition in a sale contract that the commodity should exist at the time of concluding the contract. The first exception, which does not require the commodity to exist at the time of concluding the contract, is *istisna'* as already discussed. The second exception is a **bay al-salam** or **salam** contract, which is a contract for the deferred delivery of a commodity. Though similar to *istisna'*, a *salam* contract can be defined as a contract of sale whereby the seller agrees to supply specific goods to the buyer on a deferred basis in exchange for an advance price paid in full on the spot. That is, the price for the yet-to-be-ready commodity is paid on the spot while delivery is deferred to a future date.

*Bay al-salam* or forward sale is based on the practices of farmers during the time of the Prophet (PBUH). Before interest was prohibited in commercial transactions, farmers were used to obtaining interest-based loans for the purpose of growing their crops and harvesting. This form of transaction was condemned by the Prophet because it is tainted with elements of interest, but he proffered an alternative in the form of *bay al-salam*. This was specifically meant to facilitate the farmers' commercial activities before their crops were harvested. They received money in advance of the harvest period.

The modern practice of *bay al-salam* is more formal. It has been transformed into a viable financial instrument in international trade. It has been used in contracts that involve raw materials and fungible goods through financial intermediaries—the IFIs.

### Conditions

The conditions for the validity of a *salam* contract as generally agreed upon by Muslim jurists are:

1. It is not necessary that the goods sold exist at the time of concluding the contract.

2. The purchase price must be paid in full by the buyer at the time of concluding the contract.

3. The exact delivery date and the location for delivery should be specified in the contract.

4. The actual specification of the goods including the quality, size, and description must be specified and agreed upon in the contract.

5. The quantity of the goods (and the means of measurement) must be agreed upon in absolute terms and should be carried out according to the customary method of measurement.

6. The right to demand surety from the seller is vested in the buyer in order to guarantee delivery of the goods.

7. Ownership of the goods and all the accompanying rights can only be exercised by the buyer upon receipt of the goods.

8. The buyer may nullify the contract and exercise the performance bond if the seller is unable to deliver the goods on the delivery date.

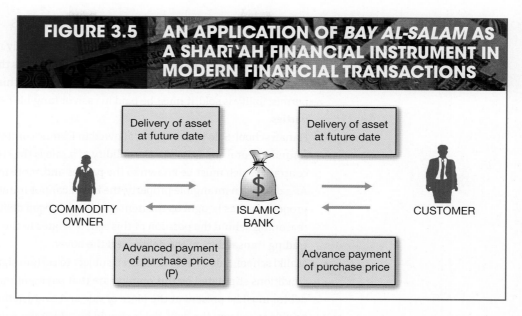

**FIGURE 3.5  AN APPLICATION OF *BAY AL-SALAM* AS A SHARĪ'AH FINANCIAL INSTRUMENT IN MODERN FINANCIAL TRANSACTIONS**

9. Delivery of the goods must be made practically regardless of the buyer's circumstances on the date of delivery.

10. The contract cannot be concluded on goods that can be delivered on the spot because the *salam* contract is specifically meant for forward sales.

## Application

Figure 3.5 illustrates the application of *bay al-salam* as a Sharī'ah financial instrument in modern financial transactions, based on the following steps:

1. A customer approaches a bank or financial institution for the purchase of certain commodities.

2. The customer and bank conclude a *salam* contract for the purchase of specified goods with full payment of the advance purchase price.

3. The bank, as the financial intermediary, concludes a different *salam* contract with a commodity owner and makes a full advance payment of the purchase price.

4. The commodity owner delivers the goods to the bank on the due date of delivery at the future date.

5. The bank in turn delivers the goods to the customer.

*Bay al-salam* is a flexible financial instrument that can be used for various financing needs.

## Bay al-Dayn (Sale of Debt)

**bay al-dayn**
(sale of debt)
A sale and purchase transaction involving an outstanding debt.

The meaning of **bay al-dayn** is sale of debt. The simple meaning of this form of contract is a sale and purchase transaction involving a quality debt. Muslim jurists are not unanimous on the permissibility of this form of sale. While some jurists of the Shafi'i school allow it, those of the Hanafi school declare it impermissible. For the Maliki school, *bay al-dayn* is allowed subject to certain important conditions.

## Position of the Four Major Muslim Schools

- Shafi'i school: Sale of debt is allowed to a third party only if the debt was initially guaranteed and was sold in exchange for goods that must be delivered immediately. When such a debt within the confines of this thin line of permissibility is sold, it must be paid in cash or tangible assets as agreed by the parties.
- Hanafi school: Sale of debt is not allowed in Islamic commercial transactions. A fundamental condition for the validity of a sale is the subject matter of the contract, which must be known to the parties and, more importantly, be tangible. As a debt is an intangible property, the buyer cannot immediately own the property he has bought as the item sold has not been delivered by the seller. The reasoning behind the position of this school relates to the potential risks of a debt trading transaction on the debtor and the buyer.
- Maliki school: Sale of debt is allowed subject to certain significant conditions. The conditions stipulated by this opinion are that payment must be expedited, the debtor must be present at the place of sale and confirm the debt, the debtor must be able to redeem the debt, debts should be sold at par value, and the goods must be saleable before they are fully possessed. This is the position of Ibn al-Qayyim, who further argued that there is no express legal text either in the Qur'an or Sunnah that forbids such a transaction.
- Hanbali school: Some jurists in the Hanbali school divide the sale of debt into two—confirmed and unconfirmed debts. Confirmed debts, which are already ascertained and reasonably quantified, can be sold on the spot. Unconfirmed debts, such as wages or fees for services during the course of the performance of a service, are not tradable whether on the spot or on a deferred basis.

## The Position of Modern Jurists

As debt is a liability on a person, many modern scholars believe there is no room for profit in debt trading. The International Islamic Fiqh Academy and the majority of contemporary scholars consider the sale or purchase of debt securities at a price other than their nominal value as impermissible in Islamic commercial transactions. *Hawalah* or assignment of debt can be made instead of *bay al-dayn*. When a relationship is established between the so-called purchaser of the debt and the original debtor, a *hawalah* contract is established. This is permissible in the Sharī'ah.

## *Bay al-Inah* (Sale with Immediate Repurchase)

**bay al-inah**
A seller sells a commodity to a buyer on a cash basis and immediately repurchases the same commodity on a deferred payment basis at a price higher than the initial cash price.

This is usually referred to as a sale-and-buyback transaction and it remains controversial in the global Islamic finance industry. **Bay al-inah** can be defined as a contract where a seller sells a commodity to a buyer on a cash basis and immediately repurchases the same commodity on a deferred payment basis at a price higher than the initial cash price.

## Views on the Validity of *Bay al-Inah*

*Bay al-inah* is a controversial Sharī'ah financial instrument. While many jurists believe it is invalid, a minority opinion upholds the validity of the transaction. The views of the jurists who validate and invalidate *bay al-inah*, respectively, are as follows.

- The Shafi'i school: *Bay al-inah* contracts are permissible in Islamic law because they are properly concluded in line with the underlying principles of a contract of sale. If the parties have any negative ulterior motive for concluding the contract, it will be considered immaterial in determining the validity of the contract. Imam al-Shafi'i considers *bay al-inah* permissible but quickly added a caveat that this conclusion is based on his own personal opinion.

- The Maliki, Hanafi and Hanbali schools: According to the jurists in these schools of thought, motive is paramount in determining the validity of a contract. Therefore, *bay al-inah* is not permissible in Islamic law because the motive of the parties in such a contract is illegal, which renders the contract void. They contend that *bay al-inah* is a move towards circumventing the mandatory prohibition of Islamic law through a legal device (**hilah**). They maintain that the prohibition of this form of transaction is based on the consensus of opinion of the jurists. Ibn al-Qayyim once quoted a relevant hadith where the Prophet is reported to have said: "A time will certainly come to mankind when they will legalise *riba* under the name of trading."

**hilah**
(pl. *hiyal*. contractum trinius)
A legal device employed by some Muslim jurists to circumvent certain prohibitive elements of the law.

*Bay al-Inah* is only used as a financial instrument in Malaysia, where it is considered permissible. The practice in Malaysia is simple; with the *bay al-inah* facility, the bank or financial institution sells the underlying asset to a client on a credit basis. The bank subsequently repurchases the asset from the customer immediately at a price lower than its earlier cost price on cash basis. A typical example is described thus:

1. A client approaches a bank and concludes a sale contract for the sale of land worth US$5,000 through a deferred sale.

2. The bank immediately concludes a separate purchase contract with the client for the sale of the same land to the bank for payment of US$6,000 in cash.

*Bay al-Inah* is used for different types of financing that involve real estate and house financing. But some scholars have suggested that alternative modes of financing that are not subject to elements of *riba*, such as **musharakah mutanaqisah** (diminishing partnership), should be used by the banks as a formidable Sharī'ah financial instrument. Note that in all other countries, including those in the Middle East, *bay al-inah* is considered to be tainted with elements of interest and thus declared impermissible under the law. According to the majority of jurists, both in the past and today, *bay al-inah* is prohibited in Islamic commercial activities. The *Global Islamic Finance* box discusses the basis for the differences of opinion among scholars and the need to downplay them, as they are often overblown unnecessarily.

**musharakah mutanaqisah**
Diminishing partnership with an embedded lease contract, where the financial institution gradually transfers the ownership of a property to the client over a period of time.

# GLOBAL ISLAMIC FINANCE

The Islamic financial instruments used in the global Islamic finance industry are the result of financial engineering through the process of product development. Originating in nominal contracts, most of the commonly used products such as *istisna'* (manufacturing contract), and *sukuk* (Islamic trust certificates or bonds) are structured from simple contracts.

While most of the contracts are practiced widely across different jurisdictions, there are some differences of opinion among scholars on the validity of some contractual arrangements. This reflects the interpretation by individual schools of thought while considering the same source evidence. The fundamental basis of Islamic law remains the same, as enunciated in the Qur'an and Sunnah, but the interpretation and deductions of Muslim scholars of diverse backgrounds and experience differ in some cases. Apart from the differences among the four major Sunni schools—Maliki, Shafi'i, Hanbali, and Hanafi—there are some modern differences in the structuring of some key Islamic finance instruments such as *bay al-inah* and *tawarruq*.

In broad terms, the scholars in the GCC countries generally believe *bay al-inah* is not totally Sharī'ah-compliant as they consider it *riba* by the back door, yet many scholars in South-East Asia, particularly in Malaysia, contend that it is permissible. In fact, it is the most widely used instrument by IFIs in Malaysia. While avoiding the controversy between scholars on *bay al-inah*, and indeed *tawarruq*, it suffices to conclude that even though they may differ in terms of their interpretation of certain evidence to justify structured instruments in the Islamic finance industry, they all evince the general spirit of Sharī'ah compliance and sincerity.

There is a commonly cited saying of the Prophet which notes the reward for a *mujtahid* (a scholar who makes independent legal deductions from the primary sources) who makes a correct reasoning and that for one who makes a wrong reasoning—both are rewarded accordingly, though the one who arrives at the correct conclusion gets two rewards while the other gets just one. The major consideration in the process of product development is sincerity of purpose, which should be the driving force of the global Islamic finance industry.

## *Tawriq* (Securitization)

**tawriq**
A process for converting an asset into its cash equivalents, issued as certificates of investment that are tradable in the secondary market.

**secondary market**
A financial market within the Islamic capital market, where previously issued instruments such as bonds are traded.

**sanadat**
Islamic commercial papers issued to raise funds in investment activities.

**usufruct**
The right to use and enjoy property or premises without causing unnecessary destruction.

The term for securitization in Islamic commercial jurisprudence is **tawriq**. Equivalent terms that imply the same meaning are *taskik* and *tasnid*. Securitization results in the issuance of *sukuk*. These are terms and concepts commonly applied to Sharī'ah financial instruments in the Islamic capital market. Bearing this in mind, *tawriq* can be defined as a process for converting an asset into its cash equivalents issued as certificates of investment that are tradable in the **secondary market**. This is the process of transforming a deferred debt into investment certificates that can be traded in the secondary market for the period between the establishment of the debt and the maturity period. In this process, the ownership of an asset is transferred to a number of investors through the issuance of *sukuk* instruments. These have also been referred to as **sanadat**, which means certificates of investment. Therefore, the end product of *tawriq* is the issuance of *sukuk* or *sanadat* to a large number of investors. As the investors cannot individually manage the underlying asset, an SPV is established to carry out two important functions—managing the assets on behalf of the *sukuk*-holders and issuance of the investment certificates. One unique aspect of Islamic finance is its asset-backed nature, which helps in securing debt. The *sukuk* certificate issued serves a special purpose. It is evidence of ownership of the underlying asset or its **usufruct**.

## Parties to *Tawriq*

A number of parties are involved in the process of Islamic securitization. These include the originator, SPV, investment banks, subscribers, obligor, the lead manager, cash administrator, legal and tax counsel, the servicer, auditor, credit enhancement provider, the custodian (registration and transfer agents or R&T agents), and the credit rating agency. Of this huge number of parties, the four most important parties in securitization are:

- ORIGINATOR OR ISSUER OF *SUKUK*: The whole process starts with the originator or issuer of the *sukuk*, which is usually a large corporation, government, or entity that intends to raise funds for a particular financial purpose. The originator sells its assets to the SPV in order to be able to use the funds.

- SPECIAL PURPOSE VEHICLE: Although the SPV is sometimes referred to as the issuer because, in practice, it issues investment certificates to the subscribers, it is usually considered as a company specifically established to undertake the twin role of managing the securitization process and handling the issuance of the certificates. The SPV purchases the underlying asset from the originator and thus commences the securitization process. The purchase price for the asset is funded through the issuance of *sukuk* to the subscribers and the individual portion of each subscriber represents their respective ownership of the underlying asset for which they will receive a return at the maturity date.

- INVESTMENT BANKS: These are needed in the process of securitization for the purpose of underwriting and bookmaking services to guarantee investors' funds. Islamic banks or Islamic windows of multinational banks can conveniently carry out this service for the purpose of guaranteeing such funds.

- SUBSCRIBERS OR INVESTORS: These are the *sukuk*-holders, who may be individuals, corporate entities such as Islamic banks, or other financial institutions who subscribe to the Islamic bonds issued by the SPV on the underlying asset.

## How it Works in the Secondary Market

- An SPV is established to manage the underlying asset and issue investment certificates (*sukuk*) to the investors (*sukuk*-holders).

- The investment certificates represent ownership of an asset or entitlement to a debt or a rental income in the case of usufruct.

- There is an initial agreement between the originator and the SPV with regard to the purchase of the underlying asset.

- There is another agreement between the SPV and the investors, whether senior or subordinate.

- Flowing from the initial agreements, the initial cash flows are effected through the purchase consideration from the SPV to the originator, and from the subscribers or investors to the SPV. Once the subscribers/investors conclude their subscription

**participation term certificate (PTC)**
A certificate that indicates a partial ownership in a joint pool of assets, usually a securitized asset, which entitles the holder to periodic returns.

through payment for their respective bonds, the SPV in turn pays the purchase price to the originator.

- The monthly cash flow of dividends follows a complex chain whereby the obligor pays the cash flows that are securitized to the servicer who monitors and maintains the asset. The servicer pays into an account where the **participation term certificates (PTC)** are issued to the SPV for the purpose of monthly payments to the investors.

- The monthly payment is made by the SPV to all classes of the investors in accordance with their respective PTC.

Figure 3.6 shows a typical process of securitization based on the above outline.

Different hybrid financial instruments have been developed by experts and Sharī'ah scholars to undertake the process of securitization to cater for modern needs in the Islamic finance industry. This has led to different categories of *sukuk*. These categories include: *muqaradah* or *mudarabah sukuk* (loans and trust financing securities), *musharakah sukuk* (equity-based securities), *ijarah sukuk* (securities on the basis of usufruct), *salam* securities, *istisna' sukuk* (securities on the basis of manufacturing contracts), *murabahah sukuk* (securities on the basis of *murabahah*). All these categories of *sukuk* can be used for different investment, developmental, and economic purposes. Chapter 7 discusses these forms of securities in greater detail.

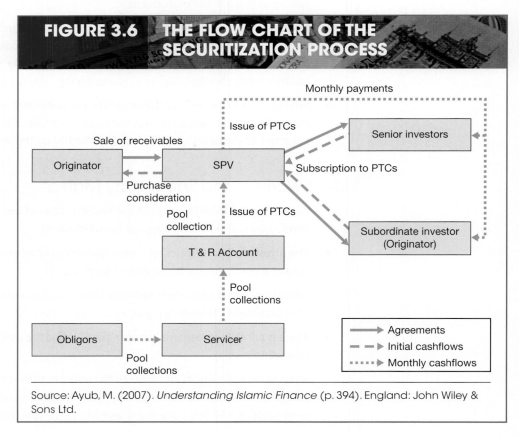

**FIGURE 3.6    THE FLOW CHART OF THE SECURITIZATION PROCESS**

Source: Ayub, M. (2007). *Understanding Islamic Finance* (p. 394). England: John Wiley & Sons Ltd.

## *Sarf* (Sale of Currency)

### Definition and Nature

*bay al-sarf*
A contract of exchange of currencies, which may either be the same kind or different kinds.

A foreign exchange contract is known as **bay al-sarf** in Islamic law. It involves the exchange of currencies, which may be either the same kind or different kinds. Initially, the traditional *bay al-sarf* mentioned in a hadith involves the exchange of gold or silver against gold or silver. The currency exchange contract is well known in Islamic law. There is a general consensus among Muslim jurists on the validity of exchange contracts for currencies of different countries provided the exchange is carried out on the spot. Possession has to be made on both sides on the spot, otherwise known as *majlis al-'aqd*. The delivery of both currencies has to be made in full at the time of concluding the contract. This is because immediate payment of the price is necessary for the validity of the contract. The majority of jurists agree that currency exchange on a forward basis is not permissible in Islamic law. This is so only when the rights and obligations of both parties to the exchange contract are deferred to a future date, but there are differences of opinion regarding a situation whereby the rights or obligations of either of the parties are deferred to a future date.

In essence, the exchange must take place at the same sitting in which the contract is drawn up. The nature of a foreign exchange contract can be explained by giving a practical example. It is permissible to sell €100 for dollars provided the exchange takes place in the same sitting as the contract is made between the parties, but it is not permissible to trade in the same currency at different rates. For instance, exchanging $100 for $200 at the same sitting is tantamount to a usurious transaction. In a situation like this, for the transaction to be valid when the exchange involves the same currency, it must be an exchange of equal amounts at the same sitting.

### Validity of Foreign Exchange Contract in Islamic Law

The validity of foreign exchange transactions is established in Islamic law according to the authority of the relevant Prophetic traditions. Ubaadah Ibn Al-Saamit narrated that the Prophet said:

> Hadith: Gold for gold, silver for silver, wheat for wheat, barley for barley, dates for dates, salt for salt, like for like, same for same, face to face. If the types are different then sell however you like, so long as it is face to face.[2]

The implication of the above narration is that trade in currency is permissible in Islamic law, as the prevailing currency during the era was gold and silver in addition to the usual barter trade. The only limitation to this permissibility is that an exchange must be made face to face in one sitting if it involves different currencies. If the exchange is not made at the same sitting and there is a delay, the transaction is not permissible because it is then tainted with elements of *riba*. On the other hand, if the currencies are the same, two conditions must be met to validate the transaction—the currencies being exchanged must be of equal amounts, and the exchange must take place at the same sitting in line with the face to face rule in the hadith.

## *Tawarruq* (Cash Financing or Reverse *Murabahah*)

**tawarruq**
A hybrid sale contract whereby a customer approaches a bank or financial institution to purchase a commodity with payment arranged in installments and in turn sells the commodity to a third party for cash.

This systematic sale contract is a reverse form of *murabahah* that was discussed earlier. ***Tawarruq*** comes from the word *wariq*, which means silver, because the customer who buys the commodity is buying for the sake of dirhams or silver coins. This is why it is called cash financing. In simple terms, *tawarruq* is a hybrid sale contract whereby a customer approaches a bank or financial institution to purchase a commodity with payment arranged in installments and in turn sells the commodity to a third party for cash.

### Justification of *Tawarruq*

The majority of jurists opine that this transaction is permissible in Islamic law based on the general principles of a typical contract of sale. The permissibility of trading emphatically mentioned in the Qur'an and Sunnah and the absence of any modicum of interest in this transaction have been the justification for *tawarruq* in the light of the primary sources of the Sharī'ah. The client who approaches the bank or financial institution has a clear intent to either benefit from the commodity itself or its price. According to Shaykh Ibn Baaz, a *tawarruq* transaction is permissible as it does not amount to *riba*.

> With regard to the issue of *tawarruq*, it is not *riba* and the correct view is that it is permissible, because of the general meaning of the evidence and because it facilitates relief and enables people to meet their current needs. As for the one who sells it to the one from whom he bought it, this is not permissible, rather this is a *riba*-based transaction, which is called *'aynah*. This is *haraam* because it is a trick aimed at getting around the prohibition on *riba*.[3]

Early scholars, such as Ibn Taimiyyah, held that *tawarruq* is impermissible because it presents a situation where one takes dirham for dirham on a deferred basis, which is against the underlying principles of financial transactions in Islamic law. According to this view, the commodity that is purported to be sold comes in between the deferred money exchange transaction to make what has been declared forbidden permissible in the eyes of the law—a form of legal device (*hilah*). Having said this, modern scholars strongly believe that *tawarruq* transactions are permissible in Islamic law because of people's growing needs and a paucity in the number of sincere lenders who will not demand interest. Therefore, *tawarruq* has been declared permissible subject to the following conditions for its validity:

1. The person must be in need of money. If the purpose of concluding a *tawarruq* contract is to lend others the money, it is not permissible.

2. There is no other permissible manner of obtaining cash financing, such as benevolent loans.

3. The contract must not include any modicum of *riba*.

4. Sale of the commodity is not allowed until the client has taken full possession of it and effectually moved it to his own place.

## Practical Application of *Tawarruq*

The International Islamic Fiqh Academy differentiates between traditional *tawarruq* and modern *tawarruq*. While traditional *tawarruq* has a purpose in nature as it solves a particular problem at the time and is thus permissible, modern *tawarruq* as practiced by Islamic banks is an organized form of reverse *tawarruq* that is not permissible. As the *Islamic Finance in Practice* box illustrates, this issue of permissibility lies in the practical application of the transaction. The original purpose of *tawarruq* is to meet the liquidity or cash needs of a person. Therefore the difference between permissible *tawarruq* and impermissible *tawarruq* lies in the sale of the item. The client must sell the item to an identified buyer who should be a different party from the original seller (in most cases, a bank). It becomes permissible if it is sold to a different third party, but if it is sold back to the original seller, the whole transaction becomes impermissible.

Figure 3.7 shows a typical example of *tawarruq* through its practical application as a Sharī'ah financial instrument. The example is summarized thus:

1. The customer approaches the bank and concludes a *tawarruq* contract.

2. The Islamic bank (financier) purchases the commodity from a seller in accordance with the customer's instructions.

3. The commodity is sold to the customer at a mark-up price.

4. The customer pays the price (or mark-up price) in installments.

5. The customer sells the commodity to an identified buyer and receives spot cash.

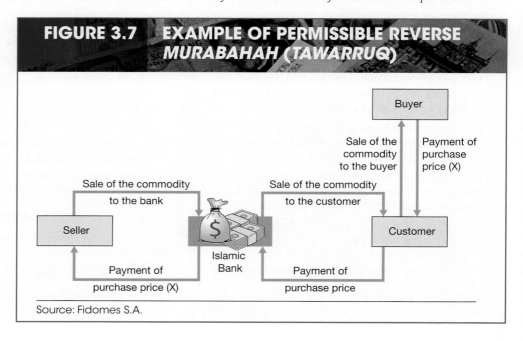

### FIGURE 3.7    EXAMPLE OF PERMISSIBLE REVERSE MURABAHAH (TAWARRUQ)

Source: Fidomes S.A.

## ISLAMIC FINANCE IN PRACTICE

# Question on *Tawarruq* Brought Before the International Islamic Fiqh Academy

*Tawarruq* has been a controversial issue within the Islamic finance industry. Different Sharīʿah supervisory boards have issued their respective rulings regarding the structuring of a *tawarruq* transaction. Notable among such bodies, and of international repute, is the International Islamic Fiqh Academy. A question was brought before it regarding the ruling of Islam on the reverse *tawarruq* generally practiced by some by Islamic banks. The reply of the Academy is presented below.

\*   \*   \*

Praise be to Allah alone, and blessings and peace be upon the one after whom there is no Prophet, our Prophet Muhammad, and upon his family and companions.

The Islamic Fiqh Council of the Muslim World League, in its nineteenth session, held in Makkah al-Mukarramah between 22–27 Shawwaal 1428 AH (November 3–8, 2007 CE) examined the subject 'products offering an alternative to depositing for a certain length of time' which are offered by some banks at present under several names, such as reverse *murabahah*, *reverse tawarruq*, direct investment, investing by *murabahah*, and other names which have been invented or may be invented. The most common form of this product is as follows:

1.  The customer appoints the bank to buy a certain product, and the customer hands over to the bank the price of the product straight away.

2.  Then the bank buys the product from the customer for a price to be paid at a later date, with a profit margin as agreed.

After listening to the comprehensive discussion on this topic, the Council determined that this transaction is not permissible, for the following reasons:

1.  This transaction is similar to the ʿinah transaction which is *haraam* according to Sharīʿah, in that the purchased product is not sought in and of itself, so it cannot come under the ruling on that type of

product, especially since the bank is committed to buying this product from the customer.

2.  This transaction comes under the heading of planned *tawarruq*. The Council has previously stated that planned *tawarruq* is *haraam*, in its second statement in its seventeenth session. The reason why planned *tawarruq* is forbidden is also present in this transaction.

3.  This transaction is contrary to the purpose of the Islamic way of financing, which is based on connecting finance to real activities which support economic growth and prosperity.

The Council appreciates the efforts of Islamic banks to protect the *ummah* from the problem of *riba*, and it emphasizes the importance of the proper application of Islamically acceptable transactions and avoidance of dubious or superficial transactions which lead to *haraam riba*. Hence it recommends the following:

1.  Banks and financial institutions should avoid *riba* in all forms, in obedience to the command of Allah (interpretation of the meaning): "O you who believe! Fear Allah and give up what remains (due to you) from *riba* (from now onward) if you are (really) believers" [al-Baqarah 2:278].

2.  The role of *fiqh* councils and independent academic bodies in correcting and guiding the course of Islamic banks should be affirmed, so as to achieve the aims and goals of the Islamic economy.

3.  A supreme committee should be set up in the central banks of all Muslim countries, independent of the commercial banks, composed of Islamic scholars and financial experts, to act as a reference point for Islamic banks and to ensure that their work is in accordance with Islamic Sharīʿah.

And Allah is the Source of strength. May Allah send blessings and peace upon our Prophet Muhammad and his family and companions.

Source: The Muslim World League. www.themwl.org/Fatwa/default.aspx?d=1&cidi=166&l=AR&cid=10.

**LEARNING OBJECTIVE 3.3**

Understand how service-based contracts are used as financial instruments in Islamic finance.

# The Concept of Service-Based Contracts

Service-based contracts involve hiring or employing another person or renting premises for a specific purpose in line with the payment of certain wages, rental fees or commissions. The service-based contracts that have been developed into efficient Shari'ah financial instruments include *ijarah* (leasing), *ijarah muntahia bittamlik* (financial lease), *ijarah thumma al-bay'* (leasing and subsequent purchase), *jarah mawsufah fi dhimmah* (forward lease), *ujrah* (fees), and *ju'alah* (commission). This section examines how these service-based contracts are used in the modern Islamic finance industry.

## *Ijarah* (Leasing)

**ijarah**
A financing mechanism that involves the rent of an asset or hire purchase where some form of rental fee is paid for a stipulated period of time mutually agreed by the parties.

The term **ijarah** literally means to give something in rent to another person. The term has been used in two different ways in Islamic jurisprudence generally. The first usage relates to hiring another person to do a particular thing. This means employing a person for a particular job for a consideration known as wages. In this contractual usage, which is found in the Qur'an, the employer is known as *musta'jir* while the employee is called *ajir*. The second usage of the term in Islamic jurisprudence relates to the transfer of usufruct in an asset for a consideration. Here, the lessor who transfers the usufruct rights is called *mu'jir* while the lessee is known as *musta'jir*. The commission or rental fee payable to the lessor is known as *ujrah*. The contract of transfer of usufruct for a consideration for a given period of time is known in Islamic law as *ijarah*. This simply means giving something in rent for a consideration. It has been defined by Muslim jurists, and all the definitions point to the fact that *ijarah* relates to the transfer of the usufruct in a property to another person for a consideration. For the purpose of this book, *ijarah* as used in the second context to refer to the transfer of usufruct is our focus because of its relevance as a mode of financing in modern Islamic banking and finance business.

The legality of the lease contract is firmly established in a number of legal texts in the Qur'an and Sunnah. It suffices to quote the following verses in the Qur'an:

> Qur'an: 28:26–27: "One of the two women said: 'O my father! Hire him! Surely the best of those that you can employ is the strong man, the faithful one.' He said: 'I desire to marry one of these two daughters of mine to you on condition that you should serve me for eight years; but if you complete ten, it will be of your own free will, and I do not wish to be hard to you; if Allah please, you will find me one of the good.'"

This verse narrates the story of Musa and how he was hired by Shuaib, who later became his father-in-law. This indicates that an *ijarah* contract is permissible in any lawful transaction, whether a hire or lease contract. In a similar vein, the Prophet was reported to have emphatically said: "Pay the hired worker his wage before his sweat dries off."[4]

The rules of a contract of sale are applicable to the lease contract because in both cases something is transferred from one party to another for a valuable consideration. While the physical object is known and ascertained in a sale contract, the benefit of the usufruct must be ascertained by the parties while concluding a lease contract. A sale contract involves the transfer of ownership in the corpus of the property, while in a lease contract the transferor remains the owner of the property and only permits the transferee the right to use the property subject to the agreement. Box 3.1 presents a summary of the basic rules regulating *ijarah* according to Mufti Muhammad Taqi Usmani, the leading Sharī'ah scholar.

According to the majority of Muslim jurists, *ijarah* is valid in objects that have a beneficial usufruct that can be effectively used or hired while their corpus is retained. In fact, a lease contract is considered a viable mode of financing in modern Islamic banking and finance as a veritable alternative to the charging of interest. Three main modern applications of *ijarah* are *ijarah thumma al-bay'* (a lease contract ending with a sale), **ijarah muntahia bittamlik** (leasing ending with ownership) and *ijarah mawsufah fi dhimmah* (forward lease).

**ijarah muntahia bittamlik**
A lease contract which culminates in a transfer of legal title and confers ownership on the lessee.

## Ijarah Muntahia Bittamlik (Financial Lease)

This is a typical lease contract which culminates in a transfer of legal title and confers ownership on the lessee. This is a modern Sharī'ah financial instrument developed by

---

### BOX 3.1: A SUMMARY OF THE BASIC RULES REGULATING *IJARAH*

1. Leasing is a contract whereby the owner of something transfers its usufruct to another person for an agreed period, for an agreed consideration.

2. The subject of a lease must have a valuable use. Therefore, things having no usufruct at all cannot be leased.

3. It is necessary for a valid lease contract that the corpus of the leased property remains in the ownership of the seller, and only its usufruct is transferred to the lessee. Thus, anything which cannot be used without consuming cannot be leased out. Therefore, the lease cannot be effected in respect of money, eatables, fuel, and ammunition, etc. because their use is not possible unless they are consumed. If anything of this nature is leased out, it shall be deemed to be a loan and all the rules concerning the transaction of loans shall accordingly apply. Any rent charged on this invalid lease shall be interest charged on a loan.

4. As the corpus of the leased property remains in the ownership of the lessor, all the liabilities emerging from the ownership shall be borne by the lessor, but the liabilities referable to the use of the property shall be borne by the lessee.

Source: Muham\mad Taqi Usmani. (1999). *An Introduction to Islamic Finance*. Karachi: Idara Isha'at-e-Diniyat: p.111.

experts in line with the principles of Sharī'ah. The phrase *al-ijarah muntahia bittamlik* contains two main words: *ijarah*, which means lease, and *tamlik*, which is ownership. *Ijarah* was explained earlier. *Tamlik* means the process of conferring ownership on another person. The ownership in question may be either of property or usufruct. Thus, *al-ijarah muntahia bittamlik* is ownership of the usufruct in an identifiable asset or property within a specified period followed by the granting of the ownership of such property at the maturity of the lease contract. Leases and purchase are combined, where the right of purchase is conferred on the lessee at the end of the lease period. It is important to add that the transfer of the legal title in the leased asset may be with or without consideration. If it is with a consideration, a sale is concluded at the end of the contract, which may be similar to *al-ijarah thumma al-bay'* (leasing and subsequent purchase). However, it is also possible for the legal title in the leased asset to be transferred without a consideration, for example, when the leased asset is given to the lessee as a gift at the end of the lease period. Two separate contracts are concluded—one is the main *ijarah* contract and the second is the ownership contract.

## Ijarah Thumma al-Bay' (Leasing and Subsequent Purchase)

**ijarah thumma al-bay'**
A contract of lease which is subsequently followed by a sale contract.

This is a lease contract that is followed by a sale contract. When a typical lease contract ends with an actual sale, it is referred to as **ijarah thumma al-bay'**. Figure 3.8 shows a good example of this contractual arrangement. In this contract, two separate contracts are concluded under this chain transaction—the *ijarah* contract and the purchase contract. As a form of hire purchase, *ijarah thumma al-bay'* is more appropriate for

**FIGURE 3.8 IJARAH THUMMA AL-BAY' CONTRACT**

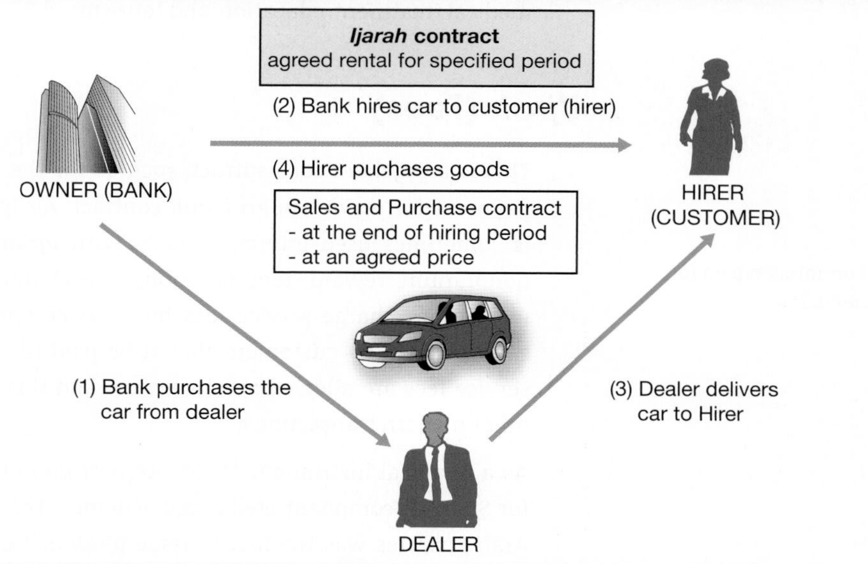

*Ijarah* contract
agreed rental for specified period

(2) Bank hires car to customer (hirer)

(4) Hirer puchases goods

Sales and Purchase contract
- at the end of hiring period
- at an agreed price

OWNER (BANK)

HIRER (CUSTOMER)

(1) Bank purchases the car from dealer

(3) Dealer delivers car to Hirer

DEALER

Source: Abdullah, N. I. and Dusuki, A. W. (2006). *A Critical Appraisal of Al-Ijarah Thumma al-Bay' (AITAB) Operation: Issues and Prospects*. Fourth International Islamic Banking and Finance Conference. Monash University of Malaysia, Kuala Lumpur. November 13–14.

financing consumer goods and durables. The procedure for the application of *ijarah thumma al-bay'* in Malaysia is described in the following steps:

- The bank purchases a car from the dealer.
- The bank rents the car to the customer, who concludes an agreement of *ijarah* with bank for a specified period.
- The bank instructs the dealer to deliver the car to the hirer (customer).
- At the end of the rental period, a sale and purchase contract is concluded by the bank and the hirer, who purchases the car for an agreed price.

## *Ijarah mawsufah fi dhimmah* (Forward Lease)

**ijarah mawsufah fi dhimmah**
A lease for specified future usufruct of an asset which is not practically in existence at the time of concluding the contract.

This is a lease for specified future usufruct of an asset that does not practically exist at the time of concluding the contract. Very different from the other forms of lease, this form of lease agreement is concluded on an asset that does not exist. The lessor undertakes to deliver the asset to the lessee in accordance with the agreed specifications. This form of contract can be concluded on a specified unavailable asset that may not be owned by the lessor. When the lease asset is under construction or being manufactured, the lessor may demand payment of a portion of the agreed rental as a forward lease. Such advance payment is considered by the lessor to be a debt subject to the successful delivery of the leased asset. The rent paid is usually used to finance the construction of the asset. One thing that must be borne in mind while discussing **ijarah mawsufah fi dhimmah** is that once the leased asset is successfully constructed or manufactured, the contract becomes an ordinary lease but it still has the tendency to become *ijarah muntahia bittamlik*, subject to the contract between the parties. The modern application of a forward lease is diverse. It is applicable to a wide range of sectors within the economy and can be used in medical treatment, education, and tourism.

## *Ujrah* (Fees)

**ujrah**
A fee or commission paid for services rendered.

This is a payment for usufruct, such as for the use of another person's property, or payment for service in an *ijarah* contract. *Ajr* (pl. *ujur*) is another related term that is sometimes used interchangeably with **ujrah**. This may mean fees, commission, honorarium, reward, remuneration, or a charge. Most Islamic banks and financial institutions charge service fees for services rendered to their customers. The bank services used by customers should be paid for through a *ujrah* scheme. Such fixed service fees are allowed in Islamic law and this concept has been adapted for many other modern transactions.

As a financial instrument, the concept of *ujrah* has been used by a number of banks for Sharī'ah-compliant credit card schemes. The Emirates Islamic Bank of the United Arab Emirates was the first to issue *ujrah* or fee-based Islamic credit cards, whereby the Islamic bank guarantees the customer's purchase and charges a fixed service fee for the guarantee. In a similar vein, the Saadiq Visa credit card scheme introduced by the multinational Standard Chartered Bank in Pakistan has a *ujrah* fee structure.

The Saadiq Visa credit card scheme introduced by the multinational Standard Chartered Bank in Pakistan has a *ujrah* fee structure.

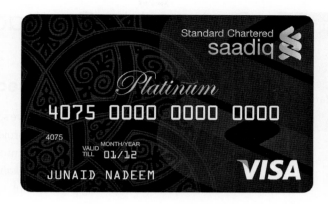

## *Ju'alah* (Reward)

**ju'alah**
(contract of commission)
A contract of promise of reward where the entitlement to compensation is contingent upon the performance of a particular act.

In the literal sense, **ju'alah** means the act of doing any job or rendering a service for a specific purpose that is uncertain if it can be accomplished. The accomplishment of the job or service will in turn attract some reward or fees. In the juristic sense, *ju'alah* is a unilateral contract whereby a reward or commission is promised for the accomplishment of a specific task. In some cases, it may involve hiring another person to perform the specific task with some consideration. The legality of the *ju'alah* contract is established in the Qur'an and Sunnah. In the Qur'an, there is reference to the announcement about a missing beaker and how whoever finds it will be given a reward of a camel load of grain, as clearly outlined in Surah Yusuf. In the Sunnah, it was reported that some of the Prophet's companions passed by some people staying at a place where there was water. One of them had been stung by a scorpion and a man from the group staying near the water came and asked the companions, "Is there anyone among you who can do *Ruqya* (exorcism) as near the water a person has been stung by a scorpion." One of the companions went to him and recited Surat-al-Fatihah (the opening chapter of the Qur'an) for a sheep as his fee. The patient was cured and the man brought the sheep to his companions, who disliked it and said, "You have taken wages for reciting Allah's Book." When they arrived at Medina, they said, "O Allah's Apostle! (This person) has taken wages for reciting Allah's Book." At that, Allah's Apostle said, "You are most entitled to take wages for doing a *Ruqya* with Allah's Book."[5] The recitation of the opening chapter from the Qur'an which cured the sick was considered to be a service for which the reward of a sheep was given. The hadith clearly explains that the Prophet gave approval for such a contract, which is tantamount to a *ju'alah* contract.

There is an element of *ju'alah* in *takaful* contracts. In the recovery of overdue debts, *ju'alah* may be useful; for instance, if the bank announces a specific reward for defaulters who redeem their debts within a specified period. There are usually two parties to a *ju'alah* contract—*ja'il* (the offerer) and the worker. While the offerer undertakes to give a particular reward or commission for whoever does a specified thing, the worker is the one who actually comes forward to undertake the task. Once the task is accomplished, the worker receives his prize, reward, or commission.

**LEARNING OBJECTIVE 3.4**

Understand how partnership contracts are used as financial instruments in Islamic finance.

# Partnership Contracts in Islamic Finance

## The Concept of Equity-Based Contracts

Equity-based contracts generally involve some sort of partnership. They are used in joint-venture project finance and trustee project finance. In this section, three partnership contracts that have been transformed into financial instruments are discussed. They are *mudarabah* (trust financing), *musharakah* (joint-venture partnership) and *musharakah mutanaqisah* (diminishing partnership).

## *Mudarabah* (Trust Financing)

### Nature and Definition of *Mudarabah*

**mudarabah**
A trust partnership contract between a capital provider and an entrepreneur where the parties share the profits but in the event of any loss, the capital provider bears the loss.

As a trust financing contract, a **mudarabah** contract is a form of investment. However, before giving the juristic definition of the term, let's look at some synonymous terms used by some jurists in the classical literature. The word *mudarabah* is used to represent a form of partnership where one party provides the funds while the other party plays the entrepreneur through effective management. The word is of Iraqi origin as it is mostly used in Abu Hanifah and Ahmad Ibn Hanbal's works. Meanwhile, the word *qirad*, which is of *hijazi* origin (Arabian Peninsula), is mainly used in the Shafi'i and Maliki works on Islamic commercial transactions.

**rabb al-mal**
Financier or capital provider who invests in a trust investment partnership.

**mudarib**
Entrepreneur who manages and runs a trust investment business.

In trust financing, the financier (**rabb al-mal**) provides the capital while the entrepreneur (**mudarib**) provides the entrepreneurial management to run the business. The former is a sleeping partner in the partnership contract, while the latter is an active partner directly involved in the day-to-day running of the business. In *Majjalah al-Ahkam*, Article 1404 defines *mudarabah* as "a type of partnership where one party supplies the capital and the other the labor. The person who owns the capital is called the owner of the capital and the person who performs the works is called the workman."[6] The parties to the partnership contract share the profit of the business venture based on an agreed percentage and they consequently bear any loss incurred. While the entrepreneur loses his livelihood, the financier loses the capital in the event of losses.

### Legality of *Mudarabah*

**ijma**
A secondary source of the Sharī'ah, which means the unanimous agreement of the Muslim scholars of a particular period on a Sharī'ah issue.

The legality of a *mudarabah* contract is established in the Qur'an, Sunnah, practices of the companions, and **ijma** (consensus of opinion of scholars). The basis of this transaction is the concept of entrepreneurship encouraged in the Qur'an.

> Qur'an 73: 30: "While others travel in the land in search of Allah's bounty."

The extrapolation of this verse reveals the importance of *mudarabah* transactions, whereby people travel for the purpose of trade and seek lawful income through permissible forms of business. This naturally includes those who work with other people's capital to earn some profits, which are shared with the financiers. The Prophet was reported to have worked with Khadijah (his first wife) as a *mudarib* when he used to go to Sham (Syria) for trade.

### Types of *Mudarabah*

There are two types of *mudarabah* transactions—restricted (*muqayyad*) and unrestricted (*mutlaq*)—and each has different legal implications.

- A restricted *mudarabah* partnership is defined in the AAOIFI Sharī'ah Standards as "a contract in which the capital provider restricts the actions of the *mudarib* to a particular location or to a particular type of investment as the capital provider considers appropriate, but not in a manner that would unduly constrain the *mudarib* in his operations." In this type of *mudarabah* transaction, the powers of the *mudarib* are restricted with regard to the kind of trade to be engaged in, where it should be carried out, and the period for same. The *rabb al-mal* may specify the type of business he wants the *mudarib* to invest his funds in and the timeframe for the business.

- In an unrestricted *mudarabah* transaction, the *rabb al-mal* does not specify the type of business in which the *mudarib* can invest and no timeframe is specified. The *mudarib* can use their discretion in respect of their experience and expertise as an entrepreneur. Their authority is absolute and they can use the capital in the manner they deem fit in accordance with the principles of the Sharī'ah.

The share of the profits of the business to be distributed between the financier and the entrepreneur must be predetermined by them and must be based on the actual profit derived through the business excluding the capital invested. The share of profit is left to the parties' mutual agreement. The Sharī'ah respects party autonomy in the distribution of profits but it must be based on a predetermined agreement. Parties are allowed to share the profits in equal proportions. The predetermined profit-sharing ratio must be just and fair in all ramifications. In the event of loss, all financial or proprietary loss must be borne by the financier while the fund manager or entrepreneur does not benefit from the labor expended in the joint venture.

As a partnership contract, either of the parties can terminate the contractual relationship at any time, subject to notice being given to the other party within a reasonable time prior to effective termination of the contract. If a profit has been realized and all the assets of the partnership contract are in cash, the parties simply distribute the profit in accordance with their predetermined profit-sharing ratio. However, if some assets have yet to be traded and one party suddenly intends to terminate the contract, some time must be given to the *mudarib* to sell the assets in order to determine the actual profit to be distributed.

The modern application of *mudarabah* in Islamic banking and finance business is beyond mere conjecture. This form of partnership contract fits well into the structure of venture capital. *Mudarabah* financing is also used in project financing, unit trusts, **general investment accounts (GIA)** and **special investment accounts (SIA)**. In addition, there is a letter of credit used in international trade transactions that is based on the *mudarabah* model.

**general investment account (GIA)**

An account based on a contract between the bank (entrepreneur) and the customer (depositor), where it is agreed that the bank will use the capital in business and any profit will be shared between the parties according to a pre-agreed ratio.

**special investment account (SIA)**

An account based on a contract between the bank and the customer (depositor), where it is agreed that the bank will use the capital in a specific business and any profit will be shared between the parties according to a pre-agreed ratio.

*musharakah*

A joint business partnership enterprise in which the parties share the profits based on the contractual ratio and losses are borne based on the equity participation ratio.

## *Musharakah* (Partnership Contract)

While **musharakah** is similar to the *mudarabah* contract, it emphasizes the practical participation of both parties in the partnership business. The term *musharakah* is not commonly found in the classical literature of *fiqh* but was introduced by later scholars who developed it from the general theory of *shirkah*, which means sharing or partnership. According to Mufti Muhammad Taqi Usmani, *musharakah* is "a word of Arabic origin which literally means sharing. In the context of business and trade it means a joint enterprise in which all the partners share the profit or loss of the joint venture."[7] Thus, *musharakah* is a form of *shirkat al-amwal* where all the partners invest some capital into the joint venture. As a mode of investment, *musharakah* is a form of partnership between two or more persons who trade with joint capital contributed by all partners. This equity-based financing envisions a situation where the return of the investors is based on the actual profit of the joint venture. Losses are shared in accordance with the capital investment of each of the partners. The profit and loss nature of this mode of financing in Islamic commercial law is the kernel of all partnership contracts. In fact, *musharakah* is considered to be the most viable Islamic financial product in the modern banking business.

The legality of a *musharakah* contract is established in the Qur'an, Sunnah and the practices of the Prophet's companions and predecessors. The oft-quoted verse to support partnership contracts is handy here:

> Qur'an 5:2: "Help one another in virtues (righteousness and piety); but do not help one another in sin and transgression."

Pooling resources in a joint venture to make lawful profits through permissible business is an act of mutual assistance in virtues. Abu Hurairah narrated that the Prophet Muhammad related that Allah said: "I am the third in a partnership of the two, but if one betrays the other, I will withdraw from the partnership."[8] The legitimacy of a *musharakah* contract is clearly established in the divine hadīth because there is emphasis on fair dealing while undertaking a joint venture. Such fair dealing automatically exerts a pull on the blessings of God as clearly emphasized in the narration, and if one partner betrays the other, God immediately withdraws His blessings from the transaction. Thus, a partnership is based on mutual trust and the positive delegation of powers to achieve the purpose of the joint enterprise.

When a joint venture is established through the financial or proprietary resources of all the partners, all the basic rules of Islamic law of contract are applicable. The characteristics of a valid contract are applicable and all parties must abide by the rules. As the *musharakah* contract is premised on voluntary mutual consent, the parties must agree at the time of initiating the contract the proportion of profit due to each partner. Failure to agree on the proportion of profit due to each partner will render the contract void from the very beginning. "The amount of profit for each partner must be determined in proportion to the actual profit accrued to the business, and not in proportion to the capital invested by the partner. It is not allowed to fix an amount in a lump sum for any one of the partners, or any rate of profit tied up with his investment."[9] In a similar vein, any loss incurred by the joint enterprise will be shared proportionally by the partners in accordance with the ratio of their respective investments.

*Musharakah* has been applied in various transactions by modern Islamic banks and financial institutions. This form of partnership could be used effectively for small and medium enterprises. In addition, the *musharakah* partnership has been adopted in the primary Islamic capital market where *sukuk* certificates are issued. The securitization of *musharakah* partnerships has enabled market players to raise more funds for *musharakah* joint ventures.

### Differences between *Musharakah* and *Mudarabah* Contracts

People often confuse these two seemingly similar but different forms of contractual arrangement, which are both considered as partnership businesses whereby two or more people agree to invest in a certain subject matter based on predetermined ratios. Mufti Taqi Usmani explicitly identified the five differences between the two forms of partnership contracts, and these are presented in Box 3.2.

### *Musharakah Mutanaqisah* (Diminishing Partnership)

Diminishing *musharakah* is mostly used by many banks and financial institutions as an effective financial instrument for house financing and fixed assets. This form of participatory partnership is a chain of three contracts. The first contract is that of joint ownership between a client and an enterprise (financier), where the client promises to purchase shares in the enterprise. The second contract is a lease contract between the financier and the client under the joint ownership whereby units of shares due to the client are given to him in the lease agreement. In the third contract the client partner concludes another contract with the financing partner and gradually purchases the financier's remaining units of ownership, based on the earlier agreement. The joint partnership gradually diminishes as the amount owed decreases until the client partner finally owns the underlying property.

Diminishing *musharakah* is a long-term financing instrument where the bank's share in the joint ownership of a designated property decreases gradually through the continuing sale of its shares to the customer for payment of predetermined installments. The bank is allowed to sell its share at a price higher than its original value in order to make a profit. This way, the bank's shares diminish gradually until the maturity period, when all its shares have been bought by the customer, who can finally take ownership of the property.

## BOX 3.2: FIVE DIFFERENCES BETWEEN *MUSHARAKAH* AND *MUDARABAH*

1. The investment in *musharakah* is made by all partners, while in *mudarabah* investment is the sole responsibility of the *rabb al-mal*.

2. In *musharakah*, all the partners can participate in the management of the business and can work for it, while in *mudarabah*, the *rabb al-mal* has no right to participate in the management, which is carried out only by the *mudarib*.

3. In *musharakah* all the partners share any losses in accordance with their ratio of the investment while in *mudarabah* the loss, if any, is suffered by the *rabb-al-mal* only, because the *mudarib* does not invest anything. The *mudarib*'s loss is restricted to the fact that their labor has been in vain and yielded no fruit for the work done. However, this principle is subject to the condition that the *mudarib* worked with due diligence, as is normally required for business of this type. If the *mudarib* has been negligent or dishonest, they are liable for any resulting losses.

4. The liability of the partners in *musharakah* is normally unlimited. Thus, if the liabilities of the business exceed its assets and it goes into liquidation, all the excess liabilities shall be borne pro rata by all partners. However, if all the partners have agreed that no partner shall incur any debt during the course of business, then the excess liabilities shall be borne only by the partner who incurred the debt in violation of the aforesaid condition. In contrast, in *mudarabah* the liability of the *rabb al-mal* is limited to their investment, unless they have permitted the *mudarib* to incur debts on their behalf.

5. In *musharakah*, as soon as the partners mix up their capital in a joint pool, all the assets are jointly owned by all of them, proportionate to their respective investments. Thus, each partner can benefit from the appreciation of the value of the assets, even if profit does not accrue through sales. The case of *mudarabah* is different. Here, all the goods purchased by the *mudarib* are owned solely by the *rabb al-mal*, and the *mudarib* can earn their share in the profits only if they sell the goods at a profit. The *mudarib* is not entitled to claim their share in the assets themselves, even if their value has increased.

Source: Muhammad Taqi Usmani. (1999). *An Introduction to Islamic Finance*. Karachi: Idara Isha'at-e-Diniyat (P) Ltd: pp. 31–32.

**LEARNING OBJECTIVE 3.5**

Know the nature of supporting contracts in Islamic finance, including the unilateral supporting contracts.

# Supporting Contracts

The supporting contracts in Islamic finance are sometimes called accessory contracts because in most cases they have been structured as subsidiary financial instruments to support the underlying Sharī'ah financial instruments. In most cases, they are usually not independent, but are used in some complex financial instruments.

## *Hawalah* (Transfer of Debt)

### Nature and Definition

**hawalah**
A contract of debt assignment whereby a debt obligation is transferred from one party to another.

**bill of exchange**
A written order that binds the issuer for making payments, usually in international trade.

**promissory note**
An instrument by which a party promises unconditionally to pay another a particular sum of money within the stipulated time.

In literal terms, **hawalah** means assignment, bill of exchange, or promissory note. A **bill of exchange** is a written order that binds the issuer to make payments, while a **promissory note** is an instrument by which one party promises to pay another party a sum of money at a certain time. In the juristic sense, the *hawalah* contract is a special type of security contract that simply means debt assignment. According to Article 673 of *Majjalah al-Ahkam, hawalah* means to transfer a debt from one debtor account to the debtor account of another.[10] This form of contract, according to the majority of scholars, requires the consent of the creditor, the debtor, and the third party to whom the debt is assigned. *Hawalah* is a contract where the debtor transfers the responsibility of payment of their debt to a third party who owes the creditor a similar debt of about the same value. During the Abbasid period (750–945 CE), the term *hawalah* was used in public finance to refer to the practice of directing claimants, whose claims could not be met by the state treasury, to occupy some regions within the state where they could legally redeem their claims through taxes they collected from the inhabitants of such regions.

### Essential Elements

The essential elements of a *hawalah* contract are as follows.

1. *Muhal.* The creditor or person to whom the transfer is made.
2. *Muhil.* The transferor or debtor who assigns the debt.
3. *Muhal 'alayhi.* The transferee of the assigned debt.
4. *Al-Muhal bihi.* The transferred debt that is assigned from one debtor to another.
5. The debt owed by the transferee to the principal debtor.
6. Form of contract. The contract is concluded by an offer from the principal debtor and acceptance by the transferee and the creditor.

In the formation of the contract, the parties involved include *muhal* (the creditor) or transferred party, *muhil* (the transferor) or debtor, and *muhal 'alayhi* (the transferee) or the third party. The transferred debt is known as *al-muhal bihi*. In such an arrangement, there is a general presumption of an existing debt owned by the transferee to the principal debtor according to the majority of the Muslim jurists.

Figure 3.9 presents the two-stage arrangement of a *hawalah* contract. In diagram A, the debtor is indebted to the creditor and the transferee is simultaneously indebted to the debtor.

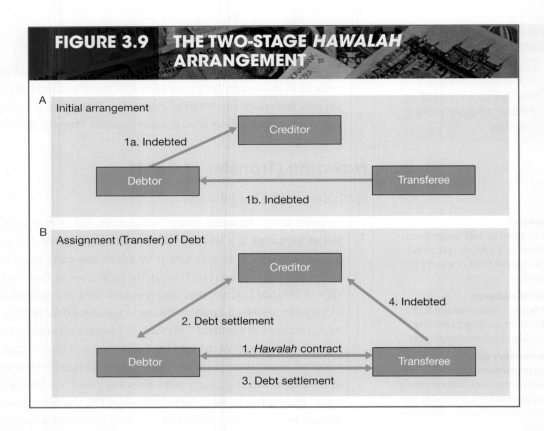

**FIGURE 3.9    THE TWO-STAGE *HAWALAH* ARRANGEMENT**

Thus, in order to transfer the debt, diagram B represents the new contractual relationship.

1.  A *hawalah* contract is concluded between the debtor and transferee.

2.  Once the creditor agrees to the contract of assignment, the debtor is discharged from their debt because the existence of the *hawalah* contract is a settlement of the debt.

3.  The assignment of the debt is also a complete settlement of the debt of the transferee owed to the debtor.

4.  Under the new arrangement, the transferee is indebted to the creditor.

    One constant variable in the above example is that the nature and amount of the debt owed among all the parties in the contract must be equal in all forms for the application of the principles of assignment of debt.

## Modern Application

The modern context of the concept of *hawalah* involves the positive transfer of debt from one debtor to another for the purpose of redeeming it. The legal implication of this debt assignment contract is that the original debtor is relieved of the debt immediately the contract takes place as it has been assigned to a third party. That is, the third party automatically becomes the debtor who is legally responsible for redeeming the debt. In most cases, a debt assignment is made with the understanding that the third party who subsequently becomes the debtor is also indebted to the original debtor, but there are situations where it may not be so. The third party, after paying the debt, has the right to claim the amount from the original debtor or offset the amount paid from any debt arrangement between them.

The debt assignment contract is carried out through an offer from the assignor and corresponding acceptance from the assignee, who agree that a particular debt should be assigned accordingly. This may be concluded without necessarily using the term *hawalah* for the contract. The *hawalah* contract can easily be deduced from an arrangement between two parties to assign a debt for the purpose of paying a particular creditor. It is considered binding once it has been concluded and none of the parties can rescind the contract at a later stage.

The modern application of *hawalah* contracts is further emphasized by the AAOIFI with its release of Sharī'ah Standard No. 7, whose scope is debt assignment and assignment of rights. The modern application of *hawalah* comprises bills of exchange (*suftajah*),[11] issuance of checks against a current account, endorsement of a negotiable instrument, and transfer of money or remittance (*al-sarf*). According to the AAOIFI Standard on *hawalah*, the following conditions must be met for the contract to be valid within the modern application of this financial instrument.

1.  All the parties involved in the contract must consent. The form of the contract must be clear enough to evince consent. Remember that in this contract, the parties are the transferor, transferee, and the payer.

2.  The transferor must be a debtor to the transferee.

3.  The payer does not necessarily need to be a debtor to the transferor.

4.  All parties must have full legal capacity to act independently in the contract.

5.  Both the transferred debt and the debt to be used for settlement must be known, ascertainable, and transferable.

6.  For restricted *hawalah* (where there is an exclusive use of the financial or tangible asset of the transferor even though in the possession of the payer to settle the transferred debt), the transferred debt must be equal in type, quality, and amount to the debt owed to the transferee.[12]

## *Rahn* (Collateral/Pledge)

### Nature and Definition

**rahn**
A collateral, pledge, or mortgage offered as a security for a debt that allows the creditor to take away the debt from such security in the event of any default on the part of the debtor.

From the contracts discussed earlier, it is clear that security contracts involve a form of undertaking to guarantee the fulfillment of certain obligations. It therefore follows that **rahn** is another Qur'anic concept of security contract established in clear injunctions. It represents collateral, a pledge, or a mortgage offered as a security for a debt that allows the creditor to take away the debt from such security in the event of any default on the part of the debtor. Although there are various definitions given to *rahn* by different scholars, one thing they all drive at is the nature of a *rahn* contract, which involves positive steps towards securing a debt through some form of mortgage. The legality of this form of mortgage contract is established in the Qur'an and Sunnah. For example, a clear instruction from the Lawgiver is given thus:

> Qur'an 2:283: "And if you are on a journey and cannot find a scribe (to document the terms of contract), then let there be a pledge taken (mortgaging); then if one of you entrust the other, let the one who is entrusted discharge his trust (faithfully), and let him be afraid of Allah, his Lord..."

In a similar vein, the Sunnah is replete with instances where the Prophet or his companions engaged in a form of mortgage contract. It was reported that the Prophet bought some food from a Jew and mortgaged his iron shield to him. Abu Hurairah narrated that the Prophet once said: "I am closer to the believers than their own selves. So if a true believer dies and leaves behind some unpaid debt, I will be responsible [as a guarantor] for him and if he leaves behind some property, it will be for his heirs."[13]

The significance of a *rahn* contract is that it is a voluntary charitable contract (*tabarru'*). The concept was developed based on the concept of mutual assistance (*ta'awun*). That is, people are encouraged to stand as guarantors to individuals who are in need of money from IFIs. It is usually not considered binding until the object of the contract is delivered. "One of the significant features of the Islamic guarantee is that the guarantor assumes to perform the principal debtor's obligation. Therefore the arrangement is essentially collateral in nature. In other words, the obligation of the guarantor is dependent upon the existence of the principal obligation. This necessarily means that in the event the principal obligation is extinguished, the guarantor would not be liable. Similarly if the principal debtor is discharged, the guarantor should also be discharged."[14] The *rahn* contract may be concluded in different forms. It may originate from a debt-generating contract, to establish a debt, or originate prior to the establishment of a debt. Once the mortgage contract has been concluded, it becomes binding on the mortgagor (debtor) and not on the mortgagee (creditor). Box 3.3 describes the specific conditions of *rahn* according to Kharofa.

## Modern Application

The modern application of a *rahn* contract is seen in contracts involving credit transactions such as a deferred sale or loans from IFIs. One may mortgage bank deposits, including current account deposits and investment account deposits, but this can only take place, according to the International Islamic Fiqh Academy, through a contractual arrangement that precludes the account holder from having access to the deposit for the agreed mortgage period. "In case the bank operating the current account is itself the mortgage, the amount must be transferred to an investment account, in such a way that the guarantee is no longer applicable in view of the conversion of the loan into a *kirad* (*mudarabah*, i.e. sleeping partnership) and the profits arising from the account are credited to the account holder so as to preclude the mortgagee (creditor) from deriving benefits from any appreciation in the mortgage value."[15] This is an example of the application of the concept of *rahn* in bank deposits.

## BOX 3.3:    SPECIFIC CONDITIONS OF *RAHN*

1. The indebted party cannot be coerced into putting up collateral.

2. An orphan's property cannot be put up as collateral by the trustee, unless under exceptional circumstances.

3. The property held as collateral must be liquid.

4. The property held as collateral must be distinct from other properties.

5. The ownership does not change, therefore the owner is responsible for the cost of maintaining the property even when it is pledged as collateral. Likewise, the owner continues to enjoy any secondary benefits to the property.

6. There is disagreement among the scholars on whether the property pledged as collateral can be used. Many scholars say that the property cannot be used by either the debtor or the borrower, while many argue that the owner (the borrower in this case) can continue to use the property.

7. If the property held as collateral is lost or damaged while in possession of the trustee, without any negligence on his part, there is no guarantee by the trustee.

8. The ownership of the property cannot be transferred until the debt is settled or the debtor allows for such a transaction.

9. If the borrower cannot pay back at the expiry of the term, the judge will order the property pledged as collateral to be sold on the open market, even if it is the residence of the borrower.

Source: Kharofa, A. (2002). *The Loan Contract in Islamic Sharī'ah and Man-Made Law (Roman-French-Egyptian): A Comparative Study.* Kuala Lumpur: Leeds Publications.

## *Muqasah* (Offsetting)

**muqasah**
A debt settlement through a counter-transaction or offsetting.

The offsetting of a debt may be necessary in some cases. This is a supporting or accessory contract that is hybridized with an underlying contract. The debt settlement through a counter-transaction is known as **muqasah**, and has been widely used in the form of a letter of offset. This is a discharge of a debt receivable against a payable debt. For instance, where A owes B $1,000 and B owes A $1,100, the parties can agree to offset the debt partially while B pays the remaining $100. Alternatively, the amount owed on both sides may be denominated in different currencies. In this case, the parties may agree on the exchange rate and offset the debt. If the two debts are discharged absolutely without any remainder after the offset, the debt is considered wholly settled. But if after the offset through the exchange rates there is still some remainder that may be paid by one of the parties, the debt will be considered to be partially settled and the remainder must be paid by the relevant party.

## Types of *Muqasah*

1.  *Muqasah al-qanuniyyah* (legal offset). This is a form of mandatory offset that may be carried out without the permission of the parties. It is effected through the operation of law. When debts are equal, this legal rule automatically operates to cancel out the obligations on both parties without their mutual consent. This may either be by a judicial decision of the court or the express operation of a statutory provision.

2.  *Muqasah al-talabiyyah* (offset on demand). This is also a mandatory offset that is not effected by the operation of law but by the express demand of the privileged creditor, whose consent is required to conclude this transaction. But an important caveat that must be taken into consideration is that an offset on demand must not bring about injustice on the part of the other party. If there is any element of injustice in the offset, the aggrieved party can approach a competent court to enforce their rights accordingly.

3.  *Muqasah al-ittifaqiyyah* (consensual offset). This is a voluntary offset where both parties mutually agree to it because the subject matter of the contract—the debts—are not identical in nature. Such a contractual offset is applicable when the debts are not similar but the parties must be cognizant of the fact that they cannot introduce any element of *riba* into the contract because party autonomy in contractual terms does not extend to violation of the law under the Sharī'ah.

## Debt Types That Can Be Offset

*Muqasah*, as a means of clearing obligations between a debtor and a creditor, is a means to facilitate contractual obligation in Islamic law. One important condition stipulated by jurists is that offset debts must be identical in nature. However, if they are different in value, the smaller debt is deducted from the larger and the balance paid. The types of debts that can be offset are:

*   *duyun al-naqd* (currency debts)
*   *duyun al-'ard* (commodity debts)
*   *manfa'a* (usufruct).

Muslims jurists have deliberated on the extent of legality of *muqasah* and three views have been expressed:

1.  *Muqasah* is an approved method of settlement of identical debts between two parties that does not necessarily fall under *bay al-dayn* in Islamic commercial transactions.

2.  *Muqasah* is merely an exception to *bay al-dayn* (sale of debts), which is permissible under certain conditions.

3.  *Muqasah* is a sale of debts by its real nature because its subject matter is debt which is intangible. However, the practice of *muqasah* is firmly established by a consensus of opinion among the scholars.

The most widely accepted view, which is also the position of AAOIFI, is that *muqasah* is a permissible method for the settlement of identical debts between two parties provided the contractual arrangement is not executed in a manner that contradicts the fundamental principles of Islamic law such as *riba* and *gharar*.

## *Kafalah* (Guarantee)

### Nature and Definition

*Kafalah* is another type of security contract in Islamic law. Lexically, *kafalah* means suretyship, sponsorship, or responsibility, but in juristic usage as a financial instrument, it means guaranteeing future obligations. Thus, *kafalah* can be defined as the amalgamation of a guarantor's liability with a debtor's liability, resulting in their joint liability. That is, *kafalah* is a form of promise to be liable for the debt of a principal debtor in case they default or fail to redeem the debt, but such liability does not relieve the principal debtor from liability. However, *kafalah* is not only used in terms of guarantee in commercial transactions, it is more applicable to the concept of guardianship in Islamic law. The other two words used interchangeably with the term *kafalah* are *himalah* and *za'amah*, which generally mean the same thing. While *kafalah* is used for individual guarantee, *himalah* is used for blood money and *za'amah* for substantial financial sums. The Qur'anic usage of the word *zaim* in a verse implies *kafil* which means guarantor.

> Qur'an 12:72: "They said, 'We are missing the measure of the king. And for he who produces it is [the reward of] a camel's load, and I am responsible (*zaim*) for it.'"

Nevertheless, the scope of this chapter is limited to its usage in commercial transactions.

### Legality

The concept of guarantee has been in practice since the time of the Prophet. The Prophet was reported to have ruled at an instance that 'a guarantor (*zaim*) holds the liability (*gharim*) of a third person'.[16] In a similar vein, Salamah bin al-Akwa' narrated: "We were seated with the Prophet when a dead person was brought and the people requested him to pray over it. He asked, 'Does the deceased have any outstanding debts?' They replied, 'No.' He asked, 'Has he left any wealth?' They replied, 'No.' The Prophet offered the funeral prayer over the deceased. Then another dead person was brought. They requested, 'O, Prophet of Allah, pray over it.' He asked, 'Does he have any outstanding debts?' They replied, 'Yes.' He asked, 'Has he left any wealth?' They replied, 'Three dinars.' The Prophet then offered the funeral prayer over the deceased. Then a third dead person was brought and they said, 'Pray over it.' He asked, 'Does the deceased have any outstanding debts?' They replied, 'Three dinars.' He said, 'Pray over your companion.' Abu Qatadah said, 'Pray over him, O Prophet of Allah, and I shall bear the burden of his debt.' The Prophet then offered the funeral prayer over him."[17] There is a wealth of evidence in the Prophetic traditions that points to the fact that guarantee has been part and parcel of Islamic law right from inception.

## Elements

There are five elements of *kafalah*:

- *makful 'anhu* (principal debtor or obligor or guaranteed)
- *kafil* (surety or guarantor)
- *makful lahu* (creditor or obligee)
- *makful bihi* (object of guarantee)
- *sighah* (expression).

Note that there are two major types of guarantee in Islamic law—*kafalah bi al-nafs* (physical guarantee) and *kafalah bi al-mal* (financial guarantee).

## Modern Application

The application of *kafalah* in modern financial transactions can be seen in the documentary credit system, which is mostly used in international trade. There are also credit card transactions based on the *kafalah* model in modern IFIs. As a security contract, *kafalah* can be used as a supporting guarantee contract for the following major contracts in Islamic finance: *mudarabah, murabahah, ijarah, salam, istisna',* and *musharakah*. The contractual guarantee used in Islamic financial transactions, particularly in the capital markets, involves the assumption of responsibilities and obligations by the guarantor on behalf of the party being guaranteed for whatever claims arise from a particular transaction. "This concept is also applicable to a guarantee provided on a debt transaction in the event a debtor fails to fulfill his debt obligation."[18] Accordingly, the classical *kafalah* has been transformed into a modern-day financial instrument in Islamic finance.

## *Wakalah* (Agency)

**wakalah**
(contract of agency)
A contract of agency whereby a party appoints an agent to act on his behalf based on certain specified terms of service.

**Wakalah** is a contract that establishes an agency relationship between two parties for a specific purpose; such authority may be general or specific. This contract gives a party the power to appoint another party to act on their behalf based on certain agreed terms and conditions. Article 1949 of *Majallah al-Ahkam* defines *wakalah* thus: "Agency consists of one person (principal) empowering another person (agent) to perform an act for them, whereby the latter stands in the stead of the former in regard to such act (an authorized act)."[19] The scope of the agency relationship is to be expressly determined in the contractual language.

A *wakalah* contract is normally considered to be an accessory contract, which is required in almost all other major commercial contracts in Islamic law. The legitimacy of the concept and practice is established in the Qur'an and Sunnah. In the story of the companions of the cave, described in the Qur'an, there was an instance where the companions authorized one of them to go out to the city and buy some food with the silver coins they had. The Qur'an says:

> Qur'an 18: 19: "So send one of you with the silver coin of yours to the town, and let him find out which is the good lawful food, and bring some of that to you. And let him be careful and let no man know of you."

There are other numerous instances of narrations in the Qur'an where power of attorney was given to a person to undertake an action on behalf of another or a group of people. This indicates that the practice was common during the early days of Islam, and there are practical precedents from the Prophetic era justifying this viewpoint.

The principal party is the *muwakkil* while the agent is the *wakil* in an agency relationship. It is, however, a fundamental requirement that the latter discharges their responsibility in accordance with the concept of trust (*amanah*). The *wakalah* relationship envisages a situation where the agent positively represents the principal in a well-defined transaction or act and may acquire rights for the principal and even subject them to certain liabilities arising. The subject matter of the contract of agency must be known to both parties. In the case of an agency for the procurement of a commodity, all necessary details such as the kind, quality, genus, and all other attributes should be included in the contract. However, it is a mandatory requirement that the subject matter of an agency must be permissible under the Sharī'ah. Any act should fall under the acts for which representation is permissible, such as commercial transactions. Representation will not be permitted for acts of worship such as prayer, fasting, performing ablutions, or a ritual bath, as acts of worship regulate the relationship between man and God, and hence must be performed by individuals without appointing any agent. In summary, the conditions for the validity of a *wakalah* agreement are that the principal should have the power and requisite competence to deal with the subject matter (property), the agent should also have the relevant legal capacity to engage in the contract, the subject matter of the contract should be known and well-defined to avoid uncertainty and excessive risk, the services to be carried out by the agent must be lawful in the eyes of the law, and the action must fall within the general scope of things for which representation is permissible.

As with other forms of contract in Islamic law, a *wakalah* agreement must include an offer and acceptance. The form and extent of the agency agreement may be specific or general depending on the agreement concluded by the parties. The principal objective of *wakalah* in Islamic commercial transactions is to facilitate economic exchanges between a principal party and third parties in situations where the former may not be able to act directly due to distance, size of transaction, or even personal conviction. As the agent merely carries out the will of the principal party in accordance with the scope of the powers delegated, *wakalah* is a typical service contract which is used to facilitate other major financial contracts.

The modern application of *wakalah* is seen in today's Islamic banking, finance and *takaful* industry where all business is carried out through certain forms of agency agreement to support the underlying contract. The application of *wakalah* is a thread running through almost all transactions. This is where the nexus between *wakalah* and *ujrah* (wages or service fees) is established. It is typical for a party to pay the agent some form of commission for agency work when carried out in accordance with the agreed terms and conditions. Another modern application is corporate *wakalah*, which banks and other financial institutions carry out on behalf of their clients in different transactions. In addition, there is a *takaful* model based on *tabarru'* (gratuitous contract) and the *wakalah* contract. There is a pure *wakalah* model of *waqf* (charitable endowment) where an agency agreement is entered into by the participants and the operators. There is also a *wakalah* based on the *waqf* model where the participants donate to the fund while the operator charges an agency fee. Some of these products will be discussed further later in this book.

## Wadi'ah (Safekeeping)

**wadi'ah**
Contract of safe custody or bailment where a sum of money or valuable property is deposited with a corporate body or individual for safekeeping.

In a **wadi'ah** contract, the bank or financial institution is deemed to be the trustee as a safekeeper of the funds or precious materials. According to the Hanafis, *wadi'ah* is entrusting someone with the responsibility of keeping one's wealth, in either explicit or implicit terms. The Malikis and Shafi'is however define *wadi'ah* as the representation in the safekeeping of a precious privately-owned property in a specific way. In light of these juristic definitions, *wadi'ah* can be defined as a contract for entrusting one's precious property or money to the care of another, usually a trusted person or a secured corporate entity.

The concept of *wadi'ah* is not directly mentioned in the Qur'an but there are a number of legal texts pointing to the importance of trust, which is the underlying principle of a *wadi'ah* contract. One of the legal texts states:

> Qur'an 4:58: "Verily, Allah commands that you should render back the trusts to those to whom they are due."

Keeping and returning entrusted property to the rightful owner, a Qur'anic concept, is further illustrated in a hadith narrated by 'Abdullah bin Dinar and Sadaqah bin Yasar of Ibn Umar, who specifically mentioned that the above verse was revealed to the Prophet while he was in Munnah during his farewell pilgrimage. The Prophet declared, among other issues: "O, you mankind! He who has been entrusted with wealth should return it to their rightful owners."[20]

In line with the indirect evidence in the Qur'an and the more direct evidence in the Sunnah, Muslim jurists are unanimous on the permissibility of *wadi'ah* contracts. The reason behind this general acceptance is because it is not possible for people to keep all their precious property, particularly gold, silver, and other currencies, with them.

The modern types of *wadi'ah* are:

- *Wadi'ah yad al-amanah* (safekeeping by a trust). This is a trust safekeeping, which is considered a charitable act and rewardable when sincerely undertaken. There is a trustee-beneficiary relationship. Any damage to the property will attract liability accordingly.

- *Wadi'ah yad al-damanah* (safekeeping with guarantee). This is safekeeping with the guarantee of funds or property deposited. This is commonly used in modern Islamic banking transactions because depositors keep their money with a bank, and this money is considered as the bank's source of funds with which it carries out its business. *Wadi'ah* is used in both current accounts and savings accounts.

## Concept of Unilateral Supporting Contract

Unilateral contracts may also be considered as supporting contracts in some cases. These contracts are made unilaterally without the usual offer and acceptance at the session of contract. The unilateral supporting contracts under consideration are *waqf* (endowment), *ibra'* (foregoing of rights), *hibah* (gift), *wa'ad* (promise) and *tabarru'* (donation). Although some of these concepts will be discussed in detail in the relevant chapters, it is appropriate to give a general overview here.

### *Waqf* (Endowment)

**waqf**
A charitable endowment in perpetuity for a specific purpose. It is meant to assist the poor and the less privileged in the society.

**Waqf** is an age-old unilateral contract introduced during the time of the Prophet. This is a process whereby a person dedicates his property to God for the benefit of a certain class of people in society. It may either be for a specific class of people or for the whole public. Hundreds of *awqaf* (plural of *waqf*) are created everyday in the Muslim world and beyond. In *waqf*, the owner of a property confers their usufruct or income for the use of either the general public or a certain class of people for a specific purpose. Once this is done, the ownership in the property, according to the majority opinion of Muslim jurists, vests in God. For more than a millennium, *waqf* has been created and developed and there has been a gradual transformation of the concept of *waqf* as a Sharī'ah financial instrument, with the revival of the concept of cash *waqf*. Property set aside for a charitable purpose may be further developed—the income realized is invested while the corpus is secured. In cash *waqf*, customers can donate cash as *waqf* to a specified account and the funds will be invested for a specific purpose. The proceeds realized from such an investment are the benefits to be distributed to the beneficiaries, while the initial amount of cash *waqf* in the account is secured. IFIs in a number of countries have designed this instrument to better serve the socioeconomic purpose of *waqf* in contemporary society.

### *Ibra'* (Forgoing of Rights)

**ibra'**
Freeing an individual or corporate entity from a financial responsibility or forgoing a right.

The term **ibra'** has featured in the discussion on debts and rights in Islamic commercial law. In order to maintain the competitiveness of the Islamic banking and finance industry, the concept of *ibra'*, which resembles the practice of rebate in the conventional banking system, was introduced. *Ibra'* can be defined as the waiving of one's financial rights or ownership that is owed to him in totality or partially. There are some situations where a bank has no choice but to waive some debts totally or partially, such as when it appears that the debtor is not able to redeem the debt. Sometimes *ibra'* is granted by an Islamic bank when the customer makes an early settlement of a debt as means to encourage such practices. It is usually at the discretion of the financier. Some scholars have justified the inclusion of *ibra'* as a contractual term to encourage early settlement of debts before the agreed period.

## Hibah (Gift)

**hibah**

A gratuitous contract where a person transfers a property to another without any formal material consideration.

**Hibah** is the gratuitous transfer of property from one person to another without any consideration whatsoever. Such a transfer of ownership confers a permanent title to the transferee, who is not required to furnish any consideration in exchange for such a benevolent gesture. In order to encourage investors, IFIs have developed the common concept of *hibah* as a supporting Sharī'ah instrument in other transactions such as *ijarah thumma al-bay'*. For instance, if customers pay their monthly installments on schedule without defaulting, this may be rewarded through the crediting of a certain amount as *hibah*.

## Wa'ad (Promise)

**wa'ad**

A unilateral promise that binds the maker alone.

**Wa'ad** can be described as a promise or undertaking by a party to carry out a unilateral contract. It is given by one party to another to signify the commitment to perform an obligation. The concept of *wa'ad* is based on the principle of fulfillment of a promise in all dispositions. In financial transactions, *wa'ad* may be a fundamental requirement through which a customer declares their intention to perform a contract that was entered into earlier. For instance, in a *murabahah* transaction where the bank is required to purchase the commodity, the customer must give an undertaking to show their commitment to perform the contract. This is because if the customer fails to perform their own part of the *murabahah* contract after the bank has purchased the commodity, the bank will definitely suffer financial loss. Therefore, a unilateral promise is required at the onset to avoid future disputes. Another example of *wa'ad* is found in a lease contract (*ijarah*) where a customer gives a binding promise to buy the leased asset upon expiry of the leasing period. This happens in a contractual arrangement known as *ijarah thumma al-bay'*, otherwise known as the Islamic hire-purchase transaction.

There is a divergence of opinion among Muslim jurists on the binding nature of *wa'ad*. The majority of jurists opine that fulfilling *wa'ad* is recommended in financial transactions. The jurists who uphold this view include those of the Shafi'i school, some Maliki jurists, and Abu Hanifah. They believe a promise is like a gift that only becomes binding after it has been delivered. On the other hand, the majority of the Maliki scholars believe that fulfilling *wa'ad* is obligatory and is usually enforceable.

On the other hand, *muwa'adah*, which is a derivative of *wa'ad*, is a bilateral promise in contractual form that may either be conditional or unconditional. In this contractual arrangement, the bilateral promise may be accompanied with or without a corresponding consideration. The nature of an unconditional bilateral promise is like that of a simple contract where a party undertakes to sell a commodity during a particular time and the other party agrees to buy it at that same time. But the conditional bilateral promise occurs when a party promises to sell a commodity and the other party agrees to buy it under certain conditions. The legality of *muwa'adah* has been affirmed by modern jurists as being binding on the orderer of the assets provided the bank owns the goods, the goods are in the bank's possession, the goods are sold to the purchase orderer with an agreed specification of profit, the bank bears the ownership risk until delivery, and the bank undertakes to accept redelivery if the goods have hidden defects. This is based on the resolution of the second conference of Islamic banking in Kuwait held in 1983. When an option is given to one of the parties, a mutual promise becomes permissible and binding.

From the above, it is clear that the concept and implications of the terms *wa'ad* and *muwa'adah* are closely related to the term *'aqd* because the former are forms of contract which are either unilateral or bilateral.

## *Tabarru'* (Gratuitous Donation)

**tabarru'**
Gratuitous contract or donation, which includes bequests and gifts.

**Tabarru'** is a gratuitous contract that is unilateral but supportive of certain underlying contracts such as *takaful*. The concept of *tabarru'* can be described as certain benefits in the form of charity given to another person either by the repayment of a debt on behalf of another or a direct grant to another person without receiving anything in exchange. Apart from the application of the concept of *tabarru'* in *takaful*, it is also applicable in *waqf* donations managed by an Islamic financial institution for the benefit of the beneficiary. Ownership in the subject matter of *tabarru'* is transferred at the time of donation from the donor to the donee. It will not be permissible if the donor subsequently wants to benefit from the subject matter of a *tabarru'* unilateral contract because the legal title in the property is now vested in the donee. In a hadith narrated by Ibn Abbad, it was reported that the Prophet said: "He who takes his gift/donation back is like a dog which takes back its vomiting."[21]

# Review

## Key Terms and Concepts

*bay al-dayn* (p. 89)
*bay al-inah* (p. 90)
*bay al-salam* (p. 88)
*bay al-sarf* (p. 95)
bill of exchange (p. 109)
debt-based financing instrument (p. 82)
dual banking system (p. 79)
equity capital (p. 79)
general investment accounts (GIA) (p. 105)
*hawalah* (p. 109)
*hibah* (p. 120)
*hilah* (p. 91)
*ibra'* (p. 119)
*ijarah* (p. 99)
*ijarah mawsufah fi dhimmah* (p. 102)
*ijarah muntahia bittamlik* (p. 100)
*ijarah thumma al-bay'* (p. 101)
*ijma* (p. 104)
Islamic capital market (p. 87)
Islamic finance windows (p. 79)
*istihsan* (p. 86)
*istisna'* (p. 85)
*ju'alah* (p. 103)
*kafalah* (p. 115)
margin of profit (p. 85)
*mudarabah* (p. 104)

*mudarib* (p. 104)
*murabahah* (p. 82)
*muqasah* (p. 113)
*musharakah* (p. 106)
*musharakah mutanaqisah* (p. 91)
participation term certificate (PTC) (p. 94)
promissory note (p. 109)
*rabb al-mal* (p. 104)
*rahn* (p. 111)
real capital (p. 79)
*sanadat* (p. 92)
secondary market (p. 92)
short-term liquidity (p. 80)
Sharī'ah supervisory council (p. 85)
special investment accounts (SIA) (p. 105)
special purpose vehicle (SPV) (p. 87)
*tabarru'* (p. 121)
*tawarruq* (p. 96)
*tawriq* (p. 92)
*ujrah* (p. 102)
usufruct (p. 92)
*wa'ad* (p. 120)
*wadi'ah* (p. 118)
*wakalah* (p. 116)
*waqf* (p. 119)

## Summary

**Learning Objective 3.1**

1. The sources and uses of funds and the operation of bank accounts in modern Islamic banks are generally based on Sharī'ah financial contracts structured as financial instruments to meet people's modern needs. The contracts have been developed, designed, and fine-tuned to meet the demands of modern Islamic finance business without compromising the underlying philosophy of such contracts.

**Learning Objective 3.2**

2. Exchange-based contracts used as financial instruments include *murabahah* (mark-up), *istisna'* (manufacture sale), *salam* (forward sale), *bay al-dayn* (sale of debt), *tawriq* (securitization), *sarf* (sale of currency), *tawarruq* (cash financing) and *bay al-inah* (sale with immediate repurchase). These instruments are widely used in both Islamic banking and Islamic capital market transactions.

**Learning Objective 3.3**

3. Service-based contracts that have been structured as financial instruments within the Islamic finance industry include *ijarah* (leasing), *ijarah muntahia bittamlik* (financial lease), *ijarah thumma al-bay'* (leasing and subsequent purchase), *ijarah mawsufah fi dhimmah* (forward lease), *ujrah* (fees), and *ju'alah* (commission). They relate to either the right to use an asset or services rendered with a fee or commission as a consideration.

**Learning Objective 3.4**

4. The partnership contracts are considered the most important financial instruments in Islamic finance. These include *mudarabah* (trust financing), *musharakah* (joint-venture partnership) and *musharakah mutanaqisah* (diminishing partnership). Muslim scholars have continuously encouraged the use of these contracts because of their inherent equity-like nature.

**Learning Objective 3.5**

5. The supporting or auxiliary contracts in Islamic finance are indispensable in the chain of transactions contained in modern financial instruments. These include *hawalah* (assignment of debt), *wakalah* (agency contract), *muqasah* (offsetting), *ibra'* (foregoing of rights), *wa'ad* (promise or undertaking), *tabarru'* (gratuitous donation), *hibah* (gift), *wadi'ah* (safe custody), and *waqf* (charitable endowment).

## Practice Questions and Activities

### Practice Questions

1. Write a short note on how Islamic banks source funds and use them in Sharī'ah-compliant business.

2. Discuss three main types of accounts in the modern practice of Islamic banking.

3. Name five exchange-based contracts and discuss any three of your choice.

4. Discuss the kind of financial instruments that can be used to purchase a car, bearing in mind that the client who is approaching a bank does not have much knowledge about the types of cars.

5. Explain the applicability of three service-based contracts of your choice to people's modern needs, such as housing, hire purchase, and teaching. Give relevant examples to support your answer.

6. Explain the basic rules of an *ijarah* contract.

7. Why do you think Sharī'ah scholars give preference to partnership-based contracts in the Islamic finance industry?

8. Differentiate between *musharakah* and *mudarabah*.

9. Briefly discuss the relevance of supporting contracts in Islamic financial instruments and explain their significance in the modern practice of Islamic finance.

10. How does *wakalah* complement the structuring of a *mudarabah* financial instrument used by an Islamic bank?

## Activities

1. Find three resolutions of the Sharī'ah Advisory Council of any Islamic bank or financial institution and identify the financial instruments analyzed in them.

2. Prepare a simple sketch of the diminishing partnership contract using relevant images of the parties involved.

3. Interview the customer service section of any Islamic bank or financial institution in your locality (or elsewhere) and identify the Sharī'ah financial instruments it adopts.

## Further Reading

Ayub, M. (2007). *Understanding Islamic Finance*. England: John Wiley & Sons, Ltd.

Hassan, H. (2002). Contracts in Islamic Law: The Principles of Commutative Justice and Liberality. 13 *Journal of Islamic Studies*: pp. 257–297.

Kharofa, A. (2002). *The Loan Contract in Islamic Sharī'ah and Man-Made Law (Roman-French-Egyptian): A Comparative Study*. Kuala Lumpur: Leeds Publications.

Mohd. Ma'sum Billah. (2006). *Sharī'ah Standard of Business Contract*. Kuala Lumpur: A. A. Noordeen.

Niazi, L. A. (1991). *Islamic Law of Contract*. Lahore: Research Cell, Dyal Sing Trust Library.

Rayner, S. (1991). *The Theory of Contracts in Islamic Law*. London: Graham and Trotman.

Razali, S. S. (2010). *Islamic Law of Contract*. Singapore: Cengage Learning Asia Pte Ltd.

Usmani, M. T. (1999). *An Introduction to Islamic Finance*. Karachi: Idara Isha'at-e-Diniyat (P) Ltd.

Usmani, T. (2006). *Islamic Finance—Musharakah & Mudarabah*. Karachi: Darul Uloom. Jamia Darul Uloom.

Vogel, F. E., and Hayes III, S. L. (1998). *Islamic Law and Finance—Religion, Risk and Return*. The Hague, The Netherlands: Kluwer Law International.

# 4

# Financial Accounting for Islamic Banking Products

# Learning Objectives

**Upon the completion of this chapter, the reader should be able to:**

1 Understand the definition of accounting from both conventional and Islamic perspectives, respectively, and its significance in financial decision-making.

2 Explain the relevance of International Financial Reporting Standards (IFRS) in international accounting regulation.

3 Understand the basic principles of accounting.

4 Understand the basic principles of Islamic accounting.

5 Differentiate between the accrual and cash flow accounting methods.

6 Draft the main financial statements for Islamic finance products.

Accounting is regarded as a product of the environment within which it operates. A number of environmental factors greatly influence a country's financial accounting system. These factors include the legal, regulatory, and political frameworks, size of ownership, and the nature of business being carried.

There is a strong relationship between Islamic financial principles and accounting. Such principles have been aligned with international financial standards with a view to establishing a formidable framework for financial accounting for Islamic banking products without compromising an inch of the fundamental requirements of Islamic financial transactions. To this end, this chapter examines financial accounting for Islamic banking products. It examines the international financial reporting standards, basic principles of conventional accounting, and basic principles of Islamic accounting. It further appraises the financial accounting standards of the Accounting and Auditing Organization for Islamic Financial Institutions (AAOIFI), which, for the purpose of this book, are considered to be the general standards for Islamic financial accounting. In order to guide the reader, the chapter also gives comparative financial statements for Islamic financial products. There is no doubt that the development of the Islamic banking sector requires a standard financial reporting framework.

**Professor Mustafa Hanefah**
*Dean, Research and Innovation*
*Universiti Sains Islam Malaysia*

**1   What accounting standards do you adopt in your organization?**

Malaysian universities are required to adopt IFRS of the International Accounting Standards Board, and Malaysian Financial Reporting Standards (MFRS) in their teaching at undergraduate and postgraduate programs. Since January 1, 2012, MFRS issued by the Malaysian Accounting Standards Board (MASB) are in congruence with the IFRS. All corporate entities, including Islamic financial institutions (IFIs), must adopt IFRS or MFRS in their reporting and disclosure practices. It is also mandatory for all Malaysian IFIs to adopt IASB recommended standards and guiding principles.

**2   Is there any conflict between IFRS, AAOIFI and IFSB recommendations regarding accounting standards for Islamic financial products?**

There are several major differences between IFRS and AAOIFI accounting standards. AAOIFI standards are mainly for IFIs, whereas the IFRS cover all entities. AAOIFI and IFSB standards are based on Sharī'ah principles, and full compliance with these principles are mandatory at all times. Sharī'ah-based standards differ in respect to time value of money (money available at this time is worth more in future as a result of its inherent potential earning capacity), legal forms, and rule-based standards. The IASB is more concerned with substance and principle-based accounting standards. Time value of money or interest is not a problem for the IFRS, but is with regard to AAOIFI and IFSB standards and guidelines. The AAOIFI and IFSB should also ensure their standards and guiding principles can be adopted by all entities, not just Islamic banks. Islamic banks in the Middle East adopt AAOIFI standards, but Malaysian ones adopt IFRS as AAOIFI standards are not mandatory. Issues of comparability and transparency arise because of these anomalies.

**3   Are the accounting standards for Islamic banks enough? Do we need to come up with more standards?**

New accounting standards are only issued when new Islamic financial instruments or products are made available by Islamic banks. In today's competitive business world, Islamic banks always try to market new financial products to their customers. This will require new standards, just like IFRS. Standards should also cover all areas of Islamic finance and banking including corporate governance, risk management, capital adequacy, and not only for the banks but also other IFIs.

## professional perspectives

**Muhammad Tariq**
*Partner, Head of Islamic Finance, KPMG UAE*

**1    What accounting standards are adopted by organizations in your jurisdiction?**

The choice of an accounting framework is almost always driven by regulatory requirements. In the United Arab Emirates, all Islamic financial institutions (IFIs) follow International Financial Reporting Standards (IFRS), except those IFIs which are domiciled in Dubai International Financial Centre (an offshore jurisdiction) and regulated by Dubai Financial Services Authority (DFSA) where the accounting framework for IFIs is Financial Accounting Standards (FAS) issued by Accounting and Auditing Organization for Islamic Financial Institutions (AAOIFI). I am aware that DFSA is currently reviewing its position on mandatory use of FAS and there is a possibility that this requirement will be removed.

**2    Is there any difference between IFRS, AAOIFI and IFSB recommendations regarding accounting standards for Islamic financial products?**

It is important to understand why FAS were created in the first place. For a very long time Islamic finance professionals have been highlighting the inadequacies of IFRS when it comes to dealing with Sharī'ah-compliant products and transactions. They believed that the true nature of Sharī'ah-compliant products and transactions was being ignored and the needs of the users of financial statements were not being fully met. In particular, the risk-sharing nature of these products and transactions was being lost because IFRS focuses on the 'economic substance' of the products and transactions rather than their legal structure. Another reason for creating FAS was to address accounting issues which are unique to Islamic finance. For example, accounting for *qard hasan*, *zakah*, profit equalization reserves, etc.

Clearly, IFRS do have an advantage because of its global reach and long history of robust standard-setting, which gives confidence to users of financial statements. However, AAOIFI has been trying to gain more jurisdictions, and much effort has gone into creating awareness of its value proposition.

**3    Are the accounting standards for Islamic Banks enough? Do we need to come up with more standards?**

The clear answers to these two questions are 'probably not' and 'yes', respectively. There are many areas which are the subject of considerable debate, and authoritative accounting guidance is lacking. This is compounded by fast-paced growth in the Islamic finance industry and the continuing evolution and complexity of many Islamic finance products. In my personal opinion, AAOIFI is struggling to cope with this and the pace of standard-setting has been relatively slow as a result. I believe a closer coordination among standard-setters in this respect will be beneficial and many more synergies can be achieved.

# Definition of Islamic Financial Accounting

The language of business is accounting. The language can only be communicated through a process that may involve a number of activities such as recording the transactions and classifying them under the appropriate heading. This process is essential for the success of a business. In this section, we shall be defining the terms 'accounting' and 'Islamic accounting' and explain the importance of accountability in Islam. Although there are different kinds of accounting, our focus in this chapter is financial accounting.

## What is Accounting?

In simple terms, accounting is a process whereby business operations and activities are measured, and the measurements are processed into information that is made available to decision-makers. This simple definition involves three main issues:

- recognizing, recording, classifying, and summarizing business transactions
- measuring, analyzing, processing, and interpreting operating results
- reporting and presenting the financial position.

The financial position presented on the business transactions is specifically meant for the decision-makers, who include both internal and external stakeholders. The internal decision-makers include the company management while the external decision-makers are mainly investors and customers.

**American Accounting Association**
A voluntary organization for people interested in accounting education and research, which was founded in 1916.

For more information on the American Accounting Association, see http://aaahq.org

**financial accounting**
A process where business operations and activities are measured, and the measurements are processed into information that is made available to decision-makers.

**Islamic worldview**
The vision of reality and truth about a phenomenon based on Islamic ideals.

According to the **American Accounting Association**, accounting can be defined as "the process of identifying, measuring, and communicating economic information to permit informed judgments and decisions by users of the information."[1] The purpose of this process is to provide necessary information that has the potential to be useful for economic decision-making by stakeholders in the financial industry. Accounting or economic information is identified and measured by creating a set of accounts in which the records of business transactions are summarized.

## What is Islamic Accounting?

Islamic **financial accounting** can be defined as "the accounting process that provides appropriate information (not necessarily limited to financial data) to stakeholders of an entity that will enable them to ensure that the entity is continuously operating within the bounds of the Islamic Sharī'ah and delivering on its socioeconomic objectives."[2] Islamic law is generally inclusive regarding issues that relate to Islamic financial transactions, with the exception of few prohibited elements. Therefore, the general definition of financial accounting remains acceptable within the Islamic financial framework provided that the underlying objective of Islamic financial accounting is an **Islamic worldview** in compliance with the Sharī'ah prescriptions. The significance of financial accounting in both frameworks is to enable stakeholders to make informed decisions about their various options when conducting business transactions. Financial accounting is directed at the needs of external decision-makers. Decision-makers include the company management, the board of directors, shareholders, investors, creditors, regulatory authorities, staff, and the general public.

## The Importance of Accountability in Islam

In the Qur'an, the generic word for accounting or accountability is *hisab*. The word *hisab* or *muhasabah* (a word derived from *hisab*) refers to the individual spiritual reckoning in Islam. It is generally used in several verses of the Qur'an to emphasize the need for accountability in every human activity. In most of the verses in the Qur'an, the word is used in its generic sense, which emphasizes the obligation on mankind to be accountable to God in every worldly disposition. There is emphasis on the importance of accountability in daily transactions regardless of whether they relate to financial or administrative matters. In order to ensure transparency in commercial dealings, there is emphasis on the accountability of parties in a partnership business. For instance, in a trust partnership contract where a capital provider provides the capital to an entrepreneur for investment in a commercial enterprise, known as a *mudarabah* transaction, one key element in the transaction is accountability and fair dealing. The Islamic worldview of accountability leaves its footprints in every page of the Qur'an. All legislative prescriptions on economic matters mentioned in the Qur'an and clearly explained in the Prophetic traditions are based on fair dealings and accountability.

Against this backdrop, a number of Islamic concepts underscore the significance of accountability in Islam with particular reference to financial transactions. These concepts include *khilafah* (vicegerency), *taklif* (responsibility), documentation of financial dealings, Islamic law of inheritance (*mawarith*), calculation of obligatory alms (*zakat*), and the underlying concept of *tawhid* (unity of God). The concept of responsibility (*taklif*) in Islam typifies the duty of people towards their God. The purpose of creation in Islam as proclaimed by God is the unparalleled worship of the Ultimate Creator. Therefore, a person is the vicegerent of God (*khalifah*) and merely the trustee of all resources provided for their benefit on earth. As a vicegerent of God, a person is accountable for their prudent management of these resources. Each person will be held accountable for their deeds involving the management of endowed resources in this world and the next. This is one reason why one of the commonest names for the **Last Day**, when all persons and *jinns* (a class of spirits that are capable of appearing in animal or human forms) will account for their deeds, is the Day of Accountability. This implies full accountability of one's deeds on earth, which accordingly attracts some form of immediate recompense.

**Last Day**
The Day of Accountability where, according to the Islamic belief, human beings and *jinns* will account for their worldly life before Almighty God.

So we can see that accountability and the need for proper accounting in whatever one undertakes is part of the Islamic ideals. This is the reason why Islamic accountants have more responsibility in their duties for they are expected to understand the underlying religious principles of their chosen profession.

LEARNING OBJECTIVE 4.2

Explain the relevance of International Financial Reporting Standards (IFRS) in international accounting regulations.

# International Financial Reporting Standards

Financial reporting is an element of documentation in financial dealings, which is a Qur'anic prescription in commercial transactions in Islam. The general approval and guideline Islam provides for recording and subsequent reporting of transactions is summarized in Qur'an 2, verse 282, which is the longest verse of the Qur'an, popularly called the 'verse on debt', or *ayat al-dain* in Arabic. The emphasis on these issues requires a standard framework for Islamic reporting of various commercial transactions in Islamic law. The recording and reporting of Islamic financial products requires different techniques. For instance, the financial reporting of *mudarabah* financing is different from that of *murabahah* financing, and so on.

**International Accounting Standards Board (IASB)**

An independent standard-setting body of the IFRS Foundation. This is the leading standard-setting body for conventional accounting and auditing practices.

The International Financial Reporting Standards (IFRS) are a set of principles-based accounting standards developed by an independent, non-for-profit organization called the **International Accounting Standards Board** (**IASB**). The IASB is the standard-setting body of the IFRS Foundation. The main goal of the IFRS is to provide globally acceptable standards for public companies in the preparation and disclosure of their financial statements. Box 4.1 outlines the principal objectives of the IFRS and IASB. The IFRS contains general guidelines for financial reporting. It does not contain industry-specific standards for individual companies. Public companies across the world are required to adopt and adapt the global standards to suit the specifics of the industry within which they operate. The IFRS is more relevant to multinational corporations with subsidiaries spread across different countries as it allows them to adopt the same set of accounting standards. This simplifies the accounting procedures as all subsidiaries can adopt the same reporting language in preparing and disclosing their respective financial statements. Both prospective investors and auditors will have the same overview of the company's finances as a single set of standards of reporting has been adopted.

## BOX 4.1: THE IFRS FOUNDATION AND THE IASB

The IFRS Foundation is an independent, not-for-profit, private sector organization working in the public interest. Its principal objectives are:

- to develop a single set of high quality, understandable, enforceable and globally accepted international financial reporting standards (IFRS) through its standard-setting body, the IASB
- to promote the use and rigorous application of those standards
- to take account of the financial reporting needs of emerging economies and small and medium-sized entities (SMEs)
- to bring about convergence of national accounting standards and IFRS.

See IFRS Foundation at www.ifrs.org.

People often confuse the International Accounting Standards (IAS) with the IFRS. These are two different accounting reporting regimes. The IAS are the old standards, which have been replaced by those of the IFRS. Nevertheless, many standards forming part of the IFRS are still known by their older name of IAS. The Board of the International Accounting Standards Committee (IASC) issued IAS between 1973 and 2001. The new IASB took over the responsibility for setting international accounting standards from the IASC on April 1, 2001. It has, however, adopted the existing IAS and the Standing Interpretations Committee (SIC). Since then, the IASB has continued to develop new standards under the new name IFRS. More than 120 countries require the adoption of IFRS for public companies in financial reporting and disclosures (see Table 4.1 on page 133).

IFRS provides broad rules and dictates specific treatments for certain aspects of financial reporting. The structure of IFRS comprises five different aspects:

- International Financial Reporting Standards (IFRS)—standards issued after 2001
- International Accounting Standards (IAS)—standards issued before 2001
- Interpretations originated from the International Financial Reporting Interpretations Committee (IFRIC)—issued after 2001
- Standing Interpretations Committee (SIC)—issued before 2001
- Conceptual Framework for Financial Reporting (IFRS Framework) (2010).

## IFRS and Islamic Banks and Financial Institutions

The applicability of IFRS to Islamic banks and financial institutions has created certain problems because its standards are intended for conventional forms of business whereas Islamic banks have their own specific requirements in terms of transactions, reporting, and disclosure. There are issues in Islamic finance for which there are no IFRS, and a number of the existing IFRS are not applicable to Islamic banks and financial institutions. Therefore, the Islamic finance industry requires its own set of accounting and financial reporting standards. This prompted the establishment of an international standard-setting body for Islamic financial institutions. The Bahrain-based **Accounting and Auditing Organization for Islamic Financial Institutions (AAOIFI)** has issued more than 81 accounting, auditing, governance, ethics, and Sharī'ah standards. AAOIFI's establishment was overdue considering the tremendous growth experienced in the Islamic finance industry within the past 20 years. This body has spearheaded the development of accounting, auditing, and Sharī'ah standards for Islamic banks and financial institutions across the world. AAOIFI operates in a competitive world where there is an increasing call for the adoption of IFRS in order to achieve harmonization in financial reporting regardless of the cultural differences between countries. The efforts made towards harmonization of the AAOIFI standards with the IFRS are given in the *Islamic Finance in the News* feature.

There is a world of difference between conventional financial instruments and Islamic ones such as *mudarabah* between two parties where they both contribute capital towards the joint venture. Therefore, their respective accounting treatments differ and, furthermore, the type of information contained in the financial statements

**Accounting and Auditing Organization for Islamic Financial Institutions (AAOIFI)** The main international standard-setting body for Islamic financial institutions.

Hint

To learn more about AAOIFI, visit its website at www.aaoifi.com.

| TABLE 4.1: Adoption of IFRS by Companies in Selected Countries | |
| --- | --- |
| Country | Status for listed companies as of December 2011 |
| Argentina | Required for fiscal years beginning on or after January 1, 2012. |
| Australia | Required for all private-sector reporting entities and as the basis for public-sector reporting since 2005. |
| Brazil | Required for consolidated financial statements of banks and listed companies from December 31, 2010 and for individual company accounts progressively since January 2008. |
| Canada | Required from January 1, 2011 for all listed entities and permitted for private-sector entities including not-for-profit organizations. |
| China | Substantially converged national standards. |
| European Union | All member states of the EU are required to use IFRS as adopted by the EU for listed companies since 2005. |
| France | Required via EU adoption and implementation process since 2005. |
| Germany | Required via EU adoption and implementation process since 2005. |
| India | India is converging with IFRS at a date to be confirmed. |
| Indonesia | Convergence process ongoing; a decision about a target date for full compliance with IFRS was expected to be made in 2012. |
| Italy | Required via EU adoption and implementation process since 2005. |
| Japan | Permitted from 2010 for a number of international companies; decision about mandatory adoption by 2016 expected around 2012. |
| Mexico | Required from 2012. |
| Republic of Korea | Required from 2011. |
| Russia | Required from 2012. |
| Saudi Arabia | Required for banking and insurance companies; full convergence with IFRS currently under consideration. |
| South Africa | Required for listed entities since 2005. |
| Turkey | Required for listed entities since 2005. |
| United Kingdom | Required via EU adoption and implementation process since 2005. |
| United States | Allowed for foreign issuers in the US since 2007; US SEC committed to global accounting standards and IFRS best placed to meet that need in the US, awaiting decision regarding use of IFRS for domestic companies. |

Source: IFRS Foundation. Available at www.ifrs.org/Use-around-the-world/Pages/Use-around-the-world.aspx.

# ISLAMIC FINANCE IN THE NEWS

## IFRS to Converge with Islamic Accounting Standards

**April 21, 2009**

Even as the Securities and Exchange Commission weighs the comments that were due this week on its proposed roadmap to International Financial Reporting Standards, IFRS could be on a convergence path of its own with Islamic accounting standards.

In addition to converging IFRS with U.S. generally accepted accounting principles, the International Accounting Standards Board is also looking to extend the standards globally, claiming that about 113 different countries have either adopted IFRS or agreed to adopt the standards. Now the IASB is looking to the Middle East to adopt the standards. Board member Robert Garnett spoke at an IFRS breakfast briefing in Dubai about the standards and how they could converge with Islamic accounting standards.

'We have to embrace all financial products so we will need to change our standards,' he said, according to *Emirates Business*. He said that the IASB would need to meet with the Middle Eastern standard-setter, the Accounting and Auditing Organization for Islamic Financial Institutions, 'to have a better understanding of their concerns and how we can accommodate those with a revised IFRS'. He sees only slight differences between the standards now and believes they can be reconciled with the help of professional judgment.

Garnett also chairs the International Financial Reporting Committee and he plans to begin holding talks with the AAOIFI this year to try to work out the differences between IFRS and the Islamic standards.

**Source:** *Accounting Today.*

### Challenge

What are the similarities of the objectives of financial accounting in both the conventional and Islamic frameworks?

also differ. Conventional accounting standards are based on a framework useful for decision-making by stakeholders who are given the relevant information. Conversely, Islamic accounting standards focus on accountability and a framework for Sharīʻah compliance that seeks fair dealing among all parties in a business transaction. That does not mean that Islamic accounting standards neglect the important objective of financial accounting, i.e. to provide useful information to the users of financial reports. But there is a more ethical perspective towards the Islamic worldview. Financial reports are made available to the users to enable them to make informed, legitimate decisions in their dealings with the IFI rather than to think of how to increase their wealth in the capitalist sense. In addition, the functions of Islamic commercial contracts, for which financial disclosure and reporting are required, are different from the functions of conventional banks' financial contracts. Whereas conventional banks aim to mobilize deposits and advance loans with interest, Islamic banks focus on investment financing and social services through joint venture contracts between the financial institutions and their customers.

# Basic Principles of Accounting

**bookkeeping**
The detailed recording of all financial transactions involved in a business.

**Hint** Remember that the users of financial information are management, potential investors, employees, lenders, suppliers and other trade creditors, customers, government and their agencies, and the general public.

**revenue**
The money received from the sale of products and services before expenses incurred are deducted. Revenue is also known as 'top line'.

**expenditure**
Amount of money or resources spent in a financial operation or in the settlement of an obligation.

**journal**
An accounting record where all financial transactions of a business are originally entered.

**T account (or ledger)**
The ledger account format that resembles the letter T, which originates from the process of using debits and credits.

**double-entry bookkeeping**
A set of rules for recording financial information where every transaction or event changes at least two different ledger accounts.

Accounting comprises two main activities that are distinct in nature but complementary in their functions. The first activity is called **bookkeeping**. In simple terms, bookkeeping is the detailed recording of all financial transactions involved in a business. This is the recording aspect of accounting, whereby all transactions are carefully documented. The second activity is the preparation of the *financial statement, or accounting*. This may be made periodically depending on the policy and accounting standards adopted by the business. Periodic statements or accounts are prepared to give a summary of the financial performance of a business. Users of this information can assess it for their needs. Regardless of the type or size of the business, the principles of accounting are the same. That is, there must be two-tier procedure for accounting, beginning with bookkeeping and ending with accounting.

## Recording Financial Information

In a business, one has to monitor the progress of transactions through appropriate records for each and every financial transaction. The information recorded must reflect both the **revenue** and **expenditure.** The accounting record where all financial transactions of a business are originally entered is known as a **journal**. However, individuals also keep records of their finances. When you receive your payslip at the end of the month, the next thing you do is plan how to use your wages. Paying the bills and rent usually comes first from your monthly pay, then a workable budget for consumables and your monthly upkeep. Keeping proper records allows you to know your financial position at every point in time, enabling you to plan for other future financial commitments. So financial information is very important to us in our daily lives. The same applies to a business, where financial information is required to make business decisions. This information can only be derived by proper record-keeping of all the business's financial transactions. The recording of financial information is formalized in a business, as opposed to that of the individuals. The reason for keeping a financial record is that it is difficult for the entrepreneur to remember all transactions; hence, the need to document everything. The basis of modern accounting systems, which became an established method of recording financial transactions in the 15th century, is double-entry bookkeeping**.**

Another relevant item in recording financial information is the **ledger**, or what is generally known as the **T account**. The ledger is a collection of financial accounts that uses both credits and debits. The format is usually in a 'T' form, where credits are presented on one side and debits are presented on the opposite, hence the name T account.

## Double-Entry Bookkeeping

The **double-entry bookkeeping** system is a set of rules for recording financial information where every transaction or event changes at least two different ledger accounts. Every financial transaction reveals two main aspects: the debit aspect and the credit aspect.

**FIGURE 4.1  THE BASICS OF THE DOUBLE ENTRY SYSTEM**

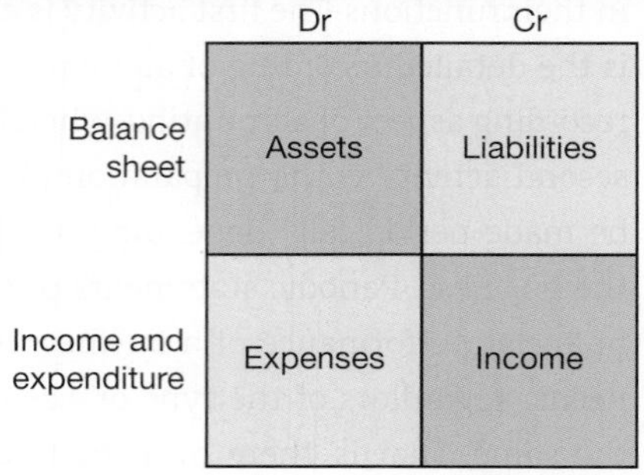

Source: Leo Isaac. Available at www.leoisaac.com/fin/fin004.htm.

**debit**

An increase in assets and expenses, and an decrease in liability, revenue, and capital.

**credit**

An increase in liability, revenue, and capital, and a decrease in assets and expenses.

The **debit** aspect is the receiving, incoming or expenses/loss aspect. Conversely, the **credit** aspect is the giving, outgoing or income/gain aspect, as shown in Figure 4.1. These two aspects form the basis of the double-entry system, which records them both. The basic principle is: *for every debit, there must be a corresponding credit of an equal amount and for every credit, there must be a corresponding debit of an equal amount.* Therefore, the accounting equation, which governs the double-entry bookkeeping, provides if revenue equals expenses, the following basic equation must be true:

$$\textbf{assets} = \textbf{liabilities} + \textbf{owners' equity}$$

To have a balanced account, total debits must be equal to total debits.

To give a practical example, suppose someone invests US$10,000 in a business. They use this capital to lease an office and buy basic office supplies to kick start the business. According to the double-entry bookkeeping, his initial journal entries might look like Table 4.2.

**TABLE 4.2: Example of a Journal Entry**

| Date | Account Name and Explanation | Debit (dr) | Credit (cr) |
|---|---|---|---|
| 1/1/2013 | Cash<br>Capital<br>  The owner contributes $10,000 to start<br>  the business | 10,000 | 10,000 |
| 1/3/2013 | Lease expense<br>Cash | 1,200 | 1,200 |
| 1/6/2013 | Office supplies<br>Computer<br>Cash | 200<br>2000 | 2,200 |

The *date* column gives the actual day when each transaction was carried out.

The *account name and explanation* gives the details of the transaction and the item either purchased or acquired.

The *debit column* provides for the assets of the business, which also signifies a decrease in the revenue or capital of the business. This is recorded on the left-hand side of a ledger or 'T' account.

The *credit column* provides information about the increase in assets and expenses. This is recorded on the right-hand side of a 'T' account.

In some cases a fifth column may be added to reflect the balance of the 'T' account. Alternatively, a line may be drawn underneath the entries to show the net balance. This is put in the appropriate side of the account.

Note how in the table each transaction is balanced accordingly. Any transaction entered on the left-hand side (debit column) equals the amount on the right-hand side (credit column). This balances the transactions and shows the double-entry system. The entries for 1/1/2013 and 1/3/2013, respectively, are single entries for each of those days. They represent two separate single journal entries for transactions on two different days. However, the entry for 1/6/2013 comprises two journal entries (office supplies and computer), where two separate accounts were credited in one single account (as cash). This is known as the **compound accounting journal entry**, which is considered to be more efficient and preferable for financial accounting.

**compound accounting journal entry**
More than one debit or credit in a single journal entry. It is is also called combined journal entry.

## The Three Branches of Accounting

Accounting covers a range of activities and related financial issues. However, the branches of accounting are broadly divided into three main categories—cost and management accounting, financial accounting, and auditing (Figure 4.2).

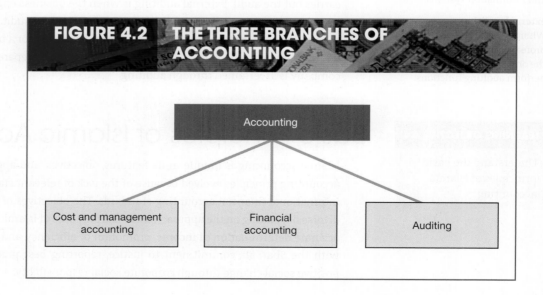

FIGURE 4.2 THE THREE BRANCHES OF ACCOUNTING

## Cost and Management Accounting

Cost and management accounting deals with the provision of relevant financial information to interested parties in the business to assist them in planning, decision-making, management, and control. The information generated must be relevant and help managers make informed decisions in the management of the business. The information is also useful for planning, control, and performance measurement. The cost component of cost and management accounting appropriately allocates costs between the costs of goods sold and inventories. This is relevant for internal and external profit reporting on the business.

## Financial Accounting

Financial accounting deals with the provision of relevant information to interested parties outside the domain of the business. Prospective investors, banks, future partners, regulatory bodies, government agencies, shareholders, and prospective buyers who will, one way or another, need financial information on the performance of the business to help them make better decisions or policies. Financial accounting allows the stakeholders in the business to make sound economic decisions that could have an impact on the populace. While cost and management accounting provides information for managers to help them make better decisions to manage the business effectively, financial accounting is directed at outsiders from the business, who are usually stakeholders in the industry at large. These stakeholders are not involved in the day-to-day running of the company but are considered to be interested parties.

**internal auditing**
This is a system designed by an organization to examine, monitor, and analyze activities related to its operation, including its business structure, employee behavior, and information systems.

**external auditing**
When an independent professional or firm outside the organization is engaged to perform auditing functions.

## Auditing

Auditing is a key branch of accounting that determines, through verification, whether the financial information recorded or disclosed is a true reflection of the business transactions that were undertaken during a financial period. There are two forms—internal auditing and external auditing. Internal auditing is where the business itself carries out the audit. External auditing is when the business engages the services of an outside company, usually an auditing firm, to conduct the audit. The modern practice is to combine both **internal auditing** and **external auditing** for a particular financial year. The validity and reliability of the financial information prepared and disclosed by the company is ascertained through auditing.

**LEARNING OBJECTIVE 4.4**

Understand the basic principles of Islamic accounting.

# Basic Principles of Islamic Accounting

Islamic accounting is unique in its features, objectives, and approach. Modern Islamic accounting principles evolved because of the lack of relevant standards in the available international financial accounting standards. The objectives of Islamic accounting are diverse depending on the approach used. The purposes of Islamic accounting include the accurate determination of income, promotion of efficiency and leadership, compliance with the Sharī'ah, commitment to justice, reporting best practices, and adapting to positive social change through corporate social responsibility.

# Consumers of Accounting Information on Islamic Banks

**Statement of Financial Accounting (SFA)**
A statement issued by the Accounting and Auditing Organization for Islamic Financial Institutions that contains financial accounting and reporting standards for Islamic finance products.

## Challenge

Compare these categories of users of financial reports with those of the conventional financial institutions. Are there any differences?

Just as in conventional accounting, the consumers of accounting information on Islamic banks consist of numerous stakeholders of the Islamic finance industry who require information to make appropriate decisions. Financial information is communicated to consumers or users through different means. The most popular method of communicating financial information is through the use of financial statements, but there are other means that can be used to communicate directly or indirectly. The type and nature of information that should be included in the financial statements is determined by the objectives of financial accounting. It is important for the financial information to focus on the information needs of diverse users. AAOIFI's **Statement of Financial Accounting (SFA)** No. 1, para 26 gives a list of the main categories of users of external financial reports for Islamic banks as:

- equity holders
- holders of investment accounts
- other depositors
- current and savings account holders
- others who transact business with the Islamic bank, who are not equity or account holders
- *zakat* agencies (in case there is no legal obligation for its payment)
- regulatory agencies.[3]

Providing financial information to the relevant stakeholders is one of the objectives of Islamic accounting. Therefore, the common information needs of users, particularly the external users, should be met by the available data in the company's financial statement. Remember that the purpose of accounting in Islam goes beyond making informed decisions but extends to aspects of accountability, transparency, fair dealing, and just policies. Thus, the information that is directed at external users should provide the following types of information as required in SFA No. 1, paras 37–42:

- Information about the Islamic bank's compliance with the Sharī'ah and its objectives and that establishes such compliance; and information establishing the separation of prohibited earnings and expenditures, if any, which occurred, and of the manner in which these were disposed.
- Information about the Islamic bank's economic resources and related obligations (its obligations to transfer economic resources to satisfy the rights of its owners or the rights of others), and the effect of transactions, other events and circumstances on its economic resources and related obligations. This information should be directed principally at assisting the user to evaluate the adequacy of the Islamic bank's capital to absorb losses and business risks, assess the risk inherent in its investments, and evaluate the degree of liquidity of its assets and the liquidity requirements for meeting its other obligations.
- Information to assist the concerned party in determining *zakat* on the Islamic bank's funds and the purpose for which it will be disbursed.

- Information to assist in estimating cash flows that might be realized from dealing with the Islamic bank, the timing of those flows, and the risks associated with their realization. This information should be directed principally at assisting the user to evaluate the bank's ability to generate income and convert it into cash flows, and the adequacy of those cash flows for distributing profits to equity and investment account holders.
- Information to assist in evaluating the Islamic bank's discharge of its fiduciary responsibility to safeguard funds and to invest them at reasonable rates of return, and information about investment rates of return on the bank's investments and the rate of return accruing to equity and investment account holders.
- Information about the Islamic bank's discharge of its social responsibilities.[4]

## An Islamic Perspective on Accounting Concepts

The Islamic perspective on accounting concepts relates to the requirement of full disclosure, and social and financial accountability. This is required for any information requested by users, in accordance with the rules of Sharī'ah. With a very few exceptions, most of the accounting concepts are not alien to key Islamic principles. The requirement for legal documentation or recording of financial transactions, as earlier explained, is the principal reason for the importance of bookkeeping and accounting in Islamic financial transactions. Within the context of modern accounting practice and the growing importance of IFRS, Islamic accounting is relevant for transactions that use alternative principles of financing based on Islamic commercial rules.

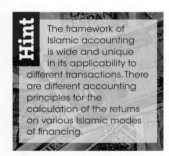

**Hint**
The framework of Islamic accounting is wide and unique in its applicability to different transactions. There are different accounting principles for the calculation of the returns on various Islamic modes of financing.

In conventional accounting, the accounting concepts are required to guide the existing practice, prescribe future directions, and identify certain fundamental issues. Conversely, the Islamic perspective on these concepts is the need for an Islamic bank or financial institution to provide the relevant information on all its transactions for the users of such information to be able to assess the level of compliance with the mandatory principles of the Sharī'ah in its daily activities. Those who patronize Islamic banks and financial institutions are greatly influenced by their ethical practices, as required by Islam. The religio-spiritual element in financial transactions is brought to bear alongside the element of profitability, which is also important in the assessment of an Islamic bank's performance. In addition, the social responsibilities specified in Islam such as obligatory charitable giving (*zakat*) and voluntary charitable endowment (*waqf*) are to be accounted for in any financial information prepared by Islamic banks and financial institutions.

There are numerous verses in the Qur'an and Prophetic precedents that emphasize accountability in commercial transactions. The strictness of the need to be accountable in a just manner in all human endeavors is emphasized in the following verse:

> Qur'an 21:47: "And We shall set up balances of justice on the Day of Resurrection, then none will be dealt with unjustly in anything. And if there be the weight of a mustard seed, We will bring it (to account). And sufficient are We to take account."

As we mentioned earlier, in Islam the Last Day, commonly known as the Day of Judgment, is also referred to as the Day of Accountability. The concept of accountability in all dealings and the need to keep a record of accounts runs through the whole body of Islamic commercial law. For instance, the main verse on the objectives of accounting in commercial transactions reads:

> Qur'an 2:282: "O you who believe! When you contract a debt for a fixed period, write it down. Let a scribe write it down in justice between you. Let not the scribe refuse to write as Allah has taught him, so let him write. Let him (the debtor) who incurs the liability dictate, and he must fear Allah, his Lord, and diminishes not anything of what he owes."

Apart from encouraging fair and just transactions among contracting parties, the verse also lays down some accounting ethics. Trustworthiness and objectivity in bookkeeping and accounting are paramount in the principles and ethics of accountants. The allusion to these ethical practices in the verses of the Qur'an explains the significance of accounting concepts in Islam. Mankind is said to be accountable before God, while in some other cases people are accountable to others, especially in transactions that involve dealings among people alone.

## The Accounting and Auditing Organization for Islamic Financial Institutions

The need to introduce international accounting standards for Islamic financial products led to the creation of the Accounting and Auditing Organization for Islamic Financial Institutions (AAOIFI). This body is an independent non-governmental organization, and is the result of the joint efforts of leading banks and financial institutions in the Muslim world. AAOIFI was established in 1990 at a meeting in Algiers based on an Agreement of Association among financial institutions from different countries. The body was registered in 1991 in Bahrain as an international, autonomous, non-profit-making institution. The vacuum that was created in international accounting and auditing standards with the proliferation of Islamic finance products was filled with the establishment of AAOIFI and the resulting relevant standards. Despite the need to standardize international financial reporting standards, as consistently advocated by the IASB, failure to fill the still-existing gaps between IFRS and the financial reporting of Islamic financial products will not allow for the much-needed convergence.

Since 1991, when AAOIFI issued the first accounting, auditing, governance and Sharī'ah standards, there has been a series of relevant standards for specific Islamic finance products. Box 4.2 on page 143 outlines the background and primary purpose of the AAOIFI accounting and auditing standards. Many sovereign nations have adopted these standards. Some countries such as Bahrain, Jordan, and Sudan have required Islamic financial institutions in their respective jurisdictions to abide by the AAOIFI reporting standards, while others allow Islamic financial institutions to adopt the standards voluntarily.

### Challenge

Why is it so important for AAOIFI to issue Financial Accounting Standards for Islamic Banks?

## BOX 4.2: BACKGROUND TO AAOIFI ACCOUNTING STANDARDS

As part of the regulatory framework for financial institutions in some countries, banks and financial institutions are required to adopt a particular standard for financial reporting. For close to two decades, Islamic financial institutions have generally adopted the IFRS for lack of Islamic alternatives. With the passage of some years and the development of more Islamic financial products in the industry, stakeholders saw the increasing need to develop Islamic accounting standards that would address the needs of these unique products. In 1987, various stakeholders met at an international forum to discuss the financial reporting by Islamic financial institutions. Participants recognized that there was a vacuum in the financial reporting of some products. The establishment of AAOIFI in 1991 was a response to this.

The objectives of financial accounting for Islamic banks and financial institutions include the need to promote consistency in financial reporting, provide a guide to the management of these institutions in making informed decisions, increase users' confidence in the institutions through proper understanding of the accounting information, and develop a new framework for international financial reporting based on the objectives of Islamic law.

Investors need to have confidence and trust in Islamic banks and financial institutions in a competitive world. This is necessary to realize the investment objectives of these institutions. So, in order to achieve this, stakeholders in the Islamic finance industry established AAOIFI, which within two years issued Islamic financial accounting standards. The new standards were adopted in October 1993.

The financial accounting standards have had far-reaching effects on the Islamic finance industry because, for the first time, issues that relate to the calculation of *zakat* (obligatory alms) surfaced in financial reporting. In addition, the role of Islamic banks and financial institutions in discharging their corporate social responsibilities was emphasized, as it is tied to the institutions' *zakat* obligations. Financial accounting, calculation, and transparent reporting is highly required in calculating the amount of *zakat* that must be paid by a bank on behalf of its shareholders or by individual shareholders.

Source: See AAOIFI. (2010). *Accounting, Auditing and Governance Standards for Islamic Financial Institutions.* Bahrain: AAOIFI.

## AAOIFI Accounting Standards

AAOIFI has issued a number of Financial Accounting Standards (FAS), which constitute a large percentage of its standards. This is due to the importance of financial documentation and reporting of commercial transactions carried out by Islamic banks and financial institutions. The objectives of financial accounting standards for Islamic banks and financial institutions as identified by AAOIFI are:

- To serve as a guide for the financial accounting standards boards for Islamic banks and financial institutions when developing financial accounting standards. This should ensure consistency in developing standards.

- To assist the Islamic banks, in the absence of accepted accounting standards, in making choices among alternative accounting treatments.

- To make available a guide and a regulator of subjective judgment made by management when preparing the financial statements and other financial reports.

- To increase users' confidence and understanding of accounting information and, in turn, their confidence in Islamic banks.

- To develop accounting standards which are likely to be consistent with each other. This should increase users' confidence in the financial reports of Islamic banks.[5]

There are two SFAs in the AAOIFI standards. SFA No. 1 is on the objectives of financial accounting for Islamic banks and financial institutions, whereas SFA No. 2 focuses on the concepts. Meanwhile, there are 25 AAOIFI standards that are relevant to Islamic accounting. These are summarized in Table 4.3.

Table 4.3 is a quick reference to the FAS. Each contains a number of paragraphs explaining the standard. For a better understanding of AAOIFI's FAS, you may need to obtain the full text of their latest standards. The uniqueness of these FAS derives from the extensive coverage of Islamic finance products, services, and issues that are not covered in IFRS. There is no doubt that Islamic banks and financial institutions and conventional banks offering Islamic financial services require specific standards for their financial reporting. AAOIFI has continued to issue guidelines or guidance statements to amend or revise existing FAS in order to address any request from the key stakeholders in the Islamic finance industry and provide a just and level playing field for financial reporting and disclosure. Therefore, in the application of the relevant FAS, any guidelines or guidance statements subsequently released by AAOIFI is effectively considered part of the standards.

**Hint**

The list of the latest AAOIFI accounting standards and their release dates is available at www.aaoifi.com/aaoifi/Publications/KeyPublications/tabid/88/language/en-US/Default.aspx.

| TABLE 4.3: AAOIFI Financial Accounting Standards | |
|---|---|
| **FAS** | **Description** |
| FAS 1 | General Presentation and Disclosure in the Financial Statements of Islamic Banks and Financial Institutions |
| FAS 2 | *Murabahah* and *Murabahah* to the Purchase Orderer |
| FAS 3 | *Mudarabah* Financing |
| FAS 4 | *Musharakah* Financing |
| FAS 5 | Disclosure of Bases for Profit Allocation Between Owners' Equity and Investment Account Holders |
| FAS 6 | Equity of Investment Account Holders and their Equivalent |
| FAS 7 | *Salam* and Parallel *Salam* |
| FAS 8 | *Ijarah* (Lease) and *Ijarah Muntahia Bittamlik* (Financial Lease Ending with a Title Deed) |
| FAS 9 | *Zakat* |
| FAS 10 | *Istisna'* (Manufacturing Contract) and Parallel *Istisna'* |
| FAS 11 | Provisions and Reserves |
| FAS 12 | General Presentation and Disclosure in the Financial Statements of Islamic Insurance Companies |
| FAS 13 | Disclosure of Bases for Determining and Allocating Surplus or Deficit in Islamic Insurance Companies |
| FAS 14 | Investment Funds |
| FAS 15 | Provisions and Reserves in Islamic Insurance Companies |
| FAS 16 | Foreign Currency Transactions and Foreign Operations |
| FAS 17 | Investments |
| FAS 18 | Islamic Financial Services offered by Conventional Financial Institutions |
| FAS 19 | Contributions in Islamic Insurance Companies |
| FAS 20 | Deferred Payment Sale |
| FAS 21 | Disclosure on Transfer of Assets |
| FAS 22 | Segment Reporting |
| FAS 23 | Consolidation |
| FAS 24 | Investments in Associates |
| FAS 25 | Investment in *Sukuk*, Shares and Similar Instruments |

Differentiate between the accrual and cash flow accounting methods.

# Accrual and Cash Flow Accounting Methods

One of the major initial decisions an entrepreneur will have to make at the start of a new business is to determine the accounting method to use. That is, the entrepreneur must decide how the financial transactions will be recorded. This is an obligation on all corporate entities, particularly Islamic banks and financial institutions. They have to present to the general public periodic reports that reflect their actual financial position as of a given date, including the results of their operations during the financial year. This enables the investing public and other interested parties to ascertain the rights and obligations of the corporate entity.

There are two main methods of accounting. The entrepreneur may either choose the *cash flow method of accounting* or the *accrual method of accounting*, depending on a number of factors. Normally, when an entrepreneur extends credit to customers by allowing them to purchase items on credit with an arrangement for **deferred payment**, they are incurring what is called accounts receivable. If an **account receivable** is recorded when it is incurred, it is regarded as accrual accounting. Conversely, if the accounts receivable are recorded when the payment is received at a later date, they are regarded as cash flow accounting.

These principles fall under the periodicity concept. The **periodicity concept** in financial accounting provides for the relationship between the income of a business and periods of time. As Islamic banks and financial institutions are required to issue periodic reports that reflect their financial position, the periodicity concept requires proper documentation of transactions within a given period of time. The AAOIFI describes the periodicity concept as follows:

**deferred payment**
A debt that has been incurred on the understanding that it will be paid back at some time in the future.

**account receivable**
Money owed to a company by a customer for products and services provided on credit.

**periodicity concept**
The concept that recognizes that each accounting period has an economic activity associated with it, which can be measured, accounted for, and reported on.

> The *periodicity concept* means that the life of the Islamic bank should be broken into reporting periods to prepare financial reports that provide interested parties with information or directions by which they can evaluate the performance of the accounting unit. This assumption also indicates the need to relate the activities of the accounting unit through the entirety of its life to the appropriate reporting periods as necessary.[6]

The periodicity concept allows the entity to properly calculate the *zakat* due and make the necessary deductions for its onward disbursement to those who are entitled to it. This is part of the obligations of the Islamic banks and financial institutions and is considered as part of their social service or corporate social responsibility.

## Cash Flow Method of Accounting

**cash flow method**
A method of accounting whereby the records are based on the flow of cash into and out of the business.

The **cash flow method** of accounting is based on the frequency of cash flow. No transaction is recorded until and unless there is an actual exchange of cash, whether the business receives it by cash, credit card or check. For instance, when a business company supplies goods to a customer in October 2011 but payment for those goods is made in December 2011, the income will not be recorded under the cash flow method until December 2011 when the payment is made. This method gives a clear account of the cash flow of the business. This cash basis of accounting is relevant in certain situations, such as upon liquidation or impending liquidation of the corporate entity.

## Accrual Method of Accounting

**accrual method**
A method of accounting whereby the records are based on the occurrence of a transaction regardless of whether there is exchange of cash or not.

The **accrual method** of accounting is based on the occurrence of a transaction regardless of whether there is exchange of cash or not. Whenever there is a transaction involving the business, a financial record is made of it immediately, whether money has changed hands or not. For example, when a business company supplies goods to a customer in October 2011 but payment for those goods is delayed until December 2011, the income is reported in October 2011 under the accrual method. This method specifically requires the use of double-entry bookkeeping. It allows the business to keep track of its assets and liabilities, even though some of its clients have yet to pay their invoices, and it gives a clear picture of the profitability of the business.

**LEARNING OBJECTIVE 4.6**

Draft the main financial statements for Islamic finance products.

# Financial Statements in Islamic Banks and Financial Institutions

A financial statement is the formal record of all the financial activities of a business entity. The end product of all financial transactions is a financial statement. The transactions recorded in the financial statements comprise any business transacted between the business entity and other corporate bodies, organizations, or individuals. This may include the receipt of a common sale contract where the price is paid in full on the spot, or a receipt of cash for goods sold on the basis of a deferred sale. All transactions are duly sorted, classified, and presented in accordance with principles of bookkeeping explained earlier. At the end of the financial year, a summary of the detailed bookkeeping is presented as the financial statement of the business entity. Figure 4.3 illustrates the simple flow of activities that begins with ordinary transactions and ends in a financial statement.

Once a transaction is concluded, the records are sorted, classified, and presented in the accounts. As we saw earlier, this procedure is known as bookkeeping. The accounts of a particular financial period are then summarized in the financial statements.

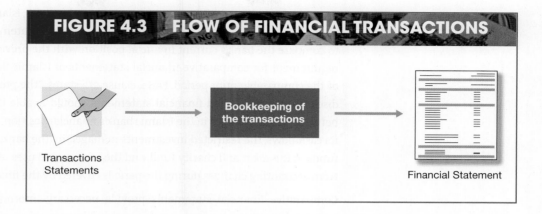

According to AAOIFI FAS 1, the financial statements of an Islamic bank should consist of the following:

- a statement of financial position (balance sheet)
- an income statement
- a statement of cash flows
- a statement of changes in owners' equity or a statement of retained earnings
- a statement of changes in restricted investment
- a statement of sources and uses of funds in the *zakat* and charity fund (when the bank assumes responsibility for the collection and distribution of *zakat*)
- a statement of sources and uses of funds in the ***qard*** **fund**
- notes to the financial statements
- any statements, reports and other data that assist in providing information required by users of financial statements as specified in the *Statement of Objectives*.[7]

**qard fund**
Interest-free benevolent loans given by Islamic banks and financial institutions.

In practice, a corporate entity often provides further details of its accounting policies in its annual report. Detailed notes and further explanations of the figures and captions presented in the financial statements provide the users of the financial statements with relevant supplementary information.

## Comparative Financial Statements of Islamic Financial Products

A corporate entity's comparative financial statements give the direction of change in the business in at least two financial periods. When changes are noted in the performance of the business in the current financial period as compared to the previous financial periods, necessary steps are taken to either sustain performance or rectify any deficiency. Comparative financial analysis involves the comparison of the figures of the current year with those of the previous year(s) to determine performance. Top management will review the major improvements or weaknesses to enable them to make informed decisions that increase or sustain performance. Comparative financial analysis is also called **horizontal analysis**.

**horizontal analysis**
A comparative analysis of financial statements of different periods or financial years.

To ensure compliance with relevant standards and policies, Islamic banks and financial institutions are required to publish comparative financial statements. This enables a user to compare the bank's current financial position with the previous year. The minimum requirement for comparative financial statements of Islamic financial products is that of the comparable prior period. FAS 1, clause 2/2 states, "the presentation methods and disclosures in published financial statements should enable the user to differentiate between actual changes in the Islamic bank's financial position, its results of operations, its cash flows, the restricted investments managed by the bank, the sources and uses of funds in the *zakat* and charity fund, and the sources and uses of funds in the *qard* fund, from accounting changes during the periods covered by the financial statements."[8]

Comparative financial statements provide necessary information about an entity's sustained or poor business performance. Changes in performance can only be determined through the availability of comparative financial figures from different periods. Box 4.3 has an example of the financial statements and disclosures of XYZ Bank as adapted from AAOIFI FAS 1. We can see that two distinct financial statements for two different financial years are compared under each item of the report. The changes in the two periods are easily noticeable when they are presented in this form side by side. The user of the information can easily identify changes in this bank's financial performance. It will also assist the bank in the decision-making process as it considers products for the next financial year.

## The Four Basic Financial Statements

There are four basic financial statements in financial reporting.

1 Balance sheet
2 Income statement
3 Cash flow statement
4 Statement of retained earnings or shareholders' equity.

The four types of financial statement are explained in AAOIFI's FAS 1.

## Balance Sheet

**balance sheet**
A summary of the financial balances of a company or business entity.

A **balance sheet** is a summary of financial balances of a corporate entity and is also known as the statement of financial position. It can be defined as a summary of the assets, liabilities, and ownership equities of a listed company as of the end of a specific financial year. FAS 1, paragraph 4/1 provides for balance sheets and sets out the specific details they should contain. The date of the statement of financial position should be disclosed. The statement of financial position should include the assets, its equivalent (prepaid, deferred and intangible assets), and owners' equity. Assets should not be offset against liabilities and liabilities should not be offset against assets unless there is a religious or legal right and an actual expectation of offset. Significant items of assets, liabilities, unrestricted investment accounts and their equivalent, and owners' equity should not be combined on the statement of financial position without disclosure. The

## BOX 4.3:    ILLUSTRATION OF A COMPANY'S COMPARATIVE FINANCIAL STATEMENT[9]

XYZ Bank

Consolidated Statement of Financial Position

As at 2011 and 2010

| | Note | 2011 $ | 2010 $ |
|---|---|---|---|
| **Assets** | | | |
| Cash and cash equivalent | 8 | 95,041,890 | 51,281,906 |
| Sales receivables | 9 | 3,804,889 | 875,556 |
| Investments: | | | |
| Investment securities | 10 | 14,850,000 | 15,000,000 |
| Mudarabah financing | 11 | 10,000,000 | 1,500,000 |
| Musharakah investments | 12 | — | 5,000,000 |
| Participations | 13 | 102,500,000 | 102,500,000 |
| Inventories | 14 | — | 2,000,000 |
| Investment in real estate | 15 | 58,500,000 | 71,750,000 |
| Assets for rent | 16 | 89,000,000 | 94,500,000 |
| Istisna' | 17 | — | 1,000,000 |
| Other investments | | | |
| — | | | |
| — | | | |
| — | | | |
| Total investments | 18 | 274,850,000 | 293,250,000 |
| Other assets | 19 | 322,000 | 15,510,000 |
| Fixed assets (net) | 20 | 24,870,500 | 26,070,000 |
| Total assets | | 398,889,279 | 386,978,462 |

The accompanying notes form an integral part of the financial statements.

amount of any allowance established to cover expected losses should be disclosed. Assets and liabilities should be combined into groupings in accordance with their nature and those groupings should be presented in the statement of financial position in the order of the relative liquidity of each grouping. The statement of financial position should present separate totals for assets, liabilities, unrestricted investment accounts and their equivalent, and owners' equity.[10]

The balance sheet should be prepared in line with the relevant paragraphs of FAS 1. The text of this standard serves to explain each and every item to be included. For instance, paragraph 41 of the standard provides that the statement of financial statement should disclose the following liabilities:

- current accounts, savings accounts, and other accounts, with separate disclosure of each category of accounts
- deposits of other banks
- *salam* payables
- *istisna'* payables
- declared but undisturbed profits
- *zakat* and taxes payable
- other accounts payable.

**equity of unrestricted account holders**
Funds received by the Islamic bank from depositors on the basis that the bank will have the right to use those funds without restriction to finance its investments within the Sharī'ah framework.

Moreover, paragraph 42 provides for the disclosure of **equity of unrestricted account holders**. It is a mandatory requirement to disclose and present the unrestricted investment accounts and their equivalent in the statement of financial position as a separate item between liabilities and owner's equity. Furthermore, paragraph 43 of the standard requires that the consolidated statement of financial position should disclose the minority interest. Such interest must be shown on the statement as a separate item between unrestricted investment accounts and owner's equity. In addition, paragraph 44 provides that disclosure of the following items should be made accordingly in the statement of financial position:

- authorized, subscribed and paid-in capital
- number of authorized ownership units (shares), number of issued ownership units, number of outstanding ownership units, par value per unit, and premiums on issued units
- legal reserve and discretionary reserves at the beginning and end of the period and changes therein during the period
- retained earnings at the beginning and end of the period and amount of retained earnings resulting from the revaluation of assets and liabilities to their cash equivalent values, where applicable, and changes therein during the period including distribution to owners and transfers to or from reserves
- other changes in owners' equity during the period
- any restrictions imposed on the distribution of retained earnings to owners.[11]

For an example of a balance sheet displaying a summary of assets in a consolidated statement of financial position, see Box 4.3. Box 4.4 reproduces an example of the financial statements and disclosures of XYZ Bank as adapted from AAOIFI FAS 1. The figure shows us that the balance sheet should also include all the bank's liabilities, unrestricted investment accounts, minority interest, and owners' equity. The usual practice, as shown in Box 4.4, is to present a consolidated statement of financial position that gives an insight into the performance of the financial institution within the most recently concluded financial year compared to the previous year. The middle column, 'Note', gives number references to detailed explanations of each item on the balance sheet. The accompanying notes form an integral part of the balance sheet as clearly shown at the foot of Box 4.4. Transparency demands the full disclosure of all these items in the balance sheet to enable users of the information such as the shareholders and even prospective investors to make informed decisions on the bank. As a bank is regarded

## BOX 4.4: ILLUSTRATION OF STATEMENT OF FINANCIAL POSITION OF A COMPANY

XYZ Bank
Consolidated Statement of Financial Position
As at 2011 and 2010

| | Note | 2011 $ | 2010 $ |
|---|---|---|---|
| **Liabilities, unrestricted investment accounts, Minority interest and owners' equity** | | | |
| Liabilities: | | | |
| Current accounts and savings accounts | 21 | 18,550,000 | 15,400,000 |
| Current accounts for banks and financial institutions | | 1,200,000 | 1,200,000 |
| Payables | 22 | 936,112 | 133,611 |
| Proposed dividends | | 5,000,000 | 5,000,000 |
| Other liabilities | 23 | 5,069,750 | 2,192,321 |
| Total liabilities | | 30,755,862 | 23,925,932 |
| Equity of unrestricted investment account holders | 24, 34 | 7,838,500 | 6,572,000 |
| Minority interest | | 3,450,600 | 3,240,550 |
| Total liabilities, unrestricted investment accounts and minority interest | | 42,044,962 | 33,738,482 |
| Owners' equity | | | |
| Paid-up capital | 25 | 350,000,000 | 350,000,000 |
| Reserves | 26 | 3,368,864 | 1,649,796 |
| Retained earnings | | 3,475,453 | 1,599,184 |
| Total owners' equity | | 356,844,317 | 353,248,980 |
| Total liabilities, unrestricted investment accounts, minority interest and owners' equity | | 398,889,279 | 386,987,462 |

(paragraphs 41 to 44 of FAS 1)

The accompanying notes form an integral part of the financial statements.

Source: AAOIFI. (2010). *Accounting, Auditing and Governance Standards for Islamic Financial Institutions*. Bahrain: AAOIFI.

**income statement**
A financial statement that measures the financial performance of a company over a specific period of time, indicating how the revenue is transformed into net income.

**net income**
The result after all revenues and expenses have been accounted for. This is also called the 'bottom line'.

as a corporate entity with a separate juristic personality, these periodic disclosures are necessary to ascertain the actual position of the bank at every material time.

## Income Statement

The **income statement** is a financial statement that measures the financial performance of a company over a specific period of time, indicating how the revenue is transformed into the result, after all revenue and expenditures have been accounted for, known as the **net income** (or 'bottom line'). The income statement may also be referred to as the profit and loss statement, statement of operations, or statement of income. The significance of the income statement is its ability to disclose the profitability of an entity during the time interval specified in its heading. This kind of financial statement discloses the investment revenues, expenses incurred, gains realized, and losses incurred in all the entity's business activities. Note that an income statement does not show cash receipts or cash disbursement. FAS 1, paragraph 49 requires the disclosure of estimated gains and losses from the revaluation of assets and liabilities to their cash equivalent values, including the general principles used by the Islamic bank or financial institution in their revaluation.

It is the responsibility of the management of the business entity to choose the period of time that the income statement covers. This varies from one company to another but the heading of the income statement must denote the period. The heading may look like any of the following options:

- for the Three Months Ended December 31, 2011 (the period of October 1 to December 31, 2011)
- the Four Weeks Ended December 31, 2011 (the period of December 3 to December 31, 2011)
- the Fiscal Year Ended January 31, 2012 (the period of February 1, 2011 to January 31, 2012).

After the heading of the income statement, it is required, according to FAS 1, paragraph 50, that the following information is disclosed, with separate disclosures of investment revenues, expenses, gains, and losses jointly financed by the Islamic bank and unrestricted investment account holders, and those exclusively financed by the bank:

- revenues and gains from investments
- expenses and losses from investments
- income (loss) from investments
- share of unrestricted investment account holders in income (loss) from investments before the bank's share as a *mudarib* (investment manager)
- the bank's share in income (loss) from investments
- the bank's share in unrestricted investment income as a *mudarib*
- the bank's share in restricted investment profits as a *mudarib*
- the Islamic bank's fixed fee as an investment agent for restricted investments
- other revenues, expenses, gains, and losses
- general and administrative expenses
- net income (loss) before *zakat* and taxes
- *zakat* and taxes (to be separately disclosed)
- net income (loss).

Box 4.5 reproduces an example of the financial statements and disclosures of Bank XYZ as adapted from AAOIFI FAS 1. We can see that all the revenues of the bank within a particular financial year are collated to determine its financial performance. More importantly, one thing that is also considered is how the revenue is transformed into net income. This can only be done when all expenses and losses are deducted from the revenue for the period under review. Taxes, *zakat,* and the usual administrative

## BOX 4.5: ILLUSTRATION OF THE INCOME STATEMENT OF A COMPANY

XYZ Bank

Income Statement

for the year ended 2011

| | Note | 2011 $ | 2010 $ |
|---|---|---|---|
| **Income** | | | |
| Deferred sales | (29A) | 97,500 | 36,389 |
| Investments | (29B) | 5,120,000 | 4,168,000 |
| | 28,29 | 5,217,500 | 4,168,000 |
| **Less** | | | |
| Return on unrestricted investment accounts before | | | |
| The bank's share as a *mudarib* | | 551,480 | 455,673 |
| Bank's share as a *mudarib* | | (110,296) | (91,135) |
| Return on unrestricted investment accounts before *zakat* | | (441,184) | (364,538) |
| **Bank's share in income from investment** | | | |
| (As a *mudarib* and as fund owner) | | 4,776,316 | 3,839,851 |
| Bank's income from its own investments | 29B | 12,000,000 | 10,000,000 |
| Bank's share in restricted investment profit as a *mudarib* | | 158,000 | 140,000 |
| Bank's fees as an investment agent for restricted investments | | 528,000 | 400,000 |
| Revenue from banking services | | 2,000 | 1,000 |
| Other revenues | | 303,000 | 2,000 |
| Total bank revenue | | **17,467,316** | **14,382,851** |
| Administrative and general expenditure | | (3,890,000) | (2,468,000) |
| Depreciation | | (2,089,500) | (2,030,000) |
| Net income (loss) before *zakat* and tax | | **11,487,816** | **9,884,851** |
| Provision for *zakat* | | (2,887,479) | (1,632,871) |
| Net income (loss) before minority interest | | 8,600,337 | 8,251,980 |
| Minority interest | | (5,000) | (3,000) |
| Net income | | **8,595,337** | **8,248,980** |

(Paragraphs 41 to 44 of FAS 1)

The accompanying notes form an integral part of the financial statements.

Source: AAOIFI. (2010). *Accounting, Auditing and Governance Standards for Islamic Financial Institutions*. Bahrain: AAOIFI.

Qatar Islamic Bank (QIB) uses Shari'ah-compliant instruments for its business activities, and generally adopts the AAOIFI Financial Accounting Standards, but it also relies on the IFRS for matters not covered by AAOIFI.

expenses must also be deducted from the revenue before you arrive at the net income. For instance, the total bank revenue for the financial year 2011 is US$17,467,316. But after making all necessary deductions such as administrative and general expenditure costs, and depreciation, the net income is reduced to US$11,487,816. And after deducting *zakat*, tax and minority interest, the total net income is now put at US$8,595,337.

The *Islamic Finance in Practice* box presents the statement of income of Qatar Islamic Bank for the six-month period ended June 30, 2011. This gives an idea of how the actual income of an Islamic bank is calculated after all the necessary deductions are made.

A brief overview of the statement of income in the Islamic Finance in Practice panel reveals that the expenses and impairment losses are deducted from the net operating income in order to arrive at the net profit before taxes. After the further deduction of the income taxes, the net profit for the period under review is arrived at. However, further deductions are presented. This includes the returns on equity of investment account holders, share of profits distributed to *sukuk* holders, etc. Therefore, once these are deducted, the net profit for the period attributable to the shareholders is arrived at. An additional item displayed in the statement of income is the earnings per share, which gives shareholders a clear indication as to the performance of their investments.

## ISLAMIC FINANCE IN PRACTICE

# Qatar Islamic Bank's Income Statement

The Qatar Islamic Bank (QIB) uses Sharī'ah-compliant instruments for its business activities. These comprise banking, investment and financing activities carried out through *murabahah, mudarabah, musharakah, musawamah* and *istisna'* on its own behalf or on behalf of its customers and/or account holders depending on the nature of the instrument used. Based on the rulings and recommendations of the Sharī'ah Board of QIB, all its activities are pursued in accordance with the principles of Islamic law, including its financial reporting. While QIB generally adopts the AAOIFI Financial Accounting Standards, it also relies on the IFRS for matters not covered by AAOIFI. In order to illustrate the practice of Islamic finance, the statement here shows the consolidated statement of QIB's income for the six-month period ended June 30, 2011. This is just one in the list of the financial statements presented in its financial report.

**Qatar Islamic Bank (S.A.Q) Interim consolidated statement of income for the six month period ended 30 June 2011** *(Amounts expressed in thousands of Qatari Riyal unless otherwise stated)*

| | Note | Three month period ended June 2011 (Unaudited) | Three month period ended 30 June 2010 (Unaudited) | Six month period ended 30 June 2011 (Unaudited) | Six month period ended 30 June 2010 (Unaudited) |
|---|---|---|---|---|---|
| Income | | | | | |
| Income from financing activities, net | | 405,935 | 485,404 | 863,256 | 906,409 |
| Income from investing activities, net | | 186,959 | 37,706 | 311,250 | 47,849 |
| Total income from financing and investing activities, net | | 592,894 | 523,110 | 1,174,506 | 954,258 |
| Commission and fees income | 9 | 60,828 | 102,734 | 125,354 | 186,322 |
| Commission and fees expenses | | (5,240) | (5,653) | (10,764) | (10,531) |
| Net commission and fees income | | 55,588 | 97,081 | 114,590 | 175,791 |
| Foreign exchange gain | | 5,654 | 7,505 | 13,361 | 13,390 |
| Net operating income | | 654,136 | 627,696 | 1,302,457 | 1,143,439 |
| Expenses and impairment losses | | | | | |
| General and administrative expenses | | (168,091) | (101,738) | (293,988) | (191,399) |
| Depreciation | | (12,109) | (10,803) | (23,147) | (20,524) |
| Impairment losses on receivable from financing activities (net) | | 7,480 | (71,809) | (20,518) | (71,809) |
| Impairment losses on financial investments | | - | - | (21,000) | (17,008) |
| Net profit from continuing operations | | 481,416 | 443,346 | 943,804 | 842,699 |
| Profit from discontinued operations | | 3,297 | - | 3,297 | - |
| Net profit before taxes | | 484,713 | 443,346 | 947,101 | 842,699 |
| Income taxes | | (4,459) | - | (4,459) | - |
| Net profit for the period | | 480,254 | 443,346 | 942,642 | 842,699 |
| Less: | | | | | |
| Return on equity of investment accountholders | | (74,786) | (137,341) | (188,450) | (236,355) |
| Minority interest | | 3,321 | - | 1,724 | (4,782) |
| Sukuk holders' share of profit | | (26,317) | (4,546) | (52,634) | - |
| Net profit for the period attributable to shareholders | | 382,472 | 301,459 | 703,282 | 601,562 |
| Earnings per share | | | | | |
| Basic and diluted earnings per share | | 1,67 | 1,39 | 3,08 | 2,82 |

The accompanying notes from 1 to 15 form an integral part of these interim condensed consolidated financial statements

Source: Qatar Islamic Bank. Unaudited Interim Condensed Consolidated Financial Statements June 30, 2011, p. 9. Available at ae.zawya.com/cm/financials/5319_20110630_6_R_C.pdf.

# Cash Flow Statements

**cash flow statement**
A financial statement that indicates how changes in the balance sheet accounts and income statements affect cash and its equivalent.

The **cash flow statement** is a financial statement that indicates how changes in the balance sheet accounts and income statements affect cash and its equivalent; the analysis is broken down into operating, investing, and financing activities. The cash flow statement may also be called a statement of cash flows or funds flow statement. The purpose of the cash flow statement is to identify the sources and uses of cash during the financial year in question. The cash flow statement derives its data from the changes in all other balance sheet items. FAS 1, paragraph 54 provides that the statement of cash flows should differentiate between cash flows from *operations*, cash flows from *investing activities*, and cash flows from *financing activities*. The statement should also disclose the main components of each of the three categories of cash flow. Paragraph 55 requires the disclosure of the net increase (or decrease) in cash and cash equivalent during the period and the balance of cash and cash equivalent at the beginning and end of the period. Paragraph 56 provides that transactions and other transfers that do not require the payment of, or do not result in the receipt of, cash and cash equivalent should be disclosed, for example, bonus shares or the acquisition of assets in exchange for shares in the equity of the company.

Box 4.6 reproduces an example of the financial statements and disclosures of XYZ Bank as adapted from AAOIFI FAS 1. We can see that the flow of funds here is derived from the previous balance sheet and income statement. The net income we saw on the income statement (US$8,595,337) in Box 4.5 for 2011 is the first item on the cash flow statement upon which the funds flow is considered. There is emphasis on the cash generated within the fiscal year under review. How this cash was used in operating, investment, and financing activities, respectively, is clearly shown in Box 4.6 on pages 157–158.

# Statement of Retained Earnings or Shareholders' Equity

**statement of retained earnings**
A financial statement that explains the changes in the retained earnings of a company over a period.

The **statement of retained earnings** is a financial statement that explains the changes in the retained earnings of a company over the period of time being reported. In a single proprietorship, the statement of retained earnings may also be called the equity statement or statement of owners' equity. In a partnership, it is called the statement of partners' equity. For corporations, it is called a statement of retained earnings and shareholders' equity. The changes in the owners' interest in the entity as well as the application of retained profit or surplus from one financial period to another are broken down. The owners' equity and retained earnings may be calculated using the following formula:

$$\text{Owners' equity} = \text{Assets} - \text{Liability}$$

As with other financial statements, the statement of changes in owners' equity or statement of retained earnings must disclose the period covered. There are specific disclosures required in the statement of changes in owners' equity and statement of retained earnings respectively.

## BOX 4.6: ILLUSTRATION OF THE STATEMENT OF CASH FLOWS OF XYZ BANK

XYZ Bank
Statement of Cash Flows
for the year ended 2011

| | Note | 2011 $ | 2010 $ |
|---|---|---|---|
| **Cash flows from operations** | | | |
| Net income (loss) | | 8,595,337 | — |
| Adjustment to reconcile net income | | | |
| **Net cash provided by operating activates** | | | |
| Depreciation | | 2,089,500 | — |
| Provisions of doubtful accounts | | 10,000 | — |
| Provision for zakat | | 2,887,479 | — |
| Provision for taxes | | — | — |
| Zakat paid | | 200,000 | — |
| Taxes paid | | — | — |
| Return on unrestricted investment accounts | | 441,184 | — |
| Gain on sale for fixed assets | | — | — |
| Depreciation of leased assets | | 8,750,000 | — |
| Provision for decline in value of investment securities | | 150,000 | — |
| Bad debts | | (6,000) | — |
| Purchase of fixed assets | | (890,000) | — |
| Net cash flows provided by operations | | 21,827,500 | — |
| **Cash flows from investing activities** | | | |
| Sale of rental real estate | | — | — |
| Purchase of rental real estate | | — | — |
| Sale of real estate | | 15,000,000 | — |
| Acquisition of investment securities | | — | — |
| Increase in mudarabah investments | | (8,500,000) | — |
| Sale of inventory | | 2,000,000 | — |
| Sale of istisna' | | 1,000,000 | — |
| Net increase in receivables | | (2,933,333) | — |
| Net cash flows from (used in) investing activities | | **6,566,667** | — |

**BOX 4.6:** *(continued)*

| | Note | 2011 $ | 2010 $ |
|---|---|---|---|
| **Cash flows from financing activities** | | | |
| Net increase in unrestricted investment accounts | | 825,316 | — |
| Net increase in current accounts | | 3,150,000 | — |
| Dividend paid | | 4,800,000 | — |
| Increase in credit balances and expenses | | 805,501 | — |
| (Decrease) in accrued expenses | | (10,050) | — |
| Increase in minority interest | | 210,050 | — |
| Decrease in other assets | | 15,188,000 | — |
| Net cash flows provided by financing activities | | 15,365,817 | — |
| Increase (decrease) in cash and cash equivalent | | 43,759,984 | — |
| Cash and cash equivalent at beginning of year | (37) | 51,281,906 | — |
| Cash and cash equivalent at end of year | | **95,041,890** | — |

The accompanying notes form an integral part of the financial statements.

Source: AAOIFI. (2010). *Accounting, Auditing and Governance Standards for Islamic Financial Institutions.* Bahrain: AAOIFI.

Paragraph 58 of FAS 1 provides that the statement of changes in owners' equity should disclose the following information.

- Paid-up capital, legal and discretionary reserves separately, and retained earnings as of the beginning of the period with separate disclosure of the amount of estimated earnings resulting from the revaluation of assets and liabilities to their cash equivalent values, where applicable.
- Capital contribution by owners during the period.
- Net income (loss) for the period.
- Distribution to owners during the period.
- Increase (decrease) in legal and discretionary reserves during the period.
- Paid-in-capital, legal and other discretionary reserves, and retained earnings as of the end of the period with separate disclosure of the estimated amount of retained earnings resulting from the revaluation of assets and liabilities to their cash equivalent values, where applicable.[12]

Paragraph 60 requires the statement of retained earnings to disclose the following information.

- Retained earnings at the beginning of the period with separate disclosure of the amount of estimated retained earnings resulting from the revaluation of assets and liabilities to their cash equivalent values, where applicable.

- Net income (loss) for the period.
- Transfers to legal and discretionary reserves during the period.
- Distribution to owners during the period.
- Retained earnings at the end of the period with separate disclosure of the amount of estimated retained earnings resulting from the revaluation of assets and liabilities to their cash equivalent values, where applicable.

Box 4.7 reproduces an example of the financial statements and disclosures of XYZ Bank as adapted from AAOIFI FAS 1. In this case, there is a focus on the assets and liability of the financial institution, which gives a true picture of the changes in its equity over the past financial year. Thus it also gives a true presentation of the current position of the financial institution to enable its stakeholders to make an informed decision regarding the plans for the coming financial year. This is usually the last portion of the balance sheet, which details the changes in shareholders' equity since the previous financial year. To calculate this, liabilities are deducted from assets to ascertain the financial position of the bank. The statement also tracks what was paid out as dividends and distributed profits.

## BOX 4.7: ILLUSTRATION OF STATEMENT OF CHANGES IN OWNERS' EQUITY OF A COMPANY

XYZ Bank
Statement of Changes in Owners' Equity
for the year ended 2011

| Description | Paid-up Capital | Reserves (NOTE 25) | | Retained Earnings | Total |
|---|---|---|---|---|---|
| | Monetary unit | Legal Monetary unit | General Monetary | Monetary unit | |
| Balance as at 2011 | 350,000,000 | — | — | — | 350,000,000 |
| Issue of () shares | | | | | |
| Net income | | | | 8,248,980 | 8,248,980 |
| Distributed profits | | | | (5,000,000) | (5,000,000) |
| Transfer to reserves | | 824,898 | 824,898 | (1,649,796) | — |
| Balance as at 2011 | 350,000,000 | 824,898 | 824,898 | 1,599,184 | 353,248,980 |
| Net income | | | | 8,595,337 | 8,595,337 |
| Distributed profits | | | | (5,000,000) | (5,000,000) |
| Transfer to reserves | | 859,534 | 859,534 | 1,719,068 | — |
| Balance as at 2011 | 350,000,000 | 1,684,432 | 1,684,432 | 3,475,453 | 356,844,317 |

The accompanying notes form an integral part of the financial statements.

Source: AAOIFI. (2010). *Accounting, Auditing and Governance Standards for Islamic Financial Institutions.* Bahrain: AAOIFI.

# AAOIFI Proposed Set of Financial Statements for Islamic Banks

## Challenge

Even though Islamic finance claims to have unique items that should appear on financial statements, what are the equivalent items for non-Islamic financial institutions, and how do you think issues such as corporate social responsibility (CSR) are reported in financial statements?

Normally, an Islamic bank would have some unique financial statements owing to the nature of businesses it undertakes as well as specific requirements that require the computation of funds such as *zakat*, *waqf*, and *qard hasan*, which are not necessarily part of the conventional framework of accounting. Besides, the way Islamic banks mobilize funds and use them, as discussed in Chapter 3, is different from conventional practice. Thus, there is a need for a different set of items in the financial statements. The *Global Islamic Finance* box on page 161 presents the raging controversy on whether the Islamic accounting framework as represented by the AAOIFI standards should be brought into the mainstream global accounting framework under the IASB. One cannot shy away from the fact that Islamic banks have unique accounting needs. This is acknowledged by all, but the controversy over who should provide the framework and what process they should follow in coming up with an Islamic accounting framework continues.

Most of the examples of financial statements presented in this chapter are based on the conventional framework but there is more to the accounting framework of Islamic banks. While it is not possible to detail all the accounting principles for each Islamic financial instrument here, as this chapter is a general introduction to Islamic accounting, it suffices to observe that AAOIFI has proposed a set of financial statements for Islamic banks and financial institutions, split into three major categories. The first category comprises the financial statements discussed and illustrated above, such as the statement of financial position, statement of income, statement of cash flows, and statement of retained earnings or statement of changes in owners' equity. These are meant to reflect the position of the Islamic bank for an investor, with the aim of recording its financial performance based on the Shari'ah-compliant investments it undertook within a given period of time.

The second category focuses on the financial reporting of restricted investments, which are managed by the Islamic bank. In most cases, the restricted investments are carried out through the facility of *mudarabah* (trust investment financing) or *wakalah* (agency) contracts, and they require a unique financial statement generally known as the **statement of changes in restricted investments**. Finally, the third category emphasizes the original value proposition of Islamic financial intermediation, which reflects the role of Islamic banks as a fiduciary of funds in providing social services, especially in situations where such services are rendered through specially designated funds. Depending on the nature of the business and the type of social services provided, the financial statements of the Islamic bank must therefore contain a statement of sources and uses of funds in the *zakat* and charity fund, and statement of sources and uses of funds in the *qard* fund.[13]

**statement of changes in restricted investments**
A unique financial statement that shows the performance of investments specifically restricted or limited by the investors, such as the restricted trust financing investment.

# GLOBAL ISLAMIC FINANCE

# Bringing AAOIFI Accounting Standards into the Mainstream Global Framework

Before the AAOIFI accounting standards were issued, Islamic banks and financial institutions used IFRS. But with the availability of relevant standards that cater for the specific financial reporting needs of Islamic finance products, most banks around the world have embraced the AAOIFI standards. One question that keeps bothering some experts is whether the available standards are sufficient to ensure best practice and transparency in financial reporting. A recent survey conducted by Deloitte showed that 93 percent of Islamic finance leaders believe the AAOIFI standards are sufficient to ensure transparency and best practice in financial reporting while a negligible 7 percent believe they are not. Furthermore, some experts have also argued that most of the standards were developed based on conventional financial reporting standards with some modifications to suit the needs of the Islamic finance industry. In response some commentators have asked whether there are no classical models of accounting in Islamic law. The recent approach adopted by AAOIFI to issue the Conceptual Framework for Financial Reporting by Islamic Financial Institutions in 2011 seems to have addressed these questions in a more proactive way. The approach adopted in developing the conceptual framework for financial reporting comprises the following:

- The identification of accounting concepts that were previously developed by other standard-setting bodies and that are consistent with the Islamic principles and ideals of accuracy and fairness.
- The identification of aspects that require disclosure and greater transparency to abide by the principles and ideals of Sharī'ah.
- The identification of concepts used by other standard-setting bodies that conflict with the Sharī'ah and the development of new relevant concepts for the purpose of financial reporting by IFIs.
- The development of concepts to address the unique nature of certain transactions, events or conditions

in IFIs. Examples include funds mobilized by IFIs under the *mudarabah* model.

- The identification of the major users, particularly those who do not have the authority or ability to obtain access to information not included in general purpose financial reports.
- The determination of the information needs of the users of financial reports that require addressing.[14]

This new approach seems to be more convincing and also sustainable as it leaves room for the adoption of best practices that do not contradict Islamic law and it also encourages the development of Sharī'ah-based principles of financial reporting. However, there is a raging controversy on the need to bring Islamic accounting standards into the mainstream global framework. While some believe that the Sharī'ah scholars and other stakeholders should work harder to make the AAOIFI accounting framework stronger in order to be considered as a serious alternative, others contend that the Islamic accounting framework should be harmonized with the global framework spearheaded by IASB. Regardless of the position of each of these groups within the Islamic finance industry, there is ongoing pressure on the Islamic finance industry to enter the global accounting mainstream. Since the International Accounting Standards Board (IASB) is the main global body setting the tone for financial reporting in conventional finance, the Islamic finance industry is under pressure to harmonize its principles under the general framework.

While it is easy to suggest that IASB introduces tailor-made guidelines exclusively for Islamic finance, only time will tell how viable such a process would be in harmonizing the global financial reporting guidelines for both Islamic and conventional financial reporting. A uniform approach may or may not be the answer but what is required is the avoidance of the rivalry that already exists with other organizations such as AAOIFI.

Source: Anjuli Davies. 'Islamic finance pressured to join accounting mainstream', *Reuters*, April 5, 2012.
Available at http://www.reuters.com/article/2012/04/05/us-finance-islamic-accounting-idUSBRE8340CA20120405.

These are items that are unique to the business of Islamic banks and financial institutions. The social services they carry out should also be disclosed to ensure transparency and accountability to shareholders. Thus, going beyond the provisions of *zakat* or any other social services in any of the above financial statements, a full disclosure in the form of a statement of sources and use of funds in *zakat* and charity funds may be necessary to sustain investors' confidence. This is why AAOIFI introduced the proposed set of financial statements.

# Review

## Key Terms and Concepts

Accounting and Auditing Organization for Islamic Financial Institutions (AAOIFI) (p. 132)

account receivable (p. 145)

accrual method (p. 146)

American Accounting Association (p. 129)

balance sheet (p. 149)

bookkeeping (p. 135)

cash flow method (p. 146)

cash flow statement (p. 154)

compound accounting journal entry (p. 137)

credit (p. 136)

debit (p. 136)

deferred payment (p. 145)

double-entry bookkeeping (p. 135)

equity of unrestricted account holders (p. 151)

expenditure (p. 135)

external auditing (p. 138)

financial Accounting (p. 129)

horizontal analysis (p. 147)

income statement (p. 151)

internal auditing (p. 138)

International Accounting Standards Board (IASB) (p. 131)

Islamic worldview (p. 129)

journal (p. 135)

Last Day (p. 130)

net income (p. 151)

periodicity concept (p. 145)

*qard* fund (p. 147)

revenue (p. 135)

statement of changes in restricted investments (p. 160)

Statement of Financial Accounting (SFA) (p. 139)

statement of retained earnings (p. 156)

T account (or ledger) (p. 135)

## Summary

**Learning Objective 4.1**

1. The definition of accounting from the Islamic perspective reflects the ethical perspective of financial transactions. The just and equitable principles of fair dealings, transparency, and accountability are significant for the users of information. These are relevant in financial decision-making.

**Learning Objective 4.2**

2. The International Financial Reporting Standards (IFRS) issued by the International Accounting Standards Board play a significant role in international accounting regulation. The Islamic banks and financial institutions adopted the standards some years ago but there has been a paradigm shift to the AAOIFI accounting standards because of the particular needs in accounting for each Islamic finance product.

**Learning Objective 4.3**

3. The basic principles of accounting are similar to the requirements for transparency and accountability in Islamic commercial law. Accounting comprises two main activities—bookkeeping and accounting (preparation of financial statements). Recording financial information is crucial to the success of any business undertaking. There are three branches of accounting: cost and management accounting, financial accounting, and auditing. This chapter provided a general introduction to financial accounting.

**Learning Objective 4.4**

4. The framework and principles of Islamic financial accounting are based on certain fundamental concepts in Islam such as *khilafah* (vicegenerecy), *taklif* (responsibility), documentation of financial dealings, Islamic law of inheritance (*mawarith*), calculation of obligatory alms (*zakat*), and the underlying concept of *tawhid* (unity of God). Compliance with the precepts of the Sharī'ah in all financial dealings must be reflected in the financial information to be communicated to the users of such information.

**Learning Objective 4.5**

5. The accounting techniques and methods adopted by modern Islamic banks and financial institutions to report Islamic financial activities are based on the AAOIFI Financial Accounting Standards. The AAOIFI standards contain exclusive provisions for the financial reporting of Islamic finance products.

**Learning Objective 4.6**

6. The main financial statements for Islamic finance products include a statement of financial position (balance sheet), an income statement, a statement of cash flows, a statement of changes in owners' equity or a statement of retained earnings, a statement of sources and uses of funds in the *zakat* and charity fund (when the bank assumes the responsibility for the collection and distribution of *zakat*), a statement of sources and uses of funds in the *qard* fund, notes to the financial statements, and any statements, reports, and other data that assist in providing information required by users of financial statements as specified in the statement of objectives.

## Practice Questions and Activities

### Practice Questions

1. Explain some underlying principles of Islamic accounting with special reference to Islamic perspectives on accounting.

2. Distinguish between the definitions of accounting as generally understood in the conventional practice of financial reporting and Islamic accounting.

3. Explain the objectives of the International Financial Reporting Standards in international financial regulation.

4. Are the International Financial Reporting Standards (IFRS) applicable to Islamic banks and financial institutions? Give appropriate reasons to justify your viewpoint.

5. What are the basic principles for recording financial information? Illustrate your answer with a simple journal entry.

6. What are the three branches of accounting and how are they related to the business of a typical Islamic bank?

7. What are the identifiable differences between the users of financial information in the conventional practice of accounting and Islamic accounting?

8. Explain the Islamic concept of accounting and list five Financial Accounting Standards issued by AAOIFI.

9. Differentiate between the accrual and cash flow methods of accounting. Support your answer with a relevant example.

10. Define the periodicity concept and explain how it is relevant to the accounting model of Islamic banks.

11. With the aid of the relevant AAOIFI Financial Accounting Standards, briefly explain the following four main financial statements: balance sheets, income statements, cash flow statements, statement of retained earnings or shareholders' equity.

12. Prepare a simple balance sheet for an Islamic bank that reflects some unique features of the types of business carried out by Islamic banks, based on the AAOIFI models explained to you in class.

## Activities

1. Prepare a chart on the main differences between conventional accounting concepts and the Islamic accounting paradigm.

2. Read the text of AAOIFI's Financial Accounting Standards and prepare a summary of them for a 15-minute class presentation.

3. Find two copies each of a statement of financial position (balance sheet), an income statement, a statement of cash flows, a statement of changes in owners' equity or a statement of retained earnings for any Islamic bank or financial institution.

## Further Reading

AAOIFI. (2010). *Accounting, Auditing and Governance Standards for Islamic Financial Institutions*. Bahrain: AAOIFI.

Abdul Rahman, A. (2010). *An Introduction to Islamic Accounting: Theory and Practice*. Kuala Lumpur: CERT Publications.

Baydoun, N. and Willett, R. (1997). Islam and Accounting: Ethical Issues in the Presentation of Financial Information. *Accounting, Commerce and Finance: The Islamic Perspective*. 1(1): 1–25.

Drury, C. (2006). *Cost and Management Accounting* (6th edn.). London: Thomson.

Gambling, T. E. and Karim, R. A. A. (1991). *Business and accounting ethics in Islam*, London: Mansell Publishing Limited.

Hamat, S. (1994). Accounting Standards and Tax Laws in Islamic Banking. *New Horizon*. Vol. 25: 8–10.

Hameed, S. (2003). Islamic Accounting—A Primer. *Akauntan Nasional (currently Accountants Today)*. Jan–Feb.

Lewis, Mervyn K. (2001). *Islam and accounting*. Oxford: Wiley-Blackwell.

Sofat, R. and Hiro, P. (2010). *Basic Accounting* (2nd edn). New Delhi: Asoke K. Ghosh.

Sultan, S. A. M. (2006). *A Mini Guide to Accounting for Islamic Financial Products—A Primer*. Kuala Lumpur: CERT Publications.

# 5

# Corporate Governance for Islamic Financial Institution

# Learning Objectives

**Upon completion of this chapter, the reader should be able to:**

1 Describe the meaning of corporate governance within the Shari`ah framework as practiced in modern Islamic financial institutions.

2 Explain the models and key principles of corporate governance, including Shari`ah governance.

3 Understand the mechanisms of corporate governance and control, including the different organs in Islamic financial institutions.

4 Understand the different models of corporate governance and Shari`ah governance, and the different approaches adopted by Islamic financial institutions.

5 Understand the dynamics of corporate governance in Islamic insurance entities.

For the proper running of a corporate entity such as an Islamic bank or financial institution, sound corporate governance is imperative to ensure effective management. Although a corporate entity is independent from its stakeholders, those entrusted with the day-to-day management of the company must ensure accountability and transparency in all their dealings. Corporate governance within the context of Islamic financial institutions (IFIs) includes Shari`ah governance, which builds and maintains a high-level of confidence in the minds of the shareholders. Corporate governance has a vital role to play in the Islamic finance industry to ensure sustainable practices that protect the rights of all stakeholders. Good corporate governance policies and practices help develop a stable financial market and spur economic growth.

This chapter examines corporate governance for Islamic financial institutions, including Shari`ah governance. It begins with the meaning of corporate governance, and then reviews models of corporate governance, mechanisms of corporate governance and control, the diverse approaches adopted by different Islamic financial institutions, and the corporate governance paradigm for Islamic insurance entities. An overview of the corporate governance in Islamic financial institutions and current practices in some countries is given, with a view to establishing the relevance of the Islamic framework in the management of these corporate entities for the best interests of all stakeholders. Although Shari`ah governance is considered to be part of the corporate governance organ of the Islamic financial institutions, we discuss this in line with the IFSB and AAOIFI guidelines on corporate governance.

UNIVERSITY OF WOLVERHAMPTON
Harrison Learning Centre

ITEMS ISSUED:

**Customer ID: WPP60974931**

Title: Introduction to Islamic Banking &
Finance : Principles and Practice
ID: 762511624X
**Due: 05/05/2015 23:59**

Total items: 1
Total fines: £2.00
27/04/2015 13:08
Issued: 8
Overdue: 0


Thank you for using Self Service.
Please keep your receipt.


Overdue books are fined at 40p per day for
1 week loans, 10p per day for long loans.

## professional perspectives

**Professor Mervyn K. Lewis**
*University of Southern Australia*

**1    Is there any conflict between Sharī'ah and corporate governance?**

Certainly not. Corporate governance is about effective decision-making, and Islamic law defines the nature of corporate responsibilities, the priorities to society, along with specific rules for decision-making. In particular, *shura*, *hisbah* and the Sharī'ah supervisory process establish the three basic building blocks of a system of Islamic corporate governance. Iqbal and Lewis (2009) argue that the basic message of the Sura Ash-Shura, to 'live true in mutual consultation and forbearance, and rely on Allah', contains the essence of governance from an Islamic perspective. Shuratic decision-making procedures provide a vehicle for ensuring that corporate activities and strategies are fully discussed and that a consensus-seeking consultative process is applied. Directors and senior managers would be expected to listen to the opinions of other executives before making a decision and *shura* members would include, as far as possible, representatives of shareholders, employees, suppliers, customers, and other interested parties. There are thus similarities with stakeholder models, with the difference being that the ultimate ends of business and economics, indeed that of any form of human activity, are to Allah, and the means employed should not deviate in any way from the sacred law of Islam. The historical institution of *hisbah* offers a framework of social ethics, relevant to monitor the corporation, with the objective of encouraging correct ethical behavior in the wider social context. Finally, the third pillar of the system is the discipline provided by Islamic religious auditing, which is a device to solicit juristic advice, monitor compliance with Islamic precepts, and collect *zakat*. This extra layer of auditing and accountability for resource use ensures that the enterprise operates as an Islamic concern in its business dealings.

**2    Should the Sharī'ah scholars be limited only to a few organizations?**

It is not difficult to explain the basis for this question. The October 2010 survey of Sharī'ah board membership by Zawya Sharī'ah scholars in partnership with Funds@Work (www.shariahscholars.com) reveals a marked concentration of board membership. This database, which focuses mainly on Sharī'ah scholars from the Gulf Cooperation Council (GCC) countries, covers 1,141 board positions in 28 countries. The top ten scholars hold 39 percent, i.e. 450 of these board positions, an average of 45 board positions each. In fact, the top two scholars (Nizam Mohammed Yacoubi and Abdul Sattar Abdul Karim Abu Ghuddah) each occupy 85 board positions. In Malaysia, as well, some scholars sit on at least 20 boards. Some observers are concerned by the high remuneration that the scholars receive (retainers paid by individual banks range from US$20,000 up to US$100,000), but the US$1 million-plus incomes earned need to be compared with those of top lawyers, for the Islamic financial institutions can't make major decisions without the scholars' advice. Perhaps of greater concern is the excessive workload of the favored scholars and, with the same names recurring on the Sharī'ah advisory boards, the lack of a fresh perspective on Sharī'ah issues.

**3    What should be the fit and proper test for Sharī'ah scholars?**

The functions of the Sharī'ah advisory board are threefold. First, the religious supervisors give advice to the board and management about the Islamic acceptability of the firm's contractual arrangements and new financial product development. Second, an independent report is provided to inform shareholders about management's compliance with Islamic principles and the extent to which the business is run Islamically. Third, there is an audit involved with the special almsgiving levy, *zakat*, to establish that the *zakat* fund is being correctly assessed, and properly administered and distributed. Scholars need to satisfy three 'fit and proper' tests. They must be well versed in *fiqh* (i.e. Islamic jurisprudence, the science of religious law, which is the interpretation of the Sacred Law, Sharī'ah). They must also have a good understanding of finance, and the shortage of scholars who possess the appropriate combination of religious and financial knowledge is one explanation for the concentration of board positions noted above. Third, in addition, the scholars should demonstrate independence of thought and, as religious auditors, independence from the banks' directors and senior management. It is in terms of independence that the present role of the scholars might be questioned.

## professional perspectives

**Volker Nienhaus**
*Adjunct Professor, International Centre for Education in Islamic Finance, Kuala Lumpur*

**1    Is there any conflict between Sharī'ah and corporate governance?**

There is no conflict between generally accepted principles of corporate governance and Sharī'ah—one can even say that Sharī'ah principles are more comprehensive than conventional corporate governance approaches. However, the practice of many Islamic financial institutions is neither in full harmony with conventional nor Sharī'ah requirements. A major problem is the treatment of investment account holders and *takaful* participants. Both are ultimate risk-bearers. Hence, they should be given significantly more information on the risk strategy and performance of 'their' institution. However, legal disclosure requirements are based on conventional corporate codes in all Muslim countries. Corporate law usually sees only shareholders as risk-bearers and ignores the special status of investment account holders and *takaful* participants, which originates from the underlying Sharī'ah contracts. Unless existing laws are modified, Islamic financial institutions may voluntarily disclose relevant data to their customers, but actually only a few go beyond the minimum requirements. Instead, many Islamic banks give investment accounts the 'look and feel' of savings or term deposits (especially by smoothing profit payouts in line with the prevailing market rate of interest). This blurs the differences between conventional and Sharī'ah-compliant savings and investment products, undermines the authenticity or distinctiveness of Islamic finance, and is hardly a best practice example for conventional or Sharī'ah-based corporate governance. Another corporate governance area with potential for vast improvement is the information given to customers on the Sharī'ah qualities of products and the rationale behind the legal opinions of Sharī'ah boards.

**2    Should the Sharīʿah scholars be limited only to a few organizations?**

The huge number of board memberships held by top scholars (some 20 scholars with 50-100 or more board positions) is incompatible with basic corporate governance principles. A very large number of board memberships make it virtually impossible for the scholars to give detailed attention to the products and procedures of each and every institution and to avoid potential conflicts of interest in competing institutions. The drawbacks of using the least accessible but most expensive scholars may be more than compensated by the signaling effect and marketing impact of the big names on the board, but the global reputation of the Islamic finance industry does not benefit from such an overconcentration. Nevertheless, only a very few countries (notably Malaysia) have limited the number of board memberships for scholars within their jurisdiction. A less radical measure would be to recommend or stipulate that each Sharīʿah board should include at least one 'junior scholar'. This would not only create employment opportunities for the next generation of Sharīʿah experts, but could also facilitate a transfer of knowledge and skills between generations, and bring in new ideas, different perspectives, and intellectual discourses. In addition to the mere number of memberships of Sharīʿah boards of industry players, it is also a matter of concern that some top names can also be found on national Sharīʿah boards or advisory councils of the regulatory authorities. To avoid the capture of the regulators by the regulated, it might be better to restrict Sharīʿah board memberships either to the private industry or to the public sector.

**3    What should be the proper fit and test for Sharīʿah scholars?**

The ideal Sharīʿah scholar is not only an expert in classical *fiqh*, but is also qualified in *ijtihad* on the basis of their profound expertise in modern finance and a commanding knowledge of socioeconomic methods and theories; they would reconcile and integrate in themselves the conflicting micro-legalistic approach of Islamic jurists with the macro-systemic perspective of Islamic economists in order to find commercially viable and *maslahah*-promoting solutions for Islamic financial institutions.

Obviously it is virtually impossible to find a single individual who meets all these demands. Nevertheless, the different qualifications and perspectives should somehow be represented on a Sharīʿah board. This should draw the regulators' attention from individual fit and proper criteria to the multidisciplinary composition of the Sharīʿah board. Giving Sharīʿah experts a majority on the board and keeping its size to a minimum implies that a board should comprise at least three Sharīʿah scholars and two additional members with a different background, preferably one expert for non-Sharīʿah commercial law and one economist.

Islamic financial institutions are embedded in secular legal systems and exposed to competition and market discipline. Therefore, it is in their own commercial interest to select fit and proper Sharīʿah experts. Otherwise, they might face not only a reputational risk but also direct claims for damages in cases of Sharīʿah faults and errors. This should lead to a kind of self-regulation of the Sharīʿah scholar profession. Therefore, regulators should not start from scratch and invent fit and proper criteria, but should consider a limitation of the number of board positions for individual Sharīʿah scholars in their jurisdictions in order to reduce conflicts of interest, meet globally accepted governance standards, and give some room for the scholars of the next generation.

# The Meaning of Corporate Governance

**Islamic finance institutions (IFIs)**
Financial institutions that offer Islamic financial services and products.

For a proper understanding of the corporate governance framework in **Islamic financial institutions (IFIs)**, it is important to begin with the meaning of corporate governance as given by major codes and best practices. To this end, this section examines the definitions of corporate governance of the Organization for Economic Cooperation and Development (OECD), International Chamber of Commerce (ICC), and the Cadbury Report of the United Kingdom. These are meant to give a general understanding of what the term 'corporate governance' implies. In addition, a brief overview of the definition of corporate governance is given from the Islamic perspective. This focuses mainly on the meaning of corporate governance within the Sharī'ah framework as defined in the *Guiding Principles on Corporate Governance for Institutions Offering Only Islamic Financial Services* issued by the IFSB.

## Defining Corporate Governance

**corporate governance**
A set of rules, processes, laws, and policies that affect the way a company is run in the overall interest of the stakeholders.

There is no generally accepted definition of **corporate governance**. It has been defined in different contexts and jurisdictions according to the goal it is designed to achieve. To this end, no single definition can be applied to all contexts. There is also a slight difference between the conceptual understanding of the meaning of corporate governance in Islamic law and the conventional conception. The term 'corporate governance' is relatively new as it gained prominence in the last three decades, but corporate entities have been performing the role since the time companies came into existence. A comprehensive definition of corporate governance is given by the Organization for Economic Cooperation and Development:

> Corporate governance is a set of relationships between a company's management, its board, its shareholders and other stakeholders. Corporate governance also provides the structure through which the objectives of the company are set, and the means of attaining those objectives and monitoring performance are determined.[1]

This all-embracing definition sets the ball rolling. The dynamics of corporate governance involves a number of parties, structures, and processes with the central goal of ensuring transparency, accountability, and fairness in the corporate entity.

The ICC definition of corporate governance also explains the mechanisms and dynamics of the stakeholders and how they work together to ensure the three-pronged objectives of transparency, fairness, and accountability in the management of the company:

> Corporate governance is the relationship between corporate managers, directors and the providers of equity, people and institutions who save and invest their capital to earn a return. It ensures that the board of directors (BoD) is accountable for the pursuit of corporate objectives and that the corporation itself conforms to the law and regulations.[2]

Another widely recognized definition of corporate governance is contained in the report of the committee chaired by Sir Adrian Cadbury:

> Corporate governance is the system by which companies are directed and controlled. Boards of directors are responsible for the governance of their companies. The shareholders' role in governance is to appoint the directors and the auditors and to satisfy themselves that an appropriate governance structure is in place. The responsibilities of the directors include setting the company's strategic aims, providing the leadership to put them into effect, supervising the management of the business and reporting to shareholders on their stewardship. The board's actions are subject to laws, regulations and the shareholders in general meeting.[3]

The definition and description given in the Cadbury Report explains the interrelationship among the stakeholders in a corporate entity and their respective responsibilities in ensuring the transparent and fair management of the company based on accountability.

Although there are other definitions, most of them, including the ones given above, have certain features in common. These include:

- a system of relationships defined by structures and processes
- relationships with different and, in some cases, conflicting interests
- all the stakeholders, one way or the other, are involved in the direction and control of the company
- rights and responsibilities are properly distributed among the stakeholders.

**Shari'ah governance**
A set of institutional and organizational arrangements through which IFIs ensure that there is effective independent oversight of Shari'ah compliance over the issuance of relevant Shari'ah pronouncements, dissemination of information, and an internal Shari'ah compliance review.

## Corporate Governance in Islam

There is not much difference between the definitions given above and the definition of corporate governance in Islam. The slight difference lies in the inclusion of **Shari'ah governance** in the corporate governance structure of IFIs. The Shari'ah governance organ ensures strict compliance with the Shari'ah in all the activities carried out by all other stakeholders in the management of the company, and is usually represented by the Sharī'ah supervisory board in the governance structure of an IFI. Corporate governance has been defined and comprehensively described by IFSB, one of the leading international standard-setting bodies:

> Corporate governance in Islam is defined as a set of organizational arrangements whereby the actions of the management of institutions offering Islamic financial services (IIFS) are aligned, as far as possible, with the interests of its stakeholders; provision of proper incentives for the organs of governance such as the board of directors, Sharī'ah supervisory board and management, to pursue objectives that are in the interests of stakeholders and facilitate effective monitoring, thereby encouraging IIFS to use resources more efficiently; and compliance with Islamic Sharī'ah rules and principles.[4]

**Sharī'ah supervisory board**
A body of Sharī'ah scholars and experts who certify proposals on Islamic finance products, services and contracts brought before them.

**Sharī'ah compliance**
When a financial product or activity complies with the precepts and requirements of Islamic law.

From the above definition, it is clear that a key organ is added to the stakeholders, and this organ is crucial in the business and continued existence of the cooperate entity. This organ is the **Sharī'ah supervisory board**, which lays down Sharī'ah-compliant rules and procedures for the smooth running of the company. The board is composed of Sharī'ah scholars who are well-versed and competent in Sharī'ah matters, particularly aspects of economics and finance. The board supervises and ensures the **Sharī'ah compliance** of new products. They have both consultative and supervisory functions. IFIs are unique in having this important organ, which sets additional rules and procedures for the management of companies apart from the conventional rules and procedures of corporate governance.

# Models of Corporate Governance: Stakeholder versus Shareholder

There are different theories or models of cooperate governance. There are two basic models of corporate governance from the conventional perspective. The first is based on the Anglo-American model, while the second is based on the Franco-German model. While the Anglo-American model emphasizes the interests of the shareholders, the Franco-German model tends to emphasize the stakeholder value system. The Anglo-American model is of great relevance for Islamic finance as it aims to align management's interests with shareholders' interests. By the nature of the modes of Islamic finance, the shareholders are considered to be important stakeholders akin to partners in a joint-venture company. Thus, a model that promotes the shareholder value system by aligning the interests of shareholders with those of management represents the underlying principle of most Islamic modes of finance, such as *mudarabah* (trust financing) and *musharakah* (joint-venture contract).

**Anglo-American model**
Any framework, model or paradigm patterned after the American or English legal, economic or political systems.

The **Anglo-American model** accomplishes its aims through a number of mechanisms, including shareholder representation on the board of directors, management compensation schemes, and external market discipline. This optimal model puts in place good governance structures that are shareholder friendly, with a high level of disclosure to achieve high standards of efficiency, accountability, and transparency. Investors are more likely to be attracted when this model is properly enshrined within the managerial role of a company as they know their interests will be adequately represented and effectively protected.

**Franco-German Model**
A framework that is based on the prevailing model in France and Germany.

Conversely, the **Franco-German model**, which is a form of a stakeholder-value system, emphasizes cooperative relations between stakeholders, and employee protection and welfare. It incorporates the interests of shareholders and non-shareholders alike with more emphasis on the latter, who are considered to be stakeholders. Staff representatives serve on the board. In some cases, conflicts of interest arise such as when the management intends to adjust the size of the workforce. Under the Islamic paradigm of corporate governance, which emphasizes the role of the financier and the entrepreneur in a joint-venture company, all stakeholders—which includes shareholders, workers, as well as executive management—should be represented on the board to ensure transparency, accountability, fairness, and mutual consultation. The OECD's Principles of Corporate Governance state:

> The corporate governance framework should promote transparent and efficient markets, be consistent with the rule of law and clearly articulate the division of responsibilities among different supervisory, regulatory and enforcement authorities.[5]

Although the Anglo-American model is closer to the Islamic theory of corporate governance, stakeholders' interests are important in corporate policies. Some have recommended integrating of the two models, yet corporate governance from the Islamic perspective is a unique model that creates a niche for Sharī'ah governance.

## The Role of Corporate Governance in Islamic Financial Institutions

Hint
Remember the difference between the frameworks of corporate governance in both conventional practice and the Islamic paradigm.

Corporate governance has an important role to play in the management of Islamic financial institutions. The Islamic perspective on corporate governance is based on Islamic business principles. Remember that some mandatory requirements of Islamic business transactions include transparency, fairness, and accountability. Thus, the role of corporate governance in IFIs is not so different from conventional companies. As noted earlier, a key aspect of corporate governance in Islamic financial institutions is the inclusion of Sharī'ah governance to emphasize compliance with the mandatory requirements of the Sharī'ah. Accountability in business transactions, whether as entrepreneurs or institutional financial entities, includes true and fair disclosure and transparency so that the interests of all stakeholders, particularly investors, are protected.

For IFIs to be able to compete globally with conventional institutions, a sound corporate governance framework is necessary. This led to the guidelines issued by some standard-setting bodies, such as the Islamic Financial Services Board (IFSB) and the Accounting and Auditing Organization for Islamic Financial Institutions (AAOIFI), specifically to guide the increasing number of IFIs around the world. This will promote the soundness and stability of the Islamic finance industry and enhance the performance of Islamic financial institutions, while stakeholders' interests will be better served. A binding factor for all stakeholders is the uniqueness of the business of the financial institution—transactions complying with the requirements of Islamic law—which motivates investors to invest in the products of the financial institutions. Therefore, the corporate governance framework must serve this important purpose to ensure principles of transparency. Without doubt, corporate governance has a vital role to play in strengthening the confidence of all stakeholders.

In a nutshell, the roles of corporate governance in Islamic financial institutions include:

- to establish a harmonious relationship among the shareholders, board of directors, management, stakeholders, and, above all, God
- to promote prudent and transparent practices in the management of Islamic financial institutions
- to protect the interest of all stakeholders including the investors, depositors, staff, and the general public
- to ensure the proper discharge of the corporate social responsibility role of Islamic financial institutions
- to promote a sound and stable Islamic financial industry that can compete globally with conventional financial institutions in ensuring standard practices.

# Mechanisms of Corporate Governance and Control

Different mechanisms and structures are put in place for corporate governance and control in banks and financial institutions to ensure proper management policies in line with the goals of the company. As we saw earlier, Sharī'ah governance and corporate governance cannot be separated when discussing IFIs. For the purpose of clarity, however, the principles of Sharī'ah governance and corporate governance are discussed separately here.

## Principles of Corporate Governance in Islam

*shura*
Mutual consultation in a
decision-making process.

The underlying premise of corporate governance from the Islamic perspective is the concept of *tawhid* (unity of God) and the principle of **shura** (mutual consultation). These are complemented by the Islamic legal rules on harmonious relationship and mutual benefits in commercial transactions. The *tawhid* framework emphasizes the need for stakeholders to unite on this concept, which implies undertaking transactions that are compliant with the will of God, while the principle of *shura* entrenches the stakeholder-oriented value system where mutual consultation prevails, based on the common goal of oneness of God. The functional roles of a corporate entity are geared towards the *tawhid* philosophy. Figure 5.1 shows how the knowledge base of corporate governance in Islam is *tawhid*. This is where the Sharī'ah governance system derives its authority, knowledge, and practices. The functional roles of Islamic banks and financial institutions are premised on Sharī'ah rules, which stem from *tawhid*. The Sharī'ah board carries out its activities through consultation (*shura*) and this involves the general participation of shareholders and other stakeholders, including the community where the corporate body carries out its business.

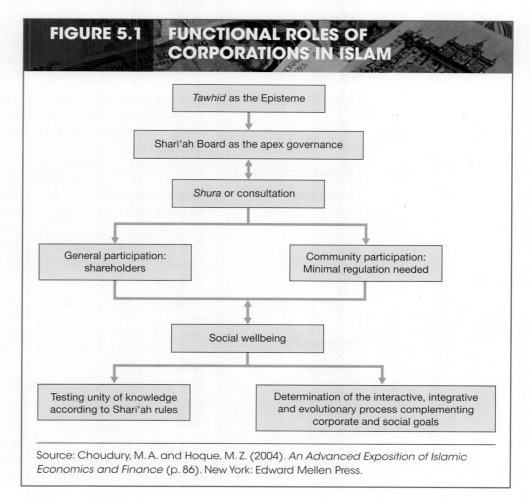

**FIGURE 5.1 FUNCTIONAL ROLES OF CORPORATIONS IN ISLAM**

Source: Choudury, M. A. and Hoque, M. Z. (2004). *An Advanced Exposition of Islamic Economics and Finance* (p. 86). New York: Edward Mellen Press.

Even though the standards and corporate governance structure of conventional financial institutions have been adopted and adapted within the Islamic framework to suit the specific needs of financial institutions that offer Islamic financial services and products, Islamic finance institutions (IFIs), as well as meeting their ethical requirements, the Sharī'ah governance system is a unique innovation in modern approaches to corporate governance. (Another common term for IFIs when specific reference is made to the banking sector of the Islamic finance industry is Islamic banking institutions (IBIs)). Table 5.1 gives the general corporate governance framework for IFIs.

**TABLE 5.1: Key Players in Corporate Governance (CG) of Islamic Financial Institutions (IFIs)**

|  | Important Issues | Objectives/Responsibilities in CG |
|---|---|---|
| **Environment** | | |
| Overall economic, financial, and legal system | Efficiency in the legal system enforceability of contracts rule of law | Promote strong business and legal environments that support CG |
| Government (laws and regulations for IFIs) | Laws facilitating operations of Islamic financial institutions | Provide clear laws and regulations that cater for the needs of IFIs |
| Accounting system | Accounting and audit standards for clear and transparent communication of information | Provide uniform, clear and transparent accounting standards |
| **Public Institutions** | | |
| Supervisors | Stability and soundness of the financial system (eliminate systemic risk) Develop internal controls, risk management procedures, and standards of transparency | Provide guidelines for financial institutions Monitor overall operations in general and risky behaviour in particular |
| Banking associations | Provide minimum standards of CG | Set Principles and Sound practices |
| **Institutional** | | |
| Shareholders | Shareholders' rights Share in profit | Elect Board Members |
| Board of directors | Ensure good management team Oversight of management Protect shareholders and investment depositors' rights | Set overall policy and strategy Accountability of the management |

*Cont'd*

**TABLE 5.1: Key Players in Corporate Governance (CG) of Islamic Financial Institutions (IFIs)**

| | Important Issues | Objectives/ Responsibilities in CG |
|---|---|---|
| **Institutional** | | |
| Senior management | Operate the institution efficiently. Right balance between risk and return Efficient incentive structure | Implement the policies set by the Board in a sound and responsible manner |
| Internal audit | Quality and quantity of information Transparency of information | Ensures that the policies set by Board are followed by the management (Compliance) |
| Employees | Skills and work ethics Right incentive structure | Meet the goals set by the Management Minimize operational risks |
| Sharī'ah boards | Set Sharī'ah related rules and principles | Oversee compliance with its verdict |
| **Others** | | |
| Depositors | Good service Comparable returns | Act responsibly Monitor the performance |
| External auditors | Quality and quantity of information Transparency of information | Evaluate the accuracy of the quality and quantity of information |
| Sharī'ah audit | Adherence to the Sharī'ah | Ensure compliance with the Sharī'ah Board verdicts. |

Source: Chapra, U. and Ahmed, H. (2002). *Corporate Governance in Islamic Financial Institutions*. Jeddah: Islamic Development Bank, IRTI: pp. 15–16.

## Sharī'ah Governance

Sharī'ah governance and corporate governance are closely related in an Islamic corporate entity, so it is important to specifically examine this additional organ of corporate governance, which is missing in the corporate governance framework of conventional financial institutions. This additional layer in the pyramidal structure of the governance framework is specifically meant to address Sharī'ah compliance. Without a Sharī'ah governance system, a supposedly incorporated Islamic financial institution cannot claim to be Islamic because the compass required for ethical business and operations is missing. With this in mind, the Sharī'ah system of governance was introduced to complement the adaptable standards of corporate governance and streamline

## ISLAMIC FINANCE IN PRACTICE

# The Corporate Governance Structure of Meezan Bank

Meezan Bank, a bank that prides itself as the primary Islamic bank in Pakistan, has built its name over the years and enjoyed sustained growth since the early 2000s. With a vision of establishing a financial institution that promotes an equitable economic system, it has carved a niche for itself through a formidable corporate governance structure that merges the best practices of conventional corporate governance models with the principles of Sharīʿah governance to produce a highly efficient, sophisticated, and resilient governance structure in order to optimize stakeholders' value. Offering a diverse range of Sharīʿah-compliant products and services, Meezan Bank can claim its position as a premier Islamic bank in Pakistan. It has approximately 4,300 full-time staff and 650 outsourced staff in its 275 branches.

Meezan Bank's corporate governance structure provides a good model of modern practice of corporate governance in an Islamic financial institution. Merging the corporate governance framework of conventional financial institutions

with the Sharīʿah governance requirements has created an integrated structure. A high level of independence is maintained among the major governance organs. The board of directors, shareholders, and the Sharīʿah supervisory board at the apex level respectively exercise their powers in the overall interest of the bank's stakeholders. The governance structure in the figure below caters for all aspects of governance required in a typical Islamic financial institution.

From the figure, it is clear that the Sharīʿah governance organ comprising the Sharīʿah supervisory board, Sharīʿah advisor, and product development and Sharīʿah compliance team, is independent even though it has been integrated into the overall corporate governance structure. The Sharīʿah supervisory board is composed of the following scholars: Justice (rtd.) Muhammad Taqi Usmani, Dr. Abdul Sattar Abu Ghuddah, Sheikh Essam M. Ishaq, and Dr. Muhammad Imran Usmani, who also acts as the Sharīʿah advisor, interacting between the board of directors and the Sharīʿah supervisory board.

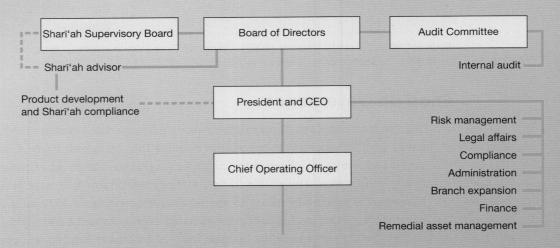

Source: Meezan Bank, *Annual Report 2011*, Karachi, p. 21. Available at www.meezanbank.com/index.aspx.

Meezan Bank provides a good model of modern practice of corporate governance in an Islamic financial institution. It merges the framework of conventional financial institutions with the Sharī'ah governance requirements, and this has created an integrated structure.

non-compatible standards according to the philosophical foundation of corporate governance in Islam. Sharī'ah governance formally emerged in the modern world with the emergence of IFIs. This was necessary to institutionalize practices and standards that enhance accountability, fairness, and transparency in IFIs, while upholding the ethical rules of business. To this end, Sharī'ah governance in modern Islamic finance business is a unique framework that adds value to the business and operations of the corporate entity and protects the interests of all stakeholders. The Islamic Finance in Practice box provides a practical description of the relationship between an IFI's general corporate governance framework and the Sharī'ah governance system. The Meezan Bank has a separate Sharī'ah governance system (on the left side of the diagram) and this includes the Sharī'ah supervisory board, the Sharī'ah executive committee and Sharī'ah auditors. The functions of each of these branches will be explained shortly.

It is important to emphasize that the scope of the Sharī'ah governance system in a jurisdiction may vary depending on the corporate governance system established by the regulatory bodies in a specific countries. We will discuss this in the next section of this chapter. It is important to reiterate that the major organ of the Sharī'ah governance system is the Sharī'ah supervisory board. In some cases the Sharī'ah board may not be able to ensure compliance with its resolutions, but the internal and external Sharī'ah review panels will point out aspects of non-compliance in practice that should be addressed in order to strengthen the Sharī'ah governance organ of the IFIs. As we saw earlier, different jurisdictions have different models, but the international standards and guidelines issued by AAOIFI and IFSB are worth exploring. The following four guidelines are related to the Sharī'ah governance system of IFIs.

1.  *Guiding Principles on Corporate Governance for Institutions Offering Only Islamic Financial Services (Excluding Islamic Insurance (Takaful) Institutions and Islamic Mutual Funds, 2006 (IFSB-3).*

2.  *Guiding Principles on Sharī'ah Governance Systems for Institutions Offering Islamic Financial Services, 2009 (IFSB-10).*

3.  *Guiding Principles on Governance for Takaful (Islamic Insurance) Undertakings, 2009 (IFSB-8).*

4.  *Guiding Principles on Governance for Islamic Collective Investment Schemes, 2008 (IFSB-6).*

Here we shall focus more on the relevant guiding principles—IFSB-3 and IFSB-10 for the Islamic banking system and IFSB-8 for the *takaful* industry.

IFSB-10 is the reference number for *Guiding Principles on Sharī'ah Governance Systems for Institutions offering Islamic Financial Services* issued by the IFSB, the international standard-setting body based in Malaysia.

According to IFSB-10, the Sharī'ah governance system "refers to the set of institutional and organizational arrangements through which an institution offering Islamic financial services (IIFS) ensures that there is effective independent oversight of Sharī'ah compliance."[6] This oversight is specifically meant to regulate the process of issuing Sharī'ah rulings or resolutions, and their dissemination to the bank personnel for implementation. An internal Sharī'ah compliance unit may also help in ensuring compliance by conducting periodic reviews to ascertain that the Sharī'ah resolutions have been complied with. This information is as necessary for stakeholders as the financial statements. These mechanisms collectively constitute the Sharī'ah governance system in IFIs.

## Functions of Sharī'ah Governance System in IFIs

**Challenge**

How can the functions of the Sharī'ah governance system complement the duties of the board of directors of an Islamic financial institution?

Sharī'ah governance systems have diverse functions within IFIs depending on the scope of the duties conferred on the Sharī'ah board and the jurisdiction within which an IFI carries out its business. IFSB-10 gives the following primary duties of the Sharī'ah board in an IFI:

1.  Advising the board of directors on Sharī'ah-related matters.

2.  Reviewing and endorsing Sharī'ah-related policies and guidelines. For this purpose, the IFI should also have a Sharī'ah process manual, which specifies the manner in which a submission or request for Sharī'ah pronouncements/resolutions should be made to the Sharī'ah board, the conduct of meetings of the Sharī'ah board, and the manner of ensuring operational compliance with any decision.

3.  Endorsing and validating relevant documentation for new products and services, including contracts, agreements, or other legal documentation used in an IFI's business transactions.

4.  Overseeing the calculation and distribution of *zakat* and any other funds to be channeled to charity.

5.  Assisting and advising relevant parties that serve the IFI, such as its legal counsel, auditor or other consultants, upon request.

6.  Put on record, in written form, any opinion that it gives on Sharī'ah-related issues.[7]

The specific functions of the Sharī'ah governance system in financial institutions offering Islamic services and products can be summarized as covering four major areas as set out below.

### Issuance of Relevant Sharī'ah Pronouncements/Resolutions

The corporate governance organs of the IFIs, including the board of directors and executive management, may raise controversial issues or policies for the approval of the Sharī'ah board before implementation. The role of the Sharī'ah board as the main arm of the Sharī'ah governance system is to review such policies or issues in line with the methodology of collective *ijtihad* and issue a resolution to that effect. *Ijtihad* is independent legal reasoning by a competent jurist (or a group of jurists) who deduces the applicable law on novel issues from the sources. This forms the basis of a Sharī'ah ruling or resolution. Such juristic opinion should be binding on all corporate governance organs of the IFI. The independence of the Sharī'ah board is emphasized in this regard because it is the only body that ensures all contracts, processes, products, and services comply with the mandatory rules and prescriptions of the Sharī'ah. Before arriving at a Sharī'ah resolution, the Sharī'ah board must consider all relevant information and views without influence from any other organ of management. Any proposed Islamic finance product or transaction must be properly scrutinized before a positive endorsement is given. The relevant documents and contracts must also be supplied for review to ensure that not only is the product Sharī'ah-compliant but the process itself is legal. For instance, we can see in Box 5.1 an example of an issue regarding Islamic banking deposits brought

### BOX 5.1: AN EXAMPLE OF A RESOLUTION OF THE SHARĪ'AH ADVISORY COMMITTEE

*As the highest Sharī'ah authority in the banking industry in Malaysia, a question was referred to the Sharī'ah Advisory Council of Bank Negara.*

**Issue**: In relation to Islamic banking deposits, is it permissible for the Islamic banking institution to accept every deposit without the need to screen its source?

*After collective deliberation by the Council comprising learned Sharī'ah Scholars, it resolved:*

**Resolution**: The council in its 58th meeting held on April 27, 2006/ 28 Rabiul Awal 1427 resolved that Islamic banking institutions may, generally, accept any application for placement of deposit or investment fund from individual or corporate customers without the need to investigate the status of the sources of fund; either Sharī'ah-compliant, non-Sharī'ah-compliant, or a mixture between the two.

*The resolution is binding on all the Islamic financial institutions in Malaysia. This is the additional and unique role of Sharī'ah governance system in the corporate structure of Islamic financial institutions.*

Source: Bank Negara Malaysia,
www.bnm.gov.my/guidelines/01_banking/04_prudential_stds/07_shariah_resolution.pdf.

before the Sharī'ah Advisory Council of the Central Bank of Malaysia. After collective deliberation among the members of the council, it issued a binding resolution for all IFIs in the country.

### Dissemination of the Sharī'ah Resolution to the Sharī'ah Review Unit

The Sharī'ah board disseminates any information on a new Sharī'ah pronouncement to the relevant department or personnel in the IFI. It is common to have a Sharī'ah review unit, which is saddled with the responsibility of monitoring the day-to-day compliance with any pronouncements or resolutions. IFIs have various different names for this compliance unit. For example, IFSB-10 refers to it as the internal sharī'ah compliance unit/department (ISCU). In some cases, a Sharī'ah compliance officer is appointed to monitor such processes and transactions. The ISCU must be independent to ensure transparency in its monitoring role. In some IFIs, an external Sharī'ah review is carried out at intervals to ascertain the level of Sharī'ah compliance in the day-to-day operations. This is outsourced to Sharī'ah audit firms.

### The ISCU to Record and Report Its Findings

The internal Sharī'ah compliance review/audit unit verifies that Sharī'ah compliance has been satisfied. In the event of any incident of non-compliance, it must be recorded and reported, and as far as possible, addressed and rectified. It is the duty of the Sharī'ah board to further present its view on how to address non-compliance and offer its opinion on how to rectify it. Its position must be made known to the board of directors and the management of the IFI for further action.

### Preparation of an Annual Sharī'ah Compliance Review Report

The ISCU in conjunction with the Sharī'ah board should prepare an annual Sharī'ah compliance review/audit report to be presented to the IFI's annual general meeting (AGM). The purpose is to keep stakeholders abreast on the level of Sharī'ah compliance. The findings of the report must be clearly enumerated and may constitute a major item of discussion at the AGM.

## Institutionalization of the Sharī'ah Governance System

When Islamic banking and finance was introduced in the last century, the Sharī'ah governance system was fluid as there was no proper structure for Sharī'ah advice and consultancy. Most advisory roles were filled by the promoters of corporate firms and, in some cases, were outsourced to Sharī'ah consultancy firms. As the practice of Islamic banking and finance crystallized, the need to embed the Sharī'ah governance system was emphasized in the legal and regulatory policies of different jurisdictions as well as by the international standard-setting bodies.

The first Sharī'ah board was established in 1976 by the Faisal Islamic Bank of Egypt and this ushered in a new regime in the embedding of Sharī'ah governance in IFIs. There are two different models for embedding—pre-modern and modern. The pre-modern society model on which the Sharī'ah governance system is premised is **hisbah**, while the modern model is collective *ijtihad*. The Sharī'ah board based on the *hisbah* model

*hisbah*
An Islamic institution that guards against infringement of the law in the economic, social, and political domains.

performs duties more related to Sharī'ah corporate control with greater emphasis on Sharī'ah compliance. The collective *ijtihad* model focuses more on Sharī'ah advice and consultancy.

In modern IFIs, the Sharī'ah board is generally responsible for product development and certification, and issuance of resolutions on matters brought before it. The Sharī'ah governance system responsible for Sharī'ah corporate control is the internal Sharī'ah review unit as identified by IFSB-10. Some IFIs use the services of external Sharī'ah audit firms who carry out Sharī'ah reviews to ascertain the level of compliance with the policies and resolutions of the Sharī'ah board. These related functions are important for the overall mission and vision of IFIs.

The whole corpus of Islamic jurisprudence is called **fiqh** (which can also mean the jurists' understanding of the Islamic law). The prominent Sharī'ah board for the Organization of Islamic Cooperation (OIC) is the International Islamic Fiqh Academy, based in Jeddah, which issues resolutions on all Islamic matters including Islamic banking and finance issues. The Fiqh Academy has resolutions on the jurisprudence of transactions regulated by Islamic law, known as *fiqh al-mu'amalat* and these cover all aspects of Islamic commercial contracts. A number of its authoritative resolutions on *fiqh al-mu'amalat* have been cited in many resolutions of the Sharī'ah boards of IFIs around the world.

## Organs of the Sharī'ah Governance System

The Sharī'ah governance system of an IFI comprises the Sharī'ah Supervisory Board, the Sharī'ah Supervisory Council, and the Internal Sharī'ah Compliance Unit.

### Sharī'ah Supervisory Board at the Micro Level

The Sharī'ah supervisory board is the highest and most visible organ of an IFI. It is part of the governance system to review processes, new products, and contracts, and consider the legitimacy of some products in the financial markets. As the heart of the Sharī'ah governance system, it is based on the traditional concept of *hisbah* (market supervisor). An official appointed to investigate complaints made by individuals against maladministration by either a public authority or in a private relationship is known as the **muhtasib** (ombudsman). Traditionally, the *muhtasib* was saddled with the responsibility of market supervision and some other religious duties, but the office has a proactive role in modern financial institutions. The concept of *hisbah* has been embedded and developed as an important organ of the Sharī'ah governance system, which led to the introduction of what is now known as the Sharī'ah supervisory board.

This new model plays both the advisory and supervisory roles in ensuring Sharī'ah compliance of procedures, products, and processes. A business cannot certify itself as 'Islamic' if it does not have a proper Sharī'ah governance system through the establishment of the Sharī'ah board. Public confidence is tied to proper Sharī'ah supervision in a company's corporate governance. Apart from the crystallized *hisbah* model, the concept of collective *ijtihad* has been explored in Islamic finance issues to establish the Sharī'ah board as the main arm of the Sharī'ah governance system. This is a new method developed by modern scholars to address novel issues in a more

**fiqh**
The whole corpus of Islamic jurisprudence. *Fiqh* may also mean the jurists' understanding of Islamic law.

**muhtasib** (ombudsman)
An official appointed by a competent authority to investigate complaints made by individuals against maladministration by either a public authority or in a private relationship.

practical and consensus-building manner. The Supreme Council of Sharī'ah Supervisory Boards for Banking and Financial Institutions in Sudan has adopted this model, where renowned scholars of Islamic law meet to deliberate and subsequently issue resolutions on particular Islamic finance issues, which are binding on all banks and financial institutions operating within the country.

The role of the Sharī'ah boards in IFIs is at the micro level because they are either engaged as a Sharī'ah committee in the corporate governance structure of an IFI or as an external Sharī'ah consultancy firm. In most jurisdictions around the world, particularly in countries where the practice of Islamic banking and finance has developed to a reasonable extent, it is a requirement in the articles of association of IFIs according to the law to establish a Sharī'ah board.

### Sharī'ah Supervisory Council at the Macro and Central Bank Level

It is widespread practice to have a Supreme Sharī'ah Supervisory Council at the macro level, and it may be in the form of a national or international set-up. For instance, the Sharī'ah board of Al Rajhi Bank Group, a multinational bank, has responsibility for implementing the bank's Islamic strategy for all its branches and subsidiaries around the world. HSBC Amanah has a Global Sharī'ah Advisory Board that operates as an advisory body for all HSBC branches and subsidiaries offering Islamic products and services. International standard-setting bodies and multinational financial institutions such as AAOIFI and the Islamic Development Bank (IDB) have their own Sharī'ah boards that were established based on mutual cooperation between the member countries.

In order to standardize the process of certifying and reviewing products, services, and operations by the Sharī'ah boards of IFIs in a country, the central bank, as the supervisory and regulatory body for the banking and financial system of a country, often establishes its own standing Sharī'ah Supervisory Council as practiced in countries such as Malaysia and Sudan. All the resolutions of the IFIs' Sharī'ah supervisory boards in such jurisdictions must comply with the general standards established by the supreme Sharī'ah Supervisory Council of a central bank. In the event of any conflict between the decisions of the Sharī'ah board of an IFI and the Sharī'ah Supervisory Council of the central bank, the resolution of the Sharī'ah Supervisory Council prevails.

### Internal Sharī'ah Compliance Unit

The internal Sharī'ah compliance unit (ISCU) or department is responsible for verifying processes, services, and transactions to ensure that the relevant departments have complied with the resolutions/pronouncements of the Sharī'ah board. It enjoys a high level of independence from all other departments of the IFIs, particularly the business unit, to ensure accountability and transparency in its verification process. Though the ISCU is part of the micro Sharī'ah governance system of IFIs, it is specifically established to ensure compliance and thus may be considered an independent body. The Islamic finance industry currently has a mix of different practices in this area, which include the use of external Sharī'ah audit firms, appointment of a sole Sharī'ah compliance officer, or the establishment of an internal Sharī'ah compliance unit or department. With the gradual move towards the standardization of best practices in the industry, Malaysia's

# ISLAMIC FINANCE IN THE NEWS

## Islamic banking seeks global standards

**November 18, 2007**

As the Islamic banking industry moves from a niche sector to the mainstream of global finance, the dearth of religious scholars with sufficient expertise to sign off on 'Islamic' products and the lack of standard opinions are emerging as key bottlenecks.

The range of Islamic scholars who have expert knowledge of finance ranges from 50 to 260, depending on estimates. But most experts agree that a few dozen scholars essentially control the industry, sitting on many of the so-called Sharī'ah boards, the bodies that banks and other institutions either employ internally or hire to judge whether products are interest-free and therefore comply with Islamic law.

'A number of institutions are being set up and transactions are raising multi billions of dollars but they are all chasing Sharī'ah fatwas [religious edicts],' says Humayon Dar, chief executive officer of London-based BMB Islamic, an advisory firm.

A group of about 12 scholars are favored by international banks that have rushed into the industry, and these religious experts are raking in millions of dollars in yearly income, say industry analysts.

'To sell products into the market, to give them credibility, you go to the tried and true guys whom everybody knows,' says Sheikh Yusuf Talal DeLorenzo, chief Sharī'ah officer at DIFC-based Sharī'ah Capital, and a leading expert on Islamic finance.

'There are 50 top Sharia scholars and hundreds of billions of dollars are decided by them,' says another industry expert who asked to remain anonymous. 'It's like having a whole industry with one regulator that has a staff of 50.'

The problem, he adds, is that 'they are a bottleneck to the growth of the market. You can't have enough discussions on products because they [the scholars] are spread very thin.'

Nasser al-Shaali, chief executive officer of the Dubai International Financial Centre Authority, says graduating Sharī'ah scholars, who reach their status through religious rather than financial education, remains a challenge. The DIFC's focus has been instead on graduating Sharī'ah technicians, who work as analysts with the scholars.

Sheikh DeLorenzo, meanwhile, cites language and culture as barriers. 'The English language is as important as Arabic, to read documentation and there's also a cultural qualification,' he says. 'Scholars often come from a relatively closed environment so they need to be able to work in an environment with which they are not comfortable and to work to a deadline.'

The Islamic finance industry has always suffered from another basic dilemma—that a product or practice that may be acceptable to one scholar could be considered un-Islamic by another, sometimes within the same jurisdiction.

But as the industry expands—the market is now estimated at $750bn—the need for standardization of fatwas is intensifying. Questions of conflict of interest have also been raised since scholars hired by banks to accredit new products give the institutions an edge vis-à-vis its competitors.

Malaysia is one of the few countries that has established a standard, government-backed Sharī'ah board. The Bahrain-based Accounting and Auditing Organization for Islamic Financial Institutions has created its own group of religious experts to issue fatwas. But it remains a voluntary body, with some banks following its standards, and many others ignoring them.

Mr Dar argues that a centralized Sharī'ah advisory board is an essential ingredient for the industry, and it should focus on issuing opinions, rather than signing off on every transaction conducted by banks.

Financial institutions, he says, should hire Sharī'ah technicians who translate opinions into practice, acting in the same way as lawyers or accountants. Insisting that there is too much hype about remuneration of scholars and that most are, in fact, poorly paid, he says the scholars on advisory boards should receive a share of what the Sharī'ah technicians make.

**Source:** Roula Khalaf, "Islamic banking seeks global standards", *Financial Times*, November 18, 2007.

IFSB model is being adopted in many jurisdictions around the world. The ISCU must prepare a report on Sharī'ah compliance audit which may be presented to the Sharī'ah board for its pronouncement or at the AGM for consumption by IFI stakeholders.

## The Sharī'ah Governance Process

The Sharī'ah governance process for IFIs comprises a number of steps and processes to sustain the underlying philosophy of the company and enhance stakeholders' confidence. The process outlined here begins with the appointment of the members of the Sharī'ah board up to the point of making the Sharī'ah resolution. This process includes a brief appraisal of the appointment, composition, qualification, Sharī'ah coordination, Sharī'ah compliance process, external Sharī'ah review, and finally the Sharī'ah resolution.

### Appointment

The appointment of Sharī'ah scholars to the Sharī'ah board is either done by shareholders at the AGM or by the board of directors (BoD) on their behalf, subject to their approval at the AGM. As there is no standard for making appointments, the power to do so is vested in the BoD in countries such as Malaysia, Jordan, and Pakistan, and some others. For instance, in Pakistan, according to *Instructions for Compliance in Islamic Banking Institutions 2008,* every IFI is required to constitute a Sharī'ah board and the appointment of its members must be approved by the BoD in the case of domestic banks, with prior written approval from the State Bank of Pakistan. However, for foreign Islamic banks with branches or subsidiaries in Pakistan, the members of the Sharī'ah board are appointed by the management. In a similar vein, section 27(a) of the Islamic Banking Law of Jordan provided for members to be appointed by the management board for a maximum period of five years. This practice was changed in 2003 with the amendment of Article 58, Law 28 of 2000, since when the power is vested in the AGM. In Malaysia, the *Sharī'ah Governance Framework for Islamic Financial Institutions 2010* requires that, upon the recommendation of the nomination committee, the BoD appoints the members for a renewable term of two years. Written pre-approval is required from the Central Bank and the Sharī'ah Advisory Council beforehand.

At the central bank level, the members of the Sharī'ah Advisory Council are appointed by the relevant government authority since the bank is under the government. For instance, members of the Sharī'ah Advisory Council of the Central Bank of Malaysia are appointed by the Yang di-Pertuan Agong (the Supreme King of Malaysia) on the advice of the Minister of Finance after consultation with the bank.[8] IFSB-10 does not expressly mention the appropriate authority responsible for appointing the members of the Sharī'ah board, but since it provides that the Sharī'ah board shall report directly to the BoD administratively, it is implied that the appointing authority is the latter depending on the model adopted by the IFI. While some may grant absolute powers to the BoD in regard to such appointments, other IFIs may prefer to subject the BoD's appointments to the AGM for approval. This latter view has been expressed in IFSB-10, albeit in the notes where the BoD is recognized as the appointing authority.[9] In a slightly different procedure, the AAOIFI governance standards provide that the members of the Sharī'ah board are appointed by the shareholders at the AGM upon the recommendation of the BoD.

## Composition

The diverse expertise and depth of knowledge of the members should cater for the different aspects of modern financial transactions. For instance, AAOIFI's Sharī'ah board is composed of experts from diverse fields with considerable expertise in their respective areas of Islamic banking and finance. Members are academics and consultants specializing in Islamic banking to broaden the expertise and capabilities of its Sharī'ah board. Generally, IFI Sharī'ah boards are composed of scholars learned in *fiqh al-mu'amalat* and *usul al-fiqh* (principles of Islamic jurisprudence). They must possess necessary practical knowledge and expertise and considerable experience in these areas. Although the composition of its Sharī'ah board is determined by each IFI and there are diverse practices in the Islamic finance industry, it has been noted that the Sharī'ah boards of international financial institutions are uniquely composed of renowned international scholars while national IFIs appoint local or regional scholars.

There is no standard practice to determine the number of scholars who sit on a Sharī'ah board, although three to six members is common. In Malaysia, there is no maximum number of members but there must be no fewer than five on the board. Pakistan does not expressly provide for the number of members on a Sharī'ah board, but its guidelines imply a minimum of one and no maximum. AAOIFI, as an international standard-setting body, has a Sharī'ah board composed of no more than 20 members appointed by the board of trustees for a four-year term. They are appointed from Sharī'ah boards of IFIs that are members of AAOIFI and the Sharī'ah supervisory boards of central banks. According to AAOIFI's governance standards, the Sharī'ah supervisory board shall be composed of at least three members and it may co-opt non-members, such as consultants, but should exclude directors and significant shareholders of the IFI.

## Qualification

The qualification of the members of the Sharī'ah board is an important consideration. The general requirements, as we saw earlier, are practical knowledge and considerable expertise in the application of *fiqh al-mu'amalat* and *usul al-fiqh* in modern financial transactions. Usually, the minimum requirement for a Sharī'ah board member is some qualification, knowledge, expertise, or experience in the two areas mentioned above. This is important because most of the issues coming before the Sharī'ah board relate to Islamic commercial law and transactions. Some IFIs in some jurisdictions want additional qualifications related to their business. For example, the Securities Commission of Malaysia requires the prospective Sharī'ah board advisors to be of good reputation and well versed in *fiqh al-mu'amalat* and *usul al-fiqh* with at least three years' experience in Islamic financial transactions. According to the guidelines of the Sharī'ah Supervisory Board of the Bank of Sudan scholars are required to have expertise in comparative law as well. Furthermore, as noted in *Islamic Finance in the News* on page 185, learned Sharī'ah scholars who are fluent in both English and Arabic should be considered. Arabic is as important as English and vice versa, and is essential for in-depth research on the extent of Sharī'ah compliance of products brought before the board, as well as legal documentation.

A brief look at the AAOIFI governance standards and IFSB-10 reveals that non-experts in *fiqh al-mu'amalat* and *usul al-fiqh* may also be appointed to strengthen the board in complex banking and finance operations as they can bring expertise in specific areas of banking and finance. A number of countries follow this model, which allows non-experts in Islamic law to sit with experts on the board for the purpose of understanding complex banking and finance operations. Examples of this can be seen in the Sharī'ah advisory councils of the Central Bank of Malaysia and State Bank of Pakistan, where experts from different fields constitute the board. Here, the members are composed of Sharī'ah scholars, judges, lawyers, chartered accountants, and a representative of the Central Bank. In the United Kingdom and North America, most of the financial institutions offering Sharī'ah-compliant products and services constitute their Sharī'ah boards with internationally renowned Sharī'ah scholars. Above all, the most important consideration should be competence with considerable experience in the field.

### Sharī'ah Coordination

Sharī'ah coordination plays a major role in the governance system of IFIs by defining the level and method of interaction among the different Sharī'ah organs of the system. A coordinator is appointed who is responsible to the Sharī'ah board as the company secretary, and reports to the BoD. As a liaison officer between the relevant Sharī'ah organs, they coordinate the Sharī'ah governance process, which mainly consists of the corporate interaction between the Sharī'ah board and the ISCU or external Sharī'ah audit review, and other organs of the IFI. They may be either a natural person (a person learned in Sharī'ah) or an artificial person (such as a Sharī'ah consultancy or advisory firm). An example of an artificial Sharī'ah coordinator is Codexa Capital LLC, which is based in New York and acts as Sharī'ah coordinator for Hyperion Australian Equity Islamic Fund. Its functions include negotiating agreements between the Sharī'ah supervisory board and the Fund, compiling periodic briefing packets for the Sharī'ah board on behalf of the Fund, and facilitating the annual Sharī'ah review meeting of the board.

In some IFIs, there is no clear demarcation between the roles of the Sharī'ah compliance officer and the coordinator and there are several models of Sharī'ah coordination in IFIs around the world. Coordination may be carried out by the secretary of the Sharī'ah board, the Sharī'ah coordination department, Sharī'ah compliance officer, an external firm such as in the example of Codexa Capital LLC above, or the internal Sharī'ah liaison officer. It is common practice for the secretary of the Sharī'ah board or the Sharī'ah compliance officer to perform the task of coordination.

### Sharī'ah Compliance Process

To ensure maximum and strict compliance with the Sharī'ah resolutions and laid-down rules in the business, products, and services of IFIs, a standard Sharī'ah review is required which includes both internal and external audits. The principal purpose of such a review is to ensure total compliance with the resolutions and specific instructions, where applicable, of the Sharī'ah board. In conducting a review, all available procedures, processes, and documents have to be reviewed to ensure compliance with the Sharī'ah and specifically the rulings of the Sharī'ah supervisory board. While it is the responsibility of the Sharī'ah board to form an opinion on the extent of an IFI's compliance with the Sharī'ah, the compliance process is carried out by a separate body. According to AAOIFI's governance standards, the internal review is an integral part of the Sharī'ah governance system. The Sharī'ah compliance process is carried out by an independent division or part of an internal audit department, depending on the organizational structure adopted by individual IFIs. According to IFSB-10, an internal Sharī'ah review/audit/unit is required to undertake the important task of effectively verifying the extent of compliance. The major difference between the functions of the internal audit department of IFIs and the internal Sharī'ah audit department is that the former reports to the audit committee while the latter reports to the Sharī'ah board. The Sharī'ah review report may make necessary recommendations to the management of the IFI to address or rectify issues of Sharī'ah compliance.

After the internal Sharī'ah review/audit team has reported, an external Sharī'ah auditor may be engaged to undertake an independent fact-finding review on the level of Sharī'ah compliance of the IFI. According to IFSB-10, the Sharī'ah board may undertake this process itself or outsource it to an external firm. Whatever choice the IFI adopts, a report has to be produced indicating whether the IFI has complied with the Sharī'ah requirements in the financial year under review. It is recommended that two sets of Sharī'ah review reports are prepared—the general statement of compliance and a detailed account of compliance work. While the former is incorporated into the IFI's annual report, the latter is directed at specific issues of compliance.

## The Sharī'ah Resolution

**fatwa** (pl. *fatawa*)
Legal ruling or Sharī'ah resolution of a scholar or group of scholars on the Sharī'ah board of an Islamic financial institution.

As we saw earlier, the Sharī'ah board functionally reports directly to the BoD, as befits its independent status. To ensure a true and fair disclosure and transparency, accurate information on the status of certain procedures, services, and transactions must be made known to all the stakeholders. A fundamental requirement in Islamic financial transactions is proper documentation of contracts and processes.[10] This is a mandatory provision in the Qur'an (2:282), and is extended to the functions of the Sharī'ah board. The board must produce a Sharī'ah report periodically or annually to explain its position on the overall business and products of the IFI, and its legal ruling, or ***fatwa,*** on matters brought before it, such as proposed products and transactions. According to IFSB-10, the Sharī'ah report may be in any of the following forms:

1.  a fact-finding report

2.  (an *ex-ante*) report in relation to product design and development

3.  (an *ex-post*) internal Sharī'ah audit/review report on the products offered to customers

4.  an annual Sharī'ah compliance report. [11]

These reports have different purposes and are submitted to different bodies in the governance of the IFIs. The fact-finding reports and product design and development reports are submitted to the IFI's management. The internal Sharī'ah audit/review report on the products offered to customers is submitted to the audit committee. The annual Sharī'ah compliance report is submitted to the BoD, which distributes it to the shareholders at the AGM. Members of the public, including investment account holders (IAH), and the supervisory authority in the jurisdiction may also have access to this report.

The Sharī'ah resolutions and reports on IFIs that have been published serve as precedents for subsequent cases in those financial institutions. For example, the Kuwait Finance House has published the resolutions of the Sharī'ah board from its inception in 1977. In fact, some other IFIs have referred to those rulings in their deliberations. The most popular body whose Sharī'ah rulings have been widely distributed is the International Islamic Fiqh Academy of the OIC. Its rulings are authoritative and are widely quoted by Sharī'ah advisory services across the world.

# A Different Approach for Islamic Financial Institutions

Despite attempts by AAOIFI to introduce a universal standard for corporate governance in IFIs, diverse approaches are adopted in different jurisdictions. With the increasing number of IFIs now adopting AAOIFI's governance standards and IFSB 10, there will be a gradual drift towards unification of standards but some countries may still require their own governance standards. Those of the IFSB and AAOIFI are similar in many aspects and complement other prudential standards issued by the two standard-setting bodies and international standards of corporate governance. The existing international standard-setting bodies that have issued guidelines on corporate governance and risk management for financial institutions include the Organization for Economic Cooperation and Development (OECD), the International Organization of Securities Commissions (IOSCO) and the Basel Committee on Banking Supervision (BCBS). These standards do not address the specifics of the Islamic finance industry, hence the need to provide standards for Sharī'ah governance for IFIs. As most IFIs operate under the regulatory regimes and banking laws of their respective jurisdictions, the corporate standards of other countries are applicable to them provided they do not contradict the Sharī'ah. As we note in the *Global Islamic Finance* panel, the IFSB and AAOIFI standards are fundamentally Sharī'ah governance standards specifically meant for the IFIs, while it is implied that the IFIs already have a standard governance structure.

## Models of Sharī'ah from Selected Countries

Here we examine different approaches to Sharī'ah governance, with a view to establishing the common trends and local variations in selected countries that have unique guidelines for Sharī'ah governance.

# GLOBAL ISLAMIC FINANCE

The need to strengthen the corporate governance framework of IFIs introduced a new dimension in modern corporate governance. Sharī'ah governance was introduced to ensure the proper supervision and monitoring of Sharī'ah compliance of IFI products. This additional layer in the general corporate governance framework with particular reference to IFIs has helped consolidate the gains of the Islamic finance industry through product development and oversight functions in financial engineering. As Sharī'ah compliance is necessary throughout the product life cycle of every IFI, conflicts or differences of opinion among Sharī'ah scholars must be carefully managed and amicably resolved. While AAOIFI issued its governance standards on Sharī'ah supervisory boards, and Sharī'ah review, most jurisdictions around the world have yet to harmonize and streamline their Sharī'ah governance structure towards achieving a universally acceptable model. The challenges of harmonization of best practices often create problems for new jurisdictions that seek to join the global Islamic finance industry. Prudential regulation, supervision and governance of IFIs must follow a set of universally acceptable standards. The usual juristic dichotomy on Sharī'ah compliance for certain Islamic financial products does not necessarily come up in issues that relate to Sharī'ah governance. AAOIFI, as a leading international standard-setting body, should at least for now be regarded as a unifying body whose standards represent best practices in the industry. This does not preclude the

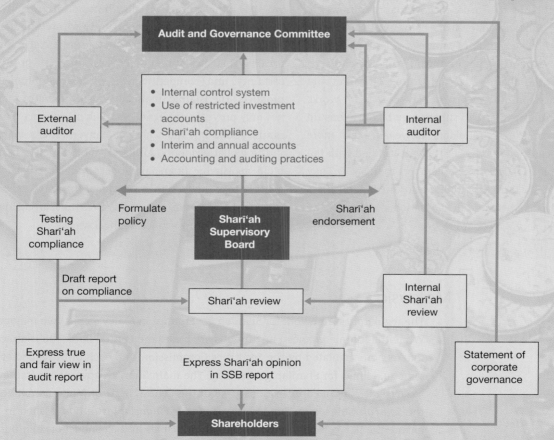

Figure source: Haniffa, R. (2010). *Islamic Finance: Instruments and Markets*. London: Bloomsbury Information Ltd: pp. 45–48

**GLOBAL ISLAMIC FINANCE (*continued*)**

powers of local regulatory bodies such as the central banks to issue directives to further clarify AAOIFI's standards through the process of domesticating them to suit the local needs of individual socioeconomic and regulatory frameworks. The complementary role of the Islamic Financial Services Board (IFSB) has further strengthened the global Sharī'ah governance framework of IFIs.

The key players in Sharī'ah governance and audit roles in IFIs do not pose any problem regarding the juristic differences occasionally experienced in substantial matters that relate to specific Islamic financial products. The diagram gives an insight into a typical structure in IFIs and the respective roles of key players in strengthening the corporate governance framework. While the Sharī'ah supervisory board is at the core of the corporate governance framework, major players in the governance structure include the shareholders, and the internal and external auditors. The audit and governance committee is part of the BoD and it works directly with the Sharī'ah supervisory board to ensure compliance. The shareholders, however, exert more power because in most cases they are saddled with the responsibility of appointing members to the BOD. They also verify the level of compliance of the IFI's business operations, as presented in the periodic reports of the Sharī'ah supervisory board.

Against this backdrop, the fortification of the global Islamic finance industry with particular reference to Sharī'ah governance requires progressive harmonization of Sharī'ah rulings and procedures of the IFI Sharī'ah supervisory boards. One positive step leads to another. When a new global model for Sharī'ah governance is introduced and accepted through effective domestication in most jurisdictions across the world, the process of harmonization will have been facilitated. As the ten leading Sharī'ah scholars occupy 39 percent of the available board positions around the world, it is expected that the process of harmonization of Sharī'ah rulings will be smooth. It may begin with the codification of universally acceptable principles, which may be compiled during a major stakeholders' meeting where leading Sharī'ah scholars from countries around the world will have the opportunity to present their views on salient governance and commercial issues for IFIs. This slick strategy is necessary to ensure the certainty and competitiveness of Islamic financial products. The Islamic financial services industry must not only prove its unfeigned Sharī'ah compliance in all ramifications but must also be conventionally viable in the global economy. All hands must be on deck to build an Islamic financial services industry that can contribute to the growth of the global economy and put in place the necessary shock absorbers that can cushion the effects of future economic shockwaves.

## Malaysia

The regulatory framework for Sharī'ah governance in Malaysia has two major aspects. While the Islamic financial institutions are under the Central Bank, the Islamic capital markets are regulated by the Securities Commission, and each of these bodies has its own guidelines for Sharī'ah governance. The main Sharī'ah governance framework in Malaysia is contained in sections 51-58 of the Central Bank of Malaysia Act 2009 and the *Sharī'ah Governance Framework for Islamic Financial Institutions* issued in 2010 to ensure the IFIs' compliance with Sharī'ah principles in the conduct of their businesses and services. This is aimed at harmonizing different Sharī'ah interpretations on Islamic financial issues to strengthen the regulatory and oversight framework. At the macro level is the Sharī'ah Advisory Council (SAC) of the Central Bank, which was established by virtue of section 51(1) of the Central Bank of Malaysia Act 2009.[12] The SAC is the highest authority for the ascertainment of Islamic law for the purpose of Islamic financial business. In more specific terms, SAC is the final authority in matters relating to:

- Islamic banking business
- *takaful* business
- Islamic financial business
- Islamic development financial business
- any other business based on Sharī'ah principles and supervised and regulated by the Central Bank of Malaysia.

Where there are disputes involving Sharī'ah issues in Islamic banking and finance and *takaful*, these are usually handled by the courts or special panels for resolving disputes through arbitration, known as **arbitration tribunals.** These are party-friendly and less formal than the normal court system and the parties are encouraged to settle the dispute amicably. Some issues may be referred to the SAC in disputes involving Sharī'ah issues in Islamic banking and finance, and *takaful*. In the case of an arbitration tribunal, a resolution from SAC is binding on the arbitrator. However, in a court case the SAC's resolution is taken into consideration and thus has a persuasive effect.[13] The banks and Islamic financial institutions can also refer matters relating to Islamic financial business to the SAC, which may be in form of requisition for a ruling or advice.[14]

At the micro level of Sharī'ah governance in Malaysia, Bank Negara Malaysia (BNM), also known as the Central Bank of Malaysia, issued the *Sharī'ah Governance Framework for Islamic Financial Institutions* in 2010, which provides that all Islamic banks, Islamic windows and *takaful* operators must have a Sharī'ah body known as a Sharī'ah committee. These committees play a complementary role to BNM's SAC. The duties and responsibilities of the Sharī'ah committee, according to the *Sharī'ah Governance Framework for Islamic Financial Institutions* are shown in Box 5.2.

**arbitration tribunals**
Special panels constituted to resolve a dispute through arbitration.

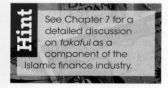

Hint

See Chapter 7 for a detailed discussion on *takaful* as a component of the Islamic finance industry.

Sharī'ah governance at Bank Negara Malaysia can be seen in its issuance of a framework that provides that all Islamic banks, Islamic windows and *takaful* operators must have a Sharī'ah body known as a Sharī'ah committee.

**BOX 5.2:** **DUTIES, RESPONSIBILITIES AND ACCOUNTABILITY OF THE SHARĪ'AH COMMITTEE ACCORDING TO THE *SHARĪ'AH GOVERNANCE FRAMEWORK FOR ISLAMIC FINANCIAL INSTITUTIONS***

1. **Responsibility and accountability**

   The Sharī'ah committee is expected to understand that in the course of discharging its duties and responsibilities, it is responsible and accountable for all Sharī'ah decisions, opinions, and views it provides.

2. **Advise the board and IFI**

   The Sharī'ah committee is expected to advise the board and provide input to the IFI on Sharī'ah matters in order for the IFI to comply with Sharī'ah principles at all times.

3. **Endorse Sharī'ah policies and procedures**

   The Sharī'ah committee is expected to endorse Sharī'ah policies and procedures prepared by the IFI and to ensure that the contents do not contain any elements not in line with the Sharī'ah.

4. **Endorse and validate relevant documentations**

   To ensure that the IFI's products comply with Sharī'ah principles, the Sharī'ah committee must approve:

   (a) the terms and conditions contained in the forms, contracts, agreements, or other legal documentation used in executing the transactions, and

   (b) the product manual, marketing advertisements, sales illustrations, and brochures used to describe the product.

5. **Assess work carried out by Sharī'ah reviews and audits**

   To assess the work carried out by Sharī'ah reviews and audits in order to ensure compliance with Sharī'ah matters. This forms part of its duties in providing an assessment of Sharī'ah compliance and assurance information in the annual report.

6. **Assist related parties on Sharī'ah matters**

   The related parties of the IFI such as its legal counsel, auditors, or consultants may seek advice on Sharī'ah matters from the Sharī'ah committee, which is expected to provide the necessary assistance to the requesting party.

7. **Advise on matters to be referred to the SAC**

   The Sharī'ah committee may advise the IFI to consult the SAC on Sharī'ah matters that could not be resolved.

8. **Provide written Sharī'ah opinions**

   The Sharī'ah committee is required to provide written Sharī'ah opinions in circumstances where the IFI makes reference to the SAC for further deliberation, or where the IFI submits applications to the bank for new product approval.

Source: *Sharī'ah Governance Framework for Islamic Financial Institutions*, 2010, pp. 34-35. Available at www.bnm.gov.my/guidelines/05_shariah/02_Shariah_Governance_Framework_20101026.pdf.

To ensure the transparency, accountability, and maximum independence of the members of the SAC and Sharī'ah committees of IFIs, certain legal restrictions have been imposed. No IFI is allowed to appoint a member of the SAC to serve on its Sharī'ah committee. Furthermore to avoid conflicts of interest and ensure confidentiality in the industry, a Sharī'ah advisor can serve as a member of the Sharī'ah committee of only one IFI in the same industry (see the Sharī'ah governance framework of BNM in Figure 5.2).[15]

Where there is conflict between the ruling given at the micro level by an IFI's Sharī'ah committee and the ruling given at the macro level by the SAC, the ruling of SAC prevails.[16] The model structure for the key bodies in the Sharī'ah governance framework for IFIs proposed by BNM is a comprehensive model worth emulating in the global Islamic finance industry. As illustrated in Figure 5.3, the model provides for the roles, functions, and relationship among those key bodies.

However, the Sharī'ah governance framework of the Islamic capital market (ICM) in Malaysia has different guidelines. The ICM has a two-tiered system consisting of the Sharī'ah Advisory Council of the Securities Commission (SAC of SC) at the macro level and Sharī'ah advisors at the micro level. The SAC of SC was established in 1996 to advise the Securities Commission on Sharī'ah matters pertaining to ICM. With the recent amendments introduced by the Capital Markets and Services Act 2010 (CMSA), the SAC of SC is established by virtue of section 316A of the CMSA. The functions of the SAC of SC are[17]:

1. To ascertain the application of Sharī'ah principles on any matter pertaining to Islamic capital market business or transactions and issue a ruling upon reference made to it in accordance with this division (Islamic Capital Market Division).

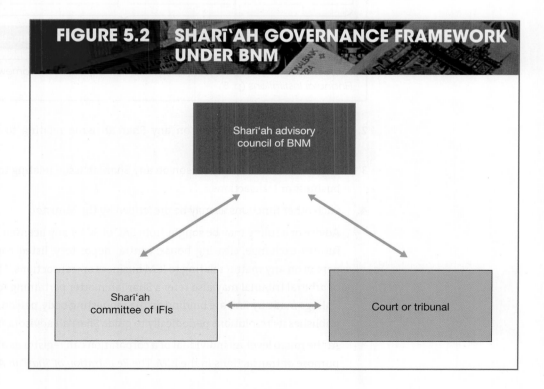

**FIGURE 5.2    SHARĪ'AH GOVERNANCE FRAMEWORK UNDER BNM**

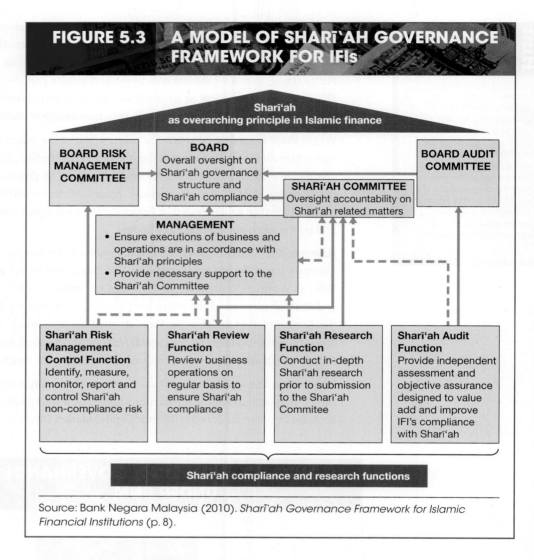

**FIGURE 5.3  A MODEL OF SHARĪʿAH GOVERNANCE FRAMEWORK FOR IFIs**

Source: Bank Negara Malaysia (2010). *Sharīʿah Governance Framework for Islamic Financial Institutions* (p. 8).

2.  To advise the commission on any Sharīʿah issue relating to Islamic capital market business or transactions.

3   To provide advice to any person on any Sharīʿah issue relating to Islamic capital market business or transactions.

4.  Such other functions as may be prescribed by the Minister.

Advice or a ruling may be sought from SAC of SC by any licensed person, stock exchange, futures exchange, clearing house, central depository, listed corporation, or any other person on any matter relating to ICM business or transactions.[18] In a similar vein, a court or arbitral tribunal may also refer a Sharīʿah matter pertaining to ICM to the SAC of SC.[19] Rulings made by SAC are binding on the requesting body, person, or firm.[20] The SAC of SC publishes its resolutions periodically to guide Sharīʿah advisors, investors and the public.

At the micro level, an individual or a corporation can register as a Sharīʿah advisor for the purpose of transactions in the ICM. The *Registration of Sharīʿah Advisors Guidelines* of SC

(RSAG), issued on 10 August 2009, provides that anybody who seeks advice on the issuance of Sharīʿah-based products or services, such as unit trust funds, real estate investment trusts, exchange-traded funds, wholesale funds, Islamic securities or bonds known as *sukuk*, asset-backed securities, structured products, and stockbroking services, must be registered as a Sharīʿah advisor.[21] The qualification for individuals seeking to become Sharīʿah advisors is a minimum of a degree in Sharīʿah, particularly in *fiqh al-muʿamalat* and Islamic jurisprudence, with a minimum of two years of relevant experience and/ or exposure in Islamic finance. Alternatively, an individual may have at least one year of relevant experience and/or exposure in Islamic finance and have attended at least five Islamic finance courses/workshops. An applicant that is a corporation must employ at least one full-time officer to be responsible for Sharīʿah matters for the products and services of ICM. A Sharīʿah officer who is an employee of the corporation must also satisfy the requirements mentioned above for the individual qualification.[22] The corporation does not need to register with the SC for the purpose of Sharīʿah advisory and consultancy on ICM products and services, but must ensure that at least one of its members meets the individual requirements for Sharīʿah advisors.[23] Where there is a conflict between a ruling given at the micro level by a registered Sharīʿah advisor and a ruling at the macro level of the SAC of SC, the ruling of the latter holds.[24]

## Pakistan

The Sharīʿah governance model in Pakistan also has two tiers, with some variations compared to the Malaysian practice. The State Bank of Pakistan (SPB) has established a Sharīʿah board at the macro level for advisory purposes in matters relating to Islamic banking and financial transactions. This board is the sole and highest authority in matters pertaining to Islamic finance. It advises the SPB on the formulation of regulations for Islamic banking and finance. With a minimum of five members, the Sharīʿah board is composed of experts drawn from different fields such as Sharīʿah, law, banking, accounting, and other relevant fields. The roles and responsibilities of the Sharīʿah board are as follows.

1. Review and approve for Sharīʿah compliance the products/instruments developed by the State Bank of Pakistan for conducting its central banking and monetary management functions under the Islamic modes.

2. Advise the State Bank of Pakistan on prudential regulations developed for the Islamic banking sector.

3. Approve the fit and proper criteria for the appointment of Sharīʿah advisors of institutions conducting Islamic banking activities.

4. Advise the State Bank on the Sharīʿah ruling in case of conflicts arising from Sharīʿah audits of the Islamic banking activities of the banks under the supervisory control of the State Bank.

5. Advise the State Bank on the Sharīʿah rulings in cases of conflicting Sharīʿah opinions on Islamic banking products.

6. Perform other functions that may be assigned from time to time, by the State Bank, to facilitate the smooth functioning of the Islamic financial system.[25]

The decisions or resolutions of the Sharī'ah Board of SBP are binding on all IFIs in the country. Although there is no specific legal cover through statutory provisions for the powers conferred on the Sharī'ah board, it is hoped that in future when the banking law is revised, these will be incorporated into law.

At the micro level, all IFIs operating in Pakistan are required to appoint a Sharī'ah advisor. The BoD is the body vested with the power to appoint the Sharī'ah advisor for domestic IFIs. For foreign banks with branches in Pakistan, the management may appoint the Sharī'ah advisor. Before such appointment can take effect, prior written approval from the SBP is required. The IFI will then appoint a Sharī'ah advisor for a renewable term of three years. In essence, the rulings or resolution of the Sharī'ah advisor in all financial matters are binding on the IFI. However, in any matter referred to them by the BoD or management, they may advise or issue guidelines. The duties and responsibilities of the Sharī'ah advisor (SA) are as follows.

1.  Ensure that all products, services, related policies, and agreements of IFIs are in compliance with Sharī'ah rules and principles. Before launching any new products and services, the related policies and agreements must be vetted by the SA, who, in coordination with management, also conducts/arranges Sharī'ah training programs for the IFI's staff. They prepare a report for the bank's annual financial statement in respect of its Sharī'ah compliance, the details of which are provided in Para C (of the SA's report).

2.  Have access to all records, documents, and information from all sources including professional advisors and IFI employees. Management is responsible for providing all information relating to the IFI's compliance with Sharī'ah.

3.  Review operations of the IFI periodically in coordination with officials responsible for Sharī'ah compliance to ensure that all the products and services offered by the IFI conform to the injunctions of the Sharī'ah. If the SA declares any income as non-compliant, it shall be credited to a charity account opened for this purpose.

4.  Provide advice to the legal counsel, auditor, or consultant of an IFI seeking guidance on Sharī'ah matters.

5.  Their decisions and rulings shall be subject to instructions, guidelines, and directives issued by SBP Sharī'ah board from time to time, notwithstanding anything contained in the instructions and guidelines for Sharī'ah compliance in IFIs.

The SPB's Sharī'ah board resolves differences of opinion on Sharī'ah issues involving Islamic banking practices between an IFI's Sharī'ah advisor and the inspection staff of the SPB or any of its departments. The decision of the SPB Sharī'ah board supersedes any ruling or resolution of other boards, as it is considered final. It is also possible for IFIs to refer any issue relating to Sharī'ah compliance directly to the SBP for the Sharī'ah board's consideration.

In situations where there is a difference of opinion on a Sharī'ah principle between an IFI and its Sharī'ah advisor, this is often resolved by referring such issue to the BoD's audit committee. Where the audit committee cannot resolve the issue it may be referred to the Sharī'ah board of the SPB for a final decision. Unlike in Malaysia, any member of the

SPB's Sharī'ah board can serve as a Sharī'ah advisor to an IFI, but can only serve one IFI at any one time.

## Kuwait

Kuwait has a different Sharī'ah governance framework compared to Malaysia and Pakistan. There is provision for Sharī'ah boards in IFIs, but no Sharī'ah board at the macro level at the Central Bank of Kuwait (CBK). However, there is a *fatwa* board in the Ministry of Awqaf and Islamic Affairs, which is considered as the final authority on matters relating to Islamic banking business and financial transactions.[26] The Sharī'ah governance framework is regulated by Article 93 of the CBK Law, which requires all IFIs to establish an independent Sharī'ah board appointed by the general assembly of the IFI. This means that the BoD does not have a role in the appointment of members of the Sharī'ah supervisory board. This can only be done at the AGM, with all stakeholders involved. The establishment of the Sharī'ah board, its formulation, powers, and workings must be clearly stated in the memorandum of agreement and the articles of association of the IFIs and there must be a minimum of three members at any given time.[27]

When there is a conflict of opinion among the members of the Sharī'ah board concerning a ruling, the BoD may refer the matter to the *fatwa* board although this is not compulsory for all issues. The *fatwa* board is considered as the final authority but it is independent of the CBK, which makes this Sharī'ah governance framework different from the models in Malaysia and Pakistan. The CBK Law does not cover the *fatwa* board rulings and whether they are binding or merely persuasive. There is no restriction on the number of members on the *fatwa* board and no legal restriction on those members serving on the Sharī'ah board of any IFI. In addition, there is no limitation on a member of the Sharī'ah board serving on more than one IFI.

The Sharī'ah board submits its report annually to the AGM as part of the IFI's annual report. The report usually contains its opinion on the IFI's operations with special reference to Sharī'ah compliance. The report is circulated to all stakeholders at the AGM to afford them the opportunity to appraise the level of Sharī'ah compliance.

## Bahrain

The Bahraini Sharī'ah governance framework is similar to the models in Malaysia and Pakistan with a two-tiered hierarchical system but some element of variation at the macro level. The Central Bank of Bahrain (CBB) established the National Sharī'ah Advisory Board to serve and verify Sharī'ah compliance of its own products only. The National Sharī'ah Advisory Board has no authority over IFIs operating in the country. There is no legal restriction on any member of the National Sharī'ah Advisory Board serving on the Sharī'ah supervisory board of any IFI and none on any Sharī'ah scholar serving on more than one Sharī'ah board.

At the micro level, all IFIs are required to establish a Sharī'ah supervisory committee, which must comply with AAOIFI's governance standards for IFIs No. 1 and No. 2.[28] Principle 9 of *The Corporate Governance Code of the Kingdom of Bahrain* emphasizes that companies that are guided by Islamic principles have additional responsibilities to their stakeholders to assure them that the company is following the Sharīʿah. To ensure compliance, every company should establish a Sharīʿah advisory committee composed of at least three Sharīʿah scholars.[29] This has been extended to IFIs through paragraph HC-9.2.1 of the CBB Rule Book, volume 2, Part A, High-level Control on Islamic Banks. IFIs are also required to have separate Sharīʿah reviews for the purpose of ensuring compliance. These are expected to be carried out in accordance with the AAOIFI governance standard No. 3. Generally, the Sharīʿah review or audit is carried out by personnel in the internal audit department.[30]

## United Arab Emirates

With the exception of Dubai, the Sharīʿah governance system of the United Arab Emirates (UAE) is governed by Federal Law No. 6 of 1985, where Article 5 provides for the establishment of a Higher Sharīʿah Authority to supervise Islamic banks, financial institutions, and investment companies at the macro level. This body is established under the Ministry of Justice and Islamic Affairs. The Authority is accorded the final authority in Sharīʿah matters pertaining to Islamic banking and finance. Its resolutions are binding on all IFIs operating in the country. The Sharīʿah advisors of the Authority are appointed by the government. A recent and welcome development in UAE is a private initiative by Sharīʿah scholars who voluntarily came together to establish a central committee of the Sharīʿah supervisory board for the purpose of harmonization, standardization, and consistency of their rulings and Sharīʿah practice generally. Currently, their resolutions are persuasive rather than binding.

At the micro level, Article 6 of the Federal Law requires all IFIs to establish a Sharīʿah supervision authority, or simply a Sharīʿah board, which should be clearly stipulated in an IFI's articles and memorandum of association, plus the manner of governance and its specific duties, including the method of appointment, functions, and responsibilities. Similar to AAOIFI's Sharīʿah governance standards, the Sharīʿah board must be composed of a minimum of three members, who are appointed by the BoD or the AGM. Proposed members must, prior to their appointment, be approved by the Higher Sharīʿah Authority.

Dubai has a different arrangement because of its unique legal framework, which established the Dubai International Finance Centre (DIFC). All IFIs must register with the DIFC and comply with the law and its regulations. IFIs are regulated under the Law Regulating Islamic Financial Business DFIC Law, No. 13 of 2004 and the DIFC Services Authority (DFSA) Rulebook on Islamic Financial Business Module (ISF). Section 13 of the Law requires IFIs to establish a Sharīʿah board but the DFSA has the power to make rules prescribing the appointment, formation, conduct, and operation of the Sharīʿah board and its members. To this end, the requirements of the Sharīʿah governance system of DFIC for IFIs registered under it are specified in the ISF. The DFSA requires all IFIs to adopt the AAOIFI governance standards for the purpose of consistency in compliance with Sharīʿah rules. In the light of this, IFI Sharīʿah boards should be composed of at least three competent members, who are appointed by the IFI's governing body.[31] As the meaning of 'governing body' may be subjectively interpreted to suit the needs of individual IFIs, in practice some Sharīʿah board members are appointed by the BoD and some IFIs allow the AGM to appoint them. There is no restriction on members of one Sharīʿah board serving on another at a different IFI, but they are restricted from serving as directors or controllers of the IFIs they serve to avoid conflicts of interest.

## Qatar

The general practice in Qatar is self-regulation, as in Kuwait. At the macro level, there is no Sharī'ah advisory board at the Qatar Central Bank (QCB) but there is a Supreme Sharī'ah Council attached to the Ministry of Awqaf. The Supreme Sharī'ah Council is the highest body and is responsible for all Sharī'ah matters including Islamic finance. Any IFI can direct any issue to the Council for clarification. The QCB only appoints Sharī'ah scholars to solve any problem encountered on a case-by-case basis. They do not constitute a permanent committee or council but only undertake such duties on an ad hoc basis.

At the micro level, there are two major regulatory frameworks for Sharī'ah governance in IFIs, namely those of the QCB and the Qatar Financial Centre (QFC).[32] The QFC also has no Sharī'ah board. For proper supervision and regulation of the banking sector, the QCB issued the prudential regulation for banking supervision in March 2009 known as Instructions to Banks (Instructions).[33] Part Seven of the instructions provides specific guidelines for IFIs. Paragraph 1 of Section D, Chapter 1 of the instructions provides that all Islamic banks operating in Qatar should establish a Sharī'ah board consisting of not less than two qualified Muslim members. Members are to be appointed by the BoD and approved by the AGM. The Sharī'ah board has the power to oversee and approve all Islamic products and services, and all contracts and documentation. IFIs are also required to adopt the AAOIFI governance standards.

The QFC Regulatory Authority periodically issues the Islamic Finance Rule Book, the latest version being ISFI 2009 (ISFI).[34] Chapter six provides for the appointment and operation of the Sharī'ah supervisory board, Sharī'ah reviews and internal Sharī'ah audits. The ISFI requires IFIs to establish a Sharī'ah board with a minimum of three members to be appointed by their governing authority. IFIs must appoint persons who are competent to perform their functions as Sharī'ah supervisory board members, taking into account their qualifications and previous experience in the Islamic finance industry. No member of the Sharī'ah supervisory board is allowed to simultaneously serve as a director or controller of the IFI.[35] The Sharī'ah review is carried out in accordance with the AAOIFI Sharī'ah governance standards.[36] Under both the QCB and QFC regulatory frameworks, there is no restriction on Sharī'ah advisors becoming a member of a Sharī'ah board in more than one IFI.

## United Kingdom

The Sharī'ah governance system for Islamic financial institutions in the UK is a one-tier system, and there is no centralized Sharī'ah authority at the national level. Individual IFIs have their own unique Sharī'ah supervisory committee, which is the final authority. There is no legal restriction on the powers of the Sharī'ah supervisory committee. Thus, in the absence of any centralized regulation, individual IFIs are free to develop their Sharī'ah governance systems.

### Challenge

Which do you prefer—a centralized Sharī'ah governance framework like that of Malaysia or an individual framework like that of the United Kingdom?

As most members of the Sharī'ah supervisory committees of leading IFIs are internationally recognized Sharī'ah scholars who also sit on the AAOIFI Sharī'ah board, the Sharī'ah governance system follows AAOIFI standards. In general, the trend is for many of the IFIs to adop AAOIFI and IFSB standards in structuring their Sharī'ah governance system.

Table 5.2 gives a general summary of the Sharī'ah governance frameworks in Malaysia, Pakistan, Kuwait, UAE, Bahrain, Qatar, and the United Kingdom.

| **TABLE 5.2: Summary of the Sharī'ah Governance System in Selected Countries** | | | | | |
|---|---|---|---|---|---|
| **Country** | **Sharī'ah Authority** | | **Governance System** | **Final Authority** | **Restriction** |
| | **Central Bank** | **IFI** | | | |
| **Malaysia** | SAC | SC | Two-tier | SAC | 1. Members of SAC cannot serve on the SC of IFIs.<br>2. One SA can only serve one IFI in the same industry (banking and *takaful*) |
| **Pakistan** | SB | SA | Two-tier | SB | 1. Members of SB can serve IFIs.<br>2. One SA can only serve one IFI (no industrial categorization of banking and *takaful*) |
| **Kuwait** | N/A | SSB | One-tier | FB | No legal restrictions |
| **UAE**<br>Dubai only | HSA<br>N/A | SSA<br>SB | Two-tier<br>One-tier | HSA<br>SB | SAs are restricted from serving as directors or controllers of IFIs they serve in |
| **Bahrain** | NSB | SSC | Two-tier | NSB | No legal restrictions |
| **Qatar** | N/A | SSB | One-tier | SSC | No legal restrictions |
| **United Kingdom** | N/A | SSC | One-tier | SB | No legal restrictions |

**Legend**

**SAC**: Sharī'ah Advisory Council      **SB**: Sharī'ah Board

**SSB**: Sharī'ah Supervisory Board      **SSC**: Sharī'ah Supervisory Committee

**NSB**: National Sharī'ah Board      **HSA**: Higher Sharī'ah Authority

**SSA**: Sharī'ah Supervisory Authority      **SC**: Sharī'ah Committee

**SA**: Sharī'ah Advisor

**FB**: Fatwa Board of the Ministry of Awqaf and Islamic Affairs

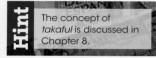

The concept of *takaful* is discussed in Chapter 8.

# Corporate Governance for Islamic Insurance

Islamic insurance (*takaful*) is part of the Islamic financial services industry. However, because of its unique nature and the need to ensure adequate Sharī'ah compliance and protection of all stakeholders' interests, separate guidelines are provided for the governance of Islamic insurance operations. This specific benchmark is necessary because of the general nature of the insurance industry and the influence of conventional insurance practice. To this end, the Sharī'ah governance framework for Islamic insurance plays a more significant role compared to other Islamic financial services. Effective Sharī'ah and corporate governance in the Islamic insurance industry ensures uniformity and standardization of prudent practices, including the harmonization of Sharī'ah rulings. The strong Sharī'ah framework complements existing corporate governance to enhance consumer confidence and create an enabling environment for flexibility on the part of *takaful* operators to innovate within the parameters of Sharī'ah standards.

**maslahah mursalah**
A branch of the secondary sources of the Sharī'ah, which means unrestricted or unregulated public interest, that is in full harmony with the letter and spirit of the Sharī'ah. An example of *maslahah mursalah* is the publication of the financial report of an Islamic bank bearing the endorsement of the Sharī'ah board.

The governance policies in internationally recognized frameworks for the insurance industry are not necessarily irrelevant to the discussion of an appropriate model for the Islamic insurance industry. This is what the IFSB undertook while preparing the guiding principles on governance for *takaful* corporate entities. The principle of **maslahah mursalah** (unrestricted public interest) allows for the adaptation of some principles and concepts that are in line with the objectives of Islamic law into the corpus of the Sharī'ah. This is one of the methods adopted by IFSB in the preparation of its standards. Therefore, all relevant principles in internationally recognized models, such as those of the International Association of Insurance Supervisors (IAIS), agree with the rules of Sharī'ah. While addressing the specifics of Islamic insurance undertaking, all relevant good governance practices in other international models for insurance companies are closely considered. In other words, IAIS's core principles of corporate governance that agree with the objectives of the Sharī'ah should be adapted in addition to the unique Sharī'ah governance principles to create a strong framework for *takaful* operators.

According to the IFSB, good corporate governance within the context of *takaful* should encompass the following three major requirements.

1. A set of organizational arrangements whereby the actions of the management of *takaful* operators are aligned, as far as possible, with the interests of its stakeholders.

2. Provision of proper incentives for governance bodies such as the BoD, the Sharī'ah supervisory board and management to pursue objectives that are in the interests of their stakeholders and facilitate effective monitoring, thus encouraging *takaful* operators to use resources more efficiently.

3. Compliance with Sharī'ah rules and principles.[37]

These three major requirements cover Sharī'ah and corporate governance, which are the two major aspects of corporate governance in Islamic financial services. *Takaful* operators must implement policies that agree with the interests of all stakeholders in the industry.

In order to achieve this, proper governance and control structures must be put in place. These structures must be empowered and granted some degree of independence to be able to develop stakeholder-oriented policies in line with the principles of public interest (*maslahah*) that will benefit all stakeholders involved in *takaful*, which has more interested parties or stakeholders than other Islamic financial services. Their interests must be recognized and protected collectively through policies and necessary Sharī'ah governance. Compliance with the Sharī'ah rules and principles is ensured and sustained through an independent Sharī'ah supervisory board whose rulings should be binding on the management of the *takaful* business.

## IFSB Guiding Principles on Governance for *Takaful* Undertakings

The *IFSB Guiding Principles on Governance for Takaful (Islamic Insurance) Undertakings* were released in December 2009. These are meant to promote the soundness and stability of the *takaful* industry, which is an important segment of the Islamic finance industry. The IFSB developed these important standards and guidelines to reflect best practices around the world while maintaining the Sharī'ah-compliance aspect. The objectives of the IFSB guiding principles are to:

1. provide benchmarks for use by *takaful* supervisors when adapting and improving regulatory regimes or, where necessary, establishing new ones

2. address regulatory issues, such as risk management and financial stability, for the *takaful* industry

3. provide appropriate levels of consumer protection in terms of both risk and disclosure

4. support the orderly development of the *takaful* industry in terms of acceptable business and operational models, and the design and marketing of *takaful* products.[38]

Such benchmarks are necessary in a business environment to ensure standard practices. As there are different models of *takaful* undertakings, it is imperative to consider the governance issues in order to effectively understand the contractual rights and obligations of all stakeholders. These prudential standards as well as optimal Sharī'ah governance are necessary for the growth and development of the *takaful* industry. The IFSB guiding principles are in three parts.

- PART I: Reinforcement of relevant good governance practices as prescribed in other relevant internationally recognized governance standards for insurance companies, while addressing the specificities of *takaful* undertakings.
- PART II: A balanced approach that considers the interests of all stakeholders and calls for their fair treatment.
- PART III: An impetus for a more comprehensive prudential framework for *takaful* undertakings.[39]

Each part has two core principles of corporate governance meant to establish specific standards for *takaful* undertakings (a summary of each part is shown in Figure 5.4), and recommendations for sound corporate governance practices in the *takaful* industry.

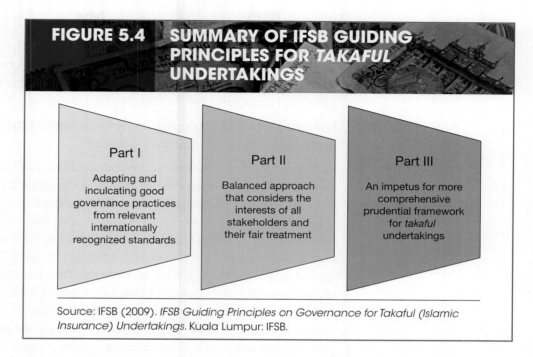

FIGURE 5.4    SUMMARY OF IFSB GUIDING PRINCIPLES FOR *TAKAFUL* UNDERTAKINGS

**Part I**

Adapting and inculcating good governance practices from relevant internationally recognized standards

**Part II**

Balanced approach that considers the interests of all stakeholders and their fair treatment

**Part III**

An impetus for more comprehensive prudential framework for *takaful* undertakings

Source: IFSB (2009). *IFSB Guiding Principles on Governance for Takaful (Islamic Insurance) Undertakings.* Kuala Lumpur: IFSB.

## Part I: Adaptation of Existing Good Governance Standards

As we have seen, good governance from the Islamic perspective has been in existence since the advent of Islam but has not been codified in a systematized manner. The need to develop standards for corporate entities began about three decades ago and efforts were made to codify standards for best practices to guide corporate entities. Specific standards were developed by the IAIS for conventional insurance companies. A number of those standards are compatible with the general spirit of Islamic law and have been assimilated into the IFSB guiding principles. These prudential and supervisory standards are specifically meant to safeguard the interests of all stakeholders in *takaful* undertakings. The applicability of the existing IAIS core principles to the regulatory and supervisory standards for *takaful* business was first examined to streamline the process of developing acceptable standards in the global *takaful* industry.

**Hint**

This part is based on the premise that the specificities of *takaful* undertakings are addressed while reinforcing relevant good governance practices.

The importance of good governance in securing and preserving public confidence is paramount in *takaful* undertakings and is one reason why separate guidelines were issued for the industry. Effective governance structures and processes need not only to be transparent but also emphasize accountability. In line with existing international standards, IFSB issued its guidelines in the belief that no single model of corporate governance can work well for every country and in all types of business, hence the need to harness relevant good governance practices and adapt them to the specificities of *takaful* undertakings. Even within the scope of Islamic financial services, the corporate governance model for other Islamic financial institutions may not be suitable. As *takaful* undertakings are not the same as those of conventional insurance, the relevant good governance practices of the IAIS and OECD can only be reinforced while addressing the specificities of *takaful* business.[40]

The two core principles in Part I are as follows.

PRINCIPLE 1.1: *Takaful* operators must manage a comprehensive governance framework appropriate for their business models, in which the independence and integrity of each organ of governance is well defined and preserved, and the mechanisms for proper control and management of conflicts of interest clearly set out.[41]

PRINCIPLE 1.2: *Takaful* operators must adopt an appropriate code of ethics and conduct to be complied with by their officials at all levels.[42]

Under Principle 1.1, the relevant international standards have been adapted to the *takaful* industry to establish a comprehensive governance framework. The powers of each organ of governance and the stakeholders are clearly defined to avoid conflicts of interest. These vary depending on the model of *takaful* being operated. In a *mudarabah* model, the *mudarib* is the *takaful* operator who administers the fund as its custodian. and their fees or commission are remunerated through the *wakalah* model. The operator is appointed by the shareholders but in some cases there is conflict between the interests of the shareholders and those of the *takaful* participants. We'll discuss this in more detail in the next subsection. For a proper governance framework, the most important thing to observe, as recommended by IFSB, is to clearly set out and document the following in the memorandum and articles of association of the firm at inception.

1. Clear identification and segregation of strategic and operational roles and responsibilities for each organ of governance, including but not limited to the board of directors and its committees, the management, Sharī'ah governance function (whether in the form of a Sharī'ah supervisory board, or a Sharī'ah advisory firm, as the case may be), as well as the internal and external auditors.

2. Mechanisms for observing and addressing the rights and interests of all stakeholders, as well as the reporting lines and accountabilities of each organ of governance.

3. A compliance mechanism for underwriting and investment activities in accordance with the legal and regulatory frameworks applicable in their respective jurisdictions.[43]

Principle 1.2 provides for the adherence to a professional code of ethics and appropriate business conduct in the observance of fiduciary duties by all parties involved in the governance and control of *takaful* undertakings. Fiduciary duties are specific professional duties that involve trust and confidence. The core principles must be explained to prospective participants and their interests, whether short term or long term, must be protected at all times. *Takaful* operators must be diligent in their duties. There should be necessary mechanisms to monitor compliance with the core principles, as any misconduct or misbehavior must be dealt with accordingly.

## Part II: Balanced Approach: Consideration of the Interests of All Stakeholders

Balancing the interests of all the stakeholders and according fair treatment to them is paramount in the corporate governance policy of any *takaful* undertaking. *Takaful* operators, as the main management organ, must adopt this balanced approach to avoid unnecessary conflicts of interest. The major two stakeholders in the *takaful* operator's

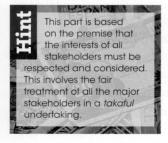
**Hint** This part is based on the premise that the interests of all stakeholders must be respected and considered. This involves the fair treatment of all the major stakeholders in a *takaful* undertaking.

business are the shareholders and the participants. A fairly balanced approach is taken where due attention is given to participants while seeking to create value for shareholders.

Such a balanced system can be achieved where all the governance structures and processes adequately represent the interests of all stakeholders. Principles of transparency and accountability require that an enabling environment for free and fair access to relevant information should be created for all stakeholders. Both shareholders and participants should be duly represented on the board as well as in all general meetings of the corporate firm. To ensure the practicability of these standards, Part II has the following principles.

PRINCIPLE 2.1: *Takaful* operators shall have in place an appropriate governance structure that represents the rights and interests of *takaful* participants.[44]

PRINCIPLE 2.2: *Takaful* operators shall adopt and implement procedures for appropriate disclosures that provide *takaful* participants with fair access to material and relevant information.[45]

The first principle emphasizes the rights and interests of the participants. An appropriate governance structure may include board representation, representation on committees, management of *takaful* undertakings, internal audits, and Sharī'ah governance and should reconcile and align shareholders' and participants' incentives to achieve the overall mission of the company. Protecting the rights and interests of stakeholders, particularly participants, involves the appointment of a recognized specialist and professional to evaluate and analyze risks, insurance and annuity premiums, reserves, and dividends. This person is known as an **actuary**, and it is their job to evaluate and analyze the risks faced by the *takaful* undertakings. To resolve conflicts of interest, the IFSB proposes a governance committee responsible for implementing the governance framework through the induction of all stakeholders. For instance, the committee may comprise an independent non-executive director (selected for their experience and ability to contribute), a Sharī'ah scholar (possibly from the *takaful* operator's Sharī'ah supervisory board), and an actuary.[46] The option of a representative of the participants on the committee would give it insight into participants' interests. According to the IFSB guidelines, the objectives of the governance committee should be as follows.

**actuary**
A recognized specialist and professional in the evaluation and analysis of risks, insurance and annuity premiums, reserves, and dividends.

1. Developing and recommending to the board of directors a set of effective corporate governance policies and procedures applicable to the *takaful* undertaking, including the formulation of appropriate business conduct and ethics codes for employees and agents.

2. Developing and recommending to the board of directors the additional governance structure and processes applicable to the *takaful* operator, and reviewing and reassessing their effectiveness.

3. Overseeing and monitoring the implementation of the governance policy framework by working with management, the audit committee, and the Sharī'ah supervisory board.

4. Monitoring the financial management of the *takaful* undertaking, particularly with respect to reserving and distribution of underwriting and/or investment profit.

5. Providing the board of directors with reports and recommendations based on its findings in exercising its functions.[47]

Necessary measures must be taken to avoid any conflict of roles and functions between the governance committee and the BOD. Duplication of roles and functions must be avoided through clear demarcation. The principal function of the governance committee is to find an appropriate balance in addressing the interest of all stakeholders, particularly participants, who are usually underrepresented in the governance structure.

Principle 2.2 provides for appropriate disclosure of and access to information, which are key elements of transparency and accountability. Participants can only have confidence in the management if they are provided with fair access to material and relevant information, which should be readily accessible to stakeholders to satisfy the requirements of best practice in corporate governance. Reliable disclosure will promote a long-term relationship based on the confidence and trust of participants towards the *takaful* undertaking and the operator. Regardless of the model adopted, strict compliance with international standards of accounting, auditing, and disclosure is necessary.

## Part III: A Comprehensive Prudential Framework for *Takaful* Undertakings

Part III has two core principles on the need for an impetus to provide a more comprehensive prudential framework for *takaful* undertakings. This implies that beyond the principles in the IFSB guidelines on corporate governance, other related guidelines and standards should be consulted for proper corporate governance. A comprehensive and hybridized prudential framework, which brings to the fore other appropriate standards and guidelines that include solvency, financial and prudential regulation, transparency and disclosure, conduct of business and the supervisory review process, is required.[48]

The two core principles in Part III are as follows.

PRINCIPLE 3.1: *Takaful* operators shall ensure that they have in place appropriate mechanisms properly to sustain the solvency of *takaful* undertakings.[49]

PRINCIPLE 3.2: *Takaful* operators shall adopt and implement a sound investment strategy and prudently manage the assets and liabilities of *takaful* undertakings.[50]

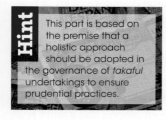

**Hint**
This part is based on the premise that a holistic approach should be adopted in the governance of *takaful* undertakings to ensure prudential practices.

Principle 3.1 provides that sustainability in terms of the solvency of *takaful* undertakings is required through appropriate mechanisms. This is fundamentally directed at protecting the interest of the participants. *Takaful* undertakings are encouraged to subscribe to a *retakaful* scheme that suits its primary requirements to avoid unnecessary loss. That is, instead of using conventional reinsurance schemes, *retakaful* operators who are Sharī'ah-compliant should be used to promote a sound and stable Sharī'ah-compliant financial system. Internal controls and risk management bodies should be strengthened by the BOD and governance committee. These measures should ensure a sound and stable business environment for the *takaful* undertakings.

Principle 3.2 provides for a sound investment strategy and prudent management of the assets and liabilities of the *takaful* undertakings. For sound corporate governance, the operator should adopt and implement these strategies in the interest of all the stakeholders. In terms of investments, there should be a standard process for the selection and purification of assets to achieve the desired level of Sharīʿah compliance. There should be an appropriate governance structure for the review of investment portfolios to ensure maximum compliance with Sharīʿah requirements and any rulings issued by the Sharīʿah board.

# Review

## Key Terms and Concepts

actuary (p. 207)

Anglo-American model (p. 173)

arbitration tribunals (p. 193)

corporate governance (p. 170)

*fiqh* (p. 183)

Franco-German model (p. 173)

*fatwa* (p. 189)

*hisbah* (p. 182)

*maslahah mursalah* (p. 203)

*muhtasib* (p. 183)

Sharīʿah compliance (p. 172)

Sharīʿah governance (p. 171)

Sharīʿah supervisory board (p. 172)

shura (p. 175)

## Summary

**Learning Objective 5.1**

1. The concept of corporate governance, although it has been part of Islamic law of transactions for centuries, has crystallized with the issuance of principles and guidelines to guide modern Islamic financial institutions. The Islamic perspective on corporate governance is unique in its character, compared to the common Anglo-American and Franco-German models. The model of corporate governance in Islam is based on certain fundamental principles that include the *tawhid* epistemology and the *shura* process. This makes the model a stakeholder-value system with mutual consultation among all stakeholders based on the purpose of implementing policies that are Sharīʿah-compliant.

**Learning Objective 5.2**

2. Although similar to the Anglo-American model, Islamic corporate governance is fortified by the Sharīʿah governance process. That is, corporate governance is not complete in Islamic corporate entities without the Sharīʿah governance arm. Therefore, Islamic financial institutions use an integrated model of Sharīʿah and corporate governance. This establishes a different model of corporate governance in the modern world specifically for Islamic banks and financial institutions.

**Learning Objective 5.3**

3. The corporate governance framework in Islamic financial institutions has been prepared by international standard-setting bodies such as AAOIFI and IFSB. Countries such as Malaysia and Bahrain also have their own corporate governance standards. While these standards are not so different from one another, the additional value they add to the existing models of corporate governance include ethical behavior in the management of the company, and prudent Sharīʿah-compliant policies.

**Learning Objective 5.4**

4. Despite the issuance of corporate and Sharī'ah governance models and standards for IFIs, some countries still have their own unique practices. While there is no difference in the conceptual dimensions, diverse approaches are adopted in the implementation of the frameworks by different IFIs. The international standards set by the standard-making bodies such as AAOIFI and IFSB are observed differently in countries with Islamic financial service industries, although the underlying principles remain the same all over the world.

**Learning Objective 5.5**

5. The corporate governance framework for Islamic insurance (*takaful*) corporate entities is not that different from other IFIs. IFSB has issued guiding principles on corporate governance that provide specific benchmarks for use in the Islamic insurance industry. The core *takaful* principles require special corporate and Sharī'ah governance rules.

## Practice Questions and Activities

## Practice Questions

1. What is corporate governance within the framework of Islamic banks and financial institutions?

2. How is Sharī'ah governance unique within the general framework of corporate governance in an Islamic financial institution?

3. How does the corporate governance model for Islamic financial institutions compare to other internationally recognized models such as the Anglo-American and Franco-German models?

4. Briefly discuss the role of corporate governance in Islamic financial institutions.

5. What are the different mechanisms and organs in Islamic financial institutions that constitute the system of Sharī'ah and corporate governance?

6. Explain the functions of the Sharī'ah governance system in Islamic financial institutions.

7. Write a short essay on the different approaches to Sharī'ah and corporate governance in Islamic banks and financial institutions in two countries of your choice.

8. Review the different approaches to Sharī'ah and corporate governance in selected countries. Which approach do you prefer? Give reasons for your answer.

9. Why are separate governance standards, and Sharī'ah and corporate guidelines issued for Islamic insurance?

10. What are the three major requirements for good corporate governance in *takaful* undertakings as outlined by IFSB?

## Activities

1.  Get the text of the AAOIFI Standards on Corporate Governance and prepare a summary of these standards for a 15-minute class presentation.
2.  Draw a comparative table of the corporate governance models of the OECD and the IFSB.
3.  Interview any staff member of an Islamic bank or financial institution about its corporate governance model. Prepare the interview report for a 15-minute class presentation.
4.  Describe the corporate governance model of any Islamic insurance (*takaful*) company you know.

## Further Reading

Bakar, M. D. (2002). The Sharī'ah Supervisory Board and Issues of Sharī'ah Rulings and Their Harmonization in Islamic Banking and Finance. In Archer, S. and Rifaat, A. A. K. (eds.), *Islamic Finance Innovation and Growth* (pp. 74–89). Euromoney Books and AAOIFI.

Chapra, U. and Ahmed, H. (2002). *Corporate Governance in Islamic Financial Institutions*. Jeddah: Islamic Development Bank, IRTI.

Choudury, M. A. and Hoque, M. Z. (2004). *An Advanced Exposition of Islamic Economics and Finance*. New York: Edward Mellen Press.

Dawud, H.Y. 1996. *Sharī'ah Control in Islamic Banks*. Herndon, Virginia: International Institute of Islamic Thought.

Grais, W. and Pellegrini, M. (2006). *Corporate Governance and Sharī'ah Compliance in Institutions Offering Islamic Financial Services*. World Bank Policy Research Working Paper No. 4054.

Hasan, A. (2007). Optimal Sharī'ah Governance in Islamic Finance. Kuala Lumpur: BNM. Available at: www.bnm.gov.my/microsites/giff2007/pdf/frf/04_01.pdf.

Hasan, Z. (2010). Regulatory Framework of Sharī'ah Governance System in Malaysia, GCC Countries and the UK. *Kyoto Bulletin of Islamic Area Studies*. Vol. 3 (2): pp. 82–11.

IFSB. (2006). *Guiding Principles on Corporate Governance for Institutions Offering Only Islamic Financial Services (Excluding Islamic Insurance (Takaful) Institutions and Islamic Mutual Funds*. Kuala Lumpur: IFSB.

IFSB. (2009). *IFSB Guiding Principles on Governance for Takaful (Islamic Insurance) Undertakings.* Kuala Lumpur: IFSB.

OECD. (2004). *OECD Principles of Corporate Governance (Revised).* Paris: OECD. Available at: www.oecd.org/dataoecd/32/18/31557724.pdf.

Rammal, H. G. (2006). The Importance of Sharī'ah Supervision in IFIs. *Corporate Ownership and Control.* Vol. 3, (3): pp. 204–208.

# 6

# Islamic Asset and Fund Management

## Learning Objectives

### Upon the completion of this chapter, the reader should be able to:

1 Understand the unique nature and fundamentals of Islamic asset and fund management.

2 Identify the criteria for the selection of Islamic stocks for investing and review Islamic fund performances.

3 Examine the structure, marketing, and distribution of Islamic funds.

4 Understand the Sharī`ah governance for Islamic funds and its importance for Islamic fund management.

5 Know the meaning and importance of risk management issues for Islamic funds, including risk-reward profile, with specific analysis of the risk-reward profile of major Islamic finance products.

Asset and fund management is sometimes used as a synonym for investment management. It generally involves managing the wealth of private individuals or corporate entities. There are firms that specialize in asset and fund management. Surplus funds and assets of corporate entities and the wealth of private individuals are monitored, managed, and maintained in a sustainable way that aims to improve and enhance their value. There is an increasing demand for Sharī`ah-compliant asset management around the world. The Islamic asset and fund management sector is a significant segment of the Islamic finance industry, and has emerged as part of the wider asset management industry. The Islamic investment sector has expanded tremendously so far this century, with various innovative finance products that are Sharī`ah-compliant. Globally, Islamic fund managers are licensed under the relevant laws of the jurisdictions where they operate. They manage mandates according to the principles of Islamic law. Fund managers offer an array of products and instruments that have been specifically designed in accordance with the principles of the Sharī`ah, for clients who choose Sharī`ah-compliant investments. This chapter examines Islamic asset and fund management in the light of current developments in the Islamic finance industry. According to Ernst & Young's Islamic Funds and Investment Report 2010, Islamic assets under management are estimated at US$52 billion.

## chapter 6

**Rushdi Siddiqui**

*Global Head, Islamic Finance, Thomson Reuters, USA*

**1   Can there be any convergence of Sharīʻah financial filters across jurisdictions?**

We need to look at the financial filters as an evolving process for investing in publicly listed companies that 'do good by avoiding the bad.' Although the Bahrain-based industry organization, Accounting and Auditing Organization for Islamic Financial Institutions (AAOIFI), has Sharīʻah-compliant screening for equities, it has not been universally accepted across all jurisdictions.

Let's start at the recent beginning. Islamic equity investing was placed on the global map with the Dow Jones Islamic Market indexes (DJIM) in 1999 (full disclosure: I lead a team at Dow Jones Indexes to launch such indexes). It was a good beginning, with the Dow Jones brand and five of the most respected scholars in Islamic finance. However, we need to continue moving forward on screening on two fronts. One, positive screens, such as environment, sustainability, and governance (ESG), as Islamic finance needs to take a more proactive approach, akin to shareholder activism.

Two, Sharīʻah-based indexes. These are publicly listed companies whose by-laws say '...operating under glorious principle of Sharīʻah...', they have a Sharīʻah board, purify impermissible income, pay *zakat*, and so on. Thus, dedicated Islamic banks, Islamic leasing companies, *takaful* operators, Islamic Real Estate Investment Trusts (iREITs), stock exchanges (Dubai's Financial Market (DFM)), etc., provide a better connection to Islamic finance and better understanding for the 'man on the street' for such companies, as many may just be, say, depositors at these banks or users of *takaful* products. A Sharīʻah-based index gives a pulse to Islamic finance, much like the Dow or S&P 500 is the pulse of the US equity markets.

Sharīʻah-compliant indexes, negatively or positively screened, will continue to have issues on some aspects of primary business (such as defense, media, etc.) and financial ratio harmonization. However, with Sharīʻah-based indexes, we do not encounter the financial ratio screening. Finally, as most Sharīʻah-based companies are in Muslim countries (with stock exchanges), there are issues concerning foreigner investor restrictions, free float, liquidity, and, at times, financial reporting.

Let's be fair about Islamic finance, generally, and investing, specifically. One needs to give this embryonic industry with historical roots more time to develop.

**2    How can Sharī'ah fund management be improved?**

First, we need more education and seminars on Islamic investing, more asset classes (including funds of funds and fund indexes), more passive investing, better distribution (funds supermarket), fund rating/ranking, lower fees, etc., as that is the only way we are going to reduce the bias that exists today on Islamic debt and depositors.

Second, as most of the Islamic equity funds are actively managed (97 percent of funds with 98 percent of Assets-Under-Management (AUMs)), it makes sense to have Islamic fund indexes, capturing the fund manager's attempt to outperform (alpha) via a corresponding Islamic index.

Third, Islamic fund management needs to build out Sharī'ah screening for other asset classes. The screening process for publicly listed companies is well accepted, and this same screening is also applied to Islamic private equity buyouts and ensuing capital structure.

Fourth, a variety of Islamic funds, including *sukuk*, should result in a more robust Islamic fund of funds strategy, which could be active, passive, and exchange-listed.

Fifth, reducing the information search cost for all investors (finding information about funds) and marketing costs for fund sponsors (finding targeted customers) is a weak link in the Islamic fund/asset management industry.

Sixth, today Islamic funds can be benchmarked (accountability) to corresponding Islamic indexes, which typically results in fund flows (new money or redemption). However, such funds also need to be compared to peer funds to get to the desired 'conventional efficiency' if the cross-sell (to conventional investors) is to materialize.

Finally, if all of the above happens, fees should go down, which will entice more investors into the industry.

**3    What is the human capital in the Islamic fund management industry and what can be done to increase capacity in this regard?**

To develop the local Islamic fund industry, it's time to bring the process of 'analyzing and investing' in-house from outsourcing. Obviously, there are large infrastructure set-up costs, hiring analysts and fund managers, and so on. However, the industry has traditionally 'bought fish' (at seller's prices), and now needs to 'learn how to fish' if it is interested in reducing some of the Sharī'ah-compliant capital flight, develop local talent (high unemployment and under-employment), innovate, build a knowledge-based economy, etc. The Islamic Development bank (IDB) can play a role here, both in providing capital to set up the infrastructure of an Islamic fund shop and launching funds with seed money.

It may make sense to start off with a quant strategy; low cost, passive (and transparent) investing via index funds. Thus the Muslim world needs to have its own Islamic vanguard (king of index funds). We already have Sharī'ah-compliant indexes—the work is pretty much done for compliant companies and their weighting in a portfolio. The Islamic index funds will set up the foundation for Islamic exchange-traded funds, which already exist, but in very few Muslim countries.

Thus, human capital has to be combined with a strategy that addresses the build-out of the Islamic equity capital market (IECM) to provide a meaningful balance with the Islamic debt capital market (IDCM).

LEARNING OBJECTIVE 6.1

Understand the unique nature and fundamentals of Islamic asset and fund management.

**legitimate investment**
Forms of business that involve investing one's wealth in transactions that comply with the prescriptions of Islamic law.

# Review and Fundamentals of Islamic Investing

Muslims believe wealth generally belongs to Allah and man can only acquire it through reasonable efforts to earn income or by inheritance. Exerting an effort to own wealth through transactions that comply with the prescriptions of Islamic law, known as **legitimate investment**, is encouraged in Islam. Business activities through trade and investment have been the most practiced profession among Muslim communities for more than 1,400 years. This is as a result of clear injunctions in the Qur'an which encourage Muslims and people generally to earn money or wealth through legitimate means, invest it and spend part of it on permissible things that are Sharī'ah-compliant. These principles have been transmitted from one generation to another through impeccable sources of law. As a result, Muslims prefer Sharī'ah-compliant investments in order to purify their wealth and comply with the religious requirements of their conviction. To ensure total compliance with the principles of the Sharī'ah in Islamic asset and fund management, the foregoing fundamentals of Islamic investing are key. Compliance with the principles of Sharī'ah is what makes Islamic asset management unique in the global finance industry.

The Qur'an documents the necessity of financial planning and asset management to prevent unforeseen economic recession at both the individual and communal levels.

The primary evidence in the Qur'an is:

> Qur'an 12:47–49: "He (Yusuf) said: You shall sow for seven years continuously, then, what you reap leave it in its ear except a little of which you eat. Then, there shall come after that seven years of hardship which shall eat away all that you have beforehand laid up in store for them, except a little of what you shall have preserved. Then there will come after that a year in which people shall have rain and in which they shall press (grapes)."

This suggestion by Prophet Yusuf was meant to properly manage the wealth of the then Egyptian state. Prophet Yusuf foretold seven years of robust harvest, which was to be followed by seven years of drought in ancient Egypt. As a result, the need for proper wealth management was very important to the King of Egypt, who decided to appoint Prophet Yusuf to help formulate standard policies for wealth management. This is the earliest example of wealth management within the realm of Islamic religion. According to the analysis of the verses quoted above, this interpretation of the dream given by Prophet Yusuf led to his appointment as the minister in charge of the state treasury. The action plan he executed to save the whole community from the potential hardship and economic recession that could have resulted from the seven-year drought was a masterpiece. The people survived the drought as a result of this planning and appropriate state policies. There are other numerous verses of the Qur'an that encourage people to plan ahead as no one knows what they will earn in the future. Wealth is regarded as a trust from God and mankind only acts as its trustee. This is why the sustainable use of resources is encouraged. But this can only be realized through proper wealth management in line with the principles in the Sharī'ah. More often than not, such planning and wealth management requires investing in Sharī'ah-compliant products in order to adequately prepare for tomorrow.

Wealth in Islam is considered as a means to an end and not the ends itself. Hence, mankind is required to manage both communal and individual wealth in line with sustainable means that cater for the interests of the current generation and do not jeopardize that of future generations. As wealth management is so important, people called **fund managers** manage investment funds on behalf of investors. These people, along with Islamic asset management firms, must be professional in the discharge of their responsibilities, and a relationship with beneficiaries should be based on trust. This is known as their **fiduciary relationship**, and it is paramount. There must be total compliance with Islamic principles to ensure absolute Sharī'ah-compliance in investing. Without proper knowledge of Islamic finance products, it would be difficult to manage the assets and funds of clients professionally in line with prudential rules. This is seen in the appointment of Prophet Yusuf as the minister in charge of the state treasury. The basic consideration referred to by the King of Egypt in making the appointment is trust, honesty, and expertise in the job, itself stemming from the dream he interpreted. This is further confirmed by the Prophet's request to be appointed to occupy the post based on his proven expertise in wealth management.[1]

**fund managers**
Entrepreneurs who manage investment funds on behalf of investors.

**fiduciary relationship**
A relationship that involves trust, particularly between a professional trustee and a beneficiary of the trust.

With robust demands for Sharī'ah-compliant investment in Muslim-dominated areas across the world, it is important to understand the fundamentals that make it unique. This form of investment management corresponds with the values of socially responsible investment based on ethical dealings. It is important to realize how Muslims regard Sharī'ah-compliant products in their daily lives. There is an increasing awareness among Muslim communities globally, including those in Europe and America, to adhere to the requirements of their religion in all facets of their lives. This has largely influenced the financial sector. It explains the growing interest in Sharī'ah-compliant products around the world and the eventual intersection between the Islamic finance industry and the **halal industry**, used to describe businesses that comply with Islamic law. Hence, fund managers should professionally assist Muslims, who constitute about a quarter of the world population, in strictly complying with their religious convictions. In order to be Sharī'ah-compliant, unethical investments are prohibited under the Sharī'ah. These include investments that deal with gambling, alcohol, pork, uncensored media/leisure, pornography, and other things that are explicitly prohibited under the Sharī'ah. In addition, Islamic investments must exclude all *ribawi* (interest-bearing) products, avoid speculative investments, be socially responsible, and ensure that contractual terms comply with Islamic law.

**halal industry**
A broad term for businesses that comply with the prescriptions of Islamic law, with particular reference to food and consumable items.

## Non-interest-bearing Products

A portfolio is a group of assets, or all the assets included in a firm's balance sheet. However, for individual investors, portfolio means stocks, bonds, shares, and rental real estate. In applying the Sharī'ah filter to these **investment portfolios**, the first fundamental consideration is the exclusion of all *ribawi* products, services, or investments. Fund managers must ensure that their clients' investments are free from all forms of interest-bearing products, whether directly, apparent, or hidden in the management of the funds. Shares and stocks must be well screened to exclude all interest-bearing securities. There is serious emphasis on **ethical investment** in Islam. All forms of deceitful dealings where one person earns multiple incomes at the expense of another are forbidden in Islam. Fair trade and ethical dealing are encouraged in Islamic investing. In selecting securities for clients who may wish to invest, fund managers must respect the specific requirements of Muslim investors who prefer Sharī'ah-compliant products. The whole process must not contain any element of interest and this is where religion plays a significant role in ethical investing. This fiduciary duty is the same as the discipline of ethical investing in conventional asset management.

**investment portfolios**
Individual investor's stocks, bonds, shares, and rental real estate.

**ethical investment**
Forms of investment that emphasize a high level of moral principles. Such investment is devoid of all forms of exploitation.

To this end, all forms of interest, whether fixed or floating, simple or compound, are prohibited. 'Nominal' or 'excessive' interest amount to the same thing and are treated alike under the prohibition rule. Regardless of whatever interest rate fixed, even if it is as low as to 0.1 percent, it is still prohibited and must be totally excluded from investment activities. Financial returns on money must bear the two inseparable features of Islamic investing, i.e., profit and loss. Islamic investment funds involve the contribution of surpluses of investors to a joint pool for the purpose of investment in order to earn lawful profits in accordance with the Sharī'ah.

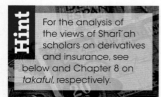

## Avoiding Speculative Investments

Speculative investment activities may involve both *gharar* (uncertainty) and *maysir* (gambling). Long-term investments in the secondary market for conventional securities may pose a serious challenge to the large number of prospective investors in the Gulf region and South-East Asia because of the speculative nature of many products, such as derivatives, futures, and options that involve excessive risks. Fund managers must ensure, as part of their fiduciary duty, that the security selection for clients who wish to invest in Sharī'ah-compliant products deserves the name. Investment activities involving excessive risk (which is different from the usual commercial risk), speculation, or uncertainty are prohibited in Islam. Risk can be defined as the variation of future price, so, it is natural for some assets to carry more risk than others. The uncertainty and contingency in contracts such as short selling and derivatives are prohibited in the Sharī'ah except when they are properly streamlined to reflect the mandatory requirements of the Sharī'ah. In addition, conventional insurance and derivatives are not permissible in Islamic investment. Let us consider the example of option trading. This form of derivatives basically involves two arrangements—an option to buy a commodity (call option) and an option to sell a commodity (put option). The speculative feature in options involves the conferment of rights without the corresponding obligations or liabilities. The exercise of the option is determined solely by the fluctuation in the market price of the underlying asset. The option-holder only exercises the right to buy or sell when the price is favorable. If by chance the price is not favorable, the option-holder abandons their promise. We shall examine options and other derivatives in more detail later in this chapter. However, it suffices to note here that the reason for the prohibition of options and other related derivatives is the speculative elements embedded in such contracts. As we saw in Chapter 2, regardless of the price movements, parties are bound by the terms stipulated in the sale contract.

## Social Responsibility

Fund managers and their clients are required by the Sharī'ah to discharge their social responsibility through their investment activities. Fund managers must bear this in mind when structuring Islamic finance products. Islam introduces certain mechanisms for wealthy people to discharge their social obligations toward the needy in society to foster community, economic empowerment, and the redistribution of resources. These mechanisms include *zakat* (compulsory alms), **sadaqah** (voluntary alms), *waqf* (charitable endowment), and even *takaful* (Islamic cooperative insurance). Each of these mechanisms plays a significant role in the redistribution of resources in society. The principles of Islamic investing require the parties to the contract to calculate the annual *zakat* due at the end of a financial year if the surpluses reach a threshold figure (**nisab**). Periodic voluntary alms, which should be part of the corporate social responsibility of the asset management firm, are also encouraged to contribute meaningfully to the immediate community within which the firm operates. This need not be in the form of cash donations but could be through the provision of basic necessities of life to poor communities. Similarly, charitable endowment is encouraged in Islamic investment.

**sadaqah**
Charity or voluntary alms encouraged by Islam to assist the less privileged in the society.

**nisab**
Amount of wealth in one's possession after meeting all vital expenses such as food, clothing, and shelter. When the wealth of a person exceeds this threshold figure and such wealth remains idle for a whole year, *zakat* becomes obligatory.

Part of the pool of funds from the surpluses may be used for endowment purposes based on the principles of *waqf*. Finally, fund managers must ensure that the assets they manage are adequately insured with the relevant *takaful* policies to avoid unnecessary exposure to any risks that may ultimately result in loss, and to protect and preserve their clients' wealth. It is considered part of prudential management of the wealth of one's clients to be properly insured against unforeseen circumstances. As wealth management involves investment and advisory services, insurance may involve dedicated advice on security issues regarding clients' property.

## Contractual Terms and Certification by Sharī'ah Experts

It is not enough for the underlying investments to be Sharī'ah-compliant. The fund manager must ensure that the contractual terms agreed with their clients conform to the principles of Islamic law. This is ensured by engaging the services of Sharī'ah experts who approve all draft contracts, processes, services, and investment activities before they are carried out or concluded as contracts. Necessary certification by Sharī'ah experts is sought for all contracts. It is common practice for a panel or board of Sharī'ah experts to do such certification and ensure the Sharī'ah compliance of all investment funds to suit the needs of the investors. This role is very important, particularly in the modern secondary markets where the tendency is to invest in conventional derivatives that may require screening.

An index is an indicator or measure representing the average value of specified prices or shares as compared with some referenced figures. Its plural is 'indexes', but in the technical usage, 'indices' is preferred.

**stock market index**
A statistical method of measuring a section of the stock market that involves a compilation of the share prices of representative stocks.

# Selection of Islamic Stocks for Investment

Selecting stocks for investment involves a process of Sharī'ah screening to ensure the stocks are compatible with the permissible forms of investment in the Sharī'ah. To guide prospective investors, a number of Islamic indices have been introduced to set benchmarks for Sharī'ah-compliant products. One of these is the Islamic Stock Market Index.

## Islamic Stock Market Indices

Islamic indices track stocks or corporations that are compatible with the Sharī'ah to enable investors and fund managers to make informed decisions on Sharī'ah-compliant products for investment.

A **stock market index** is used to measure fluctuations in the performance of stocks in a financial market. The index is likened to a thermometer but, in this case, it measures the temperature of the financial market and reveals its performance fluctuations. Bear in mind that larger companies or big corporations usually require a large amount of capital to finance their business. In most cases, such capital cannot be raised internally so the corporation, as a separate legal entity, proceeds to the securities markets to generate

### Challenge

Apart from the prominent
stock exchanges listed
in this chapter, list three
more stock exchanges
where Sharī'ah-compliant
products are traded.

### Challenge

Why must products and
stocks being offered by
Sharī'ah-compliant firms
go through the Sharī'ah
screen?

capital to finance its operations through the sale of securities. The securities are traded in a place called a **stock exchange**. Buyers and sellers of securities trade in this organized market, which may be national, regional, or international in its scope. Examples of prominent stock exchanges include the Kuala Lumpur Stock Exchange (KLSE), which uses the Kuala Lumpur Composite Index (KLCI) to measure the performance of the stock markets, including the Islamic capital market; the Hong Kong Stock Exchange; the New York Stock Exchange (NYSE); the London Stock Exchange (LSE), and the Frankfurt Stock Exchange. The most prominent Islamic indices are the Dow Jones Islamic Market Index (DJIM, see Figure 6.1 for an overview), FTSC Global Islamic Index, S&P Global Investable Sharī'ah Index and MSCI Barra.

A stock market index is a statistical method of measuring a section of the stock market by compiling the share prices of representative stocks. For instance, open a major newspaper and you will find stock market indices in the financial pages. Such major market indices are meant to guide investors on the performance of their stocks. Each of these market indices tracks certain stocks traded in the financial markets. In most cases, every sector of the economy has its own market index. For example, the DJIM was the first index created for investors seeking to invest in Sharī'ah-compliant stocks. Figure 6.1 contains the monthly performance chart of this index as of March 16, 2012.

The index in Figure 6.1 gives a one-month result of the performance of the stocks listed on the DJIM. The market movements for the four-week period are clearly shown in the graph.

## The Process of Selecting Stocks

The investment selection process of stocks for Islamic investment funds is similar to that of conventional mutual funds in many ways despite their unique features. The major requirement in Islamic investment is Sharī'ah compliance at every step of the process. This comprises all steps in the investment selection, including financial transaction modes and investment sectors. To ensure that Sharī'ah guidelines are properly followed, Islamic investment funds adhere to a systematic investment selection process, as illustrated in Figure 6.2:

* sector screen
* financial screen
* selecting Sharī'ah-compliant transactions and instruments
* purification of income distribution.

### Sector Screen or Industry Screen

The first stage of the investment process, where the underlying business activity of the company will be evaluated and certified to be compatible with Sharī'ah restrictions with respect to exposure to certain business activities, is known as the **sector screen** or **industry screen**. For Islamic funds, investment in industries that deal with prohibited goods or services, such as companies producing or selling alcohol, biotechnology firms using aborted embryos and human cloning, and conventional financial institutions, are not allowed.

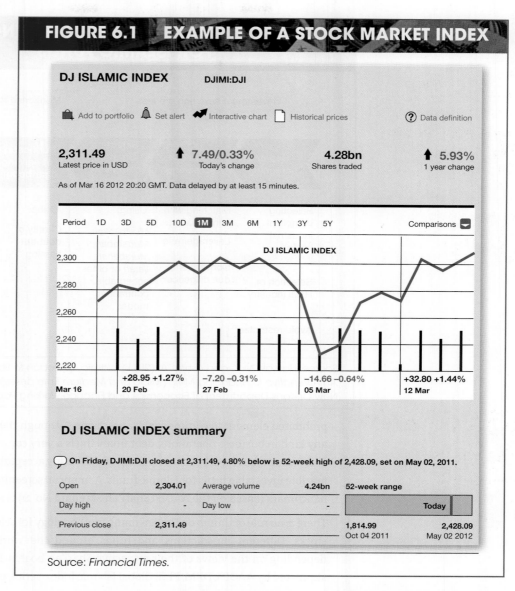

**FIGURE 6.1    EXAMPLE OF A STOCK MARKET INDEX**

Source: *Financial Times*.

As a conglomerate may have more than one business, investment in such companies and their subsidiaries is closely scrutinized. Whenever a conglomerate acquires a new subsidiary business, the mode of acquisition and target firm's business focus must also be analyzed, such as when a real estate company enters the hotel business, where some portion of its revenue comes from prohibited practices in Islam.

## Financial Screen

**financial screen**
The analysis of the nature of Sharī'ah non-compliant financial behavior of a company.

The second phase is the **financial screen**, which involves analyzing the nature of a company's Sharī'ah non-compliant financial behavior. For Islamic investments, being halal (permissible) is not enough. In addition, Sharī'ah scholars generally require that the firms under investment should operate according to Islamic financial norms, being devoid of any prohibited financial practice such as *riba*, *maysir*, and *gharar*, or any other

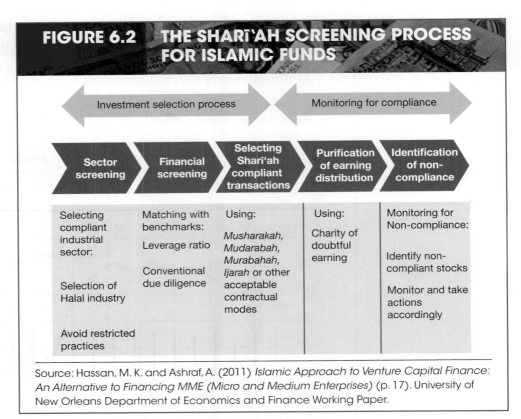

**FIGURE 6.2    THE SHARĪ'AH SCREENING PROCESS FOR ISLAMIC FUNDS**

Investment selection process — Monitoring for compliance

| Sector screening | Financial screening | Selecting Sharī'ah compliant transactions | Purification of earning distribution | Identification of non-compliance |
|---|---|---|---|---|
| Selecting compliant industrial sector:<br><br>Selection of Halal industry<br><br>Avoid restricted practices | Matching with benchmarks:<br><br>Leverage ratio<br><br>Conventional due diligence | Using:<br><br>*Musharakah, Mudarabah, Murabahah, Ijarah* or other acceptable contractual modes | Using:<br><br>Charity of doubtful earning | Monitoring for Non-compliance:<br><br>Identify non-compliant stocks<br><br>Monitor and take actions accordingly |

Source: Hassan, M. K. and Ashraf, A. (2011) *Islamic Approach to Venture Capital Finance: An Alternative to Financing MME (Micro and Medium Enterprises)* (p. 17). University of New Orleans Department of Economics and Finance Working Paper.

prohibited element in commercial transactions. Although the Sharī'ah prohibits *riba* of any kind in business operations, debt financing is a very common norm. Over the years, Sharī'ah scholars have been researching and debating acceptable debt ratios for selecting feasible investable firms for Islamic funds. A financial screening strategy often used as a benchmark (based on the AAOIFI Sharī'ah Standard No. 21) is shown in Table 6.1.

There is no rule of thumb on the screening methodology for selecting Sharī'ah-compliant stocks. Different jurisdictions and funds around the world use diverse standards depending on the views of their respective Sharī'ah boards. Different ratios have been stipulated by AAOIFI, DJIM, FTSE Global Islamic Index Series, etc.

## Selecting Sharī'ah-compliant Transactions and Instruments

Islam, as a religion, prohibits *riba, maysir,* and *gharar,* and encourages the use of profit-sharing and partnership schemes. For this reason, many conventional investment

| **TABLE 6.1: AAOIFI Ratios For Financial Screening** | |
|---|---|
| **Formula** | **Limit** |
| Conventional debt / total assets | < 30% |
| (Cash + interest-bearing deposits) / total assets | < 30% |
| (Total interest income + income from non-compliant activities) / total revenues | < 5% |
| Accounts receivable / total assets | < 45% |

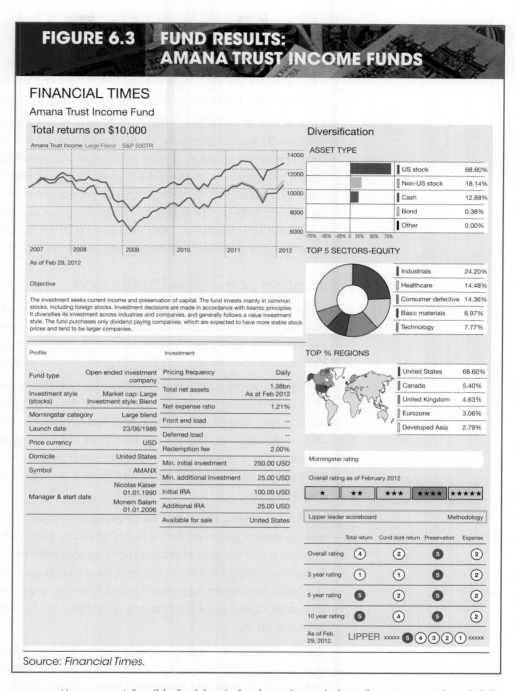

FIGURE 6.3  FUND RESULTS: AMANA TRUST INCOME FUNDS

Source: *Financial Times*.

practices are not feasible for Islamic funds as they rely heavily on interest-based debt to finance activities, which is not compatible with the spirit of Sharī'ah business. Conventional investment funds may invest in interest-bearing debt securities, preferred stocks, warrants, common stocks, and any other suitable instruments. Although Shari'ah-compliant debt certificates are currently evolving, the scope of Islamic investment funds is limited by the availability of common stocks in the halal industrial sectors. For example, Figure 6.3 illustrates the results of Amana Trust Income Funds as presented in the *Financial Times*. The investment policy clearly states that the fund seeks current income and preservation of capital, consistent with Islamic principles. Apart from the profile and investment of the mutual funds shown in the figure, the diversification column shows the asset type, the top five sectors and the top five regions. The graph shows the total returns on US$10,000 from 2007 to 2012 from these funds.

Because *riba* is prohibited, Islamic investment funds cannot invest in fixed income instruments such as corporate bonds, treasury bonds and bills, certificates of deposit (debt certificates issued by a bank or financial institution, which entitle the bearer to receive interest at the maturity date), preferred stocks, warrants, and some derivatives (such as options), etc. They cannot trade on margin or be involved in any interest-paying debt to finance their investments. It is also not permissible to engage in sale and repurchase agreements (i.e., repos or buybacks). In addition, Islamic fund managers are not allowed to speculate or undertake any unnecessary risks.

## Purification of Income Distribution

Although some Sharī'ah scholars do not allow for any sort of conventional leverage (the use of credit or borrowed capital to increase the earning potential of stock) in the investable firms, most scholars think that such investments are acceptable on the precondition that 'contaminated' earnings be cleansed or purified.

The implication of purification for Islamic funds is that if the fund observes some part of its income is doubtful, then those earnings should be foregone. Islamic funds should adopt proper financial screening as accurately as possible to figure out the composition of doubtful earnings from the common stock of a firm. For example, if an Islamic fund observes that 8 percent of its income comes from interest-related dealings, then the fund must disburse that portion of its income through charity in order to purify the fund's earnings.

Although cleansing of dividend earnings is an established practice, there is no consensus among Muslim jurists on the cleansing of capital gains. Some scholars observe that it is necessary, as the market price of the share may reflect an element of interest. Others argue that no purification is required for a capital gain, the rationale being that as the firms selected through industry and financial screenings already belong to halal industries, capital gains from trading such shares are unlikely to reflect any significant impact of interest.

*Zakat* may be used as a form of purification technique. Although the *nisab* of *zakat* for individuals is well-defined, *zakat* calculation on investment profits is still a debated issue. *Nisab* for *zakat* for investment profits is complicated because of the intricacies of the timing of the portfolio incomes and capital gains. Islamic funds may set aside a portion of profits for *zakat*, and their Sharī'ah supervisory boards may identify the recipients of this money.

Some Sharī'ah scholars associated with Islamic funds also observe that it is difficult to identify any company that pays or receives zero interest, and accordingly suggest that a fund can invest in companies with less than one-third leverage-related ratios and purify

# ISLAMIC FINANCE IN THE NEWS

## Going global from Iowa to Kuala Lumpur

August 3, 2008

Des Moines, Iowa, seems an unlikely headquarters for a major player in the Asian Islamic funds market, but Principal Global Investors, through its long-standing joint venture with Malaysia-based CIMB, has ambitions to tap into the massive demand in Asia-Pacific for Shariʿah-compliant products.

Having achieved a critical mass within Islamic accounts in their existing conventional business, the partners came to the conclusion there was a role for an Islamic specialist, according to Jim McCaughan, chief executive. 'At the same time, the Malaysian government, under the Malaysian Islamic Financial Centre, has introduced certain incentives to try to make Kuala Lumpur into a centre for Islamic finance, including Islamic asset management,' he says.

'Clearly there's a lot of potential there, because they're a tremendous economic success story and an Islamic country. For that reason, they've got a pretty good chance of being a base for what is, internationally, quite a fragmented business at the moment.'

Malaysia currently represents the main source of Islamic bond, or *sukuk*, issuance worldwide—more than 60 percent—and is the second largest market for Islamic mutual funds, with 27 percent of the market, behind only Saudi Arabia, which has 28 percent.

The monetary authorities in Singapore and Hong Kong have both made noises about attracting Islamic business, and *sukuk* issuance from Japan is on the increase as Tokyo looks to take some of this increasingly lucrative sector.

From this base, the Islamic funds industry in Asia is undergoing significant growth, driven by a number of important factors, not least the performance of Shariʿah-compliant indices. The Islamic filters preclude investment in stocks that are *haraam*—forbidden under Shariʿah law—which means they exclude financial institutions, due to Islamic restrictions on the payment of interest, as well as breweries, pornography, gambling and other activities deemed unethical. Highly leveraged stocks are also *haraam*.

The indices are consequently heavily weighted towards technology, resources, infrastructure, telecommunications and consumer goods, sectors that have been beneficiaries of the demographic and economic growth within Asia Pacific. Avoiding financial stocks in the aftermath of the subprime crisis in the US has also proved a sensible move.

It is a widespread myth, according to Datuk Noripah Kamso, chief executive of CIMB-Principal Asset Management, that the ethical filters on Islamic products mean investors have a severely restricted investment universe and cause a performance drag. The Dow Jones Asia-Pacific Islamic index consists of 1,085 stocks, with a total market capitalization in excess of US $3,500bn (£1,760bn, €2,220bn).

'So it's not a restricted universe after all,' Ms Kamso says. 'And this misconception that there is a performance drag is not right. It's not inferior to conventional performance in volatility or risk-return profile, or even in total return.'

Some markets are clearly already tailored to Islamic investing. In Malaysia itself, 85 percent of listed stocks are considered compliant—hardly surprising, given that it is a predominantly Muslim nation.

But, Ms. Kamso says: 'If you go to China, which is a non-Muslim country, and you screen the stocks, they have a lot of these stocks, manufacturing stocks, consumer goods, telecommunications; they are all Shariʿah-compliant.'

In fact, earlier this year one of the first actively managed Islamic Greater China equity funds was launched by Hong Kong-based Mayfair Pacific Asset Management, investing principally in H-shares (shares of companies based on mainland China but listed elsewhere) in the Dow Jones Islamic China Offshore index, the Dow Jones Islamic Hong Kong China Titan Index and the Dow Jones Islamic Asia-Pacific Index. Mayfair Pacific has also formed its own Shariʿah advisory board to act as a second layer of compliance checks and to assess opportunities that may arise outside of the indices through new IPOs.

With huge regional and international demand for China-focused products, particularly from Malaysia, Pakistan and the oil-rich Gulf Co-operation Council countries, the fund has generated a lot of interest, according to Christina Tung, Mayfair Pacific founder. 'I think people believe in the story and the idea,' she says.

Ms. Tung is also adamant that the fund is no gimmick and is insisting on sending every member of staff that has

*Cont'd*

contact with the fund—from senior management down to the fund accountants—for Islamic finance training, and she has made sure her Sharī'ah advisory board has respected scholars from international Islamic jurisdictions.

Products like Mayfair Pacific's mark an interesting milestone in the evolution of the Asian Islamic finance market, and challenge another misconception about Islamic finance that CIMB-Principal's Ms. Kamso is keen to dispel—that Sharī'ah-compliant products are manufactured by Muslims for Muslims.

While sukuk and fund products may attract Islamic investors, their return profile and ethical appearance has led to interest from more secular sources. Japanese investors reportedly took up 25 percent of Malaysia's last sovereign sukuk issue and both issues and advisory groups are appearing globally.

The international Islamic capital markets have some way to go before they integrate completely, but firms with a global view—whether from Kuala Lumpur, Hong Kong or Des Moines—could be best placed to profit when they do.

**Source:** Peter Guest, "Going global from Iowa to Kuala Lumpur", *Financial Times*, August 3, 2008.

its income by donating the interest-tainted income received to a charity. However, in some countries in the Middle East and South-East Asia, there is an increasing interest in Sharī'ah-compliant funds. As we can see in *Islamic Finance in the News* on page 227, 85 percent of listed stocks in Malaysia are considered Sharī'ah-compliant. In such countries, it is expected that non-compliant stocks should not dominate the market. Thus, instances of purification of income will be drastically reduced. This will place Malaysia on the world map as the hub for Islamic asset management.

## Addressing Issues of Non-compliant Stocks

One of the important functions of the Sharī'ah supervisory board is the constant monitoring of the business operations of the Islamic fund. Although firms are selected through proper industry and financial screening, constant monitoring of Sharī'ah compliance in these firms is required. At any given time, a firm may fall behind the benchmark requirement for Sharī'ah compliance. As firms may engage in mergers, acquisitions, or divestments, their Sharī'ah compliance should be re-scrutinized periodically. Sharī'ah advisors may classify the degree of non-compliance into any of the following categories.

- *Temporary non-compliance with industry or financial screens*. The Sharī'ah board may permit the transaction of stocks while benchmarks are occasionally breached up to a given approved level. However, the fund manager should report on the firm to the Sharī'ah board on a regular basis.
- *Short-term non-compliance with industry or financial screens*. The fund manager should report to the supervisory board if a stock becomes non-compliant for a longer period of time. The manager should also analyze the impact of returns from that firm on the overall return of the fund and set aside a certain portion of earnings and donate it to an appropriate charitable cause. Usually, the supervisory board reviews the status of these non-compliant stocks at regular intervals.
- *Permanent non-compliance*. When a stock falls short of compliance benchmarks of Sharī'ah approvals permanently, the Sharī'ah board may ask the fund manager to divest from such stocks.

# Structure, Marketing, and Distribution of Islamic Investment Funds

## What is an Islamic Investment Fund?

Islamic investment funds can be defined as a joint pool to which investors contribute their surplus money for the sole purpose of investment in legitimate business from which they will earn halal profits in conformity with the fundamental principles of the Sharī'ah regulating business transactions. The usual practice is for the fund manager to issue a form of certificate to the subscribers (investors) to a fund certifying their rate of subscription, which entitles them to profits earned by the fund, distributed in accordance with their respective investment portfolios and proportion of investment, known as **pro-rata profits**. The certificate or document given to the subscribers may be called 'shares', 'units', 'certificate', or 'instrument', and documents their rate of ownership in the joint fund. However, the validity of this certificate is subject to two basic conditions.

**pro-rata profits**
Profits distributed to investors in accordance with their respective investment portfolios and proportion of investment.

1. There must not be a fixed return on the certificates. Individual profits or loss must be based on the pro-rata profit actually earned by the fund in its investment. The principles of joint-venture partnership such as *musharakah* (a joint business partnership enterprise where the parties share the profits based on the contractual ratio and losses are borne based on equity participation ratio) are applicable to this form of investment.

2. The amount of funds realized from the pool should be invested in a form of investment that is acceptable under the Sharī'ah. Islamic funds cannot be channeled towards investments in illegal trades such as breweries, casinos, cafés dealing in forbidden food, and unauthorized arms and ammunition.

From its early stage, investment in common stocks has been well accepted by Sharī'ah scholars with the precondition that Sharī'ah screening is performed properly. AAOIFI defines Islamic funds as investment vehicles that should be financially independent of the institutions that establish them and be managed on the basis of either *mudarabah* (a trust partnership contract between a capital provider and an entrepreneur where the parties share the profits but in the event of any loss, the capital provider bears the loss), or agency contract or other profit-and-loss sharing contracts.[2]

## Structure of Islamic Investment Funds

The structure of Islamic funds is derived according to their different classifications, usually their respective investment style, and different categories. Most of the Islamic investment funds available in the market are similar to conventional funds but in the case of the former, they have been made to be Sharī'ah-compliant.

There are four major Islamic investment funds commonly used by an Islamic funds manager.

1. Islamic debt funds

2. Islamic equity funds

3. alternative investments

4. special asset classes.

Let us examine each of these four categories of Islamic investment funds.

## Islamic Debt Funds

**Islamic debt funds**

An arrangement where the capital of an equity-based fund is invested in fixed-income yielding activity such as an operating lease which naturally involves a debt.

As an alternative to conventional funds, the **Islamic debt funds** are created through investing the capital of the *mudarabah*-based or *musharakah*-based funds in fixed-income yielding operations that involve some sort of debt as well as a fixed income for the financial intermediary. Such fixed-income yielding operations may include *murabahah* and *ijarah*. This leads to the establishment of the *murabahah* (commodity) funds and *ijarah* (operating lease) funds. A number of steps are taken in the creation of Islamic debt funds. Figure 6.4 summarizes the five basic steps. In structuring an Islamic debt fund, the fund manager creates an equity-based special purpose contract such as *mudarabah*. Through this contract, funds are raised by issuing certificates to investors (subscribers) who contribute their surpluses to the common pool of funds as capital providers. The fund manager manages the funds and business activity by investing such funds in either *murabahah* or *ijarah* activity, which operationally involves some sort of debt. As the underlying contract is a partnership business, the percentages of revenue due to each of the subscribers are determined by the contractual ratios.

**FIGURE 6.4  THE FIVE STEPS IN THE STRUCTURE OF ISLAMIC DEBT FUNDS**

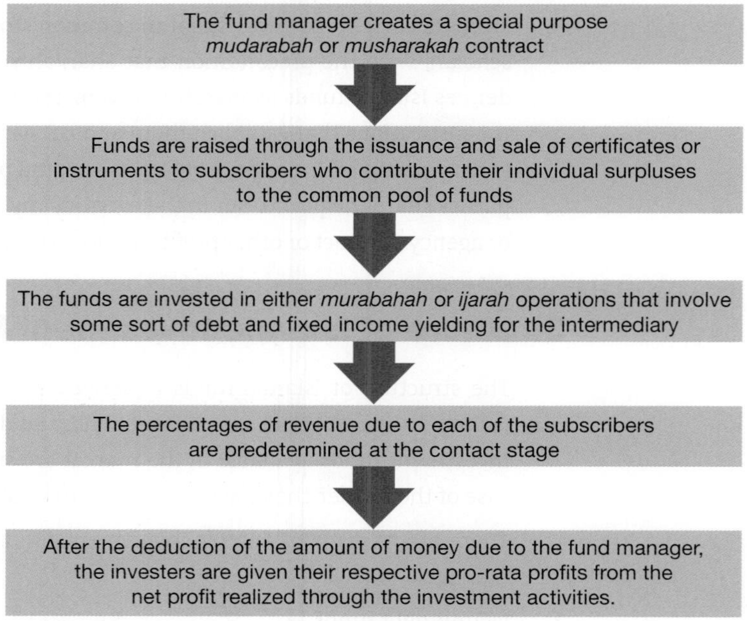

The fund manager creates a special purpose *mudarabah* or *musharakah* contract

↓

Funds are raised through the issuance and sale of certificates or instruments to subscribers who contribute their individual surpluses to the common pool of funds

↓

The funds are invested in either *murabahah* or *ijarah* operations that involve some sort of debt and fixed income yielding for the intermediary

↓

The percentages of revenue due to each of the subscribers are predetermined at the contact stage

↓

After the deduction of the amount of money due to the fund manager, the investers are given their respective pro-rata profits from the net profit realized through the investment activities.

The cost of managing the business activity is determined as fixed-income yielding for the intermediary. The fund manager may manage the business activity or outsource it to a third party who may be considered as the intermediary.

Keeping the steps taken in the creation of Islamic debt funds in mind, we will briefly examine commodity and *ijarah* funds.

## Commodity Funds

**bay' bithaman ajil**
A sale of goods where a financial institution buys a commodity on behalf of the buyer from the seller and sells the same commodity to the buyer at a profit based on a deferred payment arrangement.

Commodity funds involve *murabahah* operations or **bay' bithaman ajil** (BBA), where the fund manager uses the subscribed pool of funds to purchase different commodities for the sole purpose of resale. The amount of profits realized from the resale constitutes the main income of the fund, which is distributed among the subscribers based on their pro rata subscription to the fund. You should recall that a fundamental requirement for Islamic investment funds is compliance of the whole process of investment and the underlying asset with the precepts of the Shariʿah regulating commercial transactions. These transactions must be structured in close-ended form, which are non-negotiable in the secondary market.

## Ijarah Funds

**ijarah fund**
Lease fund where the amount realized from subscription is used to purchase an asset such as a real estate, which is leased to a third party.

A lease fund where the amount realized from subscription is used to purchase an asset such as a real estate, which is then leased to a third party, is known as an **ijarah fund**. The *ijarah* fund is created through the pool of surplus financial resources from willing investors, duly managed by a fund manager, which are used to purchase a leasable asset for the purpose of establishing a lease agreement with a third party who is the ultimate user. The underlying asset may be real estate, a motor vehicle, or special machinery that has the potential to be leased out to the ultimate user of its usufruct. Simple rules of business transactions relating to an *ijarah* contract provide that the ownership of the underlying asset still vests in the Islamic fund but the usufruct is given to the lessee up to the appointed time, as provided for in the underlying contract.

The subscribers to the fund are issued certificates that contain their individual share or unit of the underlying asset purchased with their surplus funds. The certificate is evidence of their subscriptions to the fund and guarantees their entitlement to any profit that accrues from the underlying asset leased out to the lessee. The certificates are commonly known as *sukuk* (investment certificates) in Islamic finance. The rentals that are charged from the lessee constitute the income of the fund. The income is distributed pro rata to the subscribers accordingly, after deducting the managerial expenses (see *Islamic Finance in Practice* panel for actual practice for *ijarah* funds). Unlike commodity funds, *sukuk* are negotiable instruments that can be traded in the secondary market as they represent the pro rata ownership of their holders in the tangible asset leased out.

Structuring an *ijarah* fund is similar to other Islamic debt funds. However, some additional preconditions have to be considered, as it constitutes a direct investment in business. Fund managers must take proper precautions to ensure that funds are invested in halal industry. Another issue for *ijarah* funds is the exit strategy. Usually, exit strategy options are disclosed in the fund charter that is decided before the fund is off-loaded.

## ISLAMIC FINANCE IN PRACTICE

# Ijarah Real Estate Fund, Global Investment House, Kuwait

This is a REIT investment model, which seeks to provide the unit-holders with returns between 8 percent and 10 percent per annum. The returns are payable based on the capital contributions of the unit-holders after any incentives, expenses, and fees payable to the fund manager (Global Investment House) and applicable taxes are deducted from the returns. As a REIT, the underlying property is either developed and/or acquired as real estate then leased out to ensure a stable cash inflow. Through diversified portfolios of real estate properties, Global Investment House targets countries in the Middle East, North Africa, and Turkey in its acquisition and

developmental drive. The Ijarah Real Estate Fund invests in a diverse portfolio of real estate properties in line with Sharī'ah principles to mitigate risk. The Fund operates under the standards of the Central Bank of Bahrain for Accreditor Investors.

The Ijarah Real Estate Fund made its first investment in Kuwait through a sale and leaseback arrangement with a listed firm in Kuwait. The fund invested US$10.7 million in this arrangement, which matured on December 25, 2008. Consequently, the Fund received monthly rentals at a profit of 11.50 percent. The transaction was closed in January 2009.

Source: www.globalinv.net/contentdisp.asp?pageId=56.

## Islamic Equity Funds

Equity instruments are preferred in Islamic investments because they generally agree with the true spirit of the fundamental principles of commercial transactions in Islamic law. Thus, Islamic equity funds occupy a preferential position among Islamic investment funds. Equity transactions are the oldest, enduring products, practiced since 1,400 years ago. As investments require the investor to bear the risk of the transaction to be entitled to any profits that accrue in the process, Muslim scholars prefer the returns earned through equity investment. The basic principles underlying Islamic equity funds require careful practices based on trust and transparency among the stakeholders.

In the creation of Islamic equity funds, investment firms are selected through a proper screening process to ensure that all their investments comply with Sharī'ah requirements. The underlying contract between the fund manager and the investors must also be Sharī'ah-compliant in all its ramifications. In this manner, the fund manager or firm is the financial intermediary as a result of the cardinal role it plays in managing the surpluses of investors contributed to a common pool for the purpose of investment. There is an increasing interest in Islamic equity funds in the global equity markets, particularly from among investors from the Gulf countries.

As an equity investor becomes a pro-rata shareholder of the business itself, Islamic investment principles require that the business activities of the fund manager or firm must

The Ijarah Real Estate Fund of the Global Investment House in Kuwait invests in a diverse portfolio of real estate properties, targeting countries in the Middle East, North Africa, and Turkey.

fall within the permissible category in Islamic commercial transactions. The managing firms must not engage in any debt or leverage and must avoid any prohibited financial practices. However, in reality, finding firms with such compliance may be difficult. A more liberal way to select suitable investment management firms (or equity fund firms) is to go through the systematic approach we discussed earlier, of an industry screen, a financial screen, earnings purification, and close monitoring of non-compliant shares.

The structure of an Islamic equity fund may be based on either a *mudarabah* or *musharakah* contract. For instance, in the case of a *mudarabah* contract, there are two main parties—the investors and the fund manager. The investors (*rabb al-mal*) assume the role of silent partners in the trust partnership while the fund manager (*mudarib*) as the entrepreneur performs the managerial functions. The equity fund issues securities or certificates to the subscribers and the pool of funds received is invested in Sharī'ah-compliant business, such as *mudarabah*, *musharakah*, or common stocks. In practice, the underlying contract or memorandum of association of the Islamic equity fund firm must clearly state its investment policy and it must put in place the necessary Sharī'ah governance framework that will constantly ensure Sharī'ah compliance in all the processes, procedures, services, contracts, and investment activities of the firm. It is also important that the proportion of profit sharing is clearly fixed and disclosed in the fund charter. The Islamic equity fund is the most common and widely practiced portfolio offered by Islamic fund managers around the world.

## Alternative Investments

There are three forms of funds under the alternative investment heading as commonly practiced in the Islamic finance industry. These are alternative structures for Islamic funds that are premised on key Islamic financing instruments, which are now becoming prominent in the investment sector of the Islamic finance industry. These three funds are:

- private equity fund
- Islamic venture capital fund
- real estate funds or real estate investment trusts (REITs).

These alternative investments are structured to serve as suitable substitutes to the conventional forms of investment funds.

### Private Equity Fund

Asset classes that comprise equity securities not publicly traded on a stock exchange are called **private equities.** These are generally structured as private limited companies with a few large-capital individuals or institutional investors as the stakeholders. Usually, private equity funds engage in non-exchange traded or illiquid investment strategies. The funds tend to hold their equity position in a growth company for a relatively long time horizon. Although there may be no requirement to lock in the invested capital for a specific time, the investment strategies of private equity funds essentially replicate this strategy.

Conventional private equity funds usually invest in a portfolio of growth companies and tend to hold them for a relatively long time horizon. In essence, the investment styles of conventional private equity funds do not contradict the Islamic investment framework as they focus on equity investments only. However, for a Sharī'ah-compliant private equity strategy, strict additional Sharī'ah-compliance screening is conducted. In selecting Sharī'ah-compliant investments, private equity funds can replicate the generic investment selection strategies used by Islamic funds. To ensure Sharī'ah compliance, private equity funds may ask for professional services from certified Sharī'ah scholars who are experts in Islamic finance and contemporary investment strategies. Even though private equities are not exchange-traded and much of their financial information is not disclosed, a Sharī'ah compliance audit is still put in place to guarantee investor confidence.

### Islamic Venture Capital Fund

The term **venture capital** can be defined as the capital invested in startup firms and small businesses with exceptional long-term growth potential. Apart from the usual financial capital required to set up such a firm, the managerial and technical expertise is also included in the term 'venture capital'. Like private equity, venture capital is not exchange-traded but engages in long-term investment positions in firms at different stages, such as start-ups or distressed firms in the middle of business cycles. The higher failure rate of venture capitalists is offset by the enormous return on a few successful projects. Venture capital investments may take place at any or a combination of different stages in a company's life cycle.

- *Seed-stage financing*; when venture capitalists fund startup enterprises. This usually involves the development of new business initiatives.
- *Early-stage financing*; which involves investing in companies that have received initial seed financing and have shown rapid growth potential.

---

**private equities**
Asset classes that comprise equity securities not publicly traded on a stock exchange.

**venture capital**
The money and resources made available to startup firms and small businesses with exceptional growth potential.

- *Formative-stage financing*; another step further from early-stage financing. It involves both seed-stage and early-stage financing, which support the initial development of new products and scale up capabilities.
- *Later-stage financing*; which involves financing provided after product development, manufacturing of products, and sales with a marked increase in revenue growth, but before any initial public offering.
- *Expansion-stage financing*; refers to the financing of the steps required to make the initial public offering. The expansion stage is also known as the *mezzanine* stage of financing, which naturally culminates in the initial public offering.
- *Balanced-stage financing*; which involves all the stages from seed-stage to expansion-stage financing.

After making their investments, venture capitalists usually hold the investment for a relatively long time horizon until they find a suitable time to liquidate the investment through any of the following procedures.

- Initial public offering (IPO); a company's flotation of tradable securities on a stock exchange, where its shares are sold to public investors.
- Company buyback; a company's repurchase of its own outstanding shares. This is either meant to reduce the number of shares in the market or reduce the shareholding of a single investor.
- Trade sale; a common exit route for venture capital in its early stages where a firm is sold to another company.
- Write-off; a failure for the venture capitalist, when it believes it cannot recover from its investment, although it may continue to hold shares in a non-viable enterprise.
- Secondary sale; a sale of part or all of the investment of the venture capitalist to another venture capitalist in a secondary sale without selling the shares of the entrepreneur.
- Reorganization; a restructuring of the investee company, which may include recapitalization and total reorganization of the business to enhance profitability.

Conventional venture capital funds extend from the basic idea of venture capital and portfolio diversification. They are structured as open-end funds and they are usually invested in a pool of venture capital projects, thus allowing the benefits of diversification. Islamic venture capital funds may be organized using a similar structure to pool the Sharīʿah-compliant venture capital in a portfolio and to seek investable funds from individuals.

The structure of an Islamic venture capital fund is based on a contractual arrangement between the fund manager and the institutional and individual investors. The investors are passive and act as 'limited partners'. Conversely, private equity experts, who are considered as the 'general partners', undertake the management responsibility. Although the basic set-up seems to be similar to conventional venture capital funds, there is an additional, albeit unique, requirement of Sharīʿah compliance, which must be incorporated into all contractual dealings. In addition, the sources of funds and the investment sectors must also be Sharīʿah-compliant in Islamic venture capital funds.

While analyzing the feasibility of possible ventures, an Islamic venture fund performs Sharī'ah-compliance screening in the first place and then conducts the project feasibility analysis, similar to a conventional venture capital fund.

An Islamic venture capital fund draws its funds from a wide range of investors including Sharī'ah-compliant institutions such as Islamic banks and financial institutions, *takaful* companies, and individual investors who prefer Islamic financial products. In this contractual arrangement, a *mudarabah* contract may be used to raise funds. The Islamic venture capital fund acts as the managing partner (*mudarib*), while other investors are considered to be silent partners. The fundamental principle underlying this contractual arrangement is that different clauses may be included in the *mudarabah* contract but none of them must contradict the established precepts of the Sharī'ah. The Sharī'ah principles regulating commercial transactions are inclusive in many regards. Any clause or contractual term that does not contradict the Sharī'ah, regardless of its origin, will be accepted as being Sharī'ah-compliant. To this end, the funds for Islamic venture capital may be raised in stages and locked in for a long period of time. To restrict the *mudarib*'s activities, certain clauses can be added to the *mudarabah* contract with the consent of investors. Remuneration for the *mudarib* can either be fixed or flexible. A combination of fixed and flexible compensation packages may be allowed if done in separate contracts.

### Real Estate Funds or Real Estate Investment Trusts (REITs)

**real estate investment trust (REIT)**
A company that owns and operates income-yielding real estate or items that relate to real estate.

**Real estate investment trusts (REITs)** are companies that own and operate income-yielding real estate or items that relate to real estate. REITs are structured as a limited company and the majority are listed on stock exchanges. REITs collect investable funds from investors and invest primarily in commercial and residential real estate. Although some REITs focus on only owning and managing income-generating real estate projects, some others do some lending or financing activities in the real estate sector as well. There is a third category of REITs that does both, i.e. financing others' real estate and managing their own real estate. The uniqueness of REITs lies in the way they hold their portfolios.

Conventional REITs operations are based on different modes of debt financing and lease agreements. REITs are structured in such a way to allow investors to replicate their target exposure for stock and real estate in a single contract. Thus, the REITs invest in a pool of real estate projects that allow an investor to be exposed to a diverse portfolio. Based on their investment style and income-generating sources, conventional REITs may be classified into three broad categories as identified by Mohammed Obaidullah:

- *Equity REIT*: an equity REIT acquires and develops its properties primarily to operate them as part of its own portfolio rather than to resell them once they are developed. Equity REITs engage in a wide range of real estate activities, including leasing, development of real property, and tenant services.
- *Mortgage REITs*: These focus on financing the real estate owners and operators through credit facilities. Credit facilities may be extended indirectly through the acquisition of loans or mortgage-backed securities.

- *Hybrid REITs*: An amalgam of the above two categories, whereby the REIT acquires and develops properties and at the same time lends money to real estate owners and operators.[3]

Although most REITs are exchange-traded, some REITs are not listed or traded over the counter. These are known as private REITs.

Islamic REITs are patterned after the *ijarah* contractual framework and its variations. This is different from conventional REITs, which depend wholly on debt contracts. An example of other variations of the *ijarah* contract is the *ijarah-istisna'a* contract, which is the linking of *ijarah* with *istisna'a* and popularly known as *ijarah mawsufah fi dhimmah* (forward lease). Islamic REITs are more likely to be structured as equity REITs. Investors in these may gain proportionate ownership to the underlying real estate asset and earn a stable rental.

As Islamic equity REITs may depend heavily on lease contracts, they essentially replicate a fund structure similar to the *ijarah* fund. However, there is one significant difference between them. *Ijarah* funds may have fixed maturity or may be short term. For Islamic equity REITs, the fund's maturity may be long or ideally considered as a going concern.

## Special Asset Classes

The global competitive investment market has led to market innovation within the Islamic investment sector, enabling it to compete favorably with conventional investment portfolios. This has led to new categories of funds. As the first task of fund managers is to create an optimal portfolio of existing securities, they are required to ensure their compliance with the requirements of the Sharī'ah. The inclusiveness of the Sharī'ah in commercial transactions allows the adoption of conventional investment portfolios that do not contradict any of its fundamental principles. Similarly, conventional portfolios may be restructured by purging the non-Islamic element in the contracts and streamlining them, based on the Islamic financial instruments. This is one of the methods adopted in Islamic finance product innovation. Against this backdrop, three special asset classes have been identified:

- Islamic hedge funds
- funds of funds
- mixed funds.

### Islamic Hedge Funds

**hedge funds**
Alternative investment vehicles designed for a limited number of investors, targeted at maximizing returns through different advanced investment strategies.

**Hedge funds** are alternative investment vehicles designed for a limited number of investors and targeted at maximizing returns through different advanced investment strategies. Hedge funds are acceptable in the Islamic investment sector if they are free from all forbidden elements such as short-selling and dealing in conventional options, futures, currency swaps, and other derivatives. These derivatives involve speculative elements (*gharar*), which are prohibited under the Sharī'ah. Modern Sharī'ah scholars hold different views on hedge funds. While some believe it's possible to have Islamic hedge funds, others insist that there are speculative elements in these kinds of investment portfolios. The first Islamic hedge fund launched in the world was Alfanar US Equity Hedge Fund, which was launched in 2003 by Saudi Economic and Development Company (SEDCO) and the Permal Group.[4]

### Funds of Funds

A conventional fund of funds works like a mutual fund investing in another mutual fund. The rationale behind such a fund of funds strategy is to attain broader diversification benefits. Basically, a funds of funds investment strategy is a passive strategy where the investing fund, instead of creating its own portfolio, invests in another fund with a different investment objective to diversify its exposure.

The concept of funds of funds is relatively new. It is an interesting concept in Islamic investment. Although the basic concept sounds very appealing, it may be a less efficient technique for Islamic funds. The reason for this position is the number of Islamic funds as well as the higher commissions and fees involved, because they are charged for both funds.

### Mixed Funds

Although debt funds and equity funds are the most prominent investment techniques in Islamic investment, a new fund service has evolved over the last few years. Usually, a mixed fund may invest in a pool of different assets. For Islamic funds, mixed funds require investment in both equity and debt instruments, such as equities, leases, commodities, etc. Following the decline in global markets in 2001/2002, Islamic funds moved to much safer investment objectives. Since this period, some Islamic funds have preferred a mixed funds investment style to protect their capital. As indicated in *Islamic Finance in the News* box on page 227, the resilient nature of Islamic funds was demonstrated in the recent global financial crisis.

## Distribution and Marketing of Islamic Funds

Conventional investment funds take advantage of their expansive marketing and distribution systems to ensure maximum exposure to their target investor clients. With the advent of web-based technology, conventional investment funds have restructured their distribution networks. As a result, over the years, investment in conventional investment funds has become much easier for investors in terms of access and managing investment portfolios.

Islamic fund management, as an industry still in its infancy stage, is going through a transitional phase in terms of its functional structure, marketing, and distribution systems. Although Islamic funds are structured as separate business entities by legal requirement, many Islamic funds are managed and promoted by other Islamic banks or financial institutions. One of the reasons behind this interrelationship is that the banks preceded other Islamic financial institutions. Futhermore, Islamic banks, through their direct interaction with Islamic investors, were pioneers in catering for investors' demand for Sharī'ah-compliant alternatives to conventional investment funds.

# Distributions and Marketing Strategies for Islamic Investment Funds

To promote their investment products, Islamic funds may engage in different business strategies with other Islamic banks and financial institutions. A strategic alliance with other IFIs is an effective way to promote their marketability and also minimize marketing and distribution expenses. Some of the common business strategies for distribution and marketing for Islamic investment funds include joint ventures, strategic alliances, franchising, and outsourcing.

## Joint Ventures

Islamic investment funds may enter into joint venture agreements with other Islamic banks or conventional banks to gain higher market exposure and increase the investor network at a lower cost. Joint ventures may also create new exposure to prospective investors in other geographical locations. A joint venture agreement with conventional banks is approached with some reservation compared to agreements with Islamic banks, as proper precautions must be taken to ensure the separation of fund flows. Islamic Multi-Investment Funds, offered by a joint venture between American Express Bank (AMEX) and Faisal Finance is such an example. The Dar Al-Maal Al-Islami (DMI) group manages the mutual fund but it has the benefit of AMEX's expansive distribution network of 80 offices in 36 countries.

## Franchising

Islamic investment funds may engage in franchising to promote their products in different markets although it requires the Islamic funds' products to have some brand value among the prospective investors. Franchising is preferred over joint ventures between Islamic funds and other Islamic financial institutions as branded Islamic

A joint venture between American Express Bank (AMEX) and Faisal Finance resulted in the Dar Al-Maal Al-Islami (DMI) group. DMI manages the mutual fund but benefits from AMEX's expansive distribution network.

products are basically sold through a different service provider. To ensure the sanctity of Islamic products under franchise, the Islamic fund should ensure that the buying financial institution complies with the Sharī'ah requirements.

As with a joint venture, an Islamic fund may reach out to investors from different countries. One such example is the Kuwait-based The International Investor (TII), which used this strategy to expand operations into Gulf countries such as Bahrain, Qatar, and the United Arab Emirates.

### Outsourcing

The skills and experience of the fund managers are crucial for the success of a fund. Therefore, when structuring an Islamic fund, the principal financial institution may decide to outsource management expertise rather than managing the fund itself. One example is Al-Safwa International Equity Fund, owned by Al Tawfeek Company for Investment Funds Ltd, a subsidiary of the Dallah Al Baraka Group but managed by Roll and Ross Asset Management in Philadelphia in the United States.

## Challenges in the Marketing and Distribution of Islamic Funds

**liquidity**
The ability of a business to meet its obligations without necessarily disposing of its assets.

Conventional investment funds have made the best use of web-based technologies to reach out to a wide range of investors. Their easy access and ability to meet obligations without necessarily disposing of their assets, known as **liquidity**, have made investments in conventional investment funds a preferred substitute for commercial banks' certificates of deposits (CDs).

**investable securities**
A range of bonds or stocks that can be invested in the secondary market and which attract some form of revenue.

In contrast, Islamic mutual funds face different challenges in terms of reaching out to their prospective investors. One of the main challenges is the lack of liquidity. Although interest in Islamic funds has grown significantly over the years, the number of Sharī'ah-compliant investment funds and **investable securities** is still inadequate. In most cases, Islamic markets are also much more segmented.

Lack of appropriate management skills is another major challenge. Although some Islamic funds may choose to outsource management services to other investment banks or asset management firms, it is only possible at a high cost. In addition, as the Islamic investment process is unique in many ways, outsourcing may not be a good match for the Islamic investment sector.

Another big challenge for the Islamic funds is educating their prospective customers. Although investors may be interested in Islamic investments, they may not know the Islamic investment process and its uniqueness in terms of risk features. So to ensure customer loyalty, Islamic funds have additional responsibility to create an educated investor base in the first place.

Although web-based distributions have revolutionized the distribution channels for conventional investment funds, an identical solution for Islamic funds may not be

**economies of scale**
Proportionate savings in costs
gained by an increased level of
production.

realistically feasible. One reason may be the large proportionate cost savings gained by an increased level of production (**economies of scale**) that conventional investment funds enjoy, unlike the Islamic funds for whom a web-based distribution system may not be cost-effective because of the lack of economies of scale.

Although Islamic funds may access potential markets through joint ventures, franchises, or other strategic alliances, such strategies only reach a smaller investor base and also entail the risk of losing the goodwill and confidence of investors, as the products are not delivered directly.

**LEARNING OBJECTIVE 6.4**

Comprehend Shari'ah governance for Islamic funds and the importance of Islamic fund management.

# Shari'ah Governance of Islamic Funds

The continued demand for Shari'ah-compliant investments from investors from the Middle East and South-East Asia has increased the portfolio of Islamic funds tremendously. However, one important concern for investors is the guarantee of absolute Shari'ah compliance of all products. The Shari'ah governance framework has been introduced to ensure all investment products, services, and contracts comply with the fundamentals of the Shari'ah, the supervision being provided by experts. This is essential if the investing public is to have full confidence in the Islamic funds that manage their wealth. It is not enough for investment products to be Shari'ah-compliant. Every aspect of the investment process must also be Shari'ah-compliant, right from the contract stage to the point of declaration of profits and losses, if any.

The modern practice of Islamic wealth management has copied the wider Islamic finance industry by establishing standing Shari'ah boards. An alternative is to employ the services of Shari'ah consulting firms. Some Islamic funds prefer to employ the services of independent Shari'ah scholars on an ad hoc basis to review their investment processes, services, and contracts to ensure full compliance. As there is a need to monitor the process from the contract stage onwards, the option of establishing a permanent Shari'ah board appears to be more effective for Shari'ah governance of Islamic funds.

There is another dimension—a separate Shari'ah body or officer may be entrusted to ensure all procedures, services, and contracts for investment activities comply strictly with the rulings and recommendations of the Shari'ah board, enhancing the confidence of the investing public in the management. The establishment of Shari'ah supervisory boards in Islamic banks has played a pivotal role in the understanding of Shari'ah issues and practical financial transactions. Although the Shari'ah supervisory structures for Islamic banks vary from one to another quite significantly, over the years their effective interaction with financial practitioners has enhanced innovation and ensured sustainable growth in Islamic banking as a whole. Their relative success in ensuring good governance and safeguarding Islamic investors' best interests has boosted the confidence level of average investors who yearn for Shari'ah-compliant investments.

**Challenge**

Identify the Sharī'ah supervisory board of an Islamic fund management firm and list its members.

## Composition of the Sharī'ah Supervisory Board

The composition of the Sharī'ah supervisory board should be such that the Islamic investors can trust it and its members. Ideally, the members should possess a combination of strong academic and professional backgrounds in Islamic jurisprudence. A thorough understanding of financial transactions and the financial system is also required.

To guarantee investors' confidence, Islamic funds may also include members from different demographic groups. Although AAOIFI requires a minimum of three members for the Sharī'ah supervisory board, Islamic funds may select an individual Sharī'ah scholar to assume the supervisory role. Whether an institution has a board or a single supervisor is its own choice, but the composition of a Sharī'ah supervisory board should be included in the charter of the fund and fixed before the fund's inception.

## Functions of the Sharī'ah Supervisory Board

An efficient Sharī'ah supervisory board should assume responsibility for reviewing all processes and contracts and for auditing the compliance of the fund, including its components and management. The responsibility of the board may vary for different funds based on their charter and may include, but not be limited to, the following functions:

- monitoring the fund's compliance with the Sharī'ah
- overseeing the fund's portfolio purification
- reporting on the fund's compliance status
- assisting the fund's management
- advising on *zakat* and identifying the procedures for its distribution.

## Independence of the Sharī'ah Committee and Islamic Fund Infrastructure

To ensure optimal functioning of the Sharī'ah governance body, Islamic funds should be organized in such a way that the Sharī'ah supervisory board remains independent from management influence. Independence is more likely to impart better supervision and ensure investor confidence. Islamic investors often perceive the Sharī'ah board as the safeguard of compliance as well as ensuring their best interests. As the investment activities of Islamic funds often relate to innovations in products and services from fund managers, an efficient and independent supervisory board is crucial.

The relationship between the Sharī'ah board and other management committees of the Islamic fund is another critical issue in the effectiveness of supervision. As Islamic funds engage in product innovation at frequent intervals, the operational process should include cross-checking prospective new products for compliance in the first place by the Sharī'ah board.

# GLOBAL ISLAMIC FINANCE

## Islamic Fund Management in the Global Finance Industry

The exponential growth in the global Islamic finance industry has triggered tremendous interest in Shari'ah-compliant products. Although Islamic retail banking is still struggling to compete with its conventional counterpart, the Islamic fund management component has resiliently occupied an enviable position in North America. The period between 1999 and 2009 saw the establishment of Islamic funds in the United States and Canada. It is difficult to ascertain accurate figues for the size of the Muslim population in North America because of government policies on census and the exclusion of religion on the checklist to avoid discrimination. However, researchers have estimate there are around ten million Muslims in the region. Despite living in a predominantly Christian environment, many of the growing number of Muslims prefer Shari'ah-compliant funds for investment and asset management for religious reasons.

Islamic fund management firms have mainly focused on Islamic home financing products, which is significant to the development of the Islamic finance industry in the region. There is emphasis on home ownership in investment activities and the available tax incentives have engendered the establishment of a number of Islamic fund management firms. Shari'ah-compliant asset management companies have thrived in South-East Asian and the GCC countries, and now such firms are being launched in Europe and North America to tap the latent wealth in the hands of wealthy Muslims in these regions.

According to the Islamic Finance Information Service (IFIS), the total value of Islamic funds as of 2009 was US$22.8 billion in about 556 Islamic funds. These funds comprise a variety of asset classes ranging from equities, mixed assets, money market, real estate, *sukuk*, and others.

Despite the global financial crisis in 2009, more Islamic funds have been established to cater for the increasing demand for Shari'ah-compliant funds in Muslim communities around the world. Indeed, non-Islamic financial houses have also embraced Shari'ah-compliant products. These financial houses include the National Bank of Kuwait, which launched its first Islamic KD Ijarah Fund in June 2009. Growing investor demand led to the launch of KD Ijarah Fund II in August 2009, which was fully subscribed just within a day. The bank then launched KD Ijarah Fund III a month later, which offered investors the equivalent of 6 percent per annum throughout the life of the fund, with a minimum investment of an equivalent US$100,000. Concurrently, Shamil Bank of Bahrain launched the Shamil Solid Return Fund of US$25 million, targeted at expert investors who intend to diversify their investments in the market in areas such as crude oil, Islamic equities, *mudarabah* investments, and *sukuk*. Furthermore, in September 2009, The National Investor (TNI) of Abu Dhabi and Kipco Asset Management Company (Kamco) introduced a US$150 million Islamic fund. Two months later in November, QInvest of Qatar set up a US$200 million five-year mezzanine fund with Fortis Bank Nederland.

The Islamic fund management sector of the Islamic finance industry is expected to grow in the future. According to the Ernst & Young Islamic Funds and Investment Report for 2009: "Despite this setback [the global financial crisis], the fundamentals of the Islamic fund industry remain strong. With almost US$50 billion in fund assets under management and a large, expanding and untapped Muslim population, there are likely to be considerable opportunities in the future. This is a time when strategic choices have to be made and market participants have to adapt to survive."

Source: Bank Sarasin-Alpen publication on *Islamic Wealth Management Report 2010*. Available at www.sarasin-alpen.com/internet/ieae/index_ieae/about_us_ieae/media_relations_ieae/media_release_30.03.2010.pdf.

Islamic fund management is an important sector of the global Islamic finance industry. The high demands for Sharī'ah-compliant products in Muslim majority countries as well as minority communities in western countries have contributed to the growth of the Islamic finance industry.

## Compensation and Monitoring Fees

Compensation and monitoring fees for Sharī'ah board members should be commensurate with their professional expertise and academic qualifications. They may be compensated in the same manner as the BoD on the basis of monthly remuneration. Additional payment for meetings, out-of-pocket expenses, and a special allowance for the chair of the board is also possible. However, it is important for each member of the board to be compensated in the same manner to avoid conflict.

If an individual, or even a board, is assigned with the responsibility of Sharī'ah supervision, the fund may be obliged to provide a junior assistant to work under them. Although junior assistants may be on the regular company payroll, they should only report to the Sharī'ah supervisor and not management.

## Disclosure Issues

Disclosure issues in the investment industry are gaining in importance. Newer accounting and compliance standards require better disclosure practices for all investment funds. For Islamic funds, besides the regular disclosure of financial reporting and other management information, disclosure of Sharī'ah compliance information is also crucial. Islamic investors usually consider the annual Sharī'ah-compliance reports issued by the Sharī'ah boards as the benchmark. Additional Sharī'ah-compliance reports may also be prepared on a monthly or quarterly basis.

Above all, the Sharī'ah governance framework should focus more on wealth management. Disclosure issues are important because investors will want to know the state of their wealth at any point in time. There is no doubt that the Islamic fund management sector is relatively new in the global finance industry, as indicated in the *Global Islamic Finance* box. Despite this, a high level of managerial expertise is required on the part of the fund managers.

Learn the meaning and importance of risk management issues in Islamic funds, including risk-reward profile, with specific analysis of the risk-reward profile of major Islamic finance products.

# Risk Management for Islamic Investment Funds

Fund managers of both conventional and Islamic investment funds strive to attain similar investment and risk management objectives in managing their investment portfolios. Islamic fund managers essentially replicate some of the basic risk management strategies applied in conventional investment funds. However, there are additional risk management issues because of the uniqueness of Islamic funds and their products. The Islamic fund managers consider the limitations of Islamic investments while forming their risk management strategies such as the lack of investable securities, lack of liquidity, and the lack of Sharī'ah-compliant derivatives.

## Risk-Reward Profiles of Islamic Investment Products

**risk-reward profile**
A chart of the theoretical maximum profit or loss a particular investment can have in the portfolios of investors.

A chart of the theoretical maximum profit or loss a particular investment can have in investors' portfolios is known as a **risk-reward profile**. This has been described as the ratio used by investors to theoretically compare the expected returns on an investment (reward or profits) to the amount of risk undertaken to realize such returns. This enables prospective investors to choose an appropriate investment product or portfolio. Fund managers are in the best position to proffer professional advice to their clients on the risk-reward profile of the available investment products. Let's recall that equity financing in Islamic investment involves both profit and loss. Prospective investors are encouraged to ascertain the risk-reward profile of products they intend to invest in. This is part of the prudent practices that are encouraged in the Islamic finance industry. Risk-reward theory is the cornerstone of every investment philosophy.

### How to Calculate Risk-Reward Profile

The risk-reward profile is calculated mathematically. Potential investors identify suitable finance products based on the chart. The ratio is calculated by dividing the amount of profit the investor expects to make (i.e. reward) after the close of position by the amount the investor stands to lose if a loss is recorded in the investment (i.e. the risk). This is mathematically represented as follows:

$$\text{Risk-reward profile ratio} = \frac{\$ \text{ Reward}}{\$ \text{ Risk}}$$

The most common financial instruments used in Sharī'ah-compliant investment funds are *musharakah*, *mudarabah*, *murabahah*, and *ijarah*. Each of these Islamic investment products has a unique risk-reward profile. Knowledge of each risk profile will guide potential investors in identifying the best product for investing. Fund managers must also be proactive in discharging their fiduciary duty to potential investors by guiding them on the best product according to the prevailing market indices.

## Risk Management Strategies for Islamic Funds

The risk management strategies for Islamic funds may be divided into two broad categories: market risk management and liquidity risk management.

## Market Risk Management

Market risk for investment funds arises from the price volatility of the securities under investment. To manage the market risks of their portfolios, Islamic fund managers adopt two main strategies: portfolio diversification and portfolio protection.

### Portfolio Diversification

**portfolio diversification**
A business strategy for reducing risk through the investment in a wide variety of assets.

**firm-specific risk (unsystematic risk)**
Risk in the form of uncertainty in returns due to certain factors unique to the firm such as internal management, potential labor disputes, credit issues, product liability, etc.

Like conventional fund managers, Islamic fund managers invest in a variety of assets to minimize their risk exposure. This strategy is called **portfolio diversification**. Portfolio diversification may allow fund managers to diversify the risks unique to each individual firm (**firm-specific risk** or **unsystematic risk**). However, even after diversification, the systematic risk or the market risk component remains there for the managers to manage.

Unlike conventional fund managers, the challenges for Islamic fund managers are twofold. First, they need to diversify their portfolios within a limited range of Sharī'ah-compliant asset classes. Second, as the Islamic market has relatively lower depth in terms of trading activity and lower breadth in terms of the number of asset classes traded, the market may be more volatile compared to the conventional markets.

**portfolio protection**
A strategy for managing market risk and protecting against potential losses through the use of the relevant hedging instruments.

Because of these inherent features, Islamic fund managers are more cautious about managing market risks. An effective investment strategy for Islamic fund managers is to diversify their portfolio in terms of industrial sectors or geographical concentrations. Fund managers have to be skillful to identify assets with negative or small correlations to ensure maximum benefit from such diversification.

### Portfolio Protection

**exchange-traded derivatives**
Standardized derivative contracts, such as options and futures, which are transacted on an organized futures exchange.

**over-the-counter (OTC) derivatives**
(Or off-exchange trading) Non-standardized products traded between two parties directly rather than going through a stock exchange.

*arbun*
(Or *bay' al-arbun*)
A down payment made by a buyer to the seller with an option to rescind the contract by forgoing the payment as a penalty.

The second strategy used in managing market risk is **portfolio protection**. Conventional fund managers take advantage of different **exchange-traded derivatives** (standardized derivative contracts, such as options and futures, which are transacted on an organized futures exchange) and **over-the-counter (OTC) derivatives** (a platform for non-standardized derivative contracts) to manage their risk exposures. Fund managers engage in swaps, options (call and put options), futures, forwards, or other investment strategies to minimize their risk exposures. However, as most conventional derivatives are structured on the basis of *riba* and in some cases involve excessive risk-taking (*gharar*), such derivatives are not allowed in Islamic investment. In recent times, some *murabahah*- and **arbun**-based (a down payment made by a buyer to the seller with an option to rescind the contract by forgoing the payment as a penalty) solutions have been applied to mitigate risk exposures in currency, equity, and commodity funds. However, the use of futures and short positions is widely rejected by the majority of the Sharī'ah scholars and Islamic fund managers because of the exceedingly speculative nature of such arrangements.

## Liquidity Risk Management in the Islamic Funds Market

Generally, the Islamic fund market (unlike the funds themselves) is more liquid than its conventional counterpart. This has resulted in a surplus of liquidity, which is being channeled to other investments. However, there is a low return rate on liquid assets managed by Islamic financial institutions. To this end, Islamic fund managers face managing more-constrained liquidity issues. One important liquidity issue is the investment exit strategy. As there is no secondary market in the conventional sense, fund managers may have to depend on the sponsor principal, nominated liquidity agent, or other asset management company to exit an investment.

Islamic fund managers may also be wary of balance sheet mismatches and exposure to assets that cannot be sold easily. As most investors prefer investment in more liquid asset classes, fund managers should be prepared for higher cash outflow possibilities during falling markets when individual investors may wish to liquidate their position. Under such conditions, if fund managers strive to monetize their investment portfolios, they are likely to liquidate them at a lower price and risk losing the net asset value of the fund.

To encounter such liquidity crunches, fund managers may enter agreements with other financial institutions or liquidity providers. Proper precautions should be taken as Sharī'ah scholars discourage contractual agreements conditional upon contingencies. As an immediate measure, fund managers may leave some of the short-term cash balances in interest-free current accounts.

# Review

## Key Terms and Concepts

## Summary

**Learning Objective 6.1**

1. The Islamic asset and fund management framework is unique and has specific requirements such as the prohibition of *riba*, *gharar*, and *maysir* with the strict requirement of approval of an investment fund by a Sharī'ah board, which may sometimes exclude Islamic investors from conventional investment funds.

**Learning Objective 6.2**

2. Although the criteria for the selection of Islamic stocks for investing and review of the Islamic fund performance are similar to those of conventional funds, an additional requirement for Islamic funds is strict Sharī'ah compliance of the entire investment process from the screening stage to the distribution of income stage. The Islamic investment selection process comprises sector screen, financial screen, selection of Sharī'ah-compliant transactions and instruments, and purification of income distributions.

**Learning Objective 6.3**

3. The Islamic investment funds are based on Islamic finance instruments such as *mudarabah, musharakah, murabahah, ijarah*, and other permissible instruments known to the Sharī'ah. Therefore, the structure, marketing, and distribution of Islamic funds must be based on these fundamental contractual arrangements.

**Learning Objective 6.4**

4. The Sharī'ah supervisory board is the main body in the Sharī'ah governance framework for Islamic funds. However, Islamic investment firms may engage the services of Sharī'ah consultancy firms or independent scholars to review their investment portfolios and issue relevant rulings and recommendations to guide both investors and fund managers.

**Learning Objective 6.5**

5. Risk management in Islamic investment funds is as important as in conventional funds. Prudent practices are adopted to manage the funds effectively through the use of risk-reward profiles and liquidity risk management.

## Practice Questions and Activities

## Practice Questions

1. What are the main features of Islamic wealth management?

2. Distinguish between Islamic wealth management and conventional funds management.

3. As an expert in Islamic funds management, explain the criteria for the selection of Islamic stocks for investing to an Islamic fund manager.

4. How will you address the issue of non-compliant stocks in a secondary market?

5. As an Islamic funds manager, what steps would you take to establish Islamic investment portfolios that would be acceptable to a large population of Islamic investors in a Muslim country?

6. Describe the classification of Islamic investment funds.

7. What is the significance of Sharī'ah governance for Islamic investment funds?

8. What role should the Sharī'ah supervisory boards play in ensuring Sharī'ah compliance of Islamic investment funds?

9. As an Islamic finance expert, what kind of risk management strategies would you propose for Islamic funds?

10. Explain the dynamics of liquidity funds management of the Islamic fund markets.

## Activities

**1.** Using whatever research tool is within your reach, prepare a short note on the history of the Dow Jones Islamic Market Index and explain its significance in the global Islamic finance industry.

**2.** Prepare a short note on five major Islamic mutual funds.

**3.** In the distribution and investment strategies for Islamic investment funds, there may be a need to enter into a joint venture with a conventional financial institution. Prepare a ten-minute presentation on the joint venture between the American Express Bank (AMEX) and Faisal Finance, which led to the Islamic Multi-Investment Funds.

## Further Reading

Babai, D. (1998). Islamic Project Finance: Opportunities and Limitations. Presentation at Infrastructure and Project Finance Summit, *5th Annual Islamic Banking and Finance Forum*, Manama, Bahrain.

Boocock, J. G. and Presley, J. R. (1993). Equity Capital for Small and Medium-Sized Enterprises in Malaysia: Venture Capital or Islamic Finance. *Managerial Finance*. Vol. 19 (7): pp. 82–95.

Choudhury, M. A. (2001). Islamic Venture Capital—A Critical Examination. *Journal of Economic Studies*. Vol. 28 (1): pp. 14–33.

DeLorenzo, Y. (2009). Sharī'ah Supervision of Islamic Funds. In Humayon A. Dar, Umar F. Moghul (eds). *The Chancellor Guide to the Legal and Sharī'a Aspects of Islamic Finance*. London: Chancellor Publications Limited.

Elfakhani, S., Hassan, M. K. and Sidani, Y. (2006). *Islamic Mutual Funds*. Handbook of Islamic Banking and Finance, United Kingdom.

Hassan, M. K. and Ashraf, A. (2011). *Islamic Approach to Venture Capital Finance: An Alternative to Financing MME (Micro and Medium Enterprises)*. University of New Orleans Department of Economics and Finance Working Paper. p. 17.

Islamic Finance Qualification. (2006). *Islamic Asset and Fund Management*. London: Securities & Investment Institute.

Jaffer, S. (ed.). (2004*). Islamic asset management: forming the future for Sharī'a-compliant investment strategies*. London: Euromoney Books.

Maamouri, H. (1999). Issues and Challenges of Structuring and Restructuring in Islamic Project Financing. Paper presented at *Conference on Restructuring Islamic Project Financing* organized by The Asia Business Forum, Kuala Lumpur, Malaysia.

Obaidullah, M. (2005). *Islamic Financial Services*. Jeddah: Scientific Publishing Centre, King Abdul Aziz University.

# 7

# Islamic Bonds

# Learning Objectives

## Upon the completion of this chapter, the reader should be able to:

1 Understand what *sukuk* is, its historical origin and benefits, and the distinguishing features of *sukuk* from conventional bonds.

2 Understand how Islamic bonds are structured, and distinguish between different types.

3 Be familiar with the AAOIFI standards on Islamic bonds, and the characteristics of investment *sukuk* and Sharī'ah rulings defined by these standards.

4 Differentiate between sovereign and corporate ratings of Islamic bonds, and the methodology used to rate products.

A fundamental component of Islamic finance is the Islamic capital market (ICM). One of the major products available for investors who seek to invest and transact business in the ICM is Islamic bonds, popularly known as *sukuk*. This is the Islamic alternative to conventional bonds. The *sukuk* industry experienced phenomenal growth in the first decade of the 21st century. In 2011, a record-breaking US$84.4 billion *sukuk* were issued globally. This chapter examines Islamic bonds, focusing on their types, characteristics, structuring, rating, and the AAOIFI standards on Islamic bonds. In addition, a comparison between Islamic bonds and conventional bonds is also given to highlight some key differences between them, and the underlying concepts of Islamic bonds. The chapter further examines the most important elements of *sukuk* and some of the key issues involved in the securitization of Islamic products.

## professional perspectives

**Dr. Sayd Farook**

*Global Head of Islamic Capital Markets, Thomson Reuters*

**1    Can you explain the distinction between asset-backed *sukuk* and asset-based *sukuk*?**

In very simple terms, the distinction between asset-backed and asset-based relates to the ultimate recourse for *sukuk* certificate holders. For an asset-backed *sukuk*, certificate holders ultimately rely on underlying assets to generate yield and recover their investments. Good illustrations of these are toll roads, infrastructure assets, and mortgaged property sold to *sukuk* certificate holders. In the event of non-payment by the issuer or obligor, the *sukuk* certificate holders can sell these properties to recover their investment. In contrast, an asset-based *sukuk* involves the purchase and sale of assets (hence asset-based), but ultimately relies on the creditworthiness of a particular party (for instance, a corporate or a sovereign body) to fulfill its obligations, for example under a sales receivable or lease-based obligation. Hence, a *murabahah*-based, deferred payment *sukuk* will involve the sale and transfer of assets, but the only thing that remains for *sukuk* holders is an obligation by the buyer of the assets as the assets may have been sold.

**2    What can be done to improve liquidity in the *sukuk* market?**

Numerous intertwined factors contribute to the relative illiquidity of the *sukuk* market.

- Volume, diversity and quality of issuances: first and foremost is the volume, diversity and quality of issuances in dollar terms and the relative absorption capabilities of Islamic banks and financial institutions. Because Islamic banks consume all the available investable *sukuk* in the market and hold them until maturity (due to surplus liquidity and lack of other investments), *sukuk* tends to be traded less. To counter this trend, the volume of quality issuance has to reach levels that exceed the appetite of these traditional Islamic customers by at least 30 percent, which would allow the Islamic banks to divest some of these for trading.

- GCC acceptable: there is a very liquid and substantial market for ringgit-denominated *sukuk*. Yet, most of these are not accessible to Gulf-based Islamic bank investors as they require US dollars or local currency and they need them to be compliant with the Gulf interpretation of Islamic jurisprudence, as opposed to the Malaysian interpretation. Hence, we need issuers globally to issue *sukuk* that are acceptable to investors in the most conservative markets, such as Saudi Arabia.

- Emergence of dedicated market-makers for *sukuk*: it is not enough that there are sufficient issuances. There need to be dedicated market-makers who are directly incentivized to trade actively in *sukuk* markets.
- Price discovery: linked with the requirement for market-makers is the need for efficient price discovery. Looking at a Reuters quote screen for most *sukuk* compared with a conventional bond, one notices there are fewer traders quoting *sukuk* than there are quoting bonds. This is a major factor that affects the perceived liquidity for *sukuk*, as holders see that there are not enough 'tradable' quotes, implying there is a lack of liquidity for that particular *sukuk*.

### 3    How about rating of Islamic bonds?

Rating of Islamic bonds (*sukuk*) is undertaken by the three major ratings agencies and a host of niche or localized ratings agencies, including the Islamic International Rating Agency, MARC, RAM, JCR-VIS, etc. There are at least 25 to 30 Eurobond-style *sukuk* that are investment-grade rated, while thousands of Malaysian local currency issues are investment-grade rated.

The unique aspect of rating *sukuk* lies in the fact that they are structurally complicated, as opposed to a bond, which is a mere debt obligation. Hence, the first step for a ratings agency is to analyze the structure of cash flows and payment waterfall to assess who pays who and whose rights are prioritized by the issuer.

Once this is ascertained, *sukuk* can broadly be classified into two types: asset-backed or asset-based, and the ratings analysis will depend on which type of *sukuk* it is. If it is asset-backed, then the ratings analysis will largely follow the methodology of structured finance or asset-backed securities (ABS) by dissecting the capability of the assets to generate the cash flows required to pay the certificate holders (by modeling the probability of loss under various different scenarios), taking into consideration other material risk factors such as currency, taxes, political and legal risks, among other things. If it is asset-based, then the ratings analysis will follow the methodology of a bond, i.e. a pure credit instrument, and mostly disregard the structural issues (except as these relate to enforceability of obligations) and focus on the credit quality of the obligor.

**Dr. Andreas Jobst**

*Economist, Monetary and Capital Markets Department, International Monetary Fund (IMF)*

**1  Can you explain the distinction between asset-backed *sukuk* and asset-based *sukuk* and how do sukuk compare to securitization?**

*Sukuk*, like Islamic financial instruments in general, need to comply with Sharī'ah, which discourages risk-taking *per se* but stipulates that income must be derived from profitable investment in lawful activities rather than as a guaranteed return from interest. *Sukuk* commoditize these payment obligations from the use of existing or future (contractible) assets as part of a legitimate sale and not from exchange of homogenous goods or services, making asset-backing (in the form of tangible investment) an essential structural element. Investors receive returns from the direct participation in the performance of a real or non-monetary asset. Until recently, most *sukuk* were issued as asset-based securities on reference assets (such as covered bonds) with principal guarantees provided by issuers. After widely recognized recommendations by the Accounting and Auditing Organization for Islamic Finance Institutions (AAIOFI) in February 2008, however, *sukuk* have become more akin to asset-backed, pass-through, off-balance-sheet structures, without institutional guarantees on the asset performance and perfected security interest, i.e., the securitized cash flows are fully segregated from the originator's balance sheet. Unlike ABS, however, new *sukuk* structures imply direct investor recourse to a defined portfolio of assets, with fund secured repayment from profitable investment. Thus, ownership of *sukuk* investors in religiously sanctioned, real assets generating commoditized indebtedness (rather than pre-specified returns) moves *sukuk* closer to covered bonds in terms of dual investor protection.

**2  What can be done to improve liquidity in the *sukuk* market?**

*Sukuk* cannot reach their potential as a viable funding vehicle in the absence of a supportive market-based environment for secondary trading. The development of a suitable market infrastructure would include — given the frequent absence of organized financial markets (including a stock exchange) where *sukuk* could be listed in a Sharī'ah-compliant manner — the introduction of a common trading platform or alternatively the introduction of a system of market-makers. The trading platform facility could be facilitated by the clearing and payments services commonly provided by the central bank. Alternatively, a system of market-makers could be developed whereby they are obliged to quote buy and sell prices for on-demand wholesale transactions. Also, reserving a portion of the primary *sukuk* issuance for sale to retail investors could further support secondary market trading. In countries where organized trading already exists, efforts should be aimed at increasing market liquidity. This includes collecting and disseminating the information regarding *sukuk* trading prices in a systematic and centralized manner. In addition, consideration should be given to greater flexibility of Islamic banks to redress asset-liability matching constraints by trading *sukuk* firstly as investments over different tenors (a period within which a loan matures and becomes redeemable) to avoid short-term assets and deposits funding long-term liabilities and secondly as long-term funding sources to balance (often very concentrated) long-term exposures to real estate. In particular, the latter constraint is amplified by origination and servicer risk from a currently very narrow supply of *sukuk* in the primary market, which often poses challenges to investor diversification, and thus inhibits secondary market liquidity. In addition, by offering sovereign *sukuk*, governments can help expand the range of long-term financial products available as a catalyst of capital market development.

**3    How about rating of *sukuk*?**

While rating requirements for *sukuk* should generally follow those applied to conventional asset-backed securities (ABS), *sukuk* may include additional characteristics that increase their structural complexity and complicate the valuation and risk assessment process. For instance, ownership and possession *(qabd)* of the assets (rather than the proceeds from their use by third parties) rests with investors themselves, or their agents, throughout the life of the transaction in order to ensure definite performance, which has an impact on the estimation of loss-given-default (LGD). Moreover, *sukuk* also involve additional sources of operational risk. The contribution from investors in the form of proceeds from issued notes, and any returns generated by the issuing agent from managing collateral assets, cannot be reinvested in short-term cash instruments or interest-bearing debt. Also, any form of credit enhancement and/or liquidity support (and limitations of prepayment risk) must be in a permissible form and approved by Sharī'ah scholars. Finally, the initial debt standstill imposed on *sukuk* issued by property developer Nakheel in 2009—a commercial leasehold interest-based *ijarah* transaction based on to-be-developed waterfront properties with an explicit guarantee by the parent company Dubai World (but not the government of Dubai)—has raised uncertainty about investor protection and the rule of law governing *sukuk* for purposes of dispute resolution in times of distress. Moreover, given the significant involvement of quasi-sovereign entities in *sukuk* structures, greater clarity on perceived sovereign support will influence the rating of *sukuk* going forward.

# What are *Sukuk*?

**LEARNING OBJECTIVE 7.1**

Understand what *sukuk* is, its historical origin and benefits, and the distinguishing features of *sukuk* from conventional bonds.

This section examines the meaning of *sukuk*, and their benefits and distinguishing features when compared to conventional bonds. For a good understanding of *sukuk*, a term that simply means Islamic bonds, it is important to explain the definition of *sukuk* given by AAOIFI and the Islamic Financial Services Board (IFSB). There is no doubt that the government and corporate entities require funding for major projects. Just like conventional bonds, *sukuk* also seek to provide an alternative avenue for funding while adhering to Islamic commercial principles. To this end, this section focuses on the meaning of *sukuk*, the history, the benefits as given by Muhammad Taqi Usmani, and the differences between *sukuk* and conventional bonds.

## Meaning of *Sukuk*

**sukuk**
The plural form of *sak* which is an Islamic financial certificate that is similar to a bond.

*Sukuk* is an Arabic term for financial certificate. It is the Islamic equivalent of a bond, a bond being a debt security or certificate issued to a holder to document the existence of a debt owed by the issuer to the holder. Technically, a bond means debt instruments, which are issued by an authorized issuer for the purpose of raising capital. From the Islamic commercial perspective, AAOIFI defines *sukuk* as "certificates of equal value representing undivided shares in the ownership of tangible assets, usufruct (the legal right of using and enjoying a property leased), and services, or (in the ownership of) the assets of particular projects or special investment activity; however, this is true after the receipt of the value of the *sukuk*, the closing of the subscription and employment of funds received for the purpose for which the *sukuk* were issued."[1]

This means the certificates (*sukuk*) represent equal value in the ownership of a known asset and the *sukuk* (bond) holders share in the ownership of the asset. Their respective share in the ownership cannot be divided but the certificates issued clearly stipulate the value of each of the certificate holders. The certificates indicate the partial ownership of each holder in the asset, unlike a conventional bond where it is a mere promise to repay a loan. The underlying asset can be a tangible asset (e.g. real estate, airport), usufruct (e.g. the right to the benefit derived in a property such as rent), and services (e.g. education program or technical know-how provided by a specified institution or supplier).

The IFSB defines *sukuk* in its Capital Adequacy Standard (IFSB-2) as "certificates that represent the holder's proportionate ownership in an undivided part of an underlying asset where the holder assumes all rights and obligations to such asset."[2] As explained above, *sukuk* are certificates that represent the value of an asset and the share of the holder in that asset.

*Sukuk*, as a financial instrument, are increasingly accepted and widely used in the Islamic finance industry globally. As a mandatory Sharī'ah requirement, *sukuk* holders must have interest or ownership in the underlying asset. The stipulation of an underlying asset while making the legal documentation for *sukuk* should not just be to satisfy the Sharī'ah requirements. It must be practically demonstrated that *sukuk* holders have a recognizable interest in the asset.

**Islamic capital market**
A secondary market where financial and trade activities are carried out in ways that do not contradict Islamic commercial law.

Conventional bonds that yield interest (*riba*) are prohibited in Islamic law. The need to provide a suitable and competitive alternative for the **Islamic capital market** (ICM) is borne out of the fact that conventional bonds satisfy social and economic needs, though flawed with interest-bearing and excessively risk-bearing transactions. What is being financed through the issuance of bonds must be a permissible commodity or project in an Islamic commercial transaction. Prohibited items such as setting up a piggery or brewery may not be allowed in the ICM. For this reason, the regulatory authorities of the ICM in different countries have a standing Sharī'ah advisory committee that screens the products and projects.

## A Brief History of *Sukuk*

From the classical period of Islam, the word *sak*, the singular form of *sukuk* was generally used to refer to any document or certificate representing an obligation, contract, conveyance of rights executed in conformity to the principles of Sharī'ah. During the medieval period, the use of *sak* gained more prominence as the main instrument for transferring obligations arising from commercial transactions. (The word has the same linguistic origin as check, which simply refers to a promise to pay an amount of money for certain goods that have been delivered.) This was meant to reduce the movement of money from one city to another, which may not be secured.

Even before the medieval period, there are historical references to the use of *sukuk* during the Umayyad Caliphate in the 1st century of the Islamic calendar. This earliest usage of *sukuk* relates to the method of payment of the soldiers, who were given commodity coupons in place of cash. The Prophetic narration, which documents this practice, is as follows:

> Yahya related to me from Malik that he had heard that receipts (*sukuk*) were given to people in the time of Marwan ibn al-Hakam for the produce of the market at al-Jar. People bought and sold the receipts (*sukuk*) among themselves before they took delivery of the goods. Zayd ibn Thabit and one of the Companions of the Messenger of Allah, may Allah bless him and grant him peace, went to Marwan ibn al-Hakam and said: 'Marwan! Do you make usury halal?' He said: 'I seek refuge with Allah! What is that?' He said: 'These receipts (*sukuk*) which people buy and sell before they take delivery of the goods.' Marwan therefore sent a guard to follow them and to take them from people's hands and return them to their owners.[3]

In the above passage, there is express mention of the word *sukuk*. The narration refers to a specific prohibition under the Sharī'ah on the sale of food commodities before taking possession. What instigated this swift disapproval was the practice by some soldiers to exchange their coupons for cash prior to the maturity of the commodities. They were only expected to use their coupons to collect grain upon maturity. With the exception of food commodities, there is a general permissibility for the issuance of a certificate for the value of an underlying asset where the certificate holder shares in its ownership.

In the modern practice of Islamic finance, the medieval concept of *sak* was adapted to provide alternative funding for financing projects through asset securitization. This led to a ruling by the International Islamic Fiqh Academy of the Organization of Islamic Cooperation (OIC), which clearly explains Sharī'ah-compliant investment securities and effectively legitimizes the concept of *sukuk*. The tradability of *sukuk* in the ICM may be considered a modernization of the practice during the medieval period. It is purely a re-enactment of olden day trade and commercial practices.

## Benefits of *Sukuk*

**trust certificates**
Debt investment or bonds that are backed by other assets for the purpose of collateral.

The benefits of *sukuk* depend on the various *sukuk* structures, which we will elaborate further in the next section. Meanwhile, it is important to discuss the general benefits and advantages of *sukuk*. As Islamic finance is by nature asset-backed, the uniqueness of *sukuk* is that they are an asset-backed instrument and are Sharī'ah-compatible **trust certificates** that are tradable. Box 7.1 explains the benefits of *sukuk* according to Muhammad Taqi Usmani. Many governments and financial institutions within

### BOX 7.1:    BENEFITS OF *SUKUK*

- *Sukuk* are among the best ways of financing large enterprises that are beyond the ability of a single party to do so.
- *Sukuk* provide an ideal means for investors seeking to deploy streams of capital and who require, at the same time, the ability to liquidate their positions with ease whenever the need should arise. This is because it is envisioned that a secondary market for trading *sukuk* will develop. Thus, whenever investors require cash from their investments, or from a part of the same, it will be possible for them to sell their *sukuk* holdings, or a part thereof, and receive the value of their original investment plus earnings, if the enterprise is profitable, in cash.
- *Sukuk* represent an excellent way of managing liquidity for banks and Islamic financial institutions (IFIs). When these need to dispose of excess liquidity they may purchase *sukuk*; and when they are in need of liquidity, they may sell their *sukuk* into the secondary market.
- *Sukuk* are a means for the equitable distribution of wealth as they allow all investors to benefit from the true profits resulting from the enterprise in equal shares. In this way, wealth may circulate on a broad scale without remaining the exclusive domain of a handful of wealthy persons. This is clearly among the most important of all the higher purposes sought by an Islamic economic system.

Source: Muhammad Taqi Usmani. (2007). *Sukuk and Their Contemporary Applications* (translated from the Arabic by Yusuf Talal DeLorenzo). AAOIFI: pp. 2–3.

and outside the Muslim world have used *sukuk* as an instrument for socioeconomic development. *Sukuk* can be validly adopted to finance key projects, whether in the public or private sector, such as airports, dams, bridges, and roads, etc. *Sukuk* plays a tremendous role in Islamic securitization depending on the model adopted among the varieties of target-specific *sukuk* models.

Building on the benefits described in Box 7.1, the advantages of *sukuk* include the following.

1. DIVERSIFICATION OF FUND SOURCES. Corporate bodies and governments require funds for business and capital projects respectively. *Sukuk* is a major source of revenue to undertake these projects, which also creates a wider investor base. While an opportunity is created for investors to become partners in the project, the government or corporate entity enjoys larger funding.

2. SECONDARY LIQUIDITY. The investors or *sukuk* holders are provided with a reasonable amount of liquidity, which allows them to freely trade their securities in the secondary market. The *sukuk* holder must have a legal title in the underlying asset before trading their securities. *Sukuk* also allows the banks and IFIs to manage their liquidity effectively.

3. CREATION AND ENHANCEMENT OF PROFILE ON THE INTERNATIONAL MARKET. The issuance of *sukuk* creates and enhances the profile of the issuer in international markets. *Sukuk* are accessed and rated by international rating agencies, which in turn boosts their profile on the international market. A well-managed *sukuk* issuance will enhance the profile of the issuing company in international markets and thus attract investors who seek to invest through a company of good reputation.

4. INFRASTRUCTURAL DEVELOPMENT IN MUSLIM COUNTRIES. Most Muslim-majority countries such as Malaysia, United Arab Emirates, and Qatar use *sukuk* instruments for mega-projects such as the construction of airports (Malaysia), solar and biogas plants (United Arab Emirates), and Hamad Medical City (Qatar). *Sukuk* has contributed tremendously to the infrastructural development of these countries. As illustrated in *Islamic Finance in the News*, *sukuk* is now being used in most countries to raise funds for infrastructure development.

5. PRICING BENCHMARK. The process of creating a common pool of investments in asset-backed securities allows for interbank market pricing, where the value of the units in the *sukuk* is used to determine the profit margin. The tradability of *sukuk* in the secondary market allows the market players to determine the pricing benchmark where the value of the units serves as the indicator for determining the price.

6. SIZEABLE FINANCING. The issuance of *sukuk* has a maturity horizon and investors can be confident of the security of their funds as well as the profitability of the project. The securities are in small denominations, which allows for ease of clearing and settlement at the maturity date.

## Differences Between *Sukuk* and Conventional Bonds

Even though *sukuk* may easily be likened to conventional bonds, there are a number of differences between the two forms of securities, as summarized in Table 7.1 on page 262. There are five major differences.

# ISLAMIC FINANCE IN THE NEWS

## Saudi *sukuk* success boosts bond hopes

February 8, 2012

**B**ankers expect a bumper year of bond sales in Saudi Arabia following the success of the country's first sovereign-guaranteed *sukuk* in January.

The 15bn riyal (US$4bn) Islamic instrument, issued to finance the expansion of Jeddah's international airport, was the largest single-tranche *sukuk* yet, says HSBC, which led the issuance. It was sold at a profit rate of 2.5 percent and was 3.5 times oversubscribed.

'What we saw in this issuance was extremely good prices, extremely liquid markets and extreme confidence among investors,' says Fahad al-Saif, head of the debt capital markets at HSBC in Saudi Arabia.

Mr al-Saif expects to see at least five big new Islamic bond issuances in the kingdom this year. 'Debt capital markets are now definitely an option for Saudi entities looking to diversify their funding,' he says.

The sovereign guarantee helped the 10-year bond be priced at 59 basis points above the 10-year US Treasury, and bankers expect the rate to become the new risk-free benchmark for the Saudi debt market.

'The financial system will take it as a reference point,' says Mr al-Saif, making it easier to price and evaluate future debt. 'We expect a record number of issuances.'

The Saudi debt market was largely illiquid at maturities ranging beyond five years, and the new 10-year notes will help in plotting a yield curve for the Saudi riyal, which should also encourage new issuances.

'This is a very positive development. The size is massive and it's encouraging that they got 10-year money—so the domestic market can provide liquidity and tenor as well,' says Yavar Moini, an executive director at Morgan Stanley

in Dubai. 'This all bodes well for corporate and non-government-related issuances to the market.'

Saudi borrowers have traditionally relied on bank lending but, if credit conditions remain tight, Mr Moini says more will look to the *sukuk* market. 'Ideally, Saudi would take a leaf out of Malaysia's book, with its vibrant domestic issuance market,' he says.

For investors, the debt has been assigned a zero percent risk weighting by the Saudi Arabian Monetary Agency, meaning it can be held as an investment but also used as collateral to tap liquidity from the Saudi central bank.

While the *sukuk* broke records both in the Saudi market and the Islamic finance industry, it was also the largest sovereign-guaranteed emerging-market debt issuance in a decade, HSBC said.

The Saudi government has been gradually moving to develop its capital markets as the state embarks on a US$130bn spending program, announced in 2011.

In January, its capital markets regulator announced that foreign companies listed on other regulated exchanges overseas would be allowed to list their shares on the Saudi bourse, the largest in the Arab world. The market remains closed to foreign investors, who can currently only buy stocks through unpopular swap agreements with Saudi-based intermediaries.

But that too may soon change, with growing speculation that direct foreign ownership of Saudi stocks will be permitted at some point this year, with the authorities conducting test trades and holding discussions with brokerages and asset managers.

**Source:** Tom Gara and Simeon Kerr, "Saudi *sukuk* success boosts bond hopes", *Financial Times*, February 8, 2012.

1. Conventional bonds are contractual debt securities where the authorized issuer undertakes to pay the interest and principal to the bondholders on specified dates. On the other hand, *sukuk* are not contractual debts. They represent the undivided ownership of each of the *sukuk* holders in the underlying asset.

2. The return in conventional bonds is in the form of interest (coupon) and the principal amount whereas in *sukuk*, the return is in the form of profits that are paid out pro rata in

**TABLE 7.1: Major Differences between *Sukuk* and Bonds**

|  | *Sukuk* | Bond |
|---|---|---|
| Definition | Ownership stake in asset | Issuer's pure debt |
| Certificates | Trust certificates | Debt certificates |
| Return earned | Profit | Principal and interest |
| Asset | Physical asset | Receivables, financial assets |
| Ownership | Asset or its usufruct | Debt, no ownership |
| Relationship | Partner | Creditor |

accordance with the value of shares held by each *sukuk* holder. Any revenue generated by the *sukuk* asset is shared among all investors. That is, while there is an obligation to pay interest in the conventional bond, the return on *sukuk* is generated from the underlying asset.

3. The contractual relationship between the issuer and the investors is simply a partnership and not a debtor and credit relationship, as in the case of conventional bonds.

4. *Sukuk* holders have ownership rights in the underlying asset, while conventional bonds do not usually carry ownership rights in the asset as they merely represent a debt certificate.

5. *Sukuk* must be asset-backed, while bonds may not necessarily be asset-backed. Conventional bonds may be backed by financial assets such as receivables, which are not allowed in the case of *sukuk*. That is, *sukuk* cannot be issued based on receivables, as it is not a debt, whereas bonds can be.

**Islamic financial engineering**
Principles and strategies for developing innovative Islamic financial products and solutions based on the methodology of Islamic jurisprudence.

# Structuring Islamic Bonds

In the structuring of Islamic bonds, there is a general tendency to replicate the features of conventional bonds, although with due diligence and requisite caution to exclude those characteristics that impinge on the fundamental principles of the Sharī'ah in commercial transactions, such as the prohibition of *riba* (interest) and *gharar* (excessive risk). Financial market professionals sit alongside the Sharī'ah experts to design the dynamics of Islamic bonds. The process of modeling and structuring them requires a basic knowledge of the major Islamic finance products such as *mudarabah* (trust financing), *musharakah* (joint partnership), *ijarah* (lease), *murabahah* (mark-up trade), *wakalah* (agency contract), and *istisna'* (manufacturing contract). We have discussed these in previous chapters. Islamic finance experts have developed, modeled, and structured these finance products through the process of **Islamic financial engineering** to introduce competitive products into the ICM. We will now look at the structuring of Islamic bonds and discuss relevant examples according to their type.

# Types and Structure of Islamic Bonds

Islamic bonds or *sukuk* are structured to reflect the basic requirements of the Sharī'ah for commercial and financial transactions. *Sukuk* can be of many types depending on the types of Islamic finance products used in their structuring. AAOIFI has identified 14 major *sukuk*-structured products and these are outlined in Table 7.2.

| | TABLE 7.2: The Fourteen *Sukuk* Structures of AAOIFI | |
|---|---|---|
| | *Sukuk* Structure | Explanation / Areas of Significance |
| 1 | *Sukuk ijarah* (leased asset certificates) | The owner(s) of an existing tangible leased asset may sell (securitize) such assets through *sukuk* issues. |
| 2 | *Sukuk ijarah mawsufah fi dhimmah* (forward lease certificates) | The owner(s) of a tangible asset to be acquired and subject to a lease contract may mobilize the acquisition cost of such an asset through *sukuk* issues. |
| 3 | *Sukuk manfaa ijarah* (usufruct of a lease certificate) | The owner(s) of leasehold rights of existing leased asset(s) may sell (securitize) the usufruct of such assets through *sukuk* issues. |
| 4 | *Sukuk manfaa ijarah mawsufah fi dhimmah* (usufruct of a forward lease certificate) | The owner(s) of leasehold rights of an asset to be acquired and subject to lease contract may sell (securitize) the usufruct of such an asset through *sukuk* issues. |
| 5 | *Sukuk milkiyat al-khadamat* (ownership of service certificates) | Proprietor(s) wishing to undertake specific services may mobilize the cost of such services by pre-selling the services and their expected benefits through *sukuk* issues. |
| 6 | *Sukuk al-salam* (forward contract certificates) | Proprietors wishing to produce or provide specific goods/commodities at a future date may pre-sell these through *sukuk* issues. |
| 7 | *Sukuk al-istisna'* (manufacturing certificates) | Constructors, manufacturers, and others wishing to construct, manufacture and deliver specific assets at a future date may seek the cost of such future delivery assets through *sukuk* issues. |
| 8 | *Sukuk al-murabahah* (cost-plus certificates) | Proprietor(s) wishing to acquire certain goods/commodities to be sold on under a *murabahah* agreement may mobilize the cost of such goods/commodities through *sukuk* issues. The sukuk holders shall own such goods/commodities and be entitled to their sale price. |
| 9 | *Sukuk al-musharakah* (partnership certificates) | Proprietor(s) in a business partnership may seek capital participants in the partnership through *sukuk* issues. The *sukuk* holders share in the risks and rewards of the partnership. |
| 10 | *Sukuk al-mudarabah* (trust investment certificates) | An entrepreneur (*mudarib*) with a good business idea but little or no capital may mobilize sufficient funds for a proposed business/project from capital providers through *sukuk* issues. The *sukuk* holders share in the risks and rewards of the *mudarabah*. |
| 11 | *Sukuk al-wakalah* (investment agency certificates) | Capital may be raised through *sukuk* issues to acquire certain assets, goods, or services that are then entrusted to an agent (*wakil*) to manage them on behalf of the owners. The *sukuk* holders take the risk of the underlying assets, goods, or services and are entitled to any profits they generate. |

| | **Sukuk Structure** | **Explanation / Areas of Significance** |
|---|---|---|
| **TABLE 7.2 (continued): The Fourteen Sukuk Structures of AAOIFI** | | |
| 12 | *Sukuk al-muzara'a* (sharecropping certificates) | The principal owner(s) of agricultural land (or the owner(s) of the leasehold rights to such land) may mobilize funds for the cultivation of the land through a *sukuk* issue. The subscribers to such *sukuk* are entitled to a share of the produce of the land as per original agreements with the owner(s). |
| 13 | *Sukuk al-musaqa* (irrigation certificates) | The owner(s) of mature farm trees (orchards) may mobilize funds for their irrigation, maintenance, and other uses through *sukuk* issues. The subscribers to such *sukuk* are entitled to a share of the produce of the trees as per original agreements with the owner(s). |
| 14 | *Sukuk al-mugharasa* (agricultural certificates) | The owner(s) of farmland with trees or crops thereon may mobilize funds to maintain the land as well as the trees/crops through *sukuk* issues. The subscribers to such *sukuk* are entitled to a share of the produce of the land and the trees as per original agreements with the owner(s). |

Source: Adapted from Nathif J. Adam and Abdulkader Thomas. (2004). Islamic fixed-income securities: sukuk. In Jaffer, S. (ed.), *Islamic Asset Management: Forming the Future for Shari'ah-Compliant Investment Strategies* (pp. 73–74). London: Euromoney Books.

**tradable *sukuk***
Islamic investment certificates that represent tangible assets or proportionate ownership of a business or investment portfolio.

**non-tradable *sukuk***
Investment certificates that represent receivables of cash or goods.

**equity-based *sukuk***
Partnership-based Islamic investment certificates of partnership contracts where the parties share the profits as well as any risk arising from the investment activity.

**debt-based *sukuk***
Investment certificates that are based on receivables such as debt where the rights of the certificate holders are shares in the debt.

It is important to give a brief overview of some of the popular *sukuk* in practice and their structural application in the modern capital markets. Some of the types of *sukuk* listed in Table 7.2 have been classified *tradable* while others have been classified *non-tradable*, depending on their characteristics. **Tradable *sukuk*** are Islamic investment certificates that represent tangible assets or proportionate ownership of a business or investment portfolio. These certificates are tradable in the capital market. Examples of this include *sukuk al-ijarah, sukuk al-musharakah* and *sukuk al-mudarabah*. On the other hand, **non-tradable *sukuk*** are investment certificates that represent receivables of cash or goods. Examples of these include *sukuk al-murabahah* and *sukuk al-salam*, which are generally non-tradable as they are financial assets. They cannot form the underlying asset of a tradable *sukuk* because it may amount to a sale of debt, which is not allowed in Islamic law. Table 7.3 classifies the investment certificates as tradable and non-tradable *sukuk* in accordance to the AAOIFI classification, although this is subject to the relevant rules applicable to the trading and redemption of *sukuk* in Islamic law.

Other common classifications of the types of *sukuk* structures are debt-based and equity-based, also shown in Table 7.3. **Equity-based *sukuk*** are partnership-based Islamic investment certificates of partnership contracts where the parties share the profits as well as any risk arising from the investment activity. They reflect the real essence of Islamic finance where parties are required to mutually engage in profitable business. This why equity-based *sukuk* are tradable in the ICM. On the other hand, **debt-based *sukuk*** are investment certificates based on receivables such as debt where the rights of the certificate holders are shares in the debt. Debt-based *sukuk* such as *sukuk al-salam* and *sukuk al-murabahah* are generally not tradable. AAOIFI generally encourages Islamic banks and financial institutions to use more equity-based instruments in their financing activities.

**TABLE 7.3: Classification of *Sukuk* According to Types**

| Classification | Types of *Sukuk* |
|---|---|
| Tradable *sukuk* | *sukuk al-ijarah*<br>*sukuk manfaa ijarah*<br>*sukuk ijarah mawsufah fi dhimmah*<br>*sukuk al-musharakah*<br>*sukuk al-mudarabah*<br>*sukuk al-wakalah*<br>*sukuk al-muzara'a*<br>*sukuk al-musaqa*<br>*sukuk al-mugharasa*<br>*sukuk al-istisna'*<br>*sukuk milkiyat al-khadamat* |
| Non-tradable *sukuk* | *sukuk al-murabahah*<br>*sukuk al-salam*<br>*sukuk milkiyat al-khadamat for future services*<br>*sukuk manfaa ijarah mawsufah fi dhimmah* |
| Equity-based *sukuk* | *sukuk al-ijarah*<br>*sukuk al-mudarabah*<br>*sukuk al-musharakah*<br>*sukuk al-wakalah* |
| Debt-based *sukuk* | *sukuk al-salam*<br>*sukuk al-murabahah*<br>*sukuk al-istisna'* |

In this section we discuss the most common *sukuk* in use in the industry—*mudarabah sukuk* (trust investment bonds), *musharakah sukuk* (partnership investment bonds), and *ijarah sukuk* (leased asset bonds).

## *Mudarabah Sukuk* (Trust Investment Bonds)

**mudarabah sukuk**
Investment certificates that represent the ownership of units of equal value in the equity of trust financing investment and are registered in the name of the holders.

According to AAOIFI, **mudarabah sukuk** are investment *sukuk* that represent the ownership of units of equal value in the *mudarabah* equity, registered in the names of the *sukuk* holders. The *sukuk* holders are entitled to returns according to the percentage of their respective ownership of shares. In *mudarabah sukuk*, the *sukuk* holders are the financiers, otherwise known as *rabb al-mal* (fund providers). Big investment projects may be developed using *mudarabah sukuk* to encourage wide public participation. It is usually structured as an agreement between the *rabb al-mal* who provides the capital, in this case all the *sukuk* holders. The other party is the entrepreneur, which may be an investment company or a special purpose vehicle (SPV) that is formed to manage the securities and carry out the business projects. While the SPV is the *mudarib* (fund manager), the subscribers are the *rabb al-mal*. The returns are shared in accordance with each *sukuk* holder's percentage of share ownership, based on a profit-sharing basis according to predetermined ratios. Losses are borne by the financiers but necessary measures are put in place to mitigate risks. Risk mitigation is achieved through the process of securitization, where investors make their investment decisions based on the

*Mudarabah sukuk* can be used for project financing. In order to finance the expansion of Jeddah International Airport to cater for the growing number of pilgrims visiting Mecca and Medina, the government may issue *mudarabah sukuk*.

degree of protection provided by the structure of the SPV. In addition, the securitized asset must be able to meet the principal as well as expected returns.

*Mudarabah sukuk* can be used for project financing. For example, as Jeddah in Saudi Arabia is a hub for pilgrims to Mecca and Medina, Jedda International Airport requires periodic expansion to cater for the growing number of pilgrims visiting the sanctuaries every year. In order to finance this, the government may decide to issue investment bonds using any suitable Islamic finance contract to source enough funding for the project. It may decide to use the *mudarabah* model to structure the bond. An example of *mudarabah sukuk* is illustrated in Figure 7.1.

The basic features of *mudarabah sukuk* are articulated in the Resolution of the International Islamic Fiqh Academy of the OIC in its fourth session in 1988.

1.  *Mudarabah sukuk* (MS) represent common ownership and entitle their holders to a share in the specific projects against which the MS have been issued.

2.  The MS contract is based on the official notice of the issue or the prospectus, which must provide all information required by Sharī'ah for a *qirad* (loan for financing trade) contract, such as the nature of capital, the ratio for profit distribution and other conditions related to the issue, which must be compatible with Sharī'ah.

3.  The MS holder is given the right to transfer the ownership by selling the *sukuk* in the securities market at their discretion. The market value of *muqaradah sukuk* varies with the business status and anticipated or expected profits of the concerned project. The sale of MS must follow the rules listed below:

    •   if the *mudarabah* capital is still in the form of money before the operation of the specific project, the trading of MS will be like the exchange of money for money and it must satisfy the rules of *bay al-sarf* (currency exchange contract)

- if the *mudarabah* capital is in the form of debt, it must be based on the principles of debt trading in Islamic jurisprudence

- if the capital is in the form of a combination of cash, receivables, goods, real assets, and benefits, trade must be based on the market price evolved by mutual consent.

4. The manager/SPV who receives the funds collected from the subscribers to MS can also invest his own funds. They will earn a profit for their capital contribution in addition to their share in the profit as *mudarib*.

5. Neither prospectus nor MS should contain a guarantee, from the issuer or the manager of the fund, for the capital or a fixed profit, or a profit based on any percentage of the capital. Accordingly, (i) the prospectus, or the MS issued pursuant to it, may not stipulate payment of a specific amount to the MS holder, (ii) profit is to be divided, as determined by applying the rules of Shari'ah; that is, an amount in excess of the capital, and not the revenue or the yield, and (iii) the profit and loss account of the project must be published and disseminated to MS holders.

6. It is permissible to create reserves for contingencies, such as loss of capital, by deducting from the profit a certain percentage in each accounting period.

7. The prospectus can also contain a promise made by a third party, totally unrelated to the parties to the contract, in terms of legal entity or financial status, to donate a specific sum, without any counter benefit, to meet losses in a given project, provided such commitment is independent of the *mudarabah* contract. However, it is not permissible for the issuer to guarantee the capital of the *mudarabah*.[4]

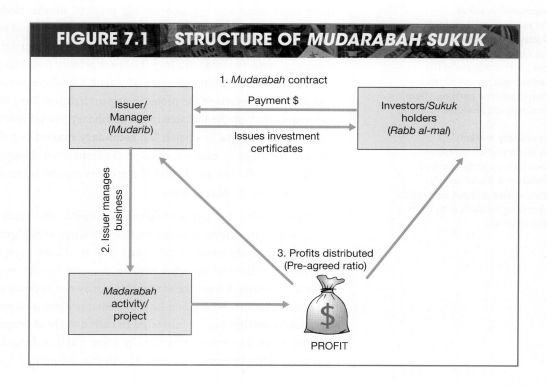

**FIGURE 7.1    STRUCTURE OF *MUDARABAH SUKUK***

In *mudarabah sukuk* structuring, an originator may decide to seek funding through the use of an SPV. The illustration given Figure 7.1 depicts a simple *mudarabah sukuk*. In practice, there are more complex structures that involve more than one financing instrument.

*Mudarabah sukuk* must be registered in the names of the *sukuk* holders as they are individually considered as owners of common shares in the capital of the business. In Figure 7.1, the following procedure is adopted.

1. An entrepreneur or company invites investors to participate in the *mudarabah* contract, which results in the issuance of investment certificates and payment for the value of shares allotted. In this case, the issuer is the manager of the venture, who provides entrepreneurial skills, while the certificate holders are the capital providers.

2. The fund generated is used as capital. The issuer manages the business on behalf of the investors in whatever business, project, or activity the parties have agreed upon in the underlying contract.

3. Any profits are distributed periodically according to the predetermined ratio as contained in the underlying contract. The issuer pays the *sukuk* holders in proportion to their individual shareholding in the capital invested. In the case of any losses, the investors are solely responsible, unless it can be proved that the loss was caused by negligence, mismanagement or fraud on the part of the entrepreneur.

## Musharakah sukuk

**musharakah sukuk**
(or *sukuk al-musharakah*)
Partnership certificates used for raising capital to widen the partnership net of the investment, where all the participants or partners share the risks and rewards.

**secondary market**
A market where investors purchase securities such as bonds and stocks among themselves without necessarily receiving funds directly from the issuers.

Where huge sums are required for big projects, **musharakah sukuk** may be more appropriate for securitization. They are investment bonds that represent the ownership of the partnership equity and can be used to mobilize funds for a new project, develop an existing project or finance a huge business activity based on joint venture contracts. The *musharakah* certificate given to all *sukuk* holders represents their proportion of ownership in the assets of the project being undertaken. They are treated as negotiable instruments that can be tradable in the secondary market (that is, they can be bought and sold in the capital markets). The **secondary market** is a market where investors purchase securities or assets such as stocks from other investors, rather than directly from the issuer. On the other hand, the primary market is the market platform for the original issuance of the certificates.

The Sharī'ah rules that apply to *mudarabah sukuk* also apply to *musharakah sukuk*, particularly in the arena of profit and loss sharing. While profit is shared according to an agreed predetermined ratio, any loss is shared according to the individual contribution of the parties/*sukuk* holders involved. Bear in mind that the capital pool of *musharakah sukuk* from the stakeholders may not necessarily be fully liquid assets. There are situations where non-liquid assets are combined with liquid assets. *Liquid assets* are items that can be converted to cash quickly or immediately such as checks, checking accounts or securities. On the other hand, *non-liquid assets* are items that cannot be easily converted to cash due to the substantial loss in value that would occur, and these include real estate, antiques, and stocks. The non-liquid assets must be evaluated accordingly to determine the ratio of contribution of each of the stakeholders. Meanwhile, every subscriber is entitled to participate in the management of the business if he or she so wills.

The structure of a *musharakah sukuk* is based on a joint venture partnership. A simple example of this is illustrated in Figure 7.2.

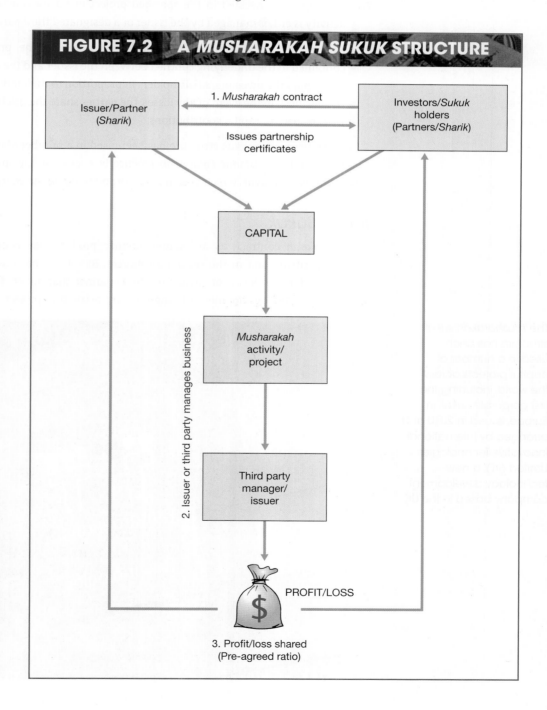

**FIGURE 7.2    A *MUSHARAKAH SUKUK* STRUCTURE**

Issuer/Partner (*Sharik*)

1. *Musharakah* contract

Issues partnership certificates

Investors/*Sukuk* holders (Partners/*Sharik*)

CAPITAL

*Musharakah* activity/ project

Third party manager/ issuer

2. Issuer or third party manages business

PROFIT/LOSS

3. Profit/loss shared (Pre-agreed ratio)

As we can see in Figure 7.2, the following procedure is adopted.

1.  A company (issuer) invites investors to participate in the partnership contract (*musharakah*), because it requires more funding. This results in the issuance of partnership certificates and payment for the value of shares allotted. In some cases, a partner, particularly the issuer, may contribute illiquid assets such as land.

2.  The capital is invested in the specified project or business activity. The *musharakah* activity is either managed by the issuer or a designated third party.

3.  Any profits are distributed periodically according to the predetermined ratio as contained in the underlying contract between the issuer and the certificate holders. The issuer pays the investors/*sukuk* holders in proportion to their individual shareholding in the business. In the event of any losses, the parties share the risk burden in proportion to their respective capital contributions.

The *musharakah sukuk* structure has been used in a number of capital projects around the world. The *Islamic Finance in Practice* box looks at the International Innovative Technologies *sukuk*, which was the first corporate *sukuk* issued in Europe.

## Ijarah Sukuk

The *ijarah* contract, as an Islamic finance product, has been transformed into a competitive bond in the secondary market. Based on the original notion of a lease contract, *ijarah* has been structured in a manner that allows for the mobilization of funds for the development of long-term infrastructure projects through the issuance

The *musharakah sukuk* structure has been used in a number of capital projects across the world, including the first corporate *sukuk* in Europe, issued in 2010 and arranged by International Innovative Technologies Limited (IIT), a new-technology development company based in the UK.

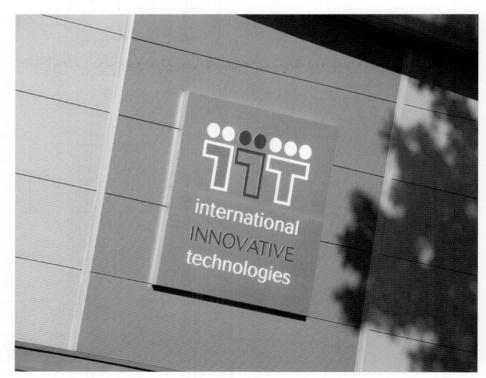

# International Innovative Technologies *Sukuk*

The first corporate *sukuk* in Europe, issued in 2010, is structured as *sukuk al-musharakah*. International Innovative Technologies Limited (IIT), a new-technology development company based in the UK, arranged the *sukuk*. This led to the establishment of a special purpose entity registered as IIT *Sukuk* Company Limited. Millenium Private Equity invested £6,1 million via *Sukuk A* and *Sukuk B*. *Sukuk A* (with a value of £3,2 million) was converted in June 2011, while *Sukuk B* (with a value of £2,92 million) has a four year maturity tenor. The *sukuk* was placed privately with Millennium Private Equity, a Sharī'ah-compliant private equity firm in Dubai, regulated by Dubai Financial Services Authority. The *sukuks* were listed on the Cayman Islands Stock Exchange on July 30, 2010. However, the *sukuk* are considered as Islamic convertible securities that may be converted to shares or redeemed based on certain performance milestones before their maturity in 2014. It is expected that the IIT *sukuk* debut will spur new Sharī'ah-compliant issuances in the global financial system. The recent controversial Goldman Sachs *sukuk* is a good example of the increasing importance of Sharī'ah-compliant securities in the west. There is potential for many western companies to embrace *sukuk* as an alternative source of funding for their business projects.

The table below shows the IIT *sukuk* issued in 2010 with a tenor of four years. *Sukuk A* was converted on January 16, 2012, as a result of the conversion of the certificates into IIT shares. *Sukuk B* continues to be listed on Caymen Islands Stock Exchange.

| | |
|---|---|
| **Current Status** | *Sukuk A* converted, *Sukuk B* listed |
| **Issuer Name** | IIT *Sukuk* Company Limited |
| ***Sukuk* Name** | International Innovative Technologies *Sukuk* |
| **Type of Structure** | *Sukuk al-musharakah* |
| **Country** | United Kingdom |
| **Currency** | GBP |
| **Closing Date** | July 30, 2010 |
| **Tenor** | 4 Years |
| **Issue Size** | £6,100,000 |
| **Listing** | Cayman Islands Stock Exchange |
| **Cancellation Date** | 2014 |
| **Reason for Cancellation** | *Sukuk A* holders exercised conversion rights |

of *ijarah sukuk*. It has also been used as a means of securitization of a tangible asset, such as a hospital or airport, which allows the issuance of *sukuk* to prospective investors. Muhammad Ayub defines *ijarah sukuk* as "the securities representing ownership of well-defined and known assets tied up to a lease contract, rental of which is the return payable to the *sukuk* holders."[5] Where a lessor (the one leasing a property) intends to recover the cost of purchasing an asset and requires liquidity or intends to make some profits from an asset, that asset may be sold wholly or partly to a number of individuals. The individuals will each own a proportion of the underlying asset based on the amount of funds they committed to it and this will be documented in the certificates issued to them. The certificates are called *ijarah* certificates or *ijarah sukuk*. The ownership of each *sukuk* holder in the underlying assets, based on the number of units they own of the undivided parts of the assets, must be clearly documented in the certificate issued to them.

There are different variations of *ijarah sukuk*.

1. *SUKUK* OF OWNERSHIP IN A LEASED ASSET. This kind of *ijarah sukuk* is issued with the sole aim of selling the asset to the *sukuk* holders through the transfer of title. Therefore, the *sukuk* holders jointly own the asset through undivided ownership and are entitled to profits and losses accordingly. This form of *ijarah sukuk* can be used for the purchase of a new asset.

2. *SUKUK* OF OWNERSHIP OF USUFRUCTS OF ASSETS. In this case, the *sukuk* holders only become the owners of the usufruct (*manfaa*) of the assets. The *sukuk* are issued with the aim of conferring the right of usufruct to the *sukuk* holders where they become joint owners. The owners of asset lease its usufruct to the *sukuk* holders through the issuance of the *ijarah sukuk*. The *sukuk* holders can sublease the usufruct of the asset to a third party.

3. *SUKUK* OF OWNERSHIP OF SERVICES. This form of *ijarah sukuk* is issued to subscribers for the purpose of conferring ownership of services to the *sukuk* holders. Such services are provided through a specified provider and the ownership transferred to the *sukuk* holders, who may also sublease the services to a third party.

An *ijarah sukuk* transaction is usually structured according to the process described in Figure 7.3.

1. The owner (originator) of an asset requires liquidity and intends to raise funds with the asset.

2. The owner establishes an SPV (issuer of the *sukuk*) and transfers the title of the asset to it.

3. A *sukuk ijarah* contract is concluded between the SPV and the certificate holders (subscribers), whereby the SPV issues *sukuk* to them and receives payment for the value of the shares allotted.

4. In return, the owner receives the *sukuk* proceeds for their own liquidity purposes. At this stage, the *sukuk* holders become the owners of the property.

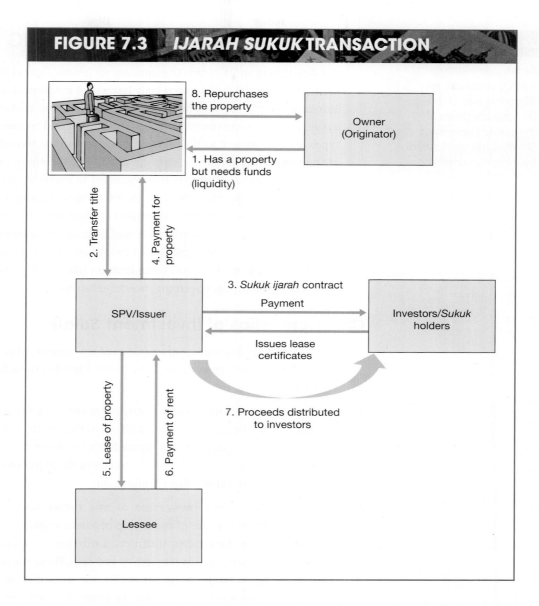

**FIGURE 7.3    *IJARAH SUKUK* TRANSACTION**

5. A lease (*ijarah*) contract is concluded between the SPV (which acts as a trustee on behalf of the investors) and the lessee (who may be the originator or a third party). The SPV leases the asset to the lessee.

6. The SPV collects the rent from the lessee.

7. The *sukuk* holders each receive a fraction of the rent in proportion to the amount of shares they own.

8. At the end of the *sukuk* period, the owner (originator) may repurchase the asset from the SPV. The proceeds of the sale are redistributed to the *sukuk* holders in proportion to their respective investments. At this stage, the SPV ceases to exist because it was established merely to accomplish a specific task.

# AAOIFI Standards for Islamic Bonds

**LEARNING OBJECTIVE 7.3**

Be familiar with the AAOIFI standards on Islamic bonds, and the characteristics of investment *sukuk* and Sharī'ah rulings defined by these standards.

The Accounting and Auditing Organization for Islamic Financial Institutions (AAOIFI) as an Islamic financial autonomous body has issued Investment *Sukuk* Standards (AAOIFI Standard No. 17) that set out the definition, types, and characteristics of investment *sukuk*. The standards contain the Sharī'ah rulings and requirements on the different types of *sukuk* as well as the prevailing practices in the secondary markets. The scope of the investment *sukuk* is clearly specified with the enumeration of the 14 types of *sukuk* structures (see Table 7.2). It is important to reiterate that the AAOIFI Investment *Sukuk* Standards do not extend to shares of stock companies, interest-based bonds as commonly traded in the conventional capital markets, certificates of funds, and investment portfolios. The focus of the standards as clearly articulated in its objectives is the IFIs or corporate entities offering Islamic financial services such as *sukuk*. To this end, this section explains the AAOIFI standards on Islamic bonds, their characteristics, and specific Sharī'ah rulings governing investment *sukuk*.

## Characteristics of Investment *Sukuk*

AAOIFI identifies five main characteristics of investment *sukuk* in its Sharī'ah Standard No. 17.[6] For easy reference, these characteristics are described below with some further explanations.

1.  CERTIFICATES REPRESENT THE RIGHTS AND OBLIGATIONS OF THE OWNER. Investment *sukuk* are certificates of equal value issued either to the owner or the bearer that establish the rights and obligations of the *sukuk* holder in respect of said certificate. It is the investment certificate that entitles the holder to the joint ownership of the underlying asset or services and also a share in any profit.

2.  COMMON SHARE IN THE OWNERSHIP OF THE UNDERLYING ASSET. Investment *sukuk* represent a common share of ownership of assets available for investments, whether they are non-monetary assets, usufructs, a mixture of tangible assets and usufructs, and monetary assets, such as receivables and cash. These *sukuk* do not represent a debt owed to the issuer by the certificate holder. The main distinguishing feature between *sukuk* and conventional bonds is that the issuer does not owe a debt to the certificate holders, but issuer and certificate holders are partners in the business venture. Thus, all the certificate holders as well as the issuer have a common share in the ownership of the underlying asset.

3.  SHARĪ'AH COMPLIANCE. Investment *sukuk* must be Sharī'ah-compliant and their issue and trading are governed by the contract's rules.

4.  TRADING OF INVESTMENT *SUKUK* AND THE RIGHTS THEY REPRESENT. Trading investment *sukuk* must be in accordance with the terms of the contract, which outlines the rights they represent. If the rights that a particular *sukuk* represent are not tradable, the *sukuk* itself will not be tradable. For example, *salam sukuk* are not tradable because the rights the certificate represents is a debt, and debts are generally not tradable in Islamic commercial law.

5.  RETURN AND LOSSES ARE COMMONLY SHARED BY CERTIFICATE HOLDERS. Certificate owners share any return or carry any loss in proportion to their share of ownership, as declared in the subscription prospectus. Based on the concept of partnership in Islamic commercial law, the parties, who in this case are the *sukuk* holders, must share the return and bear the losses of the business venture. This is, however, subject to their individual share in the ownership of the underlying asset or business venture.

## Sharī'ah Rulings and Requirements

The Sharī'ah rules and requirements as contained in the AAOIFI Standards of *Sukuk* are classified into two distinct categories:

1.  Sharī'ah requirements for the issuance of investment *sukuk*

2.  Sharī'ah rules for trading in investment *sukuk*.

For better understanding of the AAOIFI standards on *sukuk*, it is important to explain the Sharī'ah requirements and rulings on the issuance and trading of investment *sukuk*.

### Sharī'ah Requirements for the Issuance of Investment *Sukuk*

The following Sharī'ah requirements must be observed in the process of issuance of investment *sukuk*. Any of the Islamic modes of finance generally discussed in the first section of this chapter can be used to structure investment *sukuk*. Subscriptions can be made on the basis of any of the 14 types of *sukuk*. However, the certificates must be issued to securitize tangible assets, usufructs, or services. Debts owed or other receivables as a liability do not fall in the list of permissible assets. Therefore, there must be an underlying asset for the issuance of *sukuk*. The value of the assets, usufructs, or services is divided into equal shares for the purpose of issuing certificates to *sukuk* holders. The subscription funds must be used for a Sharī'ah-compliant contract.

Note that the contract of *sukuk* issuance between the issuer (SPV) and the subscribers (*sukuk* holders), who are the main parties of the contract, is governed by all the rules applicable to the contract type upon which the contract of issuance is based. For instance, in *sukuk al-musharakah*, the contract of issue has all the legal effects of a typical *musharakah* contract. So, the relationship between the issuer and the *sukuk* holders is determined and regulated by the contract upon which it is based.

### Sharī'ah Rules for Trading in Investment *Sukuk*

The Sharī'ah rules for trading in investment *sukuk* include the structuring and classifications of the 14 different types of investment *sukuk*. Some *sukuk* structures are tradable, while others are non-tradable depending on their respective characteristics. Related investment certificates are grouped together for easy reference. After the closing of the subscription, total allotment of *sukuk* to the subscribers, and consequent commencement of investment activity, certificate holders can trade their investment

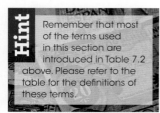

**Hint**

Remember that most of the terms used in this section are introduced in Table 7.2 above. Please refer to the table for the definitions of these terms.

certificates in the ICMs, and even redeem them. However, the rules for currency exchange (*sarf* contract) and debts must be strictly observed if trading or redemption is to be carried out, prior to the commencement of investment activity. As for **negotiable sukuk**, the issuer can purchase at market value any certificate offered to them by any certificate holder. An undertaking to purchase should be stipulated in the prospectus of issue and must be clearly contractual. The purchase is only valid if carried out after the completion of the process of issue of the *sukuk*. The tradability of investment certificates in the secondary market is permissible through any means that conforms to basic Shari'ah principles. The AAOIFI standard gives three examples of possible means of trading *sukuk*—registration, electronic means, or actual delivery by the bearer (who must be the real owner of the certificate) to the purchaser.[7]

Box 7.2 considers the tradability and consequent redemption of each of the 14 *sukuk* structures.

---

### BOX 7.2: TRADABILITY AND REDEMPTION OF THE 14 *SUKUK* STRUCTURES

*Sukuk ijarah.* After the time of issue and before the date of maturity when the ownership of the underlying asset is transferred to the certificate holder, it is permissible to trade in the certificates that represent ownership of leased assets or those to be leased on promise. Thus, before the maturity date, the issuer can redeem the certificates of ownership in the leased asset at a mutually agreed price or at the prevailing market price.

*Sukuk manfaa ijarah.* It is permissible to trade in certificates of ownership of usufructs of tangible assets but this must be done before the assets are contractually subleased. Different rules apply to the contract when a party intends to trade in certificates of ownership of a leased asset after it has been subleased. In this case, the certificate merely represents the rent, which is one of the receivables. As it has become a debt, the contract is therefore subject to the rules applicable to debts. Furthermore, a second buyer of the usufruct of an existing asset can also resell it and issue certificates for it.

*Ijarah muntahia bittamlik.* For a lease terminating in ownership, the issuer can redeem the certificate of ownership of the usufruct of tangible assets from the *sukuk* holder at the prevailing market price at the time of redemption, or at a mutually agreed price. This must, however, be done after allotment of the shares to the *sukuk* holder and payment of the subscription price. For the transaction to be valid, the subscription amount or redemption price must not be deferred.

*Sukuk manfaa ijarah mawsufah fi dhimmah.* In forward lease investment certificates, it is permissible to trade in certificates of ownership of usufructs of an asset to be made available only after the asset has been identified. The implication is that the parties cannot trade in this certificate before it is ascertained.

## BOX 7.2: *(continued)*

*Sukuk milkiyat al-khadamat.* It is generally permissible to trade in certificates of ownership of services to be provided by a specific person identified in the underlying contract before subleasing the services. However, if such services are subleased and the parties intend to trade in the certificates, then the certificates are automatically converted to receivables in the form of rent, which is then subject to the rules on the disposal of debts under the Sharī'ah. If the party who is contractually required to provide the services has not been identified in the contract, it is impermissible to trade the certificates.

*Sukuk al-istisna'.* Parties can trade in or even redeem manufacturing certificates after the funds have been converted to a tangible asset owned by the certificate holders within the period of the contract issue.

*Sukuk al-salam.* It is not permissible to trade in forward contract certificates because of the debt-like nature of the whole contract. The certificates represent a share in the debt, so they are not tradable in any manner whatsoever.

*Sukuk al-murabahah.* Trading of *murabahah* certificates is only permissible after purchase of the commodity but before transfer to the buyer. They are not tradable after delivery of the commodity to the buyer because at that stage, the certificate becomes a monetary debt against the buyer.

*Sukuk based on partnership contracts.* Investment certificates of partnership contracts, such as *mudarabah, musharakah,* and *wakalah,* are tradable after the close of subscription, allotment of certificates, and commencement of investment activity.

*Sukuk al-muzara'a and sukuk al-musaqa.* After the close of subscription, allotment of certificates to *sukuk* holders and commencement of investment activity, it is permissible to trade in certificates of ownership in irrigation and sharecropping if the *sukuk* holders are the owners of the land. However, if they are not the landowners and only participate as workers, trading is not permissible until the fruits and crops are ripe for harvest.

*Sukuk al-mugharasa.* Whether the certificate holders own the land or not, it is permissible to trade in certificates of agricultural ownership after the close of subscription, allotment of certificates, and commencement of activity.[8]

Source: AAOIFI. (2010). *Sharī'ah Standard For Islamic Financial Institutions,* Bahrain: AAOIFI. Sharī'ah Standard No. 17.

**Hint**
*Muzara'a* means a sharecropping contract. *Musaqa* is a limited form of sharecropping that relates to irrigation. *Mugarasa* is an agricultural contract.

**Hint**
For detailed information on trading of *sukuk* and their redemption, see AAOIFI Sharī'ah Standard No. 17.

## Significant AAOIFI Rulings on *Sukuk* in 2008

AAOIFI's Sharī'ah Board made some significant rulings on *sukuk* in February 2008 because of some controversies and issues surrounding *sukuk*, in order to ensure investor confidence and address issues of public interest (*maslahah*). The six key rulings are outlined in Box 7.3 and clarify further the Sharī'ah rules explained in Box 7.2, which generated controversy among Sharī'ah scholars, market players, and investors. They are not substitutes for the earlier issued guidelines presented above, but are merely clarifications and directives on the guidelines to avoid misapplication of the requirements for the issuance of investment *sukuk* and the Sharī'ah rulings for their trading in the ICMs.

---

### BOX 7.3:    AAOIFI RULINGS ON *SUKUK*

1. *Sukuk*, in order for them to be tradable, must be owned by the *sukuk* holders, together with all of the rights and obligations that accompany such ownership. The manager of a *sukuk* issuance must establish the transfer of ownership of such assets in its books and must not retain them as its own assets.

2. *Sukuk* must not represent receivables or debt except in the case of a trading or financial entity selling all of its assets or a portfolio with a standing financial obligation.

3. It is not permissible for the manager of *sukuk* to undertake to offer loans to *sukuk* holders when actual earnings fall short of expected earnings. It is permissible, however, to establish a reserve for the purpose of covering such shortfalls to the extent possible, on condition that this is mentioned in the prospectus.

4. It is not permissible for the investment manager, partner, or investment agent to agree to repurchase assets from *sukuk* holders at nominal value when the *sukuk* are extinguished on their maturity date. It is permissible, however, to agree to purchase the assets for their net value, or market value, or fair market value, or for a price agreed to at the time of their purchase, in accordance with Sharī'ah rules on partnership and modern partnerships, and on the subject of guarantees.

5. It is permissible for the lessee in a *sukuk ijarah* to agree to purchase the leased assets when the *sukuk* are extinguished for their nominal value, provided that the lessee is not also an investment partner, investment manager, or agent.

6. Sharī'ah supervisory boards should not limit their role to the issuance of *fatwa* on the structure of *sukuk*, but should also oversee implementation and compliance at every stage of the operation.

Source: AAOIFI Sharī'ah Board Pronouncement on Sukuk (2008). Available at www.aaoifi.com/aaoifi_sb_sukuk_Feb2008_Eng.pdf.

# Rating of Islamic Bonds

**LEARNING OBJECTIVE 7.4**

Differentiate between sovereign and corporate ratings of Islamic bonds, and the methodology used to rate products.

**junk bonds**
Bonds that are rated below investment grade at the time of purchase. Junk bonds are also called non-investment-grade bonds, speculative-grade bonds, or high-yield bonds.

Bond credit rating is the assessment of the creditworthiness of a corporation's debt issues or government bonds. This allows potential investors to make informed decisions before subscribing to debt securities. It is the bonds or *sukuk* issued that are rated, and not the corporation or government, and their quality is rated by letter designations. The designated grades range from 'AAA', the highest grade, to 'C', popularly called **junk bonds**. The two popular classifications of bonds for rating their quality are 'investment-grade bonds' and 'junk bonds'.

Assessment is carried out by credit rating agencies. The leading global rating agencies include Moody's, Standard & Poor's, and Fitch Ratings. Apart from these, different countries have their own rating agencies, for example, the Malaysian Rating Corporation Berhad (MARC), Indian Credit Rating Agency (ICRA), Agence d'Évaluation Financière (ADEF), and Credit Rating Agency of Bangladesh Ltd. (CRAB). Globally, there are more than 50 rating agencies. Some were established by the governments while others were established by multilateral financial agencies such as the International Finance Corporation (IFC) and the Islamic Development Bank (IDB). These agencies play a significant role in the development of capital markets around the world and help ensure competitive products are offered in the secondary markets. Some countries where Islamic financial products are offered have domestic rating agencies, including the United States, Malaysia, Poland, India, Bangladesh, and Sri Lanka.

In order to properly position the ICM and have a transnational rating agency that specifically focuses on Islamic finance products, the IDB took the initiative to establish an international rating agency known as the Islamic International Rating Agency (IIRA). The leading market players in the GCC countries and multilateral development institutions have closely supported IIRA. It began operations in 2005 and has since striven to ensure quality in the Islamic finance industry, and improve the productivity of the ICM.

Meanwhile, the three leading credit rating agencies, Standard & Poor's, Moody's, and Fitch, popularly called the Big Three—have also contributed significantly to the rating of Islamic financial products, particularly in the area of *sukuk* issuance. Looking at just one of the Big Three's impact on the global Islamic finance industry, *Global Islamic Finance* presents a snapshot of Moody's ratings of *sukuk*. Although the ratings focus on the creditworthiness of the *sukuk* structure without necessarily touching on Sharī'ah compliance, it provides a valuable guide to individual and institutional investors.

## Types of Ratings

Islamic bonds can be rated on two bases, sovereign and corporate, similar to the rating of conventional bonds.

## Sovereign Ratings

**sovereign credit rating**
The credit rating of a sovereign entity or a country.

The credit rating of a country or sovereign entity such as a national government, is called its **sovereign credit rating.** The risk level of the regulatory, political, economic, and legal environment is taken into consideration—these are the key features usually considered

# GLOBAL ISLAMIC FINANCE

## Moody's Rating of *Sukuk*

Moody's has been at the forefront of assigning ratings for Islamic financial institutions globally. Given the unique features of Islamic financial instruments, its ratings are addressed differently from conventional products. In order to ensure international credibility and enhance transparency in the global Islamic finance industry, credit ratings by reputable international agencies is important. Islamic financial instruments are not meant only for Muslims. Although grounded in faith-based values, Islamic finance is now being considered as a viable alternative mode of financing that seeks to provide more diversified funding sources for both private and public initiatives. Meanwhile, for

the issuance of debt instruments such as *sukuk* for funding purposes in the Islamic finance industry, the benefits of credit ratings to all stakeholders cannot be overemphasized, considering the increasing need for the implementation of the original value proposition of Islamic financial intermediation.

Moody's has been very active in assigning ratings for *sukuk* issued across the world. It has rated high profile deals for the benefits of investors. With a team of seven expert analysts specifically dedicated to Islamic financial products, Moody's has about 25 Islamic bank and *sukuk* ratings to guide investors across the world. The following is a list of selected *sukuk* rated by Moody's:

| COUNTRY | ISSUER | ORIGINATOR NAME | ISSUANCE AMOUNT (US$ MILLION) | ISSUE RATING/RATING OF SENIOR NOTES |
|---|---|---|---|---|
| UAE | ADIB Sukuk Co. Ltd. | Abu Dhabi Islamic Bank | 5,000 | A2 |
| UAE | DIB Sukuk Co. Ltd. | Dubai Islamic Bank PJSC | 750 | Baa1 |
| UAE | DP World Sukuk Ltd. | DP World | 1,500 | Ba1 |
| UAE | Dubai Sukuk Center Ltd. | DIFC Investments LLC | 1,250 | B2 |
| UAE | DEWA Funding Ltd* | Dubai Electricity and Water Authority | 872 | Ba2 |
| UAE | EIB Sukuk Co. Ltd. Programme | Emirates Islamic Bank PJSC | 1,000 | A2 |
| UAE | JAFZ Sukuk Ltd.* | Jebel Ali Free Zone FZE | 2,043 | B1 |
| UAE | Tamweel Sukuk Ltd | Tamweel PJSC | 272 | Baa3 |
| UAE | HBME Sukuk Company Ltd | HSBC Middle East Limited (HBME) | 5,000 | Aa3 |
| UAE | Tamweel Residential ABS CI (1) Ltd. | Tamweel PJSC | 210 | Aa2 |
| UAE | DB Sukuk Ltd | Dubai Bank PJSC | 5,000 | A3 |
| UAE | Sukuk Funding (No. 2) Ltd.* | Aldar Properties PJSC | 1,021 | Ba1 |
| UAE | TDIC Sukuk Ltd. | Tourism Development and Investment Company | 1,450 | A1 |
| UAE | Sun Finance Ltd. | Sorouh Real Estate | 1,009 | Aa3 |
| Malaysia | Malaysia Global Sukuk Inc. | Government of Malaysia | 600 | A3 |
| Malaysia | Sarawak Corporate Sukuk Inc. | State of Sarawak | 350 | Baa1 |
| Malaysia | MBB Sukuk Inc. (Subordinated) | Maybank | 300 | A3 |
| Kuwait | NIG Sukuk Ltd. | National Industries Group Holding S.A.K. | 475 | B1 |
| Qatar | Qatar Alaqaria Sukuk Co. | Qatar Real Estate Investment Co. | 300 | Baa1 |
| Malaysia | Petronas Global Sukuk Ltd. | Petroliam Nasional Berhad | 1,500 | A1 |
| Indonesia | Indonesia Global Sukuk | Republic Of Indonesia | 650 | Ba3 |
| Saudi Arabia | IDB Trust Services Ltd. | Islamic Development Bank | 850 | Aaa |
| Saudi Arabia | Dar Al-Arkan International Sukuk Company II | Dar Al-Arkan Real Estate | 450 | Ba2 |
| USA | GE Sukuk | GE Capital | 500 | Aa2 |
| USA | Al Hilal Sukuk | IFC | 100 | Aaa |
| | Total amount of *Sukuk* issuances rated by Moody's: | | 32,452 | |

*Actual Issuance in AED, USD Equivalent listed

Source: Moody's Investor Service. *Global Issuance Poised for Boost from New Legislative and Regulatory Initiatives.* Special Report, April 6, 2010.

*Continued*

It is clear that *sukuk* issuance is a global phenomenon in the Islamic finance industry. The selected *sukuk* transactions on the list include *sukuk* in the Middle East, Asia-Pacific, and North America. Alhough Moody's review of *sukuk* transactions does not offer opinion on the Sharī'ah compliance of the *sukuk* structures, it does focus on the creditworthiness of the transactions, which is meant to guide investors.

**Foreign direct investment**
Investment of foreign assets into the domestic structures, equipment, and organizations of a country.

by foreign investors in making informed decisions as these forms of risk affect the productivity and marketability of the bonds in the secondary market. The risk level of the investing environment in a country is an essential factor to be considered when planning to invest abroad. With the structuring of sovereign *sukuk*, governments of a number of countries have been able to raise funds for national development, especially when tax revenues have been insufficient. In raising funds through sovereign *sukuk*, a government seeks investment of foreign assets into the country's domestic structures, equipment, and organizations. This is known as **foreign direct investment** (FDI), and forms part of the national financial accounts. It can be secured from foreign investors if the country's risk level is low and a favorable environment exists for investment. In its country risk rating, Euromoney Country Risks consider the following factors in the ranking:

- political risk
- economic performance/projections
- structural assessment
- debt indicators
- credit ratings
- access to bank finance
- access to capital markets.

IIRA has a policy for sovereign credit ratings, rating all types of sovereign borrowers and other related financial institutions. It also assigns a credit rating to a country, for the purpose of sovereign *sukuk*, in order to establish a credit benchmark and sovereign ceiling for transactions involving foreign currency. As an example, Figure 7.4 shows the first page of the IIRA Sovereign Ratings of Turkey for 2010. The report begins with a general summary of the sovereign ratings, where the long-term and short-term credit ratings are given, followed by a SWOT analysis to give a synopsis of the ratings in order to guide investors or creditors. This one-page summary captures the numeric analysis contained in the 22-page report. The six basic categories used by IIRA to analyze sovereign *sukuk* and the likelihood of any default on debt obligations at maturity are:

- politics and policy continuity
- the economy—structure and growth prospects
- budgetary and fiscal policy
- monetary policy and flexibility
- the external accounts
- internal and external debt.

## FIGURE 7.4 FIRST PAGE OF IIRA SOVEREIGN RATING REPORT OF TURKEY, 2012

RATING REPORT

Report Date:
January 5, 2012

Rating Analyst
Sobia Maqbool, CFA
sobia.maqbool@iirating.com

Nasir Ali Merchant, CFA
nasir.ali@iirating.com

### Republic of Turkey

|  | Latest (January 5, 2012) | | Previous (October 15, 2008) | |
|---|---|---|---|---|
| Local Currency | BBB | A3 | BBB– | A3 |
| Foreign Currency | BBB– | A3 | BB+ | A3 |
| National Scale | AAA(tr) | A1+(tr) | AAA(tr) | A1+(tr) |
| Outlook | Stable | | Stable | |

### Rating Rationale

Islamic International Rating Agency (IIRA) has upgraded the long term foreign currency sovereign rating of the Republic of Turkey from 'BB+' to 'BBB–'. The long term local currency sovereign rating has also been upgraded from 'BBB' to 'BBB'. The short term credit ratingz on both foreign and local currency scale has been maintained at 'A–3'. On the rating scale, ratings have been reaffirmed at 'AAA/A-1+(tr)'. Outlook on the assigned ratings is Stable.

The upgrade reflects Turkey's improved economic fundamentals, with the country having achieved domestic demand driven recovery in 2012 and having posted GDP growth of 9% after the contraction of 4.8% in 2009. In the backdrop of fiscal and monetary tightening measures, growth rate has exhibited a quarter-by-quarter decline in 2011, though full year GDP growth is still likely to be high at around 7.5%. Moderation in GDP growth rate may be expected in the coming years. Additional monetary tightening may also be expected in the face of rising inflation, which is around 10% for full year 2011.

Turkey has undergone major changes in fiscal structure over the last decade. It has succeeded in reducing fiscal deficit as a percentage of GDP from 11.9% in 2001 to 1.8% in 2008. The ratio increased in 2009 to 5.5%, however, with the GDP growth in 2010, this again declined to 3.6%. The fiscal balance in 2011 has received support from collections against a tax restructuring scheme announced by the government, which is a temporary phenomenon and more long term, sustainable measures would be required to achieve the planned reduction in fiscal deficit in relation to GDP.

|  | 2006 | 2007 | 2008 | 2009 | 2010 |
|---|---|---|---|---|---|
| GDP (Billion $) | 526.4 | 648.6 | 742.1 | 616.7 | 526.4 |
| Current Account Deficit (%GDP) | –6.1 | –5.9 | –5.7 | –2.3 | –6.5 |
| Inflation (CPI year end, 5) | 9.65 | 8.39 | 10.06 | 6.53 | 6.40 |
| Unemployment Rate | 10.2 | 10.3 | 11.0 | 14.0 | 11.9 |
| Central Govt. Normal Debt Stock (% GDP) | 46.5 | 39.9 | 40.0 | 46.1 | 42.2 |
| International Reserves (Net, Billion $) | 63.3 | 76.4 | 74.2 | 74.8 | 86.0 |
| Exports (Billion $) | | | | | |
| Imports (Billion $) | 526.4 | 526.4 | 526.4 | 526.4 | 526.4 |

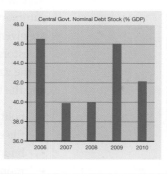

Central Govt. Nominal Debt Stock (% GDP)

Source: Islamic International Rating Agency, www.iirating.com/report/20081015_turkey_credit_report.pdf.

## Corporate Ratings

**corporate credit rating**
A financial indicator used in measuring the credit worthiness of a corporate entity.

A **corporate credit rating** is a creditworthiness rating in the form of a financial indicator to potential investors in investment certificates or securities such as *sukuk*. Prospective investors consider the credit ratings of corporate entities to ascertain whether they will be able to meet their financial obligations. The level of risk surrounding a company's business determines the confidence prospective investors will have in it. Hence, corporate credit ratings play a significant role in the economy of a country and, more importantly, promote stability and sustainability in the financial industry.

Corporate credit rating affects both the issuer and the issues. In the Islamic financial markets, corporate ratings involve bond/*sukuk* ratings, banks' financial strength ratings, Sharī'ah quality ratings, corporate governance ratings, real estate ratings, etc. The risk level of the corporate entities issuing the *sukuk* with regards to the above issues will determine the level of confidence the investing public will have in the issue. In order to win a prospective investor's confidence, corporate entities must adopt best practices by reducing their risk level and practically demonstrating their ability to meet all financial obligations.

## Rating Products and Methodology

The rating products in Islamic financial markets cover of all types of issuers and *sukuk* issues. The IIRA identified the following eight major rating products:

- sovereign rating
- issuer rating
- bond/*sukuk* rating
- insurer financial strength rating
- bank financial strength rating
- Sharī'ah quality rating
- corporate governance rating
- real estate rating.

## Sovereign Rating

This comprises issuer and issue ratings where a reliable third party gives an opinion on the feasibility of the issuer's repayment or an issue of its financial obligations within the relevant period. The rating may be carried out on all types of sovereign borrowers and relevant institutions. The general rating of a country as a sovereign entity is carried out before the rating of particular issue or institution.

*Methodology:* The methodology adopted in the rating of sovereign *sukuk* involves both qualitative and quantitative factors. When assessing the likelihood of default on debt obligations for sovereign *sukuk*, IIRA considers the following six analytical categories: politics and policy continuity, economic structure and growth prospects, budgetary and fiscal policy, monetary policy and flexibility, the external accounts, and internal and external debts.

## Issuer Rating

This involves rating the issuer of *sukuk*, where its ability to fulfill its financial obligation is considered. The rating also involves non-financial bodies such as the entity's corporate and Sharī'ah governance. The rating of a corporate entity that is an issuer is separate from the bond/*sukuk* rating.

*Methodology:* In rating the issuer, the entity is rated with particular regards to its creditworthiness and its continued ability to fulfill its debt obligations to stakeholders, particularly investors. The overall financial and institutional creditworthiness of an issuer will determine the level of confidence potential investors will have in it. Issuer rating enhances the credibility of the corporate entity.

## Bond/*Sukuk* Rating

The rating of *sukuk* in the financial market is as important to the investors as the issuer. The likelihood of receiving one's dividends in timely manner after subscribing to sukuk is an important issue that any investor must consider before deploying their surplus funds.

*Methodology:* The documented terms and covenants of the issued *sukuk* are evaluated along with the risk/return measures. The viability of the *sukuk* in the secondary market will proportionally increase the number of subscribers.

## Insurer Financial Strength Rating

The financial strength of the *sukuk's* insurer is also an important factor for prospective investors to consider when avoiding or mitigating risks. The insurer must have the corporate ability and requisite financial strength to meet its contractual obligations. According to IIRA: "The objective of an insurance company rating is to provide a reliable third-party opinion regarding an insurer's financial strength and the insurer's ability to meet contractual obligations. Islamic International Rating Agency (IIRA) is dedicated to serving the insurance marketplace in its targeted markets. IIRA aims to play a role as a source of reliable information and ratings to encourage the growth of a financially strong insurance industry. IIRA believes its role is vital in encouraging the prudent management of insurance companies and improving the industry's strength for the benefit of insurers and policyholders in particular and that of the financial system in general."[9] This is where the creditworthiness of *takaful* entities are required to effectively insure the issuers of *sukuk*.

*Methodology:* IIRA assesses the insurance company's financial strength and its capability of meeting the obligations of the policyholders and other contract holders, such as the shareholders. The sustainability of its financial strength is also included in the rating. Qualitative and quantitative factors are considered. On the qualitative side, the country risks of the domicile of a company as well as its business profile are analyzed. The quantitative assessment is premised on an evaluation of the strength of the company's balance sheet and its operating performance.

## Banks' Financial Strength Rating

IIRA rates both Islamic and conventional banks' strength. It considers global financial practices in rating financial institutions. The main issue considered in the banks' financial strength ratings is the investment quality and/or creditworthiness. The key subject headings in IIRA's asset quality analysis are: banking environment, credit or investment policies and loan administration procedures, portfolio composition and characteristics, risk management practices, lending history and performance, forecasting the portfolio and quality, and analytical conclusions regarding economic values.

*Methodology:* The methodology for assessing the financial strength of banks and financial institutions for both Islamic and conventional entities are similar but in the process of evaluation, IIRA recognizes important distinctions between the two. The following sets of fundamentals are considered during assessment: market assessment; consideration of factors that determine asset quality; liquidity and funds management; asset/liability management; capital adequacy; adjustments to achieve economic reality; finance, information systems, planning disciplines; earnings performance; ownership and management performance, reflecting all the above. Emphasis is laid on the ability of the financial institution to make profits and pay dividends.

## Sharī'ah Quality Rating

The Sharī'ah quality rating seeks to assess the level of Sharī'ah compliance of IFIs, corporate entities, and conventional financial institutions offering Islamic financial services or products such as *sukuk*. The quality rating is one of the most fundamental aspects of IIRA's assessment because the investing public wants to know the level of compliance of corporate entities in which they intend to invest. Most other rating agencies including the Big Three do not have this specialized rating product.

*Methodology:* The methodology of IIRA in assessing the level of compliance of a financial institution or corporate entity with the requirements of the Sharī'ah include the following major elements: procedure of authentication of products and services, safeguards against comingling of funds in the case of an Islamic window or branch of a conventional financial institution, code of ethics adopted by the institution, policy on the calculation of profit or loss and the consequent sharing of same, whether the types of business undertaken are Sharī'ah-compliant or not, the Sharī'ah compliance of both assets and liabilities, etc. For this purpose, a standing Sharī'ah board has been constituted by IIRA currently chaired by Justice Muhammad Taqi Usmani.

## Corporate Governance Rating

The standard of the corporate governance of a financial institution or corporate entity assigned to manage the issuance of *sukuk* is essential for the productivity of such bonds. Hence, prospective investors consider the governance rating of corporate entities before investing. The available structure and practices of the management of a company contribute to its efficiency. IIRA carries out an independent assessment of the managerial structure and practices using a variety of markers.

*Methodology:* The corporate governance rating of corporate entities is carried out through the use of key elements of corporate governance recognized at the global level. Best practices in the field are used as benchmarks for the assessment rather than using the standards of a particular country or jurisdiction, which may not represent the level of creditworthiness of the company. Above all, the level of fairness, transparency, responsibility, and accountability are considered key factors in the evaluation while recognizing and accommodating the different governance structures across jurisdictions.

## Real Estate Rating

Commercial real estate is an important product in IIRA ratings. "IIRA's rating on real estate pertains to the overall rating of the developer and is not a rating of a particular project unless a specific project rating is requested. The rating is assigned after taking into account market characteristics, the organizational structure and management quality of the developer, and finally assessing each of the projects in the portfolio the developer is executing, thereby arriving at a final credit rating for the developer."[10]

*Methodology:* The real estate rating methodology designed by IIRA "provides an independent and objective opinion on the relative financial capability of the developer in line with its commitments. The idea is to provide the stakeholders with a balanced view of the strengths and weaknesses of the developer and to create a healthy environment in the industry. IIRA will analyze all ongoing projects of the developer and arrive at an overall rating of the developer."[11] The developer's activities such as the performance of its architects, engineers, contractors, and other necessary personnel are rated accordingly.

Table 7.4 gives a summary of the general rating process for all the products. Remember that IIRA is the only rating agency offering the Sharīʿah quality rating, which assesses the extent of Sharīʿah compliance of IFIs or products.

| TABLE 7.4: IIRA Rating Process | |
|---|---|
| **Issuer/client** | Signs agreement for an initial rating. |
| | Submits preliminary information materials. |
| **IIRA** | Conducts a preliminary study. |
| | Submits a detailed questionnaire to the issuer/client. |
| **Issuer/client** | Provides detailed information in response to detailed questionnaire. |
| **IIRA** | Conducts pre due diligence meeting analysis. |
| | Conducts due diligence meeting. |
| | Conducts post due diligence analysis. |
| | Brief for committee meetings is prepared. |
| **Rating Committee** | Decides the preliminary/initial rating. |
| **IIRA** | Notifies issuer of the preliminary/initial rating. |
| **Issuer/client** | May appeal based on any new facts or information. |
| **Rating Committee** | Deliberates on appeal by issuer/client and gives decision. |
| **IIRA** | Notifies the decision of the rating committee to the issuer/client. |
| **Issuer/client** | Consents to release of the rating to the public. |
| **IIRA** | Releases the rating to media. |

Source: Islamic International Rating Agency, www.iirating.com/ratingprocess.asp.

# Review

## Key Terms and Concepts

corporate credit rating (p. 283)

debt-based *sukuk* (p. 264)

equity-based *sukuk* (p. 264)

foreign direct investment (p. 281)

Islamic capital market (p. 258)

Islamic financial engineering (p. 262)

junk bonds (p. 279)

*mudarabah sukuk* (p. 265)

*musharakah sukuk* (p. 268)

negotiable *sukuk* (p. 276)

non-tradable *sukuk* (p. 264)

secondary market (p. 268)

sovereign credit rating (p. 279)

*sukuk* (p. 257)

tradable *sukuk* (p. 264)

trust certificate (p. 259)

## Summary

**Learning Objective 7.1**

1. The liquidity of companies can be increased through securitization. Islamic bonds are necessary for the sustained growth of Islamic capital market, which helps promote sustainable practices in the Islamic banking and finance industry. Islamic bonds are different from conventional bonds in many ways, but the most striking difference is in the definition of both concepts. In Islamic bonds, investors have an ownership stake in the underlying asset, whereas conventional bonds are pure debt.

**Learning Objective 7.2**

2. The key products of the Islamic capital markets are *sukuk* or Islamic investment certificates, Sharīʻah-compliant stocks, and Islamic funds. A well-structured policy for the development of *sukuk* is required to evolve and sustain a viable Islamic capital market. The structuring, operation, and performance of Islamic bonds limits risk-taking in the capital market as all instruments in the market are based on real asset-backed economic activities.

**Learning Objective 7.3**

3. AAOIFI has provided the global Islamic finance industry with Sharīʻah standards on *sukuk*, with clear-cut rules on the tradability of each type of *sukuk*. These Sharīʻah rules must be used when structuring *sukuk* to ensure compliance, apart from the imperative need to consult Sharīʻah scholars.

**Learning Objective 7.4**

4. *Sukuk* rating is important to protect investors and guide them to make informed decisions in investing their hard-earned wealth. The two main types of rating are sovereign credit ratings and corporate credit ratings. Rating agencies have their own methodologies in rating securities, countries, and corporate entities.

## Practice Questions and Activities

### Practice Questions

1.  List 10 types of *sukuk* and explain three of them using relevant examples.

2.  XYZ Investment Company has a collection of assets that are being used in its business. It needs more liquidity and wishes to raise additional funds of up to US$100 million. The company approaches you for expert advice on how to raise the funds through the primary market. Advise the company on how to issue *sukuk* to subscribers, the relevant structures that should be created to realize the funds, and the method of payments to the *sukuk* holders.

3.  Enumerate the five characteristics of investment *sukuk* as provided in the AAOIFI Standard on Islamic Bonds.

4.  A company has a large expanse of land near the light rail train (LRT) station it owns. The company is faced with liquidity management problems and requires enough liquidity to expand its business. It therefore approaches you as an Islamic finance expert to get advice on the best method of getting liquidity through *sukuk*. What is the most appropriate *sukuk* structure you can suggest to the company to solve its liquidity problem, bearing in mind that the land near the LRT station can be converted to a car park? In addition, make a sketch of your proposed *sukuk* structure.

5.  Differentiate between the major features of *sukuk* and conventional bonds.

6.  Why do you think the issuance of *sukuk* is relevant in the global economy, whether at the governmental level or in the private sector?

7.  Differentiate between sovereign and corporate ratings of Islamic bonds and briefly explain the type that is most suited for national development at the governmental level.

8.  How can credit ratings of Islamic bonds limit risk-taking in the Islamic capital market?

### Activities

1.  Read the text of the AAOIFI Standards on *sukuk* and prepare a summary of these standards for a 15-minute class presentation.
2.  Find three newspaper cuttings on *sukuk* or the Islamic capital market of any country or corporate entity.
3.  Prepare a brief blueprint for the issuance of *sukuk* in your country.
4.  Prepare a flow chart of a mixed portfolio *sukuk* issue for any corporate body.

# Further Reading

AAOIFI. (2010). *Sharī'ah Standards for Islamic Financial Institutions*. Bahrain: AAOIFI.

Abdul Ghani, B. (2007). Survey of Current *Sukuk* Structures—Scope For Future Development of Hybrid, Exchangeable, and Derivative *Sukuk*. Presentation made at The *Sukuk* Summit 2007.

Adam, N. J. and Thomas, A. (2004). *Islamic bonds: your guide to issuing, structuring and investing in sukuk*. London: Euromoney Books.

Ayub, M. (2007). *Understanding Islamic Finance*. England: John Wiley & Sons Ltd.

Council of Islamic Fiqh Academy. (2000). *Resolutions and Recommendations (1985–2000)*, IRTI, IDB: Jeddah.

Dar Al Istithmar. (2006). *Sukuk*—An Introduction to the Underlying Principles and Structure. Dar Al Istithmar, at www.assaif.org/content/download/581/.../sukuk%20 Structures.pdf.

Dar, H. A. and Moghul, U. F. (eds.). (2009). *The Chancellor Guide to the Legal and Sharī'ah Aspects of Islamic Finance*. London: Chancellor Publications Limited.

Howlader, K. (2006). *Sharī'ah and Sukuk: A Moody's Primer*. London: Moody's Investors Service.

Lotter, P. and Howlader, K. (2007). *Understanding Moody's Approach to Unsecured Corporate Sukuk*. Dubai: Moody's Investors Service.

Securities Commission Malaysia. (2009). *The Islamic Securities (Sukuk) Market*. Kuala Lumpur: LexisNexis.

# 8

# Islamic Insurance (*Takaful*)

# Learning Objectives

## Upon completion of this chapter, the reader should be able to:

1  Understand the meaning and basic concepts of *takaful* as an alternative to conventional insurance with an insight into its historical development.

2  Describe the innovative Sharī`ah-approved models and structures of *takaful*.

3  Describe the main *takaful* products and their expansion into the global insurance market.

4  Analyze the process of determining and allocating surplus or deficit as proposed by AAOIFI.

5  Explain the relevance of reinsurance and *retakaful* in the modern practice of *takaful* business.

*Takaful*, which is a major component of the Islamic finance industry, constitutes an emerging market in the global economy. It is the Islamic alternative to conventional insurance. *Takaful* has a number of models that are patterned after some key principles of Islamic law regarding the rights, duties, and responsibilities of people towards others. The significance of *takaful* for the stability of the Islamic finance industry is beyond doubt.

This chapter presents *takaful* as a mutual or cooperative form of insurance rather than just personal gains and discusses its basic concepts, models, and structure. It further examines underwriting surplus and technical provisions. Reinsurance and *retakaful* are examined through a comparative study with particular reference to the emergence of *retakaful*. Bear in mind that *retakaful* is the Islamic alternative to the conventional practice of reinsurance. Meanwhile, aspects of Sharī`ah governance and compliance in *takaful* are also examined, with particular reference to the Accounting and Auditing Organization for Islamic Financial Institutions (AAOIFI) guidelines and the Islamic Financial Services Board (IFSB) principles. In order to complete the total framework of Islamic finance, *takaful* should be incorporated to mitigate inevitable risks and losses. *Takaful* is the third component of the Islamic finance industry, the other two being Islamic banking and Islamic capital markets.

# chapter 8

## professional perspectives

**Dr. Omar Fisher**
*Managing Director, Khidr Solutions, Bahrain*

1. **How is the conventional practice of insurance different from *takaful*?**

When one looks at what makes conventional insurance objectionable from an Islamic point of view, there are four main factors. First, commercial insurance involves gambling (*maysir*), especially for life insurance. Second, most insurance contains uncertainty and a lack of clear terms (*gharar*). Third, all insurance involves interest charges and debt investment instruments (*riba*), and fourth, most commercial insurance companies, being shareholding companies, are guided by the principle of profit maximization, not the wellbeing of the insured.

Among the characteristics of conventional insurance operations that differentiate it from *takaful*, we can note the following:

- separation of insurer (company) and insured (policyholder)
- transfer of losses using limited ownership and proprietary interests
- enterprise exists as a business for the maximization of profit
- commercial transactions dominate with investment of premiums attracting *riba* and non-Islamic securities
- no involvement or influence by policyholders in the management of the enterprise (except in a conventional mutual insurer).

By contrast, the key elements of *takaful* are:

- based upon solidarity and joint guarantee, i.e. a cooperative mechanism
- risk-sharing is spread across the community of its members
- joint ownership by the insured helps to control pricing and claims
- investments are halal (acceptable under the Shari'ah)—typically related directly to assets and avoiding debt instruments
- the overall goals are self-reliance and self-sustaining operations for community wellbeing.

In summary, there are four fundamental characteristics of a *takaful* operation. Each one is necessary to create an integrated *takaful*:

- specialty condition: joint guarantee, common risk-sharing
- partnership condition: profit-sharing, self-sustaining operations
- investment condition: using halal investments and profit-loss motivated, Islamic contracts
- management condition: the insured participate in management and review books and accounts.

291

## 2.    Is life insurance allowed in Islam?

*Takaful* insurance refers to an Islamic way of mutual guarantee by members of a group that pool their financial resources together against certain losses. Family *takaful* or life insurance can be acceptable under Islamic principles if correctly structured. It has two components: a savings element, whereby individual participants set aside a sum of money, belonging to each personally, to accumulate over time; and a risk-sharing element, which is a donation, that affords collective financial protection in the event a participant suffers disability or death. Of course, as with conventional life insurance, the true recipient (beneficiary) in the event of the death of the participant is their family, as designated in the policy terms. Here again, under *takaful* rules, the distribution of the policy benefits must adhere to Sharī'ah principles, which provide guidance on priorities assigned for distribution to nuclear family members, parents, siblings, cousins, etc, who survive the deceased.

As with conventional life insurance, a family *takaful* policy has a defined period of maturity, an identifiable savings portion, and a periodic installment portion to cover the risk protection element. There is medical underwriting, typically so that the relative health of the participant affects the total amount of contribution to adjust the risk in fairness to the risk pool. There may also be a minimum age, usually 16, and a maximum age, usually 65, limitations, occupational risk considerations, and adjustments depending upon the age at entry to the plan.

Provided that the savings element conforms to Sharī'ah investment principles, there are no serious impediments to the use of family *takaful* (life) insurance— assuming that the risk-sharing portion is operated strictly in accordance with acknowledged *takaful* principles, including the concept of *tabarru'* (donation) as a contribution towards the collective risk protection element.

Whereas the risk-sharing portion of the contribution is donated to the common risk pool, and thus belongs to the collective resources, the savings portion of the contribution remains the exclusive property of the individual participant. Under the rules of the family *takaful* policy, the savings accumulated may be withdrawn, although often subject to fees or penalties for early surrender.

# Basic Concepts of *Takaful*

## Definition of *Takaful*

***takaful***
An Arabic word, which means 'guaranteeing one another', is a mutual indemnity scheme in Islamic finance.

Although *takaful* is often translated as 'Islamic insurance', the real concept is more encompassing as it relates more to a social security system run through the collaborative efforts of the people.

***tabarru'***
Donation, gift, or charitable contribution, which is primarily meant to assist others in whatever form.

The term **takaful** is an Arabic word that originates from the root verb *kafala*—to guarantee, to secure, or to be responsible for others. In the literal sense, *takaful* means joint responsibility or guarantee based on mutual agreement. That is, guaranteeing each other through collective assurance and mutual undertaking among members of a particular group. In such a symbiotic relationship, three basic concepts of mutuality are embodied in the *takaful* model of insurance: mutual help, mutual responsibility, and mutual protection from losses.

This triangular relationship in Figure 8.1 is based on the underlying principle of the objectives of Islamic law, which seeks to bring benefit to mankind and ward off every form of harm.

*Takaful* is an alternative system of insurance whereby members contribute their financial resources to a common pool based on the principles of *ta'awun* (mutual assistance) and *tabarru'* (donation) and the group undertakes to share the mutual risk. Generally, *takaful* is premised upon the concept of *tabarru'*, which encompasses mutual assistance and mutual social security among the members. **Tabarru'** is the concept of donation in Islam and is often used to mean the premium in *takaful* although the two terms are generally used interchangeably.

In the *takaful* structure, the members jointly agree to guarantee one another against any unexpected loss or damage based on the common pool of resources. Accordingly, AAOIFI defines *takaful* as the collective undertaking by the participants to donate.

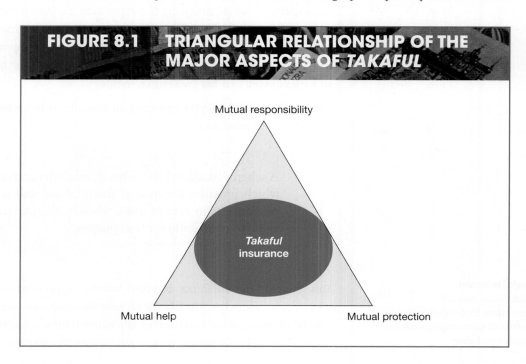

**FIGURE 8.1    TRIANGULAR RELATIONSHIP OF THE MAJOR ASPECTS OF *TAKAFUL***

Mutual responsibility

*Takaful* insurance

Mutual help                                    Mutual protection

The participants are the policyholders who own insurance policies and, in turn, are insured under the contract. The IFSB gives the following definition:

> *Takaful* is derived from an Arabic word that means joint guarantee, whereby a group of participants agree among themselves to support one another jointly for the losses arising from specified risks. In a *takaful* arrangement the participants contribute a sum of money as a *tabarru'* commitment into a common fund that will be used mutually to assist the members against a specified type of loss or damage.[1]

Mitigation of risk is permissible in Islam as many of the partnership contracts upon which the Islamic finance products are based are prone to risks and losses. There are numerous primeval risk mitigation methods that were fashionable during the time of the Prophet Muhammad (PBUH) and subsequent eras. The need to introduce certain risk management processes in whatever one is doing is gleaned from the following prophetic precedent, which continues to be familiar to many Muslims around the world. "One day Prophet Muhammad noticed a Bedouin leaving his camel without tying it and he asked the Bedouin: 'Why don't you tie down your camel?' The Bedouin answered: 'I put my trust in Allah.' The Prophet then said: 'Tie your camel first, then put your trust in Allah'."[2] Active engagement in commercial transactions is encouraged through proper entrepreneurial management, which is followed by reliance on God. In other words, appropriate measures of risk management must be put in place while carrying out commercial activities, following the expression 'tie your camel first', before relying on God. The expression typifies the importance of having insurance cover against market risks and losses. This led the Muslim scholars to develop an appropriate Sharī'ah-compliant framework to effectively manage misfortunes and risks in commercial activities as well as other civil engagements.

The Takaful Act of Malaysia also gives an appropriate definition of *takaful*. Section 2 of the Act defines *takaful* as:

> A scheme based on brotherhood, solidarity and mutual assistance which provides for mutual financial aid and assistance to the participants in case of need, whereby the participants mutually agree to contribute for that purpose.[3]

**takaful ta'awuni**
A concept of mutual cooperation that represents the true Islamic cooperative insurance scheme.

This is where the difference between Islamic cooperative insurance and commercial insurance schemes lies. The Islamic cooperative insurance scheme, otherwise known as **takaful ta'awuni**, is not a contract of sale where there is a buyer and seller, i.e., where the seller offers and sells protection and the buyer purchases the service at a certain price.

This is not what is meant by the *takaful* model. In *takaful*, the cooperative insurance scheme is adopted when there is a structured arrangement among certain people who mutually contribute a fixed amount of money to a common pool of funds from which compensation is paid to any member who suffers losses. While the cooperative insurance model is permissible and highly encouraged in Islam, the commercial model is prohibited.

All Islamic financial institutions need to undertake certain *takaful* schemes to effectively manage unpremeditated risks and losses arising from the commercial activities they carry out. This risk management role of *takaful* is unavoidable in business transactions conducted by the Islamic financial institutions. However, as a mandatory prescription of the Sharī'ah, all prohibitive elements in Islamic commercial transactions such as *riba* (interest on money), *gharar* (excessive risk), and *maysir* (gambling or speculation) are prohibited in the design of *takaful* models. These prohibited elements are contained in the conventional form of insurance, which has led to various legal verdicts on the part of modern Muslim scholars who have consistently declared that conventional insurance policies are prohibited.

## The Main Features of *Takaful*

As an alternative to conventional insurance, *takaful* has several features which make it distinct. The three main features are cooperative risk-sharing, clear financial segregation, and Sharī'ah-compliance in underwriting policies and investment strategies.

## Cooperative risk-sharing

As a well-articulated and exclusionary move to eliminate *riba* and *gharar* elements in *takaful*, cooperative risk-sharing through the means of donation was designed. This dramatic turn in the modern history of insurance is Sharī'ah-compliant as it encourages mutual assistance. *Takaful* is based on more than one contractual relationship, although the basis of it is mutual assistance. Other contractual relationships will be discussed in this chapter while considering the models of *takaful*. Social responsibility, solidarity, and the innate need to care for others are among the characteristics of such a cooperative move, and therefore, instead of premiums, the concept of donations is adopted and merged with other frameworks of Islamic commercial transactions. Although the policyholders pay some sort of premium, they are considered as donations to the common cause to assist those members who suffer any loss.

> Qur'an 5:2: "And help one another in righteousness and piety, but do not help one another in sin and rancour."

**operator or *wakil***
This term is used in *takaful* undertakings to represent the *takaful* company. Instead of using the word 'insurer', operator is used in *takaful* undertakings.

**contribution**
This is sometimes called the premium. It is the participants' payments to the *takaful* fund for the purpose of mutual protection and assistance.

## Clear financial segregation

There is a clear segregation between the participants and the **operator** (or ***wakil***). The insurance company is not considered as an insurer but merely an operator who is appointed to manage the portfolio and invest the insurance **contribution** for and on behalf of the participants. Islamic law restricts the role of the insurance company to that of an ordinary trustee who is responsible to the participants. In conventional insurance business, the insurance company is a profit-making entity that agrees to bear the financial burden and losses of its policyholders. The shareholders own the insurance company and are entitled to receive any profit and bear the burden of any deficit recorded at the end of the financial year. Conversely, in Islamic law, the role of the operator of the cooperative insurance business is clearly defined and segregated from the role of the participants. The *takaful* model determines the exact roles of the participants on the one hand and the operator on the other. These will be explained later in this chapter when we discuss the models of *takaful*.

## Sharī'ah-compliant policies and strategies

**underwriting policies**
The policies that are used to determine the extent of risk-taking of insurance operators against the payment of certain premiums.

Policies that are used to determine the extent of risk-taking of insurance operators against the payment of certain premiums are known as **underwriting policies**. The amount of liability to be accepted and the extent of coverage fall under the underwriting policies. There must be adequate measures to ensure that the underwriting policies and investment strategies are Sharī'ah-compliant. Investment of insurance funds should be made in ethical businesses that do not cause harm to people or the environment. In addition, ethical considerations in *takaful* extend to investment in businesses or products that do not contradict the Sharī'ah. Both the process and the end product must be Sharī'ah-compliant. For instance, investment in breweries and casinos are forbidden in Islam. In a similar vein, insurance underwriting policies must not contradict the Sharī'ah. These can be realized through the setting-up of a functional Sharī'ah board to guide and approve underwriting policies, investment strategies, and the operators' products. *Takaful* operators are required to put in place a standard Sharī'ah governance system to ensure absolute compliance with the Sharī'ah.

The main features of *takaful* are based on a number of core principles underlying the whole concept of mutual indemnity. As shown in Box 8.1, the core principles of *takaful* as outlined in the IFSB *Guiding Principles for Takaful* are *tabarru'* (donation) commitment, *ta'awun* (mutual assistance), and prohibition of *riba*, *gharar*, and *maysir*. Any *takaful* scheme structured upon a combination of the three core principles described satisfies the basic requirements of the Sharī'ah.

## Major Differences Between *Takaful* and Conventional Insurance

There are certain elements in conventional insurance that are unlawful in Sharī'ah and thus contradict fundamental precepts. These elements are the source of major differences between *takaful* and conventional insurance. The major differences between the two frameworks are parties to the contract, payment of premiums, and investment of insurance funds.

## BOX 8.1:     TAKAFUL CORE PRINCIPLES

Although *takaful* operators adopt different models depending on how their undertakings are structured, the general concept remains the same, as it is based on the three core principles of *takaful*.

1. ***Tabarru'* (donation/contribution) commitment**

   *Tabarru'* is an Islamic concept of donation or charitable contribution that is primarily targeted at assisting others. The objective of *tabarru'* is to donate for the benefit of others under a contractual scheme. It is the first building block in the structuring of a *takaful* transaction. Each *takaful* participant makes this commitment to fulfill the objective of mutual assistance through premiums.

2. ***Ta'awun* or mutual assistance**

   The second core principle of *takaful* is mutual assistance, which is the main reason for the initial *tabarru'* commitment. Having put together enough resources as part of the *tabarru'* commitment, the participants agree to mutually indemnify one another in the event of losses arising from an unforeseen event. Such mutual assistance is seen as an important aspect of the daily lives of Muslims, which is adapted to the needs of entrepreneurs, investors, and merchants in the Islamic finance industry. While the Islamic form of cooperative or mutual assistance is not averse to profit-making, the primary objective of the scheme is to assist one another based on the concept of *ta'awun* as chiefly documented in the Qur'an and Sunnah.

3. **Prohibition of *riba* (usury), *gharar* (excessive risk or uncertainty) and *maysir* (gambling or speculation)**

   As in all other commercial transactions, there is a general prohibition on *riba*, *gharar*, and *maysir* in *takaful* undertakings. This is because, in most cases, the pool of funds contributed by participants is invested in profitable business to increase the asset base of the *takaful* scheme. The *takaful* operator, who technically manages and oversees the *takaful* funds, must consider the mandatory prohibitions in commercial transactions when making investment decisions.

Source: Islamic Financial Services Board. (December 2009). *Guiding Principles on Governance for Takaful (Islamic Insurance) Undertakings*. Kuala Lumpur: IFSB.

## Parties to the Contract

There are two main parties in conventional insurance, i.e. the insurance company and the insured party. The insured party has nothing to do with other insured parties in terms of guaranteeing one another against any loss. The insured party is only concerned about itself. Conversely, the parties in *takaful* are many. The participants in the *takaful* scheme mutually insure one another against any loss. The *takaful* operator cannot claim to be the insurer because it only acts as the administrator of the funds in accordance with the Sharī'ah. The participants insure themselves against any loss based on mutual agreement and mutual sense of responsibility.

## Payment of Premiums

The insured party in a conventional insurance scheme pays regular installments, called premiums, in return for insurance cover. If the contingent event stated in the insurance contract occurs, the insurance company guarantees the payment of compensation. This contractual arrangement is based on probability because such an event may occur or it may not occur during the period of the insurance cover. That is, the payment of compensation is contingent on the contractual events that may or may not occur. The premiums may also be forfeited under certain circumstances in conventional insurance. As a result, issues such as *gharar*, *maysir*, and exploitation arise. However, in *takaful*, premiums are not paid as regular installments to guarantee the receipt of compensation in the event that the insured-for occurrence happens. The premiums are paid instead as a donation from the participants into the common fund in order to indemnify other participants from the agony of any eventual loss. *Takaful* premiums are considered as trust held by the operator on behalf of the participants. It would be considered an injustice for the *takaful* operator to add a clause into the insurance contract that would allow the participants to forfeit their premiums. The participants remain the owners of the premiums even though they have donated them into a pool of funds to indemnify any member of the group.

## Investment of Insurance Funds

There are no strict restrictions on the type of business in which conventional insurance companies can invest their funds. Many insurance companies invest in stocks and bonds that are prohibited under the Sharī'ah, such as companies that engage in the brewing and marketing of alcoholic drinks, or interest-bearing financial institutions. *Takaful* funds, however, are invested in Sharī'ah-compliant products and companies. The requirement for Sharī'ah-compliant products in Islamic finance has been discussed in previous chapters and is an underlying principle that runs through the whole fabric of Islamic commercial transactions, or *fiqh al-muamalat*. Profits from investment are distributed on the basis of pre-agreed ratios in the underlying *takaful* contract. The model of *takaful* adopted by the stakeholders determines the profit distribution as well as the remuneration of the *takaful* operator.

Other specific differences between *takaful* and conventional insurance are summarized in Table 8.1.

## Historical Development of *Takaful*

Different practices during the pre-Islamic era that were not contrary to the general spirit of the Sharī'ah were adapted into the law. Such practices were approved and further streamlined by the Prophet to comply with the basic precepts of the Sharī'ah. The idea of mutual assistance is innate and thus was common among the early Arabs. The ancient Arab traders had a common practice of insurance protection that was upheld and preserved by the Prophet based on Islamic ideals with the advent of Islam. The concept of shared responsibility (**aqilah**) between the Muslims of Mecca and Medina during the incident of the Prophet's migration is a classical precedent of *takaful*. It was a common

**aqilah**
An ancient Arab custom based on mutual agreement.

**TABLE 8.1:** Specific Differences between *Takaful* and Conventional Insurance

| *Takaful* | Conventional Insurance |
|---|---|
| A combination of *tabarru'* contract and agency and/or profit-sharing contract | Contract of exchange (sale and purchase) between insurer and insured |
| Participant's duty to make contributions to the scheme and expected to share the surplus mutually | Policyholder's duty to pay premium to the insurer |
| *Takaful* operator earns a fee for rendering the service of managing the *takaful* fund and from the *mudarabah* profit-sharing scheme as *mudarib* | Insurance company makes a profit when there is an underwriting surplus |
| Countervalue (*'iwad*) is effort and/or undertaking of risk | No clear valid countervalue. Source of profit is anticipating (hoping) that the uncertain future will be in the insurer's favor (that total premiums will exceed total claims) |
| *Takaful* operator acts as administrator of *takaful* fund and pays benefits from it. If the fund is insufficient, operator must provide an interest-free loan to rectify the deficiency | Insurer is liable to pay the benefits as promised from insurance funds or/and shareholder funds |
| Indemnification component is based on mutual contribution, reciprocal donation (*tabarru'*) | Indemnification component is a commercial relationship between insurance company and the insured |
| There is no insurer-insured relationship between *takaful* operator and participants. Participants act as both the insured and the insurer simultaneously | There is a clear insurer–insured relationship |
| *Takaful* funds must be invested in Sharī'ah-compliant instruments | There is no restriction in investment of funds |

Source: Dusuki, A. W. and Abdullah N. I. (2009). Takaful: Philosophy, Legitimacy and Operation. In Dar, H. A. and Moghul, U. F. (eds.), *The Chancellor Guide to the Legal and Shari'a Aspects of Islamic Finance* (p. 297). London: Chancellor Publications Limited.

practice among the ancient Arabs that when a member of a tribe unintentionally kills any member of another tribe, the paternal relatives of the accused person were obliged to pay the deceased's heirs a form of blood money (*diyah*) as a pecuniary remedy to cushion the effect of the loss of the member of the tribe. The accused's paternal relatives who paid such blood money are usually known as *al-aqilah*.

The companions of the Prophet laid down this golden precedent of mutual assistance and shared responsibility under his close supervision. This is the main Sharī'ah basis for *takaful* from the golden era of Islam although the modern application of the concept has crystallized into several models developed by Sharī'ah scholars. Figure 8.2 gives a brief timeline of the development of *takaful* in the modern Islamic finance industry from 1977 to date and how it is expected to grow in the next few years.

The modern history of *takaful* dates back to 1979 when the Islamic Insurance Company was established in Sudan. The *takaful* it offered was based on the cooperative insurance model. In the following year, the Islamic-Arab Insurance Company was established in Saudi Arabia and in United Arab Emirates. In 1984, Malaysia enacted the Takaful Act 1984, which provides for the regulation of *takaful* business in Malaysia and other incidental matters. Since then, contemporary Islamic scholars have issued numerous resolutions on the permissibility of *takaful* as a cooperative insurance. The first of these resolutions was that of the Council of Saudi Scholars in 1977. The following year, the Fiqh Council of the Muslim World League passed a similar resolution. The OIC Fiqh Academy approved the *takaful* system in 1985 but the mechanism for its operation was left to Sharī'ah scholars, who have developed certain models over time based on approved Sharī'ah contracts for the *takaful* industry.

*Takaful* products have spread all over the globe. Some multinational insurance companies have opened *takaful* subsidiaries, which has contributed significantly to the global acceptance of *takaful* products and has enhanced growth in the industry by an estimated 10-20 percent a year and could lead to a global *takaful* premium of about US$25 billion in 2015.[4] As the *Global Islamic Finance* box shows, however, there is a significant concentration in the MENA region and South-East Asia. While growth in the *takaful* industry remains promising, there is a need to further make the products conventionally viable and competitive in the light of modern developments in the global insurance industry.

## Challenge

Can you establish any relationship between the development of the Islamic financial industry and the emergence of the *takaful* component of the industry?

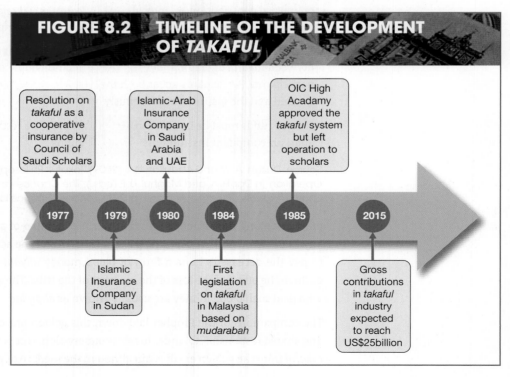

**FIGURE 8.2   TIMELINE OF THE DEVELOPMENT OF *TAKAFUL***

- **1977** — Resolution on *takaful* as a cooperative insurance by Council of Saudi Scholars
- **1979** — Islamic Insurance Company in Sudan
- **1980** — Islamic-Arab Insurance Company in Saudi Arabia and UAE
- **1984** — First legislation on *takaful* in Malaysia based on *mudarabah*
- **1985** — OIC High Acadamy approved the *takaful* system but left operation to scholars
- **2015** — Gross contributions in *takaful* industry expected to reach US$25billion

## GLOBAL ISLAMIC FINANCE

# Current Position of *Takaful* in the World

Of the three major components of Islamic finance, the *takaful* aspect has experienced slow growth in terms of range of products and expansion around the world. Despite these initial challenges, *takaful* remains a promising component of the global Islamic finance industry. From the available data, the *takaful* industry is currently concentrated in South-East Asia and the Middle Eastern and North African (MENA) countries, as shown in the figure.

Although *takaful* has been less affected by the global financial meltdown due to its concentration in emerging markets, there was a surge in the growth of the industry as a result of the paradigm shift on the part of international *takaful* giants such as the American International Group (AIG), which established AIG Takaful Enaya, headquartered in Bahrain.

According to Sameer Abdi, Head of Ernst & Young's Islamic Financial Services Group: "*Takaful* markets now span much of the globe but there still exists a large, expanding and untapped Muslim population on almost every continent. We estimate that the global *takaful*

market could be as high as US$7.7bn by the end of 2012."[5]

*Takaful* operators need to diversify their products to include new areas such as medical insurance and introduce frameworks to address complex risk issues. Partnering with international giants in offering *takaful* products in Europe and America will further expand the market rather than concentrating on the MENA and South-East Asian countries. These key strategic issues need to be closely considered in the drive towards a viable future direction and expansion of the *takaful* industry. There is much room for expansion of *takaful* products beyond the MENA region and South-East Asia. Potential markets such as Egypt, Nigeria, and Muslim minority communities in Europe and America should be the next focus. However, there is a need to restructure *takaful* products to be conventionally viable and competitive without violating any Islamic law precepts to be able to penetrate markets in Europe and America. The focus of the industry will now be turned towards the exploration of new international growth markets for *takaful*.

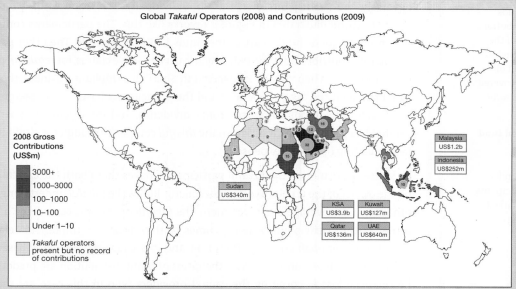

Map source: World Islamic Insurance Directory 2010; Ernst & Young analysis.

# Models of *Takaful*

**LEARNING OBJECTIVE 8.2**

Describe the innovative Sharī'ah-approved models and structures of *takaful*.

The principles of *takaful* have been applied to reflect certain models of Islamic finance products. While some of these models are based on a single Islamic product, hybrids have also been developed to reflect the modern needs and challenges of the global economy. This will be seen in the different types of *takaful* models. Meanwhile, keep in mind that the main two parties involved in the implementation of the *takaful* system are the *takaful* operator and the participants. The **_takaful_ operator** is the party who manages and administer the *takaful* fund. The party is neither the owner of the funds nor the owner of the company but the trustee of the *takaful* funds. The agents of the *takaful* operation are considered as part and parcel of the operator. They are only entitled to commissions or fees based on the terms agreed upon by the parties. The **participants** are the owners of the *takaful* fund. They are the investors or fund contributors in whatever model is adopted by the manager of the *takaful* fund.

**_takaful_ operator**
The party who manages and administer the *takaful* fund.

**participants**
The owners of the *takaful* fund.

## The *Mudarabah* Model

*mudarabah* **model of** *takaful*
An Islamic insurance model based on a trust partnership between the *takaful* operator who is appointed to manage the *takaful* business by the participants who act as the financiers, investors, or fund contributors.

**participants' risk fund (PRF)**
The common pool of funds realized from the contributions (donations or *tabarru'*) of the participants, which is used to meet claims in the event of any eventuality or loss covered under the underlying *takaful* contract.

**participants' investment fund (PIF)**
A fund derived from a portion of the pool of funds contributed by the participants, which is specially earmarked for investment or savings purposes.

The ***mudarabah* model of *takaful*** is based on the Islamic finance product known as *mudarabah* (trust financing), and is commonly used in trust financing. In this model, outlined in Figure 8.3, the *takaful* operator is the entrepreneur (*mudarib*) appointed by the participants, who act as the financiers, investors, or fund contributors (*rabb al-mal*). The funds contributed by the participants into the common pool of funds, which is used for underwriting purposes, is known as the **participants' risk fund (PRF)**, while the fund used for investment activities is known as the **participants' investment fund (PIF)**. The participants jointly own the PRF, as it is for the sole purpose of mutual indemnification. Conversely, the participants own the PIF individually. The example of a *mudarabah* model of *takaful* illustrated in Figure 8.3 works like this. The participants contribute to the common pool of funds. Part of the funds is invested as PIF. The other part of the participants' contribution is the PRF, which is used to settle claims, for *retakaful* purposes, and as reserves. When the PIF is invested in Sharī'ah-compliant business, the profit is shared between the *takaful* operator and the participants based on a pre-agreed ratio. The shareholders' funds comprise profits, dividends, and management expenses. The shareholders get their dividends from the *takaful* company through the profit it realizes after deducting operating expenses.

The strategic position of the *takaful* participants makes them both the capital provider and the owner of the whole *takaful* undertaking. But as the *takaful* undertaking involves both insurance coverage and investment, the *takaful* operator is considered a business partner of the participants when it comes to the investor-entrepreneur relationship under the *mudarabah* contract. The profit-and-loss sharing principle is based on the classical *mudarabah* contract where the ratios of profit distribution are predetermined. The financial loss is borne by the capital providers who in this case are the *takaful* participants. On the other hand, the entrepreneur, i.e. the *takaful* operator, may lose the rewards for their labor if the investment funds run into deficit.

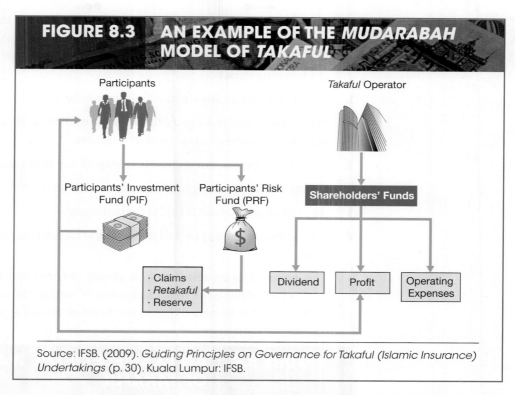

**FIGURE 8.3     AN EXAMPLE OF THE *MUDARABAH* MODEL OF *TAKAFUL***

Source: IFSB. (2009). *Guiding Principles on Governance for Takaful (Islamic Insurance) Undertakings* (p. 30). Kuala Lumpur: IFSB.

**surplus**
The amount that remains after deducting all expenses and management fees for the administration of the *takaful* fund and the claims made by the participants from the contributions to the fund. (If this amount is negative, it is called a deficit.)

In terms of the management of underwriting the risks on behalf of the participants, the *takaful* operator is remunerated from the underwriting **surplus** as agreed upon by the parties in the underlying *takaful* contract. In the underwriting of risks on behalf of the participants, any loss recorded must be borne by the participants as the capital providers, provided there is no element of negligence on the part of the *takaful* operator. According to IFSB-8 (IFSB *Guiding Principles on Governance for Takaful (Islamic Insurance) Undertakings*), in order for the *takaful* operator to make a profit in its partnership and managerial *takaful* business with the participants, it must ensure that the total share of investment profit and underwriting surplus is more than the expenses incurred in managing the *takaful* operation. It is important to observe that this *mudarabah* model is generally losing ground in the industry because many *takaful* undertakings now prefer to adopt the *wakalah* model.

## The *Wakalah* Model

**wakalah model of takaful**
An Islamic insurance model that is based on a contract of agency between the *takaful* participants and the *takaful* operator, where the former are the real owners of the fund while the latter acts as an agent.

The **wakalah model of takaful** is based on the Islamic finance product known as *wakalah* (agency). This model is widely used in the *takaful* industry. This form of *takaful*, outlined in Figure 8.4, is based on the contract of agency between the *takaful* participants and the *takaful* operator, where the former are the real owners of the fund while the latter acts as an agent. That is, the ownership of the *takaful* fund vests in the participants while the *takaful* operator merely acts as an agent in the management and administration of the fund for a contractual fee clearly specified and agreed upon by the parties. Just like the agency contract, the *takaful* operator is entitled to an agency fee or commission for their service. Any surplus realized from the investment of the participants' funds will only go to the participants. The operator only receives an agency fee based on the terms in the contract. The example of the *wakalah* model of *takaful* outlined in Figure 8.4 has the following steps.

1. Participants pay contributions into a common fund.

2. The common fund is delegated to the *takaful* operator as an agent for a mutually agreed fee, which also includes management expenses.

3. The *takaful* operator invests the PIF in Shari'ah-compliant business.

4. Claims and underwriting surpluses can be made on the PRF.

5. Any end-of-year surplus is paid to the participants.

6. A performance fee may be paid to the *takaful* operator for prudent management of the fund.

This principal–agent relationship is strictly enforced and built into the underlying contract to establish the rights and duties of each of the parties to the contract. The agency fee must be predetermined and based on mutual agreement of the parties and,

## FIGURE 8.4 AN EXAMPLE OF THE *WAKALAH* MODEL OF *TAKAFUL*

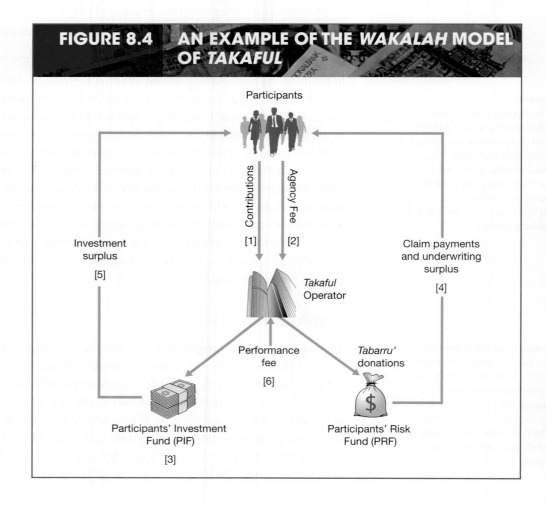

as a matter of clarity, it must be clearly stated in the contract. IFSB-8 suggests that the agency fee should cover the total sum of the following costs:

- management expenses
- distribution costs, including intermediaries' remuneration
- a margin of operational profit to the *takaful* operator.[6]

The *takaful* operator does not share in any risk borne in the investment or management of the *takaful* fund. It is in the best interest of the *takaful* operator to reduce management expenses through prudent policies, which should ordinarily attract some incentives or bonuses. Apart from the normal agency fee, which is pre-agreed by the parties and built into the contract, there can be an additional performance-related fee, where some incentives are given for good management and governance related to the underwriting output. It is always good when circumstances that may lead to the payment of such performance-related fees are made explicit in the underlying *takaful* contract. These incentives will encourage good practice in the industry and promote competitiveness and prudent management of the *takaful* funds.

## Hybrid *Wakalah-Mudarabah* Model

**hybrid *takaful* model**
An Islamic insurance model that combines and effectively uses more than one financial instrument in its structuring.

### Challenge

Why do you think the hybrid model of *takaful* is better than the single model?

This **hybrid *takaful* model** is a combination of the *wakalah* and *mudarabah* models. It uses these two specific models for two different purposes in the *takaful* fund. Under this hybrid model of *takaful*, the *wakalah* model is employed for the underwriting while the *mudarabah* model is used for the investment activities. Under the *wakalah* model adopted for the underwriting activities, the *takaful* operator is entitled to an agency fee or a mutually predetermined commission in their role as a *wakil* or agent who manages the *takaful* funds. In addition, they are entitled to a share in the profits realized for managing the investment activities of the fund in their role as an entrepreneur (*mudarib*). This twin role makes the hybrid model unique and is the reason why it is becoming more popular, as many scholars have adjudged it to be the most suitable and mutually beneficial model for all the parties concerned. The *takaful* operator's sources of income are greater in this model, being the agency fee, incentive fee, and the profit share from the investment of the funds.

AAOIFI recommends the hybrid model for *takaful* companies. In fact, the Central Bank of Bahrain (CBB), formerly known as the Bahrain Monetary Agency, only allows *takaful* companies operating in Bahrain to adopt either the *wakalah* model or the hybrid model for their business. Although the CBB does not have a specific law for regulating *takaful* operations, Volume 3 of its Insurance Rulebook summarizes the regulatory requirements for *takaful* and *retakaful* operations as part of its oversight function on financial institutions in Bahrain.

The steps in the hybrid model, as illustrated in Figure 8.5, are:

1. The participants appoint the *takaful* operator as an agent, for a mutually agreed fee.
2. The *takaful* contribution is divided into the PIF and PRF.

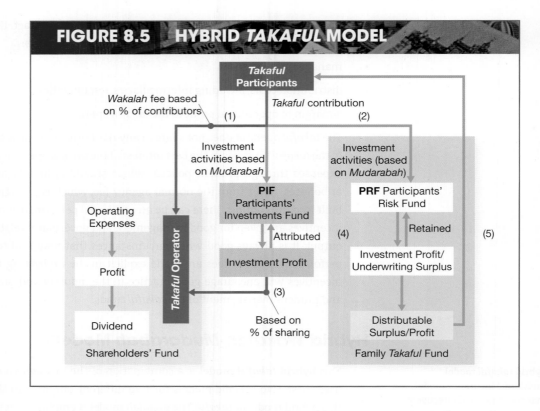

**FIGURE 8.5     HYBRID *TAKAFUL* MODEL**

3.  The investment profit from the PIF, based on the *mudarabah* model, is shared between the participants and the *takaful* operator.

4.  The investment profit from PRF is added to the PRF account, which is used for underwriting activities.

5.  Any profits and underwriting surplus may be distributed to the participants.

The hybrid model, sometimes called the mixed model, is the dominant model in the Middle Eastern markets and it is widely embraced all over the world. An important element is the clear segregation between the shareholders' funds and the participants' funds.

**Hint**

Muhammad Taqi Usmani is the Chairman of the Shari'ah Board of the Accounting and Auditing Organization for Islamic Financial Institutions (AAOIFI).

## *Waqf-Wakalah-Mudarabah* (Ultra-Hybrid) Model

The renowned Pakistani Shari'ah scholar Muhammad Taqi Usmani has introduced a new model, which is a hybrid of the *wakalah* and *waqf* models with an additional *mudarabah* element (see Figure 8.6). This is what we refer to as the ultra-hybrid model of *takaful*. *Waqf* means a charitable endowment that has been structured into an Islamic financial product for contracts that involve charitable dispositions such as *takaful* and microfinance. This new model, where *wakalah* is combined with the *waqf*, has been adopted by *takaful* companies in South Africa and some other countries, including Swiss Re *retakaful* in Malaysia. The agency contract is important in most financial transactions, hence the continued emergence of *wakalah* in most Islamic finance products.

The Central Bank of Bahrain only allows *takaful* companies operating in Bahrain to adopt either the *wakalah* model or the hybrid model.

In this model, the shareholders of a *takaful* company make donations to a common pool of funds that has been established as a *waqf*. The *waqf* funds are invested in Sharī'ah-compliant business activities. The returns from such investments plus any contributory funds (*tabarru'*) in the Participants' Special Account (PSA) are used for the benefit of the participants. It is important to note that it is only the returns from the investments that are used for the benefit of the participants. The original capital amount contributed to the common pool of funds must remain for the purpose of reinvestment in order to ensure that there is continuity in the *waqf* funds, which is one of the main features of *waqf*. In this way, cash *waqf* is used for the purpose of mutual benefit. The model described in Figure 8.6 can be summarized thus.

1. Participants pay contributions as *waqf* into the common pool of funds for **mutual indemnification**.

2. Participants enter into an agency contract with the *takaful* operator, who is paid a fixed agency fee.

**mutual indemnification**
The cooperative and collaborative element of *takaful* where the participants mutually provide insurance cover for one another in the event of any mishap.

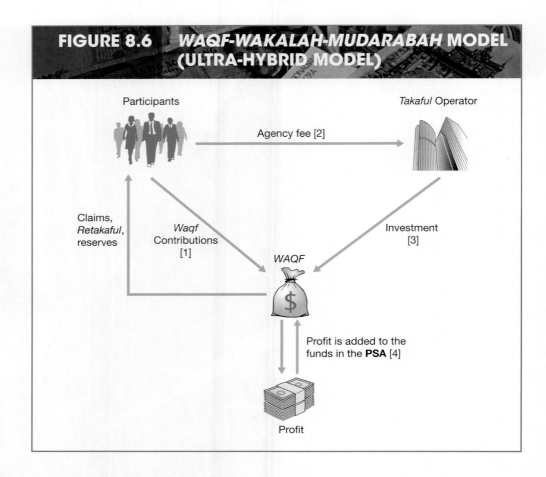

**FIGURE 8.6** *WAQF-WAKALAH-MUDARABAH* **MODEL (ULTRA-HYBRID MODEL)**

Participants

*Takaful* Operator

Agency fee [2]

Claims, *Retakaful*, reserves

*Waqf* Contributions [1]

Investment [3]

WAQF

Profit is added to the funds in the **PSA** [4]

Profit

3.  The *takaful* operator invests the funds in Sharī'ah-compliant business.

4.  The profits accruing from the investment are added to the *tabarru'* funds in the PSA and used to underwrite the risks of the participants.

    The *wakalah* element comes in to play with the role of the *takaful* operator. The shareholders of the *takaful* company make donations in order to establish a *waqf* fund. The company then becomes the shareholders' agent, delegated to manage the *waqf* funds properly and pay any valid claims. This delegation of authority is in the form of an agency contract for which the company receives an agreed fee. The company also manages the investment of the *waqf* funds as an entrepreneur, the implication being that the company is also entitled to its share in the profit realized from the investment. This ultra-hybrid model covers elements of the *waqf, wakalah*, and *mudarabah* models for *takaful*. Thus, rather than calling it a *wakalah* with *waqf* model, it is more appropriate to refer to it as **waqf-wakalah-mudarabah model**.

***waqf-wakalah-mudarabah model***
A combination of charitable endowment, agency, and trust financing contracts within the same structure for the purpose of Islamic insurance.

The key elements and differences of the four models are presented in Table 8.3.

**TABLE 8.3: Key Elements and Differences of the *Takaful* Models**

| | *Mudarabah* model | *Wakalah* model | Hybrid model | Ultra-hybrid model |
|---|---|---|---|---|
| **Contracts used** | *Mudarabah* only | *Wakalah* only | *Wakalah* and *mudarabah* | *Wakalah*, *mudarabah* and *waqf* |
| **Investment strategy** | Investment in Sharī'ah-compliant assets | Savings and investment in Sharī'ah-compliant assets | Investment in Sharī'ah-compliant assets | Investment in Sharī'ah-compliant assets |
| **Operator's responsibility** | Invests the funds and manages the whole *takaful* undertaking | Administers the *takaful* undertaking and oversees the investment of the funds | Administers the *takaful* undertaking and oversees the investment of the funds | Administers the *takaful* undertaking, oversees the investment of the funds, and manages the *waqf* fund |
| **Initial capital used** | Participants' premiums | Participants' premiums | Participants' premiums | Participants' premiums and charitable donations (*waqf*) |
| **Benefits** | Mutual guarantee for the participants. Profit to be shared between operator and participants. Surplus to be distributed to participants. | Mutual guarantee against any risk for the participants and end-of-year surplus. Agency fee for the operator. | Mutual guarantee for the participants. Profit to be shared between operator and participants. Surplus to be distributed to participants. | Mutual guarantee for the participants. Operator and participants share profit from the investment of cash *waqf* funds. Returns from *waqf* investment of the participants to be added to PRF. |

**LEARNING OBJECTIVE 8.3**

Describe the main *takaful* products and their expansion into the global insurance market.

# Main *Takaful* Products

The wide use of the *takaful* models has resulted in a number of products in the global *takaful* industry that are generally patterned on them. The available products have been classified into two main types of product—general *takaful* and family *takaful*. These are Sharī'ah-compliant alternatives to general insurance and life insurance, respectively.

## General *Takaful*

General *takaful* may also be called composite *takaful* because it embraces a wide range of products. A general *takaful* contract provides short-term *takaful* cover where the assets and other proprietary belongings of participants are protected from foreseeable material loss or any form of damage. The *takaful* participants pay certain specified contributions while the *takaful* operator undertakes to manage the risk through the administration of the underwriting activities. A general *takaful* fund is established from the participants' contributions and the money invested in Sharī'ah-compliant investments. The proceeds that accrue from these investments are returned to the fund for the purpose of indemnifying the *takaful* participants.

General *takaful* can be further categorized into a number of products according to the type of *takaful* the participants choose to invest in. The available *takaful* is divided into two further categories: motor *takaful* and non-motor *takaful*. The following are examples of general *takaful* cover:

**Challenge**

Name three examples of general *takaful* aside from the examples given in this chapter.

- motor
- employer liability
- burglary
- machinery breakdown
- health.
- fire
- fire consequential loss
- worker compensation
- marine cargo

This list is not exhaustive but represents some notable *takaful* schemes in the industry. General *takaful* is a short-term policy renewable periodically according to the terms and conditions of the *takaful* contract. Underwriting surpluses of the *takaful* funds are distributed to the participants annually. An example of general *takaful* is outlined in the *Islamic Finance in Practice* box, where one of the key *takaful* products of HSBC Amanah Takaful, which was introduced to cater for its Home Financing-i customers, is briefly examined. The Homeowner *Takaful* products covers a range of unexpected disasters that could befall any of the contributors to the *Takaful* Risk Fund.

## Family *Takaful*

Family *takaful* is the Sharī'ah alternative to life insurance, whereby people come together to mutually indemnify one another against any disaster that may befall any member of their family, such as sudden death or permanent disability. As this form of *takaful* cover involves life and family issues, it is usually offered as a long-term policy cover that may span between 10 and 30 years depending on the structure of the product.

## ISLAMIC FINANCE IN PRACTICE

# HSBC Amanah Homeowner *Takaful*

As part of the Islamic products offered by HSBC Amanah, the Homeowner *Takaful* was introduced specifically to provide Islamic insurance coverage for its Home Financing-i customers. This shows the general nature of the Islamic finance industry where each component is meant to complement each other. The symbiotic relationship is enhanced through innovative products offered by the Islamic financial institutions. While HSBC Amanah is regarded as an intermediary in the scheme, any claims and liabilities are handled directly by HSBC Amanah Takaful for consideration and onward processing. An amount of up to 10.5 percent is paid as a commission to HSBC Amanah for the service rendered. In order to protect against loss or damage to one's house, HSBC Amanah introduced this model to cover the following disasters:

- fire/lightning/thunderbolt/subterranean fire
- explosion/aircraft damage/impact damage by third-party, road vehicles, or animals
- burst or overflowing domestic water tanks, apparatus, or pipes
- theft with violent or forcible entry or exit

- hurricane/cyclone/typhoon/windstorm/ earthquake/volcanic eruption/flood
- riot /strike/malicious damage
- loss of rent
- public liability.

All these liabilities relate to the house that is covered by the policy. The basic premium costs as little as US$3.5 for cover of US$3,225 under the scheme. Thus, if the value of the cover is US$200,000, the *takaful* premium will be US$217 subject to the contractual terms. The total amount of coverage is calculated in accordance with the needs and circumstances of each person and this is usually contained in the *takaful* contract. However, the amount of coverage must necessarily reflect the full cost of reconstructing the house being covered. This form of *takaful* is more akin to mutual assistance through contributions on the basis of *tabarru'* (donations for a specific purpose, i.e. homeowner) than to the common pool known as the *Takaful* Risk Fund. The Fund is managed by HSBC Amanah Takaful while HSBC Amanah serves as the intermediary.

Source: www.hsbcamanah.com.my/1/2/amanah/personal/amanah-protection/homeowner-takaful

An example of general *takaful* is HSBC Amanah's Homeowner *Takaful*, which provides comprehensive protection against loss or damage to homes.

Examples of family *takaful* include accidental death, savings and education plans for one's dependants, retirement plans, disability plans, or *waqf* plans.

There are three types of family *takaful*:

- ordinary collaboration
- collaboration with savings
- collaboration based on specific groups.

These three categories are different in the arrangement the participants adopt in mutually indemnifying one another. Despite the fact that all three are collaborations for mutual indemnification under the management of a *takaful* operator, the scope differs.

## Ordinary Collaboration

Adopting the concept of *tabarru'*, participants mutually agree to contribute to a common pool of funds through donations. The premiums they contribute to the *takaful* fund are used for underwriting activities in the event of any mishap or disaster on the part of any of the members of the group. Any successful claim is paid directly to the participant or their beneficiaries in accordance with the underlying *takaful* contract.

## Collaboration with Savings

This second type of cover includes both collaboration through mutual indemnification and also acts as a savings account. Parties contribute through donations into a common pool of funds from which the underwriting activities are carried out. The other pool of funds constitutes individual participants' savings, held for a fixed period of time, after which they may be withdrawn by the respective owners. This second pool of funds is managed by the *takaful* operator but strategically segregated from the donations, which constitute the main *takaful* funds. Collaboration with savings has two significant advantages. First, the participants benefit from mutual indemnification from the common pool of funds they mutually contribute through *tabarru'*. Second, they benefit individually from their self-indemnification through long-term savings where they or their nominated beneficiaries can recover enough funds to cater for any eventuality, disaster, or the educational needs of orphans whose parents were participants in the fund.

## Collaboration based on specific groups

This type of family plan is usually structured in a manner that reflects communal, ethnic, or organizational needs. Participants from the same community, district, or social group may come together to establish a common pool of funds for a specific purpose expressly mentioned in the underlying contract. Contributions to the fund may be made jointly or separately by the organization and the participants. Membership of the scheme is limited to those who come from the same community or group and benefits from the common pool of funds can only be enjoyed by the participants or their beneficiaries.

If the *takaful* industry is to consolidate, the products need to make inroads into the global markets, particularly in the United States and Europe. As indicated in the *Islamic Finance in the News* box, the *takaful* industry is ripe for expansion and penetration into the global insurance market. The tremendous growth recorded in previous years justifies the need for conventional insurance companies in the western countries to further explore *takaful* products.

# ISLAMIC FINANCE IN THE NEWS

## Islamic Insurance: A global market ripe for growth

September 22, 2011

Islamic insurance has enjoyed strong growth in recent years, although the period since the global financial crisis has proved difficult for the rapidly developing industry.

Dominic Moody, senior vice-president at insurance broker Marsh in the Middle East, says the market for insurance products compliant with Islamic law—known as *takaful*—is 'growing quite phenomenally', in spite of the downturn.

Expansion is being driven by two factors: *takaful* is strongest in Muslim countries, where the take-up of insurance has been low historically; and availability is increasing, as more *takaful* insurers are established.

Ernst & Young says global *takaful* contributions totalled $9.15bn in 2010, and are on course to reach $12bn at the end of this year. The professional services firm points out they represent only 1 percent of the global insurance market, even though Muslims make up 20 percent of the world's population. The global market could reach $25bn by the end of 2015, it says.

But most Gulf Cooperation Council markets have seen a slowdown in *takaful* growth, with only Saudi Arabia's market staying strong because of the continued rollout of compulsory medical insurance.

According to Ernst & Young, Saudi Arabia, with *takaful* contributions totalling $3.86bn in 2009, Malaysia with $1.15bn, and the United Arab Emirates with $640m, were the top three markets.

Dagwood Ahmedji, head of Islamic financial advisory services at Deloitte, says there is plenty more potential in the Middle East, for example, from governments making insurance lines compulsory.

Analysts believe that for *takaful* to reach its potential, it must make inroads into Europe and the U.S., and into commercial insurance products. Many international companies have moved into the market, but more development is needed.

One challenge is to extend the insurance available for commercial lines. Mohammad Khan, a partner at PwC, and its Islamic finance leader, says that for this to happen there needs to be well-

rated Islamic reinsurance (the insurance that insurers buy) as well as so-called retrocession reinsurance (reinsurance of reinsurance).

Mr Moody says Islamic finance is radiating out from the Middle East to other parts of the world. However, this is not being matched by equivalent insurance products. 'Islamic finance is pretty much a global industry. There are challenges when it comes to provide financing for a business in Europe or the U.S., because there are limited insurance options, so they have to use regular insurance. It is not a fully Islamic financing solution,' he says.

A number of Islamic banks, he says, are setting up branches in Europe and plan to offer complementary products, for example, a personal accident insurance policy provided by the bank.

'Islamic banks are working with insurers to try to create a bancassurance product that is Shari'ah-compliant,' says Mr Moody.

In the UK, Salaam Halal insurance, the first Islamic insurance company, launched in 2008. Although it took off initially, it was operating in the ferociously competitive motor insurance market and closed to new business a year later.

PwC's Mr Khan says the tipping-point for *takaful* will come when it also appeals to non-Muslims. [*Takaful*] is ethical insurance, and that is the market to go for. The market in the U.S., in western countries isn't just Muslims, and shouldn't be restricted to Muslims,' he says.

Other hurdles include making sure that insurance contracts comply with Islamic principles and evolving regulations.

The Islamic finance industry has developed its own body, the Islamic Financial Standards Board, which has tackled issues such as solvency.

Despite the headwinds, analysts are still upbeat on prospects.

According to Mr Ahmedji, while the global financial crisis has 'damped confidence in factors such as investment returns, *takaful* is a slow-burn industry. It was never going to be an overnight phenomenon, because it is about introducing a new product to the Muslim community.'

**Source:** Andrea Felsted, "Islamic Insurance: A global market ripe for growth", *Financial Times*, September 22, 2011.

**LEARNING OBJECTIVE 8.4**

Analyze the process of determining and allocating surplus or deficit as proposed by AAOIFI.

# Underwriting Surplus and Technical Provisions

With the coming of age of many *takaful* operators and the generation of more profits, there is an increasing need to understand the appropriate manner to determine and allocate surplus in a way that is Shari'ah-compliant. This manner is premised on the origin of the surplus, which is invariably the premiums contributed by the participants. With the increasing prevalance of profit-oriented *takaful* institutions that compete strongly with conventional insurance companies, there have been some misgivings on the appropriate method for the distribution of surplus in *takaful* undertakings.

AAOIFI has issued a relevant standard, Financial Accounting Standard No. 13, to regulate the necessary disclosure of the bases for determining and allocating surplus or deficit in *takaful* companies.

## Underwriting Surplus

According to AAOIFI, "insurance or underwriting surplus is the excess of the total premium contributions paid by policyholders during the financial period over the total indemnities paid in respect of claims incurred during the period, net of reinsurance and after deducting expenses and changes in technical provisions."[7] It is common to have an underwriting surplus, particularly in *takaful* undertakings, as in most cases participants make donations to the common pool of funds for mutual indemnification. In order to properly regulate this, the underwriting surplus is calculated for a specific financial year. Accordingly, all indemnities paid for deserving claims, the *retakaful* policy and changes in technical provisions must be deducted from the total premium contributions of the participants. Total indemnities paid in respect of claims during the financial period are the underwriting activities carried out by the *takaful* company to indemnify the claims of deserving participants. Net of reinsurance implies that all *retakaful* operations must be taken into account when calculating the underwriting surplus. This should be reflected in the financial statement of the *takaful* company. Changes in technical provisions include unpaid claims and unearned premiums. All these must be adjusted in the method of accounting to reflect the actual financial position of the *takaful* fund. Changes in the technical provisions mainly relate to the method of accounting and balancing the financial statement.

## Right of Policyholders to Surplus

The policyholders or *takaful* participants have the right to the surplus. Box 8.2 quotes from AAOIFI's standard on the Shari'ah ruling on surplus.

Many Shari'ah scholars agree that the policyholders have an exclusive right to the *takaful* surplus. The surplus originated from the policyholders who made the financial contributions. The surplus belongs to the policyholders collectively, and is expected to be

### BOX 8.2: BASIS OF SHARĪ'AH RULING ON *TAKAFUL* SURPLUS

The Sharī'ah ruling on the surplus is derived from the ruling made on the origin of that surplus, i.e. the premium contributions. The ruling states that these contributions are amounts wholly or partially donated in accordance with the Islamic insurance system in which participation is considered to be an implicit acceptance of the conditions set out in the insurance policies or the by-laws relating to the disposition of the insurance surplus in the various cases, the most important of which are mentioned below. These conditions do not conflict with the Sharī'ah provisions, and Muslims are bound by their agreements, except when such agreements render the impermissible lawful or render the lawful unlawful, according to the hadith.

Sharī'ah allows that donations may be restricted by conditions and allocated for a specific purpose. They may also be made contingent upon certain conditions, according to some *fuqaha*. *Gharar* (uncertainty) in Islamic insurance is forgiven in the case of donations because according to the Maliki school of thought *gharar* does not invalidate the contracts of donations.

The shareholders in an insurance company may invest the insurance surplus for the account of the policyholders, if there is an express provision to this effect in the insurance policy or in the by-laws, provided that the Sharī'ah provisions regulating such investment (i.e., percentage of investment profit in the case of *mudarabah* or amount of fee in the case of agency) should be specified in the insurance policy, by-laws, or the notices sent to policyholders. The policy should also specify a deadline for policyholders to express any objection they may have regarding the consideration payable. Otherwise the company will assume that policyholders have no objections.

Source: AAOIFI. 2010. *Accounting, Auditing & Governance Standards (for Islamic Financial Institutions)*, Bahrain: AAOIFI. FAS 13.

**takaful policy**
An insurance policy that is based on the Islamic insurance model, which is based on mutual cooperation.

clearly stipulated in the **takaful policy**. There should be a clear segregation between the assets, obligations, and results of operations of the policyholders and the shareholders of the *takaful* company. The shareholders are not entitled to the *takaful* surplus but will be reimbursed from the profit realized from the investment activities of the *takaful* undertaking. However, some rulings by Sharī'ah boards permit the shareholders to share the surplus with the policyholders.

## Allocating the Insurance Surplus

There are numerous methods of allocating *takaful* surplus. AAOIFI identifies a number of methods:

- allocation of surplus to all policyholders, regardless of whether or not they have made claims on the policy during the financial period

- allocation of surplus only among policyholders who have not made any claims during the financial period
- allocation of surplus among those who have not made any claims and among those who have made claims of amounts less than their insurance contributions, provided that the latter category of policyholders should receive only the difference between their insurance contributions and their claims during the financial period
- allocation of surplus between policyholders and shareholders
- allocation of surplus by using other methods.[8]

A *takaful* undertaking must agree on the distribution method in the policy. Transparency is essential in these kinds of financial dealings. The methods are not cumulative but alternatives among which the *takaful* undertaking may select its specific method. AAOIFI proposes that when the *takaful* policy or by-laws is silent on the specification of allocation methods, the first method listed above should be followed, whereby all policyholders will benefit equally from the surplus.

## Covering the *Takaful* Deficit

**qard hasan**
Benevolent loan that is devoid of interest without any share in profit that accrues from the use of such funds.

In order to cover any deficit, the *takaful* operator may provide a **qard hasan** (benevolent loan) to the *takaful* fund to undertake the underwriting activities. Generally, in practice, *retakaful* companies come to the rescue of *takaful* undertakings by bailing out the *takaful* fund. As in most cases there are two main funds in the *takaful* undertaking, i.e. PRF and PIF, different frameworks exist for covering a deficit in each instance. However, AAOIFI generally proposes in its relevant standard a number of methods for covering the *takaful* deficit.

1. To settle the deficit from the reserves of policyholders, if any.
2. To borrow from the shareholders' fund or from others the amount of deficit, which should be paid back from future surpluses.
3. To ask the policyholders to meet the deficit pro rata.
4. To increase the future premium contribution of policyholders on a pro-rata basis.[9]

## Deficit in Participants' Risk Funds (PRF)

It is the duty of the *takaful* operator to rectify the deficiency and loss in the PRF. A deficit occurs when the assets of the PRF are insufficient to meet the liabilities. In other words, when the *takaful* claims of the participants are more than the pool of funds for underwriting activities, a deficit exists. While a deficit can be rectified through *qard hasan* from the *takaful* operator, there must be a sound repayment mechanism that will not affect the PRF's future obligations. It should be effectively managed by the *takaful* operator, so that such a loan can be repaid through future surpluses. In extreme situations, such as where it is clear that the deficit is due to the negligence or mismanagement of the *takaful* operator, it may be rectified through the transfer of assets from the shareholders' fund.

## Deficit in Participants' Investment Fund (PIF)

When a deficit is recorded in the PIF, the losses will be absorbed by the capital providers, especially when the *takaful* undertaking is structured on a *mudarabah* model. Therefore, the participants will bear the loss from the investment. A benevolent loan cannot be used to guarantee a deficit because it is not allowed under the Sharī'ah for the entrepreneur to guarantee the *mudarabah* capital. Thus, the *takaful* operator as the entrepreneur cannot rectify the deficit through *qard hasan*. To this end, the deficit may be made good through other means as enumerated by AAOIFI above. However, if it is proved that the deficit occurred as a result of the *takaful* operator's professional negligence or mismanagement, the deficiency should be rectified through a transfer from the shareholders' fund.

**LEARNING OBJECTIVE 8.5**

Explain the relevance of reinsurance and *retakaful* in the modern practice of *takaful* business.

# Reinsurance and *Retakaful*

The Islamic alternative to reinsurance is *retakaful*, which has been structured in a Sharī'ah-compliant model, i.e. reinsurance of *takaful* business on the basis of Islamic principles is known as *retakaful*. Ma'sum Billah explains the differences between reinsurance and *retakaful* in Table 8.4.

Within the conventional framework of insurance, collective risk management is important in the industry. In order to achieve this, insurance operators collectively share the risks they have undertaken to underwrite. Larger insurance companies play this significant role as they underwrite the risks of smaller insurance companies. The risks underwritten by most insurance companies are usually too great for them to continue with business so, reinsurance is a mechanism to mitigate them by transferring the risks to a large insurer known as a reinsurer. Thus the pool of risks of insurance companies is in practice transferred to a larger company, the reinsurer.

This risk-averse method of *retakaful* is structured so that *takaful* operators act like natural human beings who are participants in a *takaful* undertaking with a large *takaful* company. An agreed amount is paid periodically from the operator's *takaful* fund as premiums to the *retakaful company*. This way, all the underwriting risks of the *takaful* operators are insured by the *retakaful company*. Essentially, *retakaful* is a *takaful* undertaking for *takaful* operators. The *retakaful* companies play a significant role when *takaful* operators record deficits or losses. Whereas the *takaful* operator, through the *takaful* fund, underwrites the risks of the policyholders, the *retakaful* company underwrites the risks of the *takaful* operator. Figure 8.7 illustrates the *retakaful* capital flow.

The emergence of the *takaful* industry showed there was a need to reinsure the operators' risks through having them underwritten by a *retakaful* company. This was noted by the IFSB in its *Guiding Principles on Governance for Takaful Undertakings*, an excerpt of which is presented in Box 8.3. The proliferation of *takaful* companies in many Muslim countries has invariably called for the establishment of *retakaful* companies structured on Islamic principles. A large initial capital is required for *retakaful*

**Challenge**

What is the difference between *takaful* and *retakaful*?

| TABLE 8.4: Differences between Reinsurance and *Retakaful* | | |
| --- | --- | --- |
| **Differences** | ***Retakaful*** | **Reinsurance** |
| 1) *Riba* and *gharar* | A *retakaful* operation does not earn commission as a profit or interest, because this commission is subject to *riba* and dilutes the purpose of setting up a *takaful* operation. The *retakaful* operation is dependent on actual expenses spent by the *takaful* operator in the process of *retakaful*. | The conventional reinsurance operation is subject to *riba* and *gharar*, which are not in line with Sharī'ah principles, e.g. the reinsurance commission that the direct insurance company earns, from the reinsurance treaty. Because this commission is framed in such a way, it renders the commission *ribawi* and implies *gharar* to a high degree. |
| 2) Principle of insurable interest | According to Islamic law insurable interest refers to holding a specific financial interest in the subject matter of the insurance as a cardinal principle of the legality of the *retakaful* contract. The reinsured party does not get an insurable interest or to reinsure the property of the original insured party without permission from the policyholder. However, because the *retakaful* operation is based on *mudarabah*, it is vested with a right to reinsure on the insurer because permission from the policyholder is automatically inherent in the contract of *mudarabah*. | Insurable interest is vested in the reinsured party. The fact that the reinsured party has issued a policy and assumed liability for its original insured party is assumed to give it insurable interest sufficient to enable it to reinsure. The point is that although the reinsured party (direct insurance company) has no actual legal interest in the property, the subject matter of the original insurance policy, it has assumed responsibility for it, and has therefore put itself in a position, recognized by law, in which it would be prejudiced by its loss. |

Source: Dr. Mohammed Ma'sum Billah. Retakaful (Islamic Reinsurance) Paradigm. Available at www.applied-islamicfinance.com/sp_retakaful_1.htm

undertakings because of the large pool of risks involved in reinsurance. The capital of many *retakaful* companies is not large enough to attain an 'A' rating, which is mostly required for reinsurance purposes. The ratings of companies are usually conducted by designated rating agencies, as discussed in Chapter 7. Thus, many *takaful* operators opt for reinsurance policies of conventional reinsurance companies. Sharī'ah scholars have allowed *takaful* operators to reinsure this way, subject to certain conditions and

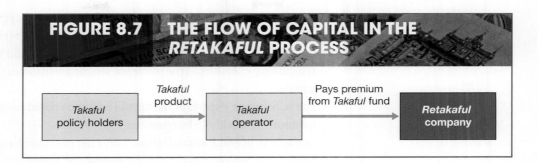

**FIGURE 8.7    THE FLOW OF CAPITAL IN THE *RETAKAFUL* PROCESS**

particularly where the available *retakaful* companies do not have the requisite capital that can cater for the large pool of risks of many *takaful* companies at an international level.

*Retakaful* operators carry out their operations in accordance with the structures and models of the *takaful* operators, which are structurally similar and based on Sharī'ah principles. While modern scholars permit *takaful* operators to undertake reinsurance policies with conventional reinsurance companies under certain conditions, they unanimously agree that preference must be given to a *retakaful* company where one is available. Wahbah Zuhaili, while approving the *retakaful* process, stipulates the following general conditions.

- Any reinsurance business between *takaful* operators and conventional reinsurers should not cause financial injury to Muslims or destabilize the financial systems of Muslim countries. If it does, the cooperation becomes unlawful for failing to serve the purpose for which it was permitted, i.e. the protection of the financial wellbeing of the *takaful* operators and participants.

---

**BOX 8.3:    IFSB-8 ON *RETAKAFUL***

As part of their risk management, *takaful* undertakings may subscribe to a *retakaful* scheme that suits the needs and requirements for primary *takaful* undertakings to protect against unforeseen or extraordinary losses. *Retakaful* can spread liability for specific risks, share liability when losses overwhelm the primary *takaful* undertakings' resources, and help them spread the risk inherent in some segments of *takaful* business.

*Takaful* operators should ensure that any *retakaful* arrangement duly serves the purpose of the *takaful* undertakings and holds the interests of *takaful* participants foremost. The pricing and protection offered by the *retakaful* operator should be consistently reviewed from time to time to ensure that it is commensurate with the needs and requirements of the *takaful* undertakings. As far as possible, *takaful* operators should strive to use *retakaful* operators, rather than conventional reinsurers, in support of a fully Sharī'ah-compliant financial system for *takaful* undertakings.

Source: Islamic Financial Services Board, *Guiding Principles on Governance for Takaful (Islamic Insurance) Undertakings*, Kuala Lumpur: IFSB, December 2009, pp. 22–23.

- *Takaful* companies must prevent capital flow from the *takaful* fund to conventional reinsurance firms. In other words, the reinsurance agreement should be designed in favor of *takaful* operations. Moreover, preference should be given to Islamic reinsurance operators in the matter of securing reinsurance protection whenever possible.
- The reinsurance experts of the *takaful* operator should carefully determine the quantum of liability to be reinsured.
- The *takaful* operator should reinsure on a net premium basis and not receive any reinsurance remunerations, profit commissions, or interest on premiums it has retained from premiums payable to its reinsurer.
- The *takaful* operator should review its reinsurance requirement annually and should progressively reduce dependence on conventional reinsurers.
- The *takaful* operator must stipulate a condition exempting it from payment of or receiving interest from a conventional reinsurance company. However, if the reinsurance company cannot adjust its management and investment methods to comply with this requirement, the *takaful* operator may accept the interest and spend it on humanitarian activities and public infrastructure projects.
- The *takaful* operator must encourage participants and shareholders to contribute to a *retakaful* fund by consenting to increase their proportion of *tabarru'*, and seek their consent to use their contribution for the purpose of reinsurance protection.
- The premium paid for securing reinsurance protection shall be as low as possible.
- *Takaful* operators should endeavor to persuade its conventional reinsurer to enter into a profit-sharing agreement and even suggest a method of management and investment compatible with Islamic principles.
- The ultimate goal of *takaful* operators must be to put an end to dealing with conventional reinsurers whenever adequate reserves, or when numerous Islamic reinsurance companies, are established.

In response to the desire of many *takaful* companies for *retakaful* operations considered to be Shari'ah-compliant, the leading global reinsurance company Swiss Re opened a dedicated *retakaful* branch in Malaysia in October 2009.

## ISLAMIC FINANCE IN PRACTICE

# Swiss Re *Retakaful*

Some conventional reinsurance companies have established *takaful* divisions, such as Swiss Re in Malaysia.

The leading global reinsurance company, Swiss Re opened a dedicated *retakaful* branch in Malaysia in October 2009. This stemmed from the increasing importance of *takaful* and the yearning of many *takaful* companies for *retakaful* operations to be Sharī'ah-compliant.

Before it made its debut in Malaysia, Swiss Re had begun offering *retakaful* solutions in the Middle East in 2006. It introduced the *wakalah-waqf* model, which was developed to embed certain sustainable elements of *waqf* into the model, beginning with the initial set up of a *waqf* fund realized through an initial donation by the *retakaful* operator. This distinctive model has now been widely adopted in South-East Asia, the Middle East and South Africa. It has also been endorsed by the Accounting and Auditing Organization for Islamic Financial Institutions (AAOIFI).

Fidrus Sukor, a client manager at Swiss Re Retakaful, explains how the model works.

- The *takaful* operator creates a cash *waqf* fund with an initial donation, for the purpose of extending financial assistance to its members in the event of losses.
- The *waqf* fund has the characteristics of a typical *waqf*. For example, it is inalienable, irrevocable, and exists in perpetuity.
- The rights and obligations of all parties are spelled out in the *waqf* deed or fund rules, and will be agreed to by all participants who wish to become a member of the fund.
- The *takaful* operator acts as a *wakil* to administer the *waqf* in accordance with the fund rules.
- Members of the fund agree to relinquish a certain amount of money without condition as *tabarru'*, and will receive benefits in accordance with the fund rules.
- Any surplus sharing and distribution will also be specified in the fund rules.

Such Sharī'ah-compliant models of *retakaful* have contributed significantly to the development of the *takaful* component of the Islamic finance industry over the years.

Source: *Islamic Finance News*. Supplement. May 2012, p. 2.

- It is incumbent upon *takaful* operators to appoint a Sharī'ah supervisory board to monitor their operations according to Sharī'ah principles.[10]

It is important to note that just as is being experienced in the Islamic banking industry, some conventional reinsurance companies have established *takaful* pools, arms, or divisions based on the active demand for capacity from the *takaful* industry. Those companies include Swiss Re, Mitsui Sumitomo, Hannover Re, Kuwait Re, Trust Re, and Labuan R (see *Islamic Finance in Practice* above for more information on Swiss Re *Retakaful*). The most prominent *retakaful* companies are presented in Table 8.5 and listed alphabetically according to the countries in which they are based.

| **TABLE 8.5:** The Most Popular *Retakaful* Companies | |
|---|---|
| **Name of *Retakaful* Company** | **Country** |
| 1. Islamic Takaful & Retakaful Co. (IRTCo.) | Bahamas |
| 2. ACR Retakaful | Bahrain |
| 3. Hannover ReTakaful B.S.C. | Bahrain |
| 4. Solidarity Islamic Takaful & Retakaful Co. | Bahrain |
| 5. PT Reassuransi Internasional Indonesia | Indonesia |
| 6. Amin Reinsurance Company | Iran |
| 7. Al Fajer Retakaful Insurance Co. | Kuwait |
| 8. ACR Retakaful | Malaysia |
| 9. Asean Re-Takaful International | Malaysia |
| 10. MNRB Retakaful Berhad | Malaysia |
| 11. Munich Re ReTakaful | Malaysia |
| 12. Swiss Re Retakaful | Malaysia |
| 13. Al Khaleej Takaful Ins & Reins Co. | Qatar |
| 14. Islamic Takaful & Re-takaful Co. | Saudi Arabia |
| 15. Malath Cooperative Insurance & Reinsurance Co. | Saudi Arabia |
| 16. Sanad Cooperative Insurance & Reinsurance | Saudi Arabia |
| 17. Saudi Reinsurance | Saudi Arabia |
| 18. Weqaya Takaful Insurance & Reinsurance | Saudi Arabia |
| 19. Tokio Marine Nichido Retakaful Pte Ltd | Singapore |
| 20. National Re-insurance Co. (NRICo.) | Sudan |
| 21. Sheikhan Insurance & Reinsurance | Sudan |
| 22. Sudanese Insurance & Reinsurance Co. | Sudan |
| 23. BEIT Iaadat Ettamine Tounsi Saoudi Re-insurance (B.E.S.T. Re) | Tunisia |
| 24. Tunis Retakaful | Tunisia |
| 25. ACR ReTakaful Holdings Limited | United Arab Emirates |
| 26. Dubai Islamic Insurance & Reinsurance Co. | United Arab Emirates |
| 27. Takaful Re Limited | United Arab Emirates |

# Review

## Key Terms and Concepts

aqilah (p. 298)

contribution (p. 295)

hybrid *takaful* model (p. 305)

*mudarabah* model of *takaful* (p. 302)

mutual indemnification (p. 307)

operator or *wakil* (p. 295)

participants (p. 302)

participants' investment fund (PIF) (p. 302)

participants' risk fund (PRF) (p. 302)

qard hasan (p. 316)

surplus (p. 303)

*tabarru'* (p. 293)

*takaful* (p. 293)

*takaful* operator (p. 302)

*takaful* policy (p. 315)

*takaful ta'awuni* (p. 294)

underwriting policies (p. 296)

*wakalah* model of *takaful* (p. 303)

*waqf-wakalah-mudarabah* model (p. 308)

## Summary

**Learning Objective 8.1**

1. *Takaful* is the Islamic alternative to conventional insurance. The underlying concepts of *takaful* include *ta'awwun* (collaboration), *tabarru'* (donations), and cooperative risk-sharing, which are based on acceptable Sharī'ah models.

**Learning Objective 8.2**

2. The innovative Sharī'ah-approved models and structures for *takaful* undertakings include the *mudarabah* model, *wakalah* model, the hybrid model which brings together the first two models, and the *waqf-wakalah-mudarabah* model. The models contain standard formulas for the management of participants' investment funds and the participants' risk funds.

**Learning Objective 8.3**

3. The available products in the *takaful* industry have been generally classified into two main products—general *takaful* and family *takaful*. These are Sharī'ah-compliant alternatives to general insurance and life insurance, respectively. A general *takaful* contract provides short-term *takaful* cover where assets and other proprietary belongings of participants are protected from foreseeable material loss or any form of damage. Family *takaful* is a long-term policy where people come together to mutually indemnify one another against any disaster that may befall any of them, such as sudden death or permanent disability.

**Learning Objective 8.4**

4. The process of determining and allocating any surplus or deficit as proposed by AAOIFI and the different guidelines issued by the regulatory bodies in some Muslim countries emphasizes the rights of the policyholders to the surplus. However, there is a current move to propose a framework that would allow the shareholders of the *takaful* company to be entitled to a share from any surplus.

**Learning Objective 8.5**

5. The relevance of reinsurance and *retakaful* to the modern *takaful* business is beyond doubt. Although some scholars allow *takaful* operators to patronize conventional reinsurance companies on the basis of necessity, preference is given to *retakaful* companies. However, there is a need for *retakaful* companies to expand their capital base to be able to give insurance cover to larger undertakings.

## Practice Questions and Activities

### Practice Questions

1. What are the underlying concepts of *takaful* in Islam?

2. Differentiate between *takaful* and conventional insurance, with special reference to their main features.

3. What are the differences between the *mudarabah* and *wakalah* models of *takaful*?

4. What do you understand as a hybrid model of *takaful*? Illustrate your answer with a suitable example.

5. Explain four main *takaful* models adopted in many countries around the world and describe the parties to the *takaful* contract.

6. What is the difference between family *takaful* and general *takaful*? Give relevant examples to support your answer.

7. How will you determine and allocate surplus in a *takaful* undertaking where surpluses have been recorded at the end of the financial year?

8. What is the AAOIFI position on the allocation of surplus in *takaful* undertakings?

9. What is the significance of *retakaful* in *takaful* undertakings?

10. What makes *retakaful* distinctive when compared to the conventional reinsurance model?

### Activities

1. Prepare a simple sketch of the *mudarabah* model adopted by most of the *takaful* operators in your country.

2. Find three newspaper cuttings on the recent development or expansion of *takaful* products in any country.

3. Prepare a brief profile of five major *takaful* operators in your country.

## Further Reading

Arboun, M. B. (2000). The Operation of Retakaful (Islamic Reinsurance) Protection. *Arab Law Quarterly*. Vol. 15, no. 4: pp. 335–362.

Archer, S., Abdel Karim, R. A., and Nienhaus, V. (eds). (2009). *Takaful Islamic insurance: concepts and regulatory issues*. John Wiley & Sons (Asia) Ltd.

Dusuki, A W. and Abdullah, N. I. (2009). Takaful: Philosophy, Legitimacy and Operation. In Dar, H. A. and Moghul, U. E. (eds). *The Chancellor Guide to the Legal and Shari'a Aspects of Islamic Finance*) (pp. 285–313). London: Chancellor Publications Limited.

Fisher, O. and Taylor, D. Y. (2000). *Prospects for Evolution of Takaful in The 21st Century*. Massachusetts: Harvard University.

Jaffer, S. (ed). (2007). *Islamic Insurance: Trends, Opportunities and the Future of Takaful*. London: Euromoney Books.

Kassar, K. and Fisher, O. C. (2008). *What's Takaful—A Guide to Islamic Insurance*. Beirut: BISC Group.

Khorshid, A. (2004). *Islamic insurance: a modern approach to Islamic banking*. London: RoutledgeCurzon.

Ma'sum Billah, M. (2003). *Islamic Insurance (Takaful)*. Kuala Lumpur: Ilmiah Publishers.

Ma'sum Billah, M. (2008). *Takaful* versus conventional insurance. In Rahali Ali (ed.), *Islamic Finance: A Practical Guide* (pp. 141–146). London: Globe Business Publishing Group.

Yusof M. F. (1996). *Takaful (Islamic Insurance) Concept And Operational System From The Practitioner's Perspective*, Kuala Lumpur: BIMB Institute of Research and Training.

# 9

# Islamic Microfinance

# Learning Objectives

**Upon the completion of this chapter, the reader should be able to:**

1  Be familiar with the history and basic components of Islamic microfinance and the benefits to society.

2  Identify key Islamic finance products that have been used for microfinance.

3  Understand the differences between Islamic microfinance institutions and conventional microfinance institutions.

4  Be familiar with the major Islamic microfinance institutions in the modern world.

5  Understand the corporate social responsibility role of Islamic banks in financing micro-enterprises.

The increasing demand for Islamic alternatives to banking and financial services has led to the development of the Islamic microfinance sector as a key sector for the provision of credit to small and medium enterprises. The diversification of Shari'ah-compliant products has created an interface between the role of Islamic banks and financial institutions, and microfinance initiatives. Supporting microfinance initiatives are part of the general functions of Islamic banks and financial institutions, triggering the rate at which Islamic microfinance institutions have developed in the 21st century. A number of traditional Islamic finance products have been structured to satisfy the immediate needs of micro-credit functions, with their principal objective being to alleviate poverty, empower the poor, and encourage financial inclusiveness in Muslim communities around the world.

Many of the planet's 2.7 billion Muslims without adequate access to credit facilities have resolutely refused to approach financial institutions that do not comply with the requirements of Islamic law for finance. As a large percentage of this disadvantaged population are low-income individuals who cannot access funds for their microbusinesses, the sudden swell in the number of Islamic microfinance institutions has been warmly welcomed by stakeholders in the Islamic finance industry. The role of Islamic banks and financial institutions in creating the favorable environment for micro-credit facilities cannot be overemphasized in the increasingly competitive financial sector. This chapter examines Islamic microfinance with its unique features and its similarities to conventional micro-credit initiatives. We focus on the role of Islamic banks and financial institutions in promoting Islamic microfinance as part of their general functions, with specific reference to corporate social responsibility.

## professional perspectives

**Professor Habib Ahmed**

*Sharjah Chair in Islamic Law and Finance, Institute of Middle Eastern and Islamic Studies, School of Government and International Affairs, Durham University, UK*

**1    What is the distinction between Islamic and conventional microfinance?**

In Islamic banking, microfinance institutions use Sharī'ah-compliant instruments and products to raise funds and use them for financing. Aside from using Sharī'ah-compliant instruments for both the liabilities and assets' side, an Islamic bank has distinct features that affect other aspects of its operations. Most microfinance institutions have a development agenda linked to financing, which is reflected in teaching clients certain behavioral and social norms. The agenda associated with Islamic microfinance institutions focuses on building moral character and strengthening family and social bonds in line with the teachings of Islam, which indirectly minimizes default and helps microfinance institutions to secure a higher recovery rate.

**2    How can Islamic microfinance specifically alleviate poverty in rural areas?**

It is widely believed that microfinance is considered a tool to cater to the needs of micro and small enterprises in rural areas that are excluded from traditional banks. However, in Muslim societies, some people do not benefit from conventional microfinance institutions because of their religious prohibition on dealing with interest. Islamic microfinance, thus, has the potential to mitigate poverty by providing financing to micro and small enterprises who are financially excluded, not only because they do not qualify for financing from traditional sources but also because of the incompatibility of conventional microfinance operations with their religious beliefs.

## professional perspectives

**Dr. Savas Alpay**
*Director General, Statistical, Economic and Social Research and Training Center for Islamic Countries (SESRIC)*

**1    How do you think microfinance can enhance entrepreneurship?**

Ideally, microfinance is expected to promote entrepreneurship and rural development. However, there is no strong evidence that microfinance is achieving this. Most households do not start a business enterprise in order to exploit a good business opportunity. To most recipients of micro-credit, the world of risk and competition is already foreign, and even frightening. They start a business for basic household economic survival. Households involved in any form of entrepreneurship suffer from lack of experience, training, and basic expertise. With the lack of basic marketing and sales techniques, they do not have access to markets for diversified goods and services, and they are forced to compete in oversupplied products but with marginal returns.

Almost all the studies on microfinance indicate that the poor people who are the main beneficiaries of microfinance services have limited ability to capitalize on investment opportunities, and face various challenges in converting microfinance funds into profitable investments with entrepreneurial value. It is true that having access to capital will allow some poor people to unleash small business opportunities and their entrepreneurial potential; however, not every borrower is a micro-entrepreneur.

On the other hand, micro-credit can be a tool for creating value networks. Social networks created between borrowers of the same lending groups can increase knowledge spillover, and business practices can be improved by sharing information, solving problems, and creating better risk-management strategies. Their ability to deal with external shocks, including disasters and market reversals, increases through these value networks, which subsequently support the entrepreneurial initiatives.

**2    How can Islamic microfinance specifically alleviate poverty in rural areas?**

Except in a few countries, there are high, and often growing, poverty rates especially in the rural parts of Muslim countries. Islamic microfinance can help alleviate poverty, firstly by including many of the poor who are currently excluded from the conventional system because of their religious values. Secondly, by redesigning the concept of microfinance into Islamic microfinance with no interest payments, it offers alternative modes of financing such as *musharakah*, *mudarabah* and *murabahah*. It also opens the doors for payment in kind, a useful alternative for rural people under various pressures. As finance will be a new, and most likely a first encounter for most of rural people, its strict compliance with the Islamic ethical and moral responsibilities and features will be an indispensable asset to attract them to the positive services it can offer. Islamic microfinance is also expected to shift the view of financiers from lending for profit only to lending for social wellbeing, while also keeping the door open to generate profit whenever possible. That is why the use of alternative funds through *zakat*, *sadaqah* and *waqf* assets in microfinance have recently been introduced in the system.

### 3    What is the distinction between Islamic and conventional microfinance?

Despite the common misconception that Islamic microfinance is like conventional microfinance less the interest, there are other fundamental differences between them. Islamic microfinance programs have access to a more diverse and expansive financial base that is not available to conventional microfinance, which usually gets its funds from foreign donors, clients' savings, and external funds. Islamic microfinance, however, as well as these sources of funds, can get funds from religious institutions such as *awqaf* and *zakat*, which are prevalent in many Islamic countries. Having an interest-free mode of operation, Islamic microfinance carries out its transactions through several Islamic modes of financing, such as *ijarah*, *murabahah*, *istisna'*, *mudarabah*, and *musharakah*.

Islamic microfinance has the potential to reach the poorest of the poor. Although the microfinance movement is meant to help the poor out of poverty, the poorest population is often left out by conventional microfinance programs because of the high costs of processing and financing, and the existence of more profitable alternatives (the not-so-poor and the not-so-in-need of assistance). However, this is not the case with Islamic microfinance. It can integrate the specifically designed poverty eradication institutions of the Islamic system such as *zakat* and *qard hasan*, and other voluntary charities (*sadaqah*) to provide the poorest people with financial services.

# Islamic Microfinance: Providing Credit to the Entrepreneurial Poor

**microfinance**
The provision of small-scale financial services to the poor who are usually excluded from formal financial services.

*Zakat, waqf,* and *qard hasan* as well as other mechanisms for promoting social security in the Muslim communities are informal tools for the socioeconomic transformation of the entrepreneurial poor.

Islamic **microfinance** can be defined as the process of providing small-scale financial services, based on Sharīʿah concepts, to the poor who may be excluded from formal financial services, without putting any burden on the parties either in the form of interest or undue benefits. There is a huge demand for Islamic microfinance in Muslim countries. With more than 44 percent of the microfinance initiatives in the modern world domiciled in Muslim countries, there is a growing need to explore Islamic microfinance initiatives that agree with the values and beliefs of people who steer clear of interest-based microfinance initiatives.[1] In addition, financial institutions in developing economies only serve 20–30 percent of the population while others are excluded from the mainstream financial system.

Microfinance initiatives based on Islamic economic principles are directed towards low-income entrepreneurs who need credit facilities for their businesses. Why should Islamic microfinance target these people? The poor or those in low-income groups may not have enough finance to engage in normal financial transactions with formal financial institutions because of the requirements for such contracts. Islamic microfinance provides a workable alternative credit facility for this target group and goes a long way to bridging the divide between rich and poor.

## The History of Islamic Microfinance Institutions

**informal savings club**
(Also known as savings and credit cooperatives)
An informal cooperative project primarily meant to help members of the group to turn small but regular cash flows into large and meaningful sums of money.

**entrepreneurial poor**
Able people who have the ability to work and carry out legitimate business activities but lack the financial wherewithal to undertake such activities.

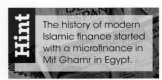

The history of modern Islamic finance started with a microfinance in Mit Ghamr in Egypt.

Early initiatives to alleviate poverty in Islam include the institution of *zakat* (compulsory alms), *waqf* (charitable endowment) and the praiseworthy benevolent loans (*qard hasan*). These worthy initiatives were vigorously pursued during the golden era of Islam, but were not called microfinance because they applied to all Muslims. Conventional microfinance initiatives were informally introduced in Europe in the 16th century through cooperative projects meant to help members of a group to turn small but regular cash flows into large and meaningful sums of money. These were known as **informal savings clubs**. They were meant to assist the poor but involved interest-bearing loans and interest-yielding deposits. Today, microfinance frameworks around the world have had their agenda institutionalized. The paradox of giving credit facilities to low-income individuals and then charging interest on the loans does not necessarily serve the real objective of microfinance as a means of assisting the **entrepreneurial poor** who lack the finance to undertake business activities.

The history of Islamic microfinance institutions (MFIs) dates back to the 1960s when the first experiment in rural finance based on profit and loss sharing was implemented in the remote village of Mit Ghamr in Egypt. This oft-cited modern origin of Islamic banking and finance was in a real sense a microfinance scheme to encourage micro-savings and micro-entrepreneurship. The model was subsequently developed into full-blown banking and financial services and, later in the 1970s and 1980s, a number of financial institutions offering Islamic products were established across the Muslim world. The 1990s and the new millennium ushered in a period of consolidation of Islamic finance products. With the pioneering efforts of the Grameen Bank in Bangladesh, there was increasing awareness in Muslim-populated countries of the need to establish inclusive financial institutions that would cater for low-income individuals in the Muslim world and beyond. The joint partnership initiative of Grameen-Jameel between the Bangladeshi Grameen Foundation and the Saudi Arabian Abdul Latif Jameel Group opened the Gulf Cooperation Council (GCC) countries to microfinance initiatives. This led to the establishment of a number of microfinance institutions across the Muslim world that practically applied Islamic finance modes to financing micro-enterprises.

As an alternative to conventional microfinance, the revival of Islamic financial services in the modern world also brought about the proper structuring of the Islamic ideals on microfinance to assist the entrepreneurial poor in the Muslim world and beyond. One major difference between conventional microfinance and the Islamic microfinance framework is the prohibition of interest-bearing credit facilities and interest-yielding deposits. This mandatory prescription in micro-credit transactions in Islamic commercial law is a general thread that runs through the fabric of all commercial transactions in Islamic law.

Islamic microfinance institutions date back to the 1960s, where the first experiment in rural finance based on profit and loss sharing was implemented in the village of Mit Ghamr in Egypt.

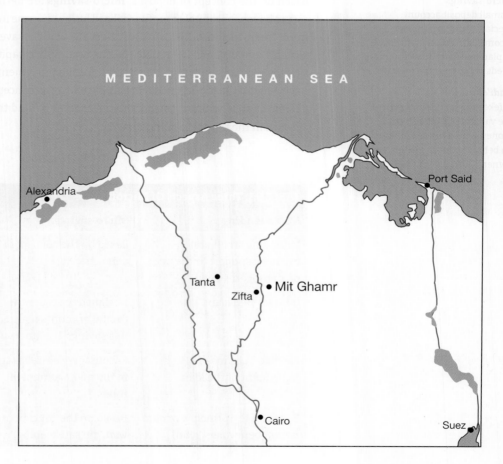

# Components of Islamic Microfinance

Islamic microfinance is an umbrella concept that consists of three main components; micro-lending, micro-saving, and micro-insurance or micro-*takaful*. These are summarized in Table 9.1. Two other terms commonly used are microfinance and micro-credit, and it is important that we understand the difference between these terms.

## Micro-lending

**micro-lending**
Provision of credit facilities for low-income people based on the principle of benevolent loans (*qard hasan*).

**Micro-lending** is also known as micro-credit schemes. It involves the provision of credit facilities for low-income people, based on the principle of *qard hasan*, meaning that they are interest-free, have a flexible repayment period, and there is no form of compensation from the borrower except for the lender to hope for the reward of God. Micro-lending assists the entrepreneurial poor in growing their income with the expectation of greater returns. It can also assist them in growing their physical asset base, for example with housing loans. Providing housing loans to the poor allows them to have a strong, income-generating, physical asset base, especially when such houses are leased to third parties.

## Micro-savings

**micro-savings**
A small deposit account specially designed for low-income earners as an incentive to plan for their future financial needs or to repay micro-loans.

**wadi'ah**
Safekeeping of deposits where the valuable commodity or money is held in trust (*amanah*) on behalf of the depositor-cum-owner.

Based on the concept of deposits, **micro-savings** are designed to provide a reasonably secure haven for capital or profits realized by low-income individuals who have benefited from credit facilities. In this way, they are able to save and manage their finances sensibly and become self-reliant. Clients accumulate capital and profits in their micro-savings account, allowing them to plan for the repayment of any micro-loan they may have benefited from. Micro-savings is based on the concept of **wadi'ah** (safekeeping) in Islamic finance, which is the underlying concept behind the introduction of the savings account in the formal banking system.

| TABLE 9.1: Three Aspects Of Microfinance | | |
|---|---|---|
| **Micro-lending** | **Micro-savings** | **Micro-*takaful*** |
| Extending small-scale financial support to the poor or low-income people | Based on the concept of deposits | Benefiting from mutual cooperation, solidarity, and protection |
| Interest-free loans | Designed to secure the capital or profits realized in a savings account | Mutual risks transfer arrangement within a group |
| Flexible in terms of repayment of the loan | Encourages self-reliance in the management of funds | Relevant for risks that are beyond the financial capacity of members |
| Based on the principle of *qard hasan* (benevolent loan) | Based on the concept of *wadi'ah* (safekeeping) | Based on the principles of *takaful* |

## Micro-takaful

**Micro-*takaful*** is a scheme established to allow members of a specified group of low-income individuals to mutually protect one another from any form of risk through collaborative *takaful*. In the event that any group member experiences some sort of mishap or encounters any financial or material risk, they will be able to benefit from the mutual cooperation, solidarity, and protection of the *takaful* scheme. The mutual risk transfer arrangement within the group ultimately benefits all the members as well as their dependants. This form of arrangement is relevant for certain risks that are beyond the financial capacity of individual members. As we saw in Chapter 8, *takaful* involves mutual risk shouldering among members of the *takaful* scheme. Micro-*takaful* may be necessary for the protection of the clients' capital in micro-lending or micro-savings.

## Microfinance and Micro-credit

It is likely that you will come across the two seemingly confusing concepts of microfinance and micro-credit, which are generally used interchangeably because what low-income individuals lack is access to credit facilities to finance their basic wants and entrepreneurial needs. However, the two terms are different in terms of meaning, scope, and application. While microfinance refers to the whole range of small-scale financial services that are provided for the benefit of the poor or low-income individuals, **micro-credit** refers to the small loans or financial assistance extended to the poor families who are practically excluded from formal financial services. In other words, micro-credit is part and parcel of microfinance.

## **Prohibition of *Riba* in Islamic Microfinance**

As we have seen in previous chapters, one recurring issue in all Islamic finance products is the prohibition of *riba* (interest). Modern microfinance schemes, even in some Muslim countries, are dominated by interest-based products that can further impoverish low-income individuals. These interest-based schemes, originally meant to provide access to credit for the poor, may end up further impoverishing them, especially when the capital and interest increase with every passing day. The impact of high interest rates on microfinance schemes will definitely be counterproductive. To combat rising interest rates, financial experts have suggested putting a cap or ceiling on interest rates in microfinance schemes.

Financial institutions that offer micro-credit facilities for low-income individuals are known as **microfinance institutions (MFIs)**. Examples include Hodeidah Microfinance Program in Yemen, Akhuwat in Pakistan, Sanduq Project in Syria, Amanah Ikhtiar Malaysia, and Islami Bank Bangladesh Limited in Bangladesh. However, it has been argued that as the MFIs' main source of income is the interest they charge and as they incur a huge amount of running costs, their interest rates are correspondingly high. Despite this, it is well known that MFIs receive concessional funds in order to finance lending. The pro-interest advocates have further argued that concessional funds are not permanent sources of finance, so MFIs must still rely on high interest rates to be able to carry out their objectives.

> ### Challenge
> Think of some other Islamic financial products that can be used as an auxiliary product for each of the three aspects of Islamic microfinance.

> ### Challenge
> Why do you think *riba* (interest) should be prohibited in all microfinance programs?

333

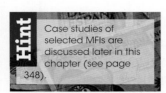

Case studies of selected MFIs are discussed later in this chapter (see page 348).

Islamic microfinance models are developed from existing Islamic finance products.

**Financial exclusion**
The direct or indirect exclusion of a certain group of people from the conventional financial system and its products.

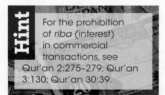

For the prohibition of *riba* (interest) in commercial transactions, see Qur'an 2:275–279; Qur'an 3:130; Qur'an 30:39.

Low-income households cannot afford micro-credit facilities because the high interest rates practically exclude them. The Islamic microfinance scheme provides a better alternative through a number of models developed from Islamic financial products. Islamic microfinance is interest-free, in line with the mandatory requirements of all Islamic products. Through partnership and entrepreneurial commercial activities between the financial institution and its clients, Islamic microfinance has developed multiple sources of income. When these sources are well managed, the returns will be more than the income generated by conventional MFIs through high interest rates. In the Islamic microfinance models that we will discuss shortly, there is an inbuilt mechanism for the operational costs. Depending on the model adopted, there is always a provision for management costs and other related expenses that may be incurred by the micro-entrepreneurs (individuals).

The Islamic approach to poverty alleviation is a holistic framework that excludes any counterproductive element such as *riba* and *gharar* (excessive risk or speculation). Whether the interest rates are high or low, they violate the fundamental basis of Islamic commercial law. Therefore, **financial exclusion** is experienced in countries where interest-based MFIs are operating because Muslims are excluded from micro-credit schemes. A fundamental requirement in Islamic commercial law is that all forms of transaction and contract must be free from *riba*. The main reason for the prohibition of *riba* is to avoid financial exploitation and oppression by the rich. There are also numerous Prophetic precedents on the prohibition of financial exclusion, exploitation, and oppression through *riba*.

The Qur'an says:

> Qur'an 2:280: "And if the debtor is in a hard time (has no money), then grant him time till it is easy for him to repay, but if you remit it by way of charity, that is better for you if you did but know."

This verse contains important lessons for the management of micro-credit schemes. When clients are not able to redeem their loans within the contractual period, it is recommended that they are given additional time and, in some extreme cases, the loans may be written off completely. Remittal of credit facilities may be considered in some extreme situations, particularly when the Islamic microfinance institution has recorded a surplus. This may be part of the corporate social responsibility role of Islamic financial institutions. The interest-free Islamic microfinance framework satisfies the need to establish user-friendly sustainable MFIs. Box 9.1 highlights some basic features of Islamic microfinance that have a direct impact on the poor and society in general. Some of the features may not be exclusive to Islamic microfinance, but they all represent its underlying spirit.

## BOX 9.1:    FEATURES OF ISLAMIC MICROFINANCE

Microfinance allows the poor to participate in the housing market

Equal opportunity, entrepreneurship, risk-sharing and participation of low-income individuals

Empowerment of the poor, particularly women, and improving access to credit facilities for social development

Interest-free micro-credit schemes where equity financing or debt financing modes are used

Compassionate treatment of poor borrowers, and in some cases debt cancellation

# Islamic Microfinance Products

Microfinance forms part of the functions of the Islamic banks and hence is part of Islamic finance. Islamic microfinance products are based on the common Islamic financial products we discussed in Chapter 3. An Islamic microfinance institution adopts debt or equity modes of finance for its financing requirements.

The debt-creating modes used by some Islamic microfinance institutions include:

- *qard hasan* (benevolent loan)
- *murabahah* (mark-up sale)
- *ijarah* (lease contract)
- *salam* (forward sale)
- *bay'-bithaman ajil* (deferred payment sales).

The equity financing mechanisms used in Islamic microfinance institutions include:

- *mudarabah* (trust partnership)
- *musharakah* (joint venture partnership)
- *musaqah* (sharecropping).

In this chapter, we have selected the most commonly used modes for further analysis.

## *Salam* as an Islamic Financial Product for Microfinancing Agriculture

**parallel *salam***
A forward contract that is concluded with a third party and which is distinct and not in any way contingent upon the first *salam* contract nor must its performance be contingent on the first contract.

One of the easiest ways to reach out to the poor in rural communities and empower them to be economically independent is through sustainable agricultural microfinance. This allows small farmers to engage in subsistence agriculture as well as offer some of their produce for sale. *Salam* (or *bay al-salam*), as the main Islamic financial product for a deferred delivery mechanism, is regarded as the most viable tool for agricultural microfinance. In this approach, *salam* is used in conjunction with **parallel *salam***, which is a forward contract concluded with a third party that is distinct and not in any way contingent upon the first *salam* contract. Nor must its performance be contingent on the first contract.

These are the most effective tools available to Islamic banks and financial institutions that support micro-credit schemes for agriculture. As a quick reminder, *bay al-salam* is a sale contract where advance payment is made for goods to be delivered later on. In other words, this is a contract where the seller undertakes to supply specific goods to the buyer at a future date in exchange of an advance price that is paid in full on the spot. Parallel *salam* is a separate contract distinct from the initial *bay al-salam* where the Islamic bank is the seller of the commodity based on deferred payment. In the ordinary *bay al-salam*, the Islamic bank is the buyer, while in the parallel *salam*, it is the seller. The two contracts must be distinguishable from each other and not dependent on each other.

With this background, when can a *salam* contract be used in Islamic commercial transactions? Two instances have been identified by the Muslim jurists where *salam* is applicable:

- to meet the liquidity needs of traders engaged in import and export business
- to meet the financial needs of small farmers who require liquidity to cultivate their land and grow their crops until harvest time.

**micro-farming**
Small-scale farming that involves the cultivation of a plot of land to grow food crops in order to be able to feed the farmer's family.

A *salam* contract is important in the financing of **micro-farming,** small-scale farming that involves the cultivation of the family's plot of land, where the farmers require some money to grow their crops and feed their family up to harvest time. Islamic banks provide micro-credit for this purpose, after entering into a *salam* contract where the bank is the buyer and the farmer is the seller who undertakes to embark on future delivery.

The micro-credit facilities provided by the Islamic banks in advance allow the farmers to sell their cash crops for a price lower than the real market price. The Islamic bank must pay the price in full to the farmer at the time of concluding the contract. The price and the date of delivery are fixed on the date of signing the *salam* contract. The quantity and quality, with an exact description or specification, must be stated in the underlying contract. This is one of the conditions for the validity of a *salam* contract. If the exact specification of the goods cannot be specified, such as precious stones, it cannot be the subject of a *salam* contract. It is also not permissible for the parties to stipulate that the *salam* contract will be effected on the produce of a particular field of farm or fruits from a particular tree. This is because of the element of uncertainty (*gharar*) in such a stipulation. There is the possibility of the destruction of the farm or the tree before harvest. Therefore, the contractual terms must be clear, certain, and specific in all ramifications. No room should be left for ambiguity that may result in an unpremeditated dispute between the parties.

After the delivery of the cash crops, the Islamic bank sells them on the open market on the basis of parallel *salam* at a price higher than the price at which it bought them from the farmer. The difference between the cost price of the crops as concluded with the farmer and the selling price on the open market is the profit realized by the Islamic bank (shown in Figure 9.1). The profits from this kind of micro-farming scheme are a major source of income for the Islamic microfinance portfolio of a financial institution.

**FIGURE 9.1    PROFITS FROM ISLAMIC MICRO-CREDIT SCHEMES FOR AGRICULTURE**

Profit parallel Salam = Cost price in Salam Contract + Selling price

# *Mudarabah* Financing for Combating Unemployment

*Mudarabah* is an Islamic finance contract whereby an Islamic bank, as the investor, exclusively provides capital for a business project while an entrepreneur provides the management expertise. *Mudarabah* as an investment partnership financing mechanism may be structured as a tool to combat unemployment in an economy. When there is a large number of skilled unemployed workers, *mudarabah* can be a good product for entrepreneurial activities. The parties share the profit in accordance with the predetermined contractual ratios. Both parties also share the risk of the partnership arrangement, where the investor risks losing the capital and the entrepreneur risks losing any reward for their labor. This contractual arrangement has been adopted in microfinance schemes for the strategic purpose of combating the increasing rate of unemployment in developing Muslim countries. *Mudarabah* does not only give jobs to the unemployed but is also a means of creating jobs. Combating unemployment and job creation are two main areas where *mudarabah* is relevant as a microfinance product.

In a *mudarabah* microfinance product, the micro-entrepreneur approaches an Islamic microfinance institution or bank for capital finance for a specific business venture. When the agreement is concluded between the parties, the bank provides the capital finance while the micro-entrepreneur is professionally responsible for the initiation and technical management of the business enterprise. As part of the underlying agreement, the parties agree to share the profits based on an agreed ratio. The parties are also individually and collectively responsible for the risk involved in the business venture. If the *mudarabah* agreement is of an open type where the particular business in which the micro-entrepreneur will invest the capital finance is not specified or restricted, the contractual arrangement is called **mudarabah al-mutlaqah** (unrestricted trust financing). When the bank or Islamic microfinance institution, which in this case is the capital provider, specifies or restricts the business in which the capital finance may be invested, this contractual arrangement is known as **mudarabah al-muqayyadah** (restricted trust financing).

**mudarabah al-mutlaqah**
Unrestricted trust financing contract where a particular business in which the entrepreneur will invest the capital finance is neither specified nor restricted.

**mudarabah al-muqayyadah**
A restricted trust financing contract where the particular business in which the entrepreneur will invest the capital finance is expressly specified.

To minimize the business risks, micro-*takaful* is put in place. Profits are shared between the micro-entrepreneur and the bank or Islamic microfinance institution. This is a good source of funds for both parties and it is sustainable for a long period of time when properly managed with the requisite risk mitigation measures. The micro-enterprise can employ sales executives and other support staff to manage the business venture while it expands. Skilled unemployed individuals who seek micro-credit approach Islamic banks or microfinance institutions with viable business proposals to set up their own micro-enterprises. The business proposals are reviewed and subsequently approved by the financial institutions and a contract is signed by the parties based on a specific mode of microfinance agreed upon by the parties. Figure 9.2 illustrates a simple six-step *mudarabah* microfinance model for tackling unemployment.

1.  Unemployed workers in the community join together to form a number of organized groups.

2.  The Islamic MFI establishes a *mudarabah* micro-credit fund.

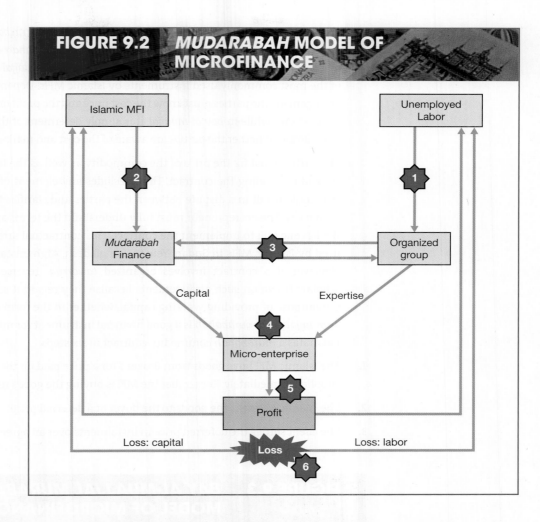

**FIGURE 9.2  *MUDARABAH* MODEL OF MICROFINANCE**

3.  Each group concludes a contract with the Islamic MFI based on *mudarabah*.

4.  The group is now the entrepreneur and contributes its expertise while the Islamic MFI provides the capital through the micro-credit scheme and a micro-enterprise is established.

5.  Profits are distributed between the Islamic MFI as the capital provider and the client as the entrepreneur, based on a predetermined ratio as contained in the underlying contract.

6.  In the event of any loss, the MFI bears the financial risk while the client bears the risk of their labor being unrewarded.

## *Bay al-Muajjal-Murabahah* Model of Providing Working Capital

**bay al-muajjal**
A sale where the parties agree to defer payment of the price to a future date.

***Bay al-muajjal*** is a sale where the parties agree to defer payment of the price to a future date. *Bay' bithaman ajil* (BBA) is another term for *bay al-muajjal*. Ordinarily, when a commodity is supplied and the parties agree to defer payment to a future date, there is already an element of *murabahah*. *Murabahah* is mark-up financing where a sale is made at a specified profit margin. When *murabahah* is combined with *bay al-muajjal*, it becomes a microfinance product. The mark-up price in the *murabahah* contract is settled as a deferred payment based on *bay al-muajjal*. In fact, *bay al-muajjal* with *murabahah* is one of the most commonly used instruments by Islamic MFIs. Depending on the contractual arrangement, the parties must know the cost price and the profit or mark-up in *murabahah* transactions, while in *bay al-muajjal*, it is simply deferment of the payment of the price regardless of whether the parties are aware of the cost and mark-up.

The parties must fix the price of the commodity as well as the terms of payment at the time of concluding the contract. This precludes any element of *gharar* in the contract that could result in a dispute between the parties and clarifies the rights and duties of each party. The entrepreneur must fully understand the terms and it should be easy for the Islamic MFI to implement the contract. This contractual arrangement is commonly used by Islamic MFIs in Sudan, Yemen, Bangladesh, Afghanistan, Indonesia, and Syria. However, if a contract involves organized *tawarruq* (reverse *murabahah*), Sharīʿah scholars frown on such arrangements because they regard it as disguised lending. For the purpose of providing working capital, whether in the form of goods or money, *bay al-muajjal* with *murabahah* is a good financial instrument for microfinancing. Figure 9.3 illustrates a *murabahah* commodity contract in six steps.

1. The Islamic MFI buys goods from Broker 1 for a price paid on the spot and the goods are supplied immediately. Remember the MFI is buying the goods requested by the client.

2. The Islamic MFI sells the goods to the buyer at a deferred price.

3. The client settles the deferred price in instalments over an agreed period.

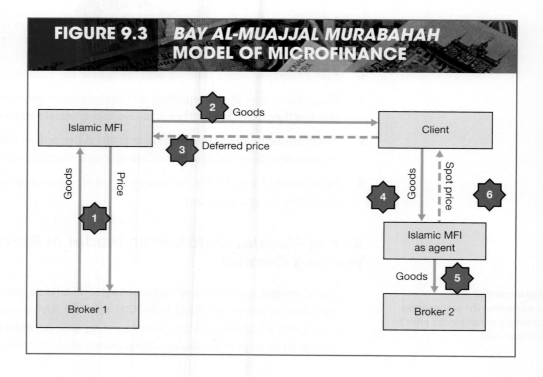

**FIGURE 9.3    *BAY AL-MUAJJAL MURABAHAH* MODEL OF MICROFINANCE**

4. In a separate contract, the client appoints the Islamic MFI as an agent to sell the goods on a spot basis.

5. The goods are sold on the spot basis to Broker 2 and the price is paid immediately.

6. The Islamic MFI remits the proceeds of spot sale to the client.

## Diminishing Partnership for Housing Microfinance

**musharakah mutanaqisah**
A diminishing partnership contract where one party's share diminishes until it is finally extinguished and complete ownership is conferred on the other party.

Housing microfinance is a means of providing shelter for low-income individuals who are either squatters or living in slums. A diminishing partnership is known as **musharakah mutanaqisah** and is an Islamic financial product structured to strategically provide access to housing for the poor. The Islamic MFI and the client enter into a partnership contract whereby they purchase a property and lease it for a specified term. While the poor client's share is minimal, the Islamic MFI provides the bulk of the capital share for the transaction. When they lease the property, the parties share the profit based on predetermined contractual ratios. The client buys a specified unit every month out of the Islamic MFI's shares, which automatically gradually decreases the MFI's capital ownership until the client has bought the total capital share in the property out of the profits over a period of time. The title then passes to the client, who fully owns the property.

In situations where poor clients do not have funds to buy a small portion of the capital share, *qard hasan* (interest-free benevolent loans with flexible repayment period), *zakat*, or *waqf* funds may be provided for the purpose. *Zakat* is the compulsory alms giving in charity in Islam, intended to redistribute wealth in society, and *waqf* is a charitable endowment in perpetuity for a specific purpose. If *qard hasan* is given, the client only needs to repay the capital amount. If it is a *zakat* or *waqf* grant, there is no need for repayment. A diminishing partnership is a useful tool for assisting the poorest homeless in society to own a property and even lease out part or the whole of the property as part of their entrepreneurial activities for sustainable economic empowerment.

## Not-for-Profit Modes of Islamic Microfinance

The not-for-profit modes of Islamic microfinance are *zakat*, *waqf*, and *qard hasan*. They are specifically meant to target the poorest in society. Unlike conventional microfinance schemes, the poorest are not excluded from benefiting from Islamic microfinance because wealth is meant to circulate among all members in society, between the rich and the poor. To realize this, Islam institutionalized a number of mechanisms, including *zakat*, *waqf*, *qard hasan* and *sadaqah* (a voluntary act of charity that is highly recommended for Muslims to assist the less-privileged and the needy in society). Combining them into a hybrid framework would drastically alleviate poverty in society. Despite the not-for-profit nature of a hybrid model, it can be easily modified to accommodate the profit-oriented modes explained earlier. Figure 9.4 illustrates the non-for-profit modes of microfinance, which can have up to 11 steps.

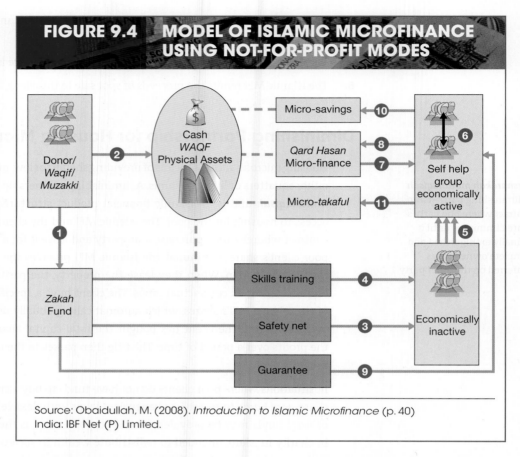

**FIGURE 9.4    MODEL OF ISLAMIC MICROFINANCE USING NOT-FOR-PROFIT MODES**

Source: Obaidullah, M. (2008). *Introduction to Islamic Microfinance* (p. 40)
India: IBF Net (P) Limited.

**muzakki**
A person who pays obligatory alms (*zakat*) in Islam.

1.  A *zakah fund* is established by the Islamic microfinance institution through funds received from donors, *zakat* payers (**muzakki**), and endowers.

2.  The donations include both monetary assets in the form of cash *waqf*, *zakat* funds, *sadaqah*, and physical assets. In most cases, the physical assets are very useful in skill acquisition programs.

3.  As the target of a microfinance initiative is the poorest of the poor, the program identifies this economically inactive group and distributes part of the *zakat* fund to them in the form of a grant.

4.  The physical assets donated as part of *waqf* are used to the maximum to provide skills training to the economically inactive group.

5.  The beneficiaries then acquire the requisite skills and managerial wit to become economically active and independent.

**kafalah**
A contract of guarantee whereby a person accepts the responsibility or undertakes to take on the liability or duty of another person.

6.  The beneficiaries are divided into groups of individuals with similar expertise whereupon they mutually guarantee one another based on a **kafalah** contract.

7.  The microfinance program provides the much-needed financing to each group, based on *qard hasan* under the general terms of a *kafalah* contract.

8.  Each group repays, entitling them to more financing from the program.

342

9. In the case of default, an additional guarantee is provided through the *zakat* fund, which is usually the last resort for paying off bad debts.

10. To encourage economic independence and ensure sustainability, micro-savings schemes are provided for group members.

11. Group members are also provided with a *takaful* fund for the purpose of micro-insurance for mutual indemnification in the case of unforeseen losses or other risks.[2]

**LEARNING OBJECTIVE 9.3**

Understand the differences between Islamic microfinance institutions and conventional microfinance institutions.

**Hint**

See the *Professional Perspectives* at the beginning of this chapter for a brief discussion on the differences between Islamic microfinance and conventional microfinance.

**Challenge**

What are the advantages of Islamic microfinance over conventional micro-credit programmes?

**Challenge**

Identify at least one more difference between Islamic microfinance institutions and conventional MFIs as practiced in your country.

# Islamic Microfinance Institutions versus Conventional Microfinance Institutions

What is so special about the Islamic framework for microfinance that is not available in the conventional practice of microfinance? This important question is relevant to the discourse on microfinance in the modern world because existing practices in the industry can be adaptable to developing Muslim countries. It is true that social programs or microfinance concepts may be adaptable to the Muslim-populated societies around the world for the purpose of poverty alleviation. However, one thing to bear in mind is the nature and purpose of Islamic finance. As discussed in the *Global Islamic Finance* box (on page 344), Islamic banking and finance, with its microfinance framework, is inclusive in its approach to reach out to the downtrodden and poor and to entrench true social justice in society. This inbuilt mechanism in Islamic finance has been practiced for more than 14 centuries, but during this long period it has sometimes been dormant, depending on the nature of society within which it was operated. The bold revival of Islamic finance services in the 20th century in a formalized form brought with it Islamic microfinance schemes. Sharī'ah scholars have structured Islamic financial products to suit the requirements of modern micro-enterprises and micro-credit schemes. This makes the case for a distinct system of microfinance that may be radically different from the conventional practice of microfinance as mostly practiced in non-Muslim communities. To this end, there are a number of operational and functional differences between the Islamic microfinance institutions and the conventional MFIs. Table 9.2 summarizes the major differences between them in their respective operational functions with regards to their clients.

The qualitative differences between the two frameworks make a case for the consideration of Islamic microfinance institutions as an alternative microfinance institutional model that may be tried out anywhere in the world and incorporated into mainstream microfinancing frameworks.

## Sources of Funds

This is where the heart of the MFI lies. Without funds, it cannot operate or discharge its key responsibilities to the entrepreneurial poor. There is a fundamental difference in the

**GLOBAL ISLAMIC FINANCE**

## Poverty Alleviation through Islamic Microfinance Programs

The rate of poverty keeps increasing geometrically. According to the *Global Employment Trends 2011* released by the International Labour Office, the number of unemployed all over the world stood at 205 million in 2010. The global economic crisis has significantly contributed to the growing number of unemployed. Microfinance seems to be the best tool for poverty alleviation because it goes beyond providing 'food stamps' but empowers the poor through meaningful projects that would enable the beneficiaries to create jobs rather than search for jobs. The multiplier effect of such job creation will drastically reduce the number of unemployed. Structuring sustainable models of microfinance is one important thing that keeps driving the industry towards achieving its objectives.

It is not only developing countries that benefit from microfinance programs; developed countries that are facing economic problems and rising rates of unemployment can also benefit from such job creation programs. The unique feature of the interest-free models introduced as Sharī'ah-compliant products is the exclusion of any element of exploitation in form of interest. Thus, the micro-entrepreneur who is just getting back on track does not face the burden of interest on loans. Instead, they simply share in the profits realized in the joint venture with the capital provider. This emphasizes the element of social benefit

for the people, particularly the less privileged, as opposed to profit maximization, which is the bane of the capitalist economy.

The solution to the socioeconomic crisis ravaging the whole world today may be found in Islamic microfinance. People do not need to be extremely rich to live a comfortable life. What they need are the basic necessities of life and this can be guaranteed when they are gainfully employed. The Islamic microfinance model not only excludes exploitative tendencies such as charging interest but it also empowers an able entrepreneur who does not need to contribute a penny at the inception of the business, just their own expertise.

It is an element of injustice for a segment of the population anywhere in the world to be excluded from traditional financial services. The Islamic philosophy of the economy is the circulation of wealth among all the citizens rather than concentrating the total wealth in the hands of a small fraction of the population that ends up controlling and exploiting the majority. Whatever it is called, whether small and medium-sized enterprise, micro-enterprise or microfinance, financial inclusion is important in any modern economy. All hands must be on deck to save the global economy. This can only be achieved when sincere efforts are made to right the wrongs that have ravaged the world economy by exploring alternative forms of financing.

sources of funds between the two frameworks. Apart from being an interest-free system, Islamic MFIs differ from conventional MFIs in a number of ways. Conventional MFIs get their funds from interest-bearing loans, foreign donors, central banks, and governments. Islamic MFIs are also funded from these sources, with the exception of interest-bearing loans, but, in addition, they get their funds from equity finance products applied in the finance of micro-enterprises, Islamic charitable sources such as *waqf*, *zakat* and *sadaqah* whose funds can be channeled to the poorest within a particular community. This takes care of the social financial mediation role of the MFIs.

| TABLE 9.2: Differences between Islamic MFIs and Conventional MFIs | | |
|---|---|---|
| **Item** | **Islamic MFIs** | **Conventional MFIs** |
| Sources of funds | External funds, clients' savings, Islamic charitable sources (*waqf* and *zakat*) | External funds, clients' savings, interest from loans |
| Assets (modes of financing) | Islamic financial instruments (equity and debt instruments) | Interest-based |
| Financing the poorest | Poorest can be included by integrating *zakat* with microfinancing | Poorest are left out |
| Funds transfer | Goods transferred | Cash given |
| Deductions at inception of contract | No deductions at inception | Part of the funds deducted at inception |
| Target group | Family | Women |
| Objective of targeting women | Ease of availability | Empowerment of women |
| Liability of the loan (when given to women) | Recipient and spouse | Recipient |
| Work incentives of employees | Monetary and religious | Monetary |
| Dealing with default | Group/center/spouse guarantee, and Islamic ethics | Group/center pressure and threats |
| Social development program | Religious (includes behavior, ethics, and social development) | Secular (or un-Islamic) behavioral, ethical, and social development |

Source: Ahmed, H. (2002). Financing Microenterprises: An Analytical Study of Islamic Microfinance Institutions. *Islamic Economics Studies*. Vol. 9, no. 2: pp. 27, 41.

## Modes of Financing

The modes of financing used by conventional MFIs are interest-based while Islamic MFIs use Islamic financial instruments that are either equity-based or debt-based. As interest is prohibited in Islam, Islamic MFIs adopt sustainable financial instruments for the financing of micro-enterprises. Various financial instruments can be used to finance different kinds of enterprises (remember the discussion on the models of Islamic finance above). While a profit-sharing mode may be used for a micro-enterprise where the micro-entrepreneur and the MFI shares the profit, *salam* and parallel *salam* may be more appropriate for micro-farming. In order to combat the scourge of unemployment, a *mudarabah* trust financing may be used.

## Financing the Poorest

Remember that Islamic MFIs are meant for all, whether lowly individuals or even the poorest in society. No segment of the population is left out of the scheme. As cases of default of repayment may be occasioned by extreme poverty, the mechanisms of *zakat* and *sadaqah* may be combined with the microfinancing activities. As a compulsory pillar of Islam, *zakat* is a means for the redistribution of income to support growth within society. The integration of *zakat* with microfinance involves the provision of grants to the poor from the *zakat* funds for consumption and granting them *qard hasan* for their entrepreneurial needs. On the other hand, the poorest are completely excluded from the microfinance net within the framework of conventional MFIs.

## Funds Transferred to Beneficiaries

In conventional MFIs, once a loan has been approved, a part of the principal is deducted by the institution for various purposes, such as group and emergency funds. Despite this, the beneficiary pays interest on the total amount approved. In addition, once cash is received, the beneficiary may divert the funds to non-productive means. These are considered as unfair practices on both sides of the contract. In contrast, it is difficult for cash to be handed out by Islamic MFIs, which precludes diversion of the funds to non-productive means. Besides, when goods are transferred by Islamic MFIs, no deductions can be made as either group funds or emergency funds.

## Guarantee and Group Dynamics

There is a difference between the two frameworks on the guarantee of repayment of the loans. In Islamic MFIs, group guarantee in the repayment of the loans takes the form of *kafalah*, which has its conditions and requirements in Islamic law. Any of the group members can stand as a guarantor for repayment of the loan. There may be an agreement among the members of a group that in the event of any default in the repayment in accordance with the installments from a member, other members agree to help. The simple way of going about this is for the group to give such a member, who is facing the problem of defaulted payment, *qard hasan*, which is interest-free, to pay his or her instalments.

## Objective of Targeting Women

The majority of MFIs' clients are women. Conventional MFIs consider this as a means of empowering them, believing it will help to raise their income level and earn them more respect in society. However, recent research suggests that men, more often than not, encourage women to take credit facilities. At the end of the day, the men spend the money and this creates problems within the family because the women are responsible for the repayment of the installments as they were given the credit facilities.

On the other hand, although women constitute an overwhelming majority of beneficiaries of Islamic MFIs' credit facilities, the objective of targeting women differs from that of conventional MFIs. According to the contract between Islamic MFIs and the beneficiary, the target group is the family. The women and their spouses both sign the contract as the target is the family and not women alone. Both parties are liable for repayment of the instalments. Women are usually the target of the Islamic MFIs schemes because of their ease of availability for weekly meetings and for social development programs.

## Work Incentives of Staff Members

The work incentive of the staff at conventional MFIs is mainly monetary gain from their salaries. Conversely, the incentives of the staff at Islamic MFIs are both monetary and religious. The staff at Islamic MFIs perform their work duties as part of their religious duty to assist the poor through facilitating access to credit facilities. They are not working in the Islamic MFIs just to earn a living but to also perform the socioreligious duty of alleviating poverty within society. This additional incentive gives the staff more zeal to work efficiently towards the achievement of the vision and mission of the Islamic MFIs.

## Social Development Programs

The social development programs of conventional MFIs are secular and in some cases go against the ideals of Islam. For instance, from the perspective of income generation for the program, there are generally no restrictions on the type of sectors conventional MFIs invests in. Conversely, Islamic MFIs put in place social development programs where the ethical, social, and behavioral aspects of Islamic ideals are brought to the fore. The Islamic content is introduced into the program and members feel comfortable in adapting to them as they consider them as part of their beliefs and acts of worship. This also helps inculcate the idea of fellowship and comradeship among beneficiaries, who are morally compelled to repay their installments regularly and when due.

## Dealing with Default

In conventional MFIs, group and center pressure is used to deal with arrears and default. In the event this pressure does not work, the MFIs resort to threats and sale of assets. These steps may be too harsh for low-income individuals within a developing society. In contrast, Islamic MFIs have more sustainable and reasonable ways to deal with defaults and arrears. Remember under the guarantee section above, we saw that members in a group guarantee one another through *kafalah*. So, in the event of default or arrears, the group may provide *qard hasan* to a defaulting member, which may be used to settle the arrears. This is motivated by the spirit of fellowship. It is also a sin in Islam to refuse to pay back a loan, motivating members to fulfill their obligations. A member's spouse may also assist in paying off arrears.

# Notable Islamic Microfinance Institutions

The number of Islamic MFIs in Muslim-populated communities around the world is increasing by the day and also growing at a fast pace in Muslim-dominated communities. While some Islamic MFIs are developmental institutions for post-war society, others specifically target poor Muslim communities. We give a brief overview on three notable institutions to glimpse what is obtainable in the practice of Islamic microfinance. Islamic MFIs in three different countries are selected for discussion in this section:

- Hodeidah Microfinance Program, Yemen
- Akhuwat, Pakistan
- Islami Bank Bangladesh Limited—Rural Development Scheme.

## Hodeidah Microfinance Program, Yemen

The Islamic banking system was formally adopted in Yemen in 1996. Consequently, the Hodeidah Microfinance Program (HMFP) was established in 1997 to satisfy the needs of the people, as a result of a market study that involved perception and acceptance in the port city of Hodeidah. Potential borrowers favored Sharī'ah-compliant micro-credit facilities such as *mudarabah* (investment partnership), *musharakah* (joint venture partnership), and *murabahah* (cost-plus financing). As a result, the HMFP was established to use Islamic financial services exclusively in its micro-credit program. These pioneering efforts to introduce a Sharī'ah-compliant microfinance project in Yemen adopted a group-based methodology in the disbursement of loans to worthy individuals. That is, credit facilities are given to individuals within a recognized group and the members of the group are required to mutually guarantee the loan. There is no need for physical collateral to secure the loans as there is what is generally referred to as a 'moral' guarantee, where defaulting members are tracked down by their colleagues in the same group to encourage them to redeem their debts.

The objectives of the HMFP were fivefold.

1. To assist the partner NGO to develop an institution that provides financial services to the poor.

2. To build institutional capacity to provide the targeted groups with sustainable financial services.

3. To reach 5,000 active borrowers by the end of the third year of operation.

4. To document the experience of the project and elicit lessons for future implementation of similar projects.

5. To use the project as an educational tool for the social fund staff to build their capacity in managing and monitoring microfinance projects.[3]

HMFP used the *murabahah* (cost-plus financing) Islamic financial mechanism to provide credit facilities for its clients. Under this scheme, HMFP (lender) purchases an item and sells it to the client (borrower) at the cost price plus a fixed mark-up cost as service charges and related administration costs. Both parties agree in the underlying contract (*murabahah* contract) that the client will pay the total cost of the commodity (cost price plus service charge) in installments over a set period of time. The HMFP micro-credit program is summarized in Table 9.3, which illustrates the main characteristics of the project as reflected in its two major streams—urban-based credit program and rural-based credit program.

### TABLE 9.3: Summary of the Hodeidah Microfinance Project

| Main Characteristics | Urban-based Credit Program | Rural-based Credit Program | |
| --- | --- | --- | --- |
| | Micro-credit | Income-generating projects | Micro-credits |
| **Target groups** | Urban slum-dwellers, men and women, but mostly male borrowers | Farmers, members and non-members of cooperatives, non-governmental organizations (NGOs), mostly male | Only women from different villages, supported by a NGO |
| **Program services** | Credit and financial advice to borrowers | Credit and veterinarian services to borrowers | Credit, savings, literacy classes, health and veterinarian services |
| **Role of social fund** | Provider of seed capital, financing of initial costs, recruitment, and payment of manager scheme | Provider of seed capital, financing of initial set-up costs. No managerial role for social fund for development (SFD) | Provider of seed capital, financing of initial set-up costs. No managerial role for SFD |
| **Target and policy** | 5,000 active borrowers, organizational and financial sustainability | Financial sustainability | 2,000 savers and borrowers, financial and organizational sustainability |
| **Identification credit proposal** | By individual | By NGO | By groups in villages |
| **Appraisal and approval** | By credit program | By SFD | By group in village but with veto of NGO |
| **Loan contract** | Promissory notes, detailed loan use, loan amount, and repayment date | Promissory notes, detailed repayment amount or condition, and repayment date | Promissory notes, detailed loan use, loan amount, and repayment date |
| **Use of loan** | Free use, as long as it is productive (no providential use permitted) | For one type of income-generating activity only, such as goat or sheep raising, cattle fattening | Free use of loan, but use should be productive |

*Cont'd*

| **TABLE 9.3: Summary of the Hodeidah Microfinance Project** | | | |
|---|---|---|---|
| **Main Characteristics** | **Urban-based Credit Program** | **Rural-based Credit Program** | |
| | **Micro-credit** | **Income-generating projects** | **Micro-credits** |
| **Duration** | Short-term from one week to maximum one year | Equal for all loans usually 10 to 12 months | Equal for all loans, up to one year |
| **Loan size** | First time borrowers up to US$93, frequent borrowers up to US$464 | Depends on loan use and market prices of cattle. Ranges from US$93 to US$464 | Same for all first time borrowers (US$42), increases for frequent borrowers up to US$93 per borrower |
| **Security** | Joint liability, no hard collateral | Joint liability, no hard collateral | Joint liability, no hard collateral or savings |
| **Repayment schedule** | In installments | In lump sum | In lump sum |
| **Repayment incentives** | New loans in higher amounts become available | None | None |
| **Repayment sanctions** | Fees, imprisonment | None | Fees |
| **Islamic banking/cost-plus rate** | *Murabahah*/2 percent per month | *Mudarabah* | *Murabahah* |
| **Savings component** | Not included | Not included | Compulsory part of loan program |
| **Insurance scheme** | Covers payment of future installments | Not included | Not included |
| **Management** | Independent from NGO | Independent from NGO | Integrated in the group, supervised by NGO |

Source: Abdulkarim Al-Arhabi. (1998). Approach of Micro-Credit and Income-Generating Projects Financed by the Social Fund for Development in Yemen. Economic Development and Poverty Reduction Workshop, Mediterranean Development Forum, Marrakech, Morocco, September, 3–6: p. 9.

From the table, it is clear that the target groups for the urban-based credit program are urban slum-dwellers, both men and women, although practically all HMFP clients in this category are male borrowers. Conversely, the rural-based credit program scheme is divided into two—income-generating projects and micro-credits. While the target groups for the income-generating projects include farmers, members and non-members of cooperatives, and non-governmental organizations (NGOs), the other category of micro-credits targets only women from different villages and they are generally supported by NGOs.

## Akhuwat, Pakistan

The idea of establishing an interest-free microfinance program was discussed by a group of friends in 2001 at the Gymkhana Club in Lahore, Pakistan. The discussion was sparked off by the displeasure of most people regarding the exorbitant interest rates being charged by existing microfinance institutions in the country. They realized that this was jeopardizing the main objective of the microfinance finance program—alleviation of poverty. Instead of engendering economic empowerment, the existing microfinance initiatives further impoverished the less-privileged. Initially, the friends were bereft of ideas on how to set up an interest-free microfinance project, but later a successful experiment was made through an interest-free loan (*qard hasan*) to a widow who returned the principal amount within six months. Based on this and drawing inspiration from the fellowship shown by the companions of the Prophet Muhammad (PBUH), especially during his travels from Mecca to Medina, the group of friends came together to establish Akhuwat, which literally means 'brotherhood' under the leadership of Dr. Amjad Saqib.

These are the objectives of the Akhuwat microfinance program.

1. To provide interest-free microfinance services to poor families, enabling them to become self-reliant.

2. To promote *qard hasan* as a viable model and a broad-based solution for poverty alleviation.

3. To provide social guidance, capacity-building, and entrepreneurial training.

4. To institutionalize the spirit of brotherhood, compassion, and volunteering.

5. To transform Akhuwat borrowers into donors.

6. To make Akhuwat a sustainable, growth-oriented, and replicable organization.[4]

The principal objective of the Akhuwat program is to disburse interest-free loans to poor families to ensure economic empowerment, through the two prongs of enhancing the standard of living of the recipients and empowering them to become entrepreneurs. When poor families are empowered, they will ultimately become donors to the common pool of funds. In essence, rather than giving poor families fish to eat, Akhuwat takes a step further and teaches them how to fish. The main model used by the program is *qard hasan*, the concept of benevolent loans, which is encouraged in Islam. Therefore, in order to ensure the maximization of the opportunity given to their clients, Akhuwat provides the necessary social guidance, capacity-building, and much-needed entrepreneurial training. Rather than working with individuals, Akhuwat has consistently worked with the whole household, that is, both husband and wife. This has contributed tremendously to the program's success rate to date.

Box 9.2 shows Akhuwat's seven guiding principles, which summarize the mission and vision of the program with particular reference to poverty alleviation. With its heavy reliance on philanthropic donations from individuals, industrialists, and institutions, Akhuwat disburses funds to deserving clients regardless of their religious or racial backgrounds. With 75 total branches, Akhuwat operates in mosques and churches to reduce overhead costs, where funds are disbursed to deserving clients. This makes the program unique, as it builds bridges across religious divides. According to the latest statistics, the repayment rate is up to 99.85 percent. Unlike other Islamic microfinance institutions, the cost structure of Akhuwat includes 0 percent profit-sharing, 0 percent loan processing fees, and of course 0 percent interest rate. However, there is a minimal

**BOX 9.2:** **THE SEVEN GUIDING PRINCIPLES OF AKHUWAT IN PAKISTAN**

## Interest-free micro-credit

Akhuwat provides the economically poor with interest-free loans so that they may acquire a self-sustaining livelihood. It also provides the skills and support they need to realize their full potential and abilities.

## Reliance on philanthropy

Since its inception, Akhuwat has relied solely upon philanthropists in extending its services to the community. However, in order to fulfill the increased credit needs of its ever-increasing clientele it is now willing to work with international donors as well.

## Spirit of volunteerism

The spirit of volunteerism that Akhuwat's management and its team members exhibit is indicative of the success Akhuwat has achieved within a short timespan.

## Family loans

A family loan is the most common type of loan that Akhuwat offers to its clients for setting up or expanding a business. Income from this business is shared jointly by the whole family. The loans are co-signed by the male and female heads of the family. Akhuwat believes in strengthening the family unit as some studies show that separate loans to the males and females in a family may result in tensions and hence cause disintegration of this important institution.

## Links with mosques and churches

An important and novel idea associated with the loan scheme is the use of the local mosque/church infrastructure as centres for loan disbursement and as an avenue for community participation.

## Combination of individual and group lending program

Diversification of the loan portfolio by offering different loan products has helped to increase outreach.

## Credit-plus approach

Akhuwat has employed a credit-plus approach by introducing the idea of social guidance for its credit beneficiaries. The purpose approach is to help borrowers grow their small enterprises so that they can lead socially healthier lives than before.

Source: *Guiding Principles of Akhuwat,* www.akhuwat.org.pk/principles.asp.

fee of about US$1.1 as the application fee. There is also an additional insurance fee of 1 percent of the loan amount, although this is voluntary. As of October 25, 2012, 200,000 families have benefited from the program since inception, with the disbursement of a total of US$30 million.

## Islami Bank Bangladesh Limited—Rural Development Scheme

The Islami Bank Bangladesh Limited (IBBL) is an Islamic financial institution established in 1983 with the principal objective of fostering an Islamic economy that ensures the just distribution of resources among the people. To further this objective, the Rural Development Scheme (RDS) of the IBBL was established in 1995 as the first Sharīʻah-compliant microfinance program in Bangladesh. The program is targeted at rural dwellers in order to alleviate poverty and empower the poor through sustainable projects that satisfy their economic needs and comply with their religious beliefs. These are the main objectives of this pioneering scheme.

1. To extend investment facilities to agricultural, other farming, and off-farming activities in rural areas.

2. To finance self-employment and income-generating activities for rural people, particularly unemployed youths and the poor.

3. To alleviate poverty through an integrated rural development approach.

4. To extend investment facilities for hand tubewells and rural housing, keeping in view the need for safe drinking water and housing facilities for rural dwellers.

5. To provide education and medicare facilities to downtrodden people.[5]

As a program established by an existing financial institution, there was no challenge to open new offices. IBBL branches around the country were designated to execute the program. The target groups include the industrious rural poor in the age bracket of 18 to 50 who must be permanently domiciled in the project area for proper monitoring; farmers who own land that can be cultivated (maximum of 0.50 acres) and sharecroppers; persons who engage in menial jobs (off-farm) in rural areas; and women who are destitute, as well as distressed people. People who have been declared bankrupt or who have some liabilities with other financial institutions are not qualified under the program.[6]

Depending on the sector or purpose of the investment, the IBBL branch may select any of the following modes of investment: *musharakah, mudarabah, murabahah, bay al-salam, ijarah* (hire purchase or lease), or *bay al-muajjal* (sale on deferred payment or credit sale). As Box 9.3 shows, the operational procedure for the IBBL's RDS is a 12-step process, from the selection of suitable villages to the manner in which the clients are expected to pay back the principal amount as well as the profit. Just like the Hodeidah and Akhuwat models of Sharīʻah-compliant microfinance, RDS does not require its clients to give collateral security. However, they are encouraged to be disciplined and ensure mutual guarantee by members of the same group. With a higher than 99 percent rate of recovery, RDS disbursed more than US$407.25 million between 1995 and 2010.

## BOX 9.3: SETTING UP THE RURAL DEVELOPMENT SCHEME

The Rural Development Scheme adopts a group approach where people of like minds are brought together to undertake the investment. In most cases, they are people of similar professions who can easily work together to realize their goal. The scheme has the following 12-step operational procedure to execute the program.

1. Select suitable villages within a 10-kilometer radius from the branch location.

2. Conduct a baseline survey to identify target groups and identify the baseline scenario.

3. Form small groups consisting of five members, preferably of similar professions/ occupations.

4. The members of the group select their leader and deputy leader to coordinate activities. The branch manager then visits the group for a discussion and then gives formal recognition of the group through the issuance of passbooks.

5. A center is formed by minimum of two and a maximum of eight groups. The group leaders under a particular center select the center leader and deputy center leader from among themselves to coordinate the center's activities.

6. The center must conduct a regular weekly meeting, held at a particular place, day, and time as decided in the meeting.

7. Center meetings are recorded in a resolution book along with members' signatures (members who do not know their signature must learn it). Attendance at centre meetings is the first requirement to become a dependable client member of the scheme.

8. The center meetings are conducted by the field officers.

9. Investment clients are selected at center meetings and supplied with the application forms and other related papers. On finalization of the application, the list of the selected clients, supported by their applications, are submitted to the branch manager, signed by the group leader, center leader, field officer, and project officer.

10. Each member of the group has to provide a guarantee against investment of the other members of their group. If any member of a particular group does not comply with the principles or rules of the group, then other members can compel them to observe group discipline, otherwise they are responsible for recovering the defaulted amount and/or loss, if any.

11. Clients are allowed to take an initial investment of US$145 maximum eight weeks after enrollment as active member in the group. The highest of amount of investment under the scheme is US$1,449.

12. The investment amount along with profit has to be paid back by the clients in 45 equal weekly installments.

Source: Modus Operandi, Rural Development Scheme, IBBL, www.islamibankbd.com/rds/modus_operandi.php.

# Financing Micro-enterprises by Islamic Banks: Rationale

**Corporate social responsibility (CSR)**
The commitment of a company to engage in capacity building for a sustainable society.

Islamic banks and financial institutions play a significant role in providing access to credit facilities to low-income entrepreneurs. As an incorporated financial entity with an organized corporate governance system, the process of financing micro-enterprises and subsequent monitoring of their progress is enhanced. There are two schools of thought regarding the financing of micro-enterprises. The first school believes this activity is part of the **corporate social responsibility (CSR)** role of Islamic banks and financial institutions. The second school believes that financing micro-enterprises requires designated MFIs rather than classifying such role as part of the CSR of the Islamic banks and financial institutions.

Before the establishment of so many MFIs across the Muslim world, the sources of credit facilities were broadly classified into two major areas: institutional and non-institutional sources. Institutional sources are the corporate financial entities such as banks and other financial institutional sources, such as cooperatives. The non-institutional sources include credit facilities from moneylenders, friends, and family members.

## Challenge

Should microfinance be excluded from the role of Islamic banks? Why?

It is often difficult for micro-entrepreneurs to obtain credit facilities for their micro-enterprises from institutional sources because of their inability to provide the physical collateral for such loans. In addition, the banks are usually reluctant to finance micro-enterprises because of the high running costs per unit of credit. In other words, micro-entrepreneurs are financially excluded from institutional sources. Likewise, the interest rates for non-institutional loans are too expensive for low-income individuals. Thus MFIs were established as a new concept in banking, lending, and financing for micro-enterprises through microfinancing. Grameen Bank in Bangladesh is one of the pioneering MFIs established to assist low-income individuals who are ordinarily

Grameen-Jameel aims to alleviate poverty through the provision of financial support, technical assistance, training, and access to best practices in the field of microfinance in the MENA region.

**Grameen - Jameel**

financially excluded from formal financial services. Although Grameen Bank's credit facilities involve some interest, it provides the entrepreneurial poor an uncommon opportunity to gain access to credit facilities without the formal requirement of physical collateral. Grameen-Jameel was launched in 2003 through a joint venture between Bangladeshi Grameen Foundation and the Saudi Arabian Abdul Latif Jameel Group. Grameen-Jameel has formed strategic partnerships with MFIs in the Middle East and North African (MENA) countries by increasing their capacity through the provision of financial support, technical assistance, training, and access to best practices in the field. Grameen-Jameel focuses on MFIs rather than the individuals but it indirectly reaches more low-income individuals through its outreach across those countries.

## Role of Islamic Banks in Financing Micro-enterprises

The functions of Islamic banks and financial institutions are more than just accepting deposits, managing savings and current accounts for their customers, and engaging in partnership financing. The social function of Islamic banking is an aspect that relates to modern CSR roles. Although microfinance may be considered as part of the general CSR functions of Islamic banks, CSR may not necessarily be part of microfinance. The social benefits of Islamic banking and finance include the ability of the industry to come up with meaningful frameworks to provide credit facilities to low-income individuals who are ordinarily shut out from conventional banking. This is the reason why Islamic banks and financial institutions are encouraged to have microfinance schemes for low-income individuals in the community. This is one of the social benefits the needy public derives from Islamic banks and financial institutions.

### Challenge

How do the key features of profit and loss sharing in Islamic finance affect Islamic microfinance?

As a means to alleviate poverty, financing small- and medium-sized enterprises (SMEs) is considered part of the social benefits derivable from the banks and financial institutions. Although there exist microfinance institutions established to provide credit facilities exclusively to the entrepreneurial poor, Islamic banks and financial institutions are not expected to exclude the less-privileged. Thus, a department or division of the bank should be dedicated to Islamic microfinance. Alternatively, a subsidiary of an Islamic bank may be established to carry out the microfinance functions, and may also have responsibility for managing the *zakat* funds of the holding company through proper channeling towards the needy within a particular society.

Although most conventional banks do not engage in microfinancing, it is part of the social role of Islamic banks to establish, manage, and consolidate the microfinance institution as part of its CSR role. In Islam, there are no separate banks for the poor and the rich. All classes of people in society are accommodated within the general sphere of financing. Therefore, the social dimension of the objectives of Islamic banks is the promotion and support of SMEs to further bridge the gap between rich and poor. As a manifestation of their social role, necessary credit facilities must be made available to the poor to increase their wealth and income for a just and fair society. This is where the relationship between Islamic finance and development is established. Islamic banks adopt sustainable practices towards developing society through the provision of credit facilities to both rich and poor alike.

The need for social intermediation by the Islamic banks to finance micro-enterprises cannot be overemphasized in a competitive world where many Muslims are excluded from conventional MFIs because of interest-bearing loans. In addition, small-scale enterprises are a means of increasing employment. In combating the increasing rates of unemployment, microfinance may be the solution. However, it will have more impact if Islamic banks undertake the great challenge of managing the schemes effectively. The poor must be able to benefit from the social role of the Islamic banks. Whatever Islamic microfinance model a bank adopts, the scheme must have the potential to provide the poor with reasonable credit facilities to finance their micro-enterprises. A social development program of this kind will go a long way to alleviating poverty. For social justice to be realized within a society, Islamic banks and financial institutions must play this cardinal role. However, proper mechanisms must be put in place to avoid high rates of defaults among their clients.

A bank that primarily functions as a formal Islamic microfinance institution was established in Bahrain in January 2010. It is known as the Family Bank (*Bank Al-Usrah*). Unlike the large Islamic financial institutions operating in Bahrain, the Family Bank targets women, youths, recent graduates, and the poor, who are normally excluded from the formal financial services offered by the existing banks. This makes the Family Bank unique in its social venture in the country. The Family Bank partners with the Grameen Trust to replicate a Sharī'ah-compliant model of the Grameen Bank in Bahrain focusing on the needs of the people. As we can see in the *Islamic Finance in Practice* box, an Islamic bank should serve both the purpose of large-scale financing as well as microfinance. The laudable efforts of Family Bank re-emphasize the original value proposition of Islamic financial intermediation, which not only responds to the financing needs of the rich but provides an equal opportunity to all.

## Financing Micro-enterprises: Microfinance Institutions versus Islamic Banks

Financing micro-enterprises requires a good framework to achieve the social objectives of the scheme through sustainable means. This has led to recurring consideration of the issue of whether it is the MFIs or banks that are better suited to finance micro-enterprises. As discussed earlier, it is part of the social role of Islamic banks to provide credit facilities to those who are inadvertently excluded from formal financial services. Does that mean there is no need for MFIs within Islamic communities? Before we consider this question further, it is necessary to take a quick look at the frameworks available in both the banks and MFIs with special reference to providing credit facilities to clients.

Although ideally an Islamic financial institution would serve the objective of both large-scale financing and serving low-income families, the reality nowadays is a separation of these functions. While banks are established to undertake large-scale financing with the objective of profit maximization, the microfinance institutions undertake social and education programs through the provision of micro-credit facilities to the less-privileged.

## ISLAMIC FINANCE IN PRACTICE

# Family Bank in Bahrain

Providing banking services to low-income families and individuals in society is part of the original value proposition of Islamic financial intermediation. This is a task Family Bank has undertaken since its establishment in January 2010. Far from just being a microfinance institution, Family Bank combines both formal banking services with microfinance initiatives based on the Grameen Bank model. The Grameen Bank model is not fully Sharīʿah-compliant, but the Family Bank is and it offers banking services and microfinance initiatives primarily targeted at the poor in order to contribute to poverty alleviation and engender economic empowerment.

Combining social developmental initiatives with the traditional banking system through Islamic financial techniques is the principal objective of the Family Bank project. This is reflected in its goals:

1. Focus on providing sustainable microfinance banking services to lower-income individuals.
2. Provide a broad community service that reaches all citizens of Bahrain.
3. Implement best practices in procedures drawn from the experience based on the Grameen Bank and other microfinance programs.
4. Focus on developing micro- and small enterprises that lead to social development as well as provide support to the economic development of Bahrain.
5. Meet all environmental and safety standards as well as social obligations.

With the above goals, the Family Bank operates as a fully Sharīʿah-compliant program through an Islamic microfinance bank licensed by the Central Bank of Bahrain. This pioneer social bank in Bahrain had more than 300 clients by the end of December 2011. With its collateral-free finance, Family Bank is a true representative of the original idea of microfinance—banking for the poor.

According to the *Annual Report of Family Bank 2010*, the bank gives credit facilities to deserving families for developmental purposes summarized as follows.

- **Income-generating activities (IGA):** Microfinance

can be used to buy equipment, raw materials, and used as capital for various income-generating activities.

- **Micro-enterprise development:** Microfinance can be used to accelerate the development of small and micro-enterprises and the shift of many of them from informal to formal.
- **Home improvement:** Small finance can be used to renovate or repair clients' rooms or houses, enabling them to work from home to pursue their income-generating activities.
- **Economic asset improvement:** Microfinance may be used to repair cars, taxis, improve a store, or other activities that enhance a client's earning potential.
- **Skills improvement:** Microfinance may be used to offset costs of education, training and other skills improvement initiatives that will result in higher earning potential for the client.
- **Livelihood finance:** To meet the various social needs arising in needy families from time to time (see page 20 of the *Annual Report 2010*).

In its bid to turn dreams into reality, the Family Bank has put smiles on the faces of a number of clients who are now in a position to serve the community. The story of a widow, Fateen Ebrahim, is instructive in this respect. After her husband died, she relied exclusively on welfare assistance provided by the government of Bahrain. Knowing her capabilities, she was not satisfied with being totally reliant on welfare. She needed to put into practice her entrepreneurial skills but could not get enough funds. She approached the Family Bank for financial support to open a restaurant and coffee shop, which had the effect of changing her status from a welfare recipient to a businesswoman. This also meant losing her welfare assistance from the government but since she was determined and received US$10,610 financing from the Family Bank for her business project, she was ready to change her social status. At last, she was able to open her cafeteria through the funding from Family Bank and became an independent businesswoman in Bahrain.

Source: *Family Bank Annual Report December 2010*, www.familybankbh.com/fb_financial_reports.asp.

Unlike the large Islamic financial institutions operating in Bahrain, Family Bank targets women, youths, recent graduates, and the poor, who are normally excluded from the formal financial services offered by the existing banks.

Table 9.4 shows the main differences between the banks and microfinance institutions in the provision of credit facilities. The Family Bank model discussed above is unique in that it focuses on low-income families. What is expected in the future is a holistic approach to Islamic financial intermediation, which should combine both the role of a normal bank and that of an Islamic microfinance institution.

| TABLE 9.4: Differences between Banks and MFIs in the Provision of Credit Facilities | |
|---|---|
| **Bank** | **Microfinance Institution** |
| A profit-maximizing firm | Non-profit governmental/non-governmental organization |
| Financial intermediary between savers and investors in the economy | Funds from external sources provided to the poor |
| Deposits form bulk of the liability | Savings (forced) of clients only deposits |
| Does not have social/educational programs | Includes social/educational programs |
| Physical/financial collateral required to access funds | Social collateral through group and center formation |
| Clients relatively well-off | Clients are poor |
| Clients come to the bank | Bank goes to the clients |
| Amount of loan: large | Amount of loan: small |
| Most clients are men | Most clients are women |
| Repayment frequency small (end of the contract period) | Repayment is frequent (weekly) |

Source: Ahmed, H. (2002). Financing Microenterprises: An Analytical Study of Islamic Microfinance Institutions. *Islamic Economics Studies*. Vol. 9, no. 2: pp. 27, 33.

Islamic banks combine both the conventional framework for financing in terms of provision of credit facilities as well as those of the MFIs. The social role of the Islamic banks comprises financing micro-enterprises. The concept of fair dealing and justice in financial matters does not allow Islamic banks to exclude a low-income class from its clients. According to suggestions by Sharī'ah scholars and financial experts in the *Islamic Finance News* box, Islamic commercial banks must encourage financial inclusion through concerted efforts to establish functional Islamic microfinance institutions in society. The best framework is the hybrid bank, which relates with all classes of individuals, both rich and poor. This is the model of an Islamic bank or financial institution that may either establish a subsidiary to handle its microfinance function or create a department within the bank saddled with the sole responsibility of administering microfinance to low-income individuals. This will solve the problem of financial exclusion and managerial inefficiency in the financing of both micro- and macro-enterprises.

# ISLAMIC FINANCE IN THE NEWS

## Microfinance: Industry urged to refocus on poverty

**December 14, 2011**

**Small start: about 40 percent of the world's microfinance clients reside in Muslim countries but Sharī'ah compliance makes up less than 1 percent of industry.**

Sharī'ah-compliant retail products now come in every shape and size.

From mortgages to insurance and even the Islamic credit card, the choice and availability for Muslims seeking religiously compliant finance has never been greater. But one sector that has continued to lag behind is microfinance.

The dearth of Islamic microfinance institutions (IMFIs) is a glaring absence in the industry, according to development specialists.

With Islamic finance now expanding its range and geographical reach, there are growing calls for Sharī'ah-compliant financial institutions to focus on what have been labeled as the 'unbankable' sectors of the Muslim world.

Muhammad Yunus, a pioneer of conventional microfinance in Bangladesh, is one of the most prominent voices to advocate a 'paradigm shift' in Islamic finance towards poverty alleviation, which is often criticized for mimicking conventional instruments and an overconcentration on capital markets.

Islamic financial institutions are required to donate a percentage of their profits in *zakat* or charitable payments every year. Although most of these funds have been concentrated in projects that provide disaster relief, *zakat* could be an untapped source of funding for microfinance initiatives.

'The big Muslim finance houses have ploughed their assistance into basic needs, but now there is a focus on longer-term development,' says Ajaz Ahmed Khan, an adviser at Care International, the aid agency.

'As the industry has grown, Islamic institutions have started developing corporate social responsibility wings and it makes no sense for them to sponsor non-Sharī'ah-compliant microfinance.'

But obstacles to the provision of sustainable Islamic micro-finance and microcredit schemes in particular are manifold.

Classic Islamic financing techniques are often costlier to administer at the micro level, making them more expensive for borrowers and unsustainable for the agencies that provide them.

Lenders are often required to locate, purchase and then resell the commodities they lend to clients—an onerous responsibility that has contributed to the limited outreach of individual institutions.

*Cont'd*

According to research by the Consultative Group to Assist the Poor (CGAP), an arm of the World Bank, IMFIs have an average client base of only 2,400 customers, a situation that can be attributed to a lack of trained practitioners and a shortage of funding.

Yet the demand for loans and services from low-income Muslim clients is high. About 40 percent of the world's microfinance clients reside in Muslim countries, but Sharī'ah compliance makes up less than 1 percent of the industry, according to the World Bank.

Large swathes of the Muslim world have no access to formal banking and up to 45 percent of respondents to a survey by CGAP in Jordan, Algeria and Syria said they refrained from financial services that do not adhere to Islamic principles.

'Islamic microfinance has been going on for a long time. It is a way a lot of traditional Muslim communities have always funded trade and the purchase of agricultural commodities,' says Aziza Atta, managing director of Alternative Finance and Marketing Consulting.

Conventional microfinance has been hit by a number of scandals recently, including accusations of extortion that has led to suicides among borrowers in parts of the Indian subcontinent.

Centered on principles of profit and loss sharing, Islamic finance is a broadly ethical approach that can act as a powerful tool in poverty alleviation by spurring new financing models, according to some in the development industry.

Al-Amal bank in Yemen is an example of successful innovation. In 2010, it won CGAP's microfinance challenge by pioneering a lease-to-purchase venture, which has borrowers work as salaried employees of the bank while also working on the project for which they receive the loan.

'Conventional microfinance agencies just [offer] one type of loan, but the needs of the poor are not [all] the same. Islamic microfinance techniques allow us to cater to the particular needs of clients,' says Mr Khan.

Demands for Sharī'ah-compliant microfinance reflect a wider push for a back-to-basics approach in Islamic finance. With the industry's rapid growth, financial engineering has given way to complex structures, such as those that underlie some Islamic bonds, introducing unwelcome risk.

Babar Khan, director of Ethos Human Capital, a Sharī'ah-compliant social enterprise, says: 'Most people in Islamic finance need to ask why they are involved: 90 percent of the industry is structured debt.'

Based in the UK, Ethos promotes equitable investment in human and venture capital. Composed of professionals with experience in conventional finance, organizations such as this are at the vanguard of the return to first principles in Islamic finance, says Ms Atta of AFM Consulting.

Generational shifts may be the catalyst for microfinance to catch up with other parts of the industry. 'It is people of my generation who have the ideas and the expertise that will drive microfinance to become more structured,' says Ms Atta.

'Islamic microfinance lags behind, but it is the not-for-profit mentality, rather than that of the big banks, that will force the breakthrough in the coming years.'

**Source:** Mehreen Khan, "Microfinance: Industry urged to refocus on poverty", *Financial Times*, December 14, 2011.

# Review

## Key Terms and Concepts

*bay al-muajjal* (p. 339)

corporate social responsibility (CSR) (p. 355)

entrepreneurial poor (p. 330)

financial exclusion (p. 334)

informal savings club (p. 330)

*kafalah* (p. 342)

micro-credit (p. 333)

micro-farming (p. 337)

microfinance (p. 330)

microfinance institutions (MFIs) (p. 333)

micro-lending (p. 332)

micro-savings (p. 332)

micro-*takaful* (p. 333)

*mudarabah al-muqayyadah* (p. 338)

*mudarabah al-mutlaqah* (p. 338)

*musharakah mutanaqisah* (p. 341)

*muzakki* (p. 342)

parallel *salam* (p. 336)

*wadi'ah* (p. 332)

## Summary

**Learning Objective 9.1**

**1.** Islamic microfinance has unique features such as interest-free loans and client-based initiatives that make it the most appropriate microfinance system for poverty alleviation.

**Learning Objective 9.2**

**2.** A number of Islamic finance products such as *mudarabah*, *murabahah*, *musharakah mutanaqisah*, and *salam* have been structured, either as debt or equity instruments, to provide the necessary credit facilities to the entrepreneurial poor. They target the specific needs of the poor depending on the nature of the product.

**Learning Objective 9.3**

**3.** There are a number of operational and functional differences between Islamic microfinance institutions and conventional MFIs. These include sources of funds, assets (modes of financing), financing the poorest, funds transfer, deductions at inception of contract, target group, objective of targeting women, liability of the loan (when given to women), work incentives of employees, dealing with default, and social development programs.

**Learning Objective 9.4**

**4.** The number of Islamic MFIs in Muslim-populated communities around the world is increasing by the day. Islamic microfinance institutions are scattered in Muslim-populated societies all over the world. These include Hodeidah Microfinance Program in Yemen, Rural Development Scheme of the Islami Bank of Bangladesh Limited and Akhuwat microfinance scheme in Pakistan.

**Learning Objective 9.5**

5. The social role of Islamic banks and financial institutions places them in the forefront in the drive towards poverty alleviation. Islamic banks must activate this corporate social responsibility role in its functions to contribute meaningfully to the economy.

## Practice Questions and Activies

### Practice Questions

1. Define Islamic microfinance and explain its three major components.

2. What are the qualitative distinguishing features between Islamic microfinance and conventional microfinance schemes?

3. Explain three major Islamic finance products that are commonly used for Islamic microfinance.

4. A poor farmer intends to cultivate three acres of paddy but lacks the necessary credit facilities for such farming. The farmer needs money to prepare and till the land and also needs money to feed the family for the next five months before the harvest. He approaches you for expert advice on how to get the necessary credit facilities. Advise the farmer on the best mode of Islamic microfinance for their needs and explain the procedure and conditions for the validity of the contract.

5. What do you understand to be the not-for-profit modes of Islamic microfinance? How are they different from other modes of Islamic microfinance?

6. Give five major differences between Islamic microfinance institutions and their conventional counterparts. Illustrate your answer with relevant examples of existing MFIs.

7. How successful are the case studies of Islamic microfinance institutions? Which microfinance model would you prefer for emerging economies? Justify your answer with relevant examples.

8. Discuss the differences and similarities (if any) of the Hodeidah Microfinance Program in Yemen and Akhuwat microfinance scheme in Pakistan.

9. What is the role of Islamic banks and financial institutions in poverty-stricken societies?

10. Can an Islamic bank run a microfinance project as part of its mandate?

## Activities

1. Select two Islamic microfinance institutions of your choice and compare them with two conventional microfinance institutions.
2. Prepare a case study on any specific microfinance project of an Islamic financial institution.
3. With the aid of relevant case studies, prepare a brief presentation on the relevance of Islamic microfinance in the post-revolution Arab countries.

## Further Reading

Ahmed, H. (March 2002). Financing Microenterprises: An Analytical Study of Islamic Microfinance Institutions. *Islamic Economics Studies.* Vol. 9, no. 2: 27–64.

Ali, S. Nazim (ed.). (2012). *Shari'a-compliant Microfinance*, London & New York: Routledge.

Chapra, U. (1992). *Islam and the Economic Challenge.* Leicester, UK: Islamic Foundation and Virginia, USA: the International Institute of Islamic Thought.

IRTI. (2007). *Framework for Developing Islamic Microfinance Services.* Policy Paper, Jeddah: IRTI, Islamic Development Bank.

Kahf, M. and Khan, T. (1992). *Principles of Islamic Financing, A Survey,* Jeddah: Islamic Research and Training Institute/Islamic Development Bank, Research Paper no. 16.

Khan, A. A. (2008). *Islamic Microfinance: Theory, Policy and Practice.* Birmingham, UK: Islamic Relief Worldwide.

Obaidullah, M. (2008). *Introduction to Islamic Microfinance.* India: IBF Net (P) Limited.

Said, P., Shafqat, M., and Ur-Rehman, Z. (2006). *Draft Guidelines for Provision of Islamic Microfinance Services and Products by Financial Institutions.* Karachi: State Bank of Pakistan.

Seibel, H. D. (April 2008). Islamic Microfinance in Indonesia: The Challenge of Institutional Diversity, Regulation, and Supervision. *Sojourn: Journal of Social Issues in Southeast Asia.* Vol. 23, no.1: 86–103.

Wilson, R. (2007). Making Development Assistance Sustainable Through Islamic Microfinance. *IIUM Journal of Economics and Management.* Vol. 15, no. 2: 197–217.

# 10 Risk Management in Islamic Finance

# Learning Objectives

**Upon the completion of this chapter, the reader should be able to:**

1 Understand the concept of risk management from the Islamic perspective, with particular reference to Islamic commercial transactions.

2 Be familiar with the types and characteristics of risk exposure and the Islamic banking risks under the IFSB's guiding principles.

3 Examine the risk management techniques in Islamic banks and how such risks can be avoided, absorbed, or transferred.

4 Understand risk management techniques such as hedging through the use of the following derivatives: forwards, futures, and swaps, based on Sharī`ah-compliant risk mitigation frameworks.

In Islamic finance, profits are associated with risks. Profits cannot be generated without bearing risks. The rapid growth experienced in the Islamic finance industry around the world has consequentially exposed Islamic financial products to a number of risks. In fact, a number of products are inherently prone to risks because a cardinal principle in Islamic commercial transactions is that earning profit is legitimized only by risk-sharing. Therefore, in order to effectively manage the risk vulnerability of the Islamic finance instruments, proper measures for risk management have been put in place based on different frameworks that are either Sharī`ah-compliant or Sharī`ah-based. There is no doubt that Islamic banks are exposed to business risk just like their conventional counterparts. In addition, Islamic banks also face risks associated with compliance with the Sharī`ah in Islamic financial transactions. The most common risks include credit risk, equity investment risk, market risk, liquidity risk, rate of return risk, and operational risk. Risks may lead to unexpected losses in commercial transactions. The impact of losses occasioned by market risks may be reduced through hedging (a contract entered or asset withheld as protection against financial loss). Understanding the risks in Islamic banking business and how they can be effectively managed is important for practitioners in the Islamic finance industry. To this end, this chapter examines risk management in Islamic finance through an analysis of key guidelines on risk management issued by internationally recognized standard-setting bodies such as the Islamic Financial Services Board (IFSB). The complementary nature of the *Guiding Principles of Risk Management for Institutions (Other than Insurance Institutions) Offering Only Islamic Financial Services* to the Basel Committee on Banking Supervision is highlighted.

## chapter 10

**Dr. Zamir Iqbal**
*Lead Investment Officer, World Bank, Washington, D.C.*

**1 How is risk management in Islamic finance different from conventional finance?**

The discipline of risk management can be divided into risk measurement, risk control, and risk management. As far as the principles and rules of risk measurement and risk control are concerned, there is no difference between Islamic finance and conventional finance. However, risk management could be very different for several reasons. First, and most important, is the nature of financial intermediation in the two systems. Whereas in the conventional system a bank's depositors are promised a predetermined fixed return irrespective of the outcome on the asset side, in the case of Islamic banks, the deposits are not guaranteed any predetermined returns. Instead, the depositors are investors who share returns (profit or loss) on the assets side. Due to this built-in 'pass-through' nature of financial intermediation, Islamic banks are not exposed to the classic 'asset-liabilities mismatch' (ALM) risk. Therefore, there is no need for Islamic banks to pursue active ALM risk management.

The second most important difference is in the fundamental approach to risk management in each system. Whereas the conventional system uses risk-shifting or risk transfer, Islamic finance strongly advocates risk-sharing. This has very strong implications for risk management. In a risk-transfer system, risk does not disappear but is shifted within the system from one party to another and therefore risk becomes concentrated, which could cause systemic risk. However, in risk-sharing systems, the risks are shared among economic agents so that there is no risk concentration at the systemic level. One may conclude from this that in a risk-sharing system, there is less need for any active risk management.

**2 Are the modern tools of risk management appropriate for Islamic finance?**

When we look at the risk measurement, risk analysis, and risk control tools of the conventional system, Islamic finance can benefit from them greatly and, as the principles and rules of quantifying risk are well established, there is no need to reinvent the wheel. One notable difference is that as conventional markets are dominated by fixed-income securities, risk management for them is much more advanced than other asset classes, i.e. equities and risk-sharing asset classes. In other words, the modern tools of risk management are designed for a risk-shifting financial system whereas the Islamic financial system is a risk-sharing system. Therefore, there is no need to apply the risk analysis framework developed in the conventional system to the asset classes and financial products practiced by Islamic finance. When it comes to risk management through hedging products, Islamic finance cannot benefit from them as derivatives are not permitted. To illustrate this point, let's take credit risk as an example. Islamic finance can use all the techniques of analyzing credit exposure to a counterparty, like a conventional institution, but when it comes to using market-based credit management tools such as credit default swaps, an Islamic institution would not be permitted to use them.

**3   How about the use of derivatives as potential tools for risk management?**

As mentioned earlier, the Islamic system is risk-sharing rather than risk-shifting. Therefore the need for derivatives would be limited. At the moment, derivatives as practiced in the conventional markets are not permitted by Islamic financial institutions on the grounds that they encourage speculative behavior and create leverage, neither of which are compatible with the core tenets of Islamic finance. There is growing debate on the issue but the consensus is that derivatives (exchange-traded or OTC) are not allowed. As we know that the concept behind derivative pricing is based on a no-arbitrage principle and that a derivative can be constructed synthetically, one could argue that through financial engineering a financial instrument that is fully compliant with Islamic finance with the sole purpose of hedging one's undesirable risk can be developed. For example, if two financial institutions decide to exchange cash flows for their respective assets or liabilities in different currencies, one could construct a return-sharing currency swap (assuming that the principle of prohibition of interest is not violated).

**LEARNING OBJECTIVE 10.1**

Understand the concept of risk management from the Islamic perspective, with particular reference to Islamic commercial transactions.

# Risk Management from an Islamic Perspective

Although risk management is a general concept in modern finance, this section focuses on risk management from the Islamic perspective. That is, we shall examine the meaning of risk and risk management, consider the affirmative evidence of risk management in Islam, and discuss the concept in the light of Islamic commercial transactions.

## The Meaning of Risk and its Underlying Principles

**Hint**

The word 'risk' derives its origin from the French word *risqué* and Italian *risc(hi)o* both of which mean something that has an obscure origin.

**risk management**

A process of identification, quantification, and understanding of business risks with a view to undertaking necessary measures to control or mitigate the risk or its impact in the overall business of a financial institution.

**Hint**

Commercial risk is recognized in Islamic law, as it is considered part of business activities especially in equity-based transactions.

**aleatory transactions**

These are transactions conditioned on uncertain events. Literally, these are transactions that depend on chance or the throw of a die.

Risk is exposure to the chance of imminent danger or loss. Such damage or loss may present itself in the form of loss of life, property, or loss of investments in commercial transactions. One thing that remains certain is the nature and effect of risk in human endeavors. That is, risk may be harmful to human transactions because of its obscure or uncertain nature. Therefore, any measures undertaken to reduce the effect of any form of risk are regarded as risk management or risk mitigation techniques. Risk is associated with uncertainty, speculation, and obscurity in business transactions. Generally, there is an element of risk in every walk of life. The financial sector has its own share of risks. Due to the significance of financial transactions in human life, the risks encountered in this sector often have ripple effects that may eventually trigger the collapse of a country's economy; hence, the need to evolve proper measures of risk management.

**Risk management** is the quantification and assessment of business risks with a view to taking the necessary measures to control or mitigate them. Islam recognizes risk while engaging in business activities. Cumming and Hirtle define risk management as "the overall process that a financial institution follows to define a business strategy, to identify the risks to which it is exposed, to quantify those risks, and to understand and control the nature of the risks it faces."[1] According to Islamic commercial principles, a business only grows by taking risks. One of the reasons for the prohibition of interest-bearing (*riba*) transactions is the unjust enrichment associated with such transactions where the lender earns multiple returns without any risk, hence the common legal maxim in financial transactions, *al-ghunm bi al-ghurm*, which means entitlement to return is related to the liability of risk. Another maxim, derived from the sayings of Prophet Muhammad (PBUH), says, *al-kharaj bi al-daman*, meaning entitlement to the return of an asset is associated with the risk resulting from its possession. This gives a preliminary glimpse into the nature of commercial transactions in Islam. There is no transaction, whether debt-based or equity-based, in Islamic finance that is not associated with risk. What is prohibited in Islam is the excessive risk of transactions based on uncertain events known as **aleatory transactions**, which is completely anticipated by the parties engaging in contracts such as games of chance or raffle draws.

## Affirmative Evidence on Risk Management in Islam

Islam encourages its followers to effectively manage risks associated with their worldly activities. There are numerous examples in the Qur'an and Prophetic precedents where instances of risk management have been reported to serve as lessons for future generations. A narration given in the Qur'an relates to the story that revolves around the family of Prophet Yaqub (Jacob). As a precautionary measure to be taken to avoid unnecessary risk, Prophet Yaqub told his sons:

> Qur'an 12:67: "And he said: 'O my sons! Do not enter (the capital city of Egypt) by one gate, but enter through different gates, and I cannot avail you against Allah at all. Verily, the decision rests only by Allah. In Him, I put my trust and let all those that trust, put their trust in Him'."

The precautionary measures must be directed towards risk management, as clearly underscored in the verse. In a similar vein, precautionary steps to be taken to reduce the effect of the risk of famine that was anticipated in the city during the time of Prophet Yusuf (Joseph) were outlined thus:

> Qur'an 12:47: "Yusuf said: 'For seven consecutive years, you shall sow as usual and that (the harvest) which you reap you shall leave it in the ears, (all) except a little of it which you may eat'."

In order to avoid the risk of rejection, the Prophet Muhammad began his call towards Islamic faith from among the members of his immediate family and friends who were closely associated with him. The Prophet also approached the people of Arabia, who are known for their truthful lives and who readily accepted his sacred mission. He did not go openly to the Sacred House of Ka'aba to preach Islam to others nor openly teach his companions the precepts during the early days of Islam. These steps were taken to mitigate instances of risks to life, loss of property, and persecution as a result of the mass exodus from paganism to Islamic monotheism, which was then prevalent in Arabia. When the instances of persecution grew by the day, in order to avoid the continuous loss of life, the Prophet immediately advised his companions to migrate to Abyssinia before the greater migration to Medina. For more than a thousand years, Muslims have continued to face all sorts of risks. Risk mitigation techniques are provided in the Qur'an and Sunnah, which Muslims have continuously used to reduce the effect of such risks.

**sadd al-dhari'ah**
Preventive measures or precautionary principles which are a secondary source of Islamic law that seeks to prevent a violation of the law.

In Islamic jurisprudence, a secondary source of the Sharī'ah is known as **sadd al-dhari'ah** (blocking the legitimate means to an evil), is designed to reduce risks in commercial and non-commercial transactions among people through the use of precautionary measures. All measures taken towards blocking the means to evil are steps towards risk management, particularly when the risk is imminent. Scholars of Islamic jurisprudence have developed this concept into a secondary source of Sharī'ah. Therefore, blocking all potential risks is important in the steps towards risk management. This tool is used to block an ostensibly legitimate means when it is being used to pursue an illegitimate end. *Sadd al-dhari'ah* resonates in the risk management techniques that we discuss later in this chapter.

# Risk Management in Islamic Commercial Transactions

All Islamic commercial transactions, particularly those that involve profit and loss arrangements, are prone to market risks. Since inception, risk has been at the front of Islamic commercial transactions. Business activities have always been exposed to risks. If a person is not ready to bear any risk, he or she does not have to undertake any business activities within the framework of Sharī'ah-based or Sharī'ah-compliant transactions. For the sake of emphasis, the general maxims in Islamic commercial transactions we mentioned earlier are:

- *al-ghunm bi al-ghurm*: entitlement to return is related to the liability of risk
- *al-kharaj bi al-daman*: entitlement to the return of an asset is associated with the risk resulting from its possession.

These two maxims mean the same thing. Profit in commercial activities means risk with responsibility. The criterion of the legality of any return on capital investment is risk. People have to bear loss if they want legitimate profits on investment. Suppose an entrepreneur gets capital investment from an Islamic financial institution on the basis of trust financing (*mudarabah*). Both the entrepreneur and the capital provider must agree on terms and conditions at the inception of the contract. The underlying contract must contain the pre-agreed ratio of capital contribution and the ratio for the distribution of profit and loss. Ordinarily, the entrepreneur risks losing any potential reward from his or her labor while the capital provider risks losing the capital in a *mudarabah* contract. The parties must agree to mutually bear the risk of business in line with the mandatory provisions of the Sharī'ah on commercial transactions. In a *musharakah* (partnership) contract, the parties make financial contributions on the basis of profit and loss sharing (PLS). The profit and, where applicable, loss are shared at predetermined ratios, as contained in the underlying contract. These examples give the idea of risk in commercial transactions. Both profit and risk go together in commercial transactions and the parties must undertake to share both. However, reasonable measures must be put in place to mitigate the effect of any risk. This has been analyzed in the affirmative evidence given above on risk management and risk prevention in human endeavors. Such gestures must be extended to commercial transactions with a view to maximizing profits and minimizing instances of market-associated risks.

The risks faced by the Islamic banking industry are more than the normal risks of the banking industry. This is because of the requirement for Sharī'ah compliance in Islamic banking business and the nature of Islamic financial products. Risk in Islamic commercial transactions is not evil in itself, but its effect on the parties' contributions and situations is what brings about any problem. Therefore, avoiding risk with zero profit in business activities is allowed in Islam. This is being applied in Islamic banking through a product known as a **wadi'ah yad damanah** (savings only) deposit. This is a contractual arrangement on the basis of trust where the parties agree that the customer deposits their money into the custody of the bank or financial institution and the latter acts as the guarantor of the funds. The safe custody of the funds deposited is guaranteed and the customer can withdraw part or the whole of the funds at anytime. The bank

**Hint**

Risk management is related to the mitigation of commercial risks, which are permissible under the law. These forms of commercial risks are different from the risks in aleatory transactions. While the former is permissible, the latter is prohibited in Islamic law.

**Challenge**

Why do you think risk is generally inherent in Islamic financial products?

**wadi'ah yad damanah**
A guaranteed bank deposit where the bank is the guarantor and undertakes to pay the whole or part of the deposit when requested by the depositor.

guarantees the repayment of the funds. Note, avoiding risk with a positive profit is not allowed because this is the same as interest (*riba*) from loans.

Remember, there cannot be any profit without risk. An attempt to obtain profit from a business without bearing any risk may result in transactions involving unjust enrichment, such as interest-bearing business activities. This is why avoidance of risk if it injures the counterparty is considered an evil action under the Sharī'ah when it involves business activities. This is only realizable through interest from loans, which is categorically prohibited in the Sharī'ah. In risk management for Islamic finance products, Islamic law has its own framework, which precludes the replication of conventional techniques of risk management.

The wide range of possibilities offered by Islam to manage risks is part of the main discourse of this chapter, as clearly described in Box 10.1. Every Islamic financial institution is required to put in place a good framework for risk management. As a prelude to other sections of this chapter, it is important to bear in mind that the IFSB's *Guiding Principles of Risk Management for Institutions (Other than Insurance Institutions) Offering Only Islamic Financial Services* (IIFS) will be the major source of reference on risk management. Throughout this chapter, direct references to the IFSB guiding principles will be made in appropriate places to explain some of the key mechanisms inherent in the Islamic traditions.

**Hint**

The first guiding principles issued by IFSB, *Guiding Principles of Risk Management for Institutions (other than insurance institutions) offering only Islamic Financial Services*, generally called IFSB-1, will be used throughout this chapter.

---

## BOX 10.1:  REQUIREMENT FOR A COMPREHENSIVE RISK MANAGEMENT PROCESS

The IFSB's *Guiding Principles of Risk Management for Institutions (Other than Insurance Institutions) Offering Only Islamic Financial Services* (IIFS) provides for the need for every Islamic financial institution to have a comprehensive risk management framework. The guiding principles, popularly known as IFSB-1, expressly prohibit the making of profit without necessarily bearing the corresponding business risks.

The general spirit of the underlying objective of IFSB-1 is given in Principle 1.0 which reads:

> IIFS shall have in place a comprehensive risk management and reporting process, including appropriate board and senior management oversight, to identify, measure, monitor, report, and control relevant categories of risks and, where appropriate, to hold adequate capital against these risks. The process shall take into account appropriate steps to comply with Sharī'ah rules and principles and to ensure the adequacy of relevant risk reporting to the supervisory authority.

The above principle connects risk management with the role of corporate governance and Sharī'ah governance in properly managing risks in order to protect the interest of all stakeholders, particularly investors who are likely to lose their money in the case of losses. Thus, it becomes imperative for every IIFS to put in place a formidable framework for risk management to protect the funds of depositors and investors.

Source: IFSB. (2005). *Guiding Principles of Risk Management for Institutions (Other than Insurance Institutions) Offering Only Islamic Financial Services*. Kuala Lumpur: IFSB: p. 1.

# Types of Risk Exposure

## Types of Risk Exposure

**LEARNING OBJECTIVE 10.2**

Be familiar with the types and characteristics of risk exposure and the Islamic banking risks under the IFSB guiding principles.

Islamic banks are exposed to a number of risks in the course of business transactions with customers. In this section, we will examine the types and characteristics of risk exposure and the specific Islamic banking risks enumerated in the IFSB guiding principles, which are unique to institutions offering Islamic financial services other than insurance companies. As Table 10.1 shows, financial institutions are exposed to a number of risks that can be broadly classified into financial and non-financial risks. The financial risks include market risk, credit risk, liquidity risk, displaced commercial risk, and rate of return risk. Non-financial risks comprise operational risk, regulatory risk, and legal or Sharī'ah risk. These are presented in the first two columns below. The third column enumerates the risks that have some features are exclusive to Islamic banking business.

Islamic financial institutions face a number of risks, some of which are specific to Sharī'ah-compliant businesses. We shall focus on the risks that are associated with the Islamic banking industry as a whole because within the global financial system, the Islamic finance industry has a unique risk profile due to the requirement of Sharī'ah compliance. The requirement to have in place a Sharī'ah board is one of the major ways of preventing operational risk. In discussing the Islamic banking risks, we shall rely on the IFSB's *Guiding Principles of Risk Management for Institutions (Other than Insurance Institutions) Offering Only Islamic Financial Services*. As shown in Figure 10.1, IFSB-1 identifies the following six risks that have some features unique to the Islamic banking business:

- credit risk
- equity investment risk
- market risk
- liquidity risk
- rate of return risk
- operational risk.

## Challenge

Name any other type of risk that is not unique to the Islamic banking business.

The IFSB guiding principles require Islamic banks and financial institutions to have in place comprehensive risk management and reporting processes. As shown in the *Global Islamic Finance* box on page 375, the framework for risk management introduced by the IFSB is not so different from the framework introduced by the Basel Committee on Banking Supervision (BCBS), which is used globally. The box sheds some light on the relationship between the IFSB guiding principles and the BCBS guidelines.

**TABLE 10.1: Risks in Business Transactions**

| Financial Risks | Non-Financial Risks | Islamic Banking Risks |
|---|---|---|
| • market risk<br>• credit risk<br>• liquidity risk<br>• displaced commercial risk<br>• rate of return risk | • operational risk<br>• regulatory risk<br>• legal or Sharī'ah risk | • credit risk<br>• market risk<br>• liquidity risk<br>• operational risk<br>• displaced commercial risk<br>• Sharī'ah risk<br>• rate of return risk |

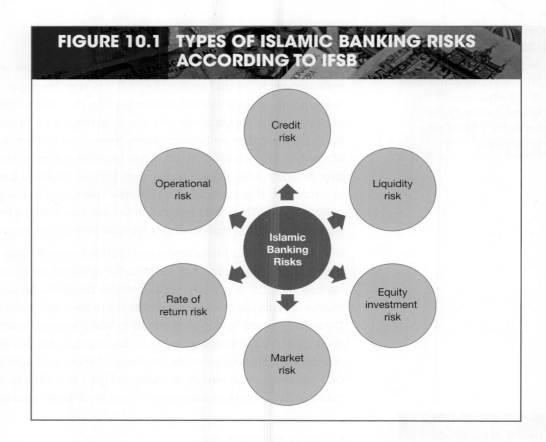

**FIGURE 10.1   TYPES OF ISLAMIC BANKING RISKS ACCORDING TO IFSB**

Credit risk

Liquidity risk

Operational risk

Islamic Banking Risks

Equity investment risk

Rate of return risk

Market risk

## Credit Risk

**credit risk**
Risk encountered in business transactions when there is potential for default on the part of a party in meeting its obligations as agreed in an underlying contract.

**counterparty**
An opposite party in a financial transaction or contract.

**credit exposure**
The amount of risk, or amount subject to loss of value, or the size of the commitment.

**Credit risk** is the risk encountered in business transactions when there is the potential for default on the part of the **counterparty** in meeting its obligations as agreed in an underlying contract. This is a common risk in Islamic banks. Whenever there is a default in the repayment of a debt or loan obligations in accordance with the agreed terms in the contract, the problem of credit risk arises. While using Islamic financial techniques such as *murababah* (mark-up cost contract), *musharakah mutanaqisah* (diminishing partnership) and *ijarah* (lease contract), which contractually involve receivables and leases, there is the potential that the counterparty may fail to meet its obligations under the contractual terms. This is also true of contracts that involve credit facilities for working capital financing projects.

Islamic banks and financial institutions also lend funds, which exposes them to credit risks. Exposure is a loose word to describe a transaction that generates some risk. **Credit exposure** refers to the amount of risk, or amount subject to loss of value, or the size of the commitment. For example, when a bank takes a position such as deciding to lend or extend financing facilities, it has an exposure. Different stages of the financing contracts in Islamic finance have different credit exposures. These potential credit exposures must be recognized and closely examined, using appropriate measures and strategies to effectively manage the resultant risks.

## GLOBAL ISLAMIC FINANCE

# Risk Management: IFSB Guidelines and Basel II Framework

Before the modern Sharī'ah-oriented framework for risk management in Islamic banks and financial institutions, these institutions used conventional risk management techniques while still trying to remain on the Sharī'ah-compliance track. In December 2005, the IFSB issued *Guiding Principles of Risk Management for Institutions (Other than Insurance Institutions) Offering Only Islamic Financial Services (Guiding Principles)*. This was not meant to replace the existing framework of Basel Committee on Banking Supervision (BCBS) guidelines. The new IFSB guiding principles were meant to complement the BCBS's guidelines, which are used in all banks and financial institutions around the world. While certain issues are of equal importance to all financial institutions, some exclusive issues need to be addressed as they affect the Islamic finance industry. The IFSB guiding principles specifically cater for the needs and unique nature of institutions offering Islamic financial services.

One of the major features of Islamic finance is the consideration of both profit and risk together that must be present in every joint venture. One is not allowed to generate profit without bearing risk. This does not imply that the Islamic financial institutions should be carefree in their dealings with their customers. The fiduciary duty they owe their customers requires

them to exercise due diligence in the management of investment funds. To this end, they are required to put in place all necessary Sharī'ah-compliant risk mitigation techniques. Pairing risk and profit in Islamic commercial transactions does not in any way imply the mismanagement of funds.

The approach adopted by IFSB in crafting its guidelines is commendable. Not every technique or mechanism that originates from the conventional banking industry is non-Sharī'ah-compliant. All the sound practices and principles that relate to risk management in the BCBS guidelines are considered in Islamic finance and are adapted to suit the needs of the industry to the extent of their consistency with the general spirit of Islamic economic theory. This is carried out without compromising the principles of Islamic finance. The internal mechanism in the principles of Islamic jurisprudence, which allows for the adaptation of such standards from whatever models that are not contrary to the Sharī'ah, remains the driving force that makes Islamic finance Sharī'ah-compliant and, at the same time, conventionally competitive. Further harmonization of regulations, guiding principles, and laws should be encouraged in a global village where the rate of financial intercourse has reached an unprecedented level.

## Nature of Credit Risk

The potential default of a bank's customer to meet their obligations on agreed terms constitute a credit risk for the bank. Credit risk is a type of banking risk that relates to the repayment of a debt at the appointed time in accordance with the terms of the loan. Failure to repay the debt within the time stipulated in the contract and in line with the terms of the contract will result in a loss and therefore constitute a risk for the bank. This is considered the most important type of risk faced by banks and financial institutions in their relationship with the owners of wealth, the reason being that default is not uncommon. Bank customers will always have one reason or the other to default on repayments, which ultimately results in a credit risk for the bank. Outright default in

---

**BOX 10.2:    IFSB GUIDING PRINCIPLES ON CREDIT RISK**

**Principle 2.1:**   IIFS shall have in place a strategy for financing, using various instruments in compliance with Sharī'ah, whereby it recognizes the potential credit exposures that may arise at different stages of the various financing agreements.

**Principle 2.2:**   IIFS shall carry out a due diligence review in respect of counterparties prior to deciding on the choice of an appropriate Islamic financing instrument.

**Principle 2.3:**   IIFS shall have in place appropriate methodologies for measuring and reporting the credit risk exposures arising under each Islamic financing instrument.

**Principle 2.4:**   IIFS shall have in place Sharī'ah-compliant, credit risk mitigating techniques appropriate for each Islamic financing instrument.

Source: IFSB. (2005). *Guiding Principles of Risk Management for Institutions (Other than Insurance Institutions) Offering Only Islamic Financial Services*. Kuala Lumpur: IFSB: p. 6.

---

debt repayment results in loss and the bank bears the credit risk. As credit risk is inherent in any business involved in lending funds, there is a need for credit risk management in order to minimize such risks. IFSB-1 provides guiding principles for the management of credit risk for Islamic banks and financial institutions, outlined in Box 10.2.

## Operational Considerations in Credit Risk Management

The operational considerations for risk management in IFI place credit risk management at the core of the integrated approach to the management of financial risks. A holistic approach is required to tackle the problems of credit risk arising from transactions involving Islamic financial instruments. In order to cushion and effectively mitigate such risks, IIFS are required to put in place proper framework towards the identification, measurement, monitoring, reporting, and control of credit risks. According to IFSB-1, the proposed framework for IIFS should include:

- an appropriate credit strategy, including pricing and tolerance for undertaking various credit risks
- a risk management structure with effective oversight of credit risk management—credit policies and operational procedures including credit criteria and credit review processes, acceptable forms of risk mitigation, and limit setting
- an appropriate measurement and careful analysis of exposures, including market- and liquidity-sensitive exposures
- a system to (a) monitor the condition of ongoing individual credits to ensure the financings are made in accordance with the IIFS' policies and procedures, (b) manage problem credit situations according to an established remedial process, and (c) ensure adequate provisions are allocated.[2]

These tools for credit risk management are meant to reduce the potential exposure of IIFS to risks. The boards of directors (BoDs) of the IIFS should be proactive in this regard to lay down a workable strategy for risk management. A good understanding of the credit risks associated with each of the Islamic financial instruments would assist in this regard.

There is also the requirement for due diligence reviews of the counterparties of the IIFS, who generally include retail/consumer, corporate, or sovereign clients. This will enable them decide on the appropriate Islamic financial instruments to be used in each case. Each case is treated on its own merit while dealing with the counterparties. A due diligence review includes the ascertainment of the eligible counterparties through a comprehensive assessment of their individual risk profiles. This process must precede the granting of any type of financing for the counterparties. The creditworthiness of the counterparties as well as the Sharī'ah compliance of newly proposed business projects should be properly reviewed and ascertained through the assistance of Sharī'ah advisors or the standing Sharī'ah advisory committee and, in some cases, the services of technical experts should be employed to determine the feasibility of certain projects.

Credit risk exposure must be properly measured and reported through standardized methodologies that are relevant to Islamic financial instruments. The IIFS are also required to manage their counterparty risks at different stages of the implementation of the contract. While carrying out risk measurement and reporting, price volatilities of the underlying asset must be taken into consideration. Furthermore, each financial instrument must have its unique credit risk mitigating technique that is Sharī'ah-compliant.

## Equity Investment Risk

**equity investment**
The money invested in a company by its owners or holders of ordinary shares in a company, which though not necessarily returned in the course of the business, can only be recouped when they decide to liquidate the assets of the company or sell their shareholdings to other investors.

**equity investment risk**
A risk that arises from a partnership investment contract whereby the capital providers share in the business risk.

**Equity investment** is the buying and holding of shares by individuals or firms of a listed company on the stock exchange in anticipation of income from dividends and capital gains. When the value of the stock rises on the stock market, the value of the investment increases. For unlisted companies, equity investment is defined as the acquisition of equity (or ownership) participation in a joint venture company or a start-up. This arrangement is otherwise called venture capital investing, which is considered to be of higher risk than that for listed companies.

Therefore, according to IFSB-1, **equity investment risk** can be defined as "the risk arising from entering into a partnership for the purpose of undertaking or participating in a particular financing or general business activity as described in the contract, and in which the provider of finance shares in the business risk."[3] Remember that the most popular Islamic finance instruments are equity-based products such as *mudarabah* and *musharakah*. These financial products are based on a joint venture through the partnership of the capital provider and the entrepreneur in the case of *mudarabah*, and joint partnership in the provision of both capital and management of the venture in the case of *musharakah*. Much as the parties hope to make a profit and share it in accordance with predetermined ratios, they also undertake to share the business risk such as a loss. It is this kind of risk that is known as equity investment risk.

## Nature of Equity Investment Risk

The nature of equity investment risk is a combination of risks connected to the entrepreneur (*mudarib*) or a partner in a *musharakah* arrangement, the underlying business activity for the partnership, and operational issues. Preventive measures must be put in place such as the consideration of the risk profiles of potential partners. This element of due diligence is significant, as the IIFS is in a fiduciary relationship with the **investment account holders (IAH)**. Investing the IAH funds in profit-sharing and loss-bearing investments with third parties requires the utmost due diligence to uphold the fiduciary relationship between the IIFS and IAH. The IIFS will have to review the risk profiles of the potential partner or entrepreneur through a careful examination of its past records, the quality of the business plan, the proposed business activity, and the human resources involved. These preventive measures are necessary to forestall instances of loss, which would take its toll on the funds of IAH. The risk evaluation should also include factors relating to the legal and regulatory environment that may affect the viability of the investment within a particular jurisdiction.

**investment account holders (IAH)**
Bank customers who opt for an investment account at an Islamic bank, which yields legitimate returns of predetermined share of profits. The funds are especially used in Sharī'ah-compliant investments.

## Operational Considerations in Equity Investment Risk Management

There are three IFSB guiding principles on equity investment risk management, summarized in Box 10.3. The first principle relates to appropriate strategies for risk management and adequate reporting processes. The second principle focuses on appropriate valuation methodologies for the purpose of profit allocation. The third principle provides for exit strategies in respect of the equity investment activities of the contracting parties.

### BOX 10.3: IFSB GUIDING PRINCIPLES ON EQUITY INVESTMENT RISK

**Principle 3.1:** IIFS shall have in place appropriate strategies, risk management and reporting processes in respect of the risk characteristics of equity investments, including *mudarabah* and *musharakah* investments.

**Principle 3.2:** IIFS shall ensure that their valuation methodologies are appropriate and consistent, and shall assess the potential impacts of their methods on profit calculations and allocations. The methods shall be mutually agreed between the IIFS and the *mudarib* and/or *musharakah* partners.

**Principle 3.3:** IIFS shall define and establish the exit strategies in respect of their equity investment activities, including extension and redemption conditions for *mudarabah* and *musharakah* investments, subject to the approval of the institution's Shari`ah board.

Source: IFSB. (2005). *Guiding Principles of Risk Management for Institutions (Other than Insurance Institutions) Offering Only Islamic Financial Services*. Kuala Lumpur: IFSB: p. 12.

There is a need for the proper stipulation of objectives for profit-sharing instruments such as *mudarabah* and *musharakah*, and the criteria for each of them should be properly structured. The applicable risks in the acquisition of, holding, and exiting from profit-sharing investments should be evaluated and managed appropriately. An appropriate management structure is required, which must include a Sharī'ah compliance body for the proper evaluation of investment activities. Adequate financial reporting standards must also be agreed upon for the purpose of transparency and accountability. The risk mitigating techniques must be Sharī'ah-compliant.

Valuation methodologies must be appropriate and consistent for the purpose of profit allocation. The IIFS is required to agree mutually on the valuation methodologies with the partner/entrepreneur to ensure the quality of the equity investment. The parties must agree on the procedure to be adopted to determine the profit of the investment. It can either be agreed that the profit should be a percentage of the gross or net profit of the underlying business, or as mutually agreed by the parties.

Risk associated with the possible manipulation of reported profit, which may manifest itself as overstatement, or understatement, of the profit should be properly addressed through adequate measures to nip this potential problem in the bud. The services of independent bodies or parties should be engaged to carry out audits and valuation of the business investments for the overall interest of the parties, including the IAH.

Finally, the parties must agree on the exit strategies and their criteria, and the period of the joint venture and the timing of the exit. The IIFS and the investing partner must also agree on the treatment of retained profits. All the agreements, contracts, and processes must be reviewed and approved by the Sharī'ah board of the IIFS to ensure the utmost Sharī'ah compliance.

## Market Risk

**market risk**
The risk arising from the potential of investors to experience losses occasioned by movements in market prices.

**restricted investment accounts**
These are account portfolios where the account holders authorize the Islamic bank to invest their funds in Sharī'ah-compliant business ventures with certain restrictions as to where, how, and for what purpose the funds are to be invested.

**Market risk** is also known as systematic risk, or generally called systematic market risk. The market risk can be defined as the risk arising from the potential of investors to experience losses occasioned by market price fluctuations. IFSB-1 defines market risk as "the risk of losses in on- and off-balance-sheet positions arising from movements in market prices, i.e. fluctuations in values in tradable, marketable, or leasable assets (including *sukuk*) and in off-balance-sheet individual portfolios (for example restricted investment accounts)."[4] **Restricted investment accounts** are account portfolios where the account holders authorize the Islamic bank to invest their funds in Sharī'ah-compliant business ventures with certain restrictions as to where, how, and for what purpose the funds are to be invested. The volatility of market values of assets results in market risk, particularly in transactions that involve future delivery or deferred payment such as a *salam* contract or *murabahah* contract. Foreign exchange rates are also not fixed. The foreign exchange market fluctuates from time to time and this volatility leads to market risk. In other words, market risk is the impact of volatility on income as a result of the changes in market price. The income of IIFS is greatly affected in this regard.

## Nature of Market Risk

The nature of market risk as it appears in some of the Islamic financial instruments is explained here. It is important to note that other types of risks are also applicable to the financial instruments discussed here but our focus here is market risk.

### *Salam* Contract

This is a commodity sale involving an advance payment where the delivery of the commodity is deferred. Risk exposure in a *salam* contract manifests in different ways. When the price expectation reverses after the bank has earlier concluded a **salam contract** for future delivery of the commodity, a market risk arises. The bank may have to pay more to obtain the commodity on or before the maturity date to fulfill the contractual terms. This commodity risk adversely affects the income of the bank. According to IFSB-1, IIFS are exposed to commodity price fluctuations on a long position after entering into a contract and while holding the subject matter until it is disposed of. "In the case of parallel *salam*, there is also the risk that the failure of delivery of the subject matter would leave the IBIs [Islamic Banking Institution] exposed to commodity price risk as a result of the need to purchase a similar asset in the spot market in order to honor the parallel *salam* contract."[5]

### *Ijarah* Contract

An **ijarah contract** is a typical lease contract where the owner (lessor) of an asset leases it to a customer (lessee) at an agreed rental fee, which is a consideration for the beneficial use of the underlying asset. In a lease arrangement, when there is a default of payment on the part of the lessee because of a price variation, the resultant effect is market risk. The bank/lessor faces market risk, which in turn may lead to credit risk and ultimately losses for the bank/lessor. In some cases, market risk in a lease contract may arise from the default on the asset delivery by the bank/lessor. If the lessee terminates the lease earlier than the contractual term, either through default in payment or some other factor, the lessor is exposed to market risk on the residual value of the leased asset. The risk exposure is more in a lease contract that offers the lessee an option to own the asset at the end of the lease period, known as **ijarah muntahia bittamlik**, because in the event of any form of default on the part of the lessee on the lease obligations, the lessor will be exposed to market risk on the carrying value of the leased asset. This commodity risk may have an adverse affect on the lessor.

### Foreign Exchange Contract

The nature of market risk in **foreign exchange contract** (*bay al-sarf*) is related to fluctuations in currency exchange rates. Foreign exchange rate risk is the risk arising from changes experienced in the currency exchange rates. This may affect the value of investment by the IIFS. An adverse movement in exchange rates will always result in currency risk or exchange rate risk. IIFS that engage in export and import business activities are usually affected by any sudden changes in exchange rates. IIFS that engage in international investments are also exposed to exchange rate risks. According to IFSB-1, IIFS are also exposed to foreign-exchange fluctuations arising from general FX spot-rate changes in both cross-border transactions and the resultant foreign currency receivables

**salam contract**
A commodity sale contract involving an advance payment where the delivery of the commodity is deferred.

**ijarah contract**
A contract where the owner of an asset leases it to a client at an agreed rental fee, which is a consideration for the beneficial use of the underlying asset.

**ijarah muntahia bittamlik**
(also known as *ijarah wa iqtina*) A form of lease contract that offers the lessee an option to own the asset at the end of the lease period either by purchase of the asset through a token consideration or payment of the market value, or by means of a gift contract.

**foreign exchange contract**
A contract of exchange of money for money, closely regulated and restricted by relevant Shari'ah rules.

and payables. These exposures may be hedged using Sharī'ah-compliant methods.[6] There is only one IFSB guiding principle on market risk, shown in Box 10.4.

## Operational Considerations in Market Risk Management

In order to mitigate or properly manage instances of market risk in financial transactions between the IIFS and a client, an appropriate framework is required. Note that these risk management policies are also applicable to the assets held on behalf of restricted IAH, based on the fiduciary relationship between the IIFS and the IAH. This framework comprises a number of strategies summarized in Figure 10.2.

These strategies for market risk management in Islamic financial institutions are explained in Box 10.5 where they are reproduced verbatim from IFSB-1.

## Liquidity Risk

**liquidity risk**
The potential loss anticipated by an Islamic financial institution that arises as a result of insufficient liquidity to meet its normal operating obligations and operating needs.

**Liquidity risk** can be defined as the potential loss anticipated by an Islamic financial institution that arises as a result of insufficient liquidity to meet its normal operating

**FIGURE 10.2   STRATEGIES FOR MARKET RISK MANAGEMENT IN ISLAMIC FINANCIAL INSTITUTIONS**

| | | |
|---|---|---|
| Appropriate market risk strategy | Sound and comprehensive market risk management process and information system | Quantification of market risk exposure |
| Appropriate definition of risk appetite for the tradable assets with adequate capital support | Detailed approach to valuing the market risk positions | Allocate funds to cover risks resulting from illiquidity, new assets and uncertainty |

Source: Based on IFSB. (2005). *Guiding Principles of Risk Management for Institutions (Other than Insurance Institutions) Offering Only Islamic Financial Services* (p. 17). Kuala Lumpur: IFSB.

## BOX 10.5: EXPLANATION OF THE STRATEGIES FOR MARKET RISK MANAGEMENT

According to IFSB-1, the framework to be implemented for the operational considerations in market risk management consists of the following strategies.

1. **Appropriate market risk strategy.** IIFS shall develop a market risk strategy including the level of acceptable market risk appetite taking into account contractual agreements with fund providers, types of risk-taking activities, and target markets in order to maximize returns while keeping exposures at or below the predetermined levels. The strategy should be reviewed periodically by IIFS, communicated to relevant staff and disclosed to fund providers.

2. **Sound and comprehensive market risk management process and information system.** IIFS shall establish a sound and comprehensive market risk management process and information system, which includes:

   a) a conceptual framework to assist in identifying underlying market risks

   b) guidelines governing risk-taking activities in different portfolios of restricted IAH and their market risk limits

   c) appropriate frameworks for pricing, valuation, and income recognition

   d) a strong MIS for controlling, monitoring and reporting market risk exposure and performance to appropriate levels of senior management.

   Given that all the required measures are in place (e.g. pricing, valuation, and income recognition frameworks, strong management information system for managing exposures, etc.), the applicability of any market risk management framework that has been developed should be assessed, taking into account consequential business and reputation risks.

3. **Quantification of market risk exposure.** IIFS should be able to quantify market risk exposure and assess exposure to the probability of future losses in their net open asset positions.

4. **Appropriate definition of risk appetite for the tradable assets with adequate capital support.** The risk exposures in investment securities are similar to the risks faced by conventional financial intermediaries, namely market price, liquidity, and foreign exchange rates. In this regard, IIFS shall ensure that their strategy includes the definition of their risk appetite for these tradable assets and that this risk appetite is adequately supported by capital held for that purpose.

5. **Detailed approach to valuing the market risk positions.** In the valuation of assets where no direct market prices are available, IIFS shall incorporate in their own product program a detailed approach to valuing their market risk positions. IIFS may employ appropriate forecasting techniques to assess the potential value of these assets.

6. **Allocate funds to cover risks resulting from illiquidity, new assets and uncertainty.** Where available valuation methodologies are deficient, IIFS shall assess the need to (a) allocate funds to cover risks resulting from illiquidity, new assets, and uncertainty in assumptions underlying valuation and realization; and (b) establish a contractual agreement with the counterparty specifying the methods to be used in valuing the assets.

Source: IFSB. (2005). *Guiding Principles of Risk Management for Institutions (Other than Insurance Institutions) Offering Only Islamic Financial Services.* Kuala Lumpur: IFSB: p. 17.

obligations and operating needs. The implication of liquidity risk is that the Islamic financial institution may find it difficult to meet its liabilities by selling assets whose market value has fallen. Liquidity risk is sometimes considered to be part of market risk but for the purpose of IIFS, liquidity risk is regarded as a separate risk. Liquidity risk involves a kind of systemic failure on the part of the financial institution where it fails to meet expected and unexpected cash flow needs as they emerge from time to time. Such cash flows include the financial institution's portfolio of assets. The inability to fund those assets at appropriate maturity and rates results in liquidity risk. Liquidity risk can be caused by incorrect judgment and complacency, unanticipated change in cost capital, abnormal behavior of financial markets, range of assumptions used, risk activation by secondary sources, breakdown of payment systems, macroeconomic imbalances, financial infrastructure deficiency, and contractual forms. In Islamic financial institutions, liquidity risk is linked with displaced commercial and Sharī'ah compliance risks.

## Nature of Equity Liquidity Risk

IIFS manage two major funds directly:

- current account holders
- unrestricted investment account holders (IAH).

The funds of these two account holders require proper management through a stable level of liquidity that regulates the cash flow process. The IIFS must meet the requirements for withdrawals of the two types of account holders through a healthy degree of liquidity. The current account holders only make cash withdrawals. They do not participate in the sharing of profits realized in investment activities. To this end, the IIFS must make readily available funds for cash withdrawal at every point in time. This requires enough liquidity in the cash flow of the financial institution. All cash withdrawal requests of the current account holders must be adequately met through a sound repayment capacity. Such repayments are guaranteed at any point in time when requests are made because the current account holders do not share in the profit or the risk of the business activities of the IIFS. However, unlike the current account holders, the IAH have a share in the profits and risk of the business of IIFS as investors. IFSB-1 provides that "apart from general withdrawal needs, the withdrawals made by IAH may be the result of (a) lower than expected or acceptable rates of return; (b) concerns about the financial condition of the IIFS; and (c) non-compliance by the IIFS with Sharī'ah rules and principles in various contracts and activities."[7] There are two IFSB guiding principles on liquidity risk, shown in Box 10.6.

## Operational Considerations in Liquidity Risk Management

The IIFS must put in place a liquidity management framework, which addresses the liquidity exposures of the financial institution with particular regards to the two types of account holders—current account holders and IAH. This involves measuring and monitoring the risk exposures at every point in time and coming up with strategies for liquidity risk mitigation. First and foremost, the IIFS are required to maintain adequate liquidity at all times to meet all their obligations.

> ## BOX 10.6: IFSB GUIDING PRINCIPLES ON LIQUIDITY RISK
>
> **Principle 5.1:** IIFS shall have in place a liquidity management framework (including reporting), taking into account separately and on an overall basis their liquidity exposures in respect of each category of current accounts and unrestricted investment accounts.
>
> **Principle 5.2:** IIFS shall assume liquidity risk commensurate with their ability to have sufficient recourse to Sharī'ah-compliant funds to mitigate such risk.
>
> Source: IFSB. (2005). *Guiding Principles of Risk Management for Institutions (Other than Insurance Institutions) Offering Only Islamic Financial Services*. Kuala Lumpur: IFSB: p. 19

The oversight functions of the BoD cannot be overemphasized in a corporate entity, especially when it comes to the challenges of liquidity risk. The failure of effective oversight functions through proper policy formulation and monitoring will lead to solvency issues in the IIFS. In order to mitigate instances of liquidity risk effectively, the IIFS should have a liquidity contingency plan.

## Rate of Return Risk

**rate of return risk**
Risk associated with the potential impact of the returns of an Islamic financial institution, arising from unexpected change in the rate of returns in business transactions undertaken by such institutions.

**Rate of return risk** is defined as the risk associated with the potential impact of the returns of an Islamic financial institution, arising from unexpected change in the rate of returns in business transactions undertaken by such institutions. This happens when the IIFS balance sheet is exposed to unexpected change in the rate of returns, which causes an inconsistency between the assets and balances of the capital providers. To fulfill its fiduciary duty to the IAHs on one part and the current account holders on the other, the IIFS must put in place a sound framework for balance-sheet risk management. There is a difference between the rate of return risk and the interest rate risk, which is prevalent in the conventional banking industry. While the rate of return risk is based on the return on investments anticipated by the IIFS at the end of the investment cycle, the interest rate risk relates to a predetermined interest rate that is fixed at the beginning of the investment cycle.

### Nature of Rate of Return Risk

The rate of return risk may lead to displaced commercial risk. This refers to the risk arising from the assets managed on behalf of the IAH that is in due course transferred to the Islamic financial institution's own capital, where the IIFS foregoes part or all of its portion of profits on a profit-sharing investment account (PSIA), in order to increase the rate of return that would otherwise be payable to the IAH.[8] The prevailing market pressure at a particular point in time may push the IIFS to pay a return that exceeds the rate that has been earned on assets financed by IAH in situations where the return on assets is underperforming compared with competitors' rates. It is strategic for the IIFS to retain their fund providers to avoid insolvency and an ultimate liquidation. Therefore, it may be ready to waive some of its rights by parting with its share of profits in the *mudarabah* arrangement with the IAH to avoid a situation where they withdraw their funds from the IIFS. Investors, who are fund providers, must be retained at all costs as a result of market competitive pressures.

Two important terminologies that are related to rate of return risk management are profit equalization reserve (PER) and investment risk reserve (IRR). The PER is the amount of funds set aside by the Islamic financial institution out of its gross income prior to the appropriation of the relevant amount due to the investment manager (*mudarib*). This step is taken to protect the interest of the investors who, in this case, are the IAH. Apart from maintaining a certain level of return on investment for the IAH, PER also increases the equity of the owners of the financial institutions.

The IRR is the reverse of PER in that it is the amount appropriated from the income of the IAH after the share of the investment manager (*mudarib*) has been allocated. This is carried out to prevent any future risk of investment losses on the part of the IAH. As a means of cushioning the effects of future losses on the part of the IAH, the IRR is very appropriate for *mudarabah* arrangements in deposit accounts at Islamic banks.

PER and IRR are important reserves maintained by IIFS to cater for situations where market pressures may result in displaced commercial risk. The IIFS maintains these reserves as part of its risk management strategy. There are two IFSB guiding principles on rate of return risk, shown in Box 10.7.

## Operational Considerations in Rate of Return Risk Management

The operational considerations in rate of return risk management relate to the necessary steps the IIFS needs to take in assessing the potential impact of market factors that affect the rates of return on assets. When these are compared with the expected rates of return

### BOX 10.7: IFSB GUIDING PRINCIPLES ON RATE OF RETURN RISK

**Principle 6.1:** IIFS shall establish a comprehensive risk management and reporting process to assess the potential impact of market factors affecting rates of return on assets in comparison with the expected rates of return for investment account holders (IAH).

**Principle 6.2:** IIFS shall have in place an appropriate framework for managing displaced commercial risk, where applicable.

Source: IFSB. (2005). *Guiding Principles of Risk Management for Institutions (Other than Insurance Institutions) Offering Only Islamic Financial Services.* Kuala Lumpur: IFSB: p. 23.

for IAHs, necessary steps are taken to mitigate any mismatch between the assets and balances from the funds of the investors.

Islamic banks must have in place appropriate management processes that cater for the identification, measurement, monitoring, reporting, and control of the rate of return risk. The factors that give rise to this kind of risk must be identified in order to put in place a proper strategy to mitigate such risk. Apart from other techniques, IIFS are encouraged to use balance-sheet techniques to minimize exposure to risks. In addition, displaced commercial risk must be properly managed through an appropriate policy and framework. The IIFS must identify their shareholders' and IAH expectations, and put in place an appropriate policy and framework to meet those expectations through the proper management of the displaced commercial risk.

## Operational Risk

**operational risk**
Risk that arises from the execution of the business functions of an Islamic bank.

**Operational risk** can be defined as a risk that arises from the execution of the business functions of an Islamic bank. These are risks arising from failures in the internal controls of a financial institution involving processes, people, and systems. Operational risk also includes risk arising from non-compliance with the Sharī'ah requirements and any failure in the fiduciary responsibilities of the financial institution towards the IAH and current account holders. This risk may lead to withdrawal of funds by the fund providers and the ultimate closure of accounts, resulting in loss of income, diminished reputation, and limited business opportunities.

## Nature of Operational Risk

Operational matters are important in the life of an Islamic bank. When the internal controls of a financial institution are not functioning well and there is exposure to risks coupled with non-compliance with the Sharī'ah, a systemic failure has occurred that may lead to eventual insolvency. Thus, operational risk must be properly handled to ensure the sustained confidence of fund providers. Relevant governance bodies are required to play their roles in properly mitigating operational risk. For instance, the Sharī'ah board must play its supervisory role to ensure total compliance with the rules and principles of Sharī'ah, as compliance is critical to the continued existence of the IIFS.

The other form of operation risk relates to fiduciary risk. Remember that every financial institution has a fiduciary relationship with its clients, which must be performed in accordance with standard practices in the industry. In managing the investments of the IAH, the financial institution must act with the utmost due care in terms of calculation of expenses and allocation of profits. Failure to uphold the fiduciary relationship may result in loss of investments. If the financial institution becomes insolvent, it is impossible to meet the frequent demands of the current account holders and protect the interest of the IAH.

There are two IFSB guiding principles on rate of return risk, shown in Box 10.8.

---

**BOX 10.8:   IFSB GUIDING PRINCIPLES ON OPERATIONAL RISK**

There are two IFSB guiding principles on rate of return risk.

**Principle 7.1:** IIFS shall have in place adequate systems and controls, including a Sharī'ah board/advisor, to ensure compliance with Sharī'ah rules and principles.

**Principle 7.2:** IIFS shall have in place appropriate mechanisms to safeguard the interests of all fund providers. Where IAH funds are commingled with the IIFS' own funds, the IIFS shall ensure that the bases for assets, revenues, expenses, and profit allocations are established, applied, and reported in a manner consistent with its fiduciary responsibilities.

Source: IFSB. (2005). *Guiding Principles of Risk Management for Institutions (Other than Insurance Institutions) Offering Only Islamic Financial Services.* Kuala Lumpur: IFSB: p. 26.

---

## Operational Considerations in Operational Risk Management

The IIFS must have an adequate system for the management of operational risks arising from its business activities. This operational risk relates to Sharī'ah non-compliance risk and fiduciary risk.

With regards to Sharī'ah non-compliance risk, the IIFS must ensure that total compliance is maintained in all contracts, procedures, processes, and services in accordance with the rulings of the Sharī'ah board or advisor or as determined by the appropriate body in the jurisdiction within which they operate. Sharī'ah compliance begins with contract documentation and, after the implementation of contracts, there should be a Sharī'ah compliance review. This should be in the form of a Sharī'ah audit to periodically determine the level of compliance of the IIFS' activities with the Sharī'ah.

Fiduciary risk can be more destructive, considering the relationship of an IIFS with its fund providers. The interest of the fund providers must be protected at all times in all business policies and investments. The fiduciary responsibilities of the IIFS towards the fund providers must be reflected in the due diligence it applies in the management of the investment funds.

**LEARNING OBJECTIVE 10.3**

Examine the risk management techniques in Islamic banks and how they can be avoided, absorbed, or transferred.

# Risk Management Mechanisms in Islamic Banks

The risk management mechanisms or systems for Islamic banks and financial institutions are meant to mitigate, transfer, avoid, or absorb the risk in a particular business undertaking. Hence, the terms risk mitigation, risk transfer, risk avoidance/

**risk-adjusted return on capital (RAROC)**
An adjustment to the return of an investment, which accounts for the element of risk. This gives decision-makers the ability to compare the returns from different projects with varying risk levels.

**gap analysis**
An accounting term that means a technique for determining the steps to be taken in moving from a current state to a desired future state.

**risk avoidance**
A technique of risk management which involves pre-emptive steps to remove moral hazards or risk-prone activities through alternative activities.

elimination, and risk absorption/management. There are two general mechanisms for risk identification and management for Islamic banks and financial institutions. The first mechanism is based on certain standard techniques that are consistent with the Sharī'ah. These include techniques such as risk reporting, internal and external audits, **risk-adjusted return on capital (RAROC)**, and internal rating. One important technique, known as **gap analysis**, determines the steps to be taken in moving from a current state to a desired future state. This tool helps companies compare actual performance with potential performance. It is also called need-gap analysis, needs analysis, and needs assessment.

The second mechanism comprises techniques that require adaptation and further development to suit the requirements of Sharī'ah compliance. The discussion here focuses on the risk management techniques available for Islamic banks and financial institutions. Figure 10.3 gives a graphic example of how the key risks in *musharakah mutanaqisah* (diminishing partnership contract) are effectively managed.

## Risk Avoidance

**Risk avoidance** is also known as risk elimination. It is a technique of risk management that involves pre-emptive steps to remove moral hazards or risk-prone activities through alternative activities. In financial businesses, it is most appropriate to set up strategic frameworks for risk avoidance. This is the best technique for risk mitigation. Most contractual terms in Islamic commercial transactions were legislated to avoid instances of risks. Therefore, measures that promote risk avoidance start from the contractual stage. All business-related documents must be standardized in line with the requirements of the Sharī'ah and endorsed by the Sharī'ah board of an Islamic bank. All processes, procedures, and services rendered by the financial institution should also be subject to the same approval to ensure that no stone is left unturned in the process of standardizing the activities of the corporate entity. There are also some risks the bank can reduce or totally eliminate through transfer or sale.

Risk avoidance or elimination techniques in Islamic banks include contractual risk mitigation, where appropriate documentation of products and proper construction of contractual terms are made. All elements of uncertainty (*gharar*) and undue enrichment through interest (*riba*) are excluded from the contract. When the counterparties bear these in mind and prepare proper documentation in compliance with the Islamic modes of finance, potential risks are avoided or totally eliminated at the contract stage. A typical example of a risk control technique in an Islamic mode of finance contract is the case of *istisna'* (manufacturing contract). The enforceability of qualitative specifications stipulated by a party is always a problem. Muslim jurists have allowed the counterparties to stipulate in the underlying contract that in the event of any default in fulfilling the qualitative specifications, a penalty fee (*band al-jaza'a*) will be imposed. This penalty fee is meant to eliminate the risk associated with non-fulfillment of the qualitative specifications in the *istisna'* contract and enhances the contract's credit quality.

## FIGURE 10.3 — MANAGEMENT OF KEY RISKS IN A DIMINISHING *MUSHARAKAH* CONTRACT

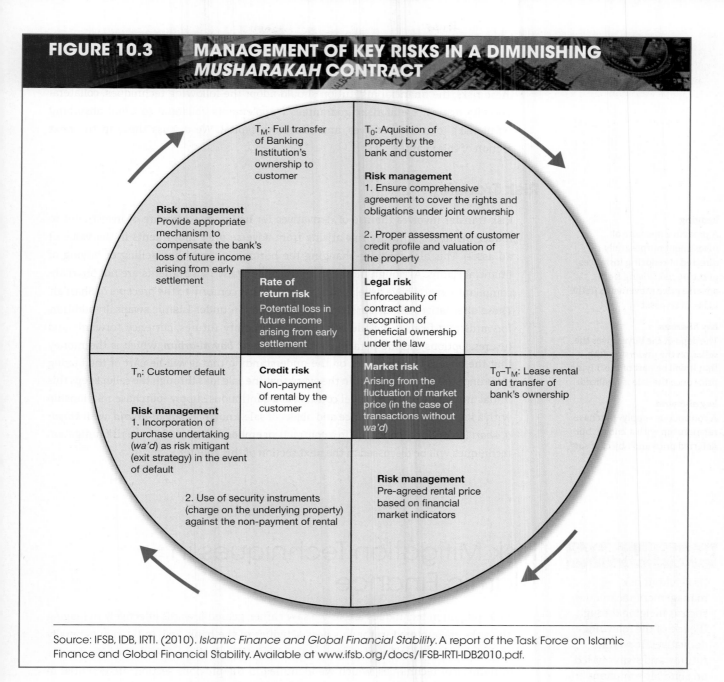

$T_M$: Full transfer of Banking Institution's ownership to customer

**Risk management**
Provide appropriate mechanism to compensate the bank's loss of future income arising from early settlement

$T_0$: Aquisition of property by the bank and customer

**Risk management**
1. Ensure comprehensive agreement to cover the rights and obligations under joint ownership

2. Proper assessment of customer credit profile and valuation of the property

**Rate of return risk**
Potential loss in future income arising from early settlement

**Legal risk**
Enforceability of contract and recognition of beneficial ownership under the law

$T_n$: Customer default

**Risk management**
1. Incorporation of purchase undertaking (*wa'd*) as risk mitigant (exit strategy) in the event of default

2. Use of security instruments (charge on the underlying property) against the non-payment of rental

**Credit risk**
Non-payment of rental by the customer

**Market risk**
Arising from the fluctuation of market price (in the case of transactions without *wa'd*)

$T_0$–$T_M$: Lease rental and transfer of bank's ownership

**Risk management**
Pre-agreed rental price based on financial market indicators

Source: IFSB, IDB, IRTI. (2010). *Islamic Finance and Global Financial Stability*. A report of the Task Force on Islamic Finance and Global Financial Stability. Available at www.ifsb.org/docs/IFSB-IRTI-IDB2010.pdf.

## Risk Absorption

**risk absorption**
Risks that can neither be eliminated nor transferred but can be absorbed and effectively managed by the financial institution due to their centrality in its business operations.

There are some risks that cannot be eliminated or transferred. Instead they must be absorbed or effectively managed by the financial institution. This is known as **risk absorption**. Some risks are so complex that they cannot be easily separated from the assets of the bank and its investors. The financial institutions must accept such risks because they are central to their business. Remember the legal maxim on profit and risk given earlier in this chapter: entitlement to return is related to the liability of risk.

Relating this maxim to risk absorption, the financial institution must decide from inception to bear some risks while hoping to maximize profits. Credit risk and market risk are the most prominent in this regard. In order to effectively absorb or manage these risks, the financial institution should adopt the following techniques: collateral (security against credit risk), guarantees (supplements collateral to avoid absorbing credit risk), loan loss reserves, and allocating capital. We discuss these in the next section of this chapter.

### Risk Transfer

**hedging**
A proactive measure of investment purposefully directed at reducing instances of future risk arising from adverse price movements in the value of an asset.

**bay al-arbun**
The deposit the buyer gives the seller, on the understanding that it will be part of the buying price once the sale is finalized.

**bay al-tawrid**
A continuous supply–purchase relationship with a known but deferred price and object of sale.

Risk transfer involves the use of derivatives for **hedging** (a measure of investment to reduce instances of future risk arising from adverse price movements in the value of an asset). This also includes changing the borrowing terms and selling or buying of financial claims. Although most conventional derivative instruments are not Sharī'ah-compliant, experts have developed alternatives that conform to the precepts of Sharī'ah. These alternatives are discussed in the next section under Islamic swaps. In addition, forwards and futures include *salam* and commodity futures, currency forwards and futures. Options include parallel contracts, such as **bay al-arbun**, which is the money that the buyer gives the seller on the understanding that it will be part of the buying price once the sale is finalized. In the event that the sale falls through the seller keeps this initial amount. Another parallel contract is a continuous supply–purchase relationship with a known but deferred price and object of sale, known as **bay al-tawrid**, with *khiyar al-shart* (an optional condition in a contract), or embedded options. These risk mitigation techniques will be discussed in the next section of this chapter.

### LEARNING OBJECTIVE 10.4

Understand risk management techniques such as hedging through the use of the following derivatives: forwards, futures, and swaps based on Sharī'ah-compliant risk mitigation frameworks.

## Risk Mitigation Techniques in Islamic Finance

Risk mitigation techniques are, as we saw earlier, geared towards effectively managing the risks encountered in the business activities of the bank. Risk mitigation generally includes risk absorption/management, risk transfer, and risk avoidance/elimination. A number of techniques, which we identified in the previous section, are essential in the risk mitigation strategy of Islamic banks. However, in this section, let us focus on risk mitigation techniques through hedging. Risks may be hedged through the use of the following derivatives, forwards, futures, and swaps, subject to the restrictions of the Sharī'ah. A brief overview of each of these techniques with relevant examples will give you an insight into how you can effectively mitigate risks in an Islamic bank. But before addressing these techniques, it is important to understand the meaning of some fundamental concepts used in risk mitigation within the framework of conventional banking.

# The Basics: Defining Derivatives

Derivatives are financial instruments or securities whose value or price depends upon or is derived from the value of one or more underlying assets, or from the value of a rate or index of asset value. Derivatives are generally used specifically as an instrument to hedge risks. This is why they are considered to be financial instruments for trading risks. They are also used for speculative purposes within the secondary market (a financial market where previously issued securities such as bonds are bought and sold). The most common types of derivatives are futures contracts, forward contracts, options, and swaps. These derivatives are contracts and can be structured in a way to serve as underlying assets. A good understanding of derivatives is necessary for better comprehension of the Islamic paradigm for risk mitigation using such derivatives that are Sharī'ah-compliant.

## Forwards and Futures

**Forward contracts** are derivatives involving a cash market transaction where the delivery of the underlying asset is deferred to a future date. This is a non-standardized contract between counterparties. The parties agree on the price on the spot but the underlying asset is delivered at a specified future time. The parties agree on the delivery price, which is the forward price at the time of entering into the contract. The parties agree the price at the time of the contract and not at the future date of delivery. This is why a forward contract is generally regarded as a contract where the parties 'lock in' the price when entering into the contract to avoid future fluctuations in the market. In essence, the price is paid before delivery. For example, it is possible for a farmer to enter into a forward contract with a bank where he locks in a price for his grain from the upcoming harvest. Forward contracts can be used as derivative securities to hedge risks, especially those associated with currency or exchange rate risks, as a means of speculation on future fluctuations in the market value.

**Futures contracts** are similar to forward contracts but there are some differences between the two. While forward contracts are non-standardized contracts, futures contracts are defined on standardization. Forward contracts are not exchange-traded, while futures are exchange-traded derivatives. To this end, a futures contract is defined as a standardized contractual agreement between two parties to exchange a specified asset with a known standardized quantity and quality at a price agreed upon by the parties on the spot while delivery is made at a specified future date. The price may be known as the futures price or the strike price. The futures contract is traded on the floor of a futures exchange, which is a centralized financial market where contracting parties can trade standardized futures contracts.

For instance, a farmer who produces wheat in commercial quantity and who supplies a biscuit factory with tonnes of wheat every season intends to secure the selling price of wheat for the next crop season. At the same time, the biscuit company seeks to secure its buying price of wheat for the next financial year to determine the exact quantity of biscuits it can produce and the corresponding realizable profits. With these similar

**Challenge**

Why are conventional derivatives considered to be non-Sharī'ah-compliant?

**forward contract**
An informal contractual transaction involving derivatives where the delivery of the underlying asset is deferred to a future date.

**futures contract**
A standardized contractual agreement between two parties to exchange a specified asset with a known standardized quantity and quality at a price agreed upon by the parties on the spot while delivery is made at a specified future date.

Farmers can enter into a forward contract with a bank where the price for grain is fixed for the season prior to harvest.

objectives, the wheat farmer and the biscuit company may decide to enter into a futures contract providing that in the next six months, 100 tonnes of wheat will be delivered to the biscuit company at a price of US$3,500 per tonne. This futures contract secures the price of wheat regardless of market fluctuations. This futures contract between the two parties can be bought or sold in the futures market. That is, it is the contract instrument that can be sold or bought and not the wheat. By entering into the futures contract, the parties have hedged or prevented future market risks. Remember, just like forward contracts, futures are used primarily by buyers and sellers in the futures market to hedge risk or speculate. A futures contract is more about hedging risks than exchanging physical commodities. This is why there are standardized contracts that may be traded on the floor of the futures exchange.

## Options

**option**
A financial derivative sold by the option writer to an option holder where there is the opportunity to buy or sell a security at an agreed price within a specified period of time.

**call (call option)**
A financial contract between a buyer and the seller where the former is given the right but not the obligation to buy an agreed quantity of an underlying commodity or financial instrument from the seller of the option at a particular time and at a fixed price.

An **option** is a financial derivative sold by the option writer to an option holder. That is, it is a contract whereby the buyer is given a right to buy (call) or sell (put) a security at an agreed price within a specified period of time. The buyer is only given the right and not an obligation, nor does the right constitute an obligation.

A **call** or **call option** is a financial contract between a buyer and the seller where the former is given the right but not the obligation to buy an agreed quantity of an underlying commodity or financial instrument from the seller of the option at a particular time and at a fixed price. The option remains with the buyer. Once they decide to buy the underlying asset through the exercise of the right, the seller is obligated to sell it at the agreed price and within the specified period of time. However, for the buyer to be able to exercise their right, they must pay a fee called a premium. For example, if an individual has a call option that gives them the right to purchase the stock of ABC Company at a price of US$80 in four months' time, they pay the premium of US$10 for the call to secure the price. If, per chance, the price of the stock increases to US$100 on the maturity date, the buyer has therefore recorded a net gain of US$10 on the investment of the initial US$10. The net gain realized by the buyer is a loss on the part of the seller. The risk of the buyer is only limited to the premium paid (in this example, US$10). In this case, the buyer would want the stock to go up so that they can benefit from the price rise.

A **put** or **put option** is a financial contract between a buyer and the seller where the holder has the right to sell, but not an obligation, at a specified period of time and at a certain price. In this case, the buyer would want the stock to go down so that they can exercise the right. In relation to risk mitigation, put can be used to limit the risk of the seller's (writer's) portfolio. For example, the shares of ABC Company are trading at US$80 at present. The price at which the put option can be exercised (the strike price) is US$5. Stephen expects the shares of ABC Company to depreciate so he bought a contract of put options of 100 shares from a seller. The premium Stephen paid is US$500 (a strike price of US$5 x 100 shares). During the expiration of the put options, the shares of ABC Company fell to US$70. Therefore, Stephen made US$1,000 ([US$80 – US$70] x 100). The total net profit made by Stephen in the put transaction is US$500 (US$1,000 – US$500), so his risk is only limited to the premium he paid.

## Swaps

The term swap is derived from its lexical meaning, i.e. to exchange certain items. In business terms, a **swap** can be defined as the exchange of one security for another for the mutual benefit of the parties. The counterparties exchange each other's financial instrument in order to enjoy the benefits of the other. This is a derivative where the parties *swap* the financial instruments. The benefits in question depend on the type of financial instruments swapped by the parties. In a case involving two firms seeking to engage in swaps involving two bonds, they may agree on the periodic interest payments on those bonds as the benefits being exchanged. The parties may swap currency, interest rates, bonds, etc. Firms may engage in swaps to change the quality of issues, either as bonds or stocks. They also engage in swaps because of a sudden change in their investment objectives. This affords them the opportunity to benefit from each other's vantage point. This may be in form of cash flow, where each of the parties exchanges their individual cash flow streams for the other in order to mutually benefit from the exchange. The cash flow streams are otherwise called the legs of swap. When they exchange the legs of swap, the swap contract is concluded and they both stand to mutually benefit from each other's stream of cash flows.

When counterparties enter into a swap agreement, the agreement must clearly stipulate the way the cash flows are calculated and the dates they will be paid. The different types of swaps include interest rate swaps, currency swaps, commodity swaps, equity swaps,

**put (put option)**
A financial contract between a buyer and the seller where the buyer has the right to sell, but not an obligation, at a specified period of time and at a certain price.

**swap**
A derivative contract where two parties exchange one financial instrument for another for the mutual benefit of the parties.

and credit default swaps. When pricing a swap, the 'fair fixed rate' is used. This means the calculation of a fixed rate whereby the parties are indifferent whether the fixed rate is fixed over time or fluctuates over time. In order to realize this, the value of the swap is set at zero at inception. The value of the two expected cash flow streams must be equal to each other to achieve this. Swaps are used to hedge certain risks. This includes interest rate risk where the counterparties agree to exchange interest payments based on a certain notional amount.

For example, ABC Bank and DEF Bank conclude a contract for an interest rate swap for one year based on a nominal value of US$100 million. In exchange for a rate of **LIBOR** (London interbank offered rate) plus 2 percent, ABC Bank offers DEF a fixed annual rate of 5 percent. While the interest rate of ABC Bank is fixed, that of DEF Bank is floating and both parties intend to swap their respective interest rates. Meanwhile, it is assumed that both parties have speculated the rate at which LIBOR will be trading at maturity to be 4 percent. If, per chance, the LIBOR rate is trading at 5 percent by the end of the year, DEF Bank is expected to pay 7 percent (5% + 2% of US$100 million) to ABC Bank, which is US$7 million. On the other hand, ABC Bank will pay 5 percent of US$100 million, which is US$5 million to DEF Bank. You will notice a difference of US$2 million, which is considered as the value of the swap transaction. Both parties initially speculated on the rate of LIBOR. As the LIBOR rate was higher than initially contemplated by the parties, ABC Bank has gained US$2 million while DEF Bank lost US$2 million. In this case, DEF Bank only needs to pay the difference (US$2 million) to ABC Bank, and rather than both banks paying the full amounts of US$5 million and US$7 million respectively.

## Hedging

The concept of hedging in business investments is meant to reduce exposure to various risks within the market environment. In simple terms, hedging may be likened to insurance where a person protects themselves or their property from unexpected death or destruction to the property as the case may be. In order to reduce the impact of such a loss, they purchase an insurance policy. The same thing applies to the financial investments. Portfolio managers, investors, and corporations use hedging to reduce the potential effects of business risks on them. To this end, hedging can be defined as a proactive measure of investment purposefully directed at reducing instances of future risk arising from adverse price movements in the value of an asset. In the literal sense, this is like insuring oneself against loss. The concept is best understood through this comparison with the notion of insurance.

### Approaches to Hedging

There are three approaches to hedging:

- economic hedging
- cooperative hedging
- contractual hedging.

Economic hedging involves a strategic arrangement by the decision-makers in a corporate entity to achieve the aim of hedging. This does not involve dealing with third

**LIBOR**
(London interbank offered rate) The basic interest rate used in interbank lending, which is common among the banks on the London market.

parties or agents to achieve their purpose. It basically involves the diversification of the investment of the corporate entity. This is a very important investment strategy, which can be independent of or complementary to other hedging strategies.

Cooperative hedging involves a strategic partnership among market players to overcome economic problems. This requires social interaction among the market players through a partnership in investment activities. Economic problems are better solved through cooperation and partnership rather than using for-profit business. Cooperative hedging is similar to cooperative insurance, which involves risk-sharing and proper management of the risk.

Contractual hedging involves contractual financial instruments, which are, in most cases, for-profit instruments. The same financial instruments can be modified to accommodate finance, risk management, and ownership together.

## How to Hedge

Investors make use of complicated financial instruments otherwise known as derivatives in order to hedge. In hedging, two prominent derivatives are used—options and futures. These investment strategies allow the investor to offset a loss in one investment through a gain in a derivative. This makes it a risk mitigation technique for investors, particularly those who have invested in the secondary market. Here is a simple example:

Jane owns shares in Immaculate Computer Corporation. In order to protect her investment from likely short-term losses in the industry, Jane may buy a derivative on the company in the form of a put option at a specified price (the strike price). This gives her the right to sell her shares in the corporation at a specific price. If Jane's stock price dips below the strike price, she can offset the losses by gains in the put option. The strategy adopted by Jane to mitigate future risk is known as married put.

## The Islamic Perspective on Hedging

Hedging can be modified to suit the requirements of the Sharī'ah. When the speculative and gambling elements are removed from the process of hedging in conventional practice, it may be adopted within the Sharī'ah framework of investments. The majority of Islamic finance experts have agreed that hedging is allowed in order to reduce risk and protect investments provided the fundamental prohibitions in Islamic commercial transactions are excluded. This is applicable if the sole purpose of hedging is to protect against loss of value as a result of various factors such as currency fluctuation, etc. in the transaction involving an underlying real asset. Market speculators are not allowed to deliberately expose themselves to risk in order to gain profit from currency fluctuations. That is tantamount to gambling because speculations that involve any type of derivative have elements of *gharar* (uncertainty) and *maysir* (gambling), which invalidate them totally from the Sharī'ah perspective. Any futures, forwards, swaps, or options contracts involving market speculation are not Sharī'ah-compliant.

It should be borne in mind that in conventional hedging, speculation in derivatives is often carried out to maximize profit rather than to facilitate business activity. This is why it is not common to see the actual delivery of the underlying asset in the contract. The speculative elements gradually creep in, which are prohibited in the Sharī'ah.

## Forwards, Futures, Options, Swaps and Other Derivatives from the Islamic Perspective

As the concept of hedging involves the use of the different types of derivatives to reduce potential risks, this section examines the Islamic perspectives on the main derivatives we discussed earlier.

### Islamic Promissory Forward Contract

**Islamic promissory forward contract (IPFC)**

A tool for risk management where binding promise (*wa'ad*) in Islamic law is used in structuring forward contracts for the purpose of hedging risks.

An **Islamic promissory forward contract** (**IPFC**) is also used as a tool for risk management in Islamic financial transactions where a binding promise (*wa'ad*) in Islamic law is used in structuring forward contracts for the purpose of hedging risks. IPFC is structured in a manner that reflects the concept of *wa'ad* (promise) in forward contracts. The concept of *wa'ad* plays an important role in the evolution of derivatives in Islamic finance. Its binding nature has been extended from *murabahah* transactions to other Islamic finance structures. AAOIFI allows the extension of the enforceability of *wa'ad* in currency exchange transactions within the Islamic framework. As demonstrated in the *Islamic Finance in the News* box, Sharī'ah scholars have adapted the dynamics of conventional derivatives in Sharī'ah-compatible terms through the use of relevant Islamic finance instruments.

When the Islamic forward contracts such as *salam* or *murabahah* are backed with a promise, an IPFC is established. This is used for hedging risks associated with contracts such as commodity *murabahah*. It is important to emphasize that conventional futures in which payment and delivery of goods are postponed are not allowed under the Sharī'ah due to the presence of elements of *gharar* and *riba*.

### Islamic Swap

**Islamic swap**

A derivative contract where two parties exchange one financial instrument for another backed with an underlying asset and excluding all prohibitive elements under the Sharī'ah for the mutual benefit of the parties.

Islamic swaps are different from the conventional swaps. An **Islamic swap** is a derivative contract where two parties exchange one financial instrument for another backed with an underlying asset and excluding all prohibitive elements under the Sharī'ah for the mutual benefit of the parties. Apart from the exclusionary rules on all prohibited elements such as *riba*, *gharar*, and *jahl* (ignorance), the Islamic swaps are linked to asset-backed transactions such as *ijarah*, *murabahah*, *bay' bithaman ajil*, etc. The three main instruments of a Islamic swap have been structured in a manner that complies with the precepts of the Sharī'ah. They are FX swap, cross currency swap, and profit rate swap.

### Islamic Foreign Exchange Swap (Islamic FX Swap)

**Islamic FX swap**

A contract that has been designed as an Islamic hedging mechanism to minimize the exposure of market participants to the volatile and fluctuating market currency exchange rate.

An **Islamic FX swap** is a contract that has been designed as an Islamic hedging mechanism to minimize the exposure of market participants to the volatile and fluctuating market currency exchange rate. The Islamic FX swap functions like its conventional counterpart but there is a great deal of effort to maintain absolute Sharī'ah compliance in the contract. The FX swap generally involves the exchange and re-exchange of foreign currency.

# ISLAMIC FINANCE IN THE NEWS

## Islamic finance embraces derivatives

**May 4, 2010**

Few took notice outside certain coteries of specialist bankers and lawyers, but the launch of a 42-page master documentation for derivatives that comply with Muslim religious principles could have a far-reaching impact on the Islamic finance industry.

The International Islamic Financial Market (IIFM), a Bahrain-based Islamic capital markets body, and the International Swaps and Derivatives Association (ISDA) have for the past four years been working on standardized documentation for derivative instruments that comply with Sharī'ah, or Islamic law.

On March 1 the two industry bodies finally presented their 'Tahawwut Master Agreement' and are now embarking upon a series of workshops to encourage Islamic banks to adopt its standardized documentation.

If widely adopted, the new standards could encourage more Islamic banks to hedge more of their risk, and thereby help the Islamic finance industry meet its potential, bankers say.

Islamic institutions that operate across country borders—such as Saudi Arabia's Al Rajhi Bank, which also operates in Malaysia—will benefit from easier currency hedging and all could gain from better risk management on credit exposures and interest rate movements.

The Tahawwut documentation has been drafted to closely resemble existing standardized documentation for derivatives used widely in western markets, which was drafted by ISDA in 1992, according to Priya Uberoi, head of Islamic derivatives at Clifford Chance, who worked on the Islamic version for ISDA.

The new Sharī'ah-compliant master agreement should therefore appeal to conventional banks with Islamic arms, such as HSBC, Citigroup, and Standard Chartered. The launch of the Sharī'ah-compliant master agreement is timely. The Islamic finance industry has continued to grow despite the financial crisis—to about US$950bn last year according to Moody's—but its increasing size and maturity means that risk management is becoming more pressing.

While conventional banks can easily hedge themselves

against an array of risks, Islamic banks have often been prevented from doing the same, due to the reluctance of clerics to approve derivatives that could contravene religious bans on interest, gambling, and unnecessary risk.

Many Sharī'ah scholars have moderated their position in recent years. While using Islamic derivatives to 'speculate' or enhance returns is forbidden, Sharī'ah-compliant financial institutions are now allowed to hedge against currency moves, credit exposures, interest rate movements, and even *sukuk* bonds through 'Islamic credit default swaps'.

'Blending Islamic principles with derivatives only started four to five years ago, but a lot is going on now,' says Ms Uberoi. 'The recent turmoil has made many people in Islamic finance realize the value of risk management tools. For the industry to develop further we need these products.'

Islamic investors are already able to mimic the effects of conventional derivatives by using a complex combination of existing Islamic contracts and concepts.

The most common products used are *wa'ad*, a type of unilateral promise, and *murabahah*, comparable to a conventional 'sale and deferred payment' structure. But products such as *arbun* and *bay salam* can also be used. *Arbun* is similar to a conventional option, and *bay salam* resembles forward contracts.

However, the development of such instruments has been piecemeal and fragmented, and each bank often uses its own structures and documentation, hampering their usage by increasing the complexity and cost. The potential for Islamic derivatives is significant, particularly in the Middle East, where Islamic finance is relatively less developed than in Malaysia.

'In theory, the potential market size is several billion dollars per annum of structured investment products and hedging instruments, but we're barely scratching the surface today,' says Harris Irfan, head of Islamic products at Barclays Capital.

**Source:** Robin Wigglesworth, "Islamic finance embraces derivatives", *Financial Times*, May 4, 2010.

There are two stages in the FX swaps. At the beginning, there is the foreign exchange of monetary currencies and, at the expiry date, there is another exchange. This may be differentiated from a FX forward contract, which is only a one-stage contract, i.e. it only requires the initial exchange and that concludes the contract. For instance, suppose that Bank Istithmar, a British bank intends to invest in Saudi Arabia, which results in an initial conversion of £50 million to SAR 307.5 million in accordance with the current spot price. One important step the parties would take at the beginning of the contract is to agree on a future exchange rate, which is the exchange rate fixed by the parties for the second stage of the contract regardless of market volatility or fluctuations in the value of the currency. To this end, at the maturity date, the parties would convert the SAR back to GBP based on the future exchange rate mutually agreed at the initial stage of the contract, and not at the prevailing market rates. This swap is meant to avoid the effects of market volatility with regard to currency fluctuations in the future.

## Islamic cross currency swap

**Islamic cross currency swap (ICSS)**

A bilateral contractual arrangement between two parties to exchange a series of profit and/or principal payments denominated in one currency for another series of profit and/or payments denominated in another currency, based on a notional principal amount, over an agreed period of time.

The **Islamic cross currency swap** (**ICSS**) is a bilateral contractual arrangement between two parties to exchange a series of profit and/or principal payments denominated in one currency for another series of profit and/or payments denominated in another currency, based on a notional principal amount, over an agreed period of time. This allows the Islamic banks to hedge the interest and currency exchange risks of their investments in foreign-denominated assets. Through this arrangement, the parties are able to exchange a series of profit-principled payments in one currency for another denominated in a different currency based on a notional principal amount over an agreed period of time. The underlying asset for these transactions is commodity *murabahah*. A mutually agreed commodity is used as the underlying asset to legitimize the transactions. The ICSS performs many functions, just like conventional cross currency swaps. It serves as a tool for risk management, reduces the cost of raising resources, and helps identify appropriate investment opportunities. Better asset-liability management is also derived from ICSS when properly implemented.

## Islamic profit rate swap

**Islamic profit rate swap (IPRS)**

A bilateral contract to exchange profit rates between a fixed rate party and a floating rate party or vice versa.

**fixed rate party**

A party who intends to swap its fixed rate profits in the profit swap arrangement.

**floating rate party**

A party who intends to swap its floating rate profits in the profit swap arrangement.

The **Islamic profit rate swap** (**IPRS**) is a bilateral contract to exchange profit rates between a fixed rate party and a floating rate party or vice versa. It is implemented through a number of underlying contracts to trade certain assets based on the Islamic modes of contract. IPRS can be defined as a contract to exchange profit rates between a **fixed rate party** and a **floating rate party** or vice versa, implemented through the execution of a series of underlying contracts to trade certain assets under the Sharī'ah principles of *bay'* and *bay' bithaman ajil*. A fixed rate party is a party who intends to swap its fixed rate profits with a floating rate in the profit swap arrangement, while a floating rate party is a party who intends to swap its floating rate profits with a fixed rate in the profit swap arrangement.

Funding rates are matched with the return rates of investment to have a healthy profit rate swap. This provides a risk control mechanism for the Islamic financial institutions, which are also protected from fluctuating borrowing rates through the implementation of IPRS. This is a Sharīʿah-compliant version of the interest rate swap. As Islamic financial institutions cannot deal in transactions involving interest, IPRS serves as an appropriate Sharīʿah-compliant mechanism to reduce risk exposures.

A good example of IPRS in practice is the Commerce International Merchant Bank (CIMB) in Malaysia's Islamic profit rate swap, outlined in the Islamic Finance in Practice box.

## ISLAMIC FINANCE IN PRACTICE

# CIMB Islamic Profit Rate Swap

CIMB Islamic entered into an agreement that allowed it to swap its profit rate obligation from fixed rate to floating rate. In order to legitimize the transaction, the profit rate swapped must be of the same currency. In this case, the currency was the Malaysian ringgit (RM). The transaction was carried out in three distinct but related stages. The transaction must have a tenor or what is generally called the maturity date. While the first two stages of the IPRS transaction involved a swap of fixed profit rate between CIMB and the counterparty, the second stage involved the swap of the floating profit rate, respectively. The third stage involved the repetition of the floating profit rate swap every six months to mitigate risks until the contractual maturity date.

There were three stages in CIMB's IPRS.

## Stage 1: Fixed Profit Rate

1. CIMB sells asset to Islamic swap counterparty at the notional principal of RM500,000.

2. Islamic swap counterparty sells asset to CIMB at the notional principal of RM500,000 + profit based on fixed profit rate.

3. The notional principal amount of RM500,000 owed by both CIMB and Islamic swap counterparty to each other is offset.

4. The net difference, i.e. the fixed profit rate in Step 2, is paid to Islamic swap counterparty by CIMB at the agreed interval payment date of six months.

## Stage 2: Floating Profit Rate

1. CIMB sells asset to Islamic swap counterparty at the notional principal of RM500,000 + floating profit rate.

2. Islamic swap counterparty sells asset to CIMB at the notional principal of RM500,000.

3. The notional principal amount of RM500,000 owed by both CIMB and Islamic swap counterparty to each other is offset.

4. The net difference, i.e. the floating rate profit in Step 1, is paid to CIMB by the Islamic swap counterparty at the agreed interval payment date of six months.

## Stage 3: Determination of Subsequent Floating Rate

The floating profit rate (Stage 2) is repeated every six months until maturity.

Source: Badlisyah Abdul Ghani. (24 June 2004). Islamic Profit Rate Swap—its Mechanics and Objectives. Seminar on Derivatives in Islamic Finance. Kuala Lumpur, Malaysia.

A good example of IPRS in practice is the CIMB Islamic Profit Rate Swap, which gave it the opportunity to swap its profit rate obligation from fixed rate to floating rate.

## Islamic Options

**Islamic option**

A contract of promise to buy or sell an asset at a predetermined price within a stipulated period of time with the condition that such options cannot be traded in the financial market.

**Islamic option** is a contract of promise to buy or sell an asset at a predetermined price within a stipulated period of time. Within the framework of Islamic finance, these promises cannot be traded and no premium should be charged for such options. In Islamic jurisprudence, there is a reference to options in commercial transactions under the doctrine of contractual stipulations (*al-khiyarat*). Reference to options is also found in *bay al-arbun*, which is a transaction in which a buyer pays a deposit to secure the underlying asset as well as the price at the time of concluding the contract. This is a kind of risk management technique where the buyer tries to avoid or eliminates future market volatility. However, it should be borne in mind that *bay al-arbun* is only permitted by the Hanbali jurists (one of the four major schools of Islamic jurisprudence). The three other doctrines do not allow it as they consider it a void contract. This influenced the ruling of the OIC International Islamic Fiqh Academy in 1992 when it held: "Option contracts as currently applied in the world financial markets are a new type of contract which do not come under any of Sharīʻah denominated contracts. Since the subject of the contract is neither a sum of money nor a utility nor a financial right, which may be waived, the contract is not permissible in Sharīʻah."[9] Therefore, Muslim scholars are not unanimous with regards to the validity of options as a derivative for the purpose of hedging within the Islamic financial market. As trading in options is prohibited by the resolution of the OIC Fiqh Academy, it therefore has a limited scope of utility in Islamic banks as a risk management technique.

# Review

## Key Terms and Concepts

aleatory transactions (p. 369)

*bay al-tawrid* (p. 390)

*bay al-arbun* (p. 390)

call (call option) (p. 392)

counterparty (p. 374)

credit exposure (p. 374)

credit risk (p. 374)

equity investment (p. 377)

equity investment risk (p. 377)

fixed rate party (p. 398)

floating rate party (p. 398)

foreign exchange contract (p. 380)

forward contract (p. 391)

futures contract (p. 391)

gap analysis (p. 388)

hedging (p. 390)

*ijarah* contract (p. 380)

*ijarah muntahia bittamlik* (p. 380)

investment account holders (IAH) (p. 378)

Islamic cross currency swap (ICSS) (p. 398)

Islamic FX swap (p. 396)

Islamic option (p. 400)

Islamic profit rate swap (IPRS) (p. 398)

Islamic promissory forward contract (IPFC) (p. 396)

Islamic swap (p. 396)

LIBOR (p. 394)

liquidity risk (p. 381)

market risk (p. 379)

operational risk (p. 386)

option (p. 392)

put (put option) (p. 393)

rate of return risk (p. 384)

restricted investment accounts (p. 379)

risk absorption (p. 389)

risk-adjusted return on capital (RAROC) (p. 388)

risk avoidance (p. 388)

risk management (p. 369)

*sadd al-dhari'ah* (p. 370)

*salam* contract (p. 380)

swap (p. 393)

*wadi'ah yad damanah* (p. 371)

## Summary

**Learning Objective 10.1**

1. The concept of risk management in Islamic finance is different from the conventional practice of risk management. The unique characteristics of the Islamic framework include the prohibition of *gharar* (uncertainties) and speculation, *riba* (interest) and *jahl* (ignorance) in risk mitigation techniques. Once these elements have been successfully isolated from the conventional risk management framework, it becomes Sharī'ah-compliant and has the potential to be replicated in the Islamic finance industry.

**Learning Objective 10.2**

2. The basis of the IFSB guiding principles on risk management is to standardize the Sharī'ah risk mitigation techniques while considering adaptable guidelines of the Basel Committee on Banking Supervision (BCBS). The IFSB guiding principles provide the Sharī'ah mitigation techniques to cater for the specificities of the Islamic finance industry.

**Learning Objective 10.3**

3. The most common risks in the Islamic banking industry as identified by IFSB-1 include credit risk, equity investment risk, market risk, liquidity risk, rate of return risk, and operational risk. These risks have specific features in the Islamic finance industry given its unique nature. They can be measured and controlled through Sharī'ah-compliant risk mitigation techniques.

4.  Risk transferring techniques such as hedging through the use of derivatives have been adapted to suit the fundamental requirements of the Islamic finance industry. Forwards, futures, and swaps that are based on Islamic modes of financing are now considered as Sharī'ah-compliant and can be used as tools for risk mitigation in the Islamic finance industry.

## Practice Questions and Activities

## Practice Questions

1.  Define risk and risk management. How are the two concepts related?

2.  How can you distinguish between the main features of risk management in Islamic finance from the conventional practice of risk management?

3.  What is the relevance of the IFSB guiding principles on risk management for Islamic financial institutions?

4.  Are the guidelines of the Basel Committee on Banking Supervision on risk management unsuitable for Islamic financial institutions?

5.  Explain the six major risks faced by Islamic banks and financial institutions.

6.  What are the appropriate risk mitigation strategies for the six major risks faced by Islamic banks and financial institutions?

7.  Explain the risk transferring techniques in the Islamic finance industry with special reference to the use of derivatives as a tool for hedging risks?

8.  What do you understand as the Islamic profit rate swap (IPRS)?

## Activities

1.  Prepare a 10-minute presentation on the Islamic framework of risk management and its relevance to the 2007–2009 global financial crisis.

2.  Prepare a short summary for presentation on the six major risks faced by Islamic financial institutions as given in the IFSB *Guiding Principles of Risk Management for Institutions (Other than Insurance Institutions) Offering Only Islamic Financial Services*.

3.  Identify an Islamic financial institution within your city and explain its framework for risk management.

# Further Reading

Ahmed, H. and Khan, T. (2007). Risk Management in Islamic Banking. In M. Kabir Hassan and Mervyn K. Lewis. *Handbook of Islamic Banking* (pp. 144–158). Cheltenham, United Kingdom: Edward Elgar Publishing Limited.

Al-Amine, M. A. (2008). *Risk Management in Islamic Finance: An analysis of derivatives instruments in commodity markets* (Brill's Arab and Islamic Laws series). Leiden & Boston: Brill Academic Publishers.

Al-Suwailem, S. (2006). *Hedging in Islamic Finance.* Occasional Paper No. 10. Jeddah: Islamic Development Bank.

Greuning, H. V. and Iqbal, Z. (2008). *Risk Analysis for Islamic Banks.* Washington, DC.: The International Bank for Reconstruction and Development/The World Bank.

IFSB. (2005). *Guiding Principles of Risk Management for Institutions (Other than Insurance Institutions) Offering only Islamic Financial Services.* Kuala Lumpur: IFSB.

IFSB, IDB, IRTI. (2010). *Islamic Finance and Global Financial Stability.* A report of the Task Force on Islamic Finance and Global Financial Stability. Available at www.ifsb.org/docs/IFSB-IRTI-IDB2010.pdf.

Khan, T. and Ahmed, H. (2001). *Risk Management: An Analysis of Issues in the Islamic Financial Industry.* Occasional Paper No. 5. Jeddah: IRTI-IDB.

Mahlknecht, M. (2009). *Islamic Capital Markets and Risk Management Global Market Trends and Issues.* London: Risk Books.

Obaidullah, M. (2002). Islamic Risk Management: Towards Greater Ethics and Efficiency. *International Journal of Islamic Financial Services.* Vol. 3, no. 4: 1–18.

Vogel, F. and Hayes, S. (1998). *Islamic Law and Finance: Religion, Risk, and Return.* Netherlands: Kluwer Law International.

# Endnotes

## Chapter 1

1. Related by Al-Bukhari. See Muhammad Muhsin Khan. (1997). *The Translation of the Meanings of Sahih Al-Bukhari* (Arabic–English). Riyadh: Darussalam. Vol. 3, p. 216 (book 34, chapter 78, hadith no. 2177).

2. Related by Muslim. See Imam Abu Al-Husain Muslim bin Al-Hajjaj. (1998). In Ahmad Shams al-Din (ed.). *Sahih Al-Muslim*. Beirut: Dar al-Kutub al-'Ilmiyyah. Vol. 3, p. 51 (book 22, chapter 15, hadith no. 1584).

3. Related by Al-Bukhari and Muslim. See Muhammad Muhsin Khan. (1997). *The Translation of the Meanings of Sahih Al-Bukhari* (Arabic–English). Riyadh: Darussalam. Vol. 3, p. 54 (book 22, chapter 18, hadith no. 1594).

4. Ibn Hisham. *Al-Sirah al-Nabawiyah*, Beirut: Dar al-Ma'rifah, n.d. Vol. 2, p. 603.

5. Islamic Development Bank and Islamic Fiqh Academy. (2000). *Resolutions and Recommendations of the Council of the Islamic Fiqh Academy (1985–2000)*. Jeddah: IRTI-Islamic Development Bank: pp. 15–16.

6. This hadith was related by Ibn Majah. See Muhammad bin Yazid Al-Qazwini. (1998). In Hasan, M. M. M. (ed.). *Sunan Ibn Majah*. Beirut: Dar al-Kutub al-Ilmiyyah. Vol. 3, pp. 163–164.

7. The hadith was related by Al-Bukhari. See Muhammad Muhsin Khan. (1997). *The Translation of the Meanings of Sahih Al-Bukhari* (Arabic–English). Riyadh: Darussalam. Vol. 3, p. 167 (book 34, chapter 14, hadith nos 2068 and 2069).

8. This hadith was related by Al-Bukhari and Muslim. Ibid. Vol. 3, p. 244 (book 35, chapter 1, hadith no. 2239). See also Imam Abu Al-Husain Muslim bin Al-Hajjaj. (1998). In Ahmad Shams al-Din (ed.). *Sahih Al-Muslim*. Beirut: Dar al-Kutub al-'Ilmiyyah. Vol. 3, pp. 62–63 (book 22, chapter 25, hadith no. 1604).

9. The hadith was related by both Al-Bukhari and Muslim in their respective collections. For instance, see Muhammad Muhsin Khan. (1997). *The Translation of the Meanings of Sahih Al-Bukhari* (Arabic–English). Riyadh: Darussalam. Vol. 3, pp. 224–225 (book 34, chapter 89, hadith nos. 2201 and 2202).

10. The hadith was related by both Al-Bukhari and Muslim in their respective collections. See Imam Abu Al-Husain Muslim bin Al-Hajjaj. (1998). In Ahmad Shams al-Din (ed.). *Sahih Al-Muslim*. Beirut: Dar al-Kutub al-'Ilmiyyah. Vol. 3, p. 51 (book 22, chapter 15, hadith no. 1584).

11. Zakariyau I. Oseni. (2012). *Al-Hajjaj Ibn Yusuf Al-Thaqafi: A Formidable Umayyad Viceroy in Iraq*. Kuala Lumpur: A.A. Noordeen: pp. 116–117.

12. Islamic Development Bank. www.isdb.org/irj/portal/anonymous?NavigationTarget=navurl://24de0d5f10da906da85e96ac356b7af0.

13. Hassan, M. K. and Lewis, M. (2007). *Handbook on Islamic Banking*. United Kingdom: Edward Elgar Publishing: pp. 1–17.

14. Caplen, B. and DiVanna, J., "Top 500 Islamic Financial Institutions", In *The Banker*, November 2011 Supplement, www.thebanker.com/Markets/Islamic-Finance/Top-500-Islamic-Financial-Institutions2.

15. Top 500 Islamic Financial Institutions. In *The Banker*, November 2011 Supplement, p.9

16. Kuwait Finance House Profile. See www.kfh.com/pdf/kfh-profile-en.pdf.

17. David Oakley. The Future of Islamic Finance. In *Financial Times Special Report*, December 14, 2010, pp. 1–2.

## Chapter 2

1. This hadith was narrated by Ahmad and classed as authentic by Al-Albani. See Ahmad bin Muhammad bin Hanbal, *Musnad Al-Imam Ahmad bin Hanbal*. (1998). Beirut: Alam Al-Kutub. 1st edn.

2. This hadith was related by Al-Bukhari. See Muhammad Muhsin Khan. (1997). *The Translation of the Meanings of Sahih Al-Bukhari* (Arabic–English). Riyadh: Darussalam. Vol. 3, p. 168 (book 34, chapter 15, hadith no. 2072).

3. *The Mejelle* Being an English Translation of *Majallah el-Ahkam-l-Adliya* and a Complete Code of Islamic Civil Law, trans. C. R. Tyser, D. G. Demetriades, and Ismail Haqqi Effendi. (2007). Kuala Lumpur: The Other Press: p. 16.

4. Abdurrazzaq Al-Sanhuri. (1997). *Masadir al-Haqq fi al-Fiqh al-Islami*. Cairo: Dar al-Nahdah al-'Arabiyah. Vol. 1, p. 32.

5. *Resolutions and Recommendations of the Council of the Islamic Fiqh Academy (1985–2000)*. (2000). Jeddah: Islamic Fiqh Academy and Islamic Development Bank: p. 86. See Resolution 40–41 (2/5 and 3/5) concerning discharging of promises and *murabahah* for the orderer of a purchase. The Council of Islamic Fiqh Academy issued this resolution at its fifth session in Kuwait, held between December 10 and 15, 1988.

6. *Ibid.,* p. 87.

7. Related by Al-Bukhari. Muhammad Muhsin Khan. (1997). *The Translation of the Meanings of Sahih Al-Bukhari* (Arabic–English). Riyadh: Darussalam. Vol. 3, p. 169 (book 34, chapter 15, hadith no. 2074).

8. Abdul-Aziz Al-Bukhari. (1997). *Kashf al-Asrar 'an Usul Fakhr al-Islam al-Bazdawi*. Beirut: Dar al-Kutub al-'Ilmiyyah: p. 335.

9. Abdurrahman Al-Sabouni. (1978). *Al-Madkhal Li dirasat Al-Fiqh Al-Islami*. (4th. edn). Damascus: Al-Matba'ah Al-Jadidah. Vol. 2, p. 24.

10. Ahmad M. Al-Zarqa'. (1959). *Al-Madkhal Al-Fiqh Al-'Am*. Damascus: Matba'ah Jaamiah Damascus. (6th edn). vol. 2, p. 733.

11. Muhammad Muhsin Khan. (1997). *The Translation of the Meanings of Sahih Al-Bukhari* (Arabic–English). Riyadh: Darussalam. Vol. 3, pp. 170–171 (book 34, chapter 18, hadith no. 2078).

12. Related by Muslim, Tirmidhi and Ahmad. See Imam Abu Al-Husain Muslim bin Al-Hajjaj. (1998). In Ahmad Shams al-Din (ed.). *Sahih Al-Muslim*. Beirut: Dar al-Kutub al-'Ilmiyyah. Vol. 3, p. 57 (book 22, chapter 19, hadith no. 1598).

13. Related by Muslim and Ahmad. See Abu'l Husain Muslim. (1955). *Sahih Muslim*. Cairo: 'Isa al-Babi al-Halabi Co. Vol. 2, p. 889.

14. Related by Al-Bukhari and Muslim. See Muhammad Muhsin Khan. (1997). *The Translation of the Meanings of Sahih Al-Bukhari* (Arabic–English). Riyadh: Darussalam. Vol. 3, p. 216 (book 34, chapter 78, hadith no. 2177).

15. Ibid., p. 54 (book 22, chapter 18, hadith no. 1594).

16. Related by Ahmad and Ibn Majah. See Muhammad bin Yazid al-Qazwini. (1998). *Sunan Ibn Majah*. Beirut: Dar al-Kutub al-Ilmiyyah: pp. 36–37 (book 12, chapter 24, hadith no. 2196).

17. Muhammad Ayub. (2007). *Understanding Islamic Finance.* England: John Wiley & Sons Ltd: p. 60.

18. Ibid., p. 58.

19. Franz Rosenthal. (1975). *Gambling in Islam.* Leiden: Brill Academic Publisher: p. 2.

20. Muhammad Muhsin Khan. (1997). *The Translation of the Meanings of Sahih Al-Bukhari* (Arabic–English). Riyadh: Darussalam. Vol. 6, pp. 324–325 (book 65, chapter 2, hadith no. 4860).

## Chapter 3

1. Mustapha Ahmad Al-Zarqa. (1995). 'Aqd al-Istisna'a wa madaa Ahammiyyatuhu fi al-Istithmaraat al- Islaamiyyaah al-Mu'aasira (Lecture Series of Renowned Scholars No. 12). Islamic Development Bank, Jeddah: p. 21.

2. Related by Muslim. See Imam Abu Al-Husain Muslim bin Al-Hajjaj. (1998). In Ahmad Shams al-Din (ed.). *Sahih Al-Muslim.* Beirut: Dar al-Kutub al-'Ilmiyyah. Vol. 3, p. 51 (book 22, chapter 15, hadith no. 1584).

3. Abdul Aziz Ibn Baaz. (2002). *Majmu'u al-fatawa.* Vol. 19, p. 245.

4. This hadith was related by Ibn Majah. See Ibn Qudamah. 1972.

5. This hadith was narrated by Ibn Abbas and related by al-Bukhari. Vol. 7, no. 663.

6. *The Mejelle* Being an English Transalation of *Majallah el-Ahkam-l-Adliya* and a Complete Code of Islamic Civil Law. Trans. C. R. Tyser, D. G. Demetriades, and Ismail Haqqi Effendi. (2007). Kuala Lumpur: The Other Press: p. 233.

7. Muhammad Taqi Usmani. (1999). *An Introduction to Islamic Finance.* Karachi: Idara Isha'at-e-Diniyat (P) Ltd: p. 17.

8. This hadith is related by Abu Dawud. See Abu Dawud, Sulayman ibn al-Ash'ath al-Sijistani. (1998). *Sunan Abu Dawud*, Jeddah: Dar al-Qiblah li al-Thaqafah al-Islamiyyah.

9. Muhammad Taqi Usmani. (1999). The Concept of Musharakah and Its Application as an Islamic Method of Financing. *Arab Law Quarterly.* Vol. 14 (3), p. 206.

10. *The Mejelle*, ibid., p. 102.

11. The Hanafi school considers this form of transaction as *makruh tahrimi*, which means a practice that is reprehensible to the level of prohibition.

12. Accounting and Auditing Organization for Islamic Financial Institutions. (2010CE/1432 AH). *Sharī'ah Standards for Islamic Financial Institutions*, Bahrain: AAOIFI: p. 100.

13. Ahmad Ali Ibn Hajar al-Asqalani. (1987CE/1407 AH). *Fath al-Bari.* Dar al-Rayyan li-al-Turath. Vol. 4, p. 478.

14. Mustafa Anas al-Zarqa'. (1967). *al-Madkhal al-Fiqhi al-'Am*, Damascus: Dar al-Fikr li al-Tiba'a. Vol. 1, p. 326,

15. Islamic Fiqh Council of the Muslim World League. (2006CE/1427 AH). *Majallat al-Majma' al-Fiqh al-Islami*: (22), p. 189.

16. This hadith was related by Ibn Majah. See Abu Bakr Ahmad bin al-Husayn al-Bayhaqi, *al-Sunan al-Kubra*, Beirut: Dar al-Ma'rifah. Undated, vol. 6, p. 72.

17. Related by Al-Bukhari. Muhammad Muhsin Khan. (1984). *The Translation of the Meaning of Sahih al-Bukhari* (Arabic–English). New Delhi: Kitab Bhavan. Vol. 3, p. 247.

18. Securities Commission Malaysia. (2004). *Guidelines on the Offering of Islamic Securities*, p. A3.

19. Ali Haidar. (1925). *Durar al-Hukkam fi Sharh Majallat Al-Ahkam*. Haifa: Abasid Press. Vol. 1.

20. Related by Tirmidhi. Al-Tirmidhi. (2009). 'Isa Muhammad ibn Sawrat, *Shama'il al-Muhammadiyyah*. Beirut: al-Yamamah lil-Tiba'ah wa al-Nashr wa al-Tawzi'. Hadith no. 1264.

21. Abu Dawud, Sulayman ibn al-Ash'ath al-Sijistani. (1998). *Sunan Abu Dawud*. Jeddah: Dar al-Qiblah li al-Thaqafah al-Islamiyyah. Book 23, hadith no. 3532.

## Chapter 4

1. Sofat, R. and Hiro, P. (2010). *Basic Accounting* (2nd edn). New Delhi: Asoke K. Ghosh: , p. 3.

2. Shahul Hameed. (2003). Islamic Accounting—A Primer. *Akauntan Nasional (Currently Accountants Today)*, Jan–Feb.

3. AAOIFI. (2010). *Accounting, Auditing and Governance Standards for Islamic Financial Institutions*. Bahrain: AAOIFI: p. 13.

4. Ibid., pp. 17–18.

5. These objectives of financial accounting for Islamic banks are adapted from AAOIFI (2010). *Accounting, Auditing and Governance Standards for Islamic Financial Institutions*. Bahrain: AAOIFI: para 19, p. 11.

6. Amended from AAOIFI *Statement of Financial Accounting* No. 2, paragraph 5, Clause 3.

7. AAOIFI (2010). *Accounting, Auditing and Governance Standards for Islamic Financial Institutions*. Bahrain: AAOIFI: paragraph 2 of FAS 1.

8. Ibid., p. 67.

9. Ibid., p. 93.

10. This part of this chapter is fully adapted from AAOIFI FAS 1, paragraph 4/1. See AAOIFI (2010). *Accounting, Auditing and Governance Standards for Islamic Financial Institutions*. Bahrain: AAOIFI.

11. Ibid.

12. AAOIFI. (2010). *Accounting, Auditing and Governance Standards for Islamic Financial Institutions*. Bahrain: AAOIFI, para 58, p. 78–79 and para 60, p. 79.

13. Ibid.

14. Accounting and Auditing Organisation for Islamic Financial Institutions (AAOIFI), *Exposure Draft: Conceptual Framework for Financial Reporting by Islamic Financial Institutions.* Retrieved from www.aaoifi.com/aaoifi%20-%20conceptual%20framework%20for%20 financial%20reporting%20(draft%20for%20public%20hearing).pdf.

## Chapter 5

1. OECD. (2004). *OECD Principles of Corporate Governance (Revised).* Paris: OECD. Available at www.oecd.org/dataoecd/32/18/31557724.pdf, p. 11.

2. Guler Manisali Darman. (2004). *Corporate Governance Worldwide: A Guide to Best Practices and Managers.* Paris: ICC Publishing: p. 9.

3. Committee on the Financial Aspects of Corporate Governance. (1992). Report with Code of Best Practice, [Cadbury Report], London: Gee Publishing: p. 14.

4. IFSB. (2006). *Guiding Principles on Corporate Governance for Institutions Offering Only Islamic Financial Services (Excluding Islamic Insurance (Takaful) Institutions and Islamic Mutual Funds.* Kuala Lumpur: IFSB: p. 27.

5. OECD. (2004). *OECD Principles of Corporate Governance (Revised).* Paris: OECD. Available at: www.oecd.org/dataoecd/32/18/31557724.pdf.

6. IFSB. (2009). *Guiding Principles on Sharī'ah Governance Systems for Institutions Offering Islamic Financial Services.* Kuala Lumpur: IFSB: pp. 2–3.

7. Ibid., p. 23.

8. Section 53(1) of the Central Bank of Malaysia Act 2009 states: "The Yang di-Pertuan Agong may, on the advice of the Minister after consultation with the bank, appoint from amongst persons who are qualified in the Sharī'ah or who have knowledge or experience in the Sharī'ah and in banking, finance, law or such other related disciplines as members of the Sharī'ah Advisory Council."

9. IFSB-10, p. 23.

10. Qur'an 2: 282 states: "O you who have believed, when you contract a debt for a specified term, write it down. And let a scribe write [it] between you in justice. Let no scribe refuse to write as Allah has taught him. So let him write and let the one who has the obligation dictate. And let him fear Allah, his Lord, and not leave anything out of it."

11. IFSB. (2009). *Guiding Principles on Sharī'ah Governance Systems for Institutions Offering Islamic Financial Services,* Kuala Lumpur: IFSB: p. 25.

12. Section 51(1) of the Central Bank of Malaysia Act 2009 states: "The Bank may establish a Sharī'ah Advisory Council on Islamic Finance which shall be the authority for the ascertainment of Islamic law for the purposes of Islamic financial business."

13. Section 56(1) of the Central Bank of Malaysia Act 2009 states: "Where in any proceedings relating to Islamic financial business before any court or arbitrator any question arises concerning a Sharī'ah matter, the court or the arbitrator, as the case may be, shall:

    (a) take into consideration any published rulings of the Sharī'ah Advisory Council; or

    (b) refer such question to the Sharī'ah Advisory Council for its ruling."

14. Section 55 of the Central Bank of Malaysia Act 2009 states:

    (1) The Bank shall consult the Sharī'ah Advisory Council on any matter:

(a) relating to Islamic financial business; and

(b) for the purpose of carrying out its functions or conducting its business or affairs under this Act or any other written law in accordance with the Sharī'ah, which requires the ascertainment of Islamic law by the Sharī'ah Advisory Council.

(2) Any Islamic financial institution in respect of its Islamic financial business, may:

(a) refer for a ruling; or

(b) seek the advice, of the Sharī'ah Advisory Council on the operations of its business in order to ascertain that it does not involve any element which is inconsistent with the Sharī'ah.

15. For this purpose, Islamic banking and *takaful* are considered as two distinct industries.

16. Section 58 of the Central Bank of Malaysia Act states: "Where the ruling given by a Sharī'ah body or committee constituted in Malaysia by an Islamic financial institution is different from the ruling given by the Sharī'ah Advisory Council, the ruling of the Sharī'ah Advisory Council shall prevail."

17. See section 316B of the Capital Markets and Services Act 2010 (CMSA).

18. Ibid., section 316E.

19. Ibid., section 316F.

20. Ibid., section 316G.

21. Registration of Sharī'ah Advisers Guidelines (RSAG), paragraphs 1.02 and 3.01, respectively.

22. Ibid., paragraph 4.05.

23. Ibid., paragraph 4.07.

24. CMSA, section 316H (1).

25. *Strategic Plan for Islamic Banking Industry in Pakistan*, p. 6, available at www.sbp.org.pk/departments/pdf/StrategicPlanPDF/Appendix-C%20Shariah%20Compliance.pdf.

26. See Article 93 of CBK Law, Section 10, Chapter 3, Law 32/1968 (as amended).

27. Section 93 states: "Each Islamic bank shall have an independent Sharī'ah Supervisory Board, comprised of not less than three members appointed by the bank's General Assembly. The Memorandum of Agreement and Articles of Association of the bank shall specify the establishment of the Board as well as its formulation, powers, and workings.

In case of a conflict of opinions among members of the Sharī'ah Supervisory Board concerning a Sharī'ah rule, the BoD of the designated bank may transfer the matter to the Fatwa Board in the Ministry of Awqaf and Islamic Affairs, that shall be the final authority on the matter.

The Sharī'ah Supervisory Board shall annually submit to the bank's General Assembly a report comprising its opinion on the bank's operations in terms of their compliance with the Islamic Sharī'ah principles and any comments it may have in this respect. This report shall be included in the bank's Annual Report."

28. See HC-9.2.6. of Central Bank of Bahrain Rulebook, *High-Level Controls*, volume 2, Islamic Banks, October 2010.

29. Ibid., HC-9.2.1. Principle 9.1 of *The Corporate Governance Code of the Kingdom of Bahrain* states: "Companies which are guided by the principles of Islamic Sharī'ah have additional

responsibilities to their stakeholders. Companies which refer to themselves as 'Islamic' will be subject to additional governance requirements and disclosures to provide assurance to stakeholders that they are following Sharī'ah principles. In ensuring compliance with Sharī'ah principles, each company should establish a Sharī'ah Supervisory Board consisting of at least three Sharī'ah scholars."

**30.** Ibid., HC-9.2.6.

**31.** See paragraph 5.1.1. of the ISF.

**32.** This was established in 2005 with the purpose of creating a separate regulatory body for the financial sector.

**33.** Qatar Central Bank, *Instructions to Banks—March 2009* (11th edition). The latest edition of the instructions is the *Instructions to Banks—May 2010* (12th edition) although it focuses on a different subject matter. Despite this, the latest instructions are considered as an integral part of the 11th edition. See www.qcb.gov.qa/English/Legislation/Instructions/Pages/BankInstructions.aspx.

**34.** QFC Regulatory Authority, *Islamic Finance Rule Book (ISFI)*, Version No. 3, 6 December 2009. Two previous editions have been issued.

**35.** Ibid., Chapter 6, paragraph 6.1.1.

**36.** Ibid., Chapter 6, paragraph 6.2.

**37.** IFSB. (2009). *IFSB Guiding Principles on Governance for Takaful (Islamic Insurance) Undertakings*, Kuala Lumpur: IFSB, p. 26.

**38.** IFSB Guidelines on *Takaful*, para 79, p. 1.

**39.** IFSB. (2009). *IFSB Guiding Principles on Governance for Takaful (Islamic Insurance) Undertakings*, Kuala Lumpur: IFSB. www.ifsb.org/standard/ED8Takaful%20 Governance%20Standard.pdf.

**40.** The differences between *takaful* undertakings and the conventional insurers have been identified in the IFSB Guiding Principles:

(i) *Takaful* undertakings are generally structured as 'hybrids' between mutual and proprietary entities; thus, they may face various conflicts of interest that ordinarily would not arise in conventional insurance.

(ii) *Takaful* undertakings must adhere to the core principles of *ta`awun* and *tabarru'* and the prohibition of *riba*.

(iii) An inherent component that adds value and differentiates between *takaful* undertakings and conventional insurers is the sharing of risks among the *takaful* participants, rather than the transfer of risks from the participants to the *takaful* operator. This becomes part of the rationale for the practice of creating a separate account for underwriting activities on behalf of the *takaful* participants, while shareholders of *takaful* operators will not bear any implications in the event of deficit or loss suffered by the *takaful* fund, other than having in place a *qard* facility to enable the participants' risk fund (PRF) to meet its obligations in the event of a deficiency. However, the capital of the *takaful* operators is exposed in extreme cases where the PRF suffers a loss on such a scale that the *qard* once made cannot be recovered from contributions over any reasonable period.

41. IFSB Guidelines on *Takaful*, para 20, p. 8.

42. Ibid., para 28, p. 10.

43. Ibid., para 27, p. 9.

44. Ibid., para 44, p. 12

45. Ibid., para 55, p. 15

46. Ibid., para 49, p. 14.

47. Ibid., para 50, p. 14.

48. Ibid., para 79, p. 21.

49. Ibid., para 81, p. 21.

50. Ibid., para 92, p. 23.

## Chapter 6

1. See Qur'an 12: 54.

2. AAOIFI (2010). *Accounting, Auditing and Governance Standards for Islamic Financial Institutions*. Bahrain: AAOIFI, Standard No. 16.

3. Mohammed Obaidullah. (2005). *Islamic Financial Services*, Jeddah: Scientific Publishing Centre, King Abdul Aziz University: p. 209.

4. Rushdi Siddiqui. (2006). Islamic Investment Opportunities in the OIC: Alternative Investments to Reverse Capital Flight. In Sohail Jaffer (ed.), *Islamic Retail Banking and Finance: Global Challenges and Opportunities* (pp. 98–106). London: Euromoney Books: p. 102.

## Chapter 7

1. AAOIFI. (2008). *Sharī'ah Standards for Islamic Financial Institutions*. Bahrain. AAOIFI, p. 307.

2. IFSB. (2005). *Capital Adequacy Standards for Institutions (Other than Insurance Institutions) Offering Only Islamic Financial Services*. December 2005, p. 47.

3. This hadith is in *Al-Muwatta'*. Book 31, no. 31.19.44.

4. IDB and Islamic Fiqh Academy. (2000). *Resolutions and Recommendations of the Council of the Islamic Fiqh Academy 1985–2000*. Jeddah: Islamic Development Bank.: pp. 61–66.

5. Muhammad Ayub. (2007). *Understanding Islamic Finance*.England: John Wiley & Sons Ltd., pp. 400–401.

6. AAOIFI. (2010). *Sharī'ah Standard For Islamic Financial Institutions*, Bahrain: AAOIFI. Sharī'ah Standard No. 17, pp. 309–310.

7. Ibid., p. 315.

8. Ibid., pp. 315–317.

9. IIRA's Insurance Financial Strength Rating Methodology at www.iirating.com/methodologies/insurance_eng.pdf.

10. Rating Methodology—Commercial Real Estate, at www.iirating.com/methodologies/commercial_real_estate_eng.pdf.

11. Ibid.

## Chapter 8

1. Islamic Financial Services Board. (2009). *Guiding Principles on Governance for Takaful (Islamic Insurance) Undertakings* (IFSB-8). Kuala Lumpur: IFSB.

2. This hadith was related by Al-Tirmidhi. Muhammad Isa Al-Tirmidhi. (2006). *Sunan Al-Tirmidhi (Al-Jaami' Al-Sahih)*, Beirut: Dar al-Kutub al-Ilmiyyah.

3. Takaful Act (Act 312) of 1984, Laws of Malaysia.

4. Ernst & Young. 'Global Takaful market to reach US$25 Bn in 2015: Ernst & Young'. www.ey.com/EM/en/Newsroom/News-releases/MENA-_Global-Takaful-market-to-reach-_US-25-Bn-in-2015--Ernst---Young.

5. Global *takaful* market could touch US$7.7bn in 2012, reports Ernst and Young, ameinfo.com, www.ameinfo.com/192579.html.

6. IFSB (2009). *Guiding Principles on Governance for Takaful (Islamic Insurance) Undertakings*. Kuala Lumpur: IFSB, p. 4.

7. Accounting and Auditing Organization for Islamic Financial Institutions. (2010). *Accounting, Auditing & Governance Standards (for Islamic Financial Institutions)*, Bahrain: AAOIFI, p. 409.

8. Ibid., FAS 13.

9. Ibid., Financial Accounting Standard 13.

10. M. B. Arboun. (2000). The Operation of *Retakaful* (Islamic Reinsurance) Protection. *Arab Law Quarterly*. Vol. 15, No. 4, pp. 335, 350.

## Chapter 9

1. Nimrah Karim, Michael Tarazi, and Xavier Reille. (2008). Islamic Microfinance: An Emerging Market Niche. *Focus Note*. CGAP, No. 49: p. 5.

2. M. Obaidullah. (2008). *Introduction to Islamic Microfinance*, India: IBF Net (P) Limited: pp. 40–41.

3. Abdulkarim Al-Arhabi. Approach of Micro-Credit and Income-Generating Projects Financed by the Social Fund for Development in Yemen. *Economic Development and Poverty Reduction Workshop*, Mediterranean Development Forum, September 3–6, 1998, Marrakech, Morocco: p. 11.

4. Akhuwat website. www.akhuwat.org.pk/objectives.asp.

5. Islami Bank Bangladesh Limited. www.islamibankbd.com/rds/objectives.php.

6. Ibid., www.islamibankbd.com/rds/target_group.php.

## Chapter 10

1. Christine M. Cumming and Beverly J. Hirtle. (2001). The Challenges of Risk Management in Diversified Financial Companies. *Economic Policy Review*. Federal Reserve Bank of New York. Vol. 7, no. 1 (March 2001): p. 3.

2. IFSB. (2005). *Guiding Principles of Risk Management for Institutions (Other than Insurance Institutions) Offering Only Islamic Financial Services*. Kuala Lumpur: IFSB: p. 7.

3. Ibid., p. 12.

4. Ibid., p. 16.

5. Ibid., p. 16.

6. Ibid.. p. 16.

7. Ibid., p. 19.

8. IFSB. (2005). *Capital Adequacy Standard for Institutions for Institutions (Other than Insurance Institutions) Offering Only Islamic Financial Services*. Kuala Lumpu: IFSB. p. 19. This is generally referred to as IFSB-2.

9. Islamic Fiqh Academy of the Organization of Islamic Conference. Seventh session, May 9–14, 1992.

**Accounting and Auditing Organization for Islamic Financial Institutions (AAOIFI)**
The main international standard-setting body for Islamic financial institutions headquartered in Bahrain. Since inception, it has issued more than 81 accounting, auditing, governance, ethics, and Sharī'ah standards.

**account receivable**
Money owed to a company by a customer for products and services provided on credit.

**accrual method**
A method of accounting whereby the records are based on the occurrence of a transaction regardless of the fact whether there is an exchange of cash or not.

**active legal capacity**
The capacity of a person to acquire rights, responsibilities and discharge obligations absolutely with full capacity.

**act of God**
Legal description of an event that is outside human control, usually a destructive type that prevents the performance of a duty under a contract. An example of this is a natural disaster.

**actuary**
A recognized specialist and professional in the evaluation and analysis of risks, insurance and annuity premiums, reserves and dividends.

**al-aqidan**
The two contracting parties in a transaction.

**aleatory transactions**
Transactions conditioned on uncertain events. Literally, these are transactions that depend on chance or throw of a die.

**al-ma'qud alaih**
The subject matter of the contract which is usually the object of sale.

**al-rida**
Mutual consent of the parties in a contract. This is known as 'consensus ad idem' in the conventional contract law.

**American Accounting Association**
A voluntary organization for people interested in accounting education and research, which was founded in 1916.

**Anglo-American model**
Any framework, model or paradigm patterned after the American or English legal, economic or political systems.

**'aqd**
A contractual transaction involving two or more parties.

**'aqd infiradi**
A unilateral contract where a single party, who intends to establish a form of legal relationship with another party, makes a promise which is considered binding to the initiating party alone.

**'aqd thuna'i**
A bilateral contract between two parties where the legal terms and conditions are binding for both parties.

**aqilah**
An ancient Arab custom based on mutual agreement.

**arbitration tribunals**
Special panels constituted where a dispute is resolved through the arbitration process.

**arbun** (or bay al-arbun)
A down payment made by a buyer to the seller with an option to rescind the contract by forgoing the payment as a penalty. It is the deposit the buyer gives the seller, on the understanding that it will be part of the buying price once the sale is finalized.

**Bait al-mal**
The state treasury who deals with all economic matters, including the revenue and expenditure of the Islamic state.

**balance sheet**
A summary of financial balances of a company or business entity.

**bay'**
Any transaction in which the ownership of a property is transferred to another party.

**bay al-dayn** (A sale of debt)
A sale and purchase transaction involving a quality debt.

**bay al-inah**
A seller sells a commodity to a buyer on cash basis and immediately repurchases the same commodity on a deferred payment basis at a price higher than the initial cash price.

**bay al-muajjal**
A sale where the parties agree to the deferment of the payment of the price to a future date.

**bay al-salam** (or salam)
A forward sale contract where advance payment is made for goods to be delivered later.

**bay al-sarf**
A contract of exchange of currencies, which may either be the same kind or different kinds.

**bay al-tawrid**
A continuous supply—purchase relationship with a known but deferred price and object of sale.

**bay' bithaman ajil**
A sale of goods where a financial institution buys a commodity on behalf of the buyer from the seller and sells the same commodity to the buyer at a profit based on a deferred payment arrangement.

**bilateral contract**
A contract between two parties with the necessary legal effect that makes their terms and conditions binding on them.

**bill of exchange**
A written order that binds the issuer for making payments, usually in international trade.

**bookkeeping**
The detailed recording of all financial transactions involved in a business.

**call (call option)**
A financial contract between a buyer and the seller where the former is given the right but not the obligation to buy an agreed quantity of an underlying commodity or financial instrument from the seller of the option at a particular time and at a fixed price.

**cash flow method**
A method of accounting whereby the records are based on the flow of cash into and out of the business.

**cash flow statement**
A financial statement that indicates how changes in the balance sheet accounts and income statements affect cash and its equivalent.

**compound accounting journal entry**
More than one debit or credit in a journal entry. A compound accounting journal entry is also called combined journal entry.

**consensus of opinion**
A secondary source of the Sharī'ah, which means the unanimous agreement of the Muslim scholars of a particular period on a Sharī'ah issue. The Arabic term for this concept is *ijma*.

**consideration**
Something that has a value given by one party to a contract in return for a benefit or promise from the other party of the contract.

**contribution**
This is sometimes called a premium. It is the participants' payments to the *takaful* fund for the purpose of mutual protection and assistance.

**corporate credit rating**
A financial indicator used in measuring the credit worthiness of a corporate entity.

**corporate governance**
A set of rules, processes, laws, and policies that affect the way a company is run in the overall interest of the stakeholders.

**corporate social responsibility (CSR)**
The commitment of a company to engage in capacity building for a sustainable society.

**counterparty**
An opposite party in a financial transaction or contract.

**credit**
An increase in liability, revenue, and capital, and a decrease in assets and expenses.

**credit exposure**
The amount of risk, or amount subject to loss of value, or the size of the commitment.

**credit risk**
Risk encountered in business transactions when there is potential of default on the part of a party in meeting its obligations as agreed under an underlying contract.

**debit**
An increase in assets and expenses, and a decrease in liability, revenue, and capital.

**debt-based financing instruments**
Financial instruments that create a debt-like relationship between the parties.

**debt-based *sukuk***
Investment certificates that are based on receivables such as debt where the rights of the certificate holders are shares in the debt.

**deferred payment**
A debt that has been incurred on the understanding that it will be paid back at some time in the future.

**dhimmah**
Fitness of a person to warrant the application of Islamic law through either acquisition of rights or discharge of obligations.

**double-entry bookkeeping**
A set of rules for recording financial information where every transaction or event changes at least two different ledger accounts.

**dual banking system**
A banking system of a country or territory that incorporates both the conventional and Islamic financial systems.

**economies of scale**
Proportionate savings in costs gained by an increased level of production.

**enforceable contract**
A contract where a party has the legal remedy to execute the contract.

**entrepreneurial poor**
Able people who have the ability to work and carry out legitimate business activities but lack the wherewithal to undertake such activities.

**equity-based *sukuk***
Partnership-based Islamic investment certificates of partnership contracts where the parties share the profits as well as any risk arising from the investment activity.

**equity capital**
Funds invested to acquire real capital. This generally includes the funds of shareholders and investors.

**equity investment**
The money invested in a company by its owners or holders of ordinary shares in a company, which although not necessarily returned in the course of the business, can only be recouped when they decide to liquidate the assets of the company or sell their shareholdings to other investors.

**equity investment risk**
A risk that arises from a partnership investment contract whereby the capital providers share in the business risk.

**equity of unrestricted account holders**
Funds received by the Islamic bank from depositors on the basis that the bank will have the right to use those funds without restriction to finance its investments within the Sharī'ah framework.

**ethical investment**
Forms of investment that emphasize a high level of moral principles that satisfy the natural state of man. Such investing is devoid of all forms of exploitation.

**exchange-traded derivatives**
Standardized derivative contracts, such as options and futures, which are transacted on an organized futures exchange.

**expenditure**
Amount of money or resources spent on a financial operation or in the settlement of an obligation.

**external auditing**
When an independent professional or firm outside the organization is engaged to perform auditing functions.

***fatwa*** (pl. *fatawa*)
Legal ruling or Sharī'ah resolution of a scholar or group of scholars on the Sharī'ah board of an Islamic financial institution.

**fiduciary relationship**
A relationship that involves trust, particularly between a professional trustee and a beneficiary of the trust.

**financial accounting**
A process where business operations and activities are measured and processed into information that is then made available to decision-makers.

**financial exclusion**
The direct or indirect exclusion of a certain group of people from the conventional financial system and its products. Financial institutions that offer micro-credit facilities for low-income individuals.

**financial screen**
The analysis of the nature of non-Sharī'ah-compliant financial behavior of a company.

***fiqh***
The whole corpus of Islamic jurisprudence. *Fiqh* may also mean the jurists' understanding of the Islamic Law.

***fiqh al-mu'amalat***
The jurisprudence concerning transactions regulated by Islamic law. This covers all aspects of Islamic commercial contracts.

**firm-specific risk (unsystematic risk)**
Risk unique to each individual firm in the form of uncertainty on returns because of certain factors unique to the firm such as internal management, potential labor disputes, credit issues, product liability, etc.

**fixed rate party**
A party who intends to swap its fixed rate profits in the profit swap arrangement.

**floating rate party**
A party who intends to swap its floating rate profits in the profit swap arrangement.

**foreign direct investment**
Investment of foreign assets in the domestic structures, equipment, and organizations of a country.

**foreign exchange contract**
A contract of exchange of money for money closely regulated and restricted by relevant Sharī'ah rules.

**forward contract**
An informal contractual transaction involving derivatives where the delivery of the underlying asset is deferred to a future date.

**Franco-German Model**
A framework that is based on the prevailing model in France and Germany.

**fund managers**
Entrepreneurs who manage investment funds on behalf of investors.

**fund mobilization**
The process of raising funds to establish a viable financial institution through the sale of shares to investors and receiving funds from depositors.

**fund utilization**
The process of using the funds realized in Sharī'ah-compliant business.

**futures contract**
A standardized contractual agreement between two parties to exchange a specified asset with a known standardized quantity and quality at a price agreed upon by the parties on the spot while delivery is made at a specified future date.

**gap analysis**
An accounting term that means a technique for determining the steps to be taken in moving from a current state to a desired future-state.

**general investment account (GIA)**
An account based on a contract between the bank (entrepreneur) and the customer (depositor), where it is agreed that the bank will use the capital in business and profit will be shared between the parties according to a pre-agreed ratio.

**gharar**
Excessive risk or absolute uncertainty relating to major elements of a contract, for example, sale of a commodity that is not present at the time of concluding the contract.

**hadith**
The sayings, acts, or tacit approvals and disapprovals of the Prophet Muhammad (PBUH).

**hajj**
The annual pilgrimage to the Holy Sanctuary in Mecca by Muslims. This is the fifth pillar of Islam.

**halal industry**
A broad term for forms of businesses that comply with the prescriptions of Islamic law, with particular reference to food and consumable items.

**haram**
Strictly forbidden acts, practices or transactions in Islam, which are considered as sins.

**hawalah**
A contract of debt assignment whereby a debt obligation is transferred from one party to another.

**hedge funds**
Alternative investment vehicles designed for a limited number of investors that are targeted at maximizing returns through different advanced investment strategies.

**hedging**
A proactive measure of investment purposefully directed at reducing instances of future risk arising from adverse price movements in the value of an asset.

**hibah**
A gratuitous contract where a person transfers a property to another without any formal material consideration.

**hilah** (pl. *hiyal.* contractum trinius)
A legal device employed by some Muslim jurists to circumvent certain prohibitive elements of the law.

**hisbah**
An Islamic institution that guards against the infringement of the law whether in economic, social, or political domains.

**horizontal analysis**
A comparative analysis of financial statements of different periods or financial years.

**hybrid *takaful* model**
An Islamic insurance model that combines and effectively uses more than one financial instrument in its structuring.

**ibra'**
Freeing an individual or corporate entity from a financial responsibility or forgoing a right.

**ijarah**
A financing mechanism that involves the rent of an asset or hire purchase where some form of rental fee is paid for a stipulated period of time mutually agreed by the parties.

**ijarah contract**
A contract where the owner of an asset leases it to a client at an agreed rental fee, which is a consideration for the beneficial use of the underlying asset.

**ijarah fund**
Lease fund where the amount realized from subscription is used to purchase an asset, which is leased to a third party.

**ijarah mawsufah fi dhimmah**
A lease for specified future usufruct of an asset which is not practically in existence at the time of concluding the contract.

**ijarah muntahia bittamlik** (also known as *ijarah wa iqtina*)
A form of lease contract that offers the lessee an option to own the asset at the end of the lease period either by purchase of the asset through a token consideration or payment of the market value, or by means of a gift contract.

**ijarah thumma al-bay'**
A contract of lease which is subsequently followed by a sale contract.

**ijma**
A secondary source of the Sharī'ah, which means the unanimous agreement of the Muslim scholars of a particular period on a Sharī'ah issue.

**ijtihad**
Independent legal reasoning by a competent jurist (or a group of jurists) who deduces the applicable law on novel issues from the sources of the Sharī'ah.

**income statement**
A financial statement that measures the financial performance of a company over a specific period of time, indicating how the revenue is transformed into net income.

**informal savings club**
(also known as savings and credit cooperatives) An informal cooperative project among a like-minded group, primarily meant to help members of the group to turn small but regular cash flows into large and meaningful sums of money.

**interest-bearing (*ribawi*)**
Any product or transaction that has an element of usury or interest that is considered as unearned and undeserving income.

**internal auditing**
This is a system designed by an organization to examine, monitor, and analyze activities related to its operation, including its business structure, employee behavior, and information systems.

**International Accounting Standards Board**
An independent standard-setting body of the IFRS Foundation. This is the leading standard-setting body for conventional accounting and auditing practices.

**International Islamic Fiqh Academy (IIFA)**
The central rule-making body of the Organization of Islamic Cooperation (OIC), composed of learned Sharī'ah scholars who are entrusted with the duty of issuing legal rulings on contemporary issues, which generally include commercial transactions.

**invalid contract**
A transaction where the basis of the contract itself is valid but there are defects in its attributes that make it invalid and thus unenforceable under the Sharī'ah.

**investable securities**
A range of bonds or stocks that can be invested in the secondary market which attract some forms of revenue.

**investment account holders (IAH)**
Bank customers who opt for the investment account of the Islamic bank, which yields legitimate returns of a predetermined share of profits. The funds are especially used in Sharī'ah-compliant investments.

**investment portfolios**
Individual investor's stocks, bonds, shares, and rental real estate.

**Islamic capital market**
A secondary market where financial and trade activities are carried out in ways that do not contradict Islamic commercial law.

**Islamic cross currency swap (ICSS)**
A bilateral contractual arrangement between two parties to exchange a series of profit and/or principal payments denominated in one currency for another series of profit and/or payments denominated in another currency, based on a notional principal amount, over an agreed period of time.

**Islamic debt funds**
An arrangement where the capital of an equity-based fund is invested in fixed-income yielding activity such as an operating lease which naturally involves a debt.

**Islamic financial institutions (IFIs)**
Financial institutions that offer Islamic financial services and products. Another common term for IFIs when specific reference is made to the banking sector of the Islamic finance industry is Islamic banking institutions (IBIs).

**Islamic finance windows**
Subsidiaries or branches of a conventional financial institution that are specifically established to operate Sharī'ah-compliant banking and finance.

**Islamic financial engineering**
Principles and strategies for developing innovative Islamic financial products and solutions based on the methodology of Islamic jurisprudence.

**Islamic FX swap**
A contract that has been designed as an Islamic hedging mechanism to minimize the exposure of market participants to the volatile and fluctuating market currency exchange rate.

**Islamic hire-purchase contract (*al-ijarahthumma al-bay'*)**
A lease agreement where the lessee gives a binding commitment or promise to purchase the underlying asset upon expiry of the lease period.

**Islamic option**
A contract of promise to buy or sell an asset at a predetermined price within a stipulated period of time with the condition that such options cannot be traded in the financial market.

**Islamic profit rate swap (IPRS)**
A bilateral contract to exchange profit rates between a fixed rate party and a floating rate party or vice versa.

**Islamic promissory forward contract (IPFC)**
A tool for risk management where a binding promise (*wa'ad*) in Islamic law is used to structure forward contracts for the purpose of hedging risks.

**Islamic swap**
A derivatives contract where two parties exchange one financial instrument for another backed with an underlying asset and excluding all prohibitive elements under the Sharī'ah for the mutual benefit of the parties.

**Islamic worldview**
The vision of reality and truth about a phenomenon based on the Islamic ideals.

*istihsan*
A secondary source of Islamic law that simply means juristic preference or equity, used as a legal adaptation mechanism to address people's emerging needs while upholding the general philosophy of the Qur'an and Sunnah.

*istisna'*
A manufacturing contract for a made-to-order asset based on a deferred delivery basis.

**journal**
An accounting record where all financial transactions of a business are originally entered.

*ju'alah* (contract of commission)
A contract of promise of reward where the entitlement to compensation is contingent upon the performance of a particular act. It is the performance of an act, the accomplishment of which attracts some form of reward.

**junk bonds**
Bonds that are rated below investment grade at the time of purchase. Junk bonds are also called non-investment-grade bonds, speculative-grade bonds, or high-yield bonds.

*kafalah*
A contract of guarantee whereby a person accepts the responsibility or undertakes to take the liability or duty of another person. It is a binding promise to be liable for the debt of a principal debtor in case they default or fail to redeem the debt but such liability does not relieve the principal debtor from liability.

**Last Day**
The Day of Accountability where, according to the Islamic belief, human beings and jinns will account for their worldly life before Almighty God.

**leasing mode**
A financing mechanism that involves the rent of an asset or hire purchase where some form of rental fee is paid for a stipulated period of time mutually agreed by the parties.

**legal capacity**
Ability to acquire and exercise rights and at the same time accept duties and perform them accordingly.

**legitimate investment**
Forms of business that involve investing one's wealth in transactions that comply with the prescriptions of Islamic law.

**LIBOR (London interbank offered rate)**
The basic interest rate used in interbank lending, which is common among the banks on the London market.

**liquidity**
The ability of a business to meet its obligations without necessarily disposing of its assets.

**liquidity risk**
The potential loss anticipated by an Islamic financial institution that arises as a result of insufficient liquidity to meets its normal operating obligations and operating needs.

***Majallah al-ahkam al-adliyyah*** (also known as the *Mejelle*)
The famous, oft-cited Islamic civil code of the Ottoman Empire, which also contains a number of provisions relating to Islamic commercial transactions.

*majlis al-'aqd*
The session of contract where the parties conclude the terms and conditions of the contract.

**margin of profit** (also net margin)
A ratio that determines the amount of profit to be realized, generally calculated by dividing net profits by sales.

**market risk**
The risk arising from the potential of investors to experience losses occasioned by movements in market prices.

**maslahah mursalah**
A branch of the secondary sources of the Sharī'ah, which means unrestricted or unregulated public interest that is in full harmony with the letter and spirit of the Sharī'ah. An example of *maslahah mursalah* is the publication of the financial report of an Islamic bank bearing the endorsement of the Sharī'ah board.

*maysir*
A game of chance or gambling that involves the acquisition of wealth by chance of winning the game or speculation without any form of consideration or compensation for such wealth.

**micro-credit**
Small loans extended to poor families or individuals who are excluded from the formal financial services.

**micro-farming**
Small scale farming that involves the cultivation of the family's plot of land to grow food crops in order to be able to feed the farmer's family.

**microfinance**
Provision of small-scale financial services to the poor who are usually excluded from the formal financial services.

**microfinance institutions (MFIs)**
Financial institutions that offer micro-credit facilities for low-income individuals.

**micro-lending**
Provision of credit facilities for low-income people based on the principle of benevolent loans (*qard hasan*).

**micro-savings**
A small deposit account specially designed for low-income earners as an incentive to plan for their future financial needs or to repay micro-lending.

**micro-*takaful***
The Sharī'ah-compliant micro-insurance model where members of a specified group of low-income individuals to mutually protect one another from any form of risk.

*mu'allaq*
A contingent contract where the contract is only effective upon the actualization of an event or condition that will occur in the future.

*mu'amalat*
Commercial transactions between people regulated under the principles of Islamic law.

*mudarabah*
A trust partnership contract between a capital provider and an entrepreneur where the parties share the profits but, in the event of any loss, the capital provider bears the loss.

*mudarabah al-muqayyadah*
Restricted trust financing contract where a particular business in which the entrepreneur will invest the capital finance is expressly specified.

*mudarabah al-mutlaqah*
Unrestricted trust financing contract where a particular business in which the entrepreneur will invest the capital finance is neither specified nor restricted.

*mudarabah* **model of *takaful***
An Islamic insurance model based on a trust partnership between the *takaful* operator who is appointed to manage the *takaful* business by the participants who act as the financiers, investors, or fund contributors.

**mudarabah sukuk**
Investment certificates that represent the ownership of units of equal value in the equity of trust financing investment and are registered in the name of the certificate holders.

**mudarib**
An entrepreneur who manages a trust investment business on behalf of the capital partner or financier. The entrepreneur and financier agree on a predetermined profit-sharing ratio.

**muhtasib** (ombudsman)
An official appointed by a competent authority to investigate complaints made by individuals against maladministration of either public authority or in a private relationship.

**mukallaf** (*sui juris*)
A person who is competent enough to acquire rights and discharge obligations accordingly without any encumbrance, and as a result is a subject of the law. To conclude a valid contract, the general rule is that a person must be *sui juris*.

**multilateral contracts**
Contracts involving more than two parties such as a bank, the client and the agent.

**muqaradah**
Another term for *mudarabah*, which means a trust financing contract.

**muqasah**
A debt settlement through a counter-transaction or offset.

**murabahah**
Cost-plus financing contract where a sale is made at a specified profit margin.

**musharakah**
A joint business partnership enterprise where the parties share the profits based on the contractual ratio and losses are borne based on the equity participation ratio.

**musharakah mutanaqisah**
Diminishing partnership with an embedded lease contract, where the financial institution gradually transfers the ownership of a property to the client over a period of time.

**Musharakah sukuk** (or sukuk al-musharakah)
Partnership certificates used for raising capital to widen the partnership net of the investment, where all the participants or partners share the risks and rewards.

**mutual indemnification**
The cooperative and collaborative element of *takāful* where the participants mutually provide insurance cover for one another in the event of any mishap.

**muwa'adah**
A bilateral promise in commercial transactions that binds both parties when inculcated into a contract.

**muzakki**
A person who pays the obligatory alms (*zakat*) in Islam.

**negotiable *sukuk***
Securities that are transferable from one person to another at a mutually agreed price.

**net income**
The result after all revenues and expenses have been accounted for. This is also called the 'bottom line'.

**nikah**
The marital union between a male and female in accordance with the rules of Islamic law.

**nisab**
Amount of wealth in one's possession after meeting all vital expenses such as food, clothing, and shelter. When the wealth of a person exceeds this threshold figure and such wealth remains idle for a whole year, *zakat* becomes obligatory.

**non-tradable *sukuk***
Investment certificates that represent receivables of cash or goods.

**operation of law**
A right or liability created by law irrespective of the intention of the party or parties involved.

**operational risk**
Risk that arises from the execution of the business functions of an Islamic bank.

**operator or *wakil***
This is the term used in *takaful* undertakings to represent the *takaful* company. Instead of using the word 'insurer', operator is used in *takaful* undertakings.

**option**
A financial derivative sold by the option writer to an option holder where there is the opportunity to buy or sell a security at an agreed price within a specified period of time.

**over-the-counter derivatives (OTC)**
(also off-exchange trading) Non-standardized products traded between two parties directly rather than going through a stock exchange.

**parallel *salam***
A forward contract that is concluded with a third party and which is distinct and not in any way contingent upon the first *salam* contract. The performance of the second *salam* contract must not be contingent on the other *salam* contract.

**participants**
The owners of the *takaful* fund.

**participants' investment fund (PIF)**
A fund derived from a portion of the pool of funds contributed by the participants, which is specially earmarked for investment or savings purposes.

**participants' risk fund (PRF)**
The common pool of funds realized from the contributions (donations or *tabarru'*) of the participants, which is used to meet claims in the event of any eventuality or loss covered under the underlying *takaful* contract.

**participation term certificate (PTC)**
A certificate that indicates a partial ownership in a joint pool of assets, usually a securitized asset, which entitles the holder to periodic returns.

**periodicity concept**
The concept that recognizes that each accounting period has an economic activity associated with it, and that activity can be measured, accounted for, and reported upon.

**portfolio diversification**
A business strategy for reducing risk through the investment in a vast variety of assets.

**portfolio protection**
A strategy for managing market risk and protecting against potential losses through the utilization of the relevant hedging instruments.

**power of attorney**
An authorization by one person to another to act on his behalf or represent him in business or other legal affairs such as a contract.

**private equities**
Asset classes that comprise equity securities not publicly traded on a stock exchange.

**prodigal**
A thoughtless person who exhibits a lack of good sense or judgment.

**product development**
A systematic process of developing and structuring Islamic finance products, which are generally used in Islamic financial transactions.

**promissory note**
An instrument where a party promises unconditionally to pay another a particular sum of money within the stipulated time.

**pro-rata profits**
Profits distributed to investors in accordance with their respective investment portfolios and proportions of investment.

**put (put option)**
A financial contract between a buyer and the seller where the buyer has the right to sell, but not an obligation, at a specified period of time and at a certain price.

**qard fund**
The interest-free benevolent loans given by Islamic banks and financial institutions.

**qard hasan**
Benevolent loan that is devoid of interest without any share in profit that accrue from the use of such funds.

**qimar (or maysir)**
A game of chance or gambling that involves the acquisition of wealth by chance of winning the game or speculation without any form of consideration or compensation for such wealth.

**quasi contract** (*shibh al-'aqd*)
An arrangement or obligations created by the law despite the absence of a contract.

***rabb al-mal***
Financier or capital provider who invests in a trust investment partnership.

***rahn***
A collateral, pledge, or mortgage offered as security for a debt that allows the creditor to take away the debt from such security in the event of any default on the part of the debtor.

**rate of return risk**
Risk associated with the potential impact of the returns of an Islamic financial institution arising from an unexpected change in the rate of return in business transactions undertaken by such institutions.

**real capital**
Original assets of financial institutions, such as machinery, equipment, and real estate.

**real estate investment trust (REIT)**
A company that owns and operates income-yielding real estate or items that relate to real estate.

**receptive legal capacity**
The capacity of every human being to acquire rights and obligations subject to certain limitations.

**restricted investment accounts**
These are account portfolios where the account holders authorize the Islamic bank to invest their funds in Sharī'ah-compliant business ventures with certain restrictions as to where, how, and for what purpose the funds are to be invested.

***retakaful***
The Islamic alternative to reinsurance. It is structured in a Sharī'ah-compliant model.

**revenue**
The money received from the sale of products and services before expenses incurred are deducted. Revenue is also known as 'top line'.

***riba***
Interest—a condition in a debt transaction where the lender seeks to get more than the amount or better quantity than what was initially lent to the borrower.

***riba al-buyu'u***
Interest in trade and commercial transactions where there is a difference in the quantity or quality of the counter values. It is also known as *riba al-fadl*.

***riba al-duyun***
Interest on loans usually for the purpose of deferment in payment. It is also known as *riba al-nasi'ah*.

***riba al-fadl***
Interest of an increase in the quantity of one of the countervalues, which is clarified in the Sunnah.

**riba al-jali**
Obvious interest charged because of delay in the repayment of a loan. It is also known as *riba al-nasi'ah*.

**riba al-khafi**
Hidden interest which is shrouded in the counter values of a trade transaction. It is also known as *riba al-fadl*.

**riba al-nasi'ah**
An unjustifiable increase for the deferment of repayment of a loan mentioned in the Qur'an.

**riba al-mubashir**
Direct interest charged because of a delay in repayment. It is also known as *riba al-nasi'ah*.

**riba ghayr al-mubashir**
Indirect interest embedded in the counter values of a trade transaction. It is also known as *riba al-fadl*.

**risk absorption**
Risks that can neither be eliminated nor transferred but can be absorbed and effectively managed by the financial institution because of its centrality in its business operations.

**risk-adjusted return on capital (RAROC)**
An adjustment to the return of an investment, which accounts for the element of risk. This is meant to give decision-makers the ability to compare the returns from different projects with varying risk levels.

**risk avoidance**
A technique of risk management that involves pre-emptive steps to remove moral hazards or risk-prone activities through alternative activities.

**risk management**
A process of identification, quantification, and understanding of business risks with a view to undertaking necessary measures to control or mitigate the risk or its impact in the overall business of a financial institution.

**risk-reward profile**
A chart of the theoretical maximum profit or loss a particular investment can have in the portfolios of investors.

**Sa'a**
An ancient measure of volume, equivalent to 3 kg, that was widely used in Muslim communities.

**sadaqah**
An act of charity which is voluntary but highly recommended for the Muslims to assist the less privileged and the needy in the society.

**sadd al-dhari'ah**
Preventive measures or precautionary principles which are a secondary source of Islamic law that seeks to prevent a violation of the law.

**salam** (or *bay al-salam*)
A forward sale contract where advance payment is made for goods to be delivered later.

**salam contract**
A commodity sale contract involving an advance payment where the delivery of the commodity is deferred.

**sale mode**
A mechanism where the bank purchases an item on behalf of the client and resells it to them, whether on a deferred basis or immediately.

**sanadat**
Islamic commercial papers issued to raise funds in investment activities.

**sarf**
A contract of exchange of money subject to the mandatory rules of Islamic law.

**secondary market**
A financial market within the Islamic capital market, where previously issued instruments such as bonds are traded. It is a market where investors purchase securities such as bonds and stocks among themselves without necessarily receiving funds directly from the issuers.

**sector screen (industry screen)**
The first stage of the investment process where the underlying business activity of the company will be evaluated and certified to be compatible with Sharī'ah restrictions.

**Sharī'ah**
Embodiment of divine prescriptions in form of faith and belief, and laws and moral norms, which are meant to guide the affairs of Muslims. It is often translated as Islamic law even though it is conceptually broader in its meaning.

**Sharī'ah compliance**
When a financial product or activity complies with the precepts and requirements of Islamic law.

**Sharī'ah governance**
A set of institutional and organizational arrangements through which IFIs ensure that there is effective independent oversight of Sharī'ah compliance over the issuance of relevant Sharī'ah pronouncements, dissemination of information, and an internal Sharī'ah compliance review.

**Sharī'ah supervisory council** (board or committee)
A body of Sharī'ah scholars and experts who certify proposals for Islamic finance products, services, and contracts brought before them.

**sharing modes**
Partnership where the funds initially mobilized are invested in a Sharī'ah-compliant business and the parties share the profits or loss, whichever is applicable.

**shibh al-'aqd**
Semblance of a contract or a quasi contract which, although it creates an obligation, lacks elements of a valid contract.

**shirkah**
Any form of business partnership between two or more individuals.

**short-term liquidity**
Degree by which a corporate body or an individual can meet its short-term cash obligations.

*shura*
Mutual consultation in a decision-making process.

*sighah*
The form of any contract in Islamic law expressed as an offer and an acceptance.

**sovereign credit rating**
The credit rating of a sovereign entity or a country.

**special purpose vehicle (SPV)**
A corporate entity incorporated for the sole purpose of carrying out a specified investment within a particular period of time. This entity manages the securitization process and handles the issuance of the certificates.

**specific investment account (SIA)**
An account based on a contract between the bank and the customer (depositor), where it is agreed that the bank will use the capital in a specific business and profit will be shared between the parties according to a pre-agreed ratio.

**statement of changes in restricted investments**
A unique financial statement that shows the performance of investments specifically restricted or limited by the investors, such as the restricted trust financing investment.

**Statement of Financial Accounting (SFA)**
A statement issued by the Accounting and Auditing Organization for Islamic Financial Institutions that contains financial accounting and reporting standards for Islamic finance products.

**statement of retained earnings**
A financial statement that explains the changes in the retained earnings of a company over a period.

**stock exchange**
A market in which securities are bought and sold. Securities, whether as stocks, bonds, or derivatives, are often floated on the stock exchange.

**stock market index**
A statistical method of measuring a section of the stock market that involves a compilation of the share prices of representative stocks.

*sukuk* (Islamic bonds)
These are certificates of equal value representing undivided shares in the ownership of tangible assets of certain identified projects, services or usufruct.

**Sunnah**
The second primary source of the Sharī'ah, which comprises the sayings, practices and tacit approvals of the Prophet Muhammad (PBUH).

**surplus**
The amount that remains after all expenses and management fees for the administration of the *takaful* fund have been deducted and the contributions are more than the claims made by the participants.

**swap**
A derivative contract where two parties exchange one financial instrument for another for the mutual benefit of the parties.

*tabarru'*
Donation, gift, or charitable contribution that is primarily meant to assist others in whatever form.

*tabarru'at*
Gratuitous contracts or donations which include bequests and gifts.

**T account**
The ledger account format that resembles the letter 'T' which originates from the process of using debits and credits.

*Tabung Haji*
The Malaysian Hajj Pilgrims Fund Board.

*takaful*
Islamic form of cooperative insurance, which is based on mutual cooperation. It is a mutual indemnity scheme in Islamic finance.

*takaful* operator
The party who manages and administer the *takaful* fund.

*takaful* policy
An insurance policy that is based on the Islamic insurance model, which is based on mutual cooperation.

*takaful ta'awuni*
A concept of mutual cooperation that represents the true Islamic cooperative insurance scheme.

*talaq*
The legal dissolution of marriage in accordance with Islamic law.

*tawarruq*
A hybrid sale contract where a customer approaches a bank or financial institution to purchase a commodity with payment arranged on an installment basis and the customer in turn sells the commodity to a third party for cash.

*tawriq*
A process of converting an asset into its cash equivalents, issued as certificates of investment that are tradable in the secondary market.

**tradable *sukuk***
Islamic investment certificates that represent tangible assets or proportionate ownership of a business or investment portfolio.

**trade by barter**
A simple trade where goods or services are exchanged for a certain amount of other goods or services subject to the exceptions and general rules of the Shari'ah.

**trust certificates**
Debt investment or bonds which are backed by other assets for the purpose of collateral.

*ujrah*
Fee or commission paid for services rendered.

**underwriting policies**
The policies that are used in determining the extent of risk taking of insurance operators against the payment of certain premiums.

**unilateral contract**
A contract initiated and concluded by a single party which involves some form of benefit being transferred to another party usually without consideration.

**usufruct**
The right to use and enjoy property or premises without causing unnecessary destruction.

**venture capital**
The money and resources made available to start-up firms and small business with exceptional growth potential.

**vicegerency**
The concept of the representation of God's ruling on Earth, conferred on mankind.

**void contract**
An unenforceable contract that is invalid from the very beginning, which cannot be remedied by addressing any missing element in such transaction.

*wa'ad*
A unilateral promise or undertaking by a party to carry out a unilateral contract. Usually, it binds the maker alone.

*wadi'ah*
Contract of safe custody or bailment where a sum of money or valuable property is deposited with a corporate body or individual for safekeeping.

*wadiah yad damanah*
A guaranteed bank deposit where the bank is the guarantor and undertakes to pay the whole or part of the deposit when requested by the depositor.

*wakalah* (contract of agency)
A contract of agency whereby a party appoints an agent to act on his behalf based on certain specified terms of service. It is a contract that establishes an agency relationship between two parties for a specific purpose though such authority may be general or specific.

*wakalah* model of *takaful*
An Islamic insurance model that is based on a contract of agency between the *takaful* participants and the *takaful* operator, where the former are the real owners of the fund while the latter acts as an agent.

*waqf*
A charitable endowment in perpetuity for a specific purpose. It is meant to assist the poor and the less privileged in society. The ownership of the property vests in God while the benefits of it are meant for the less privileged in society.

*waqf-wakalah-mudarabah* model
A combination of charitable endowment, agency, and trust financing contracts in the same structure for the purpose of Islamic insurance.

*wasiyyah*
The statement or will of a Muslim testator where it is stipulated how a limited portion (up to one-third) of the testator's estate is to be disposed after their demise.

*zakat*
Obligatory charitable alms in Islam. Every able Muslim individual, including juristic persons, are obliged to pay this due on one's wealth.

Emboldened terms can be found in the glossary. Letters 'b', 'f' or 't' following page numbers refer respectively to box, figure or table.

**Text**